EARLY CHILDHOOD CURRICULUM RESOURCE HANDBOOK

A Practical Guide for Teaching Early Childhood (Pre-K–3)

CORWIN PRESS, INC.
A Sage Publications Company
Thousand Oaks, California

Consulting Editors:

Joanne Hendrick
Professor Emeritus,
University of Oklahoma

Sydney Schwartz
Professor, Early Childhood Education
Queens College, City University of New York

Carol Seedfeldt
Professor, Institute for Child Study
University of Maryland at College Park

Editorial and Production Staff:

L. Meredith Phillips, *Managing Editor*
Joy E. Runyon, *Senior Editor*
Liza Pleva, *Production Editor*
Lois Hilchey, *Editorial Assistant*

Cover design:
Sonja Originals; adapted by Pat Tanner

Cover illustrations:
Rick Powell

First Printing 1993
Printed in the United States of America

Library of Congress Cataloging-in-Publication Data
Early childhood curriculum resource handbook: a practical
    guide for teaching early childhood (pre-K–3).
        p.   cm.
    Includes bibliographic references (p.) and index.
        1. Early childhood education—United States—
Curricula—Handbooks, manuals, etc. 2. Curriculum
planning—United States—Handbooks, manuals, etc.
LB1139.4.E175   1993   92-46194
372.19—dc20

CONTENTS

PART III: TEXTBOOKS, CLASSROOM MATERIALS, AND OTHER RESOURCES

PUBLISHER'S FOREWORD

THE *Early Childhood Curriculum Resource Handbook* is one of a new series of practical references for curriculum developers, education faculty, veteran teachers, and student teachers. The handbook is designed to provide basic information on the background of early childhood curriculum, as well as current information on publications, standards, and special materials for early childhood, kindergarten through grade 3. Think of this handbook as the first place to look when you are revising or developing your early childhood curriculum—or if you need basic resource information on early childhood any time of the year.

This handbook does not seek to prescribe any particular form of curriculum, nor does it follow any set of standards or guidelines. Instead, the book provides a general grounding in the early childhood curriculum, so that you can use this information and then proceed in the direction best suited for your budget, your school, and your district. What this handbook gives you is a sense of the numerous *options* that are available—it is up to you to use the information to develop the appropriate curriculum or program for your situation.

How To Use This Handbook

There are various ways to use this resource handbook. If you are revising or creating an early childhood curriculum, you should read the Introduction (for an overall sense of the different philosophies of curriculum and how this will affect the program you develop), chapter 1 (for basic background on the trends and research in early childhood), and chapter 2 (for a how-to guide to developing curriculum materials). With this background, you can go through the other chapters for the specific information you need—ranging

from topics to be covered at various grade levels (chapter 4) to state requirements (chapter 5) to publishers and producers (chapter 11).

If you know what type of information you need, then check the Table of Contents for the most appropriate chapter, or check the Index to see where this material is covered. For instance:

1. If you are looking for ideas on developing special projects, turn to chapter 9.
2. If you are looking for a new textbook or supplementary materials (book, video, or software), turn to chapter 11.
3. If you need to contact state departments of education for early childhood curriculum documents, check the list provided in chapter 6.

What's in the Handbook

The *Introduction* provides an overview of the ideologies and philosophies that have affected American curriculum through the years. This will acquaint you with the various ideologies, so that you can determine whether your school is following one such philosophy (or a combination), and how this might influence the development of your curriculum. The Introduction is generic by design, since these ideologies pertain to all subject areas.

Chapter 1 provides an overview of *Recurring Themes and Current Issues.* This chapter discusses the history and development of present-day curriculum and looks at the directions the curriculum is taking. The major research works are cited so that you can get more detailed information on particular topics.

Chapter 2 is a step-by-step description of *Curriculum Process and Design: Pre-K through Grade Three.* It is meant to be a practical guide to creating or revising early childhood curriculum guides.

Chapter 3, *Funding Curriculum Projects*, lists funding for programs that are studying or developing curriculum. Along with addresses and phone numbers, the names of contact persons are provided (wherever possible) to expedite your gathering of information.

Chapter 4 outlines *Important Topics and Integration in Early Childhood Education.* This is not meant to be a pattern to follow, but instead is a reflection of what most schools cover and what current research recommends.

Chapter 5, *State-Level Curriculum Guidelines: An Analysis,* describes the statewide frameworks and discusses the various emphases, philosophies, and coverage among the state materials.

Chapter 6, *State-Level Curriculum Guidelines: A Listing,* supplements the previous chapter by listing addresses of state departments of education and their publication titles.

Chapter 7, *How To Develop an Assessment Program,* discusses the considerations and methods involved in developing a program to assess the effectiveness of your early childhood curriculum.

Chapter 8 consists of *Annotated Lists of Curriculum Guides: Kindergarten–Grade 3.*

Chapter 9 discusses *Projects in the Early Childhood Curriculum.* The chapter discusses projects, their goals, and the methods used to create them.

Chapter 10 gives information on *Recommended Trade Books* that can be used as supplementary texts in early childhood classrooms. This chapter discusses the bibliographic tools to use in finding these trade books; it also cites the various published lists of children's books for early childhood education.

Chapter 11 is an annotated list of *Curriculum Material Producers* of textbooks, videos, software, and other materials for use in early childhood education.

Chapter 12, *Statewide Text Adoption,* lists the early childhood textbooks and materials adopted by the states that have such an adoption policy.

Chapter 13 is an *Index to Reviews* of early childhood textbooks and supplementary materials. Since these items are reviewed in a wide variety of publications, we have assembled the citations of appropriate reviews in index form (cited by title, author, publisher/distributor, subject, and grade level).

Chapter 14 provides a list of *Kraus Curriculum Development Library* (KCDL) subscribers; KCDL is a good source for models of curriculum guides in early childhood education.

The Appendix reprints large sections of two exemplary curriculum guides in early childhood education.

Acknowledgements

The content of this handbook is based on numerous meetings and discussions with educators and curriculum specialists across the country. Our thanks go to the curriculum supervisors in schools across the United States; the faculty at education departments in the colleges and universities we visited; and curriculum librarians. Special thanks go to the members of the Curriculum Materials Committee (CMC) and the Problems of Access and Control of Education Materials (PACEM) committee of the Association of College and Research Libraries' Education and Behavioral Sciences Section (ACRL/EBSS). Our meetings with the committees during American Library Association Conferences continue to provide Kraus with valuable ideas for the handbooks and for future curriculum projects.

We also acknowledge with thanks the assistance of Ruth Eisenhower, Marjorie Miller Kaplan, Barbara Meyers, Thomas Wolfe, and the indexers at AEIOU.

Your Feedback

We would like to make a request of our readers. At the back of this handbook is a user survey that asks your opinions about the book, its coverage, and its contents. Once you have used this book, please fill out the questionnaire—it should only take a minute or so—and mail it back to us. If the form has already been removed, please just send us a letter with your opinions. We want to keep improving this new series of handbooks, and we can do this only with your help! Please send questionnaires or other responses to:

Kraus International Publications
358 Saw Mill River Road
Millwood, NY 10546-1035
(914) 762-2200 / (800) 223-8323
Fax: (914) 762-1195

SERIES INTRODUCTION

P. Bruce Uhrmacher

Assistant Professor of Education
School of Education, University of Denver, Denver, Colorado

WHEN I travel by airplane and desire conversation, I inform the person sitting next to me that I'm in education. Everyone has an opinion about education. I hear stories about teachers (both good and bad), subject matter ("The problem with the new math is . . ."), and tests ("I should have gotten an A on that exam in seventh grade"). Many people want to tell me about the problems with education today ("Schools aren't what they used to be"). Few people are apathetic about schooling. When I do not wish to be disturbed in flight, however, I avoid admitting I'm in education. "So, what do you do?" someone trying to draw me out asks. I reply matter-of-factly, "I'm a curriculum theorist." Unless they persist, my retort usually signals the end of the dialogue. Unlike the job titles *farmer*, *stockbroker*, or even *computer analyst*, for many people *curriculum theorist* conjures few images.

What do curriculum theorists do? The answer to this question depends in part on the way curriculum theorists conceive of curriculum and theory. The term *curriculum* has over 150 definitions. With so many different ways of thinking about it, no wonder many curriculum theorists see their task differently. In this introduction, I point out that curriculum theorists have a useful function to serve, despite the fact that we can't agree on what to do. In short, like economists who analyze trends and make recommendations about the economy (and, incidentally, who also

agree on very little), curriculum theorists generate a constructive dialogue about curriculum decisions and practices. Although curricularists originally fought over the word *curriculum*, trying to achieve conceptual clarity in order to eliminate the various differences, in time educators recognized that the fight over the term was unproductive (Zais 1976, 93). However, the problem was not simply an academic disagreement. Instead, curricularists focused on different aspects of the educational enterprise. At stake in the definition of curriculum was a conceptual framework that included the nature of the role of the curricularist and the relationships among students, teachers, subject matter, and educational environments. Today, most curricularists place adjectives before the term to specify what type of curriculum they're discussing. Thus, one often reads about the intended, the operational, the hidden, the explicit, the implicit, the enacted, the delivered, the experienced, the received, and the null curriculum (see glossary at the end of this chapter). Distinctions also can be made with regard to curricularist, curriculum planner, curriculum worker, and curriculum specialist. I use the terms *curricularist* and *curriculum theorist* to refer to individuals, usually at the college level, who worry about issues regarding curriculum theory. I use the other terms to refer to people who actually take part in the planning or the implementation of curriculum in schools.

In order to trace the development that has

brought the field of curriculum to its present state, I will begin with a brief overview of the progression of curriculum development in the United States. First, I examine issues facing the Committee of Ten, a group of educators who convened in 1892 to draft a major document regarding what schools should teach. Next, I focus on the perennial question of who should decide what schools teach. Curriculum was not a field of study until the 1920s. How were curriculum decisions made before there were curriculum specialists? How did curriculum become a field of study? We learn that the profession began, in part, as a scientific endeavor; whether the field should still be seen as a scientific one is a question of debate. Finally, I provide a conceptual framework that examines six curriculum "ideologies" (Eisner 1992). By understanding these ideologies, educators will discern the assumptions underlying various conceptions of curriculum. Then they should be able to decide which ideology they wish to pursue and to recognize its educational implications.

What Should Schools Teach?

In the nineteenth century, curriculum usually meant "the course of study," and what many educators worried about was what schools should teach. Under the theoretical influence of "mental discipline" (derived from the ideas of faculty psychologists), many educators believed that certain subjects strengthened the brain, much like certain exercises strengthened body muscles. Greek, Latin, and mathematics were important because they were difficult subjects and thus, presumably, exercised the brain. By the 1890s, however, with the great influx of Italian, Irish, Jewish, and Russian immigrants, and with the steady increase of students attending secondary schools, a concern grew over the relevance and value of such subjects as Greek and Latin. Why should German or French be any less worthy than Greek or Latin? In addition, students and parents raised further questions regarding the merits of vocational education. They wanted curricula that met their more practical needs.

While parents pressed for their concerns, secondary school principals worried about preparing students for college, since colleges had different entrance requirements. In 1892 the National Education Association (NEA) appointed

the Committee of Ten to remedy this problem. Headed by Charles W. Eliot, president of Harvard University, the committee debated and evaluated the extent to which a single curriculum could work for a large number of students who came from many different backgrounds with many different needs. In its final report, the committee suggested that colleges consider of equal value and accept students who attended not only the classical curriculum program, but also the Latin scientific, the modern language, and the English programs.

By eliminating the requirement of Greek for two of the programs and by reducing the number of required Latin courses, the committee broke with the traditional nineteenth-century curriculum to some degree. Yet, they were alert to the possibility that different kinds of curriculum programs taught in different ways could lead to a stratified society. Eliot had argued that the European system of classifying children into "future peasants, mechanics, trades-people, merchants, and professional people" was unacceptable in a democratic society (Tanner and Tanner 1975, 186). The committee believed all should have the opportunity for further studies under a "rational humanist" orientation to curriculum, a viewpoint that prizes the power of reason and the relevance and importance of learning about the best that Western culture has to offer.

The committee's report met with mixed reviews when it came out. One of its foremost opponents was G. Stanley Hall, a "developmentalist," who argued that the "natural order of development in the child was the most significant and scientifically defensible basis for determining what should be taught" (Kliebard 1986, 13). According to Hall, who had scientifically observed children's behavior at various stages of development, the committee did not take into account children's wide-ranging capabilities, and it promulgated a college-bound curriculum for everyone, even though many high school students would not go to college. Rather than approaching curriculum as the pursuit of a standard academic experience for all students, Hall and other developmentalists believed that knowledge of human development could contribute to creating a curriculum in harmony with the child's stage of interest and needs.

Thus far I have indicated two orientations to curriculum: the rational humanist and the developmentalist. We should understand, however, that at any given time a number of interest groups struggle for power over the curriculum. Historian Herbert Kliebard observes:

> We do not find a monolithic supremacy exercised by one interest group; rather we find different interest groups competing for dominance over the curriculum and, at different times, achieving some measure of control depending on local as well as general social conditions. Each of these interest groups, then, represents a force for a different selection of knowledge and values from the culture and hence a kind of lobby for a different curriculum. (Kliebard 1986, 8)

Who Should Decide What Schools Teach?

Thinking about curriculum dates back in Western culture to at least the ancient Greeks. Plato and Aristotle, as well as Cicero, Plutarch, and Rousseau, all thought about curriculum matters in that they debated the questions of what should be taught to whom, in what way, and for what purposes. But it wasn't until 1918 that curriculum work was placed in the professional domain with the publication of *The Curriculum* by Franklin Bobbitt, a professor at the University of Chicago. Although supervisors and administrators had written courses of study on a piecemeal basis, "Professor Bobbitt took the major step of dealing with the curriculum in all subjects and grades on a unified and comprehensive basis" (Gress 1978, 27). The term *curriculum theory* came into use in the 1920s, and the first department of curriculum was founded at Teachers College, Columbia University, in 1937. Of course, the question arises: If curricularists (a.k.a. curriculum specialists, curriculum theorists, and curriculum workers) were not making decisions about what should be taught in schools prior to the 1920s, then who was?

As we have seen, national commissions made some of the curricular decisions. The NEA appointed the Committee of Ten to address college–high school articulation in 1892 and the Committee of Fifteen to address elementary school curriculum in 1895. In the early 1900s the NEA appointed another committee to develop fundamental principles for the reorganization of secondary education. Thus, university professors, school superintendents, and teachers made some curricular decisions as they acted in the role of acknowledged authorities on national commissions.

Along with commissions, forces such as tradition have shaped the curriculum. One long-time student of curriculum, Philip Jackson, observes:

> One reason why certain subjects remain in the curriculum is simply that they have been there for such a long time. Indeed, some portions of the curriculum have been in place for so long that the question of how they got there or who decided to put them there in the first place has no answer, or at least not one that anyone except a historian would be able to give. As far as most people are concerned, they have just "always" been there, or so it seems. (Jackson 1992, 22)

Jackson also notes here that subjects such as the three R's are so "obviously useful that they need no further justification"—or, at least, so it seems.

Texts and published materials have also been factors in shaping the curriculum. Whether it was the old *McGuffey Readers* or the modern textbooks found in almost any classroom in the United States, these books have influenced the curriculum by virtue of their content and their widespread use. According to some estimates, text materials dominate 75 percent of the time elementary and secondary students are in classrooms and 90 percent of their time on homework (Apple 1986, 85). Textbook writers are de facto curriculum specialists.

National Commission committees, tradition, textbooks, instructional materials, and the influence from numerous philosophers (e.g., Herbart and Dewey) were focal in deciding what schools should teach. Of course, parents, state boards of education, and teachers had their own convictions as to what should be in the curriculum. However, as the United States moved toward urbanization (30 percent of 63 million lived in cities in 1890; over 50 percent of 106 million lived in cities in 1920 [Cremin 1977, 93]), new factors influenced schooling. In particular, the industrial and scientific revolutions commingled in the minds of some to produce new ways of thinking about work. Franklin Bobbitt applied these new ideas to education. Influenced by Frederick Winslow Taylor, the father of the scientific management movement, Bobbitt assumed that the kinds of accomplishments that had been made in business and industry could be made in education. What was needed was the application of scientific principles to curriculum.

Briefly, Bobbitt believed that "educational engineers" or "curriculum-discoverers," as he called them, could make curriculum by surveying the array of life's endeavors and by grouping this broad range of human experience into major fields. Bobbitt wrote:

> The curriculum-discoverer will first be an analyst of human nature and of human affairs. . . . His first task . . . is to discover the total range of habits, skills, abilities, forms of thought . . . etc., that its members need for the effective performance of their vocational labors; likewise the total range needed for their civic activities; their health activities; their recreations, their language; their parental, religious, and general social activities. The program of analysis will be no narrow one. It will be as wide as life itself. (Bobbitt 1918, 43)

Thus, according to Bobbitt, curriculum workers would articulate educational goals by examining the array of life's activities. Next, in the same way one can analyze the tasks involved in making a tangible object and eliminate waste in producing it, Bobbitt believed one could streamline education by task analysis, by forming objectives for each task, and by teaching skills as discrete units.

Bobbitt's push for the professionalization of curriculum did not replace other factors so much as it added a new dimension. By arguing that schools needed stated objectives and that curricularists should be chosen for the task since they were trained in the science of curriculum, Bobbitt opened up a new line of work. He and his students would be of direct help to practitioners because they would know how to proceed scientifically (analyze the range of human experience, divide it into activities, create objectives) in the making of curriculum, and this knowledge gave curricularists authority and power. The world was rapidly changing in communications, in agriculture, in industry, and most of all in medicine. Who could argue with the benefits of science?

If Franklin Bobbitt created the field of professional curriculum activities, Ralph Tyler defined it. In his short monograph, *Basic Principles of Curriculum and Instruction* (1949), Tyler offered a way of viewing educational institutions. He began his book by asking four fundamental questions that he believed must be answered in developing curriculum:

1. What educational purposes should the school seek to attain?
2. What educational experiences can be provided that are likely to attain those purposes?
3. How can these educational experiences be

effectively organized?
4. How can we determine whether these purposes are being attained? (Tyler 1949, 1)

Tyler devoted one chapter to each question. Unlike some curricularists, Tyler did not say what purposes a school should seek to attain. He recognized that a school in rural Idaho has different needs from an urban one in Boston. Rather, Tyler suggested that schools themselves determine their own purposes from three sources: studies of the learners themselves, studies of contemporary life, and studies from subject matter specialists.

Tyler, like Bobbitt before him, wished to bring order to the complex field of education. Although there are differences between the two men, both believed there was work to be done by professional curricularists. Both men trained students in the field of curriculum, and both believed in the liberal ideals of rationality and progress. Curricularist Decker Walker summarizes the tradition that Bobbitt and Tyler started as follows:

> Since Bobbitt's day, planning by objectives (PBO) had developed into a family of widely used approaches to curriculum improvement. As a method of curriculum materials design, PBO focuses early attention on developing precise statements of the objectives to be sought. If the process is to be fully scientific, the selection of objectives must be rationally justifiable and not arbitrary. (Walker 1990, 469)

While Bobbitt and Tyler taught students how to become professional curricularists and encouraged them to conduct research, to write, and to attain university positions, differences of opinion on what curricularists should be doing soon mounted. At issue was not only the utility of scientific curriculum making, but also the specific endeavors many curricularists pursued.

A Framework for Thinking about Curriculum

Tyler produced a seminal work that provided curriculum workers with a way of thinking about curriculum. While some elaborated on his ideas (Taba 1962), others wondered whether indeed Tyler provided the best questions for curricularists to think about. During the 1970s, numerous educators began to seek other ways of thinking about curriculum work. William Pinar, for example, asked, "Are Tyler's questions . . . no longer pertinent or possible? Are they simply cul-de-sacs?" (Pinar 1975, 397). Reconceptualizing the term *curriculum* (race course) from the verb of the Latin root, *currere* (to run a race), Pinar goes on to argue:

> The questions of *currere* are not Tyler's; they are ones like these: Why do I identify with Mrs. Dalloway and not with Mrs. Brown? What psychic dark spots does the one light, and what is the nature of "dark spots," and "light spots"? Why do I read Lessing and not Murdoch? Why do I read such works at all? Why not biology or ecology? Why are some drawn to the study of literature, some to physics, and some to law? (402)

More will be said about Pinar's work later. My point here is that curriculum theorists do not necessarily agree on how one should approach thinking about curriculum. By trying to redefine curriculum entirely, Pinar drew attention to different aspects of the educational process.

Out of this continuing discussion among curricularists, various ideologies—beliefs about what schools should teach, for what ends, and for what reasons—have developed (Eisner 1992). In this section, I present six prominent curriculum ideologies that should prove useful in thinking about developing, adapting, or implementing curriculum. While these ideologies are important, they are not the only ones. Elliot Eisner writes of religious orthodoxy and progressivism and excludes multiculturalism and developmentalism. Some authors may include constructivism rather than developmentalism.

I remind the reader that few people actually wear the labels I describe. These conceptualizations are useful in helping one better articulate a set of assumptions and core values. They help us see the implications of a particular viewpoint. They also help us understand issues and concerns that may otherwise be neglected. Sometimes ideologies are specified in mission statements or some other kind of manifesto; at other times, ideologies are embedded in educational practice but are not made explicit. Rarely does a school adhere to one curriculum ideology—though some do. More often, because public schools are made up of people who have different ideas about what schools should teach, a given school is more likely to embrace an array of curricular ideas. While some readers may resonate strongly with a particular ideology because it expresses their inclinations, some readers may appreciate particular ideas from various ideolo-

gies. In either case, it may be a good idea to examine the strengths and weaknesses of each one. Later in this chapter I argue that one does not need to be ideologically pure in order to do good curriculum work.

Rational Humanism

We have already seen, in the historical example of Charles Eliot and the Committee of Ten, an early exemplar of rational humanism. During Eliot's day, rational humanists embraced the theory of mental discipline, which provided a handy rationale for traditional studies. Why study Greek and Latin? Because these subjects exercised the mind in ways that other subjects did not. While mental discipline fell by the wayside, rational humanism did not. From the 1930s through the 1950s, Robert Maynard Hutchins and Mortimer Adler championed the rational humanistic tradition, in part by editing *The Great Books of the Western World*. Hutchins argued that the "great books" offer the best that human beings have thought and written. Thus, rather than reading textbooks on democracy, science, and math, one ought to read Jefferson, Newton, and Euclid.

Today, one may find the rational humanist ideology in some private schools and in those public schools that have adopted Adler's ideas as represented in the *Paideia Proposal* (Eisner 1992, 310). In short, the Paideia plan provides a common curriculum for all students. Except for the choosing of a foreign language, there are no electives. All students learn language, literature, fine arts, mathematics, natural science, history, geography, and social studies.

While Adler endorses lecturing and coaching as two important teaching methods, the aspect of teaching Adler found most engaging was maieutic or Socratic questioning and active participation. In essence, maieutic teaching consists of a seminar situation in which learners converse in a group. The teacher serves as a facilitator who moves the conversation along, asks leading questions, and helps students develop, examine, or refine their thinking as they espouse particular viewpoints. This process, according to Adler, "teaches participants how to analyze their own minds as well as the thought of others, which is to say it engages students in disciplined conversation about ideas and values" (Adler 1982, 30).

Another important educational feature of these seminars is that one discusses books and art but not textbooks. In a follow-up book to *The Paideia Proposal*, Adler (1984) provides a K–12 recommended reading list in which he recommends for kindergarten to fourth grade Aesop, William Blake, Shel Silverstein, Alice Walker, Jose Marie Sanchez-Silva, Langston Hughes, and Dr. Seuss, among other authors. I indicate these authors in particular because the charge that Adler's program embraces only the Western European heritage is not entirely accurate. While Adler would argue that some books are better than others, and that, in school, students should be reading the better ones, one can see that Adler includes authors who are not elitist and who are from culturally diverse backgrounds.

Developmentalism

Another approach to curriculum theory, which was discussed briefly in the historical section of this chapter, is developmentalism. Although a range of scholars falls under this heading, the basic point is that, rather than fitting the child to the curriculum, students would be better served if the curriculum were fitted to the child's stage of development. Why? One argument is that doing otherwise is inefficient or even detrimental to the child's development. It would be ridiculous to try to teach the Pythagorean theorem to a first grader, and it could be harmful (to use a fairly noncontroversial example) to teach a fourth grader to master throwing a curve ball. By understanding the range of abilities children have at various ages, one can provide a curriculum that meets the needs and interests of students. Of course, while the stage concept cannot pinpoint the development of a particular child at a given age, it serves as a general guide.

One might also pay attention to the idea of development when creating or adapting curriculum because of the issue of "readiness for learning." There are two ways of thinking about readiness. Some educators, in their interest to hurry development, believe that encouraging learners to perform approximations of desired behaviors can hasten academic skills. In this case, one tries to intervene in apparently natural development by manipulating the child's readiness at younger and younger ages. The research findings on whether one can greatly enhance one's learning processes are somewhat mixed, but, in my opinion, they favor the side that says "speed learning" is inefficient (Duckworth 1987, Good and Brophy 1986, Tietze 1987). I also think

the more important question, as Piaget noted, is "not how fast we can help intelligence grow, but how far we can help it grow" (Duckworth 1987, 38).

A different way of thinking about readiness for learning concerns not how to speed it up, but how to work with it effectively. Eleanor Duckworth, who studied with Piaget, believes the idea of readiness means placing children in developmentally appropriate problem situations where students are allowed to have their own "wonderful ideas." She believes that asking "the right question at the right time can move children to peaks in their thinking that result in significant steps forward and real intellectual excitement" (Duckworth 1987, 5). The challenges for teachers are to provide environmentally rich classrooms where students have the opportunity to "mess about" with things, and to try to understand children's thought processes. Students should have the opportunity to experiment with materials likely to afford intellectual growth, and teachers should learn how their students think. In this approach to curriculum, mistakes are not problems; they are opportunities for growth.

The developmental approach to curriculum teaches us to pay attention to the ways humans grow and learn. One basic idea underlying the various theories of human development in regard to curriculum is that the curriculum planner ought to understand children's abilities and capabilities because such knowledge enables one to provide worthwhile educational activities for students.

Reconceptualism

As noted earlier with Pinar's use of the term *currere*, during the 1970s numerous individuals criticized the technical aspects and linear progression of steps of the Tyler rationale. Loosely labelled as reconceptualists, some educators felt the following:

> What is missing from American schools . . . is a deep respect for personal purpose, lived experience, the life of imagination, and those forms of understanding that resist dissection and measurement. What is wrong with schools, among other things, is their industrialized format, their mechanistic attitudes toward students, their indifference to personal experience, and their emphasis on the instrumental and the out of reach. (Pinar 1975, 316)

Reconceptualists have focused on Dewey's

observation that one learns through experience. Given this assertion, some important questions arise. For example, how can teachers, teacher educators, or educational researchers better understand the kinds of experiences individual students are having? To answer this question, reconceptualists employ ideas, concepts, and theories from psychoanalysis, philosophy, and literature.

Another question that arises when one reflects on understanding experience is, How can teachers provide worthwhile conditions for students to undergo educational experiences? Maxine Greene divides educational experiences into two types: "an education for having" and "an education for being." Education for having is utilitarian—for example, one may learn to read in order to get a job. Some students need this kind of experience. Education for being is soulful—one may learn to read for the sensual qualities it can provide. All students, she says, need the latter kind of experience. One problem is that the latter has often been neglected or, if not, often provided for the talented or gifted at the expense of others (Green, 1988a).

In their effort to reperceive education, reconceptualists such as Maxine Greene, Madeleine Grumet, and William Pinar do not usually offer specific educational ideas that are easily implemented. In part, this is because the kind of education with which they are concerned is not easy to quantify or measure. In general, reconceptualists do not believe their theories and ideas need quick utilization in schools in order to validate their worth. If in reading their writings you think more deeply about educational issues, then I think they would be satisfied.

Nevertheless, I can think of two practical challenges for education that stem from their writing. First, how could you write a rigorous and tough-minded lesson plan without using objectives? What would such a lesson plan look like? Second, if you wanted to teach students a concept such as citizenship, how would you do it? Rational humanists would have students read Thomas Jefferson or Martin Luther King, Jr. Reconceptualists, however, would wonder how teachers can place students in problematic situations (i.e., in the classroom or on the playground) where students would grapple with real issues concerning citizenship.

Critical Theory

The idea of critical theory originated at the Institute for Social Research in Frankfurt ("the Frankfurt school") in the 1920s. Today, scholars who continue to recognize the value and importance of Marxist critiques of society and culture draw from and build on ideas from critical theory. In education they reveal, among other things, that schooling comprises a value-laden enterprise where issues of power are always at play.

For instance, while many people perceive schools as neutral institutions, places that will help any hard-working student to get ahead in life, critical theorists suggest that, on the contrary, schools do not operate that way. Michael Apple points out, "Just as our dominant economic institutions are structured so that those who inherit or already have economic capital do better, so too does cultural capital act in the same way" (Apple 1986, 33). According to Apple, schools reflect the general inequities in the larger society. Rather than changing society through cultural transformation (teaching students to question or to be independent thinkers), schools actually maintain the status quo through cultural reproduction.

Unlike some curricularists who try to appear neutral in exercising judgments about curriculum matters, Apple's values are well known. He believes in John Rawls's insight that "for a society to be truly just, it must maximize the advantage of the least advantaged" (Apple 1979, 32). Apple encourages curricularists to take advocacy positions within and outside of education. While critical theory makes for a powerful theoretical tool, one question frequently asked of critical theorists is how this information can be used in the classroom. Teachers point out that they may not be able to change the school structure, the kinds of material they must cover, or the kinds of tests that must be given. Although admittedly application is difficult, one high school English educator in Boston who employs the ideas of critical theory is Ira Shor.

In an activity called "prereading," for example, Shor tells students the theme of a book they are about to read and has them generate hypothetical questions the book may answer. At first students are reluctant to respond, but after a while they do. Shor believes this kind of exercise has numerous functions. First, it provides a bridge for students to decelerate from the "rush of mass culture" into the slow medium of the printed word. Habituated to rock music and MTV, students need a slow-down time. Also, after creating a list of questions, students are curious how many will actually be addressed. Students may still reject the text, says Shor, but now it won't be a result of alienation. Perhaps most importantly, prereading demystifies the power of the written word. Rather than approaching the text as some kind of untouchable authority, "students' own thoughts and words on the reading topic are the starting points for the coordinated material. The text will be absorbed into the field of their language rather than they being ruled by it" (Shor 1987, 117).

Critical theory offers a radical way of thinking about schooling. Particularly concerned with students who are disenfranchised and who, without the critical theorists, would have no voice to speak for them, critical theory provides incisive analyses of educational problems.

Multiculturalism

In some ways, multiculturalists have an affinity with the critical theorists. Though critical theory traditionally is more concerned with class, most critical theorists have included race and gender in their analyses and discussions. Multiculturalism, however, deserves its own category as a curriculum ideology because it is rooted in the ethnic revival movements of the 1960s. Whether the purpose is to correct racist and bigoted views of the larger community, to raise children's self-esteem, to help children see themselves from other viewpoints, or to reach the child's psychological world, the multicultural ideology reminds educators that ethnicity must be dealt with by educators.

One major approach to multicultural education has been termed "multiethnic ideology" by James Banks (1988). According to Banks, Americans participate in several cultures—the mainstream along with various ethnic subcultures. Therefore, students ought to have cross-cultural competency. In addition to being able to participate in various cultures, Banks also suggests that when one learns about various cultures, one begins to see oneself from other viewpoints. The multiethnic ideology provides greater self-understanding.

When teaching from a multiethnic perspective, Banks advises that an issue not be taught from a dominant mainstream perspective with other points of view added on. This kind of teaching still suggests that one perspective is the "right one," though others also have their own points of view. Rather, one should approach the concept or theme from various viewpoints. In this case, the mainstream perspective becomes one of several ways of approaching the topic; it is not superior or inferior to other ethnic perspectives. In addition to what takes place in the classroom, Banks also argues that a successful multiethnic school must have system-wide reform. School staff, school policy, the counseling program, assessment, and testing are all affected by the multiethnic ideology.

Cognitive Pluralism

According to Eisner, the idea of cognitive pluralism goes back at least to Aristotle; however, only in the last several decades has a conception of the plurality of knowledge and intelligence been advanced in the field of curriculum (Eisner 1992, 317). In short, cognitive pluralists expand our traditional notions of knowledge and intelligence. Whereas some scientists and educators believe that people possess a single intelligence (often called a "g factor") or that all knowledge can ultimately be written in propositional language, cognitive pluralists believe that people possess numerous intelligences and that knowledge exists in many forms of representation.

As a conception of knowledge, cognitive pluralists argue that symbol systems provide a way to encode visual, auditory, kinesthetic, olfactory, gustatory, and tactile experiences. If, for example, one wants to teach students about the Civil War, cognitive pluralists would want students not only to have knowledge about factual material (names, dates, and battles), but also to have knowledge about how people felt during the war. To know that slavery means by definition the owning of another person appears quite shallow to knowing how it feels to be powerless. Cognitive pluralists suggest students should be able to learn through a variety of forms of representation (e.g., narratives, poetry, film, pictures) and be able to express themselves through a variety of forms as well. The latter point about expression means that most tests, which rely on propositional language, are too limiting. Some students may better express themselves through painting or poetry.

One may also think about cognitive pluralism from the point of view of intelligence. As I mentioned, some scholars suggest that intelligence may be better thought of as multiple rather than singular. Howard Gardner, a leading advocate of this position (1983), argues that, according to his own research and to reviews of a wide array of studies, a theory of multiple intelligences is more viable than a theory about a "g factor." He defines intelligence as follows:

> To my mind, a human intellectual competence must entail a set of skills of problem-solving—enabling the individual to resolve genuine problems or difficulties that he or she encounters and, when appropriate, to create an effective product—and must also entail the potential for finding or creating problems—thereby laying the groundwork for the acquisition of new knowledge. (Gardner 1983, 60–61)

Gardner argues that there are at least seven distinct kinds of human intelligence: linguistic, musical, logical–mathematical, spatial, bodily–kinesthetic, interpersonal, and intrapersonal. If schools aim to enhance cognitive development, then they ought to teach students to be knowledgeable of, and to practice being fluent in, numerous kinds of intelligences. To limit the kinds of knowledge or intelligences students experience indicates an institutional deficiency.

Applying Curriculum Ideologies

While some teachers or schools draw heavily on one particular curriculum ideology (e.g., Ira Shor's use of critical theory in his classroom or Mortimer Adler's ideas in Paideia schools), more often than not, a mixture of various ideologies pervade educational settings. I don't believe this is a problem. What Joseph Schwab said in the late 1960s about theory also applies to ideologies. He argued that theories are partial and incomplete, and that, as something rooted in one's mind rather than in the state of affairs, theories cannot provide a complete guide for classroom practice (1970). In other words, a theory about child development may tell you something about ten-year-olds in general, but not about a particular ten-year-old standing in front of you. Child developmentalists cannot tell you, for example, whether or how to reprimand a given child for failing to do his homework. Schwab suggested one become eclectic and deliberative when working in the practical world. In simpler terms, one should know about various theories and use them when applicable. One does not need to be ideologically pure. One should also reflect upon

one's decisions and talk about them with other people. Through deliberation one makes new decisions which lead to new actions which then cycle around again to reflection, decision, and action.

To understand this eclectic approach to using curriculum ideologies, let's take as an example the use of computers in the classroom. Imagine you are about to be given several computers for your class. How could knowledge of the various curriculum ideologies inform your use of them?

Given this particular challenge, some ideologies will prove to be more useful than others. For example, the rational humanists would probably have little to contribute to this discussion because, with their interests in the cultivation of reason and the seminar process of teaching, computers are not central (though one of my students noted, that, perhaps in time, rational humanists will want to create a "great software" program).

Some developmentalists would consider the issue of when it would be most appropriate to introduce computers to students. Waldorf educators, who base their developmental ideas on the writings of philosopher Rudolf Steiner (1861–1925), do not believe one should teach students about computers at an early age. They would not only take into account students' cognitive development (at what age could students understand computers?), but they would also consider students' social, physical, and emotional development. At what age are students really excited about computers? When are their fingers large enough to work the keyboard? What skills and habits might children lose if they learned computers at too early an age? Is there an optimum age at which one ought to learn computers? Waldorf educators would ask these kinds of developmental questions.

Developmentalists following the ideas of Eleanor Duckworth may also ask the above questions, but whatever the age of the student they are working with, these educators would try to teach the computer to children through engaging interactive activities. Rather than telling students about the computer, teachers would set up activities where students can interact with them. In this orientation, teachers would continue to set up challenges for students to push their thinking. Sustaining students' sense of wonder and curiosity is equally important. In addition to setting new challenges for students, teachers would also monitor student growth by trying to understand student thought processes. In short, rather than fitting the child to the curriculum, the curriculum is fitted to the child.

Reconceptualists' first impulse would be to consider the educational, social, or cultural meaning of computers before worrying about their utility. Of course, one should remember that there isn't one party line for any given ideological perspective. Some reconceptualists may be optimistic about computers and some may not. Although I don't know William Pinar's or Madeleine Grumet's thoughts on computers, I imagine they would reflect on the way computers bring information to people. Pinar observes that place plays a role in the way one sees the world (Pinar 1991). The same machine with the same software can be placed in every school room, but even if students learn the same information, their relationship to this new knowledge will vary. Thus, to understand the impact of computers one needs to know a great deal about the people who will learn from and use them. Having students write autobiographies provides one way to attain this understanding. Students could write about or dramatize their encounters with technology. After such an understanding, teachers can tailor lessons to meet student needs.

Critical theorist Michael Apple has examined the issue of computers in schools. Though he points out that many teachers are delighted with the new technology, he worries about an uncritical acceptance of it. Many teachers, he notes, do not receive substantial information about computers before they are implemented. Consequently, they must rely on a few experts or pre-packaged sets of material. The effects of this situation are serious. With their reliance on purchased material combined with the lack of time to properly review and evaluate it, teachers lose control over the curriculum development process. They become implementers of someone else's plans and procedures and become deskilled and disempowered because of that (Apple 1986, 163).

Apple also worries about the kind of thinking students learn from computers. While students concentrate on manipulating machines, they are concerned with issues of "how" more than "why." Consequently, Apple argues, computers enhance technical but not substantive thinking. Crucial political and ethical understanding atrophies while students are engaged in computer proficiency. Apple does not suggest one avoid computers because of these problems. Rather, he wants

teachers and students to engage in social, political, and ethical discussions while they use the new technology.

Multiculturalists would be concerned that all students have equal access to computers. Early research on computer implementation revealed that many minority students did not have the opportunity to use computers, and when they did, their interaction with computers often consisted of computer-assisted instruction programs that exercised low-level skills (Anderson, Welch, Harris 1984). In addition to raising the issue that all students should have equal access to computers, multiculturalists would also investigate whether software programs were sending biased or racist viewpoints.

Finally, cognitive pluralists, such as Elliot Eisner, would probably focus on the kinds of knowledge made available by computers. If computers were used too narrowly so that students had the opportunity to interact only with words and numbers, Eisner would be concerned. He would point out, I believe, that students could be learning that "real" knowledge exists in two forms. If, however, computers enhance cognitive understanding by providing multiple forms of representation, then I think Eisner would approve of the use of this new technology in the classroom. For example, in the latest videodisc technology, when students look up the definition of a word, they find a written statement as well as a picture. How much more meaningful a picture of a castle is to a young child than the comment, "a fortified residence as of a noble in feudal times" (*Random House Dictionary* 1980, 142).

In addition to learning through a variety of sensory forms, Eisner would also want students to have the opportunity to express themselves in a variety of ways. Computers could be useful in allowing students to reveal their knowledge in visual and musical as well as narrative forms. Students should not be limited in the ways they can express what they know.

Each curriculum ideology offers a unique perspective by virtue of the kinds of values and theories embedded within it. By reflecting on some of the ideas from the various curriculum ideologies and applying them to an educational issue, I believe educators can have a more informed, constructive, and creative dialogue. Moreover, as I said earlier, I do not think one needs to remain ideologically pure. Teachers and curricularists would do well to borrow ideas from the various perspectives as long as they make sure

CURRICULUM IDEOLOGIES

Ideology	Major Proponent	Major Writings	Educational Priorities	Philosophical Beliefs	Teachers, Curriculum, or Schools Expressing Curriculum Ideology	Suggestions for Curriculum Development
Rational Humanism	R. M. Hutchins M. Adler	The Paideia Proposal (Adler 1982) Paideia Problems and Possibilities (Adler 1983) The Paideia Program (Adler 1984)	Teaching through Socratic method. The use of primary texts. No electives.	The best education for the best is the best education for all. Since time in school is short, expose students to the best of Western culture.	Paideia Schools. See Adler (1983) for a list of schools.	Teach students how to facilitate good seminars. Use secondary texts sparingly.
Developmentalism	E. Duckworth R. Steiner	Young Children Reinvent Arithmetic (Kamii 1985) "The Having of Wonderful Ideas" and Other Essays (Duckworth 1987) Rudolf Steiner Education and the Developing Child (Aeppli 1986)	Fit curriculum to child's needs and interests. Inquiry-oriented teaching.	Cognitive structures develop as naturally as walking. If the setting is right, students will raise questions to push their own thinking.	Pat Carini's Prospect School in Burlington, VT.	Allow teachers the opportunity to be surprised. Rather than writing a curriculum manual, prepare a curriculum guide.
Reconceptualism	W. Pinar M. Grumet	Bitter Milk (Grumet 1988) Curriculum Theorizing (Pinar 1975) Curriculum and Instruction (Giroux, Penna, Pinar 1981)	Use philosophy, psychology, and literature to understand the human experience. Provide an "education for having" and an "education for being."	One learns through experience. We can learn to understand experience through phenomenology, psychoanalysis, and literature.	See Oliver (1990) for a curriculum in accordance with reconceptualist thinking.	Write lesson plans without the use of objectives. Curriculum writers ought to reveal their individual subjectivities.
Critical Theory	M. Apple I. Shor P. Freire	Ideology and Curriculum (Apple 1979) Teachers and Texts (Apple 1986) Pedagogy of the Oppressed (Freire 1970) Freire for the Classroom (Shor 1987)	Equal opportunities for all students. Teaching should entail critical reflection.	A just society maximizes the advantage for the least advantages. Schools are part of the larger community and must be analyzed as such.	See Shor's edited text (1987) for a number of ideas on implementing critical theory.	Curriculum writers ought to examine their own working assumptions critically and ought to respect the integrity of teachers and students.
Multiculturalism	J. Banks E. King	Multiethnic Education (Banks 1988) Multicultural Education (Banks and Banks 1989)	Students should learn to participate in various cultures. Approach concept or theme from various viewpoints.	Students need to feel good about their ethnic identities. All people participate in various cultures and subcultures.	See King (1990) for a workbook of activities teaching ethnic and gender awareness.	Make sure that text and pictures represent a variety of cultures.
Cognitive Pluralism	E. Eisner H. Gardner	"Curriculum Ideologies" (Eisner 1992) The Educational Imagination (Eisner 1985) Frames of Mind (Gardner 1983)	Teach, and allow students to express themselves, through a variety of forms of representation. Allow students to develop numerous intelligences.	Our senses cue into and pick up different aspects of the world. Combined with our individual history and general schemata, our senses allow us to construct meaning.	The Key School in Indianapolis.	Curriculum lesson plans and units ought to be aesthetically pleasing in appearance. Curriculum ought to represent a variety of ways of knowing

they are not proposing contradictory ideas.

The chart on page 11 summarizes the major proponents, major writings, educational priorities, and philosophical beliefs of each curriculum ideology covered in this chapter. (Of course, this chart is not comprehensive. I encourage the reader to examine the recommended reading list for further works in each of these areas.) In the fifth column, "Teachers, Curriculum, or Schools Expressing Curriculum Ideology," I indicate places or texts where readers may learn more. One could visit a Paideia school, Carini's Prospect School, or the Key School in Indianapolis. One may read about reconceptualism, critical theory, and multiculturalism in the listed texts. Finally, in the sixth column, "Suggestions for Curriculum Development," I also include interesting points found in the literature but not necessarily contained in this chapter.

Recommended Reading

The following is a concise list of recommended reading in many of the areas discussed in this chapter. Full bibliographic citations are provided under *References*.

Some general **curriculum textbooks** that are invaluable are John D. McNeil's *Curriculum: A Comprehensive Introduction* (1990); William H. Schubert's *Curriculum: Perspective, Paradigm, and Possibility* (1986); Decker Walker's *Fundamentals of Curriculum* (1990); and Robert S. Zais's *Curriculum: Principles and Foundations* (1976). These books provide wonderful introductions to the field.

The recently published *Handbook of Research on Curriculum* (Jackson 1992) includes thirty-four articles by leading curricularists. This book is a must for anyone interested in research in curriculum.

For a discussion of **objectives** in education, Tyler (1949) is seminal. Also see Kapfer (1972) and Mager (1962). Bloom refines educational objectives into a taxonomy (1956). Eisner's (1985) critique of educational objectives and his notion of expressive outcomes will be welcomed by those who are skeptical of the objectives movement.

Good books on the **history of curriculum** include Kliebard (1986), Schubert (1980), and Tanner and Tanner (1975). Seguel (1966), who discusses the McMurry brothers, Dewey, Bobbitt, and Rugg, among others, is also very good.

Some excellent books on the **history of**

education include the following: Lawrence Cremin's definitive book on progressive education, *The Transformation of the School: Progressivism in American Education, 1876–1957* (1961). David Tyack's *The One Best System* (1974) portrays the evolution of schools into their modern formation; and Larry Cuban's *How Teachers Taught: Constancy and Change in American Classrooms, 1890–1980* (1984) examines what actually happened in classrooms during a century of reform efforts. Philip Jackson's "Conceptions of Curriculum and Curriculum Specialists" (1992) provides an excellent summary of the evolution of curriculum thought from Bobbitt and Tyler to Schwab.

For works in each of the ideologies I recommend the following:

To help one understand the **rational humanist** approach, there are Mortimer Adler's three books on the **Paideia school**: *The Paideia Proposal: An Educational Manifesto* (1982), *Paideia Problems and Possibilities* (1983), and *The Paideia Program: An Educational Syllabus* (1984). Seven critical reviews of the Paideia proposal comprise "The Paideia Proposal: A Symposium" (1983).

For works in **developmentalism** based on Piaget's ideas see Duckworth (1987, 1991) and Kamii (1985). Among Piaget's many works you may want to read *The Origins of Intelligence* (1966). If you are interested in Waldorf education see Robert McDermott's *The Essential Steiner* (1984) and P. Bruce Uhrmacher's "Waldorf Schools Marching Quietly Unheard" (1991). Willi Aeppli's *Rudolf Steiner Education and the Developing Child* (1986), Francis Edmunds's *Rudolf Steiner Education* (1982), and Marjorie Spock's *Teaching as a Lively Art* (1985) are also quite good.

A general overview of the developmental approach to curriculum can be found on pages 49–52 of Linda Darling-Hammond and Jon Snyder's "Curriculum Studies and the Traditions of Inquiry: The Scientific Tradition" (1922).

Two books are essential for examining **reconceptualist** writings: William Pinar's *Curriculum Theorizing: The Reconceptualists* (1975) and Henry Giroux, Anthony N. Penna, and William F. Pinar's *Curriculum and Instruction* (1981). Recent books in reconceptualism include William Pinar and William Reynolds's *Understanding Curriculum as Phenomenological and Deconstructed Text* (1992), and William Pinar and Joe L. Kincheloe's *Curriculum as Social Psychoanalysis: The Significance of Place* (1991).

Some excellent works in **critical theory** include Paulo Freire's *Pedagogy of the Oppressed* (1970) and *The Politics of Education* (1985). Apple's works are also excellent; see *Ideology and Curriculum* (1979) and *Teachers and Texts* (1986). For an overview of the Frankfurt School and the application of Jürgen Habermas's ideas, see Robert Young's *A Critical Theory of Education: Habermas and Our Children's Future* (1990).

For an application of critical theory to classrooms see the Ira Shor–edited book, *Freire for the Classroom* (1987) with an afterword by Paulo Freire.

In **multicultural education** I recommend James Banks's *Multiethnic Education: Theory and Practice* (1988) and Banks and Banks's *Multicultural Education: Issues and Perspectives* (1989). Also see Gibson (1984) for an account of five different approaches to multicultural education. Nicholas Appleton (1983), Saracho and Spodek (1983), and Simonson and Walker (1988) are also important. Edith King's *Teaching Ethnic and Gender Awareness: Methods and Materials for the Elementary School* (1990) provides useful ideas about multicultural education that could be used in the classroom. John Ogbu's work (1987) on comparing immigrant populations to involuntary minorities is also an important work with serious educational implications.

Important works in the field of **cognitive pluralism** include Elliot Eisner (1982, 1985, 1992) and Howard Gardner (1983, 1991). Some philosophical texts that influenced both of these men include Dewey (1934), Goodman (1978), and Langer (1976).

For $20.00, the Key School Option Program will send you an interdisciplinary theme-based curriculum report. For more information write Indianapolis Public Schools, 1401 East Tenth Street, Indianapolis, Indiana 46201.

Glossary of Some Common Usages of Curriculum

delivered curriculum: what teachers deliver in the classroom. This is opposed to Intended curriculum. Same as operational curriculum.

enacted curriculum: actual class offerings by a school, as opposed to courses listed in books or guides. *See* official curriculum.

experienced curriculum: what students actually learn. Same as received curriculum.

explicit curriculum: stated aims and goals of a classroom or school.

hidden curriculum: unintended, unwritten, tacit, or latent aspects of messages given to students by teachers, school structures, textbooks, and other school resources. For example, while students learn writing or math, they may also learn about punctuality, neatness, competition, and conformity. Concealed messages may be intended or unintended by the school or teacher.

implicit curriculum: similar to the hidden curriculum in the sense that something is implied rather than expressly stated. Whereas the hidden curriculum usually refers to something unfavorable, negative, or sinister, the implicit curriculum also takes into account unstated qualities that are positive.

intended curriculum: that which is planned by the teacher or school.

null curriculum: that which does not take place in the school or classroom. What is not offered cannot be learned. Curricular exclusion tells a great deal about a school's values.

official curriculum: courses listed in the school catalogue or course bulletin. Although these classes are listed, they may not be taught. *See* enacted curriculum.

operational curriculum: events that take place in the classroom. Same as delivered curriculum.

received curriculum: what students acquire as a result of classroom activity. Same as experienced curriculum.

References

Adler, Mortimer J. 1982. *The Paideia Proposal: An Educational Manifesto*. New York: Collier Books.

———. 1983. *Paideia Problems and Possibilities*. New York: Collier Books.

———. 1984. *The Paideia Program: An Educational Syllabus*. New York: Collier Books.

Aeppli, Willi. 1986. *Rudolf Steiner Education and the Developing Child.* Hudson, NY: Anthroposophic Press.

Anderson, Ronald E., Wayne W. Welch, and Linda J. Harris. 1984. "Inequities in Opportunities for Computer Literacy." *The Computing Teacher: The Journal of the International Council for Computers in Education* 11(8):10–12.

Apple, Michael W. 1979. *Ideology and Curriculum.* Boston: Routledge and Kegan Paul.

———. 1986. *Teachers and Texts: A Political Economy of Class and Gender Relations in Education.* New York: Routledge and Kegan Paul.

Appleton, Nicholas. 1983. *Cultural Pluralism in Education.* White Plains, NY: Longman.

Banks, James A. 1988. *Multiethnic Education: Theory and Practice.* 2d ed. Boston: Allyn and Bacon.

Banks, James A., and Cherry A. McGee Banks, eds. 1989. *Multicultural Education: Issues and Perspectives.* Boston: Allyn and Bacon.

Bloom, Benjamin S., ed. 1956. *Taxonomy of Educational Objectives: The Classification of Educational Goals, Handbook 1: Cognitive Domain.* New York: McKay.

Bobbitt, Franklin. 1918. *The Curriculum.* Boston: Houghton Mifflin.

Cremin, Lawrence A. 1961. *The Transformation of the School: Progressivism in American Education, 1876–1957.* New York: Vintage Books.

———. 1977. *Traditions of American Education.* New York: Basic Books.

Cuban, Larry. 1984. *How Teachers Taught: Constancy and Change in American Classrooms 1890–1980.* White Plains, NY: Longman.

Darling-Hammond, Linda, and Jon Snyder. 1992. "Curriculum Studies and the Traditions of Inquiry: The Scientific Tradition." In *Handbook of Research on Curriculum: A Project of the American Educational Research Association,* ed. Philip W. Jackson, 41–78. New York: Macmillan.

Dewey, John. 1934. *Art as Experience.* New York: Minton, Balch.

Duckworth, Eleanor. 1987. *"The Having of Wonderful Ideas" and Other Essays on Teaching and Learning.* New York: Teachers College Press.

———. 1991. "Twenty-four, Forty-two, and I Love You: Keeping It Complex. *Harvard Educational Review* 61(1):1–24.

Edmunds, L. Francis. 1982. *Rudolf Steiner Education.* 2d ed. London: Rudolf Steiner Press.

Eisner, Elliot W. 1982. *Cognition and Curriculum: A Basis for Deciding What to Teach.* White Plains, NY: Longman.

———. 1985. *The Educational Imagination.* 2d ed. New York: Macmillan.

———. 1992. "Curriculum Ideologies." In *Handbook of Research on Curriculum: A Project of the American Educational Research Association,* ed. Philip W. Jackson, 302–26. New York: Macmillan.

Freire, Paulo. 1970. *Pedagogy of the Oppressed.* Trans. Myra Bergman Ramos. New York: Seabury Press.

———. 1985. *The Politics of Education.* Trans. Donaldo Macedo. South Hadley, MA: Bergin and Garvey.

Gardner, Howard. 1983. *Frames of Mind.* New York: Basic Books.

———. 1991. *The Unschooled Mind: How Children Think and How Schools Should Teach.* New York: Basic Books.

Gibson, Margaret Alison. 1984. "Approaches to Multicultural Education in the United States: Some Concepts and Assumptions." *Anthropology and Education Quarterly* 15:94–119.

Giroux, Henry, Anthony N. Penna, and William F. Pinar. 1981. *Curriculum and Instruction: Alternatives in Education.* Berkeley: McCutchan.

Good, Thomas S., and Jere E. Brophy. 1986. *Educational Psychology.* 3d ed. White Plains, NY: Longman.

Goodman, Nelson. 1978. *Ways of Worldmaking.* Indianapolis: Hackett.

Greene, Maxine. 1988a. "Vocation and Care: Obsessions about Teacher Education." Panel discussion at the Annual Meeting of the American Educational Research Association, 5–9 April, New Orleans.

———. 1988b. *The Dialectic of Freedom.* New York: Teachers College Press.

Gress, James R. 1978. *Curriculum: An Introduction to the Field.* Berkeley: McCutchan.

Grumet, Madeleine R. 1988. *Bitter Milk: Women and Teaching.* Amherst: Univ. of Massachusetts Press.

Jackson, Philip W. 1992. "Conceptions of Curriculum and Curriculum Specialists." In *Handbook of Research on Curriculum: A Project of the American Educational Research Association,* ed. Philip W. Jackson, 3–40. New York: Macmillan.

Kamii, Constance Kazuko, with Georgia DeClark. 1985. *Young Children Reinvent*

Arithmetic: Implications of Piaget's Theory. New York: Teachers College Press.

Kapfer, Miriam B. 1972. *Behavioral Objectives in Curriculum Development: Selected Readings and Bibliography.* Englewood Cliffs, NJ: Educational Technology.

King, Edith W. 1990. *Teaching Ethnic and Gender Awareness: Methods and Materials for the Elementary School.* Dubuque, IA: Kendall/Hunt.

Kliebard, Herbert M. 1986. *The Struggle for the American Curriculum, 1893–1958.* Boston: Routledge and Kegan Paul.

Langer, Susanne. 1976. *Problems of Art.* New York: Scribners.

McDermott, Robert A., ed. 1984. *The Essential Steiner.* San Francisco: Harper & Row.

McLaren, Peter. 1986. *Schooling as a Ritual Performance: Towards a Political Economy of Educational Symbols and Gestures.* London: Routledge and Kegan Paul.

McNeil, John D. 1990. *Curriculum: A Comprehensive Introduction.* 4th ed. Glenview, IL: Scott, Foresman/Little, Brown Higher Education.

Mager, Robert. 1962. *Preparing Instructional Objectives.* Palo Alto, CA: Fearon.

Ogbu, John. 1987. "Variability in Minority School Performance: A Problem in Search of an Explanation." *Anthropology and Education Quarterly* 18(4): 312–34.

Oliver, Donald W. 1990. "Grounded Knowing: A Postmodern Perspective on Teaching and Learning." *Educational Leadership* 48(1): 64-69.

"The Paideia Proposal: A Symposium." 1983. *Harvard Educational Review* 53 (4): 377–411.

Piaget, Jean. 1962. *Play, Dreams and Imitation in Childhood.* New York: Norton.

———. 1966. *Origins of Intelligence.* New York: Norton.

Pinar, William F., ed. 1975. *Curriculum Theorizing: The Reconceptualists.* Berkeley: McCutchan.

Pinar, William F., and Joe L. Kincheloe, eds. 1991. *Curriculum as Social Psychoanalysis: The Significance of Place.* Albany: State Univ. of New York Press.

Pinar, William F., and William M. Reynolds, eds. 1992. *Understanding Curriculum as Phenomenological and Deconstructed Text.* New York: Teachers College Press.

The Random House Dictionary. 1980. New York: Ballantine.

Saracho, Olivia N., and Bernard Spodek. 1983. *Understanding the Multicultural Experience in Early Childhood Education.* Washington, DC: National Association for the Education of Young Children.

Schubert, William H. 1980. *Curriculum Books: The First Eight Years.* Lanham, MD: Univ. Press of America.

———. 1986. *Curriculum: Perspective, Paradigm, and Possibility.* New York: Macmillan.

Schwab, Joseph J. 1970. *The Practical: A Language for Curriculum.* Washington, DC: National Education Association.

Seguel, M. L. 1966. *The Curriculum Field: Its Formative Years.* New York: Teachers College Press.

Shor, Ira, ed. 1987. *Freire for the Classroom: A Sourcebook for Liberatory Teaching.* Portsmouth, NH: Heinemann.

Simonson, Rick, and Scott Walker, eds. 1988. *The Graywolf Annual Five: Multi-Cultural Literacy.* St. Paul, MN: Graywolf Press.

Spock, Marjorie. 1985. *Teaching as a Lively Art.* Hudson, NY: Anthroposophic Press.

Taba, Hilda. 1962. *Curriculum Development: Theory and Practice.* New York: Harcourt Brace Jovanovich.

Tanner, Daniel, and Laurel N. Tanner. 1975. *Curriculum Development: Theory into Practice.* New York: Macmillan.

Tietze, Wolfgang. 1987. "A Structural Model for the Evaluation of Preschool Effects." *Early Childhood Research Quarterly* 2(2): 133–59.

Tyack, David B. 1974. *The One Best System: A History of American Urban Education.* Cambridge: Harvard Univ. Press.

Tyler, Ralph W. 1949. *Basic Principles of Curriculum and Instruction.* Chicago: Univ. of Chicago Press.

Uhrmacher, P. Bruce. 1991. "Waldorf Schools Marching Quietly Unheard." Ph.D. diss., Stanford University.

Walker, Decker. 1990. *Fundamentals of Curriculum.* New York: Harcourt Brace Jovanovich.

Young, Robert. 1990. *A Critical Theory of Education: Habermas and Our Children's Future.* New York: Teachers College Press.

Zais, Robert S. 1976. *Curriculum: Principles and Foundations.* New York: Thomas Y. Crowell.

RECURRING THEMES AND CURRENT ISSUES

Helen Freidus
Graduate Faculty
Bank Street College of Education, New York, New York

W HEN we are young, we rarely question the methods by which we are taught, nor do we wonder who decides what we should learn in school. We see curriculum and the ways it is implemented as "the way things are." It is only when we grow older and begin to sense the all-pervasive influence of education that we are likely to question how schools are organized or curriculum is shaped. We soon realize that curriculum and methodology are parts of society created by and for the communities in which they exist. We see that education is a social institution; we recognize that the form and content of curriculum are intertwined with the social and intellectual values of the people they serve. They are shaped by political and economic concerns and molded by physical and ideological realities. We learn that this is as true of early childhood curriculum as it is of the curriculum of universities. Whether early childhood education is considered play or work, a safe, warm place to be until real learning begins, or a place where real learning is ongoing, is directly related to a community's vision of children and of learning. Early childhood curriculum is grounded in the thoughts and needs of the times. This is true today and was true in times past.

The Beginning of Early Childhood Education: Johann Heinrich Pestalozzi

There was a time when cities were in decay. Family structures had broken apart, leaving the adult population unable to assume its traditional responsibilities to the young. Poverty and destruction seemed to exist everywhere. Large numbers of children were forming together in bands, looting and pillaging for survival. The government, believing that hope lay in the future of the young people, called for educational reform.

This description, sounding so much like the plight of urban centers in today's world, refers to the Swiss city of Stans during the last decade of the eighteenth century. Religious wars had decimated the country. The quality of life was abysmal. Then, as has happened in times of turmoil throughout history, hope was placed in the education of young children. In this case, the educational visionary who came forth was Johann Heinrich Pestalozzi (1746–1827), the "grandfather" of modern early childhood education.

Pestalozzi was the intellectual heir to Rousseau and Locke (Weber 1984). Like Rousseau, he believed that children were naturally good; they became corrupt through the influence of society. The role of education was to nurture and preserve this innate innocence. To do this, teachers must break with the traditional methodology of rote learning and look to the spontaneous activities of the child as seeds for curriculum. They must acknowledge and nurture individual differences. Just as gardeners must respect the inherent qualities of the plants with which they work, teachers must respect the needs and concerns of their students. Only in this way can their innate goodness and beauty bloom.

Pestalozzi's vision of education did not suggest that children should be allowed to pursue their individual paths. His methodology was quite teacher-directed, and the substance of curriculum was the same for one and all. However, within this teacher-directed curriculum, there was room for individual differences in experience, style, and pacing. Pestalozzi sought to create an educational environment in which diversity added interest but in which the primary focus was on the whole community.

Individuals, according to Pestalozzi, may be ignorant without being degenerate. Social reform could be attained by helping children to help themselves. This, in turn, would facilitate their ability to become economically self-sufficient when the time came for them to make their way in the world. To reach these goals, education must address the moral, intellectual, and physical needs of the child. By "moral," Pestalozzi meant what we would consider the affective, social, and emotional needs of the child. By "intellectual," he referred to what we would consider cognitive development. Pestalozzi was the first to see that the nature and needs of the child must bear a direct influence on the form and substance of curriculum.

In his novel, *How Gertrude Teaches Her Children,* published in 1801, Pestalozzi articulated his belief that the roots of moral education lie in the parent–child relationship.

Education begins in the home; emotional security and moral instruction, coupled with a well-established work ethic, enable children to resist the evils of society. Only those children with strong moral foundations are likely to become successful members of their communities. For children who do not have parents or whose parents cannot fulfill these needs, schools must fill the gap. In order to break the chain of socially induced degeneracy, schools need to incorporate the dynamics of successful mother–child relationships.

Pestalozzi practiced what he preached. He turned his farm into a school for fifty poor children aged 6–18. By teaching vocational skills in a family atmosphere, he worked to develop self-respect and independence in his students. He led the school not as a pedantic but as a loving father. This role was consonant with the views of his Pietist religion, but was unheard of in the field of eighteenth-century education. His first effort failed for economic reasons, but served as the foundation for his later schools in Stans, Burgdorf, and Yverdon.

In all of his schools, Pestalozzi developed and implemented instructional methodology that was in accord with his respect for the nature of the child and his philosophy of life and learning. He saw childhood as a uniquely valuable stage of development. He saw the world as a continuity of experience, "a widening circle of mankind." Knowledge of the immediate world formed the basis for higher-level understandings. Learning from the home was encompassed in the environment of the school, the school in the community, the community in the state, ad infinitum. Learning about that which was near and concrete spiraled into abstract learning. With these principles in mind, Pestalozzi believed instruction must follow a specific sequence. It must progress from the simple to the complex, the concrete to the abstract, the gross to the fine, and the specific to the general.

The format Pestalozzi used was called the "object lesson." It always included three elements: form, number, and language. An object lesson might take the form of a trip to the woods for the purpose of collecting leaves. Form would involve observation of the leaves, sorting and classification, noting consistencies and variations. Number would involve counting the leaves, placing them in sets, identifying and numbering the parts, the points, the colors on a given leaf or groups of leaves. Language would involve discussions of the leaves, articulating observations, and connecting these observations to prior knowledge. Students would then return to the classroom and write in their notebooks about their learning. Throughout the process, the search for patterns predominated. Pestalozzi's world view of a universe created in harmony and order and his principles of instruction were consistent.

Embedded in the philosophy and curriculum of Pestalozzi's schools we see many of today's concerns about the form and content of early childhood education. How to make classrooms meet the needs of the whole child, how to make learning developmentally appropriate without sacrificing the substance of academic content and skills, how to identify and meet individual needs, how to integrate curriculum across the content areas, how to acknowledge and incorporate the role of parents in early childhood classrooms are all questions that fill the pages of current popular and educational journals. Many of the responses are very similar to those demonstrated by Pestalozzi two hundred years ago.

The Father of Early Childhood Education: Friedrich Froebel

Pestalozzi's influence on education is of great significance. However, he left no explicit body of writing that systematically described his philosophy and practice. Much of what we know about his work has been gleaned from the writings of philosophers and educators who visited his schools. Perhaps the most notable of these is Friedrich Froebel (1782–1852), considered by many to be the father of early childhood education.

Froebel combined the optimism of the Enlightenment with the spirit of nineteenth-century German romanticism. From the former he took the belief that through scientific knowledge all things could be possible. From the latter he took a belief in the harmony and interconnectedness of the universe and all its parts, a belief in the doctrine of idealism, and a

little bit of mysticism. Together these shaped his vision of children and his philosophy of education. His curriculum, like that of Pestalozzi, emerged from a sense of connection with nature that was both scientific in its emphasis on observation and spiritual in its interpretations (MacCormac 1991).

Froebel was an innatist, believing in the doctrine of preformation so widely espoused in the religious and philosophical writings of nineteenth-century Germany. He saw children, like plants, coming into this world holding the seeds of their own later development. He believed that when the emerging capacities of children were acknowledged and exercised, they might attain higher and higher levels of physical, moral, and intellectual development. It was the teacher's role to stimulate this growth, to enable children to become aware of and able to use that which they understood intuitively.

Froebel was the first to recognize that the learning styles of young children were unique and to design and implement a curriculum utilizing materials and methods directly related to his perceptions of their needs and interests (Williams 1987). Many of his methods were adapted from Pestalozzi, but Pestalozzi had worked with children of all ages. For these reasons, it is Froebel who is considered to be the father of early childhood education.

Play was the medium of instruction in Froebel's curriculum. It was not play as generally perceived in today's world. The goal was not free expression of inner thoughts and needs, but, rather, active engagement with materials in order that prior knowledge might be demonstrated and new learning pursued. Play meant the use of manipulative materials through which children might observe, imitate, and reconstruct the instruction of their teachers. Rigid as this definition of play might sound by today's standards, it was revolutionary in the nineteenth-century classroom. Even more revolutionary was Froebel's intent that play as a medium of instruction would bring joy into the classroom.

Manipulative materials were designed by Froebel as vehicles through which children's implicit understanding of universal principles could be made explicit. These manipulatives took the form of a carefully sequenced set of ten "Gifts," a set of geometric forms made from natural materials. The Gifts were enriched by an equally carefully sequenced set of "Occupations," a series of handwork projects involving such materials as clay, lacing, paperfolding and -cutting, parquetry, and weaving. Each activity in which these materials were used built on the prior activity. Children reinforced prior learning by identifying familiar shapes and patterns, comparing and contrasting new learning with prior knowledge, and making connections to the world at large. They used the same materials over and over in order to develop increasingly higher levels of cognitive sophistication.

Gifts were used in three carefully prescribed series of activities. Through Forms of Life, children used the blocks to build objects from the everyday world. They created tables, chairs, houses, churches, and many other concrete forms found in the real world. Through Forms of Knowledge, children applied mathematical reasoning. They created geometric shapes, had opportunities for counting and making calculations, and paid careful attention to pattern recognition. Through Forms of Beauty, children made symmetrical designs embodying the principles of symmetry, proportion, rhythm, and balance. For each activity, children were expected to observe, imitate, and reconstruct that which their teacher modeled. They analyzed and synthesized their accomplishments on an ongoing basis. This process was intended to help them recognize the interconnectedness of all things.

> In life we find no isolation. One part of the cube, therefore, must never be left apart from or without relation to the whole. The child will thus become accustomed to treat all things in life as bearing a certain relation to one another. (Boelte and Drauss in MacCormac 1991, 102)

Continuity and order pervaded every aspect of Froebel's curriculum, both in theory and implementation. Froebel saw the goal of education as the development of the children's understandings of themselves and their relationship to the members of their families, their community, the natural and external world, and God. Home and school must work together; their teachings were mutually supportive. The first gifts were designed to be used by mothers in the warm environment of their homes. In

kindergarten, these activities would be reinforced by teachers who were viewed as extensions of their students' mothers. Valuing a mother's role as teacher, Froebel created a place for women in the teaching profession, a profession that had historically been the province of men. In so doing, he acknowledged nurturing as an essential component of early childhood education.

The symbol of continuity in myth and art has always been the circle. With this in mind, the circle became an important part of the Froebelian kindergarten. Circle time and circle games originated in Froebel's classrooms. The valuing of harmony, the cultivation of the senses, and cultural awareness made music, art, and story telling important tools for classroom learning. Games provided opportunities for the cultivation of skills as well as for the development of community. Classrooms were large open spaces with adjacent grassy areas and gardens where children could learn about their environment. Elizabeth Palmer Peabody brought Froebel's teachings to the U.S. in the 1860s. Here, these activities were adapted into the mainstream of early childhood education (Roopnarine and Johnson 1987).

In the U.S., the Froebelian kindergarten flourished for several decades. However, removed from the social and cultural environment in which it was rooted and having no leader with the charismatic nature of the man who had formulated both its theory and methodology, the Froebelian kindergarten gradually began to lose its driving energy. Many of its practices became increasingly formalized, and the importance of child and community as center of the curriculum was forgotten. Gradually, there came a call for early childhood curriculum and materials that were more relevant to the world of the twentieth-century child. At the same time, educational theorists began to advocate a new form of instructional methodology, one that was less teacher-directed, one that allowed for greater nurturance of individual differences and democratic values. By the turn of the century, the Froebelian kindergarten was considered outdated. However, it left behind a legacy of materials and practice as well as a vision of the capabilities of the young child that have continued to influence early childhood practice to this day.

Maria Montessori: Origins of the Montessori Method

The educational influence of Froebel was felt not only in Germany and the United States but throughout Europe and Asia as well. Maria Montessori (1870–1952) observed Froebel's schools and shared his concern for the education of the whole child. Like Froebel, she saw the child as innately good, the process of learning as a process of unfolding, and the key to this unfolding as self-activity through play in which self-discipline, independence, and self-direction could be attained (Spodek, Saracho, and Davis 1991). However, in 1859, a book was published that changed the nature of intellectual thought. *The Origin of Species* irrevocably altered the way scholars viewed the natural world. With Darwin's discoveries came a change in the vision of childhood. No longer did theorists depend solely on philosophy and religion for insights into the nature and needs of children. Henceforth, the study of children and the philosophy of education would be greatly influenced by scientific methodology.

Montessori was a physician by training. She spent time during her studies at the psychiatric clinic of Rome and at city asylums for the insane. There, she began to work with mentally retarded children using sensorimotor materials and techniques developed by Itard and Seguin, two pioneers in the education of severely mentally and sensory-impaired children. Her efforts to teach them reading and writing were so successful that these "idiots" from the asylum outscored the majority of "normal children" on state tests. This experience proved to be a watershed in Montessori's career; she found a new calling in the world of education. If impaired children could learn so successfully using a sensorimotor approach, it stood to reason, according to Montessori, that all children might come closer to fulfilling their potential through a similar form of education. The key to success could be found in a program that respected children and their innate abilities, a program that provided "Liberty in a Prepared Environment" (Montessori in Orem 1965, 25). Bringing from her medical training an awareness of the importance of careful observation and insight into the connections between health and performance, Montessori devoted herself to the education of the whole child.

In 1899, Montessori was given the opportunity to put her ideas into practice. She accepted the offer made by officials of Rome to direct an experimental school, Casa Dei Bambini ("House of Children"), located in a housing project within the slums of Rome. The area was plagued by the problems of poverty that characterized the Industrial Revolution. Parents working all day in factories left their children to the streets. Unsupervised, they ran in all directions, fighting and destroying property. Here Montessori began to develop her first program for young children, "not simply a place where the children are kept, not just an asylum, but a true school for their education with methods inspired by the rational principles of scientific pedagogy" (Montessori in Hunt 1964).

Montessori's educational practice emerged from her theory of child development. She saw children as going through different stages characterized by different forms of intellectual and emotional sensitivity. Two of these stages applied to early childhood; these stages serve as the foundation for all subsequent growth and development. The years from birth to three she describes as a period of intense physical, emotional, and intellectual growth at the unconscious level. She sees this growth as becoming conscious during the years from three to six. These are years when children have an extraordinarily high degree of "sensitivity" to sensorial stimulation. It is a time when active engagement in motor skills and use of the senses as pathways to intellectual development are most important (Carter in Roopnarine and Johnson 1987; Williams 1984b).

Children's natural interest in learning, their need and right to develop at different rates, and their need to be independent from the very earliest stages of development are fundamental aspects of Montessori's philosophy. Her curriculum and methodology were developed in accord with a series of principles clearly related to her practice:

1. Children are capable of sustained mental concentration when truly interested in their work.

2. Children prefer order and enjoy repetition of actions they have already mastered.
3. Children prefer work to play.
4. Children do not need rewards and punishments to motivate them when the environment is properly structured.
5. The child has a profound sense of personal dignity that is easily offended. (Standing in Williams 1984b)

Montessori transformed her philosophy into forms of instruction through careful observation of individual children and groups of children.

"In the 'Children's Houses,' the old-time teacher, who wore herself out maintaining discipline of immobility, and who wasted her breath in loud and continual discourse, has disappeared" (Montessori in Hunt 1964, 370). The role of the teacher, according to Montessori, was not that of disciplinarian or taskmaster but that of guide. The teacher helps children to help themselves by carefully preparing the learning environment, modeling appropriate practice, and using specifically designed, carefully sequenced "didactic" materials. "Didactic," to Montessori, meant materials that are self-teaching and self-correcting. The teacher provides instruction by demonstrating how materials are to be used. Very few words are used in this process. The child is then asked to imitate the teacher's model. If he or she has problems in doing this, the teacher simply repeats the instruction or introduces a different material. There is no need to point out errors; when the child is developmentally ready to learn, the teacher's model and the sensory input of the materials will enable the child to correct errors and identify success. Once materials have been introduced, children are free to pick and choose their activities according to individual needs and interests.

Montessori's classroom was the first to look at things from a child's perspective. Everything was scaled to the size of the child. Neatly organized low tables and chairs where children could sit and work with their feet firmly reaching the floor, mats on which they could organize their floor work, low shelves where children could reach attractively displayed materials without the help of a teacher, and sideboards where they could prepare their own snacks invited children to engage in and take

responsibility for their own learning. The respect manifested by the thoughtfulness with which the teacher prepared the classroom and the neat patterns in which things were laid out was intended to encourage the children to act courteously toward each other, to care and interact with the environment, and to respect accuracy and order in their own work.

The physical layout of the classroom reflected the division of the curriculum into four major areas: motor education, sensory education, language education, and academic learning. In the area devoted to motor education, one found activities related to "practical life." Here children practiced buttoning, pouring rice from one container to another, and polishing shoes. They learned to sweep floors, polish glass, and wash soiled classroom objects as well as to take care of plants and animals. In so doing, they increased their self-sufficiency and developed self-esteem as they increased their mastery of fine motor skills.

The area of sensory education included an array of intriguing materials, each designed to train one of the five senses. Many materials were designed so that they might be taken apart and reassembled. Others required children to match objects that contributed to the development of concepts of form, size, color, weight, and texture. Frequently, materials were designed to focus a child's attention on subtle gradations of the sensory stimuli. Color tablets were sequenced from darkest to lightest, sound cylinders were organized from loudest to softest, and the pink tower was created from carefully proportioned blocks ordered from large to small. In each case, Montessori believed that the child would develop his or her observation skills while developing the ability to recognize and use all five senses in a careful, methodical way.

The curriculum of language development in Montessori's classroom was very different from that of language arts in today's early childhood curriculum. No formal efforts were made to teach children language, nor were children encouraged to talk among themselves as they worked. Language was tightly focused on articulation of the sensory experiences. Language lessons had three parts. In the first part, the teacher identified the essential quality of the activity. For example, shaking a sound cylinder, she would say, "This is loud." In the second part of the lesson, she would say to the child, "Please give me the loud cylinder." By the child's response, she could observe his or her ability to recognize the quality. Finally, she would ask, "What is this?" The child would then respond, "This is a loud cylinder." The child's response here demonstrated awareness of the sensory quality and the ability to label the quality accurately. These three areas of the curriculum—motor, sensory, and language— were seen as underpinnings of the academic curriculum consisting of reading, writing, and arithmetic. Each of the academic components of the curriculum was taught through equally systematic, carefully sequenced instruction.

During the first half of this century, the Montessori curriculum was much criticized by many influential American early childhood educators. They objected to the lack of opportunities for free play, the limited opportunities for language development, and the adherence to a predetermined sequence of activities, all perceived as stifling the creativity and emotional development of the young child. As with Froebel, they felt that the Montessori curriculum was not relevant to the world of the modern American child.

However, the 1960s saw a significant resurgence of interest in Montessori methods and materials that continues today. Many Montessori schools in the U.S. have modified the form and content of the traditional Montessori curriculum. In the classrooms of these schools, one finds more opportunities for dramatic play, a much broader range of activities related to language development, and a more diverse array of materials, including many that foster collaborative play. These modifications have been made in response to the findings of contemporary educational research, and they maintain the Montessori vision of early childhood education within the context of the changing world of the twentieth century.

Montessori materials are not limited to Montessori schools. They can be found in many early childhood settings where children are actively engaged in their own learning and where autonomy is a goal. Whether or not one accepts Montessori's philosophy, one cannot underestimate the contributions, both in form and structure, that Montessori has made to the world of early childhood education.

John Dewey: Progressivism and Social Change

At the beginning of the twentieth century, John Dewey (1859–1952) began to shape a new theory of education, one that departed significantly from the theories of his predecessors. Born in New England and educated at the universities of this country, Dewey belonged to the world of American intellectual thought. He shared the vision of G. Stanley Hall and the Child Study Movement that observation must be a primary tool for understanding and educating young children, the belief of the "reform Darwinists" that education could and should be an instrument of social change, and the faith of the Transcendentalists in the importance of humanistic values. Dewey became a strong critic of existing models of early childhood education, including those of Froebel and Montessori. He saw how quickly and dramatically the world was changing. Traditional approaches to education, he felt, would not be adequate to prepare men and women to meet the challenges of the twentieth century. Children must be educated in ways that were relevant to the needs and culture of their times, ways that would enable them to act responsibly as adults in an industrialized society that was becoming increasingly complex and interdependent, and ways that would allow them to fulfill the promise of American democracy.

Traditionally, the goal of education has been construed as the transmission of preidentified bodies of information and skills, standards, and rules of conduct from one generation to the next. Pestalozzi, Froebel, and Montessori opposed the manner in which early childhood education was being developed and implemented, but did not disagree with this basic goal of cultural transmission. Dewey's argument was with both the form and purpose of traditional education. Calling for a curriculum of problem solving to replace that of rote learning, he envisioned teachers as facilitators or guides rather than as directors or inculcators. The role of teachers should be to foster the social and intellectual skills of their students by nurturing their interest in the world around them. In Deweyan classrooms, children would be taught how to think, not what to think.

Like Froebel and Montessori, Dewey believed that education must consider the nature and needs of the child, but Dewey saw individual variation as even greater than that served by Froebelian or Montessori methodology. No one set of methods and materials could be right for all children. Curriculum must be inductive rather than deductive, child-centered rather than task-centered. The population of the United States was becoming increasingly diverse and the needs of the growing nation differed from those in times gone by. Adults could not always know the best way for all children to learn, nor could they predict the knowledge base that would be needed in the changing world. American society in the twentieth century would very probably call for new ways of looking at the world, new standards, and even new rules of conduct.

Because, according to Dewey, intellectual growth and development emerge from personal experience, schools need to look to their students as well as to their subject content when shaping curriculum. Teachers must be classroom professionals, thoroughly knowledgeable both about subject matter and about children. They help children to recognize what they already know, structure learning activities that begin with and extend existing knowledge along an "experiential continuum," provide students with opportunities to recreate these activities, and teach children to reflect upon and analyze their own learning. Teachers are curriculum makers rather than implementers of predesigned series of activities.

In Dewey's approach to education, the work of the school was seen as continuous with the work of the home. This was important to Dewey for two reasons. It ensured that teachers might begin their instruction by reinforcing the child's preexistent knowledge and skills. Furthermore, in Dewey's words, "the same motives which keep the child at work and growing should be used in the school as in the home, so that he shall not feel that he has one set of reasons which belongs to the school and another which is used at home" (Mayhew and Edwards in Tanner and Tanner 1990, 130). In this way, home and school could work together in building a democratic community

Both at home and at school, the intellectual growth of young children emerged from active engagement in purposeful activities. In classrooms, activities would begin with that which was familiar to the children and would gradually extend the complexity and breadth of their understanding. Dewey created the Laboratory School at the University of Chicago as a place where he might put his theory into practice. Here, for example, young children's natural interests in food and clothing might lead to trips to a farm. They would see orchards and fields and observe the ways in which fruit and vegetables were harvested. Returning to the classroom, they might recreate their experience by "constructing" a farm and a grocery store. Some children would act as farmers; others would purchase crops from the farmers. Taking real fruit, children could learn to turn it into jam and applesauce and "sell" it to the grocery store. Embedded in their play were myriad opportunities for the teachers to offer instruction in math, reading, writing, and science as well as opportunities for discussions, songs, and movement games. All were related to the direct experience of the children; all provided opportunities for the children to develop an understanding of the connections between their homes and the economic institutions of the community at large. As the children developed their academic skills, they also developed insight into the ways in which people and institutions in an industrial society depended on one another.

Dewey's curriculum and methodology have made a lasting contribution to the debate over what constitutes good education. Lazerson (1984) expressed the views of decades of progressive educators when he wrote: "The Dewey teacher was flexible, experimental, knowledgeable of child development and of subject matter. But I believe this became more than the definition of a progressive teacher. It became the language which defined the best teachers, an ideal to aim for" (176).

Developmental and Cognitive Psychology: Theoretical Support for Deweyan Curriculum

Beginning with Freud, scholars in the field of psychology began to look at the child in a new way. They began to become increasingly aware of and more involved in the study of children as thinking, feeling beings whose nature and needs differed from those of the adults in the world around them. Among these psychologists, three—Erikson, Piaget, and Vygotsky—have had significant influence upon the field of early childhood education in the twentieth century. The work of all three of these men has meshed frequently with and supported Dewey's influence on early childhood curriculum.

Erikson, deeply schooled in Freudian theory, accepted the fundamental tenets of psychoanalytic thought. Like Freud, he identified a series of developmental conflicts through which each child must pass and which each child must resolve. At each stage of development, cognitive growth was related to the child's ability to balance these emotional conflicts. To the dynamic of internal conflict Erikson added the perspective of social and historical context. The expectations and values of a society at a given point in historical time could facilitate or impede the child's natural growth and development (Erikson 1950, 63).

Erikson's writing added strength to Dewey's position that the school must attend to the whole child. If emotional well-being impacts on intellectual growth, then emotional well-being must become a classroom concern. If the realities of home and society impact on the child's school performance, then these too need be considered when curriculum is being designed. Effective teaching can take place only when both the nature and needs of the child and those of society were considered.

Moreover, according to Erikson, young children use symbolic play to represent and work through their conflicts. Play that evolved from children's interests and fantasies began to be perceived as integrally related to and necessary for subsequent academic growth and development. Consequently, new importance and increased dignity were attached to childhood play. Most early childhood curriculum, influenced by the writings of Erikson, would now include an area in which familiar events and objects could become the focus of play and learning in the classroom.

From yet another perspective, Piaget gave added credence to a Deweyan vision of education. Like Freud and Erikson, Piaget describes a series of developmental stages through which all children pass. His focus, however, was on the cognitive rather than the emotional. Individual children may vary in the pace of their progress through these stages, but the stages themselves are sequential and hierarchical. The characteristics of Piagetian stages characterize the ways in which children learn at each point in their growth and development. Because Piaget believed that children must actively construct meaning by integrating prior knowledge with new information, his theory has come to be known as a constructivist approach to education.

Young children, according to Piaget, learn only through direct experience. Knowledge of the natural world comes through interaction with the physical world. Social knowledge develops from interactions with others. Young children cannot learn in a rote fashion; they are not developmentally ready to internalize abstract information. They may be able to imitate the teacher's performance, but they do not develop true understanding in so doing. To really learn and develop a firm foundation for higher-level reasoning, young children need to be allowed to actively explore and manipulate materials in their environment. They are concrete in their reasoning and need opportunities to make sense of the world through participatory experiences. Dramatic play, manipulative materials, field trips, and cooking are examples of learning experiences through which young children can extend and integrate—in Piaget's terms, "assimilate" and "accommodate"—new information, thus "constructing" increasingly higher levels of knowledge.

Piaget's theory has had significant implications for early childhood curriculum. By introducing the concept of developmental readiness, it has led most early childhood educators to view traditional forms of paper and pencil instruction as scientifically unsound for young children. It has encouraged teachers to use children's natural interest in the world and their proclivity for play as vehicles for curriculum development. Activities involving hands-on learning have come to be seen as important ways of facilitating children's abilities to make sense of their world. In addition, Piaget's description of the stages of cognitive development has enabled teachers to have greater insight into the ways in which the minds of young children work. Acknowledging that all children are not at the same place at the same time—individual style as well as family and cultural values impact on performance—it is nonetheless easier for teachers to implement sound early childhood practice when they have a better sense of what the range of anticipated behaviors might be. Piaget provides a theoretical context for a child-centered curriculum.

Yet a third theory that has had significant influence upon early childhood classrooms is that of Lev Vygotsky. Vygotsky and, later, Jerome Bruner and Dan Stern subscribe to a vision of learning that has come to be known as "social interactionist." They agree with aspects of the developmental school of thought. However, whereas Erikson and Piaget see each stage of development as superseding the earlier stages in a hierarchical way, the social interactionists see these stages as diverse ways of understanding and interacting with the world. As each stage develops, it forms a part of an individual's ever-growing repertoire of knowledge. "Earlier or more 'primitive' modes of organization are not eradicated, but become integrated into the more advanced modes of organization" (Biber and Franklin in Shapiro and Biber 1972, 65). New stages impact upon earlier stages and styles, but they do not replace them.

Whereas Piaget sees learning as emerging from within the child as he or she interacts with the environment, the social interactionists do not believe that intellectual development arises primarily from within the child. Rather, they see development as guided and shaped by the values and culture of the home and community (Bruner 1966; Vygotsky 1978; Stern 1985). Motivation for learning emerges from a child's innate desire to make sense of experience. However, the ways in which this motivation is realized are determined by the nature of the child's world.

These differences between constructivist theory and social interactionist theory have some important implications for early childhood curriculum. Piagetian theory suggests that the teacher can prepare a classroom atmosphere that is conducive to learning, but that learning is primarily a developmental process. The child's readiness for cognitive development emerges from internal growth rather than external motivation. Like Piaget, Vygotsky and the social interactionists believe that the learning environment must be developmentally appropriate. It must be experiential and interactive. However, social-interaction theory suggests that teachers can play a more active role in scaffolding children's cognitive development. By providing instruction within what Vygotsky calls the "zone of proximal development"— that is, instruction that meets and extends a child's demonstrated competence—teachers can actually stimulate children's motivation and achievement. By providing developmentally appropriate instruction, teachers can effect change.

An Integrated Model of Progressive Education: The Developmental-Interaction Approach

One approach to early childhood education that integrates the theory of twentieth-century developmental and cognitive psychology with Dewey's theory of educational psychology is the developmental-interaction approach implemented by Lucy Sprague Mitchell in the Bank Street School for Children and used as a model for teacher education at Bank Street College. This approach emerges from the belief that cognitive growth and personal and interpersonal development are interdependent and inseparable. Early childhood curriculum at Bank Street is concerned equally with cognitive development, the development of self-esteem, and the development of attitudes and skills that enable children to respect and deal effectively with the world in which they live.

> It is a basic tenet of the developmental-interaction approach that the growth of cognitive functions—acquiring and ordering information, judging, reasoning, problem solving, using systems of symbols—

cannot be separated from the growth of personal and interpersonal processes—the development of self-esteem and a sense of identity, internalization of impulse control, capacity for autonomous response, relatedness to other people. (Shapiro and Biber 1972, 61)

The developmental-interaction approach sees all learning—learning at home, at school, and in the community—as interrelated. Within the classroom, academic content areas are viewed not as distinct disciplines but as mutually reinforcing sources of knowledge. Academic experiences in one content area support and extend learning in other content areas. Consequently, the developmental-interaction approach advocates the implementation of integrated curriculum.

The developmental-interaction approach views the role of the teacher as designer of curriculum and creator of a positive classroom environment. Teachers stimulate and scaffold learning by establishing a climate of mutual trust between themselves and their students. Curriculum is dynamic rather than preestablished. Guided by their knowledge of child development, their understanding of the learning opportunities inherent in materials like blocks, clay, and paint, and their ongoing observations of their students' interests and concerns, teachers shape and reshape the content of their curriculum to meet the needs and interests of the classroom community.

In accordance with their Deweyan roots, teachers at Bank Street see themselves as both teachers and learners. They seek to weave connections between school, home, and the community at large. They collaborate with parents and colleagues. They listen to and learn from their students. As they participate in dialogue, they gather information that enables them to make the kinds of curriculum decisions that engage children's interests. For example, diversity of family backgrounds and the reality of children's concerns about such community issues as problems of the homeless or the effects of pollution upon the environment serve as resources for the social studies curriculum. Folktales and the recounting of family stories and experiences connect social studies with reading and writing. Collecting materials to be recycled provides opportunities for sorting, counting, measuring, estimating, and numerous

other math activities. Curriculum makes connections between disciplines as it makes connections between the classroom, the home, and the community.

Work and play are interrelated in the developmental-interactionist perspective. Both are viewed as serious endeavors in which learning occurs in a developmentally appropriate and culturally sensitive way. Play is seen as a reflection of children's relationship to the world around them, "a natural medium for exploration, discovery, and consolidation of learning" (Shapiro and Biber 1972, 72). Play also facilitates the building of bridges between the work of school and the work of home. It brings the real-life world of the child into the classroom by providing an arena in which children can play out their fantasies and recreate real-life experiences. Opportunities for play are viewed as important parts of a learning environment that nurtures affective, social, and cognitive growth.

In its developmental vision of the child as learner, its positive vision of the teacher as active participant in the learning process, and its vision of education as the wedding of individual growth and development to social change, the developmental-interactionist approach combines the theory of Dewey, developmental psychology, and social-interaction theory. Like its predecessors in this century and the past, the developmental-interaction approach evolved out of and responsed to the needs and values of the society to which it belongs.

The Behaviorists: An Alternative Paradigm for Early Childhood Education

There was and is, however, another voice as influential upon the world of education in the twentieth century as the voice of Dewey and the voices of developmental and cognitive psychology. This voice also emerged from the scientific approach of Darwin and was shaped by the paradigms of twentieth-century scientific thought. This voice, however, takes issue with the vision of learning as intrinsically motivated and self-directed. This is the voice of the Behaviorists coming forth from the halls of experimental psychology. The Behaviorists believe learning is extrinsic and other-directed. They see children as neither self-motivated nor self-directed in their quest for knowledge. According to behavioral theory, learning is shaped by the environment in which the child is nurtured. Early childhood curriculum is, therefore, most effective when it is systematically controlled to elicit desired responses. The ideas, feelings, past experiences, and present concerns of the child are not necessarily significant factors in the learning process; rather, the ways in which content material is presented and reinforced are what determine how much or how little growth and development occur.

Behavioral theory began with the laboratory experiments of Pavlov (1928) and Watson (1930). By ringing a buzzer before a dog was given food, Pavlov "taught" a dog to salivate as soon as the buzzer rang. Gradually, the dog came to salivate whenever the bell was rung— even in the absence of food. Watson subsequently documented ways in which Pavlov's techniques could be useful in shaping responses to a broad variety of stimuli. Thorndike and Skinner then extrapolated this theory from animal learning and applied it to human learning. The work of these men forms the core of what today is known as learning theory.

From Skinner's work emerged the theory of operant conditioning. Beginning his work with animals and extending it to the rearing of his own daughter, he found that behaviors that are rewarded are likely to repeated; those that go unrewarded are likely to be extinguished. Reinforcement shapes behavior through a series of "successive approximations" that lead the learner from where he is to the acquisition of the skills and knowledge that are to be mastered. It is from this theory that both Programmed Learning of the 60s and today's concept of Mastery Learning have evolved. This vision of learning has also had a significant impact on the form and substance of standardized testing.

Those who advocate a behavioral vision of learning see children as born neither good nor bad. Children are a "mass of original tendencies," much like Locke's *tabula rasa*; they are shaped by their environments to develop the attitudes and behaviors valued by the communities in which they live. Through a more scientific approach to teaching and learning,

this process can be made more effective. Learning is seen as sequential and hierarchical. One piece of knowledge builds on another in a fixed order. When the Developmentalists speak of sequence and hierarchy, they are referring to stages of child development. The Behaviorists see the learning process as constant throughout the life process: small pieces of knowledge that must be learned in proper sequence. Definitions of school readiness have been strongly influenced by behavioral theory, for, according to behavioral theory, children cannot succeed at complex learning activities until they are able to demonstrate success on more fundamental ones.

For the Behaviorists, the role of the teacher involves identifying the entry-level skills and knowledge of one's students, and then designing and implementing a series of carefully structured activities that will move the student closer and closer to the desired outcome by systematically reinforcing each successful move forward. Observable objectives for learning must be carefully articulated, for only in this way will teachers and students know what the goal is and when it has been reached. Classroom instruction is always teacher-directed. Neither play nor free exploration is viewed as an essential part of the learning process.

Many commercial educational programs have been designed to make classroom implementation of the behavioral model more consistent and less onerous to the individual teacher. Perhaps the best known of these has been Bereiter and Engelmann's Distar Program (1966). Designed for Head Start programs in the 60s, Distar provided a learning program that was highly structured, work-oriented, and academic. It was designed to allow young, "disadvantaged" children to compensate for the absence of mainstream language experiences in their homes. Immediate feedback provided through a variety of rewards, ranging from food to teacher praise, was used to move children along the learning pathways that were thought to be essential precursors to school success in reading and writing. The lessons were carefully structured and carefully scripted. Teachers needed only to implement them as guided by the teacher's manual (Roopnarine and Johnson 1987).

Educational programs grounded in behavioral theory are consonant in many ways with traditional visions of education. Teachers are seen as directors. Both the form and content of the curriculum are fully determined by adults: teachers, curriculum specialists, and researchers. Children are recipients of, not partners in, the educational process. Depending upon the program, they may move at their own individual pace or, as a group, with starting points that differ according to their preexistent knowledge and skills. However, all move along the same course with little room, if any, for individual choice. To this vision of education, behavioral programs add the use of clearly articulated objectives, objective measurement, and both concrete and symbolic rewards. There are few "pure" behavioral programs in today's early childhood programs, but the influence of behavioral theory and methodology on early childhood curriculum is widespread both in this country and throughout the world.

Common Themes in Early Childhood Curriculum

The approaches to early childhood curriculum that have been discussed in this chapter have differed in their philosophy, their methodology, and their vision of the role of the teacher. None has been universally accepted, but each has left a legacy that is carried on consciously and unconsciously in early childhood classrooms throughout the world. As diverse as these approaches have been, they do share some traits. These may explain the long-standing influence of these models of early childhood education. Each approach includes the following factors:

1. Classroom practice has been grounded in a clearly articulated theoretical framework. This framework has included a vision of how children learn, how teachers should act or interact with their students, and what should be the focus of classroom content.
2. In each case, the goals of curriculum have been clearly articulated. In some cases, these goals have been the transmission of beliefs and skills; in others, it has been the breaking of constricting mind-sets and the nurturing of divergent thought. However, in each case, early childhood curriculum has been shaped by a clear vision of desired outcomes.

3. The kinds of activities and materials that accompany each approach to early childhood curriculum have been intentionally chosen to be consistent with its theory and goals.
4. Teachers have understood and shared the theory and goals of the chosen approach. They have been carefully trained to develop and/or implement appropriate classroom practice.
5. Teachers form a community of believers. They believe in the curriculums they are implementing. They work together, collaborating, supporting, and reinforcing each other's practice.
6. Teachers are knowledgeable about children, about content, and about pedagogy. Whether the approach is child-centered or curriculum-centered, teachers have a thorough understanding of the learner, that which is to be learned, and the ways to facilitate this learning.
7. There is a fundamental respect for the child implicit or explicit in each approach to early childhood curriculum. In some cases, the respect is for the child as agent of his or her own learning. In others, it is as a malleable being waiting to be shaped. However, in each case, there is a respect for the child as learner.
8. Each of these approaches to early childhood curriculum agrees that early childhood curriculum must be pleasureful for young children. Froebel spoke of joy; the Behaviorists speak of positive reinforcement. All refer to children engaged in positive learning experiences.

Current Research in Early Childhood Education

There are still many unanswered questions about what constitutes good early childhood curriculum. In an ongoing quest for greater understanding of unresolved issues, we turn to research in the field. Contributions to our pool of knowledge have emerged from the disciplines of anthropology, psychology, and sociology, as well as from the classroom practice of teachers. These offer new insights and diverse perspectives from which to consider the development of children, the influence of society upon this growth and development, and the form and content of good teaching. Yet, answers are still elusive. Growing concern that, in many communities, our children are not learning motivates new research and leads us to look more carefully at the assumptions that underlie early childhood practice.

The Question of Readiness

One issue that is currently of great interest to parents, educators, and policy makers is the question of readiness. The concept of readiness dates back to the practice of Pestalozzi. Although he did not use the term itself, Pestalozzi's belief that teaching must be attuned to the needs and interests of the child—that not all children are able to learn in the same way at the same time—foreshadows current notions of readiness.

In this country, two constructs of readiness have influenced the educational community: readiness for learning and readiness for school (Kagan 1990). Readiness for learning has emerged from the research of cognitive psychology and child development. It refers to the time when a child has developed the capacity to engage in specific kinds of learning and, by extension, to successfully learn certain kinds of knowledge and skills. Readiness for learning is a holistic concept involving motivation, cognitive ability, emotional maturity, physical development, and the child's physical and mental health. It suggests that what goes on in classrooms should emerge from and be relevant to the nature and needs of the children in that classroom. No one curriculum is appropriate for all children of a given age. Readiness for learning has had significant impact on the nature of curriculum in early childhood classrooms.

Readiness for school has emerged from the research of experimental and behavioral psychology. It is part of a hierarchical vision of learning. This vision suggests that children must possess certain information and skills before they can be expected to engage successfully in the traditional curriculum of elementary schools. Whereas readiness for learning suggests that it is the school's responsibility to provide appropriate curriculum for all children, readiness for school suggests that it is the child's responsibility to meet the demands of a traditional curriculum.

In recent years, this concept of readiness has led to the expectation that children will have reached a specified level of maturational development in language, visual motor organization, gross motor skills, and social development before entering the public school classroom (Kagan 1990). To assess a child's development in these areas, tests are given before entering kindergarten and/or before entering first grade. It is often recommended that children who have not yet attained these specified levels be given "the gift of time" (Ilg and Ames 1965). Although this recommendation is consistent with a maturationist perspective, which sees children's growth and development as innately determined, there is little empirical data that show a significant correlation between "the gift of time" and later school success. Moreover, the expectation that readiness will emerge from time in and of itself is at odds with the social-interactionist position that appropriate curriculum motivates and stimulates intellectual development.

The debate between these two perspectives gains even greater importance when considered in the context of equity. It is often the children of the poor who perform least successfully on traditional tests of school readiness. Will time alone make them "more ready" when they are one year older? How the needs of all children can best be met, and educational success ensured, is one of the most critical issues in current research in early childhood education.

The Assessment of Young Children

Related to issues of readiness and how one tests for readiness is the more general concern about what constitutes meaningful assessment of young children. In today's world, where education is failing greater and greater numbers of students, parents and administrators feel a need for some kind of accountability. Teachers agree that in order to be effective, they must understand how their students learn and what they know. The question in debate is, What kinds of assessment tools provide the most accurate and the most meaningful information about what young children do know and should know?

Many parents and administrators feel that there is a need for the objective measurement provided by standardized testing. However, whereas standardized tests provide certain pieces of information, they are not always sensitive to the nature of the young child. We know that the growth and development of young children is episodic, highly individualized, and rapidly changing. A measure at any point in time can be likened to a snapshot, which freezes a moment. Sometimes it is accurate; sometimes it distorts. Moreover, the performance of young children is frequently context-dependent. Their ability to relate to the person administering the assessment instrument or their momentary mood can impact significantly on their performance. Consequently, standardized tests—particularly group tests or tests given in one sitting—do not always provide accurate measures of what children really know.

Secondly, early childhood researchers have some serious concerns with the tests themselves. Few tests of early childhood development are valid, reliable, and carefully standardized (Meisels in Kagan 1990). Few consider the cultural patterns and knowledge of diverse populations. Few allow assessors to use a range of strategies to elicit a child's understanding. The information they seek to elicit is frequently irrelevant to the world of the child. Consequently, the true profile of the child is not captured.

Current research indicates that assessment is more likely to be accurate when it is embedded in the curriculum itself. This form of assessment, often called "authentic assessment," calls for teachers to monitor their students' progress on an ongoing basis and to make curriculum decisions that are responsive to their findings. This premise has not changed since the time of Froebel and Montessori. However, there are now increased efforts to familiarize teachers with systematic ways of observing, recording, and communicating children's progress. These methods include portfolios, interviews with parents, caretakers, and other professionals, as well as anecdotals, and checklists. Children are often made partners in the assessment process, learning at a very young age to reflect upon their work and articulate their learning. One tool that has proven to be particularly effective in this way is the Primary Language Record (ILEA/Centre for Language in Primary Educa-

tion 1988). The PLR was designed to involve parents and children, along with teachers, in the assessment process and to provide valuable information about those children both for whom English is their native language and those for whom it is a second language.

The growing support for authentic assessment is consistent with the belief that early childhood education is socially constructed. "It takes a whole community to educate a child," is an African proverb often quoted by early childhood educators. Authentic assessment provides formal and informal opportunities for the insights of all those involved with the education of young children. In so doing, it affirms the social context of learning and helps to make the curriculum of early childhood education relevant to the real world of young children.

Authentic assessment documents a renewed commitment to the belief that all children can be effective learners throughout their school career (University of the State of New York, 1991). Children learn in different ways and at different rates. Consequently, no one form of measurement can be valid for all children, especially all children in their early childhood years. There is a place for standardized tests in the assessment process, but if the goal of early childhood curriculum is to acknowledge and affirm diversity, standardized tests cannot constitute the whole process.

The Role of the Home in Early Childhood Education: Collaboration and Multiculturalism

Perhaps not since the time of Froebel has there been such an emphasis on the role of the home as an active agent in early childhood education. The growing diversity of cultures in urban America and the realization that the customs and values of these cultures impact on a child's school performance have led early childhood educators to a new recognition of the need for communication between home and school. Multicultural curriculum and family–teacher collaboration are two important constructs derived from the early childhood research of the last decade.

This research has documented both the goals families and schools hold in common and the ways in which these goals can disappear when mistrust and miscommunication prevail (Bredekamp 1987; Derman-Sparks 1989). In the field of early childhood special education, research has led to legislation mandating the creation of interdisciplinary and community-based agencies to identify and meet the needs of young children. This policy validated the importance of shared authority and decision making in shaping programs for the education of all children. It allowed parents a voice in setting priorities and establishing goals for their children's education. In so doing, it opened doorways for diverse perspectives emerging from multicultural vantage points and created new pathways for communication between parents and professionals. The positive effects of this legislation have significantly influenced the recent early childhood education policy.

Many historical obstacles to communication between home and school have been highlighted by recent research in early childhood education. Stress and frustration have been shown to affect both parents and teachers, making each insensitive to the caring and concern of the other (Galinsky 1988). Traditionally, many parents and teachers have seen each other as "the enemy" instead of as a mutual support system. Accounts of anxiety relating to parent-teacher conferences have been shared by parents and teachers from diverse social classes and ethnic backgrounds (Clinton 1992). These have demonstrated a need for schools to create opportunities for more positive dialogue by informing parents about classroom practice, using them as resources for curriculum ideas and activities, and viewing them as partners in the process of education.

Research has also pointed out how important it is for home and school to work together to shape the attitudes of young children. It has been shown that by the age of four or five, children have internalized traditional stereotypes of gender roles and racial bias and are reluctant to act in ways that depart from these stereotypes (Derman-Sparks 1989). These attitudes and expectations create barriers to growth and development for children of all ages, classes, and ethnic backgrounds. They inhibit their willingness to take risks, to think critically, and to solve problems. Schools alone

cannot reverse these stereotypes. The need for home–school collaboration and for the development of a bias-free curriculum has been clearly documented.

As we move into the twenty-first century, the problems we face are as bewildering to us as the problems of the twentieth century were to Dewey. We know that schools can make a difference, but we also know that this difference can become reality only when schools implement curriculum that is relevant to the needs of all children. In order to do this, teachers, parents, and community institutions must work together to identify and teach those attitudes and skills that will enable students to deal effectively with challenges yet unknown.

How Young Children Learn To Read: A Question of Philosophy and Practice

The question that has probably stimulated the most research in the field of twentieth-century education is, How do young children learn to read? Traditionally, literacy—like all forms of education—has been viewed as a single body of knowledge that is transmitted to students by their teachers. This view, accepted on faith for generations, found a theoretical grounding in the literature of behavioral psychology. Consistent with the precepts of behavioral psychology, reading has been taught by identifying that which needs to be learned, breaking down the task into a series of subskills, providing appropriate stimuli, and reinforcing correct responses until the desired habit—in this case, proficient reading—is developed. Reading is thus seen as a linear process that proceeds from part to whole, each part building on those skills that have already been learned. Within this context, skills acquisition precedes the process of reading for meaning (Chall 1987).

However, in the latter part of this century, an alternative approach to reading has emerged from the teachings of cognitive psychology. This approach, called "whole language," views reading as a process of problem solving integrally related to all learning. It is an extension of the development of oral language and a counterpart of, rather than a precursor to, the process of writing. It is part of a lifetime effort to make meaning of one's world

(Holdaway 1979). According to the philosophy of whole language, the desire to engage in meaningful activity scaffolds the acquisition of early reading skills.

Whole language views the development of a "set" for literacy as the foundation of reading success. Whole-language instruction teaches young children to understand the connections between written and spoken language. They learn to value speaking, reading, and writing as important components of home life as well as of school life. Children are provided with many pleasurable experiences with words, both oral and written. Through these experiences they come to understand the significance and utilize the conventions of print. They listen to stories, rhymes, and songs. They learn to pay attention to print in their environment—on signs, in stores, on the boxes that house their toys, and in the experience charts that describe their activities. They begin to write, at first in scribbles, then with some phonetic correlations, and finally with orthographic and grammatical accuracy. Skills are an important part of the reading process, but they are taught only within a meaningful context (Noyce and Christie 1989).

In the traditional approach to early reading, the teacher sequences and orders the acquisition of skills. Worksheets and drills are an important part of the daily routine. Reading instruction utilizes basal readers with controlled vocabulary. Children progress individually, in small groups, or as a whole class through a prearticulated sequence of activities.

In the whole-language approach, teachers work with children to create a print-rich environment. They design language-based activities that engage children's active participation. Each activity provides opportunities for the development of a myriad of skills. Teachers observe children's performance and then draw on their own knowledge of language and reading to articulate and extend the child's experience. Reading instruction uses trade books, poems, and the children's own writing. The learning sequence is not the same for all children; it varies with their needs, interests, and preexistent knowledge.

There are many misconceptions about the differences between traditional models of reading instruction and that of whole language. Often, people equate whole language with a maturationist approach. They see whole-language advocates as describing reading and writing as naturally unfolding processes. Hence, there is no need to teach the component skills. In reality, whole language emerges from a social-interactionist perspective. Through their choice of materials, their selection of activities, and their careful observations of classroom dynamics, whole-language teachers make instructional decisions that scaffold their students' growing ability to read and write.

Contrary to popular belief, whole language is a philosophical approach rather than one specific way of teaching. It incorporates many different methodologies. Like more traditional models of reading, whole language includes the teaching of phonics. However, phonic skills are taught as children need them to make sense of what they are reading and writing. Teachers provide cues for children who are writing or draw the attention of readers to graphophonic cues. They provide minilessons to individuals or small groups of children. Unlike more traditional forms of instruction, lessons in phonics are not taught first and applied later.

In a similar vein, spelling, grammar, and handwriting play an important role in whole-language classrooms. Whole language is predicated upon the assumption that communication is a primary goal of reading and writing. Spelling, grammar, and handwriting facilitate communication; therefore, they are important. However, it is the communication that is the primary goal; skills are means to that end.

The debate between academically oriented classrooms and developmentally appropriate/culturally sensitive practice is directly related to the debate between the traditional and the whole-language approaches to reading. Each side believes that what goes on in the early childhood years is critical for subsequent learning. Their differences emerge from the different belief systems underlying their practice. Advocates of academic programs in early childhood education believe that the teaching of academic subjects involves a hierarchically ordered set of skills. Most children need to be taught these skills in a carefully structured, systematic way (Chall 1987; Adams 1990). Advocates of developmentally appropriate/culturally sensitive practice believe that children learn subject matter through a process of social construction. The order in which skills are acquired can vary from child to child. What does not vary is the need for children to be actively involved in learning that relates to and extends their prior knowledge. Developmentally appropriate/culturally sensitive curriculum differs from academically oriented curriculum in both form and content. The goals of the two approaches are similar; the paths they follow to achieve these goals are different.

There are no easy answers to the long-standing debates in early childhood education. What we learn from the lessons of history and the findings of research is that we, as educators, must be clear about what we value and about what is valued by the communities with whom we work. We must design our curriculum and implement our practice in a way that is consistent with these values. Only then can we hope to fulfill our goals and help all children to become successful learners.

References

Adams, M. J. 1991. *Beginning To Read.* Cambridge: MIT Press.

Aries, P. 1962. *Centuries of Childhood.* Trans. R. Balkick. New York: Knopf.

Bereiter, C., and S. Engelmann. 1966. *Teaching Disadvantaged Children in the Preschool.* Englewood Cliffs, NJ: Prentice-Hall.

Braun, S., and E. Edwards. 1972. *History and Theory of Early Childhood Education.* Worthington, OH: Charles A. Jones.

Bredekamp, S., ed. 1987. *Developmentally Appropriate Practices in Early Childhood Programs Serving Children from Birth through Age 8.* Washington, DC: National Association for the Education of Young Children.

Bruner, J. 1966. *Toward a Theory of Instruction.* Cambridge: Harvard Univ. Press.

Chall, J. 1987. "Reading and Early Childhood Education: The Critical Issues." *Principal* 66 (May): 6-9.

Clinton, Hillary. October 1992. Speech given at Bank Street College of Education, New York.

Cremin, L. 1964. *The Transformation of the School.* New York: Vintage.

Derman-Sparks, L. 1989. *Anti-Bias Curriculum.* Washington, DC: National Association for the Education of Young Children.

Dewey, J. 1963. *Experience and Education.* 1938. New York: Collier.

Erikson, E. 1963. *Childhood and Society.* 1950. New York: Norton.

Froebel, F. 1887. *The Education of Man.* Trans. W. Hailman. New York: Appleton.

Galinsky, E. 1988. "Parents and Teacher Caregivers: Sources of Tension, Sources of Support." *Young Children* 43(3): 4-11.

Gutek, G. L. 1972. *A History of the Western Educational Experience.* New York: Random House.

Holdaway, D. 1979. *The Foundations of Literacy.* Portsmouth, NH: Heinemann.

Hunt, J. M., ed. 1964. *The Montessori Method.* New York: Schocken.

ILEA/Centre for Language in Primary Education. 1988. *Primary Language Record.* Portsmouth, NH: Heinemann.

Ilg, F., and L. B. Ames. 1965. *School Readiness: Behavior Tests Used at the Gesell Institute.* New York: Harper & Row.

Kagan, S. L. 1990. "Readiness 2000: Rethinking Rhetoric and Responsibility." *Phi Delta Kappan* (Dec.): 272-79.

Kessen, W. 1965. *The Child.* New York: Wiley.

Lazerson, M. 1984. "If All the World Were Chicago: American Education in the Twentieth Century." *History of Education Quarterly* 24 (Summer).

MacCormac, R. 1991. "Form and Philosophy: Froebel's Kindergarten Training and the Early Work of Frank Lloyd Wright." In *Frank Lloyd Wright: A Primer on Architectural Principles,* ed. R. McCarter. Princeton: Princeton Architectural Press.

Manson, G. C. 1958. *Frank Lloyd Wright to 1910.* New York: Van Nostrand Reinhold.

A New Compact for Learning. 1991. New York: Univ. of the State of New York, State Education Department.

Noyce, R., and J. Christie. 1989. *Integrating Reading and Writing Instruction.* New York: Allyn & Bacon.

Orem, R. C., ed. 1965. *A Montessori Handbook.* New York: Putnam.

Pestalozzi, J. H. 1915. *How Gertrude Teaches Her Children.* Trans. L. Holland and F. Turner. 1801. Syracuse, NY: Bardeen.

Piaget, J. 1962. *Play, Dreams, and Imitation in Childhood.* New York: Norton.

Powell, R. E. 1992. "Goals for the Language Arts Program: Toward a Democratic Vision." *Language Arts* 69(5): 342–49.

Roopnarine, J., and J. Johnson. 1987. *Approaches to Early Childhood Education.* Columbus, OH: Merrill.

Rousseau, J. J. 1984. *Emile.* London: Everymans Books.

Shapiro, E., and B. Biber. 1972. "The Education of Young Children: A Developmental-Interaction Approach." *Teachers College Record* 74(1): 56–79.

Spodek, B., O. Saracho, and M. Davis. 1991. *Foundations of Early Childhood Education.* Englewood Cliffs, NJ: Prentice-Hall.

Stern, D. 1985. *The Interpersonal World of the Child.* New York: Basic Books.

Tanner, D., and L. Tanner. 1990. *History of the School Curriculum.* New York: Macmillan.

Vygotsky, L. 1978. *Mind and Society.* Ed. M. Cole and S. Scribner. Cambridge: Harvard Univ. Press.

Weber, E. 1984. *Ideas Influencing Early Childhood Education.* New York: Teachers College Press.

Williams, L. R. 1984a. "The Froebelian Kindergarten: History, Theory, and Practice." In *International Encyclopedia of Education*, ed. T. Husen and T. N. Paselthwaite, 1982–84. Oxford: Pergamon.

———. 1984b. "Montessori Method." In *International Encyclopedia of Education*, ed. T. Husen and T.N. Paselthwaite, 3403-06. Oxford: Pergamon.

———. 1987. *Determining the Curriculum in the Early Childhood Curriculum.* Ed. C. Seefeldt. New York: Teachers College Press.

CURRICULUM PROCESS AND DESIGN: PRE-K THROUGH GRADE THREE

Diane Lynch Fraser
Assistant Director
School for Language and Communication Development, North Bellmore, New York
Assistant Professor
St. John's University, Jamaica, New York

VERY simply, curriculum is a way of helping teachers think about children and organize their experiences. The term *curriculum* has many definitions: it can mean all the experiences that happen at school; a written plan for learning; a syllabus that lists learning topics in the order in which they will be presented; or a specific program, such as a whole language curriculum, that describes an itinerary of activities. The goals contained in any learning program's rationale are explicitly defined in terms of *curriculum planning*. Curriculum plans include activities, teaching–learning approaches, and materials used in implementation. A curriculum plan usually specifies *scope* (what will be learned) and *sequence* (the order in which the learning will take place). Yet, because young children learn from so many experiences both in and out of school, early childhood curriculum can also be defined more broadly as the "actual membrane between the world and the child" (Weikart 1989).

Psycho-Philosophical Differences in Curriculum

Two major psycho-philosophical views have evolved. One way to look at curriculum is to conceive it based upon the requirements for success in the adult world. Education is seen as skill development for meeting cultural demands. In this view, early childhood curriculum is designed to facilitate young children's success in later school programs—an orientation in which fragments of an idea are presented with the goal of fitting these pieces into a whole. In order to achieve academic success, this kind of orientation recommends teacher-directed and narrowly defined basic skill, particularly in the area of reading and mathematics. Published programs, which often include isolated verbal and "paper-and-pencil," seat-work activities, are used for "training" homogeneous, "ability-grouped" children. This is the curriculum view held by *behaviorists*, theorists who believe that behavior can be shaped by the response or reinforcement that follows any particular action.

Another way to view early childhood curriculum is the developmental perspective. In this view, consummate adulthood is realized by cultivating a child-centered curriculum. Curriculum planning begins with observation and analysis of children's developmental characteristics—a design in which the whole idea is presented first and the specifics are addressed later. This early childhood curriculum, instead of being determined by the demands of later school content, views children's current developmental experiences as being essential in their own right—not merely for how they might benefit children's later schooling or later life experiences. This approach supports the children's construction of knowledge through child-initiated learning. This curriculum view is held by *interactionists,* theorists who believe children learn through their personal experiences with the environment and their subsequent interpretations of those experiences.

Position Statements

Some recent trends in early childhood education, most especially the more formal academic emphasis embraced by the behaviorists, are a cause for concern. *The Public School Early Childhood Study* (Marx and Seligson 1988), which found most public-school kindergartens highly academic, teacher-directed, rigidly scheduled, and dependent upon workbooks, is a good example.

Most professionals in early childhood education and child development characterize these trends as being at cross purposes with understanding how young children learn. Educational scholars have discovered that academically oriented early childhood programs actually hinder children's potential to evolve as literate, problem-solving adults. The National Association of State Boards of Education (1988) stated that the academic curriculum is "shockingly unstimulating to children and fails to stimulate their thinking."

There is also concern regarding the social results of such academic programs. In his ten-year study of early childhood programs, Weikart (1989) found that although the different curricula produced essentially the same academic results, the social results were very different. Children involved in child-initiated curriculum were self-directed and able to follow through on long-term goals during adolescence. Conversely, children enrolled in teacher-prescribed programs often experienced alienation from home, school, and even society during adolescent years.

These concerns and others have led to support for a curriculum based upon sound developmental theory, often referred to as *developmentally appropriate curriculum.* Such

curriculum focuses upon observation and knowledge of how children develop, and thus is a tailored progression from birth through age eight.

Developmental Theory and Implications for Curriculum

This section provides very brief outlines of the four developmental components—*physical, social, emotional,* and *intellectual*—with suggestions for curriculum developed in each of these specific areas for pre-K–3. The purpose of describing development in these four segments is to make studying child development easier. It must be noted that the separation of real-life experiences into physical, social, emotional, and intellectual components is clearly artificial: Children learn all four developmental components simultaneously, not individually.

Physical Development

All young children need vigorous physical activity each day. No child should be deprived of this opportunity because he has other school tasks to complete or because he is being punished. There is a growing concern that children in the United States are less physically fit than previous generations of children (Zigler and Finn-Stevenson 1987). This trend seems to reflect the passive time American children spend watching television or sitting motionless at desks.

Children also need opportunities to engage in fine-motor activities: painting, cutting with scissors, manipulating clay, stringing beads, sewing, puzzles, pegboards, and so on. The following suggestions can help teachers plan gross- and fine-motor activities that encourage the physical development of children.

Three- and four-year-olds
- Outdoor play: Provide enough space for children to move about freely: running, jumping, and skipping. Many children can ride tricycles. As children learn to throw and catch, provide soft rubber balls.
- Indoor play: Indoor equipment can now include rocking boats, foam cubes, individual steps, and low slides. As children now tire easily after periods of vigorous

activity, there should be a balance between quiet and active play: vigorous activity followed by a story, discussion, or snack. Children can be encouraged to draw, assemble puzzles, and cut with scissors.

Five- and six-year-olds

- Outdoor play: Provide opportunities to demonstrate movement and/or impulse control, such as "statues," run-and-stop, or seeing how long they can stand on one foot. Five-year-olds can use hula hoops and jump ropes. They will also need durable rubber balls for kicking.
- Indoor play: Make certain children have many opportunities to experiment with representation using fine motor control. Five- and six-year-olds have a keen interest in the alphabet, words, drawing, and making collages. Paper, markers, crayons, watercolors, fingerpaints, glue, stickers—any and all arts and writing materials should be plentiful and available.

Seven- and eight-year-olds

- Outdoor play: Children have a highly developed large- and small-muscle control, in some cases: skill and coordination. Deviations from the traditional racelike and competitive games of this developmental period should be implemented to support physical competence. Jump rope, hula hoops, yoga, t'ai chi-like movement, and dance games with music are optimal choices.
- Indoor play: Although writing becomes the primary focus of fine-motor coordination for children this age, writing should not replace the earlier developing skill, drawing. Sketching and painting offer unique opportunity for visual representation that writing cannot. If gymnastic equipment is available indoors, it can offer children opportunities to develop strength, balance, and flexibility.

Social Development

Teachers do not normally develop specific activities whose sole purpose is social development. Instead, teachers use existing classroom routines to support development in this area. Social activities should encourage children to cooperate, develop self-esteem, and gain skill in interacting with other children. The following are a few suggestions of ways to promote social development:

Three- and four-year-olds

- Children's ability to accept group life, to cooperate, and to take turns is in its earliest phase. Provide many creative experiences that initially coax, but do not force, children into group experiences. Allow children to do things for one another.
- Set up costume corners where children can use dress-up clothes to stimulate dramatic play.
- Have an assortment and quantity of the most desired playthings available. Children cannot wait too long for a turn at this age, and this strategy avoids the inevitable conflict.
- Use puppets to model social interactions. Understand that all social interactions will need to be modeled rather than merely discussed at this stage of development.

Five- and six-year-olds

- Provide experiences where children are asked both to take turns and request turns of other children.
- As children are beginning to respond with empathy to others' feelings, provide them with extensions of these experiences using literature that depicts individuals in social predicaments.
- Children are beginning to demand more realism in play. Provide them with time to play-act situations they have actually experienced.
- Children are beginning to form their first real friendships. Although they should experience the company of all or most class members, accommodations should be made so children can be special friends at certain points during the day.
- Use role-playing games to solve social problems in the classroom. Encourage children to display empathetic behavior by displaying this yourself.

Seven- and eight-year-olds

- Children are now capable of complying with social rules and expectations. Provide play-acting activities that will help them understand when social rules need to be exercised and when it would be important to break them.

- Children are interested in what other people think and do. Allow them to see, hear, and experience other points of view. Encourage the exchange of ideas.
- Set aside time each day for children to work in pairs or small groups. Once they have become facile here, it is easier for them to work in larger groups.

Emotional Development

Emotional development progresses as children evolve from expressing undifferentiated emotional responses to being able to express their emotions divergently, in socially acceptable ways, and to control their impulses. Children grow more capable of understanding how others might feel in a particular situation and have developed a sense of right and wrong.

The following are examples of classroom activities that can enhance children's emotional development:

Three- and four-year-olds
- Recognize children's feelings and fears, including anger and sadness, through stories and discussion. Make certain that children feel secure and safe when expressing emotions.
- Children's emotional states are affected by feelings of competence. As children can often feel powerless and insecure, opportunities to succeed and develop self-esteem and belonging are primary. Teachers need to comfort children when necessary, integrate each child's name and their life experiences into the curriculum. When an activity appears difficult, break it down into smaller pieces.
- Children are most concerned with events that affect them personally. Children should be encouraged to bring in pictures of themselves and their families, to make their own books about their own lives. Curriculum should initially reflect the feelings and ideas most familiar to the children.

Five- and six-year-olds
- Children are able to talk about their strengths and weaknesses now. They want to know that it is permissible to make a mistake, and need opportunities to repair their errors.
- Children are particularly interested in receiving adult attention at this stage. Some may "show off." See that children receive attention for tasks both big and

small; try not to relegate attention to the big moments.
- Humor is a newly developing skill. Allow children to create and tell their own humorous stories.
- Provide opportunities for children to handle emotionally charged situations with less intervention from adults.

Seven- and eight-year-olds
- Children understand and have experienced a wide range of emotions. Provide opportunities for children to acknowledge true feelings appropriately.
- Provide opportunities for children to redefine and explore who they are. Have them keep journals and diaries, write poetry, draw pictures, and take photographs.
- Children are learning to forgo immediate reward for delayed gratification. Provide opportunities to plan and execute long-term projects whose themes are developed over the course of several weeks.

Intellectual Development

Children progress intellectually from the sensorimotor phase of development, in which infants and toddlers organize their universe through direct physical interaction with people and objects, to the preoperational phase, in which preschool and young elementary-grade children develop representational skills such as language and mathematics using real-life experiences.

The following are examples of classroom activities that can enhance intellectual development:

Three- and four-year-olds
- Children are naturally curious and still learn best through active involvement and their senses. Whenever possible, provide firsthand experiences. If you want to talk about the ocean, bring in sand, seaweed, and seashells.
- Provide opportunities for children to explore familiar objects such as water, soap, and paint.
- Children's strengths at this period include their rapidly expanding language and skill and their ability to classify and seriate. Capitalize on these developing abilities by providing opportunities to use new vocabulary and materials to manipulate.
- Provide opportunities for children to develop a sense of time. Although children are primarily concerned with the

	SAMPLE CURRICULUM	
	KINDERGARTEN	
Characteristics	*Needs*	*Classroom Suggestions*
Can often be fearful or frustrated	Opportunities for positive reinforcement	Use positive statements. Refrain from negative comments.
Becoming more independent	Self-help skills	Provide practice and just the needed assistance in skills such as dressing, toileting, and eating.
Beginning to make friends	Opportunities to form friendships	Allow children to select their own playmates and form their own play groups.
Are curious about their environment	Opportunities to discover the properties of objects	Provide materials children can manipulate in order to discover various object attributes.
Developing gross and fine motor control	Opportunities to develop motor skill	Provide adequate equipment to climb on, "vehicles" to ride on, and balls to throw and catch. Provide small manipulatives to handle and problem solve.
Developing and expanding language skill	Opportunities to use language	Converse, read aloud, dramatize stories, and use singing games to stimulate language. Write children's dictated stories. Have classroom charts and other print available to children. Provide materials for children to draw, write, paint, etc.
Developing creative expression	Opportunities to express themselves creatively	Provide opportunities to learn basic skills (e.g., mathematics) and content area material (e.g., social studies and science) in integrated ways (i.e., while working on theme-oriented projects instead of isolated tasks in each area).
Becoming familiar with symbols.	Opportunities to use representational forms	Provide props and costumes for dramatic play and plenty of good children's literature to stimulate story telling.
Like to make choices and use their ideas.	Independent thinking skills	Permit children to select as many of their own activities as possible. Provide a physical setting which encourages individual or small, informal groups rather than large group time for most of the day.

present, they can be coaxed to plan and organize activities and to recall experiences. At mid-morning, children can be asked what they did earlier in the day.

- As children are developing the ability to symbolize experience, provide many opportunities to express ideas in a variety of forms such as stories and music.
- Children are developing the ability to deal with complex abstract ideas. Provide opportunities for children to note similarities and differences between objects around them. Children can be asked to compare or contrast any two familiar items in terms of color, size, or function.

Five- and six-year-olds

- Plan activities that encourage children to have a personal reason for problem solving and exchanging their perspectives with other children. Arguing and debating become important mechanisms for sharing points of view. Cooperative learning can also be fostered as children work together

at a meaningful task such as serving a snack (Tudge and Caruso 1988; Williams and Kamii 1986).

- Children are developing concentration and can now pay attention to a single activity for as long as 15–20 minutes. Give children time to develop their emerging concentration by allowing them to explore materials for longer and longer periods.
- Provide opportunities for children to engage in activities that involve the handling of simple directions up to three or four sequenced steps: recipes, origami, and so forth.

Seven- and eight-year-olds

- Children can concentrate on selected activities for indefinite periods. Provide opportunities for children to select and complete chosen projects.
- Provide opportunities for children to represent internal events. Children can now place themselves mentally into situations they have never actually experienced. Ask

	SAMPLE CURRICULUM	
	KINDERGARTEN AND PRIMARY GRADES (ages six, seven, and eight years)	
Characteristics	*Needs*	*Classroom Suggestions*
Can be impulsive	Opportunities to demonstrate self control	Set clear limits in a positive way and have children participate in rule making. Use group problem solving to resolve discipline problems.
Like more and can accept more independent activity	Opportunities to demonstrate self-sufficiency	Allow children to make suggestions regarding classroom improvement. Support children in their decision making.
Enjoy working with other children	Opportunities to cooperate and assist each other	Provide small-group activity for children to cooperate with and help other children.
Continue to be curious about their world	Opportunities to investigate the world around them	Arrange for field trips and people in the community to enhance classroom projects.
Are using language as a means of communicating thinking and problem solving	Opportunities for verbal expression	Provide reading and writing actvities that will enhance ongoing projects. Use quality literature by reading aloud stories and poetry each day and asking the children to share in this oral reading. Plan class projects such as book making or preparing a class newspaper.
Like to express themselves creatively	Opportunities to explore their creativity	Plan ways to integrate art, music, dance, and drama into ongoing projects.
Are using symbol systems	Opportunities to use symbols	Assist children in developing reading, writing, and mathematics skills when these are needed to explore or solve meaningful problems.
Are able to make choices and monitor their decisions	Opportunities to exercise decision-making skills	Provide opportunities to work individually and in small groups with self-selected projects for a greater part of the time. Involve children in their own self-management (e.g., setting their own goals, budgeting their time, evaluating their work, and cooperating with each other.

children to represent fantasies: What do you think it would be like to fly, to visit another planet, to tap dance on mustard, or to turn into clay?

· Children are able to give more thought to decisions. Have children go back to earlier projects, reconstruct them, make them better.

· Remember that reading and writing are best supported when activities are contextual or are the result of meaningful experiences.

Young children are concrete thinkers, which means they are able to think with seemingly adult logic as long as they can manipulate objects at the same time. Concrete thinkers need curriculum experiences that do not demand extensive application of abstract reasoning. Using manipulatives, concrete thinkers are able to understand many sophisticated mathematical and scientific concepts. For exam-

ple, the concrete thinker can solve the problem of mixing all the possible combinations of primary colors if allowed to use the colors and create the combinations, but cannot mentally construct all the possible combinations.

Activities do not need to be designed to teach children "thinking." Thinking and reasoning should be part of every child's experience. When children are provided with opportunities to explore objects, formulate hypotheses, gather information, and draw their own conclusions, they are already thinking and do not need to be taught.

Other considerations for curriculum planning may include:

1. Preparing children for the complexities of modern-day life and the future. Hartmann (1977) suggests ways to help young children develop (*a*) focusing skills necessary to deal with a highly stimulating world, (*b*) decision-making skills, (*c*) independence, and (*d*) curiosity.

2. Multicultural education should be integrated throughout the curriculum; however, the *Early Childhood Public School Study* (1988) found culturally relevant activities to be isolated in the form of special events, even in schools serving predominantly minority students. Programs such as the *Anti-Bias Curriculum* (Derman-Sparks and ABC Task Force 1989) propose that different methods be used to achieve these goals of ability, gender, and racial equality.

3. Assist children in exploring computer and related technologies through manipulation of (as opposed to being manipulated by) the computer, and use the computer to broaden other learnings.

Curriculum Organization

The most common approaches for organizing curriculum for young children are the *facts approach* and the *skills approach*. With a facts approach, children learn given sets of factual information, such as the days of the week, the alphabet, or the names of colors. With a skills approach, children acquire knowledge by engaging in developmentally appropriate experiences such as cutting on a line, sharing materials with one another, or discovering information in reference books.

The most common curriculum organization in elementary schools has been the *subject matter approach*, in which children learn specific subjects such as reading, math, or social studies. Another approach is *thematic organization*, in which knowledge is integrated around a unifying theme, such as a study of insects, time, or Native American cultures (Schwartz and Robison 1982). In the 1960s, Bruner (1960) and other curriculum theorists helped curriculum designers cluster classroom activity around key concepts in the various discipline areas. The broadest curriculum organizers are the basic human needs shared by all people: friends, social responsibility, and so on.

The Developmentally Appropriate Curriculum: An Integrated Thematic View

The most productive organizer for developmentally appropriate curriculum is the *thematic approach*, where learning experiences are arranged around a chosen topic. Carefully selected themes allow children to learn facts in a meaningful context while simultaneously developing and applying skills from various subject areas.

Objectives in the thematic approach are rather broad (in comparison to objectives used in subject matter approaches.) The broader the objectives, the wider the range of activities that can be offered. Varying skill levels and interests can then be accommodated, and a variety of performance measures utilized.

The idea of using an integrated curriculum is not new. John Dewey (1902) advocated the organization of curriculum around common interests that would involve children. Even so, the most common curriculum approach in the United States today continues to be a subject matter organization, in which learning is segmented into lessons for math or science or language arts (Jacobs 1989). In elementary school you have reading in the morning, math before lunch, and science in the afternoon. Yet, children do not learn in fragments like this; instead, they learn in wholes. Contexted learning is not the enemy of understanding but rather a resource for gaining insight into how children learn in their everyday lives outside of school.

For children (or anyone) to learn optimally, they must consider the information personally useful, not something learned to please someone else.

Themes must be carefully selected, planned, and monitored to make certain children are truly involved and continue to expand upon the original theme.

Selecting a Theme

Katz and Chard (1989) list the following criteria for selecting a theme:

- Relevance: Why would this child want to learn about this topic?
- Opportunities for application of skills: Are children using their language and computational skills in activities that are motivating for them?
- Availability of resources: Are there community and library resources that can contribute adequately to this topic?

- Teacher interest: Why choose a topic if you are not personally interested in it? (There are too many other alternatives.)
- Time of year: How are children's previous experiences going to affect their acceptance of this theme? (The earliest topics presented should be ones that the teacher knows the children are familiar with but that will still spark their interest.)

Katz and Chard (1989) group topics of study in the following way:

1. The children themselves: homes, babies, families, food, school bus, television shows, toys, games.
2. The local community: people, hospital, shops, building site, transport services, waterworks, fish market.
3. Local events and current affairs: annual carnival or county fair, important anniversary, Independence Day, visit by famous person.
4. Place: neighborhood, roads, directions, landmarks, rivers, hills, woods.
5. Time: clocks, seasons, calendar, festivals, holidays, historical events, historical objects.
6. Natural phenomena: weather, water, wind and air, plants, animals, rocks, the sea, dinosaurs.
7. Content-free concepts: opposites, pattern, color, symmetry.
8. General knowledge: deserts, ships and other vehicles, inventions, space travel, river.
9. Miscellaneous: hats, black holes, puppets, math or book week.

There are many different topics available and certainly many different ways of grouping these topics. Teachers will want to balance their program by alternating emphases, such as science with social studies and/or language with creative arts. For example, plant study typically has a science focus, and map study a social studies focus.

The main reasons for implementing a thematic approach is so children have the opportunity to explore particular topics in depth rather than superficially. Yet using a thematic organization does not guarantee developmentally appropriate curriculum. Thematic organization can be trivialized, so that a potentially rigorous study of bears, their habits, the hibernation process, and famous bears in literature (Winnie the Pooh, Paddington) and history (Teddy Roosevelt) can be reduced to making teddy bear cookies and paper cutouts.

Child-Centered Themes

Whatever theme is selected, it needs to be initiated by the children. Teachers need to be mindful of informal discussions, items children bring from home, and favorite television programs and performers. These naturally evolving interests are the stuff themes are made of. For example, if Ninja Turtles or the like are found in lunch boxes and cubbies, a theme on turtles may prove engrossing.

Implementing the Theme

Once a topic has been selected, the teacher and children can brainstorm using a web format, such as the one shown here:

Grouping Subtopics and Developing Activities

After ideas are generated, subtopics can be combined into larger units and activities developed to help children learn content and apply skills in meaningful contexts.

1. Author study: A. A. Milne, author and illustrator of Winnie the Pooh
   - Read aloud and discussion
   - Dramatization and videotaping of story segments
   - Discussion of personality types (compare and contrast Pooh, Eeyore, and Christopher Robin)

2. Honey
   - How and why bears make honey
   - The uses of honey in ancient times
   - Recipes with honey
   - Visit to a bee farm
   - Commercial uses of honey
3. Hibernation
   - How, why, and where bees hibernate
   - Investigation of other animals who hibernate
   - Visit to a national forest
   - Viewing of National Geographic films on various bear groups
4. The polar bear
   - Life in the Arctic Circle
   - Other polar-region animals
   - Compare and contrast nutritional habits and care of polar bear babies with those of the American brown bear.

After subtopics have been grouped and discussed, children can volunteer additional activities to use in the study. Teachers will need to make certain that language and computational skills are applied throughout: Children can write haiku about the endangered panda and learn to measure ingredients for porridge. Topics and/or activities not related to particular curriculum goals will need to be revised by the teacher.

A teacher can work with the children to devise ways to introduce the topic. For example, the bear study can begin with each child bringing his or her (or a friend's) teddy bear from home and then writing an invented biography of the teddy. Learning centers can be outfitted with objects and materials that support the bear study. The library corner should be replete with Paddington, Berenstain Bears, Pooh, and many informational books on bear anatomy, family care, and environmental adaptation.

The following is a list of additional activities related to bears.

1. Create a web about bears with the children. Determine what they already know.
2. Invite a zoologist to the classroom and have her bring film about the real bear habitats, habits, and life cycles.
3. Use reference and other informational books to find information about bears living throughout the world: pandas, polar bears, brown bears, etc.
4. Create a chart comparing the characteristics of bears and other animal groups that children may know about.
5. Construct a habitat for a specific bear.
6. Dramatize one of the Paddington stories.
7. View a film about bears. Create a chart summarizing the facts presented in the film.
8. Create a booklet describing the life cycle of a bear.

Delivery System

Teachers must also plan the delivery system for prearranged activities using *learning centers* or *learning episodes*. Learning centers are places where equipment and materials are arranged for child-selected dramatic play, library, science, art, or music activities. In contrast, learning episodes are teacher-directed activities involving one child, a small group, or the entire class.

The delivery system is determined by the psycho-philosophical approach. The behaviorist approach emphasizes learning episodes. The interactionist approach uses learning centers and episodes, the emphasis remaining on learning centers. Spodek (1985) suggests that the unit of instruction for early childhood is the activity. *Activity* differs from *lesson* in that it does not have a formal beginning, middle, and end; it is often open-ended; and it is not teacher-prescribed. Children, rather than teachers, drive and designate its content.

Prearranging Activities for Learning Centers

In some early childhood programs, children are permitted to use any materials in the learning center in any way they wish. There are no planned activities, and, as a result, children's needs can remain unrealized.

The specific objectives of the program determine the appropriate equipment and materials selected and arranged in learning centers; if the objective is for children to be able to name primary colors, materials that will help achieve this objective are prearranged in the learning centers. The following are some examples:

1. In the art center, red, yellow, and blue collage materials are provided.

2. In the manipulative and/or mathematics center, sorting boxes of primary-colored objects are left on the carpet.
3. In the block center, primary-colored building blocks and Lego materials are available.
4. In the library corner, stories, posters, and mobiles emphasizing primary colors are displayed.

Designing a Learning Episode

In developing a learning episode emphasizing the same objective (naming the primary colors), a teacher could read *Colors To Talk About* by Leo Lionni, followed by discussion; hold a color-naming contest; or devise a playlet with crayons as the leading characters. Learning episodes have a separate purpose from learning centers. They are used to determine the appropriateness of equipment and materials, and are effective when introducing new concepts to children. In addition, inexperienced teachers can often become familiar with a concept more easily during a learning episode rather than during activities in learning centers.

Learning centers and episodes can be used simultaneously to achieve similar objectives. Often, learning episodes complement the individualized practice offered in the learning centers by emphasizing the contributions of the entire class and the teacher.

Learning Plans

A *learning plan* differs from a *lesson plan* in that a lesson plan generally outlines prepares one lesson at a time. Learning experiences are not usually confined to one lesson in early childhood programs. As Elkind (1987) reminds us, "Clearly children learn in many different ways and what mode of learning is employed depends very much upon what is to be learned." As a teacher in a program, you may not have much control over program goals. In the best case, these are developed with the collaboration of teachers, but most often they are established by the administration at the school-district level. Even so, program goals do not describe how objectives are to be achieved. The *hows* are left to the teacher and should reflect her own unique strengths and interests as well as her particular knowledge of

the children's abilities as evidenced in her classroom. Each day's activities should contribute to the overall focus of the program.

A daily learning plan may contain a list of the equipment and materials available in the learning centers, suggest plans for evaluation, and include notes on specific children's development.

Learning plans should always be as complete as possible, but should never be so rigid that *incidental learning*, learning that occurs in addition to what is written into the learning plan, cannot be included in the day's schedule. The point of using a learning plan is to take advantage of what the children want to know on a day-to-day basis as you keep the overall program goals in mind.

Learning Plan (3- to 4-year-olds)

Program goals. Enhance problem-solving skills and language and fine-motor development.
Theme. Trees.
Objectives. Children will be able to distinguish various species of local trees. Children will learn vocabulary of leaf, trunk, roots, acorn. Children will learn the various foods trees bear: nuts, berries, fruit.
Activity time. **Discovery:** Visit an orchard for apple picking. **Art:** Use leaves collected from local trees for printing (cover leaf with paint and press paper over it). **Library:** Display information books about trees.
Small groups. Take a walk around the school to observe different kinds of trees. Gather leaves, acorns, pine cones, and so on for use in collages. Each child has a small bag or box for collecting.
Cooking. Mr. Turner (parent volunteer) will help children pare and dice apples gathered at orchard to make apple butter.
Movement. Pretend to be trees swaying in the wind.
Evaluation. Teacher will observe children's responses to apple picking activity and will record evidence of tree knowledge on walk.

Learning Plan (6- to 7-year-olds)

Program goals. Enhance ability to communicate, and increase literacy and problem solving.
Theme. Fairy tales.

Objectives. Children will be able to note similarities and differences between and among folktales. Children will be able to describe a round character versus a flat character. Children will devise original endings to traditional fairy tales. *Activity time.* **Social studies:** Have children gather folktales from different countries. Organize oral reading of this literature. Make a chart that lists the similarities and differences between and among various folktales. **Language arts:** After oral readings of several fairy tales and/or fables, children will draw pictures of round and flat characters. They will use captions to describe their pictures. **Writing:** Children will select a favorite fairy tale and write an original ending to the story. Children will share these endings with one another. *Movement.* Stage several ethnic tales using traditional music and dances. *Evaluation.* Teacher will evaluate contributions to folktale chart, originality of story endings, and character drawings.

Evaluation

When focusing on a given theme, teachers record each child's progress and how the program goals were met. One recording method is the evaluation checklist, constructed for each child for each theme of study, as in the following example:

SAMPLE EVALUATION CHECKLIST

Child's Name:_____

Theme: Fairy Tales

Reads a variety of materials:
reference materials, narrative stories, poetry

Participates in writing process:
personal writing, narratives, expository writing

Uses problem-solving skills

Contributes ideas to group planning

Rarely can a theme be repeated in the same form from year to year. Different groups of children vary considerably. Themes that work well with one group of children are not at all

exciting to others. Even if topics are repeated, the activities chosen are likely to vary so that one year's implementation will not be the same as the previous year's. If a teacher simply supplies a theme to the children, rather than applying children to a theme, the process becomes mechanical, and the contexted learning is lost in the routine.

Individualizing the Curriculum

According to Hendricks (1992), the teacher can ask three questions in order to determine whether the curriculum is sufficiently individualized:

1. Are there some recent instances where curriculum was based on a child's specific interests?
2. Can examples be identified where a child was deliberately provided with opportunities to learn what evaluations had indicated that he especially needed to know?
3. Can examples be cited where curriculum plans were changed because a child revealed an unanticipated interest or enthusiasm during the day?

Current Trends in Curriculum

Whole language and cooperative learning are having widespread application of late in the early childhood curriculum. Even so, many teachers remain unfamiliar with the basic philosophy of these approaches.

Whole Language

Like many other curriculum entities, language cannot be treated as an isolated entity. There is virtually no portion of any person's day that does not include some form of language use. The theory behind the whole language approach is confirmed by Goodman (1986):

> Language learning is easy when it is whole, real, and relevant; when it makes sense and is functional; when it is encountered in the context of its use; and when the learner chooses to use it.

Halliday (1978) says this of the whole language philosophy:

Language comes to life only when it is functioning in some environment. We do not experience language in isolation—if we did, we would not recognize it as language—but always in relation to a scenario, some background of periods and actions and events from which the things are said to derive their meaning.

In other words, the less integrated or collaborative the educational model, the more difficult language learning becomes for the child. Language learning should do the following:

- Focus upon meaningful experiences and meaningful language in context rather than upon isolated skill development.
- Provide language experiences as an integrated part of the broader communications process, which involves sensory experiences including art, movement, music, and play.
- Encourage children to be active participants in the learning process rather than passive recipients of knowledge by using activities that allow for experimentation and self-direction.

What Goodman coined the "whole language" philosophy is built on the premise that the development of language must be understood as interdependent and reciprocal in nature.

Cooperative Learning

It is apparent that children learn as much (if not more) from one another as they do from teachers and other adults. Like whole language, which simply articulates and reinforces the natural learning environment for language, cooperative learning establishes the natural learning context for social development, and uses this phenomenon as a motivational tool for assimilating academic content and working successfully with diverse groups of children.

Teachers can use cooperative learning in all content areas, with all ability groupings, and with all developmental levels. This learning technique frees the teacher from direct instruction and management of large groups of children and allows her more time to observe individuals and bolster students with specialized needs. Children can work in pairs or smaller or larger groups depending on the task. Student teams are devised by the teacher so that groups

contain a good balance of various personality types for fruitful interaction (Foyle, Lyman, and Thies 1992).

Scheduling

Scheduling greatly influences the children's feeling of security, the accomplishment of objectives, and the staff's effectiveness. Scheduling involves planning the length of the session and timing and arranging activities during the session.

Timing and Arranging Activities

Regardless of whether the session is full-day or half-day, as is the case for preschool and kindergarten, good schedules for early childhood programs have certain characteristics:

1. A good session begins with a friendly, informal greeting of the children. Staff members should make an effort to speak with each child individually during the first few minutes of each session. A group activity such as a greeting song also helps children feel welcome.
2. Children's physical needs, such as toileting and eating, should be cared for at regular intervals in the schedule. Special times should be set aside for toileting early in the session, before and after each meal or snack, and before and after resting. Meals should be served every four or five hours, and snacks should be served midway between meals; however, each child's individual needs must be considered.
3. The schedule must provide a balance between physical activity and rest. Young children are prone to become overtired without realizing their need for relaxation.
4. The schedule should fit the psycho-philosophical view of the program and the needs of the children as individuals and a group. There should be a balance between indoor and outdoor activities, group and individual times, and activities selected by children and staff.
5. The schedule must be flexible under unexpected circumstances, such as inclement weather, children's interests different from those planned for, and emergencies.

6. A good schedule should be readily understandable to the children so they will have a feeling of security and will not waste time trying to figure out what to do next.

7. A good session ends with a general evaluation of activities, straightening of indoor and outdoor areas, a hint about the next session, and a farewell. Children need to end a session with the feeling they have achieved something and with a desire to return. These feelings are important to staff members, too!

Every program should have its own schedule. Programs that serve children of different age groups, such as infants and toddlers, must have more than one schedule so that each group's needs will be met.

Schedules must fit the length of the program day, week, and year. However, scheduling usually refers to the timing of daily activities. In general, schedules are often referred to as "flexible" or "fixed." *Flexible schedules* permit children to choose how to spend their time, and require children to participate in group activities for only a few routines during the day, such as the morning greeting and short periods of group instruction. Infant programs must have perhaps the most flexible schedules of all early childhood programs because infants stay on their own schedules, regardless of adults. Day care programs often have flexible schedules due to their longer hours of operations, the children's staggered arrivals and departures, and the varying ages of the children the center serves. Programs adhering to the interactionist view also have long, flexible time periods.

Other programs place more emphasis upon group conformity by having *fixed schedules*, by expecting children to work and play with others at specified times, and by taking care of even the most basic human differences—appetites and bodily functions—at prescribed times except for emergencies. Often programs for primary grade–level children have fixed schedules. Behaviorist programs are very time-oriented. The National Association for the Education of Young Children states that flexible schedules are developmentally appropriate (Brendekamp 1984).

The following schedule examples for different age groups are only suggestions; they are not prescriptive. Examples are not given for public school programs adhering to state regulations regarding scheduling (i.e., state departments of education often specify the total length of school day and the number of minutes of instruction in each of the basic subjects).

Prekindergartens and kindergartens can be either half- or full-day, with children arriving and departing at approximately the same times. Kindergartens usually schedule longer group times than pre-K because kindergartens have more structured activities.

Primary grade schedules tend to be the most highly structured.

Sample Schedules

Half-day program for pre-K

Times	Activities
9:00-10:00	Activity Time
10:00-10:20	Music and Movement
10:20-10:40	Group Time (calendar, weather, discussions)
10:40-11:00	Outdoor Play
11:00-11:10	Snack
11:10-11:30	Story, Poetry

Full-day kindergarten

Times	Activities
9:00-9:15	Opening, singing, planning for the day
9:15-10:15	Activity Time
10:15-10:45	Snack
10:45-11:15	Outdoor Play (gross motor play indoors in bad weather)
11:15-11:45	Story Time, Literature Study
11:45-12:30	Lunch and Recess
12:30-1:30	Rest Period
1:30-1:40	Group Time (discussion, planning for afternoon)
1:40-2:15	Activity Time
2:15-2:45	Library, Music, Art, or Physical Education
2:45-3:00	Evaluation of Activities, Dismissal

Primary children

Times	Activities
9:00-9:15	Opening, planning for the day
9:15-10:30	Activity Time
10:30-11:00	Physical Education
11:00-11:30	Math Activities
11:30-12:30	Lunch, Recess

12:30-1:00	Literature Activities (read aloud, drama)
1:00-2:00	Activity Time (theme studies)
2:00-2:20	Recess
2:20-2:45	Library (alternating with art or music)
2:45-3:00	Sharing events of the day, discussions, plans for the next day, dismissal

Details of the Schedule

Activity Time

If the theme were a study of insects, children could work puzzles depicting insects in the manipulatives area; observe insects on display in the science area using a magnifying glass and record their observations; read or look at pictures in books about insects; sort pictures of insects; examine sequence board showing the life cycle of insects; and play with puppet and flannel board cut-outs of insects in the language arts area. Children might paint or draw insects or build insect homes in the art area. Whatever the theme, it should be incorporated into as many areas as possible and reasonable.

Group Time

Some additional group-time experiences are not especially meaningful to children. Three- and four-year-olds probably do not need group time at all. Trying to get them to learn about the calendar is not the best use of their time. Five- and six-year-olds can review the calendar and daily weather, but these should be brief reviews, not extended drills. Other activities appropriate for group time for fives and sixes include planning and evaluating their experiences during activity time, participating in some short group experiences such as viewing a video tape that relates to a theme topic, listening to a resource person, discussing a problem in the room, having specific instruction in fire safety, and so on. Whole-group instruction is not an appropriate teaching strategy for content area; lecturing on a topic to children of this age is of little value.

Group time with primary children may be used for some of the same activities as those suggested for fives and sixes. It may also be used to help children recognize the choices they can make for their theme studies and do more formal planning of their day. Some limited group instruction with primary children is useful. For example, the teacher may teach the whole group to recognize story structure or to recognize particular strategies that an author has used in a story the children are reading. Group discussions of books the children are reading are also important. Having children present work they have completed can also be an important component of group time in the primary grades.

Show and tell, or sharing, is often a regular part of group time, especially with five- to eight-year-olds. Show and tell often becomes "bring and brag" as children bring their newest toy to show off. The teacher usually controls the audience for the speaker and directs the children while they speak or ask questions. If sharing time is to achieve the goal of promoting more effective communication, however, teachers must structure the time so that children do the talking and organizing rather than the teacher. One technique is to have the sharing focus on the children's work, rather than on objects brought from home.

Children may also need to share something everyday. Another technique is to organize sharing time into small groups so that children share with three or four other children and do not have to sit while twenty-five children share. It is important to evaluate sharing experiences on the basis of what the children are actually learning, rather than simply to state glibly that sharing is important for the children to learn to communicate more effectively.

Snack Time

Very young children need a snack during the morning or afternoon. Snack time should be considered a teaching time as children learn about new foods, learn to carry on conversations, and learn how to help prepare and serve the snack. Snacks should always be nutritious and help children learn about nutrition. Snack time for fives and sixes can be quite time-consuming in a half-day program when time is so limited. By the time all the children wash their hands, are served, eat their snack, and clean up, twenty to thirty minutes out of a two-and-a-half-hour day have been used up. Therefore, some teachers prefer to have snacks available on a table so that two or three children can serve themselves and then go back to their activities. Other teachers prefer to incorporate snack time into activity time by making food preparation one of the activities. In this way the activity time can be extended.

Program Assessment

The purpose of program assessment is twofold: (1) to determine whether the program is appropriate for the children currently enrolled in it; and (2) to ascertain the program's effectiveness in terms of growth in the program. The following questions can help teachers evaluate their programs:

1. Why would you like to be a child in your classroom?
2. How are small-group, whole-group, and individual activities balanced throughout the day?
3. How is children's time balanced between self-selected and teacher-prescribed activities?
4. How are children's interests used to develop new activities and learning experiences?
5. How can each child in your classroom find success and challenge each day?
6. How are the intellectual, social, emotional, and physical aspects of growth integrated across the curriculum?
7. How are specific skills taught in meaningful contexts?
8. How can children withdraw from an activity without penalty? What alternatives are offered in this circumstance?
9. How do program goals influence the activities and learning experiences of individual children as well as the group?
10. How is information from observations and assessment used for curriculum planning?
11. How do individual children demonstrate their learning?
12. How do interactions with parents support the children's growth?

Summary

When one looks at the unique ways young children mature and develop, it is clear why early childhood education is best seen as a progression from birth to eight years of age. Educators are encouraged to observe young children's development in order to plan programs and activities that apply knowledge of child development and thus are *developmentally appropriate*. Developmentally appropriate programs speak to the variations on the theme of human development yet still address the larger needs of the group. The following developmentally appropriate practices for curriculum planning and scheduling were highlighted in this chapter.

1. Curriculum coincides with and fosters natural development. Skills and concepts are not only age-/stage-appropriate, but are integrated (as opposed to isolated or artificial), and introduced as relevant activities clustered around meaningful themes and projects. The individual needs of each child are met as small-group activities are often selected by the child and hence represent his or her unique interests within the larger interest of the group.
2. The planning of schedules should reflect the same developmentally appropriate practice as curriculum planning. Scheduling needs of the group and individuals must be considered simultaneously while providing a balance of activities.

Recommended Further Reading

Brown, J. F. 1982. *Curriculum Planning for Young Children.* Washington, DC: National Association for the Education of Young Children.

Katz, L. G., and S. C. Chard. 1989. *Engaging Children's Minds: The Project Approach.* Norwood, NJ: Ablex.

Schwartz, S. L., and H. F. Robison. 1982. *Designing Curriculum for Early Childhood.* Boston: Allyn and Bacon.

References

Brendekamp, S. 1984. *Accreditation Criteria and Procedures of the National Academy of Early Childhood Programs.* Washington, DC: National Association for the Education of Young Children.

Bruner, J. 1960. *The Process of Education.* New York: Vintage Books.

Derman-Sparks, L., and ABC Task Force. 1989. *Anti-Bias Curriculum Tools for Empowering Children.* Washington, DC: National Association for the Education of Young Children.

Dewey, J. 1902. *The Child and the Curriculum.* Chicago: Univ. of Chicago Press.

Elkind, D. 1987. *Miseducation: Preschoolers at Risk.* New York: Knopf.

Foyle, H. C., L. Lyman, and S. A. Thies. 1992. *Cooperative Learning in Early Childhood Education.* West Haven, CT: NEA Professional Library.

Goodman, J. 1986. *What Is Whole in Whole Language.* Glenview, IL: Scott Foresman.

Halliday, M.A.K. 1978. *Language as a Social Semiotic.* Baltimore: University Park Press.

Hartmann, K. 1977. "How Do I Teach in a Future Shocked World?" *Young Children* 32(3): 32–36.

Hendrick, J. 1992. *The Whole Child.* New York: Macmillan.

Jacobs, H. 1989. *Interdisciplinary Curriculum: Design and Implementation.* Alexandria, VA: Association for Supervision and Curriculum Development.

Katz, L. G., and S. C. Chard. 1989. *Engaging Children's Minds: The Project Approach.* Norwood, NJ: Ablex.

Lynch-Fraser, D. 1991. *Playdancing: Discovering and Developing Creativity in Young Children.* Pennington, NJ: Princeton Books.

Marx, F., and M. Seligson. 1988. *The Public School Early Childhood Study.* New York: Bank Street College.

National Association of State Boards of Education. 1988. *Right from the Start. The Report of the NASBE Task Force on Early Childhood Education.* Alexandria, VA: National Association of State Boards of Education.

Spodex, B. 1985. *Teaching in the Early Years.* Englewood Cliffs, NJ: Prentice-Hall.

Tudge, J., and D. Caruso. 1988. "Cooperative Problem Solving in the Classroom. Enhancing Young Children's Cognitive Development." *Young Children* 44 (Nov.): 46–52.

Weikart, D. P. 1988. "Hard Choices in Early Childhood Care and Education: A View to the Future." *Young Children* 44 (Nov.): 25–30.

Williams, C. K., and C. Kamii. 1986. "How Do Children Learn by Handling Objects?" *Young Children* 42 (Nov.): 23–26.

Zigler, E. F., and M. Finn-Stevenson. 1987. *Children: Children and Social Issues.* Lexington, MA: D. C. Heath.

FUNDING CURRICULUM PROJECTS

THE greatest challenge curriculum developers often face is locating money to finance their projects. We hear that such money is available but are at a loss to find how it can be accessed. Frequently, it requires as much creativity to locate financing as it does to generate the curriculum. This chapter includes information on three types of funding available for education projects:

1. Federal programs that provide money for special school projects
2. Foundations that have recently endowed early childhood education projects or programs that focus on parent involvment in education
3. Foundations that either identify education, including special projects, as a mission, or have granted money to education-related projects in the past.

This chapter highlights funding available for projects that include early childhood education. Some of them, however, target a specific population. It is important to keep your specific goal in mind when seeking backing for your project. Think of all the areas your program will include. Does it focus on developing language skills in children who are economically disadvantaged? If so, include in your search foundations that support language acquisition projects and programs that benefit economically disadvantaged groups. Consider other areas that may be applicable, such as children who are gifted/handicapped, volunteer programs, bilingual education, improving parenting skills, and specific immigrant groups, minorities, and academic areas (e.g., math, science, social studies). Brainstorming with your colleagues will enable you to develop a complete list of all possible areas.

When referencing a potential funding source, review any information that is available about the foundation. Specifically look at the following areas:

- *Purpose*: Is providing money for education a mission of the foundation?
- *Limitations*: Are there specific geographic requirements? Are there some regions that are disqualified?
- *Supported areas*: Does the foundation provide funding for special projects?
- *Grants*: After a review of the education projects that have been funded, does it appear that these organizations and projects are similar to yours?

Your search will be most useful if you also keep these questions in mind:

- Has the foundation funded projects in your subject area?
- Does your location meet the geographic requirements of the foundation?
- Is the amount of money you are requesting within the grant's range?
- Are there foundation policies that prohibit grants for the type of support you are requesting?
- Will the foundation make grants to cover the full cost of a project? Does it require costs of a project to be shared with other foundations or funding sources?
- What types of organizations have been supported? Are they similar to yours?
- Are there specific application deadlines and procedures, or are proposals accepted continuously?

Detailed information can be found in the foundation's annual report or in *Source Book Profiles.* Many of the larger public libraries maintain current foundation directories. If yours does not, there are Foundation Center Libraries at the following locations:

79 Fifth Avenue
New York, NY 10003-3050
(212) 620-4230

312 Sutter Street
San Francisco, CA 94180
(415) 397-0902

1001 Connecticut Avenue, NW
Suite 938
Washington, DC 20036
(202) 331-1400

1442 Hanna Building
1442 Euclid Avenue
Cleveland, OH 44115
(216) 861-1934

Identifying appropriate foundations is the first step in your quest for money. The next step is initiating contact with the foundation, either by telephone, letter, or proposal. It is a good idea to direct your inquiry to the person in charge of giving; otherwise, you run the risk of your letter going astray. As this position changes often, a phone call to the foundation will provide you with the current name.

Federal Programs Providing Money for Special School Projects

Chapter 1 Programs—Local Educational
  Agencies
Compensatory Education Programs
Office of Elementary and Secondary Education
Department of Education
400 Maryland Avenue, SW, Room 2043
Washington, DC 20202-6132
(202) 401-1682
Provides 80% funding for "follow-through" projects related to parent participation from kindergarten to grade 3. Also available are discretionary matching funds to operate family-centered education projects involving parents in

the education of their children (including migratory children).

Jacob B. Javits Gifted and Talented Students
Research Applications Division
Programs for the Improvement of Practice
Department of Education
555 New Jersey Avenue, NW
Washington, DC 20202-5643
(202) 219-2187
Provides grants for establishing and operating model projects to identify and educate gifted and talented students.

The Secretary's Fund for Innovation in
  Education
Department of Education
FIRST
Office of Educational Research and
  Improvement
Washington, DC 20208-5524
(202) 219-1496
Funding for educational programs and projects that identify innovative educational approaches and for demonstration family–school partnership projects designed to improve educational achievement of children in prekindergarten through grade 12.

Division of State and Local Programs
Office of Bilingual Education and Minority
  Languages Affairs
Department of Education
330 C Street, SW, Room 5086
Washington, DC 20202
(202) 732-5700
Contact: Director
Funding for projects to improve bilingual education, ESL, and English proficiency programs at all levels from preschool to adult education.

Transition Program for Refugee Children
Office of Bilingual Education and Minority
  Languages Affairs
Department of Education
330 C Street, SW, Room 5086
Washington, DC 20202
(202) 732-5708
Provides funding for programs meeting the special needs of refugee children in elementary and secondary schools.

Emergency Immigrant Education
Office of Bilingual Education and Minority
    Languages Affairs
Department of Education
330 C Street, SW, Room 5615
Washington, DC 20202
(202) 732-5708
Funding for immigrant children in grades K-12.

Division of Educational Support
Office of Elementary and Secondary Education
Department of Education
400 Maryland Avenue, SW, Mail Stop 624
Washington, DC 20202-6438
(202) 401-1342
Funding to projects that demonstrate effective
elementary and secondary school dropout and
reentry programs.

International Reading Association
800 Barksdale Road
P.O. Box 8139
Newark, DE 19714-8139
(302) 731-1600; (800) 336-READ
A small grants division provides money for
reading programs and projects.

National Council of Teachers of English
Grants Office
1111 Kenyon Road
Urbana, IL 61801
(217) 328-3870
Funding for language arts programs and
projects.

Reading Research Education
University of Illinois
Champaign, IL 61820
(217) 333-2452
Provides grants for reading projects.

Foundations that Have Recently Supported Early Childhood Education Projects and Programs Focusing on Parent Involvement in Education

Altman Foundation
220 East 42d Street, Suite 411
New York, NY 10017
(212) 682-0970
Contact: John S. Burke, President

• $20,000 to Northside Center for Child
  Development, New York City, to support
  Early Childhood Learning Center.
Giving limited to New York, with emphasis on
the New York City boroughs. Initial approach
through letter.

ARCO Foundation
515 South Flower Street
Los Angeles, CA 94104
(415) 421-2629
Contact: Eugene R. Wilson, President
• $50,000 to High/Scope Educational Re-
  search Foundation, Ypsilanti, MI, for
  teacher-trainer project for early childhood
  education in day care centers.
• $15,000 to Mi Escuelita Preschool, Dallas,
  TX, for early childhood education
  program.
• $10,000 to Pacific Oaks College, Pasa-
  dena, CA, for evaluation of early childhood education in Pasadena.
Giving primarily in the San Francisco Bay area.

Mary Reynolds Babcock Foundation, Inc.
102 Reynolda Village
Winston-Salem, NC 27106-5123
(919) 748-9222
Contact: William L. Bondurant, Executive
    Director
• $40,000 to State of North Carolina,
  Department of Public Instruction, Raleigh,
  for early childhood education program
  incorporating parent education, health
  services, and prenatal care.
Will not support educational institutions outside
of North Carolina.

The Blandin Foundation
100 Pokegama Avenue, North
Grand Rapids, MN 55744
(218) 326-0523
Contact: Paul M. Olson, President
• $125,500 to Grand Rapids Independent
  School District 318, Rapids Quest Pro-
  gram, Grand Rapids, MN, to continue
  imaginative enrichment programs for
  Grand Rapids students.
• $15,000 to Family Resource Center of
  Southern Chisago County, Chisago City,
  MN, to expand training and ensure
  quality, comprehensive early childhood

education for rural children and youth at risk in Isanti County.

Limited to Minnesota, with an emphasis on rural areas.

Eva L. & Joseph M. Bruening Foundation
627 Hanna Building
1422 Euclid Avenue
Cleveland, OH 44115
(216) 621-2632
Contact: Janet E. Narten, Executive Secretary

- $25,000 to Marotta Montessori School, Cleveland, OH, for operating support.

Giving limited to the greater Cleveland area. Initial approach through proposal.

The Cargill Foundation
P.O. Box 9300
Minneapolis, MN 55440
(612) 475-6122
Contact: Audrey Tulberg, Program and Administrative Director

- $12,500 to Saint Davids School, Minnetonka, MN.

Giving primarily in the seven-county Minneapolis–St. Paul metropolitan area.

Carnegie Corporation of New York
437 Madison Avenue
New York, NY 10022
(212) 371-3200
Contact: Dorothy W. Knapp, Secretary

- $159,000 to National Academy of Sciences, Washington, DC, for production and disemination of Spanish-language version of an elementary school mathematics kit for parents and children.

The Greater Cincinnati Foundation
Star Bank Center
425 Walnut Street, Suite 1110
Cincinnati, OH 45202-3915
(513) 241-2880
Contact: Ruth A. Cronenberg, Program Officer

- $15,000 to Kennedy Heights Parent Cooperative Nursery School, Cincinnati, OH.
- $15,000 to O. W. Motivational, Cincinnati, OH.

Giving limited to the greater Cincinnati area. Initial approach through letter or by telephone.

Liz Claiborne Foundation
119 West 40th Street, 4th Floor
New York, NY 10018
(212) 536-6424

- $10,000 to Harmony Early Learning Center, Secaucus, NJ.

Giving limited to Hudson County, NJ, and the metropolitan New York area.

The Cleveland Foundation
1422 Euclid Avenue, Suite 1400
Cleveland, OH 44115-2001
(216) 861-3810
Contact: Steven A. Minter, Executive Director

- $15,000 to Family Network, Minneapolis, MN, for Minneapolis Center Therapuetic Preschool for At-Risk Children.
- $95,000 to Marotta Montessori Schools of Cleveland, OH, for support of three sites.

Giving limited to the greater Cleveland area. Initial approach through letter.

The Collins Foundation
1618 SW First Avenue, Suite 305
Portland, OR 97201
(503) 227-7171
Contact: William C. Pine, Executive Vice President

- $24,000 to Tucker-Maxon Oral School, Portland, OR, for preschool program.
- $25,000 to YWCA of Portland, OR, for preschool.

Giving limited to Oregon, with emphasis on Portland. Initial approach through letter.

Communities Foundation of Texas, Inc.
4605 Live Oak Street
Dallas, TX 75204
(214) 826-5231

- $15,000 to Creative Learning Center, Dallas, TX.

Giving primarily in the Dallas area. Write letter requesting guidelines.

Dade Community Foundation
200 South Biscayne Boulevard, Suite 4770
Miami, FL 33131-2343
(305) 371-2711
Contact: Ruth Shack, President

- $12,500 to LeJardin Head Start, Homestead, FL.

Funding limited to Dade County, FL.

The Aaron Diamond Foundation
1270 Avenue of the Americas, Suite 2624
New York, NY 10020
(212) 757-7680
Contact: Vincent McGee, Executive Director
- $10,000 to Institute for Schools of the Future, New York City, for development and documentation of early childhood mathematics program.

Giving limited to New York City.

Geraldine R. Dodge Foundation, Inc.
163 Madison Avenue
P.O. Box 1239
Morristown, NJ 07962-1239
(201) 540-8442
- Support to various programs benefitting disadvantaged children.
- $30,000 to Planned Parenthood of Greater New Jersey, Morristown, to help schools and child care centers develop policies and programs regarding early childhood sexuality education.
- $50,000 to University of Virginia, Curry School of Education, Charlottesville, to restructure the school day of two K–8 schools in Jersey City in order to raise math scores.

Giving primarily in NJ, with support for local projects limited to the Morristown–Madison area.

Exxon Education Foundation
225 East John W. Carpenter Freeway
Irving, TX 75062-2298
(212) 444-1104
Contact: E. F. Ahnert, Executive Director
- Funding to multiple school districts throughout U.S. to implement math programs in early grades.

The Ford Foundation
320 East 43d Street
New York, NY 10017
(212) 573-5000
Contact: Barron M. Tenny, Secretary
- $127,000 to Bank Street School of Education, New York City, to plan curriculum and training methods emphasizing young children's social interactions with peers and adults.

- $162,000 to National Learning Center, Washington, DC, to develop model of public school early childhood education collaboration.

The Gold Family Foundation
159 Conant Street
Hillside, NJ 07205
(908) 353-6269
Contact: Meyer Gold, Manager
- $10,000 to Mason Early Education Foundation, Princeton, NJ, to enhance the elementary school math and expository writing programs.

Support primarily for Jewish organizations.

The Greater Kansas City Community Foundation and Its Affiliated Trusts
1055 Broadway, Suite 130
Kansas City, MO 64105
(816) 842-8079/0944
Contact: Janice C. Kreamer, President
- $15,000 to Learning Exchange, Kansas City, MO, for early childhood education planning.

Giving primarily in the five-county greater Kansas City, MO, area. Initial approach through letter or proposal.

Hall Family Foundations
Charitable and Crown Investment—323
P.O. Box 419580
Kansas City, MO 64141-6580
(816) 274-8516
Contacts: Wendy Burcham, Peggy Collins, John Laney, or Margaret Pence, Program Officers
- $52,430 to KCMC Child Development Corporation, Kansas City, MO, for New Start/Head Start Program.

Giving limited to the Kansas City area of Missouri and Kansas. No support for religious organizations. Initial approach through letter.

Hartford Foundation for Public Giving
85 Gillett Street
Hartford, CT 06105
(203) 548-1888
Contact: Michael R. Bangser, Executive Director
- $12,500 to New Dawn Pre-School Educational Center, Hartford, CT, for educational and recreational supplies to

enhance the quality and affordability of preschool services.
Giving limited to the greater Hartford area. No support for tax-supported agencies. Initial approach by telephone.

The Hitachi Foundation
1509 22d Street, NW
Washington, DC 20037
(202) 457-0588
Contact: Robin L. James, Vice President of Programs
  - $150,000 to Americans All for support of a new multicultural program in third, fifth, eighth, and eleventh grades of Washington, DC, public schools.
Initial contact through letter of no more than three pages.

Walter S. Johnson Foundation
525 Middlefield Road, Suite 110
Menlo Park, CA 94025
(415) 326-0485
Contact: Kimberly Ford, Program Director
  - $110,146 to Foundation for Clovis Schools to provide literacy and parent education to 40 parents of preschoolers and to develop preschool program.
  - $125,397 to Children's Television Resource and Education Center, San Francisco, CA, to produce and market materials nationally for classroom use, and to train and support teachers in Richmond Unified School District in use of Getting Along program.
Giving primarily in Alameda, Contra Costa, San Francisco, San Mateo and Santa Clara counties in California and in Washoe, NV; no support to private schools.

W. Alton Jones Foundation, Inc.
232 East High Street
Charlottesville, VA 22901
(804) 295-2134
Contact: John Peterson Myers, Director
  - $70,000 to Episcopal School of New York City for general school development and teacher professional development.

Lyndhurst Foundation
Suite 701, Tallan Building
100 West Martin Luther King Boulevard
Chattanooga, TN 37402-2561
(615) 756-0767
Contact: Jack E. Murrah, President

  - $90,000 to Chattanooga Public Schools, TN, to develop innovative early childhood school.
Limited to southeastern U.S., especially Chattanooga, TN.

The Medtronic Foundation
7000 Central Avenue, NE
Minneapolis, MN 55432
(612) 574-3029
Contact: Jan Schwarz, Manager
  - $12,500 to Minneapolis Public Schools, MN, to work with the community on general curriculum development.
Giving primarily in areas of company operations.

Richard King Mellon Foundation
P.O. Box 2903
Pittsburgh, PA 15230-2930
(412) 392-2800
  - $43,000 to Bethesda Center, Pittsburgh, to expand Early Childhood Development Program.
Giving primarily in Pittsburgh and western Pennsylvania. Initial approach through proposal.

The Ralph M. Parsons Foundation
1055 Wilshire Boulevard, Suite 1701
Los Angeles, CA 90017
(213) 482-3185
Contact: Christine Sisley, Executive Director
  - $10,000 to Mothers Club Community Center, Pasadena, CA, for teaching staff in preschool serving multicultural clientele.
Giving limited to Los Angeles County, with the exception of some grants to higher education. Does not support programs where other funding is readily available.

Z. Smith Reynolds Foundation, Inc.
101 Reynolda Village
Winston-Salem, NC 27106-5197
(919) 725-7541; Fax (919) 725-6067
Contact: Thomas W. Lambeth, Executive Director
  - $10,000 to Children's Grammar School, Asheville, NC, for equipment and to develop curriculum outline for language arts program for preschool and elementary school programs.
  - $25,000 to Washington County Public Schools, Plymouth, NC, for establishment

of Communications Skills Learning Centers in kindergarten classrooms using role play to stimulate verbal development and language competence.
Limited to NC. Will provide funding for special projects for K–12.

Rockefeller Brothers Fund
1290 Avenue of the Americas
New York, NY 10104
(212) 373-4200
Contact: Benjamin R. Shute, Jr., Secretary
• $53,000 to Cape Educational Trust, Belhar, South Africa, for Early Learning Resource Unit, second-language curriculum development program for preschool children.
Initial approach through letter of no more than two or three pages.

San Diego Community Foundation
525 B Street, Suite 410
San Diego, CA 92101
(619) 239-8815
Contacts: Helen Monroe, Executive Director; Pamela Hall, Assistant Director
• $15,000 to San Diego Innovative Pre-School, San Diego, for general support.
Giving limited to San Diego County. Initial approach by telephone or letter.

The Schumann Fund for New Jersey, Inc.
33 Park Street
Montclair, NJ 07042
(201) 783-6660
Contact: Patricia A. McCarthy, Secretary
• $45,000 to Babyland Nursery, Newark, NJ, for early childhood education program.
Giving limited to New Jersey. Initial approach through proposal.

T.L.L. Tempee Foundation
109 Tempee Boulevard
Lufkin, TX 75901
(409) 639-5197
Contact: M.F. Buddy Zeagler, Assistant Executive Director and Controller
• $86,557 to Lufkin Independent School District, TX, for early childhood learning center.
Giving primarily in counties constituting the East Texas Pine Timber Belt.

Turrell Fund
111 Northfield Avenue
West Orange, NJ 07052
(201) 325-5108
Contact: E. Belvin Williams, Executive Director
• $10,000 to El Primer Paso, Dovcer, NJ, for preschool progrâm for Hispanic children.
Giving limited to New Jersey, particularly the northern urban areas centered in Essex County. Also giving in Vermont.

Dewitt Wallace—Reader's Digest Fund, Inc.
261 Madison Avenue, 24th Floor
New York, NY 10016
(212) 953-1201; Fax (212) 953-1279
Contact: Donna V. Dunlop, Program Director
• $50,000 to High/Scope Educational Research Foundation, Ypsilanti, MI, for teacher-trainer project for teachers in preschool programs in New York City.
Initial approach through letter of no more than three pages.

Weingart Foundation
P.O. Box 17982
Los Angeles, CA 90017-0982
(213) 482-4343
Contact: Charles W. Jacobson, President
• $10,000 to Pasadena Unified School District, CA, toward new early childhood intervention program for prekindergarten children.
Giving limited to southern California. No support to religious programs.

U.S. West Foundation
7800 East Orchard Road, Suite 300
Englewood, CO 80111
(303) 793-6661
Contact: Larry J. Nash, Director of Administration
• $112,710 to Hispanic Policy Development Project, Washington, DC, as part of a two-year grant to create Building Blocks, handbooks to guide early education projects.
• $40,000 to Osage/Auraria Child Care Center, Denver, for parent involvement in early childhood programs.
Limited to states with US WEST calling areas.
Address applications to local US WEST Public

Relations Office or Community Relations Team.

The Zellerbach Family Fund
120 Montgomery Street, Suite 2125
San Francisco, CA 94104
(415) 421-2629
Contact: Edward A. Nathan, Executive Director
 • $77,500 to Beginning Oral Language
   Development (BOLD), Sacramento, to
   develop and field test curriculum and
   materials for use in child care, preschool,
   and early elementary school sites.
Giving primarily in the San Francisco Bay area.

Foundations and Organizations that Provide Funds for Education, Including Special Projects, as a Mission

The Abell Foundation, Inc.
116 Fidelity Building
210 North Charles Street
Baltimore, MD 21201-4013
(301) 547-1300
Contact: Robert C. Embry, Jr., President
Giving limited to Maryland, with a focus on
Baltimore.

Aetna Foundation, Inc.
151 Farmington Avenue
Hartford, CT 06156-3180
(203) 273-6382
Contact: Diana Kinosh, Management Information Supervisor

The Ahmanson Foundation
9215 Wilshire Boulevard
Beverly Hills, CA 90210
(213) 278-0770
Contact: Lee E. Walcott, Vice President and
 Managing Director
Giving primarily in southern California.

Alcoa Foundation
1501 Alcoa Building
Pittsburgh, PA 15219-1850
(412) 553-2348
Contact: F. Worth Hobbs, President
Giving primarily in areas of company
operation.

The Allstate Foundation
Allstate Plaza North
Northbrook, IL 60062
(708) 402-5502
Contacts: Alan F. Benedeck, Executive Direc-
 tor; Allen Goldhamer, Manager; Dawn
 Bougart, Administrative Assistant

American Express Minnesota Foundation
c/o IDS Financial Services
IDS Tower Ten
Minneapolis, MN 55440
(612) 372-2643
Contacts: Sue Gethin, Manager of Public
 Affairs, IDS; Marie Tobin, Community
 Relations Specialist
Giving primarily in Minnesota.

American National Bank & Trust Co. of
Chicago Foundation
33 North La Salle Street
Chicago, IL 60690
(312) 661-6115
Contact: Joan M. Klaus, Director
Giving limited to the six-county Chicago
metropolitan area.

Anderson Foundation
c/o Anderson Corp.
Bayport, MN 55003
(612) 439-5150
Contact: Lisa Carlstrom, Assistant Secretary

The Annenberg Foundation
St. Davids Center
150 Radnor-Chester Road, Suite A-200
St. Davids, PA 19087
Contact: Donald Mullen, Treasurer

AON Foundation
123 North Wacker Drive
Chicago, IL 60606
(312) 701-3000
Contact: Wallace J. Buya, Vice President
No support for secondary educational institutions or vocational schools.

Atherton Family Foundation
c/o Hawaiian Trust Co., Ltd.
P.O. Box 3170
Honolulu, HI 96802
(808) 537-6333; Fax (808) 521-6286
Contact: Charlie Medeiros
Giving limited to Hawaii.

Metropolitan Atlanta Community Foundation, Inc.
The Hurt Building, Suite 449
Atlanta, GA 30303
(404) 688-5525
Contact: Alicia Philipp, Executive Director
Giving limited to the metropolitan area of Atlanta and surrounding regions.

Ball Brothers Foundation
222 South Mulberry Street
Muncie, IN 47308
(317) 741-5500; Fax (317) 741-5518
Contact: Douglas A. Bakker, Executive Director
Giving limited to Indiana.

Baltimore Gas & Electric Foundation, Inc.
Box 1475
Baltimore, MD 21203
(301) 234-5312
Contact: Gary R. Fuhronan
Giving primarily in Maryland, with emphasis in Baltimore.

Bell Atlantic Charitable Foundation
1310 North Courthouse Road, 10th Floor
Arlington, VA 22201
(703) 974-5440
Contact: Ruth P. Caine, Director
Giving primarily in areas of company operations.

Benwood Foundation, Inc.
1600 American National Bank Building
736 Market Street
Chattanooga, TN 37402
(615) 267-4311
Contact: Jean R. McDaniel, Executive Director
Giving primarily in Chattanooga area.

Robert M. Beren Foundation, Inc.
970 Fourth Financial Center
Wichita, KS 67202
Giving primarily for Jewish organizations.

The Frank Stanley Beveridge Foundation, Inc.
1515 Ringling Boulevard, Suite 340
P.O. Box 4097
Sarasota, FL 34230-4097
(813) 955-7575; (800) 356-9779
Contact: Philip Coswell, President
Giving primarily to Hampden County, MA, to organizations that are not tax-supported.

Borden Foundation, Inc.
180 East Broad Street, 34th Floor
Columbus, OH 43215
(614) 225-4340
Contact: Judy Barker, President
Emphasis on programs to benefit disadvantaged children in areas of company operations.

The Boston Foundation, Inc.
One Boston Place, 24th Floor
Boston, MA 02108
(617) 723-7415; Fax (617) 589-3616
Contact: Anna Faith Jones, President

The Boston Globe Foundation II, Inc.
135 Morrissey Boulevard
Boston, MA 02107
(617) 929-3194
Contact: Suzanne Watkin, Executive Director
Giving primarily in the greater Boston area.

The Buchanan Family Foundation
222 East Wisconsin Avenue
Lake Forest, IL 60045
Contact: Huntington Eldridge, Jr., Treasurer
Giving primarily in Chicago, IL.

The Buhl Foundation
Four Gateway Center, Room 1522
Pittsburgh, PA 15222
(412) 566-2711
Contact: Dr. Doreen E. Boyce, Executive Director
Giving primarily in southwestern Pennsylvania, particularly the Pittsburgh area.

The Bush Foundation
East 900 First National Bank Building
332 Minnesota Street
St. Paul, MN 55101
(612) 227-0891
Contact: Humphrey Doermann, President
Giving primarily in Minnesota, South Dakota, and North Dakota.

Edyth Bush Charitable Foundation, Inc.
199 East Welbourne Avenue
P.O. Box 1967
Winter Park, FL 32790-1967
(407) 647-4322
Contact: H. Clifford Lee, President
Giving has specific geographic and facility limitations.

California Community Foundation
606 South Olive Street, Suite 2400
Los Angeles, CA 90014
(213) 413-4042
Contact: Jack Shakley, President
Orange County:
13252 Garden Grove Boulevard, Suite 195
Garden Grove, CA 92643
(714) 750-7794
Giving limited to Los Angeles, Orange, Riverside, San Bernadino, and Ventura counties.

H. A. & Mary K. Chapman Charitable Trust
One Warren Place, Suite 1816
6100 South Yale
Tulsa, OK 74136
(918) 496-7882
Contacts: Ralph L. Abercrombie, Trustee;
   Donne Pitman, Trustee
Giving primarily in Tulsa, OK.

The Chatlos Foundation, Inc.
P.O. Box 915048
Longwood, FL 32791-5048
(407) 862-5077
Contact: William J. Chatlos, President

The Edna McConnell Clark Foundation
250 Park Avenue, Room 900
New York, NY 10017
(212) 986-7050
Contact: Peter Bell, President

The Coca-Cola Foundation, Inc.
P.O. Drawer 1734
Atlanta, GA 30301
(404) 676-2568

The Columbus Foundation
1234 East Broad Street
Columbus, OH 43205
(614) 251-4000
Contact: James I. Luck, President
Giving limited to central Ohio.

Cowles Media Foundation
329 Portland Avenue
Minneapolis, MN 55415
(612) 375-7051
Contact: Janet L. Schwichtenberg
Limited to the Minneapolis area.

Cray Research Foundation
1440 Northland Drive
Mendota Heights, MN 55120
(612) 683-7386
Contact: William C. Linder-Scholer, Executive
   Director
Giving primarily in Minnesota and Wisconsin
for science and engineering education.

The Frances L. and Edwin L. Cummings
Memorial Fund
501 Fifth Avenue, Suite 1208
New York, NY 10017-1602
(212) 286-1778
Contact: Elizabeth Costas, Administrative
   Director
Giving primarily in the metropolitan New York
area, including New Jersey and Connecticut.

The Cullen Foundation
P.O. Box 1600
Houston, TX 77251
(713) 651-8835
Contact: Joseph C. Graf, Executive Secretary
Limited to Texas, with emphasis on Houston.

Dewitt Families Conduit Foundation
8300 96th Avenue
Zelland, MI 49464
Giving for Christian organizations.

Dodge Jones Foundation
P.O. Box 176
Abilene, TX 79604
(915) 673-6429
Contact: Lawrence E. Gill, Vice President,
   Grants Administration
Giving primarily in Abilene, Texas.

Carrie Estelle Doheny Foundation
911 Wiltshire Boulevard, Suite 1750
Los Angeles, CA 90017
(213) 488-1122
Contact: Robert A. Smith III, President
Giving primarily in Los Angeles area for non-
tax-supported organizations.

The Educational Foundation of America
23161 Ventura Boulevard, Suite 201
Woodland Hill, CA 91364
(818) 999-0921

The Charles Engelhard Foundation
P.O. Box 427
Far Hills, NJ 07931
(201) 766-7224
Contact: Elaine Catterall, Secretary

The William Stamps Farish Fund
1100 Louisiana, Suite 1250
Houston, TX 77002
(713) 757-7313
Contact: W. S. Farish, President
Giving primarily in Texas.

Joseph & Bessie Feinberg Foundation
5245 West Lawrence Avenue
Chicago, IL 60630
(312) 777-8600
Contact: June Blossom
Giving primarily in Illinois, to Jewish
organizations.

The 1525 Foundation
1525 National City Bank Building
Cleveland, OH 44114
(216) 696-4200
Contact: Bernadette Walsh, Assistant Secretary
Giving primarily in Ohio, with emphasis on
Cuyahoga County.

Fireman's Fund Foundation
777 San Marin Drive
Novato, CA 94998
(415) 899-2757
Contact: Barbara B. Friede, Director
Giving primarily in San Francisco, Marin, and
Sonoma counties.

The Flinn Foundation
3300 North Central Avenue, Suite 2300
Phoenix, AZ 85012
(602) 274-9000
Contact: John W. Murphy, Executive Director
Giving limited to Arizona.

Ford Motor Company Fund
The American Road
Dearborn, MI 48121
(313) 845-8712
Contact: Leo J. Brennan, Jr., Executive Director
Giving primarily in areas of company opera-
tions nationwide, with special emphasis on
Detroit and Michigan.

George F. & Sybil H. Fuller Foundation
105 Madison Street
Worcester, MA 01610
(508) 756-5111
Contact: Russell E. Fuller, Chairman
Giving primarily in Massachusetts, with emphasis in Worcester.

The B. C. Gamble & P. W. Skogmo
Foundation
500 Foshay Tower
Minneapolis, MN 55402
(612) 339-7343
Contact: Patricia A. Cummings, Manager of
Supporting Organizations
Giving primarily for disadvantaged youth, handi-
capped, and secondary educational institutions
in the Minneapolis–St. Paul metropolitan area.

Gates Foundation
3200 Cherry Creek South Drive, Suite 630
Denver, CO 80209-3247
(303) 722-1881
Contact: F. Charles Froelicher, Executive
Director
Giving limited to Colorado, especially the
Denver area, except for foundation-initiated
grants.

The George Foundation
207 South Third Street
PO Drawer C
Richmond, TX 77469
(713) 342-6109
Contact: Trustees
Giving primarily in Fort Bend County, TX.

General Motors Foundation, Inc.
13-145 General Motors Building
3044 West Grand Boulevard
Detroit, MI 48202-3091
(313) 556-4260
Contact: D. R. Czarnecki

The George Gund Foundation
1845 Guildhall Building
45 Prospect Avenue West
Cleveland, OH 44115
(216)241-3114; Fax (216) 241-6560
Contact: David Bergholz, Executive Director
Giving primarily in northeastern Ohio.

The Greenwall Foundation
Two Park Avenue, 24th Floor
New York, NY 10016
(212) 679-7266
Contact: William C. Stubing, President

GTE Foundation
One Stamford Forum
Stamford, CT 06904
(203) 965-3620
Contact: Maureen Gorman, Secretary and Director, Corporate Social Responsibility

The Haggar Foundation
6113 Lemmon Avenue
Dallas, TX 75209
(214) 956-0241
Contact: Rosemary Haggar Vaughan, Executive Director
Giving limited to areas of company operations in Dallas and south Texas.

Gladys & Roland Harriman Foundation
63 Wall Street, 23d Floor
New York, NY 10005
(212) 493-8182
Contact: William F. Hibberd, Secretary

Hasbro Children's Foundation
32 West 23d Street
New York, NY 10010
(212) 645-2400
Contact: Eve Weiss, Executive Director
Funding for children under the age of 12 with special needs.

The Hearst Foundation, Inc.
888 Seventh Avenue, 27th Floor
New York, NY 10106-0057
(212) 586-5404
Contact: Robert M. Frehse, Jr. Executive Director
West of the Mississippi River:
90 New Montgomery Street, Suite 1212
San Francisco, CA 94105
(415) 543-0400
Contact: Thomas Eastham, Vice President and Western Director

Vira I. Heinz Endowment
30 GNC Tower
625 Liberty Avenue
Pittsburgh, PA 15222-3115
(412) 391-5122
Contact: Alfred W. Wishart, Jr., Executive Director
Giving limited primarily to Pittsburgh and western Pennsylvania; support to other areas will be considered for projects on a national or international basis.

The Martha Holden Jennings Foundation
710 Halle Building
1228 Euclid Avenue
Cleveland, OH 44115
(216) 589-5700
Contact: Dr. Richard A. Boyd, Executive Director
Giving limited to Ohio.

The Humana Foundation, Inc.
The Humana Building
500 West Main Street
P.O. Box 1438
Louisville, KY 40201
(502) 580-3920
Contact: Jay L. Foley, Contribution Manager
Giving primarily in Kentucky.

International Paper Company Foundation
Two Manhattanville Road
Purchase, NY 10577
(914) 397-1581
Contact: Sandra Wilson, Vice President
Giving primarily in communities where there are company plants and mills.

The James Irvine Foundation
One Market Plaza
Spear Tower, Suite 1715
San Francisco, CA 94105
(414) 777-2244
Contact: Luz A. Vega, Director of Grants
Southern CA office:
777 South Figueroa Street, Suite 740
Los Angeles, CA 90017-5430

Island Foundation, Inc.
589 Mill Street
Marion, MA 02738
(508) 748-2809
Contact: Jenny D. Russell, Executive Director
Giving primarily in the northeastern U.S.
Application form required.

W. K. Kellogg Foundation
400 North Avenue
Battle Creek, MI 49017-3398
(616) 968-1611
Contact: Nancy A. Sims, Executive Assistant,
    Programming

Donald P. & Byrd M. Kelly Foundation
701 Harger Road, No. 150
Oak Brook, IL 60521
Contact: Laura K. McGrath, Treasurer
Giving primarily in Illinois, with emphasis on
Chicago.

Carl B. & Florence E. King Foundation
5956 Sherry Lane, Suite 620
Dallas, TX 75225
Contact: Carl Yeckel, Vice President
Giving primarily in the Dallas area.

Knight Foundation
One Biscayne Tower, Suite 3800
Two Biscayne Boulevard
Miami, FL 33131
(305) 539-2610
Giving limited to areas where Knight-Ridder
newspapers are published. Initial approach
through letter.

Thomas & Dorothy Leavey Foundation
4680 Wiltshire Boulevard
Los Angeles, CA 90010
(213) 930-4252
Contact: J. Thomas McCarthy, Trustee
Giving primarily in southern California to
Catholic organizations.

Levi Strauss Foundation
1155 Battery Street
San Francisco, CA 94111
(415) 544-2194
Contacts: Bay Area: Judy Belk, Director of
    Contributions; Mid-South Region: Myra

Chow, Director of Contributions; Western
Region: Mario Griffin, Director of Contributions; Rio Grande: Elvira Chavaria, Director
of Contributions; Eastern Region: Mary Ellen
McLoughlin, Director of Contributions
Giving generally limited to areas of company
operations.

McDonnell Douglas Foundation
c/o McDonnell Douglas Corp.
P.O. Box 516, Mail Code 1001440
St. Louis, MO 63166
(314) 232-8464
Contact: Walter E. Diggs, Jr., President
Giving primarily in Arizona, California, Flor-
ida, Missouri, Oklahoma, and Texas.

James S. McDonnell Foundation
1034 South Brentwood Boulevard, Suite 1610
St. Louis, MO 63117
(314) 721-1532

Meadows Foundation, Inc.
Wilson Historic Block
2922 Swiss Avenue
Dallas, TX 75204-5928
(214) 826-9431
Contact: Dr. Sally R. Lancaster, Executive Vice
    President
Giving limited to Texas.

Eugene and Agnes E. Meyer Foundation
1400 Sixteenth Street, NW, Suite 360
Washington, DC 20036
(202) 483-8294

The Milken Family Foundation
c/o Foundation of the Milken Families
15250 Ventura Boulevard, 2nd Floor
Sherman Oaks, CA 91403
Contact: Dr. Jules Lesner, Executive Director
Giving limited to the Los Angeles area.

The Morgan Guaranty Trust Company of NY
Charitable Trust
60 Wall Street
New York, NY 10260
(212) 648-9672
Contact: Roberta Ruocco, Vice President, Mor-
    gan Guarantee Trust Co. of NY
Giving limited to New York City, except for
selected institutions of higher education.

The New Hampshire Charitable Fund
One South Street
P.O. Box 1335
Concord, NH 03302-1335
(603) 225-6641
Contact: Deborah Cowan, Associate Director
Giving limited to New Hampshire.

The New Haven Foundation
70 Audubon Street
New Haven, CT 06510
(203) 777-2386
Contact: Helmer N. Ekstrom, Director
Giving primarily in greater New Haven and the
lower Naugatuck River Valley.

The New York Community Trust
Two Park Avenue, 24th Floor
New York, NY 10016
(212) 686-0010; Fax (212) 532-8528
Contact: Lorie A. Slutsky, Director
Giving limited to the New York metropolitan
area.

The Northern Trust Company Charitable Trust
c/o The Northern Trust Co., Corp. Affairs Div.
50 South LaSalle Street
Chicago, IL 60675
(312) 444-3538
Contact: Marjorie W. Lundy, Vice President,
    The Northern Trust Co.
Giving limited to the metropolitan Chicago
area.

The David and Lucile Packard Foundation
300 Second Street, Suite 200
Los Altos, CA 94022
(415) 948-7658
Contact: Colburn S. Wilbur, Executive Director

The Pittsburgh Foundation
30 CNG Tower
625 Liberty Avenue
Pittsburgh, PA 15222-3115
(412) 391-5122
Contact: Alfred W. Wishart, Jr., Executive
    Director
Giving limited to Allegheny County, PA; no
support to private schools.

The Principal Financial Group Foundation, Inc.
711 High Street
Des Moines, IA 50392-0150
(515) 247-5209
Contact: Debra J. Jensen, Secretary
Giving primarily in Iowa, with emphasis on the
Des Moines area.

Sid W. Richardson Foundation
309 Main Street
Forth Worth, TX 76102
(817) 336-0497
Contact: Valleau Wilkie, Jr., Executive Vice
    President
Giving limited to Texas.

R.J.R. Nabisco Foundation
1455 Pennsylvania Avenue, NW, Suite 525
Washington, DC 20004
(202) 626-7200
Contact: Jaynie M. Grant, Executive Director

The Winthrop Rockefeller Foundation
308 East Eighth Street
Little Rock, AR 72202
(501) 376-6854
Contact: Mahlon Martin, President
Funding primarily in Arkansas, or for projects
that will benefit Arkansas.

The San Francisco Foundation
685 Market Street, Suite 910
San Francisco, CA 94105-9716
(415) 495-3100
Contact: Robert M. Fisher, Director
Giving limited to Alameda, Contra Costa,
Marin, San Francisco, and San Mateo counties.

Community Foundation of Santa Clara County
960 West Hedding, Suite 220
San Jose, CA 95126-1215
(408) 241-2666
Contact: Winnie Chu, Program Officer
Giving limited to Santa Clara County, CA.

John & Dorothy Shea Foundation
655 Brea Canyon Road
Walnut, CA 91789
Giving primarily in California.

Harold Simmons Foundation
Three Lincoln Center
5430 LBJ Freeway, Suite 1700
Dallas, TX 75240-2697
(214) 233-1700
Contact: Lisa K. Simmons, President
Giving limited to the Dallas area.

Sonart Family Foundation
15 Benders Drive
Greenwich, CT 06831
(203) 531-1474
Contact: Raymond Sonart, President

The Sosland Foundation
4800 Main Street, Suite 100
Kansas City, MO 64112
(816)765-1000; Fax (816) 756-0494
Contact: Debbie Sosland-Edelman, Ph.D
Giving limited to the Kansas City areas of
Missouri and Kansas.

Community Foundation for Southeastern
Michigan
333 West Fort Street, Suite 2010
Detroit, MI 48226
(313) 961-6675
Contact: C. David Campbell, Vice President,
    Programs
Giving limited to southeastern Michigan.

Springs Foundation, Inc.
P.O. Drawer 460
Lancaster, SC 29720
(803) 286-2196
Contact: Charles A. Bundy, President
Giving limited to Lancaster County and/or the
townships of Ft. Mill and Chester, SC.

Steelcase Foundation
P.O. Box 1967
Grand Rapids, MI 49507
(616) 246-4695
Contact: Kate Pew Wolters, Executive Director
Giving limited to areas of company operations.
Initial contact by letter.

Strauss Foundation
c/o Fidelity Bank, N.A.
Broad & Walnut Streets
Philadelphia, PA 19109
(215) 985-7717
Contact: Richard Irvin, Jr.
Giving primarily in Pennsylvania.

Stuart Foundations
425 Market Street, Suite 2835
San Francisco, CA 94105
(415) 495-1144
Contact: Theodore E. Lobman, President
Giving primarily in California; applications
from Washington will be considered.

Travelers Companies Foundation
One Tower Square
Hartford, CT 06183-1060
(203) 277-4070/4079
Funding for school programs limited to
Hartford.

Westinghouse Foundation
c/o Westinghouse Electric Corporation
11 Stanwix Street
Pittsburgh, PA 15222
(412) 642-3017
Contacts: G. Reynolds Clark, President; C. L.
    Kubelick, Manager, Contributions and Com-
    munity Affairs
Giving primarily in areas of company
operations.

Philip L. Van Every Foundation
c/o Lance, Inc.
P.O. Box 32368
Charlotte, NC 28232
(704) 554-1421
Giving primarily in North Carolina and South
Carolina.

Joseph B. Whitehead Foundation
1400 Peachtree Center Tower
230 Peachtree Street, NW
Atlanta, GA 30303
(404) 522-6755
Contact: Charles H. McTier, President
Giving limited to metropolitan Atlanta.

Winn-Dixie Stores Foundation
5050 Edgewood Court
Jacksonville, FL 32205
(904) 783-5000
Contact: Jack P. Jones, President
Giving limited to areas of company operation.

This chapter includes a sampling of foundations that can be contacted for funding for your curriculum project. By no means are these all the resources that can be tapped. Remember, think creatively! Are there any community service organizations for you to contact, such as the Jaycees, Lions Club, or Rotary International? Does the local Community Fund support education projects? Ask friends and neighbors which organizations they belong to or support. Ask if you can use their names as references—and be sure to get the names of the people to contact. Make many initial contacts and don't be discouraged by rejections. The money is there for you. All you need to do is be persistent!

References

Source Book Profiles. 1992. New York: Foundation Center.
Information on the one thousand largest U.S. foundations.

The Foundation Grants Index. 1992. New York: Foundation Center.
Provides funding patterns and other information about the most influential foundations in the U.S.

The Foundation Directory. 1992. New York: Foundation Center.
Information about private and community grantmaking foundations in the U.S.

Government Assistance Almanac. 1992. Detroit: Omnigraphics.
A comprehensive guide to federal programs that provide financial assistance.

THE CONTENT OF INTEGRATED EARLY CHILDHOOD EDUCATION

Doris Pronin Fromberg
Professor of Education and Director, Early Childhood Teacher Education
Hofstra University, Hempstead, New York

E ARLY childhood education is an ethical practice because young children are vulnerable and malleable. The teachers of young children, therefore, cannot be merely technical or eclectic without the danger of exposing children to potential developmental and educational abuses. Although teachers might use similar labels in order to identify a topic for study, children taught in different ways learn different content. A teacher's methodology, therefore, becomes part of the context for teaching.

This chapter, written from the perspective of early childhood education as ethical intellectual practice, provides a context for teaching in the form of six conditions for learning in early childhood education. With this context in mind, effective teachers of young children ideally plan and begin by understanding how young children learn. Teachers then translate their own mature conceptions of knowledge into activities that young children can perceive as meaningful within the context of their personal development and culture.

The scope of worthwhile learning, however, may be different from the full scope of what children can learn. Indeed, young children are capable of learning much that is trivial,

limiting, and possibly harmful to their development of strong self-concepts, intelligent, independent thought, social responsibility, and a sense of competence. In this chapter, worthwhile learning denotes learning that has significant meaning to each child and takes place in ways that help each child feel competent. Worthwhile learning might also contribute to ethical social interaction.

When children are active in constructing connections between their experiences and understandings, they might acquire significant knowledge. The best early educators try to teach in ways that help children construct significant knowledge. The children they teach perceive significant knowledge as meaningful because it supports their motivation to learn and to become caring, civilized, ethical human beings.

Children arrive at school with some significant knowledge and strengths that have grown out of their varied experiences. They are active connection makers, capable of responsible choices and social behavior. Effective teachers appreciate the strengths that children bring to school and build upon these strengths in planning activities and experiences that children might find meaningful. Learning activities that are meaningful influence changes in children's perceptions and understandings.

Worthwhile learning about ideas and social and personal experiences can occur when teachers adapt to the ways that young children learn. Such learning might qualify as "intellectual" education. In contrast, however, are "academic" teachers who often feel satisfied that they have taught content after using workbooks and engaging young children in single-correct-answer recitation of isolated, memorized facts. It is unclear that children in such academic classrooms have had worthwhile learning experiences. Typically, such academic settings decimate the powerful cultural strengths with which children come to school.

This chapter deals mainly with "intellectual" early childhood curriculum. When teachers and children plan together, rich, integrated learning develops as they participate in solving real problems by asking and answering authentic questions and as they pursue a variety of active learning opportunities. Six conditions for learning, in particular, contribute to rich learning. A discussion of these six conditions for learning in early childhood education follows. Then there is a look at dynamic themes as a way to develop curriculum, along with a discussion of related issues concerning ways in which exemplary teachers offer wholesome content that is significant and worthwhile in early education.

Conditions for Learning

Young children learn best when six interconnected conditions of learning are present: (1) inductive experiences, (2) cognitive dissonance, (3) social interaction, (4) physical experiences, (5) play, and (6) competence (Fromberg 1987). Brief examples of each of these conditions follow.

Inductive Experiences

Inductive learning takes place when teachers provide active contrasts for children. The focus of instruction and learning might include the contrasting of properties, objects, measurements, poems, or stories. When two or more contrasts are present, children can perceive the impact of the similarities or differences. An

isolated instance, however, demands rote memorization, difficult to achieve and retain without a meaningful framework or context. When the learner's attention moves between one or two familiar variables, it is easier to perceive a newly present variable.

Children perceive concepts and connections more easily, for example, when they find a contrast between two concrete quantities rather than the presentation of a lone quantity. Instead of telling children what the teacher already knows, the teacher provides several pairs of contrasts, whether different quantities or graphic symbols. Consider the instances of large, medium, and small jars and jar covers; large, medium, and small boxes and their covers; three covered, opaque containers that children can shake, each filled with objects of large, medium, or small size; and three children of different heights. These contrasts would model the same underlying seriation relationship that is repeatedly present in different surface forms.

Children also learn to speak, read, and write by perceiving contrasting patterns. They might hear stories, for example, that deal with families who live in different geographic terrains, yet exhibit similar nurturing relationships or solutions to social issues.

The practice of isolating a letter of the day or a number of the day is rooted in the process of rote memorization and is not an inductive process. Those who knew the letter or number are wasting their time, and those who have not learned it yet are receiving the least amount of perceptual help in an isolated exposure. Often, children who are taught in rote ways are the ones who enter remediation programs and continue the cycle when remediation programs continue the rote teaching.

When children create surveys together, however, they are using the inductive process while they collect data and then compare their findings. They are also able to learn when cognitive dissonance is an integrated condition of learning.

Cognitive Dissonance

Cognitive dissonance takes place when teachers encourage children to predict-experience-compare within the context of different activities. This condition works effectively in varied activities such as reading comprehension, estimation in mathematics, science, or social science, and social studies and multicultural education. In a similar way, children experience feedback naturally as they explore the use of artistic media.

In the case of surveys, children might predict whose family was the largest: their parents' families, their grandparents' families, or their own family. They would then collect data (experience) for each of four, separate surveys; chart their findings in bar graph form using one-to-one correspondence; and compare the results with their predictions. In this way, they are also able to pool data, thereby integrating social interaction. Examples of other uses for cognitive dissonance are present in later sections of this chapter.

Social Interaction

Social interaction with other children provides a natural form of feedback through contrasts and comparisons, stimulates the development of self-awareness, and provides varied models and feedback for using language and solving problems. Researchers have found that children improve their intellectual development when they talk with peers (Dyson 1987; Johnson, Johnson, Holubec, and Roy 1984; Piaget et al. 1965; Slavin and Madden 1989). Teachers can stimulate extended attention to intellectual activities and critical thinking by planning collaborative projects with children. In these ways, they build on a strength that children bring to school—their interest in making friends.

Effective teachers often plan for children to work in dyads or in small groups in order for the children to collect observational data, tally findings in surveys, create puppet plays, plan class presentations about a famous person, or share their drawings or writings with one another. In this way, children who have acquired different skills or degrees of skill can make relevant contributions and learn to appreciate one another during a cooperative undertaking.

Physical Experiences

Physical experiences—those times when children manipulate concrete materials, observe concrete events, and enjoy direct experiences— become an entry point and the basis for symbolic representation. Such experiences also provide basic ways of knowing in the arts, mathematics, and sciences.

Young children need to engage in physical experiences much of the time. As contrasted with functioning as an entire class, working in small groups that offer social interaction and individual participation facilitates direct physical activity. For example, when exploring sinking and floating or magnetic attraction of objects, children themselves can handle the materials. In an "intellectual" classroom, as contrasted with a primarily "academic" or "socialization" classroom, such physical experiences integrate the six conditions of learning. After exploring and playing (play) with materials, children predict, engage in the activity, and then compare their predictions with their findings (cognitive dissonance).

Teachers often encourage children to repeat the process, whether or not they found the "correct" answer that the teacher had expected. For example, "Let's see if this happens each time. What might happen if we use this material or that shape?" Children have the opportunity to induce the underlying patterns by observing the surface contrasts (inductive experiences). Rather than ending a discussion after a child states the "correct" answer, therefore, it is useful to ask children how they arrived at their findings and who found a different method (competence). Physical experiences and data collections that expose children to cognitive dissonance are authentic opportunities for children to construct knowledge, unlike the act of memorizing a teacher's verbalized conclusions.

Play

Play is an integral part of early childhood classroom activities throughout the primary grades. It serves as a forum in which children control events. By entering into the rule-bound nature of this integrative experience, they are able to extend their learning and reduce impulsivity (see Fromberg 1992).

Pretend play in general, and sociodramatic play in particular, contribute rich deposits to children's store of learning. Reviews of research have found that there is a correlation between children's pretend play and their development of language, cognition, associative fluency (creativity), and social competence (Bergen 1988; Fein and Rivkin 1986; Fromberg 1992). Indeed, play is the ultimate integrator of learning. Play also contributes to the development of imagery and metacognitive skills that children coordinate when they engage in problem solving and critical thinking.

A teacher's playful attitude helps to engage and keep children involved in learning activities. In addition, teachers provide space, long blocks of time, and opportunities for dyads and small groups of children to engage in imaginative, sociodramatic play. Children of kindergarten and primary age are able to engage responsibly in such activity with relative independence from the teacher. It is useful, therefore, to provide a sociodramatic play area during extended activity periods so that teachers, in addition to participating in and extending play experiences, can circulate and simultaneously engage in instructional activities with other small groups of children.

Children's play is largely oral. Kieran Egan (1988) reminds us of the powers inherent in oral traditions and cautions us to retain these powerful ways of knowing. In the context of our culture's thirst for visual literacy, educators need to maintain these strengths that children bring to school. Moreover, consider that when children engage in sociodramatic play, they are engaging in perspective taking, a necessary skill for any writer who is learning to communicate with an audience.

Play is not a reward for work nor the work of young children; it is activity that is valuable in itself. It is a legitimate part of being a joyful human being. To minimize its significance in early childhood is to limit opportunities for learning and to risk abetting child abuse.

Competence

Competence grows when children feel successful enough to keep trying and to risk challenges. Teachers help children feel competent when they ask significant questions for which they legitimately need answers, and when they appreciate the children's efforts and progress. Significant questions focus on finding out what children have to say rather than expecting them to guess a preconceived

response correctly. If a teacher needs to use specific information, she or he can offer it to children to use during the discussion.

The content for writing grows out of children's oral experiences. When teachers solicit children's ideas and ask children to organize and share their experiences, the writing process has begun, even if it is initially oral. Rather than asking the yes–no question "Do you have something to add?," attempt a descriptive question: "What else can you tell us?" The positive experiences that take place when children perceive that others value their views contribute to the children's sense of accomplishment and competence. When children feel good about themselves and about what happens at school, they are likely to behave in cooperative and civilized ways.

Intellectual Education

These conditions of learning work to support "intellectual" education: the match between what teachers understand about the physical, social, representational, and aesthetic nature of human experience and the personal experiences of each child. As a teacher interacts with children, there is an opportunity for that teacher to see the underlying connectedness between the child's possible perceptions and the teacher's understandings. Upon seeing these connections, the teacher can then plan a sequence of activities and offer resources that have potential meaning and relevance to each child.

Teachers also build plans that are based upon the strengths of each child's sociocultural and personal background. When such a match occurs, children have the opportunity to feel valued and successful. They begin to feel comfortable with teachers, gain a sense of their own power, and build the potential for enjoyment of worthwhile, meaningful learning.

Having stated these principles, therefore, suggests that broad, dynamic themes can help teachers provide opportunities for children to develop varied interpretations and learn an array of forms in which to represent their learnings. Finite, rote pastimes for children in grades K–3 are less helpful.

Children whose teachers plan activities with dynamic themes in mind might potentially connect ideas when similar imagery underlies activities that take the different forms of children's physical, emotional, social, or aesthetic experiences. This intellectual view of early childhood education contends that young children learn while refining their models of perceiving dynamic, isomorphic content in different forms as they engage in the six conditions for learning.

Skills such as representational ability, language literacy, mathematical literacy, and problem solving serve to support content rather than exist for their own sake. In order to see dynamic themes in contrast with other possible ways to plan content, definitions of the terms *units, topics,* and *dynamic themes* follow.

Units

The unit often exists only within a self-contained one- or two-week period during which teachers expect children to acquire specific information. Typical unit content includes a particular holiday, introduction to a new season, a study of "me," families, pets, community helpers, houses, food groups, transportation, zoo animals, sea life, the beach, farms, dinosaurs, a book character, or subject matter such as popcorn, peaches, or hats.

Teachers often label the unit as "social studies" and plan an activity for each of the disciplines of language, mathematics, visual art, music, and science. Children read or hear stories focusing on the subject matter. They draw, use uniform craft materials, write about, sing songs about, and learn games or dances for that subject or topic. They play with related props in the sociodramatic area. They measure or do a science study or categorization of the subject or topic. There might be bulletin boards or posters for the subject. There might be a culminating activity that celebrates the week's focus, such as a parade, visit, party, mural, film, puppet show, voting booth, or sampling of related food.

Teachers who use the unit curriculum typically repeat the same units, during the same weeks of successive school years, with different populations of children. There is minimal involvement, if any, of children in the planning process. Teachers usually expect all children to engage in all of the activities and produce

similar products. "Since learning in the unit curriculum means that teachers transmit information to learners, teachers treat the curriculum as a product and teaching as a prescription for what occurs in classrooms. In turn, the role of the teacher mainly is that of a technical implementor (Goodwin 1992)." Examples of units follow:

Unit—Transportation to School
· Survey and chart routes that children take to school.
· Measure the school bus.
· Draw vehicles and label parts.
· Cut out pictures of vehicles and create collages.
· Draw and write about related travel experiences.
· Read about varied forms of transportation.
· Sing transportation songs.
· Add wheels to the woodworking area.
· Use puzzles with transportation pictures.

Unit—Winter
· Read related stories.
· Sing songs about winter.
· Draw and/or write about a winter walk or play activities in the snow.
· Make collages with white cotton balls.
· Bring snow into the classroom for observation.

Topics

The topic takes place during varied periods of time or weaves throughout the year. At the same time narrower, broader, or similar to the domains of units, topics differ in that children and teachers pursue the content in depth, without necessarily requiring a plan that represents each discipline. It is conceivable that teachers and children might pursue the topic of insects, for example, without singing about mosquitos or asking children to count groups of bees on a picture, as they might do when adhering to a unit plan. Typical topics have been a study of tools, weather, shopping, homes, school bus, birds, pets, underwater life, prehistoric animals, families, hospitals, seeds, bones, working women, great art classics, and insects.

Topics differ from units in that they evolve from direct planning with a particular group of children. Teachers might use some of the same—or different—activities with children during different years or they might develop different topics. If similar topics are present in different years, they might consume more or less class time, depending upon the children's concerns as the teacher assesses them. Different children may engage in different activities and produce different products. Examples follow:

Topic—Weather

- Identify seasons (across the school year) and chart them.
- Develop language experience charts about characteristics of each season, listing types of weather and conditions of air and water.
- Measure and chart temperature.
- Chart wind directions.
- Adopt a tree and visit it throughout the year.
- Label and read about other planetary bodies.
- Read fiction and nonfiction trade books.
- Sing songs.
- Provide varied paint and paper colors in the arts center that represent trees in different seasons.

Topic—Construction Site

- Create an illustrated and narrated timeline of events.
- Survey on-site vehicles and functions.
- Identify and interview workers.
- Draw and/or write about observed construction events or personnel.
- Read fiction and nonfiction books about related careers and construction sites.
- Read about vehicles, tools, and other related materials.
- Draw and/or write about reactions to and experiences after the shared or personal construction events within or outside of school.
- Use varied construction tools within the classroom.

Dynamic Themes

The dynamic theme takes place during varying periods of time or weaves throughout the school year. Dynamic themes develop when the teacher takes into account the forms of similar imagery that children might experience as they make connections between experiences. Teachers use dynamic, isomorphic images to identify the varied activity forms that children might perceive or the connections that children might make. Activities based on dynamic themes build on the child's potential for constructing and integrating the similar models of perception, the imagery, that underlie different forms of experience—physical, social, personal, representational, and aesthetic (Fromberg 1987; 1992).

The activities that potentially represent possible connections and similar perceptions might vary for children who have had different experiences and come from diverse multicultural backgrounds. In this way, different children doing different things for different periods of time might have equivalent experiences.

Activities that reflect dynamic themes welcome children to participate in a problem-centered, active approach to curriculum development. Teachers who plan activities with dynamic themes in mind can support children's natural ways of making connections. As teachers plan activities with children, each year's content will vary, as will the duration of activities from year to year. The broad scope of such planning might subsume some variations of the type of child-centered activities that topic-oriented teachers might use. Themes in general "can promote and reflect the cohesiveness of the curriculum, curricular integration across subject matter and/or developmental domains" (Chaille 1992, 318).

The sections that follow describe some dynamic themes that have the potential to integrate varied aspects of children's experiences as teachers identify the relevant moment in which to create a match between particular children and activities, while employing the six conditions of learning. Please note that content is significant, not in itself, but when children have potential exposure to it while engaging in the six conditions of learning with varying degrees of predominance. Examples of diverse experiences that might serve to unravel the study of each dynamic theme follow below. For the first Dynamic Theme, Conflict/Contrast (Dialectical Model), predominant conditions of learning are present in the parentheses.

Dynamic Theme—Conflict/Contrast

(Dialectical Model)
- Children argue about sharing limited numbers of a favorite piece of equipment, and discuss and predict alternative solutions. (Cognitive dissonance; Social interaction; Induction; Play; Competence)
- Hear, tell, or read stories about sibling rivalry or acceptance/rejection by a friend. Relate the stories to personal experiences, and draw/write about them. (Cognitive dissonance: Predict-experience-compare; Inductive contrasts; Social interaction; Play; Competence)
- Measure the most and the least in size—or happiness—depending upon the medium. (Cognitive dissonance: Predict-experience-compare; Physical; Inductive contrasts; Social interaction; Competence)
- Estimate and compare rolling/tossing various objects and marking distances after varying one factor at a time, such as the angle of the starting point, distance from the floor, and impetus. (Cognitive dissonance: Predict-experience-compare; Play; Social interaction; Physical; Competence)
- On the floor, with chalk, trace the path of gyroscopes and/or tops as they spin. (Cognitive dissonance: Predict-experience-compare; Social interaction; Inductive contrasts; Play; Competence)
- Observe magnets as they repel/attract objects. Record findings on a picture-word or word chart, depending on age. (Cognitive dissonance: Predict-experience-compare; Play; Physical; Social interaction; Competence)
- Observe objects as they float or sink or behave differently depending upon manipulation of variables, such as amount of light, water, other additives, and temperature. Record findings on a picture-word or word chart, depending on age. (Cognitive dissonance: Predict-experience-compare; Play; Physical; Social interaction; Competence)
- Categorize materials that are water soluble and insoluble. Compare the solubility of materials in various solutions. Record findings on a picture-word or other

language-experience chart, depending on age. (Cognitive dissonance: Predict-experience-compare; Induction; Play; Physical; Competence)
- Watch waves along a shoreline and/or erosion along a gully. Vary the flow as relevant. (Cognitive dissonance: Predict-experience-compare; Physical; Induction; Social interaction; Competence)
- Observe wind action on a planted field and identify or devise variable factors for study. Draw/write about predictions and findings. (Cognitive dissonance: Predict-experience-compare; Physical; Induction; Social interaction; Competence)
- Explore part singing and counterpoint rhythms. Explore opposites and mirror imaging in movement education/dance. Discuss movement alternatives and collaborative contrasts. (Social interaction; Inductive contrasts; Play; Physical; Cognitive dissonance; Competence)
- Represent conflict through role play, play writing, chants, drawing, dancing, writing, and graphing. (Social interaction; Play; Cognitive dissonance: Predict-experience-compare; Physical; Competence)

Dynamic Theme—The Sum Exceeds the Parts (Synergy)
- Adopt a construction site and document events and the roles of construction participants by such means as drawing, writing, creating a timeline, and interviewing the workers.
- Create an immigration map of the children in the class and their families; include parents and others in sharing immigration stories as well as multicultural meals or celebrations.
- Read stories and poems about people in varied cultural settings who have varied practices and perceptions.
- Role play voting and outcomes at adult election times. Predict, vote for activities within the classroom or the school, chart the outcomes, and compare with predictions.
- Develop a student-elected school governance structure that deals with children's real concerns.

- Cook transformative food products, such as popcorn or scrambled eggs, or make whipped cream or butter. Develop picture-word or word recipes, depending on age.
- Measure changes of volume and shape of foods that are cooking or decomposing. Feel and smell foods at different stages, tasting as relevant. Draw and/or write about findings.
- Collaborate in movement education or dance productions around themes of interest to the children. For example, if you consider dance as a form of symbolic representation, children working together might create an extended activity involving dance, role play, creative dramatics, and writing.
- Separately, small groups create melodies, as well as dances or pantomimes, to children-selected poems and then share their products.
- Observe a school orchestra rehearsal, and/or view films/videos of orchestras at work.
- Use tonal bells to create a group melody.
- Read, tell stories/write, or draw about events in which people collaborated—for example, *Stone Soup* (Brown 1972).
- Represent collaboration through role play, drawing, dancing, writing, graphing.
- Create a classroom quilt to commemorate special events of relevance to the children.
- Explore color mixing directly with paints, crayons, and/or a color wheel.

Dynamic Theme—Cyclical Change
- Adopt a tree. Visit it in various seasons and weather. Study its shadows. Enjoy its shade. Measure it, draw, sculpt, write, and fantasize about it.
- Estimate and chart shadows throughout the day.
- When growing seeds, control one variable at a time, such as temperature or amount of light, water, or other nourishment. Draw or write about predictions and findings. Feel, smell, and taste the plants, as relevant and safe.
- Create a photographic timeline of school residents, including pets, children, teachers, and administrators.
- Play a guessing game of class groups in the school. Children vote, as a class group, and guess about the match between contemporary photographs and baby pictures of children as well as of adults in the school. Record votes.
- Classify dinosaurs for characteristics such as ears, tails, and paws; relative capacity to move quickly; and food choices. Repeat with contemporary animals, comparing present-time and extinct animals.
- Small groups share their performance of movement activities that use different spatial dimensions, such as: high/low, wide/ narrow, and small/large movements.
- Observe and create evaporation and condensation with varied materials. In addition, when boiling water, weigh it before and after.
- Explore and develop battery-powered electrical circuits in sociodramatic play by wiring lights, buzzers, or bells, using easy-to-open clamps that are attached to a board.
- Survey human growth throughout the school year, using nonstandard, and then standard, measures of children's own bodies and of an invited baby. Graph and chart findings. Write up summaries. Class members bring in baby clothes they once wore.
- Measure changes in classroom pet and plant growth, using nonstandard measures and, with older children, standard measures.
- Survey family sizes of the present generation, the parents' generation, and the grandparents' generation. This activity involves parents. With the older children, complete a survey to compare findings between generations.
- Survey the food cycle from growth to reaping, transporting to markets, and sales, using field trips, readings, and interviews.
- Read or tell stories (also poems and songs) about mythic beings.
- Read and tell stories and poems about changes in nature and objects as well as among human beings.
- Read, tell stories, and see films about people from other times and varied cultures. Also include structured interviews (children plan questions together beforehand) and oral history.

- Represent by drawing, writing, or photographing, when possible, the evolution of block constructions. Older children might also record the stages of diorama development and carpentry development.
- Represent changes through role play, drawing, dancing, writing, and graphing; use audiotaping and photographing as relevant.

Adaptive Teaching

Dynamic themes or topics lend themselves to adaptive teaching and multilevel teaching. This means that different children doing different things at different times and for differing amounts of time might have equivalent experiences. If children, for example, participate in one or two surveys each week during the school year, even with different surveys, they will learn similar things about graphic representation and social science or science research. If children have daily art and writing opportunities each week, they will learn about organizing their experiences in order to communicate with others. If children have daily opportunities to engage in sociodramatic play, they will have experience in negotiating script development, communicating with an audience, and solving problems with others. If children engage in at least three or more opportunities each week to question, predict, experience, and compare things in the physical world, they will add to their repertoire of scientific strategies and concepts. If children read trade books and hear stories daily, they will add to their joy in literature and their store of vocabulary, alternative grammatical structures, and writing styles.

Exemplary early childhood education settings offer children options that relate to their capacity to choose. Most of the time during the day, there are provisions for small-group activity and social interaction. In this way, the teacher can circulate; teach small groups; engage in in-depth conversations, questioning, and problem solving; and assess individual children's development and needs. When teachers provide varied, simultaneously integrated activities, children can work independently at their own pace.

Peer feedback is often instructive. The teacher therefore creates opportunities for social interaction among children through cooperative learning projects in which children need one another and in which they need to negotiate in order to solve problems. Children can also acquaint each other with favorite readings, one another's stories, experiments with materials, and attainable models.

Children who have had varied cultural experiences, or who have special learning needs, can find opportunities for successful learning when they work in classrooms where instruction takes place mainly in small groups and between individuals. Teachers in decentralized settings—that is, settings organized mainly around small-group instruction—find it easier to mainstream children with special learning needs than do those teachers in settings where whole-group instruction and predetermined outcomes predominate. In turn, children who have special learning needs encounter more opportunities to feel successful and competent when working in decentralized settings.

Multicultural Education and Diversity

Children bring to school distinctive strengths that reflect their family and community cultures. When curriculum development takes place around dynamic themes, the teacher consistently adapts to the needs of children from diverse backgrounds.

Exemplary teachers provide varied instruction that is egalitarian and antibias. They provide opportunities for children to learn about the significance of celebrations that commemorate events from different cultures and times. Some educators in early education challenge the Eurocentric catalog of holidays and a form of calendar-worship curriculum that organizes topics or units around European holidays. Their study of holidays increasingly reflects the experiences of children who trace their roots to Africa, Asia, South America, and North America before Europeans arrived. In addition to Thanksgiving, for example, there are harvest festivals in many cultures (Ramsey 1987).

Focusing on the social significance of holidays—rather than the empty, often trivialized routine handling of holidays as a cut-and-paste pattern in ritual color—is as important as acknowledging the diversity in holiday celebrations. Teachers increasingly are helping young children relate the social celebration of holidays to their own life experiences. Multicultural activities commemorate struggles against the oppression of tyrants or the oppression of natural elements, as well as celebrate the victories over these phenomena. Underlying normal human interaction are parallel, isomorphic experiences that include disappointments, power struggles, successes, and feelings of celebration.

The younger the child, the less time teachers need to allot to holidays. The day before, or the day of, a holiday is sufficient attention. A particular food, story, or guest celebrant often is sufficient attention. It is not necessary for a teacher to cut out patterns in a ritual color of paper. It is more worthwhile to use the time to help children inductively identify with the dynamic theme underlying the holiday, whether it be a dialectic process in overcoming tyranny (all children know about power and bullies) or a celebration of a plentiful harvest after years of famine (all children know about unlimited wants and limited resources).

Sociodramatic play is an ultimate integrator of diverse cultural event knowledge. Children, in the course of entering, leaving, organizing, and reentering the play frame, negotiate underlying dynamic themes within their play scripts. They collaboratively play out their personally varied and distinctive cultural backgrounds as they represent their experiences in this oral and physical social activity. In these ways, sociodramatic play is a kind of oral play writing that is preliminary to writing down plays. As children receive peer feedback, they can learn about voice and audience and how to communicate with others.

Part of emergent literacy, sociodramatic play is a multicultural form of representation. Other forms of emergent literacy pervade the curriculum and are present in the discussion that follows.

Emergent Literacy in Language, the Sciences, Mathematics, the Arts, and the Social Sciences

An ideal literacy program begins with children's daily spoken language. Language develops in part as children participate in sociodramatic play and its oral composition, as

well as in language-experience dictation and inventing spellings. In addition to beginning to read by using written records of their own ideas, children can learn to read by using fine-quality trade books that include short passages, high predictability, and plentiful repetition. Folk-song and folk-tale formats also embody these criteria. The potential conditions for learning about such materials include inductive contrasts, cognitive dissonance, and competence.

By comparison, the controlled vocabulary and trivialized content of traditional basal readers do not serve the multicultural needs of children today, nor do they reflect current research concerning the inductive processes by which young children learn language skills. Using a broader view of emergent literacy, it is worthwhile to consider how literacy pervades the content of early curriculum.

Literacy about the physical world in early childhood practice has often consisted mainly of studying natural science. Children first measure plant or classroom pet growth using nonstandard measures such as yarn or tape, and later, using standard measuring tools. They draw and write their findings in personal booklets and on collaborative survey charts. Trips just beyond the classroom or the school, as well as farther afield, provide other phenomena upon which to practice nonstandard and standard measurement and varied forms of symbolic representation (see Russell 1990).

Teachers of young children typically have paid less attention to the domains of physical sciences, tools, and machines. Scientific literacy, however, also consists of studying the physical world in direct, active, and concrete ways. For example, children who roll balls down ramps set at different angles are also engaging in cognitive dissonance by predicting–experiencing–comparing; inductive contrasts between two ramps set at different angles; social negotiation of the setups; and physical manipulation of the materials. Having marked and/or measured with nonstandard or standard measures (depending upon age), children are seeing direct uses for mathematical skills. Comparing how much farther or nearer the balls have rolled calls for addition and subtraction that have meaning to children. Another way to practice addition and subtraction is by estimating–measuring–comparing (cognitive dissonance) how many unifix cubes (or how many inches) are equal to the height of a favorite dinosaur or truck toy. Children estimate and then record their estimates. They measure two or more toys (always provide a contrast), record their findings, and compare their findings with their estimates. They subtract from, or add to, the difference between the two, a meaningful use of skills. Children also use tools and take apart/put together simple machinery (see Sprung, Froschl, and Campbell 1985).

Along with writing, children represent their experiences by using various art media. Visual and spatial art media are the early forms in which children can represent their meanings symbolically. Teachers in early childhood classrooms have tended to offer a preponderance of two-dimensional representation. Three-dimensional representations, however, are also important; these in particular affect the visual-spatial skills that contribute to comfort in learning mathematics. Therefore, exemplary teachers provide opportunities for three-dimensional representations and constructions with such media as clay, woodwork, building blocks for the floor as well as the tabletop or mat, and mobile structures. Accompanying these three-dimensional materials, writing and drawing materials are always available, along with cameras on occasion, in order to record and celebrate children's accomplishments.

Music is another form in which children might represent their experiences. Dance and movement education, as forms of spatial sculpture, sometimes includes props, obstacles, and climbing apparatus. Children also tell stories and represent emotions through movement. When children work together in pairs, they create new collaborative forms.

Singing, sometimes with the words in view on a "big book" or a chart, is part of the musical literacy experience. The musical analog to children hearing stories in trade books and then writing their own text is for children to hear music and then write their own poems/songs. As with young children's products, in general, the younger the child, the more episodic will be the product. Acknowledgment and appreciation of the effort are often all that children need in order to feel competent as poet-composers. All children come to school having heard contemporary poet-composers in

the popular, country and western, and folk music of their times. Poetic musical composition rests on the writing continuum. Some schools, recognizing the literary value of such experience, engage folk musicians to work with children. Children's early participation might reasonably consist of humming and singing along before oral composition, and then writing of lyrics, might occur.

Sociodramatic play with multiple themes appears to support and extend children's language literacy (Christie 1991) as well as their increased interest and achievement in mathematics (Jennings et al. 1992). Teachers encourage young children to write more and to increase their range of oral and mathematical language skills when they provide varied literacy materials within thematic classroom centers. At different times throughout the school year, they provide children with varied props that represent a myriad of children's life experiences, along with reading and writing materials, paced such that children can integrate them as a part of their play. Among the props are books, writing materials, receipt books, checkbooks, appointment lists, order pads, price lists, road maps, restaurant menus, and veterinary/medical forms.

Multi-level Instruction and Grouping

Grouping for instruction comprises part of the context in which learning takes place. Increasingly, schools are finding that heterogeneous grouping increases the opportunities for children to improve their achievement (Steinberg and Wheelock 1992). Inter-age grouping is one variation of heterogeneous grouping.

Exemplary teachers in heterogeneous settings provide diversified activities that deal with similar subject matter although they require different levels of skills. Teachers adapt activity-based projects to children's learning needs, for example, by providing readings about the same subject that are written at different ability levels. Subject matter for five- and six-year-olds might include issues concerning different types of family dwellings—urban, suburban, and rural—or the variety of occupations in which female and male parents engage today. Subject matter for seven- and eight-year-olds might include issues concerning the relation between different terrains and dwellings or the variety of occupations in which grandparents engaged. Teachers also provide research problems to solve that invite children to engage in varied forms of data collection and mathematical representation.

Learning Centers. On the first day of school, teachers provide a few learning centers for small groups to use, inasmuch as young children acquire most new learning that is worthwhile when they work in smaller groups or individually rather than during whole-group instruction. These centers/areas provide the spatial context for small-group organization as well as spaces in which children can work independently and, from time to time, privately. Teachers add to, and change, learning centers and their content focus throughout the school year. They might include such centers as the arts, writing, reading, mathematics, science, sociodramatic play—including floor blocks, listening, and a teacher's instructional area. Within these generic areas there might be computers and earphones as well as many manipulatives. Changing props in the sociodramatic area might include provisions for a hotel, hospital, restaurant, zoo, farm, airport, garage, school office, shoe store, food market, bicycle shop, dentist's–physician's–veterinarian's office, beauty parlor, post office, or toy store

During different intervals of time throughout the school year, teachers might offer puppetry, roller movies, shadow play and research, hat constructions, varied baking/cooking activities, sand/water play and research, and tunnel or other construction variants. Children can profit from studying new classroom pets for six to ten weeks, while a puppet stage might be in kindergarten for two weeks but in a second-grade classroom for ten to twelve weeks. Changing or rotating subject matter and resources maintains fresh perspectives and the delight of novelty. It seems as if there is never enough time during a school year to pursue all of the worthwhile content that might appropriately take place in a classroom.

Projects in which small groups participate lend themselves to more than one solution, provide active participation for children with different abilities, and provide opportunities for participants to build mutual respect. They also potentially create a sense of competence for each child who participates. Children have opportunities to engage in many ways of knowing, whether poetic, musical, or narrative appreciation and composition (both oral and written); visual or kinetic appreciation and representation; measurement, surveys, and graphic represention; obtaining, sorting, and interpreting historical, economic, or sociological data; or measuring objects as they move in space or grow; and documenting/measuring plant growth, animal growth, or other natural phenomena.

The particular mix of materials, activities, and ways of knowing depend upon the unique fingerprint created by each group of teachers and children who plan together on a specific site at a particular time. The most gregarious activities for a group to pursue are those that are most likely to generate children's continuing development and sense of competence.

Competence

Children who feel competent within their early education are willing to risk learning about new things. They are likely to be independent thinkers who can question ideas. They are less apt to engage in antisocial or disruptive activities. We would do very well in early education if teachers helped children feel competent about meaningful learning.

In turn, teachers need to feel comfortable and competent in order to teach in ways that empower children to feel competent and successful. Each teacher might ask herself/himself what would be the next step in moving toward teaching dynamic themes, using the six conditions for learning, and then reflect on ways to take that single, next step—and then the next one.

References

Bergen, D., ed. 1988. *Play: A Medium for Learning and Development*. Portsmouth, NH: Heinemann.

Brown, Marcia, illus. 1972. *Stone Soup*. New York: Scribner.

Chaille, C. 1992. "Projects, Topics, and Themes." In *The Encyclopedia of Early*

Childhood Education, ed. L. R. Williams and D. P. Fromberg, 318. New York: Garland.

Christie, J. F., ed. 1991. *Play and Early Literacy Development*. Albany, NY: State University of New York Press.

Dyson, A. H. 1987. "The Value of 'Time off Task': Young Children's Spontaneous Talk and Deliberate Text." *Harvard Educational Review* 57(4): 396–420.

Egan, K. 1988. "The Origins of Imagination and the Curriculum." In *Imagination and Education*, ed. K. Egan and D. Nadaner, 91–127. New York: Teachers College Press.

Fein, G. G., and M. Rivkin, eds. 1986. *The Young Child at Play*. Washington, DC: National Association for the Education of Young Children.

Fromberg, D. P. 1987. *The Full-Day Kindergarten*. New York: Teachers College Press.

———. 1992. "Play." In *The Early Childhood Curriculum*: *A Review of Current Research*, ed. C. Seefeldt. New York: Teachers College Press.

Goodwin, A. L. 1992. "Unit Curriculum." In *The Encyclopedia of Early Childhood Education*, ed. L. R. Williams and D. P. Fromberg, 318. New York: Garland.

Jennings, C. M., et al. 1992. "Increasing Interest and Achievement in Mathematics through Children's Literature." *Early Childhood Research Quarterly*, 7(2): 263–76.

Johnson, D. W., et al. 1984. *Circles of Learning*: *Cooperation in the Classroom*. Alexandria, VA: Association for Supervision and Curriculum Development.

Piaget, J., et al. 1965. *The Moral Judgment of the Child*, trans. M. Gabain. New York: Free Press.

Ramsey, P. G. 1987. *Teaching and Learning in a Diverse World*. New York: Teachers College Press.

Russell, H. R. 1990. *Ten-Minute Field Trips*. 2d ed. Washington, DC: National Science Teachers Association.

Slavin, R. E., and N. A. Madden. 1989. "What Works for Students at Risk: A Research Synthesis." *Educational Leadership* 46(5): 4–13.

Sprung, B., M. Froschl, and P. B. Campbell. 1985. *What Will Happen If . . .* : *Young Children and the Scientific Method*. New York: Educational Equity Concepts.

Steinberg, A., and A. Wheelock. 1992. "After Tracking—What? Middle Schools Find New Answers." *Harvard Education Letter* 8 (5): 1-4.

STATE GUIDELINES FOR EARLY CHILDHOOD EDUCATION

Diane Lynch-Fraser
Assistant Director
School for Language and Communication Development, North Bellmore, New York
Assistant Professor
St. John's University, Jamaica, New York

T HE goal of this chapter is to provide assistance to school districts, administrators, classroom teachers, and day-care providers in planning programs for young children through appropriate analysis and application of state guidelines for early childhood education. Educators involved in the design of local curriculum guides can draw valuable information from their respective state guidelines, particularly in the areas of continuity, evaluation, and accountability. State guidelines can also be a valuable barometer for assessing which areas of the current curriculum need modification, enhancement, or change.

Determining your own particular program needs should precede any investigation of state guidelines. Needs should be assessed in terms of your program's history, its current status, and the direction administrators and teachers seek for the future. Once this information has been gathered, curriculum writers can then determine how closely their focus fits in with state curriculum mandates. This kind of analysis permits administrators and teachers involved in curriculum design to reflect upon their school's overall philosophy for early childhood

education. All state guidelines encourage such analysis in order to develop the strong theoretical foundation necessary for sound curriculum design and subsequent implementation.

It is important to remember that although some states do provide specific recommendations for activities, materials, and curriculum resources, these recommendations are not the express purpose of state guidelines. Responsibilities for devising lesson plans, selecting materials, and implementing activities rest with curriculum planners in individual school districts and in private or publicly funded programs.

Common Features of State Curriculum Guides

Many states that provide guidelines for early childhood education emphasize the concept of *developmental appropriateness*. With developmental appropriateness, learning activities are matched with children's age, individual tastes, and abilities. Developmental appropriateness is often discussed in two dimensions: age appropriateness and individual appropriateness. The concept of *age appropriateness* rests on the idea that there are predictable milestones of growth and change during the first nine years of life that should be reflected in the learning environment and learning experiences of children. The concept of *individual appropriateness* suggests that within the general pattern of human development, there are considerable individual variations. Each child is a unique person with an individual timing and pattern of growth. Many states recommend that the generation of curriculum goals and the evaluation of these goals be considered within these two dimensions of developmental appropriateness.

Although developmental appropriateness can be viewed as the underlying philosophy of most mandated curriculum guides, many states describe specific theoretical models, such as the interactionist model (see chapter 2) or specific curriculum implementations such as a Montessori or High Scope curriculum upon which individual programs can base their learning plans and activities.

Almost all states providing early childhood guidelines address two developmentally appropriate elements of practice: the learning environment and the integrated curriculum. The term *learning environment* refers to the scheduling of time, the organization of space, and the utilization of learning tools and materials in the classroom. The term *integrated curriculum* reflects the fact that children's learning is experientially based and holistic. According to this concept, a good curriculum must provide interaction between content areas in any learning situation. Isolating knowledge into separate disciplines is an artificial way of learning. When states make specific recommendations for the implementation of the integrated curriculum, they often suggest the use of learning centers and a theme approach to learning.

In the theme/unit approach, a topic or unifying theme is presented for specific learning objectives. The topics that are covered in a given year reflect a balance of various content areas. The topics provide opportunities for children to spend concentrated amounts of time exploring subjects that link content areas such

as mathematics and social studies or science and the creative arts.

A classroom with learning centers is divided into separate interest areas that enable children to learn at their own pace and in their own way. The variety in the type of learning centers provided caters to individual styles and interests in learning. Such centers may include areas for dramatic play, blocks, library, reading and writing, mathematics games, puzzles, sand, water, and woodworking. Activities in the centers are at different ability levels so that each child can find both challenge and success. Some activities enable children to discover new ideas through exploration, experimentation, and trial and error. Some encourage children to demonstrate what they know, while still others enable children to express themselves creatively.

A number of states discuss the concept of home–school–community connections in terms of the administrators' and teachers' sensitivity to each child's individual family pattern, cultural heritage, and special needs. In addition, members of the local community are used as resources for children to enhance their learning through understanding people's roles within society.

Discussions of family and community are often further reflected in two more curriculum aspects: multiculturalism and parental involvement. Multiculturalism is a philosophy of racial and ethnic pluralism in which awareness is focused on the atmosphere created within the school and the nonverbal messages that this atmosphere sends to children, parents, and teachers toward people of differing backgrounds. Emphasis is placed on the classroom teacher's understanding of and sensitivity to children representing various cultural backgrounds. The concept of parental involvement is based on the idea that young children thrive when their families are part of the life of the school. Individual teachers can initiate efforts to involve parents by extending classroom activities. Parents are a teacher's most important resource in reinforcing what teachers want children to learn, and the teacher's task is made easier when parents help develop learning skills at home.

Many states provide goals for specific content areas. These goals reflect the following philosophic orientations:

- *Creative Arts:* When integrated into the overall curriculum, the creative arts help children deal with abstractions, express their own uniqueness, listen with understanding, make decisions, and gain an appreciation of the values and the intellectual and artistic achievements of their culture.
- *Physical Education:* Motor experiences are a primary source of learning for the young child. Therefore, the physical education program should include opportunities for children to develop healthy minds and bodies by integrating movement and other aspects of health and safety into the curriculum.
- *Language Arts:* The ability to understand and use the spoken and written language is crucial to learning in all other areas. Language ability affects not only intellectual and cognitive development, but also children's social and emotional development.
- *Mathematics:* The development of mathematical knowledge involves the discovery of relationships, many being constructed from physical observations. Mathematics provides us with a language and a way of organizing information to solve problems.
- *Science:* Development of a quality science program for young children should encourage curiosity and exploration as children strive to understand the physical and biological world in which they live. Teachers should be prepared to capitalize on informal science inquiry as children question phenomena in their natural environment.
- *Social Studies:* As an essential learning aspect in early childhood, social studies curriculum should support children's total development as responsible citizens, family members, friends, and classmates, while simultaneously enabling them to explore the human experience, past and present, and various cultural heritages.

It is important to understand that although states may specify curriculum goals by addressing individual content areas, they do this primarily as a means of identifying the contributions of each discipline area, not to splinter curriculum into separate disciplines for isolated study.

Finally, most states, perhaps as an extension of their philosophy of developmental appropriateness or their implementation of an integrated curriculum, recognize the concept of "the whole child": the child as a thinking, feeling, social, and creative being—not simply as a being who learns. Thus, the child's cognitive development is not the only developmental aspect to be addressed. A child's affective and social development also influences her educational experience. States expect teachers to create learning environments that provide for children's self-esteem, self-acceptance, recognition as valued members of society, appreciation and acceptance of other people, and potential achievement.

To summarize, most state-mandated guidelines for early childhood education reflect the following curriculum aspects:

1. Developmental appropriateness
   - age appropriateness
   - individual appropriateness
2. Developmentally appropriate practice
   - the learning environment
     - use of time and space
     - use of learning tools
   - the integrated curriculum
     - theme/unit approach
     - learning centers
3. Home–school–community connections
   - multiculturalism
   - parent involvement
4. Content areas
   - creative arts
   - physical education
   - language arts
   - mathematics
   - science
   - social studies
5. Affective–social development

Evaluation and Assessment of Classroom Performance

All states providing guidelines for early childhood education provide a mechanism for evaluating whether these guidelines have been met in an individual classroom. These evaluations take the form of a checklist of behavioral objectives, which may be expressed as curriculum goals or as descriptive statements such as "The child uses language to communicate desires and needs to an adult," or "The child constructs, identifies, and names sets of objects one through ten." The teacher must respond to these goals by stating yes or no or by indicating the degree to which the goal has been met. For example, the teacher may be asked to evaluate students' performance of the objectives using the following criteria:

1 = not yet/rarely
2 = sometimes
3 = usually/frequently

Some assessments shift focus away from the child's behavior and focus on teacher behavior. In these cases, goals are formulated in the first person, For example:

- I structure interactive learning play by providing specific materials in organized activity centers.
- I work to identify and respond to children's special needs and different learning styles.

Here, instead of solely monitoring the child's responses, the teacher takes into direct account her own behavior and how she facilitates learning. The evaluations may include room for anecdotal information in which teachers record specific activities, desires for future objectives, and what new materials may help achieve certain objectives.

Included in the evaluation section of many state guidelines is a portion devoted to specific methods of recording and observing children's behaviors. The methods used for data collection affect the quality of any evaluation. The methods include spending at least ten minutes each day recording observations, keeping dated samples of each child's work, and recording in photographs or on videotape the nonpermanent products of learning such as block constructions or dramatic play.

Specific State Guidelines

The criteria used here to evaluate state guidelines are, at best, descriptive. Although there are the broad commonalities discussed

earlier, the specific contents of the guidelines vary so dramatically that an objective comparison becomes difficult and unrealistic. Ten states currently offer no guidelines for early childhood education, and three are in the process of developing guidelines. The remaining thirty-seven states do address at least one of the five curriculum aspects mentioned earlier. There are several states that address all five.

The most noticeable difference in state guidelines is the ages or grades included in the state's definition of early childhood education. Some states include guidelines for children from birth through age nine, others for prekindergarten through third grade, some for prekindergarten and kindergarten, and others simply for kindergarten. One state, Tennessee, offers a nongraded curriculum.

Accordingly, this evaluation of specific state guidelines will lead off with a chart indicating the ages and/or grades included by each state and the presence or absence of the five curriculum aspects in each state's guidelines. Then the quality of each state's guidelines will be assessed by describing how well each curriculum aspect is presented and developed.

The fifty states are divided into seven regions:

1. New England Region
   Connecticut
   Maine
   Massachusetts
   New Hampshire
   Rhode Island
   Vermont

2. Middle Atlantic Region
   Delaware
   Maryland
   New Jersey
   New York
   Pennsylvania

3. Southeast Region
   Alabama
   Florida
   Georgia
   Kentucky
   Mississippi
   North Carolina
   South Carolina

Tennessee
Virginia
West Virginia

4. South Central Region
   Arkansas
   Louisiana
   Oklahoma
   Texas

5. North Central Region
   Illinois
   Indiana
   Iowa
   Kansas
   Michigan
   Minnesota
   Missouri
   Nebraska
   North Dakota
   Ohio
   South Dakota
   Wisconsin

6. Mountain West Region
   Arizona
   Colorado
   Idaho
   Montana
   Nevada
   New Mexico
   Utah
   Wyoming

7. Pacific States Region
   Alaska
   California
   Hawaii
   Oregon
   Washington

New England Region

	Connecticut	Maine	Massachusetts	New Hampshire	Rhode Island	Vermont
NEW ENGLAND REGION						
Age/grades addressed	K–3 (1990)					
Developmental appropriateness	X					
- age appropriateness	X					
- individual appropriateness	X					
Developmentally appropriate practice	X	no state guidelines	unavailable	no state guidelines	no state guidelines	no state guidelines
- the learning environment	X					
use of time and space	X					
use of learning tools	X					
- the integrated curriculum	X					
theme/unit approach	X					
learning centers	X					
Home-school-community connections	X					
- multiculturalism	X					
- parent involvement	X					
Content areas	X					
- creative arts	X					
- physical education	X					
- language arts	X					
- mathematics	X					
- science	X					
- social studies	X					
Affective-social development	X					

Connecticut

Early Childhood Program, A Guide to Program Development for Kindergarten: Part I, 174p. *A Guide to Program Development for Kindergarten: Part II*, 112p.

A. Developmental appropriateness
1. Extensive discussion of development from historical, theoretical, and practical perspectives
2. Concepts of age appropriateness and individual appropriateness discussed and applied

B. Developmentally appropriate practice
1. Thorough review of aspects of the learning environment: scheduling, classroom organization, and application of learning tools
2. Comprehensive examination of various aspects of the integrated curriculum from both theoretical and practical perspectives
3. Extensive recommendations for application of theme/unit and learning-center approaches

C. Home–school–community connections
1. Directly addresses issues of family involvement and multiculturalism
2. Provides specific goals both for helping families participate in classroom activities and for helping teachers recognize, respond appropriately to, and integrate aspects of cultural diversity within the curriculum

D. Content goals
1. Provides extensive commentary and procedures for implementing content areas into an integrated curriculum

E. Affective–social development
1. Provides extensive information regarding social and emotional development from a theoretical perspective
2. Provides goals and recommendations for their implementation

Summary of the Region

Maine, New Hampshire, Rhode Island, and Vermont have no state-mandated guidelines for early childhood education. Massachusetts's guidelines are unavailable. Guidelines for early childhood education are generated by and are the responsibility of each individual school district.

Connecticut provides an extensive, exemplary, comprehensive program for early childhood education. There is a self-study instrument to help teachers identify objectives for a developmentally appropriate program. This instrument becomes invaluable in the evaluation process, as well as in the needs assessment process.

Extensive information on the historical and theoretical foundations of early childhood education is provided, along with specific descriptions of several developmental domains: cognitive, emotional, and social.

Specific recommendations for the learning environment are given in tables and graphs. Sample schedules, suggestions for classroom organization, and implementation of learning tools are all carefully examined.

Although the recommendations for parent involvement and multiculturalism do not match the extensive knowledge shared in other curriculum aspects, Connecticut clearly presents the tools necessary to any curriculum writing team.

Middle Atlantic Region

MIDDLE ATLANTIC REGION					
	Delaware	Maryland	New Jersey	New York	Pennsylvania
Age/grades addressed		Pre-K (1989)		Pre-K–3 (1987)	
Developmental appropriateness - age appropriateness - individual appropriateness		X			

Developmentally appropriate practice
- the learning environment
  use of time and space
  use of learning tools
- the integrated curriculum
  theme/unit approach
  learning centers
	unavailable	X
		
		X
		X
		X
			no state guidelines		unavailable

Home-school-community connections - multiculturalism - parent involvement		X		X X X	
Content areas - creative arts - physical education - language arts - mathematics - science - social studies					
Affective-social development					

Maryland

Learning Process: Process of Learning Curriculum: Theoretical Framework for Kindergarten, 38p.

A. Developmental appropriateness
1. Adequate discussion of development based on theoretical framework of child's learning process being influenced by context
2. No direct reference to concepts of age and developmental appropriateness provided

B. Developmentally appropriate practice
1. No direct references to scheduling or classroom organization; some suggestions for learning tools
2. Adequate discussion of theme unit and learning center approaches without direct reference to integrated curriculum

C. Home-school-community connections
1. Parent involvement cited as one of the basic theoretical assumptions for a sound early childhood program
2. Although no direct reference to multiculturalism is provided, some suggestions for examination of various cultures are made within individual curriculum units

D. Content area
1. Concept addressed within description of learning center approach

E. Affective-social development
1. Concept addressed within a brief discussion of the importance of self-esteem

New York

A Multicultural Early Childhood Resource Guide, 40p.

A. Developmental appropriateness
1. No direct reference to this concept provided

B. Developmentally appropriate practice
1. No direct reference to this concept

C. Home-school-community connections
1. Provides extensive information on implementation of a multicultural curriculum for early childhood
2. Includes philosophy of racial/ethnic pluralism, concepts of classroom and

school ecology, and strategies for parental involvement

D. Content areas
1. No direct reference to this concept
E. Affective-social development
1. No direct reference to this concept

Summary of Region

New Jersey has no state-mandated guidelines for early childhood education. Pennsylvania's guidelines are unavailable.

Maryland's guidelines provide an adequate overview of the theoretical foundations for prekindergarten programming. Although the guide does provide some brief information on the use of learning tools, the implementation of theme/unit and learning center approaches, parental involvement, and teaching the content areas through the use of learning centers, only the most experienced curriculum writers could use this guide without supplementary help. Apparently, this limitation is recognized, and two pages of additional resources are suggested.

New York's guidelines emphasize the application of a multicultural curriculum. The New York document is not expected to have the broad application expected of other curriculum guides. Considering that the curriculum aspect of multiculturalism is regarded as a foundation for early childhood programming, this guide manages to articulate well the crucial nature of this concept. The guide provides comprehensive information on integrating a multicultural perspective within an existing curriculum and gives excellent strategies for helping parents to become involved in their children's education.

Southeast Region

SOUTHEAST REGION										
	Alabama	Florida	Georgia	Kentucky	Mississippi	North Carolina	South Carolina	Tennessee	Virginia	West Virginia
Age/grades addressed					Pre-K–2			nongraded (1990)		
Developmental appropriateness				currently developing guidelines		no state guidelines			no state guidelines	
- age appropriateness								X		
- individual appropriateness								X		
Developmentally appropriate practice										
- the learning environment					X			X		
use of time and space	unavailable	unavailable	unavailable		X		unavailable	X		unavailable
use of learning tools					X			X		
- the integrated curriculum					X			X		
theme/unit approach								X		
learning centers					X			X		
Home-school-community connections	available	available	available				available			available
- multiculturalism								X		
- parent involvement								X		
Content areas										
- creative arts										
- physical education										
- language arts										
- mathematics										
- science										
- social studies										
Affective-social development					X			X		

Mississippi

A Promise To Keep: The Mississippi Kindergarten and Primary Instructional Planning Guide, 97p.

A. Developmental appropriateness
 1. No specific reference to this concept
B. Developmentally appropriate practice
 1. References to scheduling, organization of classroom space, and use of learning tools and equipment made within curriculum goal framework
 2. Extensive goals and activities provided, with detailed procedures for implementation within a unit/theme and a learning center approach
C. Home–school–community connections
 1. No specific reference to this concept
D. Content areas
 1. No specific reference to this concept
E. Affective–social development
 1. References to self-concept, self-esteem made throughout

Tennessee

Tennessee Nongraded Elementary Education Program, 40p.

A. Developmental appropriateness
 1. Provides adequate discussion of development and makes reference to age and individual appropriateness
 2. Discussion of development has evolved into the orientation of a nongraded curriculum
B. Developmentally appropriate practice
 1. Provides adequate discussion of scheduling and use of classroom space, learning tools, and equipment; does not provide format for implementation
 2. Provides adequate discussion of theoretical framework for an integrated curriculum, and discusses implementation via a unit/theme approach or use of learning center; does not make recommendations for implementation

C. Home–school–community connections
 1. No reference to multiculturalism
 2. Mentions parental involvement as critical to child's success in school
D. Content areas
 1. No reference to this concept
E. Affective–social development
 1. Makes references to child's social adjustment and self-esteem throughout

Summary of the Region

North Carolina and Virginia do not provide mandated guidelines for early childhood education. Guidelines for Alabama, Florida, Georgia, South Carolina, and West Virginia are unavailable. Kentucky is currently developing guidelines.

Mississippi provides extensive curriculum goals, detailed activities with visuals and suggested learning tools, and sample tests for use within the theme/unit and learning centers approaches. Thus, it represents a highly practice-oriented guide that is useful to classroom teachers. What is absent and yet equally significant for curriculum writers is a discussion of the theoretical framework upon which these goals and activities are based.

In contrast, Tennessee provides the theoretical framework that Mississippi does not. Tennessee's guide provides an adequate discussion of development, with references to age and individual appropriateness. This theoretical orientation evolves into an interesting discussion for the foundation of a nongraded curriculum for early childhood. There is adequate commentary on such aspects of the learning environment as scheduling, organization of classroom space, learning tools, and equipment. However, the guide lacks suggestions for implementation. Considering that the concept of a nongraded curriculum, although developmentally sound, is relatively unfamiliar, recommendations for practical application would be helpful both to curriculum writers and to classroom teachers.

South Central Region

SOUTH CENTRAL REGION				
	Arkansas	**Louisiana**	**Oklahoma**	**Texas**
Age/grades addressed	K (1991)		Pre-K–3 (1990)	
Developmental appropriateness - age appropriateness - individual appropriateness		n o s t a t e	X	
Developmentally appropriate practice - the learning environment 　　use of time and space 　　use of learning tools - the integrated curriculum 　　theme/unit approach 　　learning centers	X X X X	g u i d e	X X X X	u n a v a
Home-school-community connections - multiculturalism - parent involvement	X X X	l i n e s		i l a b l
Content areas - creative arts - physical education - language arts - mathematics - science - social studies	X X X X X X	(uses informal curriculum guide)	X X X X X X X	e
Affective-social development	X		X	

Arkansas

Kindergarten Course Content Guide, 30p.
A. Developmental appropriateness
　1. No specific reference to this concept
B. Developmentally appropriate practice
　1. Adequately describes scheduling, classroom organization, and use of learning tools and equipment
　2. No mention of integrated curriculum
C. Home-school-community connections
　1. Mentions concepts of multiculturalism and parental involvement
D. Content areas
　1. Discusses each content area in detail, with goals and activities for each
E. Affective-social development
　1. Reinforces this concept throughout document, but provides no specific recommendations

Oklahoma

Suggested Learner Outcomes: Developmental Four Year Olds, Kindergarten, First Grade, 73p. *Crossroads: A Handbook for Effective Classroom Management*, 191p.
A. Developmental appropriateness
　1. Adequate discussion of development, emphasizing concepts of age and individual appropriateness
B. Developmentally appropriate practice
　1. Specifically describes scheduling, classroom organization, and use of materials and equipment as aspects of the social climate within the school
　2. Does not make reference to concept of integrated curriculum
C. Home-school-community connections
　1. No specific reference to this concept
D. Content areas
　1. Describes each content area's philosophic orientation and provides goals and activities for each

E. Affective–social development
   1. Extensive discussion of social climate, with numerous suggestions for implementation in the classroom

Summary of the Region

Louisiana has no mandated guidelines for early childhood. Texas guidelines were unavailable.

Arkansas offers an adequate activity guide for kindergarten teachers, but its guide lacks theoretical underpinnings that could enhance professional understanding of early childhood development.

Oklahoma's guidelines are unique in their emphasis on the social climate in which learning takes place. There is adequate discussion of development, with a more thorough focus on implementation. Included are detailed discussions of classroom organization, suggestions for materials and equipment, and recommendation for specific content-area goals and activities.

North Central Region

NORTH CENTRAL REGION (PART I)						
	Illinois	Indiana	Iowa	Kansas	Michigan	Minnesota
Age/grades addressed		K (1989)	Birth–Grade 3 (1991)		Pre-K (1987)	Birth–Grade 3 (1990)
Developmental appropriateness	no guideline for mainstream	X	X	unavailable		X
- age appropriateness		X	X			
- individual appropriateness		X	X			
Developmentally appropriate practice		X			X	X
- the learning environment		X			X	
use of time and space		X			X	
use of learning tools		X				X
- the integrated curriculum		X				X
theme/unit approach					X	X
learning centers						
Home-school-community connections		X	X		X	X
- multiculturalism		X				X
- parent involvement		X	X		X	X
Content areas		X				
- creative arts		X				
- physical education		X				
- language arts		X				
- mathematics		X				
- science		X				
- social studies						
Affective-social development		X	X		X	X

Indiana

Kindergarten Guide, 77p.
A. Developmental appropriateness
1. Adequately discusses principles of development and learning
2. Acknowledges concepts of age appropriateness and individual appropriateness as significant in planning kindergarten curriculum
B. Developmentally appropriate practice
1. Discusses specific use of time, space and learning materials
2. Emphasizes use of learning centers and provides suggestions for setup, materials, and activities in these centers
3. Discusses concept of integrated curriculum as an overall philosophy for early childhood education and provides activities for implementation
C. Home–school–community connections
1. Provides specific recommendations in terms of activities and materials that support multiculturalism
2. Discusses parents as crucial to successful kindergarten programming and lists

specific activities for promoting parent involvement
D. Content areas
1. Discusses each content area from a developmental perspective
2. Provides specific activities for using each content area within an integrated curriculum
3. Suggests specific objectives for implementing content-area curriculum
E. Affective–social development
1. Does not mention this concept specifically but incorporates this idea within an overall discussion of development

Iowa

Iowa Early Childhood Guidelines, 38p.
A. Developmental appropriateness
1. Emphasizes developmental and curriculum theory
2. Provides detailed information on the concepts of age and individual appropriateness

NORTH CENTRAL REGION (PART II)						
	Missouri	Nebraska	North Dakota	Ohio	South Dakota	Wisconsin
Age/grades addressed		K (1984)		Birth–Grade 3 (1991)	K–Grade 3 (1986)	Birth–Grade 3 (1992)
Developmental appropriateness				X		X
- age appropriateness				X		X
- individual appropriateness	unavailable		unavailable	X		X
Developmentally appropriate practice		X		X	X	
- the learning environment						X
use of time and space						X
use of learning tools				X	X	X
- the integrated curriculum				X		
theme/unit approach				X		
learning centers						X
Home–school–community connections				X	X	X
- multiculturalism				X		X
- parent involvement				X	X	X
Content areas		X		X	X	
- creative arts				X	X	
- physical education		X		X	X	
- language arts		X		X	X	
- mathematics				X	X	
- science				X	X	
- social studies						
Affective–social development				X	X	X

B. Developmentally appropriate practice
1. Suggests goals for curriculum planning but does not discuss concepts of the learning environment or integrated curriculum
C. Home-school-community connections
1. Provides principles for home, school, and community partnerships but does not discuss implementation
2. No direct reference to multiculturalism
D. Content areas
1. No direct reference to content areas
E. Affective-social development
1. Mentions social and emotional development within the framework of developmental and curriculum theory

Michigan

Curriculum Resource Book for Preschool Programs, 70p. *The Standards of Quality and Curriculum Guidelines*, 55p.
A. Developmental appropriateness
1. No direct reference to developmental appropriateness
B. Developmentally appropriate practice
1. Provides specific recommendations for scheduling of activities, organization of classrooms, and selection of learning tools and equipment
2. Discusses application of learning-center approach in detail
C. Home-school-community connections
1. Provides specific goals for parents to improve parenting skills and extend child's learning at home
2. No direct reference to multiculturalism
D. Content areas
1. No direct reference to content areas
E. Affective-social development
1. Mentions this concept within various curriculum goals

Minnesota

Model Learner Outcomes for Early Childhood Education, 165p.
A. Developmental appropriateness
1. Although there are no specific references to age or individual appropriate-

ness, there is extensive information on six learning domains: personal, social, cognitive, etc.
B. Developmentally appropriate practice
1. The learning environment and the integrated curriculum are discussed, and specific goals are provided
2. Implementation of goals is not discussed
C. Home-school-community connections
1. Multiculturalism and parent involvement are adequately discussed in terms of philosophical overview and goals in curriculum planning
D. Content areas
1. No direct reference to content areas
E. Affective-social development
1. Provides extensive information on this concept in terms of philosophical orientation and goals for curriculum planning

Nebraska

Position Statement on Kindergarten, 9p.
A. Developmental appropriateness
1. No direct reference to developmental appropriateness
B. Developmentally appropriate practice
1. Provides limited information on scheduling of time, use of space, and selection of learning materials
C. Home-school-community connections
1. Mentions parent involvement
D. Content areas
1. Mentions content areas of language arts and mathematics
E. Affective-social development
1. No direct reference to this concept

Ohio

The Ohio Early Childhood Curriculum Guide, 193p. *Parent Involvement*, 78p. *Rules for Preschool Program*, 23p. *The Early Childhood Identification Process*, 47p.
A. Developmental appropriateness
1. Provides extensive information on the nature of development in the early childhood years

2. Included in this discussion are specific references to age and individual appropriateness

B. Developmentally appropriate practice
   1. Provides detailed information and recommendations for scheduling, organization of classroom space, and selection and use of specific learning materials and equipment
   2. Discusses concept of the integrated curriculum at length, providing both goals and ideas for their implementation, along with specific activities for both theme and learning center approaches
   3. Provides useful anecdotal information based on actual classroom observations to assist teachers' and administrators' comprehension of the integrated learning concept

C. Home-school-community connections
   1. The concept of multiculturalism is discussed in terms of family diversity
   2. Extensive information is provided to help teachers encourage parent participation at home and in school
   3. A thorough parent education program is provided

D. Content areas
   1. All content areas are addressed within the framework of three learning domains: the cognitive, language-literacy, and affective-communicative
   2. Goals and activities are provided for each domain

E. Affective-social development
   1. Although this aspect is addressed specifically within the affective-communicative learning domain, it is also addressed as a philosophical foundation for early childhood education

South Dakota

Kindergarten Today: A Guide to Curriculum Development, 27p. *Developmental Guidance and Counseling Plan for Kindergarten through Sixth Grade*, 180p.

A. Developmental appropriateness
   1. No specific mention of this concept

B. Developmentally appropriate practice
   1. Discusses the learning environment in terms of scheduling, classroom organization, and use and selection of learning tools and materials
   2. No mention of concept of integrated curriculum

C. Home-school-community connections
   1. Discusses parental involvement within the guidance and counseling plan
   2. No mention of multiculturalism

D. Content areas
   1. Addresses specific content areas, providing goals and activities for each

E. Affective-social development
   1. Discusses this concept extensively within guidance and counseling plan

Wisconsin

Opening Doors through Integration, 182p. *An Invitation To Play: Teacher's Guide*, 86p. *An Invitation To Play: Activities for Parents*, 20p. *Early Childhood: Exceptional Educational Needs,* 33p.

A. Developmental appropriateness
   1. Extensive discussion of development is presented through numerous philosophical models and approaches
   2. The concepts of age and individual appropriateness are discussed as foundations for practice
   3. Emphasis is placed on concept of mainstreaming: handicapped and nonhandicapped children learning together in integrated classrooms; thus, developmental theory becomes central to curriculum planning

B. Developmentally appropriate practice
   1. Concepts of the learning environment and the integrated curriculum well articulated
   2. Extensive goals and activities for implementation described in detail

C. Home-school-community connections
   1. No direct reference to multiculturalism
   2. Provides extensive material addressing parental involvement: activity guides for parents and curriculum planning guides for teachers implementing parent-education programs

D. Content areas
   1. No direct reference to content areas
E. Affective–social development
   1. The concept is addressed throughout the four documents reviewed

Summary of the Region

Illinois has no state-mandated guidelines for early childhood education. The guidelines for Kansas, Missouri, and North Dakota are unavailable.

Both Indiana and Michigan emphasize the design and implementation of learning centers. Indiana also outlines specific objectives for content areas, operating within an integrated curriculum. Iowa and Wisconsin both provide a strong background in developmental and curriculum theory, but Wisconsin provides much more information on how to implement these ideas in the classroom. Wisconsin also provides a unique planning guide for mainstreaming in early childhood. Minnesota provides extensive information on the concept of affective–social development, gives a philosophic orientation, and suggests goals for curriculum planning. Nebraska and South Dakota, on the other hand, merely mention the five curriculum aspects without giving much detailed theoretical or practical assistance.

Ohio's documents represent the most extensive set of guidelines. There is detailed discussion on development in the early years, as well as elaborate information on scheduling, classroom organization, and use of learning materials. The guidelines also include a thoroughly comprehensive presentation of the integrated curriculum, including goals, activities, theme approaches, and learning center approaches. Multiculturalism is addressed, and content areas are described within specific learning domains.

Mountain West Region

MOUNTAIN WEST REGION	Arizona	Colorado	Idaho	Montana	Nevada	New Mexico	Utah	Wyoming
Age/grades addressed			K (1990)					
Developmental appropriateness - age appropriateness - individual appropriateness	no state guidelines	no state guidelines		unavailable	unavailable	currently developing guidelines	unavailable	no state guidelines

Developmentally appropriate practice
- the learning environment
  use of time and space
  use of learning tools
- the integrated curriculum
  theme/unit approach
  learning centers
	no state guidelines	no state guidelines	X
			X
			X
			
			X
				unavailable	unavailable	currently developing guidelines	unavailable	no state guidelines

Home-school-community connections - multiculturalism - parent involvement	no state guidelines	no state guidelines	X X X	unavailable	unavailable	currently developing guidelines	unavailable	no state guidelines
Content areas - creative arts - physical education - language arts - mathematics - science - social studies	no state guidelines	no state guidelines	X X X X X X X			currently developing guidelines		no state guidelines
Affective-social development			X					

Idaho

Idaho Kindergarten Guide, 125p.

A. Developmental appropriateness
1. Provides general sketch of development but does not make reference to concepts of age appropriateness or individual appropriateness

B. Developmentally appropriate practice
1. Provides adequate discussion of scheduling, classroom organization, and use of materials and equipment
2. No direct reference to integrated curriculum
3. Extensive discussion of learning-center approach, with suggested procedures and materials

C. Home-school-community connections
1. No direct reference to multiculturalism
2. Brief description of parental involvement

D. Content areas
1. Discussion of content-area goals and suggestions for implementation included in description of learning center approach

E. Affective-social development
1. Included in discussion of developmentally appropriate practice

Summary of the Region

Arizona, Colorado, and Wyoming do not have mandated guidelines for early childhood education. The guidelines for Montana, Nevada, and Utah are unavailable.

Idaho's guidelines provide an adequate discussion of developmentally appropriate practice, with an extensive description of the learning-center approach.

Pacific States Region

PACIFIC STATES REGION					
	Alaska	**California**	**Hawaii**	**Oregon**	**Washington**
Age/grades addressed	K (1985)			Pre-K (1991)	
Developmental appropriateness - age appropriateness - individual appropriateness				X	c u r r e n t l y

Developmentally appropriate practice
 - the learning environment
    use of time and space
    use of learning tools
 - the integrated curriculum
    theme/unit approach
    learning centers
	X
	X
	X
	X
	X
		u n a v a i l a b l e	u n a v a i l a b l e		d e v e l o p i n g

Home-school-community connections - multiculturalism - parent involvement				X X	g
Content areas - creative arts - physical education - language arts - mathematics - science - social studies	X X X X X X X				g u i d e l i n e s
Affective-social development	X			X	

Alaska

Kindergarten Curriculum Guide, 27p.
A. Developmental appropriateness
   1. Brief discussion of development provided, but no direct reference to this concept
B. Developmentally appropriate practice
   1. Mentions use of time, space, and learning tools, with brief reference to integrated learning
C. Home–school–community connections
   1. No direct reference to this concept
D. Content areas
   1. Content areas are discussed within the framework of goal generation. Goals are presented within specific learning domains such as the cognitive, social, and emotional.
E. Affective–social development
   1. Included as one learning domain with goals and short description of appropriate activities

Oregon

Oregon Pre-kindergarten Program Requirements, 47p.
A. Developmental appropriateness
   1. Brief discussion of development, but no specific references to age appropriateness or individual appropriateness
B. Developmentally appropriate practice
   1. No specific reference to this concept
C. Home–school–community connections
   1. The entire document emphasizes parent involvement in the school
   2. No direct reference to multiculturalism
D. Content areas
   1. The document emphasized this aspect of development, especially the importance of parental involvement in it

Summary of the Region

Washington is currently developing guidelines for early childhood education. Guidelines for California and Hawaii were unavailable.

Alaska's guidelines briefly mention development, developmentally appropriate practice, and the various content areas. Oregon also briefly addresses these aspects, with a strong emphasis on parental involvement.

Conclusion

The following state curriculum guides are recommended to those professionals responsible for writing curriculum at the local level. Two are comprehensive and two have specific strengths. It is important to remember that no one guide thoroughly reflects the five curriculum aspects addressed. When writing curriculum, it is also a good idea to keep in touch with colleagues and professional organizations and to read current journals and commercially produced curriculum materials.

Connecticut

The three Connecticut documents reviewed clearly provide an excellent framework for curriculum writers at the district level. *Early Childhood Program* is a thorough self-study tool, one that could be used in the evaluation process as well. *A Guide to Program Development for Kindergarten: Part I* provides comprehensive information on the historical and theoretical foundations of early childhood education along with invaluable insights in the nature of development itself. This document sets the stage for *A Guide to Program Development for Kindergarten: Part II*, which addresses aspects of practice. This issue of practice unfolds first within clearly articulated aspects of the learning environment and then as a series of units on the various content areas presented within the framework of an integrated curriculum. The strength of these three documents lies in their comprehensive review of relevant information and their organization: focusing first on program review, then on theoretical foundations and, finally, on practice.

New York

New York's *Multicultural Early Childhood Resource Guide* can be a model for curriculum planners wishing to integrate a multicultural perspective within existing curriculum. This guide provides a theoretical framework by discussing the philosophy of racial-ethnic pluralism. The document addresses a wide range of topics including curriculum objectives, the concept of classroom and school ecology, the nonverbal communication patterns of people from differing ethnic backgrounds, and aspects of social, emotional, cultural, and physical development. Specific methods, instructional materials, and ideas for parent involvement are described and developed. An excellent bibliography is provided.

Oklahoma

Oklahoma's unique focus on the social climate of the school suggests most clearly the ecology of early childhood: young children are products of their interactions with people, the social environment, and the physical environment. Although these guidelines reinforce a strong theoretical perspective, they also give ideas for implementation. Here, theory and practice are wed by a focus on classroom ecology. As a result, the Oklahoma guidelines provide the strongest representation of the benefits of integrating affective-social development throughout the curriculum.

Ohio

Rather than present a unique focus, as the New York and Oklahoma guides do, the Ohio guidelines are comprehensive, like Connecticut's, and make a strong presentation for each curriculum aspect. What makes the Ohio guidelines unique is their interjection of useful anecdotal material, based on actual classroom observation, directly into discussions of development and multiculturalism. This framework makes the guidelines very readable and even enjoyable.

Implications

There remains a great deal of work to be done in devising guidelines for early childhood education. It is apparent that many states do not consider early childhood education enough of a priority to develop such guidelines. Several states are still in the process of developing guidelines, and several others provide such poorly developed materials that it is impossible to know the purpose of such documents.

On a positive note, many states have chosen to place the aspect of development itself first and foremost in their guidelines. This position is commendable, since placing early childhood education firmly within a developmental frame-

work reflects the findings of researchers and professionals in the field. Accordingly, those documents supporting developmental theory also embrace aspects of developmentally appropriate practice, namely, the integrated curriculum and the learning-center approach. It is interesting to note that those states supporting developmental theory and practice also tend to embrace the home-school-community connections of parent involvement and multiculturalism.

In contrast, other state guidelines, rather than focusing on the whole child and the child's relationship to home and the world, look only at the child in school. Some of these documents are quite valuable to teachers, giving them detailed directions for implementing objectives. However, without a strong theoretical foundation for early childhood education, curriculum can never be more than a series of exercises to be accomplished, rather than processes to be acquired and learned. Those activity-oriented documents tend also to emphasize separate, rather than integrated, content areas.

States that fragment the child, looking only at development occurring in school, tend to continue this fragmentation in their discussion of curriculum itself. On the other hand, in states whose philosophical orientation is to examine the child as an integrated member of society, discussion of the curriculum also reflects this orientation, presenting the curriculum as integrated and crossing discipline boundaries rather than separating them.

States can and should vary their curriculum plans and theoretical overviews for early childhood education. Differential thinking can encourage creativity and innovation. Yet it is time for curriculum writers to begin to see the young child, and all children, in fact, as members of a greater whole and not simply persons who learn or persons who are in a school building for six hours a day. Developmental theory offers the soundest framework for thinking about children as interactive beings. Therefore, those states not firmly committed to developmental thinking might begin to adjust their guidelines to reflect the current research.

STATE-LEVEL CURRICULUM GUIDELINES: A LISTING

HIS chapter provides bibliographic information on the state curriculum documents discussed in chapter 5. The publications are organized by state; for each state, we have provided the full address for that state's department of education, including the office to contact regarding curriculum publications (if such an office has been specified by the state department). The phone number shown is the best number to use for ordering the publications or for getting further information on the publications. We have also provided the addresses and phone numbers for states whose departments of education do not publish statewide curriculum frameworks. These states may produce curriculum materials on specific topics in early childhood education and in other disciplines, but they are not statewide guides as described in chapter 5.

For each publication, the listing provides the full title, document number or ISBN (if available), number of pages, year of publication or reprinting (or "n.d." if no date is available), and price. Pricing is given on those publications for which Kraus had information; note that the prices shown are taken from the department's order form. Shipping and handling are often extra, and some states offer discounts for purchasing multiple copies. If a document is listed in ERIC, its ED number is shown as well.

Alabama

State Department of Education
Gordon Persons Office Building
50 North Ripley Street
Montgomery, AL 36130-3901

Division of Student Instructional Services
Coordinator, Curriculum Development/Courses
 of Study
(205) 242-8059

The Alabama State Department of Education produces a course of study that is set up by subject area and that covers K-12. A separate kindergarten guide, which corresponds to the course of study, provides suggestions, ideas, and activities for the kindergarten classroom.

Alaska

State Department of Education
Goldbelt Building
P.O. Box F
Juneau, AK 99811

Division of Education Program Support
Administrator, Office of Basic Education
(907) 465-2841, Fax (907) 463-5279

Kindergarten Curriculum
n.d.

The Alaska State Department of Education is
developing guidelines for early childhood; no
availability date has been set.

Arizona

State Department of Education
1535 West Jefferson
Phoenix, AZ 85007

Education Services
Instructional Technology
(602) 542-2147

The Arizona State Department of Education
does not produce statewide curriculum frameworks for early childhood education.

Arkansas

Department of Education
Four State Capitol Mall
Room 304 A
Little Rock, AR 72201-1071

Instructional Services
Early Childhood Education Specialist
(501) 682-4475

Kindergarten. Arkansas Public School Course
Content Guide
30p., n.d.

Arkansas Learner Outcomes: A Vision for
Outcomes-Based Education
9p., 1991.

The Arkansas Department of Education is
currently developing a new curriculum framework for Arkansas schools which will be
available in mid-1993.

California

State Department of Education
P.O. Box 944272
721 Capitol Mall
Sacramento, CA 95814

California Department of Education
Bureau of Publications
(916) 445-1260

Early childhood guidelines are treated in each
subject area curriculum framework developed
by the California State Department of
Education.

Colorado

State Department of Education
201 East Colfax Avenue
Denver, CO 80203-1705

The Colorado State Department of Education
does not produce statewide curriculum frameworks for early childhood education.

Connecticut

State Department of Education
P.O. Box 2219
165 Capitol Avenue
State Office Building
Hartford, CT 06106-1630

Program and Support Services
Division of Curriculum and Professional
  Development
(203) 566-8113

The Teacher's Ongoing Role in Creating a
Developmentally Appropriate Early Childhood
Program
34p., 1990.

A Guide to Program Development for Kindergarten: Part I
184p., 1988.

A Guide to Program Development for Kindergarten: Part II
112p., 1988.

Delaware

State Department of Public Information
P.O. Box 1402
Townsend Building, #279
Dover, DE 19903

Instructional Services Branch
State Director, Instruction Division
(302) 739-4647

The Delaware State Department of Public Information is currently developing curriculum frameworks.

Florida

State Department of Education
Capitol Building, Room PL 116
Tallahassee, FL 32301

Office of Early Intervention and School
   Readiness
(904) 922-5300

The Florida State Department of Education does not produce statewide curriculum frameworks for early childhood education. (Curriculum frameworks are in specific subject areas, and cover grades 6-12). The local school districts develop their own early childhood education curriculum which must be developmentally appropriate.

Georgia

State Department of Education
2066 Twin Towers East
205 Butler Street
Atlanta, GA 30334

Office of Instructional Programs
Director, General Instruction Division
(404) 656-2412

Georgia's Quality Core Curriculum (K-12)
25-diskette set (AppleWorks version) $100.00,
17-diskette set (IBM WordStar version)
$68.00, 1989.

Hawaii

Department of Education
1390 Miller Street, #307
Honolulu, HI 96813

Office of Instructional Services
Director, General Education Branch
(808) 396-2502

The Hawaii Department of Education is revising its statewide frameworks; the new publications are scheduled to be available in 1993.

Idaho

State Department of Education
Len B. Jordan Office Building
650 West State Street
Boise, ID 83720

Chief, Bureau of Instruction/School
   Effectiveness
(208) 334-2165

Idaho Kindergarten Guide
126p., January 1990.

Illinois

State Board of Education
100 North First Street
Springfield, IL 62777

School Improvement Services, Curriculum
  Improvement
(217) 782-2826, Fax (217) 524-6125

*Request for Proposals (RFP) for the
Prekindergarten Program for Children at Risk
of Academic Failure*
33p., 1992.

The Illinois State Board of Education does not
produce frameworks covering early childhood
programs for mainstream children.

Indiana

State Department of Education
Room 229, State House
100 North Capitol Street
Indianapolis, IN 46024-2798

Center for School Improvement and
  Performance
Manager, Office of Program Development
(317) 232-9157

Kindergarten Guide
90p., 1989.

Iowa

State Department of Education
Grimes State Office Building
East 14th and Grand Streets
Des Moines, IA 50319-0146

Division of Instructional Services
Bureau Chief, Instruction and Curriculum
(515) 281-8141

Iowa Early Childhood Program Guidelines
43p., January 1991.

Kansas

State Department of Education
120 East Tenth Street
Topeka, KS 66612-1182

Early Childhood Specialist
(913) 296-4951

The Kansas State Department of Education
does not produce statewide curriculum frameworks for early childhood education.

Kentucky

State Department of Education
1725 Capitol Plaza Tower
500 Mero Street
Frankfort, KY 40601

Office of Learning Programs Development
Division of Curriculum Development
(502) 564-2106

Kentucky is developing curriculum frameworks
that local school districts may use as a guide to
develop their own curriculum (these frameworks will not be state-mandated). Frameworks will be available in late September 1993.

Louisiana

State Department of Education
P.O. Box 94064
626 North 4th Street
12th Floor
Baton Rouge, LA 70804-9064

Office of Academic Programs
Elementary Education (504) 342-3366
Secondary Education (504) 342-3404

The Louisiana State Department of Education
uses the following commercial curriculum
which is not state-mandated:

The Creative Curriculum for Early Childhood,
by Diane Trister Dodge and Laura J. Colker.
(Washington, DC: Teaching Strategies) 380p.,
1992 (3d ed.), ISBN 1-879537-06-0

Maine

State Department of Education
State House Station No. 23
Augusta, ME 04333

Bureau of Instruction
Director, Division of Curriculum
(207) 289-5928

The Maine State Department of Education does not produce statewide frameworks for early childhood education.

Maryland

State Department of Education
200 West Baltimore Street
Baltimore, MD 21201

Language Development and Early Learning
  Branch
Division of Instruction
(410) 333-2336

Learning Process: Processes of Learning Curriculum: Theoretical Framework for Prekindergarten
38p., 1989.

Massachusetts

State Department of Education
Quincy Center Plaza
1385 Hancock Street
Quincy, MA 02169

Bureau of Early Childhood Programs
Division of Schools Programs
(617) 770-7289

Early Childhood Initiatives
4p., n.d.

Guidelines for Chapter 188 Kindergarten Programs
#16153, 18p., n.d.

Chapter 188 Early Childhood Standards for Programs for Three and Four Year Olds
30p., 1988.

Hand in Hand: Integrating Young Children in Need of Substantial Special Education Supports
#16606, 31p., 1991.

Planning Integrated Preschool Programs
#16632, 10p., n.d.

Working Together: An Ethnographic View of Interagency Collaboration. Report on Future Trends in Early Childhood Programs
#17063, 53p., 1992.

Michigan

State Board of Education
P.O. Box 30008
608 West Allegan Street
Lansing, MI 48909

Early Childhood Education Office
(517) 373-8483

Standards of Quality and Curriculum Guidelines for Preschool Programs for Four Year Olds
55p., n.d.

Curriculum Resource Book for Preschool Programs for Four Year Olds
70p., n.d.

Minnesota

State Department of Education
712 Capitol Square Building
550 Cedar Street
St. Paul, MN 55101

Minnesota Curriculum Services Center
(612) 483-4442

Model Learner Outcomes for Early Childhood Education
E712, 4072, 491500, 165p. 1990.

Mississippi

State Department of Education
P.O. Box 771
550 High Street, Room 501
Jackson, MS 39205-0771

Bureau of Instructional Services
(601) 359-2791

The Kindergarten Guide for Instructional Planning
100p., 1989.

Primary Guide for Instructional Planning
600p., 1990.

Missouri

Department of Elementary
and Secondary Education
P.O. Box 480
205 Jefferson Street, 6th Floor
Jefferson City, MO 65102

Center for Educational Assessment, University of Missouri—Columbia (source for documents)
(314) 882-4694

The Missouri Department of Elementary and Secondary Education does not produce statewide curriculum frameworks for early childhood education.

Montana

Office of Public Instruction
106 State Capitol
Helena, MT 59620

Department of Accreditation and Curriculum Services
Curriculum Assistance and Instructional Alternatives
(406) 444-5541

Montana Kindergarten Handbook
179p., 1989 (revised)

Nebraska

State Department of Education
301 Centennial Mall, South
P.O. Box 94987
Lincoln, NE 68509

Position Statement on Kindergarten, Adopted October 1984
9p., 1984.

The Iowa and Nebraska State Departments of Education are currently developing the Nebraska-Iowa Primary Curriculum Project; it will be available Spring 1993.

Nevada

State Department of Education
Capitol Complex
400 West King Street
Carson City, NV 89710

Federal Programs
Early Childhood Specialist
(702) 687-3187

The Nevada State Department of Education does not produce statewide frameworks for early childhood education.

New Hampshire

State Department of Education
101 Pleasant Street
State Office Park South
Concord, NH 03301

Division of Instructional Services
General Instructional Services Administrator
(603) 271-2632

The New Hampshire State Department of Education does not produce statewide curriculum frameworks for early childhood education.

New Jersey

Department of Education
225 West State Street, CN 500
Trenton, NJ 08625-0500

Division of General Academic Education
(609) 984-1971

The New Jersey State Department of Education does not produce statewide curriculum frameworks for early childhood education.

New Mexico

State Department of Education
Education Building
300 Don Gaspar
Santa Fe, NM 87501-2786

Learning Services Division
Instructional Materials
(505) 827-6504

The New Mexico State Department of Education is revising its Student Competencies. The department is also working on a resource guide for early childhood education, which will be available in 1993.

New York

State Education Department
111 Education Building
Washington Avenue
Albany, NY 12234

The University of the State of New York
The State Education Department
Publications Sales Desk
(518) 474-3806

A Multicultural Early Childhood Resource
  Guide
40p., 1987.

North Carolina

Department of Public Instruction
Education Building
116 West Edenton Street
Raleigh, NC 27603-1712

Publications Sales Desk
(919) 733-4258

The North Carolina Department of Public Instruction does not produce statewide curriculum frameworks for early childhood education.

North Dakota

State Department of Public Instruction
State Capitol Building, 11th Floor
600 Boulevard Avenue East
Bismarck, ND 58505-0440

Office of Instruction, Supplies
(701) 224-2272

The North Dakota Department of Public Instruction does not produce statewide curriculum frameworks for early childhood education.

Ohio

State Department of Education
Columbus, OH 43266-0308

Stark County Board of Education
(216) 875-1431

The Ohio Early Childhood Curriculum Guide
001-1890-6969, 193p., 1991.

Oklahoma

Department of Education
Hodge Memorial Education Building
2500 North Lincoln Boulevard
Oklahoma City, OK 73105-4599

School Improvement Division
Instructional Programs
(405) 521-3361

Early Childhood Suggested Learner Outcomes: Developmental, Four-Year-Olds, Kindergarten, First Grade
73p., 1990.

Adaptive Skills for Developmental First
3p., n.d.

Creative Skills for Developmental First
2p., n.d.

Language Arts for Developmental First
3p., n.d.

Mathematics for Developmental First
3p., n.d.

Motor Skills for Developmental First
1p., n.d.

Science for Developmental First
2p., n.d.

Social Studies for Developmental First
2p., n.d.

Adaptive Skills Four-Year-Olds
3p., n.d.

Creative Skills Four-Year-Olds
1p., n.d.

Language Skills Four-Year-Olds
3p., n.d.

Mathematics Four-Year-Olds
2p., n.d.

Motor Skills Four-Year-Olds
2p., n.d.

Science Four-Year-Olds
1p., n.d.

Social Studies Four-Year-Olds
1p., n.d.

Adaptive Skills Kindergarten
3p., n.d.

Creative Skills Kindergarten
1p., n.d.

Language Arts Kindergarten
4p., n.d.

Mathematics Kindergarten
2p., n.d.

Motor Skills Kindergarten
1p., n.d.

Science Kindergarten
2p., n.d.

Social Studies Kindergarten
1p., n.d.

Crossroads: A Handbook for Effective Classroom Management
191p., 1981.

Oregon

State Department of Education
700 Pringle Parkway, SE
Salem, OR 97310

Publications Sales Clerk
(503) 378-3589

Oregon Prekindergarten Program Requirements
58p., 1991.

Head Start Program Performance Standards
45-CFR 1304, 64p., 1984.

Pennsylvania

Department of Education
333 Market Street, 10th Floor
Harrisburg, PA 17126-0333

Early Childhood and Family Education
(717) 772-2813

Learning Resource Units for Young Children: A Curriculum for Preschool Children
207p., 1991

Growing Together. . .
176p., 1991.

Rhode Island

**Department of Education
22 Hayes Street
Providence, RI 02908**

Division of School and Teacher Accreditation
(401) 277-2617

The Rhode Island Department of Education does not produce statewide frameworks for early childhood education.

South Carolina

**State Department of Education
1006 Rutledge Building
1429 Senate Street
Columbia, SC 29201**

Division of Curriculum
Education Design
(803) 734-8366

The South Carolina State Department of Education is revising its statewide frameworks; the revised publications will be issued in 1993.

South Dakota

**Department of Education
and Cultural Affairs
435 South Chapelle
Pierre, SD 57501**

Office of Educational Services
Elementary Curriculum (605) 773-3261
Secondary Curriculum (605) 773-4670

Kindergarten Today: A Guide to Curriculum Development
108p., 1986.

Developmental Guidance and Counseling Plan for Kindergarten through Sixth Grade
112p., n.d.

Tennessee

**State Department of Education
100 Cordell Hull Building
Nashville, TN 37219**

Curriculum and Instruction
(615) 741-0874

Tennessee Nongraded Elementary Education Program
40p., n.d.

Tennessee Comprehensive Curriculum Guide,K-8
194p., 1992

Texas

**Texas Education Agency
William B. Travis Building
1701 North Congress Avenue
Austin, TX 78701-1494**

Division of Curriculum Development
(512) 463-9744

State Board of Education Rules for Curriculum—Essential Elements (includes *Subchapter B. Essential Elements— Prekindergarten–Grade Six*)
AD202101, 545p., 1991.

Utah

**State Office of Education
250 East 500 South
Salt Lake City, UT 84111**

Division of Instructional Services
Coordinator, Curriculum
(801) 538-7774

Early childhood guidelines are treated in each subject area core curriculum outline developed by the Utah State Office of Education. However, there are rules and regulations relating to young children with disabilities.

Vermont

State Department of Education
120 State Street
Montpelier, VT 05602-2703

Basic Education
Chief, Curriculum and Instruction Unit
(802) 828-3111

The Vermont State Department of Education does not produce statewide frameworks for early childhood education.

Virginia

Department of Education
P.O. Box 6-Q, James Monroe Building
Fourteenth and Franklin Streets
Richmond, VA 23216-2060

Instruction and Personnel
Administrative Director of General Education
(804) 225-2730

The Virginia Department of Education does not produce statewide frameworks for early childhood education.

Washington

Superintendent of Public Instruction
Old Capitol Building
Washington and Legion
Olympia, WA 98504

Curriculum/Student Services and Technology
 Service
Curriculum Support
(206) 753-6727

The Office of the Superintendent of Public Instruction is developing early childhood education modules, scheduled to be available May 1993.

West Virginia

State Department of Education
1900 Kanawha Boulevard, E.
Building G, Room B-358
Charleston, WV 25305

Division of Instructional and Student Services
(304) 348-7805

West Virginia Programs of Study: Instructional Goals and Objectives, Early Childhood Education K-4
152p., 1992.

Wisconsin

State Department of Public Instruction
General Executive Facility 3
125 South Webster Street
Post Office Box 7841
Madison, WI 53707-7841

Publication Sales
(608) 266-2188

An Invitation to Play
Bulletin No. 7295, 20p., 1986.

Early Childhood: Exceptional Educational Needs Program Review Guide, by Jenny Lange
Project no. 88-9909-75, 33p., 1988

An Invitation to Play: Teacher's Guide, by Connie Zieher
Bulletin no. 7044, 86pp, 1986

The Wisconsin State Department of Public Instruction also uses the following publication:

Opening Doors Through Integration: An Early Childhood Resource Guide for Teachers of General and Exceptional Education Students, by Kathy Lake (West Allis, WI: Cooperative Educational Service Agency) 187p., 1992

Wyoming

State Department of Education
2300 Capitol Avenue, 2nd Floor
Hathaway Building
Cheyenne, WY 82002

Division of Certification, Accreditation and
   Program Services
Accreditation/Special Services Unit
(307) 777-6808

School Accreditation
6p., n.d.

HOW TO DEVELOP AN ASSESSMENT PROGRAM

by Meridene Grant
Hermosa Vista Elementary School, Mesa, Arizona

TEACHERS entering the field of early childhood education (K–3) today have some definite advantages. For example, more is known about how children learn, how the brain processes information, and how a variety of learning activities can access a student's strengths. The challenges a teacher faces, however, come right along with the advantages—how to use this information to help children learn in the best ways possible and how to find out, or help students show, what they know and can do. The challenge of assessment is at the heart of good teaching. One reason for this is that even very good instruction, separated from ongoing assessment, can be ineffective with some students.

Many teachers, even some who feel successful as instructors, still feel uneasy about the assessment process. They may use paper-and-pencil tests to generate grades for the grade book, but they feel dissatisfied when these grades reflect, for the most part, lower-level thinking skills. They know that their students enjoy higher-level applications activities, but they are not sure how to assess and record the learning that is occurring in these activities.

Teachers may plan creative ways to connect student learning to the world outside the classroom but then test only for recall of information, which can trivialize a great learning experience. To satisfy the very real need for scores in a grade book, teachers may turn to end-of-chapter test questions or other commercially prepared tests. They do this, not because these tests accurately measure the most important kinds of learning that are occurring in the K–3 classroom, but because they generally haven't been shown, either in education or in-service programs, how to develop an assessment program that will evaluate these kinds of learning experiences. In these situations, teachers are not fully empowered, and a vital part of the education process is shortchanged.

Fortunately, the whole area of assessment, especially day-to-day, teacher-initiated assessment, is being examined thoroughly with great energy and interest. Valuable information, comprehensive models, and results from field testing are available. This chapter will focus on important elements of classroom assessment based on current research. It will discuss types of assessment that are a part of the learning process. Most importantly, it will provide assistance to the new or experienced teacher in the K–3 classroom or to the administrator who is looking for an expanded selection of strategies and tools to measure student performance.

Areas of General Agreement

Although many approaches to reform in classroom assessment have been reported in recent publications, some areas of general agreement have emerged, nine of which will be looked at in this section.

There is widespread endorsement of criterion-referenced testing, as opposed to norm-referenced testing, in the K–3 classroom. Norm-referenced testing should be limited to its appropriate use as a selection or sorting tool for a specific purpose, such as student placement in special services. Classroom assessment should be criterion-referenced, with the expectation that all students, given adequate time and support, are capable of achieving mastery of the learning criteria or making significant growth in that direction.

Curriculum, instruction, and assessment must be closely matched. To do this, the teacher must think through the projected learning unit, identify the three or four most meaningful learning outcomes, and then simultaneously devise assessment and instructional strategies so that they match not only in content but also in levels of difficulty and types of student practice and performance.

Most of the assessment done in the classroom should be integrated into the instruction. In fact, assessment should be an ongoing part of instruction. Ongoing or formative assessment is the supportive feedback during practice time that allows students to take risks, make errors, and improve without penalty. In contrast, a summative assessment, given after instruction is over, provides a summary of a student's achievements at the end of a unit.

School districts should formulate a list of five or six major outcomes for all students in the district. A teacher could then determine whether a contemplated line of teaching would fit into the bigger picture. These outcomes would provide continuity across the district and a framework to guide curriculum, instruction, and assessment (see figure 1).

FIGURE 1.

AURORA PUBLIC SCHOOLS' FIVE OUTCOMES

A Self-Directed Learner

1. Sets priorities and achievable goals.
2. Monitors and evaluates progress.
3. Creates options for self.
4. Assumes responsibility for actions.
5. Creates a positive vision for self and future.

A Collaborative Worker

6. Monitors own behavior as a group member.
7. Assesses and manages group functioning.
8. Demonstrates interactive communication.
9. Demonstrates consideration for individual differences.

A Complex Thinker

10. Uses a wide variety of strategies for managing complex issues.
11. Selects strategies appropriate to the resolution of complex issues and applies the strategies with accuracy and thoroughness.
12. Accesses and uses topic-relevant knowledge.

A Quality Producer

13. Creates products that achieve their purpose.
14. Creates products appropriate to the intended audience.
15. Creates products that reflect craftsmanship.
16. Uses appropriate resources/technology.

A Community Contributor

17. Demonstrates knowledge about his or her diverse communities.
18. Takes action.
19. Reflects on role as a community contributor.

Source: Nora Redding, "Assessing the Big Outcomes" (*Educational Leadership* 49,8 (May 1992): 50). Reproduced with permission.

Teachers must be directly involved in the development of the assessment programs they will be using. They need to understand how these programs fit into the big picture of student outcomes. They must visualize what a successful student should know and be able to do at the end of a unit of learning, and devise strategies to enable every student in the class to reach or show substantial growth toward that goal.

Students must be actively involved in the assessment process. They must be encouraged to reflect on what they have learned or hope to learn. Students are actively involved when they select items for a portfolio, tape record their own stories, provide self-assessments, and contribute items for class quizzes, for example.

Students' chances for success are greatly enhanced when teachers provide them with simple checklists of assessment components and exemplary samples to identify learning and performance expectations.

Results from a variety of assessment types (at least three) provide a more accurate profile of a student's achievements than a single assessment method. Types of assessment could include work samples, projects, teacher notes, and quizzes, to name just a few. Assessments given over a span of time provide better evidence of student growth than can any single assessment.

"Assessment should anticipate action." When considering giving an assessment, ask the question, What action will result from this assessment? If the answer is "none," then don't give the assessment (Clarke 1992). Assessment anticipates action when it provides feedback to the student. This feedback tells the student what has been successfully mastered and what remains to be practiced and learned.

The Many Uses of Assessment

Teachers must be aware of the ways in which assessment results are used. Teachers should ask themselves not only what action will result from an assessment, but also what effect an intended assessment will have on a student's self-concept. The following are some of the ways assessment is used.

Teachers use assessment to:
- diagnose students' learning needs
- adjust instruction and curriculum
- reinforce learning
- group students for instruction
- control student behavior
- prepare and report grades
- select students for special services

Students use assessment to:
- define their classroom performance
- discover teacher expectations
- set personal academic goals
- make decisions about self-concept
- gauge effort levels
- clarify learning concepts

Parents use assessment to:
- plan for future educational expenses
- determine need for extra tutoring
- structure after-school activities
- compare student's perceived ability with actual achievement

Principals, district personnel, and other officials use assessment to make decisions about curriculum needs, program funding, and special services, among other things.

It is critical for a teacher to determine the appropriate use of an assessment. A student's

relationship with learning may be harmed, for example, if an assignment meant just for practice is reported to parents as a graded assessment. In such a case, the student is denied the opportunity for a penalty-free phase of learning in which risk taking is allowed and encouraged. The teacher must decide ahead of time how an assessment will be used and what action will result from the assessment.

Types of Classroom Assessment

In addition to determining how an assessment will be used, the teacher must decide what types of classroom assessment will provide the kind of information that is needed. If, for example, the teacher wants to assess a student's recall of terms and facts, then a paper-and-pencil quiz would be adequate and appropriate. If thinking skills or processes are to be assessed, an essay format or performance model could be used. To evaluate projects and performances, specific criteria must be developed to guide teacher observation and judgment. Affective behaviors could be assessed through a structured annotation process. As mentioned earlier, at least three different assessment types should be used to obtain a more complete and accurate reading of a student's achievement in any area of learning.

Classroom assessments can be divided into three general categories:
- Paper-and-pencil tests
- Performance assessments
- Student/teacher interviews

Each category contains objective and subjective formats (see table 1).

The above assessments can be teacher-made or textbook-supplied and can serve as assignments as well as evaluations. It is important to let students know ahead of time when an assignment is going to be used as a graded assessment.

Paper and Pencil Tests

Objective paper and pencil tests and quizzes are appropriate for testing recall of information and are efficient in terms of scoring. When properly constructed, they can test more complex thinking as well. Essay questions are efficient to construct and allow students to demonstrate thinking skills, but they are time-consuming to

TABLE 1.

Assessment Type	Objective Format	Subjective Format
Paper-and-pencil tests	Multiple choice, matching, fill in the blanks, true/false	Short-answer essay
Performance assessment	Checklists for required components	Rating scales, diagnostic rubrics
Student/teacher interview	Yes/no questions, correct/incorrect responses	Interviews, open-ended discussions that allow for multiple responses

complete and to evaluate. Construction of paper and pencil tests will be considered later in the chapter.

Performance Assessments

Performance assessments are gaining widespread recognition as a valuable way to let students show what they know and can do in a variety of inviting ways. Some of the performance formats that teachers use to evaluate student growth include work folders; journals; learning logs; portfolios; audio, video, and laser disc recordings; computer projects; photographs; drawings, paintings, or other artwork; charts and graphs; mindmaps; creative writing; dramatizations; presentations; inventions; experiments; projects; and reports. The challenge comes in structuring these learning activities so that they can be used as sound assessment opportunities. Structured performance activities or products are successful to the degree that they are carefully planned, completed, and evaluated according to clearly specified criteria, such as a checklist or rating scale. A copy of the checklist or evaluation criteria is commonly given to the student at the outset of the learning unit to identify and clarify learning expectations. Spontaneous and naturally occurring student performance can also be a valuable source of assessment when the teacher has in place a system for annotation of significant but unplanned events.

Authentic Tasks

Authentic tasks have been differentiated from other forms of performance assessments. Carol A. Meyer (1992) illustrates this by comparing two schools' direct writing assessments. The first school has a structured writing sample assessment in which students participate in a standardized series of activities to produce a writing sample during the designated testing week. According to Ms. Meyer, this qualifies as a performance assessment, but not as an authentic task. In the second school, the students produce portfolios of writing samples collected throughout the year. These samples have been written using varying amounts of teacher and peer help, editing, and rewriting in the normal course of instruction. During the designated test week, a selection of these writing samples is used to evaluate each student's progress. Meyer considers these writing samples to be authentic performance tasks because they were produced in context as a part of the actual or real-life learning process. Other authentic tasks would include learning logs, group projects, experiments, surveys, inventions, self-assessments, or other products or performances occurring in the natural course of instruction.

Student/Teacher Interviews and Teacher Observation

Student/teacher interviews, oral questions, and teacher observation give the teacher an indication of a student's understanding of a given topic, but generally are not structured enough to be used for grading purposes. It is possible to add structure by devising an annotation system to record significant events. Many systems have been used successfully, depending on individual teacher preference. One method is to photocopy a stack of daily seating charts. Attendance and significant observations are easily recorded in the appropriate square labeled with the student's name. Another strategy is to use a weekly annotated class list (see figure 2). The space across from the name can be used for significant comments. At the end of the week a teacher can see which students still need comments, and these can be added so no child is left out. Other successful methods include computer labels that can be written on and transferred to a child's folder, spiral-bound 3×5 cards with labeled index tabs, flip-style photograph albums, steno notebooks, and file

FIGURE 2.

Annotated class list			
Week beginning August 3	COMMENTS (Aberrations and Insights)	ACTION	
		REQUIRED	TAKEN
Bostow, Barry	No concept of odd and even	✳	
Carlton, Donna	Showed leadership in the group		
Carss, Marjorie			
Clements, Ken			
Coughey, Wendy			
Del Campo, Gina	Thought 63 and 36 the same	✳	✓
Ganderton, Paul	Really tried		
Grace, Neville	Squaring problems	✳	
Howe, Peter			
Lee, Beth	Spatial thinker		
McDonough, Andrea	Recognised significance of a counter example		
McIntosh, Alistair			
Moule, Jim			
Mulligan, Joanne			
Nener, Kevin			
O'Connor, Fay			
Olssen, Kevin			
Palm...eal	M.A.B ...ed...tens		

Source: David J. Clarke, "Activating Assessment Alternatives in Mathematics" (*Arithmetic Teacher* (Feb. 1992): 25). Reproduced with permission.

boxes. When a teacher has a structured annotation system in place, significant student/teacher communication and teacher observation, whether planned or naturally occurring, can be part of a complete portrait of a student's progress.

Knowledge Level Assessment

Consider the following approach to assessment:

The local zoo initiates a project to build a breeding complex for endangered gray wolves and intends to help reintroduce wolves into the wild. Teachers and students in the community are invited to participate in fund-raising efforts and a wolf awareness week at the zoo. Teacher A decides to get her class involved. She purchases a thematic activity book about wolves and selects the activities that she thinks her class will enjoy. Although many of the activities are paper-and-pencil exercises, the students willingly complete them because they are interested in learning about wolves. The class does most of the pages together because the information is new and the reading level is challenging for some of the students. The teacher arranges for the class to visit the zoo to see the two gray wolves that the zoo has acquired. When it is time to stop the study of wolves and begin another topic, the teacher looks back through the activity booklet for a summary test or selects some basic terms, facts, and concepts for a quiz. She assures the class that tests are necessary, but she senses that the fun has just gone out of wolf awareness.

Assessment Development and the Empowered Teacher

Taking active control of assessment design and implementation empowers a teacher as no other factor can. Consider the following example, developed in detail.

Teacher B also decides to get her class involved in the zoo's project to build a breeding complex and promote wolf awareness. She knows that this study will fit into the district's big picture under community involvement. She asks herself this question, "What three or four significant things do I want my students to remember about wolves after they have forgotten everything else we may study about them?" Even though Teacher B will be learning about wolves along with her class, she is able to pull out of her own thinking four concepts that seem worthwhile and meaningful. If she is working with a colleague or team, these ideas would be worked out together, but would still be limited to the three or four most significant ones.

Limit of Three or Four Significant Concepts

1. Zoos do much more than just keep animals in confined areas; they have programs to help animals, including the endangered wolf.
2. Wolves are valuable and fascinating animals.
3. Wolves live together in packs.
4. Literature influences our feelings about wolves.

Next, Teacher B chooses the assessment formats that will give her the evaluation information she needs. She also chooses or creates instruments to score the assessments.

Choose Appropriate Assessment Formats and Scoring Instruments

Concept 1: Zoos do much more than just keep animals in confined areas; they have programs to help animals, including the endangered wolf.
Assessment: Student letters to the zoo
Scoring Instrument: Seven-item checklist
Concept 2: Wolves are valuable and fascinating animals.
Assessment: Mindmaps
Scoring Instrument: Rating Scale
Concept 3: Wolves live together in packs.
Assessment: Detailed and labeled drawings
Scoring Instrument: Five-item checklist
Concept 4: Literature influences our feelings about wolves.
Assessment: Venn diagram to compare wolves in a fairy tale and a Native American legend, noting how stories influence students' feelings about wolves in each case
Scoring Instrument: Simple rating scale

Concept 1: Zoos help wolves. To evaluate this concept, Teacher B will ask students to write letters to the official at the zoo who is in charge of the wolf project. Among other things, the letters will need to include sentences that tell at least two specific things that the class is doing to support wolf awareness and other sentences that express how the student feels about what the zoo is doing to help wolves and other endangered animals. One sentence will be a vote for or against reintroducing gray wolves into the wild.

Checklist for Letters to the Zoo (shared with students)

____ Sentences telling two things our class is doing to support wolf awareness

____ Sentences expressing how you feel about the zoo's wolf project

____ A sentence voting for or against reintroducing wolves into the wild

____ Proper form of a letter

____ Spelling

____ Capitalization, punctuation

____ Neatness

Scoring: 7 points possible

Outstanding = 7 points

Mastery = 6 points (86%)

Improving = 5 points

Needs practice = 4 points or below

This graded assignment should include a prewriting activity to generate ideas and vocabulary. The checklist should be given to students to refer to while writing the letters. Exemplary models of letters should be posted for student reference and quality standards.

Concept 2: Wolves are valuable and fascinating animals. This concept will be assessed with a pre- and posttest mindmapping activity. As a pretest, students will construct mindmaps showing what they already know about wolves. At the end of the unit, students will construct mindmaps showing what they have learned. Growth will be measured by comparing the two mindmaps.

```
Rating Scale for Wolf Mindmaps

Possible scores:

     1          2          3          4
Student showed               Student showed
limited growth in            outstanding
knowledge about              growth in
wolves                       knowledge about
                             wolves


Scoring: 4 points possible

Outstanding = 4 points
Mastery = 3 points
Progressing = 2 points
Limited growth = 1 point
```

During the posttest, students should have access to the classroom resources that have been used during the study of wolves. The class could brainstorm together a list of possible categories for the mindmaps. Students should be encouraged to combine pictures, words, and shapes to make mindmaps that are individualized.

Concept 3: Wolves live in packs. This concept will be assessed using detailed drawings, labeled to show how wolves live in packs. Certain elements, such as wolf habitat and care for the young, are concepts that must be included in the drawings.

```
Checklist for the Detailed Wolf Pack Drawings
____ Shows four or more ways wolves help each other
____ Drawings have details
____ Drawings are labeled
____ Drawings are neatly colored
____ Wolf habitat is included
Scoring: 5 points possible
Outstanding = 5 points
Mastery = 4 points (80%)
Needs practice = 3 points or below
```

Students should be given a copy of the checklist as they begin their drawings. Students should also have access to resources used during the study of wolves. Exemplary models of detailed drawings on other subjects could be posted for reference and to establish quality standards. Students should be assured that their drawings don't have to look like anyone else's drawing in order to be successful.

Concept 4: Wolves in Literature. This concept will be evaluated by having students work in cooperative groups to compare the role of a wolf in a fairy tale with the role of a wolf in a Native American legend. Students should include their personal reactions and feelings about the wolves in each case. Comparisons will be written on a Venn diagram (see figure 3). Groups could also be asked to act out these stories. Exemplary models of completed Venn diagrams on other topics could be posted for student reference.

To score the Venn diagram, prepare a teacher-made diagram that would demonstrate what mastery of the assessment might look like taking into consideration the roles of the wolves and students' reactions to these roles. Simple Scale for Assessing a Venn Diagram Above goal: Group exceeds performance standard Reaches goal: Group demonstrates performance standard Below goal: Group falls below performance standard

The assessments described above would give ample evidence for reporting purposes. Many other assessments could be devised to measure student growth for this learning unit, depending on the skills being worked on in the classroom. Other assignments and activities for the unit on wolves could be graded, or they could be simply checked off for completion or correction without being graded.

By preplanning assessment and adding appropriate evaluation instruments, Teacher B gave direction to her instruction, brought in complex thinking tasks, and was able to record scores that reflected authentic and significant student achievement.

FIGURE 3. EXAMPLE OF A VENN DIAGRAM

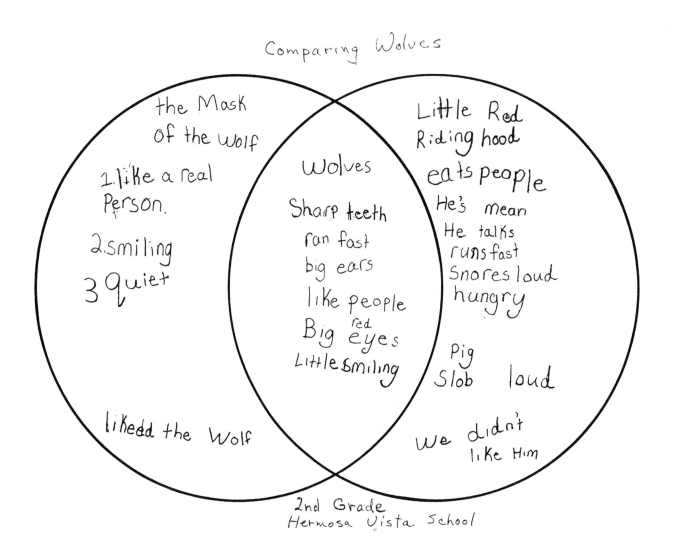

Adapting Textbook Assessments

The foregoing strategies for expanding assessment opportunities can also be applied to a textbook series of lessons that have traditionally been tested with end-of-chapter questions. By creating and using checklists, rating scales, and rubrics, a wide range of performance assessments can be used for evaluation. The same steps need to be followed:

1. Generate a list of the three or four most significant concepts to be mastered (not necessarily what the textbook has identified).

2. Choose the assessment formats that will produce the information needed. Use a variety of formats, such as paper-and-pencil quizzes, performance assessments, and annotated observations.

3. Create scoring instruments to measure the performance assessments.

In choosing the assessment format that will produce the information needed, the choice is often a paper-and-pencil task. Paper-and-pencil tasks can quickly assess a student's knowledge of content and provide feedback to students in a timely manner. For these reasons, it is important for a teacher to know how to construct a good paper-and-pencil test.

How To Construct Paper-and-Pencil Tests for Levels K–3

Multiple Choice:
1. Ask the question in a complete sentence.
2. Limit choices to three or four items.
3. Have only one clearly correct or best answer.
4. Avoid using negatively stated items.
5. Avoid using "All of the above" or "None of the above."
6. Make all choices plausible and of similar length.
7. All choices should be grammatically consistent with the test question.

Matching:
1. Don't mix types of items in one set. For example, if the items in the left column are events, then the options in the right column should be all dates or all names or all places.
2. Use short lists of items for young children, beginning with one item and two options or two items and two options. For older children, have more options than items.
3. Place the shorter words or phrases in the right column.
4. State whether options can be used more than once.
5. Label the options with letters or numbers.
6. Place all items and options on the same page.

Fill in the Blanks:
1. Use one blank per statement.
2. Place the blank at the end of the statement.
3. Make all blanks of equal length.
4. Blanks should allow enough room to write the answers.
5. Include an answer bank for young children.

True/False:
1. Test only significant concepts.
2. Measure only one concept per statement.
3. The statement must be clearly correct or clearly false.

4. Use positive statements—avoid double negatives.
5. Use a nearly equal number of true and false statements, distributed randomly.
6. Keep statements similar in length.

Short Answer:
1. Use a direct question instead of an incomplete statement.
2. Directions should clearly indicate what will be needed in the response.

Essay:
1. For young children, use a prewriting activity, such as mindmapping or webbing, to share ideas and to create a vocabulary bank on the board.
2. Create and share with students a simple checklist to identify necessary elements of the finished essay.
3. Use the checklist to score completed essays by converting the checklist into a rating scale. This is done by adding point values to each item on the checklist. In this way, items of emphasis could receive more weight by being assigned more points.

It is easy to create checklists, rating scales, and rubrics once you know how. They are very

FIGURE 4.

Name_____   Date_____

Portfolio Checklist

_____ Letters

_____ Poetry

_____ Creative stories

_____ Personal narratives

_____ Descriptive paragraphs

_____ How-to paragraphs

_____ Computer work

_____ Self-assessments

_____ Puppet shows

_____ Research reports

_____ Journals and logs

_____ Book reports

_____ Rebus stories

_____ Jokes and riddles

Other items:

_____

useful and are often the only way to score performance assessments.

How To Create Performance Assessment Scoring Instruments

Checklists

Use a checklist to determine the presence or absence of specific elements in a product or performance. A checklist may be created to score a single performance, such as whether a student has correctly included the necessary parts of a friendly letter. A checklist may also be used to verify the completion of a variety of required course components.

To construct a checklist, list in logical or sequential order all of the elements that need to be included in a product or performance. Mastery level could be set at 80 percent (eight items present out of a possible ten) or mastery could be set at 100 percent if all items need to be there. It is important to give copies of the checklist to students at the beginning of the assignment. The shared checklist should be in simple form for K–3 students. Sharing the checklist with students increases their chances to be successful in reaching learning targets by identifying and clarifying teacher expectations. Figures 4–7 are examples of checklists used for K–3 students.

Rating Scales

Use a rating scale to provide a continuum along which to place a student's performance. A rating scale differs from a checklist in that it requires the rater to judge qualities of performance. While a checklist determines whether certain elements are present, a rating scale compares a student's performance or product against predetermined standards or benchmarks. Benchmarks are actual samples of student work at various levels of competency.

To construct a rating scale, choose one of the areas to be assessed. Describe a poor performance of it. Then describe an excellent performance of the same assessment. These descriptions will give the range of the assessment. Each student's performance will be placed somewhere between these two descriptions. To complete the rating scale, place the

FIGURE 5.

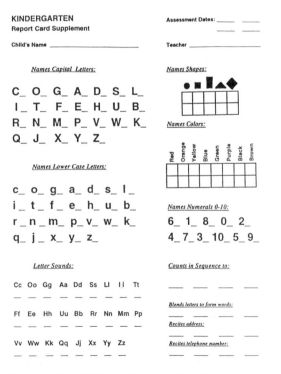

FIGURE 6.

EMERGENT READING CHECK		
NAME: _____	AGE ON ENTERING SCHOOL: _____	
	COMMENT	DATE
Enjoys listening to stories.		
Chooses to read from various resources.		
Can sit for a time and read a book.		
Participates confidently in Shared Reading.		
Participates confidently in Shared Writing.		
Retells stories and rhymes.		
Likes to write.		
Understands that writers use letter symbols to construct meaning.		
Can show the front cover of a book.		
Understands that from the print comes the message.		
Uses pictures as clues to the story line.		
Knows where to start reading the text.		
Knows which way to go, L→R, and to return.		
Can point and match 1–1 as teacher reads.		
Checks 1–1 when reading alone.		
Can indicate a word.		
Can indicate a letter.		
Can indicate the space between the words.		
Can recognize some high-frequency words both in and out of context.		
Can write some high-frequency words independently.		

Source: Nanci Withee (Hermosa Vista Elementary School, Mesa, AZ), "Kindergarten Report Card Supplement." Reproduced with permission.

Source: Avelyn Davidson, *Emergent Reading Check, Stages 1 and 2. Literacy 2000 Teachers' Resource* (Auckland: Shortland, 1990). Reproduced with permission.

FIGURE 7.

Checklist - Personal Narrative

Name_____ Date_____

Title_____

2 or 3 paragraphs_____

Indenting_____

Characters and setting_____

Told events in order_____

Something serious_____

Something funny_____

Stayed with one story_____

Ending--how it all turned out_____

Spelling_____

Exciting words_____

Capitals and end punctuation_____

FIGURE 8.

Rating Scale for the Detailed Wolf Pack Drawings

_____ Shows four or more ways wolves help each other (8 points)

_____ Drawings have details (4 points)

_____ Drawings are labeled (3 points)

_____ Drawings are neatly colored (3 points)

_____ Wolf habitat is included (2 points)

Scoring: 20 points possible

Outstanding = 18 points or better

Mastery = 16–17 points (80%)

Improving = 14–15 points

Needs practice = 12 points or below

description of poor performance at the left and the description of excellence at the right. Then add a range of numbers from one to four or six. Use an even number to avoid the tendency to cluster scores in the center. Identify the mastery level, usually around 80 percent.

Figure 8 is an example of a rating scale.

Rubrics

A rubric looks like two or three rating scales combined, and is used to assess various components of the same performance. To construct a rubric, choose as many factors as you need to assess (three may be enough) and create descriptions for the ratings; from poor to excellent, with point values for each. A diagnostic evaluation scale is a type of rubric (see figures 9 and 10). A checklist can become a rating scale or a rubric by assigning point values to each item on the list. When teacher judgment is introduced, the objective checklist becomes a subjective rating scale. For example, the above Checklist for the Detailed Wolf Pack Drawings can be changed into a rating scale, as shown below:

Assessment in the K–3 Mathematics Program

Criterion-referenced district tests are an important way to provide evidence for accountability in the mathematics program. They are efficient as paper-and-pencil pre- and posttests to measure yearly student achievement and to guide instruction. Student achievement in mathematics has traditionally been one of the easiest areas to assess through paper-and-pencil tests. However, as the use of math manipulatives has grown in the K–3 classroom, so have alternative ways to assess students' understanding of mathematical processes. Teacher observation and annotation, math logs and journals, math portfolios, writing about math, reflective logs, problem solving, and open-ended questions are some of the alternatives teachers are using to assess student growth in mathematics. Rubrics that assess thinking processes as well as final products are being developed.

First-grade teachers Earlene Hemmer and Terri Goyins (1992) from Montana report tips for using portfolios in a mathematics program: We collect samples from the beginning to the end of the year, looking especially for those that show:

how students think and learn;

how they process information;

how they feel about math;

how they communicate mathematically;

how they work in a group; and

how they are doing in all areas of our math curriculum.

FIGURE 9.

Student _____

Date _____

Teacher _____

School _____

| | 1st Grade |

Diagnostic Evaluation

FALL (required)   **SPRING** (optional)

Low 1-2	Middle 3-4	High 5-6	**Organizational Factors**	Low 1-2	Middle 3-4	High 5-6
			Maintains a topic/story (some relationship among sentences)			
Low 1-2	Middle 3-4	High 5-6	**Language Factors**	Low 1-2	Middle 3-4	High 5-6
			Fluency (sentence & word production)			
			Originality (engaging)			
			Vocabulary (descriptive, mature)			
Low 1-2	Middle 3-4	High 5-6	**Mechanics**	Low 1-2	Middle 3-4	High 5-6
			Legibility (spacing, letter formation)			
			Spelling (appropriate for grade level -- invented spelling)			

Source: Bev Merrill, "Diagnostic Evaluation—1st Grade"
(Gilbert, AZ: Gilbert Public Schools, 1990). Reproduced with permission.

Keep samples of open-ended problem-solving activities that show students' individual approaches, strategies, and thinking processes. Train children to date their work. Keep samples in sequential order as you collect them.

Hemmer and Goyins suggest storing portfolio files in an accessible place, such as hanging file folders, spiral binders with pockets for storage, or accordion files. Students are asked to evaluate themselves by writing and drawing pictures to illustrate their feelings about math and what they have been learning. These self-evaluations, along with teacher observations, are added to the portfolios. A few well-chosen samples are preferable to a large random collection. Hemmer and Goyins advise teachers to start slow and to find a colleague who is willing to collaborate with them on math portfolio assessment.

David J. Clarke (1992) encourages the use of annotated class lists to record significant events and student work folders. He also suggests practical tests (hands-on tasks), student-constructed tests, and student self-assessments. He agrees that it is important to use a variety of assessment types (three or four) to measure a student's abilities.

Commercially prepared mathematics series are now including ideas and samples of alternative assessments. *Heath Mathematics Connections* (Halloran, Gatanti, and Adcock 1992) has a portfolio assessments guide that includes a list of suggested items that could be included in a math portfolio: an informal

FIGURE 10.

Student _____

| 3rd Grade |

Diagnostic Evaluation

FALL (required)   **SPRING** (optional)

High 5-6	Middle 3-4	Low 1-2	**Organizational Factors**	High 5-6	Middle 3-4	Low 1-2
			Paragraphing (ideas arranged in paragraph form)			
			Unity (stays on subject)			

High 5-6	Middle 3-4	Low 1-2	**Language Factors**	High 5-6	Middle 3-4	Low 1-2
			Fluency (flow)			
			Originality (engaging)			
			Vocabulary (descriptive)			
			Varied sentence patterns			

High 5-6	Middle 3-4	Low 1-2	**Mechanics Factors**	High 5-6	Middle 3-4	Low 1-2
			Capitalization			
			Punctuation			
			Legibility			
			Spelling			
			Form			

Source: Bev Merrill, "Diagnostic Evaluation—3rd Grade"
(Gilbert, AZ: Gilbert Public Schools, 1990). Reproduced with permission.

mathematics inventory to test everyday mathematical concepts and decision making, samples of homework and in-class assignments, prizes and awards, photographs of math projects or group work, standardized tests, self-assessments, and attitude inventories. All papers should be dated so that progress can be shown. The portfolio assessments guide provides an informal learning inventory, a format for student attitude assessment, formats for student self-assessment of individual and group work, teacher observation checklists, and performance inventories (see figures 11 and 12).

The following publishers have also included alternative assessment components in their mathematics programs: Scott, Foresman's *Exploring Mathematics*; Silver Burdett and Ginn's *Informal Assessment: Development Benchmarks*; Harcourt Brace Jovanovich's *Mathematics Plus*; and Houghton Mifflin's portfolio and alternative assessment suggestions.

Assessment in the K–3 Language Arts Program

Achievement in the K–3 language arts program is being assessed in many ways. District- and teacher-prepared criterion-referenced tests, standardized tests, basal series assessments, writing portfolios, direct writing assessments, commercial and student-generated spelling lists, student book reading lists, and

FIGURE 11.

Name _____ Date _____

9 Performance Inventory

OBJECTIVES To measure the length of an object using an inch ruler.
To measure the length of an object using a centimeter ruler.

Materials Punchout customary ruler, centimeter ruler

Activities

☐ 1. Give the child the customary ruler and a variety of classroom objects with lengths greater than and less than 5 inches (pencils, scissors, crayons, chalk, and others). "Which objects are longer than 5 inches? Check your guesses. Use the inch ruler to measure." Repeat the activity using the centimeter ruler. "Which objects do you think are longer than 7 centimeters? Check your guesses. Use the centimeter ruler to measure."

☐ 2. Give the child the customary ruler and a variety of classroom objects of different lengths. "Use the inch ruler to measure each object." *(Check the length of each object as the child measures it.)* Give the child the centimeter ruler. "Now use the centimeter ruler to measure each object."

OBJECTIVE To estimate the weights of familiar objects as less than, about, or more than a pound.

Materials A balance with a 1 pound weight

Activity

☐ 3. Set up the balance on the table. Give the child the weight and a bottle of glue or paint that weighs 2 or more pounds. "This weight is 1 pound. Estimate whether the bottle weighs less than 1 pound, more than 1 pound, or about 1 pound?" *(Answers may vary.)* "Use the balance to compare." *(more than 1 pound)* Additional Items: a pencil *(less)*, scissors *(less)*, a heavy book *(more)*, a 1-pound book *(about 1 pound)*, a piece of paper *(less)*

OBJECTIVE To compare capacities measured in customary units.

Materials 4 quarts of uncooked rice; containers of the following sizes—5 one cup containers—3 one-pint containers, 4 one-quart containers, and 1 one-gallon container

Activity

☐ 4. Show the child 2 cups of rice and an empty pint container. "Will 2 cups of rice fill 1 pint? Measure to find out." *(yes)* Now show the child 5 cups of rice. Have the child measure to find the answers to the questions that follow. "Is 5 cups more than or less than 1 quart?" *(more)* "Is 5 cups more than or less than 1 gallon?" *(less)* Give the child 3 pint containers filled with rice. "Is 3 pints more than or less than 1 quart?" *(more)* "How many pints fill a quart?" *(2)* Give the child 4 one-quart containers filled with rice and the empty gallon container. "How many quarts fill a gallon?" *(4)*

OBJECTIVE To estimate capacities of familiar containers as less than, about, or more than a liter.

Materials Containers of the following sizes: 1 liter, 1 cup, 1 pint, 1 quart, 2 quarts, 1 gallon

Activity

☐ 5. Show the child the containers. Have the child point to the container or containers that answer the following questions: "Which containers are more than 1 liter?" *(gallon, 2 quart)* "Which are less than 1 liter?" *(cup, pint)* "Which are about the same as 1 liter?" *(quart)*

Source: Portfolio Assessments, Level 2, Heath Mathematics Connections
(Lexington, MA: D. C. Heath, 1992). Reproduced with permission.

audio- and videotape recordings are some of the ways that progress in the language arts is being assessed. The influence of thematic instruction and the whole language movement is being felt across the nation. Basal series are integrating themes and whole language approaches into reading and other language arts. Commercially prepared thematic books featuring whole language and integrated curriculum activities are proliferating in stores that carry teaching supplies. The above factors, plus a recognition of the importance of accessing individual learning styles and strengths, have led to a more activity-based instruction and assessment program. One of the best ways to assess such a program is with a language arts portfolio.

According to Sheila Valencia (1990) of the University of Washington, a portfolio

> is like a large expandable file folder that holds (a) samples of the student's work selected by the teacher or the student, (b) the teacher's own observational notes, (c) the student's own periodic self-evaluations, and (d) progress notes contributed by the student and teacher collaboratively. The range of items to include in a portfolio is almost limitless and may include written responses to reading, reading logs, selected

FIGURE 12.

Name _____ Date _____

9 ▶ Observation Checklist

DIRECTIONS: Give each child a copy of the problem-solving activity at the bottom of this page. Have children work independently to solve the problem. Complete the checklist for each child by reading each criterion statement and checking the box next to each criterion the child demonstrated while solving the problem.

These are units of measure:
inch	centimeter
pound	kilogram
cup	liter

Match each unit of measure with an object
   that is the same size.
Draw the objects on a piece of paper.
Write the name of the unit of measure.

Make available the following materials:
Inch ruler, centimeter ruler, scale, pound weight, kilometer measure, cup and liter containers

The child:
☐ 1. showed an understanding of the problem.
☐ 2. tried appropriate solutions.
☐ 3. used problem-solving techniques to arrive at a solution.
☐ 4. modeled the problem appropriately with objects.
☐ 5. was persistent in trying to solve the problem.
☐ 6. reviewed his or her work.
☐ 7. exhibited an understanding of measurement.
☐ 8. appropriately recorded information through drawing.

Circle any that apply.
The problem was solved:

with originality   outstandingly   coherently   logically   satisfactorily   inadequately

- -

These are units of measure:
inch	centimeter
pound	kilogram
cup	liter

Match each unit of measure with an object
   that is the same size.
Draw the objects on a piece of paper.
Write the name of the unit of measure.

Source: Portfolio Assessments, Level 2, Heath Mathematics Connections
(Lexington, MA: D. C. Heath, 1992). Reproduced with permission.

daily work, pieces of writing at various stages of completion, classroom tests, checklists, unit projects, and audio or video tapes, to name a few. The key is to ensure a *variety* of types of indicators of learning so that teachers, parents, students, and administrators can build a complete picture of the student's development.

The Literacy Portfolios Project in Manchester, New Hampshire, helps students know themselves better. In this project, students have a large say in what goes into their portfolios. They also include items from outside of school that have significance to them. When students select items for their portfolios, they weight each item's significance. They determine the relevance of an item in terms of these questions: Who am I? Who am I as a reader-writer? How does this item show my growth? The focus of the Literacy Portfolios is on self-evaluation. An interesting part of this project involves sharing the portfolio with others at home. After the portfolio is shared, someone at home writes personal comments on a special place in the portfolio. These sharing experiences and comments are self-validating for the students. Personal goal setting is a natural result of this shared portfolio process (Hansen 1992).

An innovative portfolio project in Wyoming involves using a multimedia system to assess the total child. Large amounts of information, including videotapes and scanned student work from kindergarten through the grades, can be stored on a laser disk small enough to slide into a student's permanent record file. These laser disks will be maintained from year to year to give students, parents, and school a tool to evaluate growth in many areas (Campbell 1992).

Assessment in the K–3 Science Program

Assessment in science fits easily into the performance assessment category. Science notebooks, logs and journals, drawings, experiments, embedded assessments, inventions, and projects are just a few examples of performance assessments that can be used in the K–3 science program. Teacher observation and annotation, and paper-and-pencil quizzes, are

all tools to be used when appropriate. Student knowledge before and after instruction can be shown in a variety of ways, such as mindmapping, drawings, charts, and reflective statements.

Embedded assessment is an excellent way to assess students in science because it is an authentic task performed in context during the learning process. Figure 13 is an example of a science lesson for second grade.

Assessment is a powerful tool in the classroom. It has great potential for shaping instruction and for affecting how students feel about school and themselves as learners. Teachers become empowered as they develop and use appropriately a wide range of assessment strategies and scoring instruments. Students, teachers, and the community benefit when sound assessment policies are in place.

Glossary

authentic task: a task performed by students that is a close approximation of a real-life task.
checklist: an objective instrument that is used to determine the presence or absence of specific and usually required elements of a performance assessment.
criterion-referenced test: a measure of student achievement in which levels of mastery are determined in relation to specific testing criteria instead of in relation to how others performed on the test, as in a norm-referenced test.
diagnostic test: an in-depth measurement of an area of performance, whose purpose is usually to discover an individual student's strengths and deficiencies to guide regular instruction or remediation.
embedded assessment: an authentic task performed in context during the learning process.
informal test: a nonstandardized test, often teacher-made, used to assess a student's knowledge or achievement level.
inventory: an assessment that gives an overview of a student's abilities, decision-making skills, attitudes, and preferences in a particular area.
item: an individual question or exercise in a test.
norm: a performance standard that has been established by evaluating a reference group and

FIGURE 13.

| *Oil and Me* | *Activity 8* |

❦ The students will be able to give a variety of examples of products that are made from petroleum.

Materials Provided in Kit:
* *Energy* student booklet page 13
* 1 piece of foam rubber
* 1 plastic bag from the materials in the kit
* 1 piece of styrofoam
* 1 candle

Teacher provides:
* lipstick, record, plastic toy, crayons
* old magazines
* scissors and glue

Procedure:
A. Display all the items that have been provided by the teacher or sent with the kit. Have the students name the things they believe come from oil. Write their suggestions on the chalkboard. Count the objects on the table, count the objects they have named. Surprise! Everything on the table is a petroleum product!

Use this to lead into a discussion of how many things in our lives are by-products of oil. The list on page 11 will be useful and may contain items even YOU did not realize were petroleum products.

If your class needs alphabetizing practice, here's a list that can be edited down to a reasonable size for A through Z alphabetizing. Note how many products start with C, if you would like for your students to do alphabetizing to the 2nd or 3rd letter.

B. Distribute magazines for the students to use in locating and cutting out pictures of products made from oil. Remind them that anything with plastic in it is made from oil. On SB page 13 have the students paste in the selected pictures.

❦ *Embedded Assessment Opportunity*
Spot check the students' work to make certain they understand which products are made from oil.

Source: An Introduction to Energy (Mesa, AZ: Science/Social Sciences Resource Center, Mesa Public Schools, 1991). Reproduced with permission.

---

then determining the average performance for that group.

norm-referenced test: an objective test that can be used to compare the scores of test takers to the scores of the reference group.

percent score: the percent of items answered correctly.

performance assessment: a test that can measure a wide variety of student products or processes. Performance assessments, paper-and-pencil tests, and oral interviews are three main categories of testing. Performance assessments are usually scored with a checklist, rating scale, or rubric.

rating scales: subjective assessment instruments that are used to evaluate a performance assessment. A student's performance score is placed on a continuum between a description of unsatisfactory performance and a description of superior performance. Another type of rating scale gives a description of performance for each point on the scale from low to high. A simple rating scale might be: *Unacceptable/ Acceptable/Outstanding.* Descriptors would be written for each level of performance in a specific assignment.

reliability: the extent to which a test is dependable and consistent when given to the same individual on different occasions.

standardized test: Standardization is achieved by administering a test to a targeted population. Means, standard deviations, standardized scores, and percentiles are calculated. Then test scores of individuals can be compared to test scores of the norm group.

validity: the extent to which a test measures what it was intended to measure.

Resource Reading

Association for Supervision and Curriculum Development. 1992. "Using Performance Assessment." *Educational Leadership* 49(8): 7-95

Farr, Roger. 1992. "Putting It All Together: Solving the Reading Assessment Puzzle." *The Reading Teacher* 46 (September): 26-37.

Guskey, Thomas R. 1985. *Implementing Mastery Learning.* Belmont, CA: Wadsworth.

Harrington-Lueker, Donna. 1991. "Beyond Multiple Choice: The Push To Assess Performance." *The Executive Educator* 13 (April): 20-22.

Hoskisson, Kenneth, and Gail E. Tompkins. 1987. *Language Arts: Content and Teaching Strategies.* Columbus, OH: Merrill.

Hymes, Donald L., with Ann E. Chafin and Peggy Gonder. 1991. *The Changing Face of Testing and Assessment Problems and Solutions.* Arlington, VA: American Association of School Administrators.

Jasmine, Julia. 1992. *Portfolio Assessment for Your Whole Language Classroom.* Huntington Beach, CA: Teacher Created Materials.

Krechevsky, Mara. 1991. "Project Spectrum: An Innovative Assessment Alternative." *Educational Leadership* 48 (February): 43-48.

Northwest Regional Education Laboratory. June 1991. *Classroom Assessment Training Program.* Portland, OR.

Perrone, Vito. 1991. *Expanding Student Assessment.* Alexandria, VA: Association for Supervision and Curriculum Development.

Spady, William G. 1989. Key Messages from the High Success Program on OBE: Parts I and II. *Outcomes.*

Stiggins, Richard J. 1987. "NCME Instructional Module on Design and Development of Performance Assessments." *Educational Measurement: Issues and Practice* 6(3): 33-42.

———. 1991. "Assessment Literacy." *Phi Delta Kappan* 72(7): 534-39.

Wilde, Sandra. 1991. "Learning to Write about Mathematics." *Arithmetic Teacher* 38(6): 38-43.

Winograd, Peter, Scott Paris, and Connie Bridge. 1991. "Improving the Assessment of Literacy." *The Reading Teacher* 45 (October): 108-16.

References

Blood, Sue. 1992. *Rating Scale for a Descriptive Paragraph.* Mesa, AZ: Field Elementary School.

Campbell, Jo. 1992. "Laser Disk Portfolios: Total Child Assessment." *Educational Leadership* 49 (May): 69-70.

Clarke, David J. 1992. "Activating Assessment Alternatives in Mathematics." *Arithmetic Teacher* 39(6): 24-29.

Davidson, Avelyn. 1990. "Emergent Reading Check, Stages 1 and 2." *In Literacy 2000 Teachers' Resource*, 180. Auckland, New Zealand: Shortland.

Halloran, P., J. L. Gatanti, and D. P. Adcock. 1992. "Portfolio Assessments, Level 2." In *Heath Mathematics Connections.* Lexington, MA: D. C. Heath.

Hansen, Jane. 1992. "Literacy Portfolios: Helping Students Know Themselves." *Educational Leadership* 49 (May): 66-68.

Hemmer, Earlene, and Terri Goyins. 1992. "Portfolio, Please." *Instructor* 101 (April): 49.

Merrill, Beverly. 1987. "Diagnostic Evaluation—3rd Grade." Gilbert, AZ: Gilbert Public Schools.

———. 1990. "Diagnostic Evaluation—1st Grade." Gilbert, AZ: Gilbert Public Schools.

Meyer, Carol A. 1992. "What's the Difference between Authentic and Performance Assessment?" *Educational Leadership* 49 (May): 39–40.

Redding, Nora. 1992. "Assessing the Big Outcomes." *Educational Leadership* 49 (May): 49–53.

Science/Social Sciences Resource Center. 1991. "Oil and Me, Activity 8." In *An Introduction to Energy*. Mesa, AZ: Mesa Public Schools.

Valencia, Sheila. 1990. "A Portfolio Approach to Classroom Reading Assessment: The Whys, Whats, and Hows." *The Reading Teacher* 43 (January): 338–340.

Withee, Nanci. 1992. *Kindergarten Report Card Supplement*. Mesa, AZ: Hermosa Vista Elementary School.

8

ANNOTATED LISTS OF CURRICULUM GUIDES: PREKINDERGARTEN–GRADE 3

Eileen Tracy Borgia
Doctoral Student in Early Childhood Education
University of Illinois Urbana–Champaign, Urbana, Illinois

THE best curriculum for young children is constructed by children and teachers together, and is built on worthwhile topics of interest to the children. The teacher leads the way toward learning experiences based on the children's existing knowledge and skills. The younger the children, the more informal the learning setting should be. The content of the curriculum should be integrated so that reading, writing, or mathematics, for example, are skills that children use to learn about phenomena in their world.

While some of the experiences should involve systematic instruction in large or small groups, most learning occurs when children act on materials and interact with other people. There should be a balance of open-ended experiences, in which children are active learners who initiate activities, and others that are systematic, structured, or teacher-initiated. Learning experiences should be designed to build on or extend concepts introduced and understood previously. Experiences should offer opportunities for children to acquire knowledge, skills, and positive attitudes toward learning. Concepts should be presented in ways that move children forward from what they already

know or can do to greater levels of knowledge and understanding.

Learning should be viewed as an ongoing process, involving reading, writing, drawing, construction, dramatic play, and other forms of active representation. Holistic learning experiences involve all of the domains of development—physical, cognitive (including language), social, and emotional—and utilize as many of the five senses as possible in the process. Cultural, linguistic, and individual diversity should be respected.

Having described what the curriculum should be, the following list of curriculum guides should not present contradictions to the above description. Teachers should think of them as guides—that is, sources for ideas and a framework from which to begin—not as prescriptions for learning nor plans to be adopted. No curriculum guide will teach itself, and no curriculum guide need be used exclusively. The role of the teacher is to be informed and to make decisions based on the ages and individual needs and interests of the children and the teacher. It is hoped that educators will use the resources listed below but not consider them to be the only sources. It is further hoped that they will guide, not drive, decisions about the education of primary-grade children. It is believed that many of the above values for a curriculum are found within the curriculum guides listed on the following pages.

A Position Statement

To address the complicated issue of curriculum choice, The National Association for the Education of Young Children and the National Association of Early Childhood Specialists in State Departments of Education (1991) published *Guidelines for Appropriate Curriculum Content and Assessment in Programs Serving Children Ages 3 through 8*. The following twenty questions are reprinted from the document to guide the selection of curriculum components.

1. Does it promote interactive learning and encourage the child's construction of knowledge?
2. Does it help achieve social, emotional, physical, and cognitive goals?
3. Does it encourage development of positive feelings and dispositions toward learning while leading to acquisition of knowledge and skills?
4. Is it meaningful for these children? Is it relevant to children's lives? Can it be made more relevant by relating it to a personal experience children have had or can they easily gain direct experience with it?
5. Are the expectations realistic and attainable at this time or could the children more easily and efficiently acquire the knowledge and skills later on?
6. Is it of interest to children and to the teacher?
7. Is it sensitive to and respectful of cultural and linguistic diversity? Does it expect, allow, and appreciate individual differences? Does it promote positive relationships with families?
8. Does it build on and elaborate children's cultural knowledge and abilities?
9. Does it lead to conceptual understanding by helping children construct their own understanding in meaningful contexts?
10. Does it facilitate integration of content across traditional subject areas?
11. Is the information presented accurate and credible according to the recognized standards of the relevant discipline?
12. Is this content worth knowing? Can it be learned by these children efficiently and effectively now?
13. Does it encourage active learning and allow children to make meaningful choices?
14. Does it foster children's exploration and inquiry, rather than focusing on "right" answers or "right" ways to complete a task?
15. Does it promote the development of higher order abilities such as thinking, reasoning, problem solving, and decision making?
16. Does it promote and encourage social interaction among children and adults?
17. Does it respect children's physiological needs for activity, sensory stimulation, fresh air, rest, nourishment/elimination?
18. Does it promote feelings of psychological safety, security, and belonging?
19. Does it provide experiences that promote feelings of success, competence, and enjoyment of learning?
20. Does it permit flexibility for children and teachers?

Integrated Curriculum Guides

The Big Book for Educators: Developmentally Appropriate Practice—A Guide to Change, by Maizie Argondizza, Jenifer Van Deusen, et al. 1988. ED 309 856. Available from the Maine Department of Educational and Cultural Services, Big Book Orders, Maine Department of Education, State House Station #23, Augusta, ME 04333. 207-289-5981. $3.00 per copy.

The Maine Department of Education has developed an evaluation tool for teachers designed to encourage self-reflection on the alignment between philosophy, research, and practice; and to provide a springboard to planning changes in the classroom environment, instructional strategies, role of the teacher, classroom management, and role of the administrator. Teachers who need assistance in making changes from traditionally structured academic programs might benefit from this self-study guide as they attempt to reevaluate and adjust teaching strategies.

Children in the Primary Years . . . A Time of Wonder, and *Year 2000: A Framework for Learning,* by Ministry of Education, Province of British Columbia. 1992. Available through Crown Publications, 546 Yates Street, Victoria, British Columbia, Canada.
The Province of British Columbia has introduced educational reforms that embrace the highest principles of learning espoused by leading educators from around the world. A key feature of the primary program is that it is ungraded. Most students are expected to take four years to complete it. It has four implied strands within which subjects are to be integrated: humanities, sciences, fine arts, and practical arts. Goals are based on the knowledge, skills, attitudes, and learning dimensions of the "Framework for Learning."

Five goals for children are outlined: aesthetic and artistic development, emotional and social development, intellectual development, physical development/well being, and development of social responsibility. Several education groups in the United States are beginning to adopt the principles of this innovative and promising program for primary education.

Circle of Childhood. 1990. North Carolina Department of Public Instruction, Instructional Services, Education Building, Raleigh, NC 27603. 157p.
Based on the NAEYC position statement on guidelines for developmentally appropriate practices, the state of North Carolina developed and implemented a curriculum which includes planning and assessing, for 3-, 4-, and 5-year-old children. It is designed around the child—surrounded by circles of school, home, and community. The handbook begins with a holistic overview of young children's growth and development. Cooperative relationships between home and school are highlighted. The curriculum is presented through generic goals and integrated, exploratory activities. Concept webs are suggested as an effective planning strategy. Planning arises from the observed interests and needs of children. Assessment

strategies, based on observation and recording, are included for children, teachers, environments, materials, and the home–school partnership. Samples of assessment checklists and other forms are included, along with a bibliography.

Creative Activities for Young Children, by Mimi Brodsky Chenfeld. 1983. New York: Harcourt Brace Jovanovich. 299p.
This guide reads like a comfortable conversation with a wise friend: "You are the heart of the activity. . . . When you mix your days with love and respect for children and when you do your best, you cannot help but succeed" (p. 7). It is organized first around the child's first world—the child's body and feelings—then goes on to include family, friends, classmates, the community, our colorful world, shapes, words, and numbers. Each chapter has the following sections: The Basics (e.g., we must be interested and excited about the ideas we share with our students), Discovery Times (important concepts to be introduced through varied and enjoyable discussions and activities), Suggested Vocabulary, Some Beginning Activities, Talk Times (to express themselves and form healthy relationships but also to learn the language), Art Times, Music Times, Movement and Play Times, Visitors and Field Trips, and Selected Bibliography (hundreds of children's books and poems, and resources for teachers).

The Creative Curriculum for Early Childhood, 3d ed., by Diane Trister Dodge, Marilyn Goldhammer, and Laura Colker. 1992. Creative Associates, Inc. Available through Gryphon House, Inc., P.O. Box 275, Mt. Rainier, MD 20712. 379p. $39.95 per copy.
The Creative Curriculum provides teachers with a middle ground between "the precise, prescriptive curriculum guide with step-by-step daily lessons and the more loosely described models in which curriculum is everything children do" (p. vii). This guide encourages creativity in both teachers and children. The authors state, "Being creative means thinking of new ideas, obtaining information by asking questions, learning through trial and error, and benefitting from mistakes" (p. ix).

Teachers are challenged to be innovative and responsive to children. The guide begins with the themes of the learning environment, and includes blocks, house corner, table toys, art, sand and water, library corner, and outdoors. Within each section are discussions of philosophy and learning theory, goals and objectives, setting up the environment, strategies for interacting with children in the area, suggestions for encouraging parent support in each area, and a list of resources for further reading.

Although this guide was written for three- to five-year-olds, and has been validated in Head Start and other preschool programs, it presents basic early childhood information in a thorough manner. It would serve as a useful guide to kindergarten and primary teachers who need to start at the beginning with an interactive curriculum in which the focus is on the learning of both the teacher and the child.

Explorations with Young Children: A Curriculum Guide from the Bank Street College of Education, by Anne Mitchell and Judy David, eds. 1992. Mt. Rainier, MD: Gryphon House. $19.95. 309p.

Explorations offers a framework for thinking and decision making—"guidelines and recommendations—not fail-safe recipes"—and encourages teachers to plan appropriate learning experiences based on the following principles:

- Work with children is based on knowledge of child development, especially the interdependence of social, emotional, physical, and intellectual growth.
- We learn about children through observation and recording, their works or projects, and their families.
- We should create a physical environment that encourages their active participation in their own learning.
- We should create a social/emotional environment that encourages a sense of community and demonstrates the value of each individual in the community.

Three chapters introduce principles of the Bank Street Approach, child development, and observing and recording children's behavior. The approach is explained further in chapters on learning environment, valuing diversity, developing curriculum, integrating curriculum, emerging literacy, mathematics, science, and art, working with families, fulfilling the teacher role, and conducting assessment. Each chapter includes a definition of the topic, a rationale,

"how-to" suggestions, examples of what teachers can do at various age levels, a series of exercises to try, and a list of resources. Respect for ethnic, cultural, and gender diversity is reflected throughout the book. The guide represents state-of-the-art thinking on curriculum development in early childhood, and is consistent with the *Guidelines for Appropriate Curriculum Content and Assessment in Programs Serving Children Ages 3 through 8* published by NAEYC in 1991.

Explorers' Classrooms: Good Practice for Kindergarten and the Primary Grades, by Elizabeth F. Shores. 1992. Available from Southern Association on Children under Six, P.O. Box 5403, Little Rock, AR 72215-5403. 95p. $10.00 per copy.

Smaller than a curriculum guide, mightier than a resource book, this publication features a celebration of children and teachers in five southern states as they explore the dimensions of developmentally appropriate practice in kindergarten and primary classrooms. This book sends a positive message to the skeptics who assert that once children are in first grade they must "get down to work" and leave behind whole language, interest centers, the Project Approach, cooperative learning, integrated curriculum, research, and exploration. Narratives describe teachers whose classrooms are alive with learning centers, flexible schedules, books and manipulatives, parental involvement, projects, multi-age grouping, and even play.

The children described in *Explorers' Classrooms* practice the real-world skills of writers, researchers, scientists, artists, business executives, and decision makers. A special whole-language activity, "Exploring the Newspaper," is also featured. This new, fresh, and enthusiastic publication will motivate teachers who know about the integrated curriculum but have been afraid to try it.

A Guide to Program Development for Kindergarten, Parts I and II. 1988. ED 301 356. Available from the Connecticut State Department of Education, Bureau of Early Childhood Education, 25 Industrial Park, Middletown, CT 06457.

This two-volume book is an exceptional curriculum guide and resource on current trends in early childhood education. Although the title implies it is for kindergarten, the authors intend the information to be relevant and useful throughout the primary grades. Part I provides teachers with a comprehensive overview of the history and philosophy of early childhood education, the principles and components of a high-quality program, the role of social and emotional development in a child's education, a description and explanation of the integrated curriculum, building a home-school-community partnership, and the early childhood education continuum.

In Part II, each subject that might be included in an integrated curriculum is described. Chapters cover exploring the arts (dramatics, movement, music, visual arts); investigating foreign languages; communicating through language arts; growing through mathematics; developing through physical education, health, and safety; discovering the world of science; and examining the social studies.

The document is more than a curriculum guide; it is also a resource on the current trends in early childhood education. Its attractive format—including charts and graphic representations of themes, photographs of children, wide margins, and glossy paper—also gives the guide a pleasant sensory appeal.

High/Scope K–3 Curriculum Series. 1991. For more information, contact High Scope Press, 600 North River Street, Ypsilanti, MI 48198. 313-485-2000. $22.00 each volume.
High/Scope Educational Foundation has expanded its cognitively oriented curriculum for preschool children, and has developed a version for kindergarten through third grade. Building on its original constructivist framework (based on the beliefs of Jean Piaget) and drawing on the most recent developmental research, the K-3 curriculum series includes separate volumes on language and literacy, mathematics, science, and the learning environment.

The curriculum guides include background information, providing teachers with an introduction to, and review of, current trends in the field. Learning activities are built around the key experiences—detailed developmental sequences of experiences that teachers can use as a process-oriented guide to children's learning.

The key experiences differ from traditional teaching objectives, which are usually focused on discrete concepts or skills, in that they are broad, build on previous learning, and continue to be refined as children develop. The key experiences form the basis for three essential teaching tasks in this curriculum:(1) planning large- and small-group activities (called workshops); (2) interacting with children during independent plan–do–review activities; and (3) assessing the children's levels of development through observation and recording. Each guide includes suggested experiences that involve interactive learning with manipulatives, construction, and a list of selected computer software and activities.

In addition to resources included in each content area guide, High/Scope Press publishes a library of videotapes for preschool and primary teachers, including *Active Learning*; *Classroom Environment*; *Language and Literacy;* and *Mathematics* ($35.00 rental, $90.00 purchase).

The High/Scope preschool curriculum manual, *Young Children in Action* (1979), has received wide acceptance in prekindergarten settings for its developmentally appropriate, interactive approach to education in the preschool years. Extension of the approach to elementary-age children gives children an opportunity for needed continuity in learning experiences, and gives primary teachers specific guided strategies for teaching in ways suited to the educational and developmental levels of children from five to eight years of age. A word of caution: there might be a tendency for those using this curriculum guide to become dependent upon one pedagogy and to develop an orthodoxy about its use.

Model Learner Outcomes for Early Childhood Education: Birth to Nine, by Corinna Moncada. 1990. For more information, contact the Minnesota Department of Education, Curriculum Services Section, 626 Capitol Square, 550 Cedar Street, St. Paul, MN 55101.
Teachers and administrators unfamiliar with the goals, issues, and philosophy of early childhood education will appreciate the thoroughness with which this exceptionally valuable document is written. It is not only a useful resource for

decision making but also a course in applying the principles of child development and education in the early years. It summarizes the mission and goals of the Minnesota Department of Education, and provides a broad framework for planning based on learner outcomes in the domains of personal, social, physical, aesthetic/ creative, cognitive, and communication development. Sections include translating learner outcomes into learning opportunities; outcomes and indicators for assessing development and learning; and cross referencing of learner outcomes, developmental domains, and units of learning within domains. Information on appropriate learning environments, components of an effective early childhood program, and bibliographies make this a unique guide to planning.

Play at the Center of the Curriculum, by Judith Van Hoorn, Patricia Nourot, Barbara Scales, and Keith Alward. 1993. New York: Merrill/ Macmillan. 273p.

This book asks not only "How can play support curriculum?" but also "How can curriculum support play?" Based on the belief that there is a natural connection between play and development and learning, the authors demonstrate how the power of play in children's lives can be draw upon to improve developmentally based early childhood education. It is "a resource for those who want to engage children in a developmental zone where both children and teachers are learning. . . . The teacher becomes the architect and gardener of the environment, using play as both structure and nutrient" (p. iv).

Four chapters provide a theoretical and developmental foundation. In chapters 5 through 9, the authors present practical ideas for including play in the curriculum areas of the arts, science, mathematics, language and literacy, and socialization. Anecdotes of children in real situations show how a potential curriculum is embedded in children's spontaneous play. Chapter 10 examines how play, toys, and technology affect children's learning, and includes commentary on the role of computers, television, and games. Chapter 12 offers an in-depth look at the relationship between developmental theory and play, intended to help the reader integrate thought and experience. The final chapter is a conversation with teachers on how to implement a play-centered, integrated curriculum.

A Practical Guide to Early Childhood Curriculum, by Claudia Eliason and Loa Jenkins. 1990. 4th ed. New York: Merrill/Macmillan. 580p.

This text is designed to help preservice and beginning teachers of children from ages three to seven plan and prepare developmentally appropriate, meaningful learning experiences. Part I introduces the philosophy and history of early childhood, developmental characteristics of children and how they learn, and an in-depth discussion of the value of play and the physical environment. Each chapter consists of a theoretical framework, an approach to teaching, sample lesson and unit plans, references, and suggested resources (children's nooks, records, pictures, kits, films, and videos). Chapters include: planning the curriculum, language and literacy, socioemotional skills (myself and other people), sensory experiences (nutrition and food experiences, the five senses), aesthetic development (music and movement, creativity and art), science and critical thinking, and math and problem solving. Additional chapters address working with parents, children with special needs, teacher-made learning materials, resources and organizations, and additional readings. More experienced teachers will forgo the day-by-day structure of the suggested lessons and unit plans, instead taking cues from the children's interests and abilities and choosing among the wide variety of suggested resources and activities.

Project Construct—A Curriculum Guide: Understanding the Possibilities, by Deborah G. Murphy and Stacie G. Goffin. 1992. ED 324 114. Available from the Center for Educational Assessment, University of Missouri-Columbia, 403 South Sixth Street, Columbia, MO 65211. $25.00 per copy.

The developmental theories of Jean Piaget have significantly influenced the field of early-childhood education. *Project Construct* is a curriculum and assessment guide that draws heavily on Piaget's theory that, as explorers and discoverers, children actively seek new knowledge and understanding that is meaningful for them; they are not viewed as passive recipients of information. The curriculum framework consists of twenty-six goals that reflect current knowledge about how children learn. Each goal is defined by a curriculum and assessment specification.

Consistent with the philosophy that knowledge is constructed by the individual while interacting with his or her environment, the guide is written so that the teacher also constructs her/his own knowledge of this approach to early childhood education. This is neither a cookbook-style "how-to" nor an activities manual. It consists of a series of chapters framed as questions. It is hoped that reading and reflecting on the thoughtfully developed texts will lead the reader to realize the teacher's potential for autonomy in designing the learning environment and in choosing experiences and that are most meaningful to the children.

Introductory chapters provide a rationale for the constructivist framework and a description of the initiative in the state of Missouri that resulted in publication of the document. More than twenty-five questions frame the discussions of the approach. Among the questions from which teachers are encouraged to make curriculum decisions are: Why is play so important for children? What should children know before entering school or going to first grade? How do I integrate the curriculum? How do I integrate the curriculum using the Project Approach? How do I choose good activities? How do I use literature as a framework for planning? Will discipline be a problem? How can I be sure children are learning? Can a constructivist approach work with special needs children? What does my principal need to understand if I want to become a constructivist teacher? How can parents understand the constructivist approach? There are also opportunities for teachers to receive training and support to implement Project Construct.

Recent developments in the understanding of how young children learn place more emphasis on the role of social interaction in children's learning. Although Piagetian theory emphasizes the individuality of learning, the concepts described in this document provide teachers with insights they can use to guide interactive curriculum planning. The recommended use of integrated learning, the Project Approach, children's literature, and play, imply

that children will be involved in social interaction during their learning process. The rich, thoughtful conceptual chapters provide teachers with information and a sense of empowerment to make their own curriculum decisions.

Reaching Potentials: Appropriate Curriculum and Assessment for Young Children. Volume 1, by Sue Bredekamp and Teresa Rosegrant, eds. 1992. Washington, DC: National Association for the Education of Young Children.
The purpose of this book is to make meaningful the *Guidelines for Appropriate Curriculum Content and Assessment*, a joint position statement of the National Association for the Education of Young Children and the National Association of Early Childhood Specialists in State Departments of Education.

The book introduces a new paradigm for the "mindful curriculum," or "transformational curriculum," based on the assumption that, not only does a curriculum change the learner, but the learner also affects and changes the curriculum. The child is at the center of the curriculum, is transformed by the interaction with the curriculum, but influences and transforms it in return. The transformational approach is conceptually organized, draws on the knowledge base of the disciplines, considers child development information in all domains, and considers the developmental/learning continuum of each individual. Two chapters deal with implementing the transformational curriculum. Three chapters on reaching potentials of all children focus on children with special needs, antibias, multicultural curriculum, and linguistically diverse children. The latter two chapters help teachers and administrators reach their potentials for embracing the appropriate curriculum and assessment guidelines. This is an important and significant publication that will stimulate discussion and lead toward more appropriate curriculum for young children.

Resources for Creative Teaching in Early Childhood Education, by Bonnie Mack Flemming, Darlene Softley Hamilton, and JoAnne Deal Hicks. 1990. ED 135 482. Orlando, FL: Harcourt Brace Jovanovich. 634p.

As its title suggests, this comprehensive guide provides teachers with resources that support teaching and learning through the use of themes. It is organized around the themes of self-concept, families, family celebrations, seasons, animals, transportation, and the world we live in. It provides beginning teachers with information on planning and offers suggestions on how to incorporate learning experiences into various learning centers. Background information is included for teachers as well as lists of books and resources that support each theme. This was one of the first books if its kind for preschool teachers, but it has value for kindergarten and primary teachers as well.

The Teacher's Ongoing Role in Creating a Developmentally Appropriate Early Childhood Program: A Self-Study Process for Teachers of Children Ages 5–8. 1990. ED 319 520. Hartford, CT: Connecticut State Department of Education. 44p. 203-566-5409.

This self-study instrument was designed to support teachers' efforts to implement an early childhood program that reflects the qualities of developmentally appropriate programming for children of five to eight years of age. The program focuses on the learning environment, the integrated curriculum, the roles of players in the program, evaluation, and partnerships among home, school, and community.

Teaching Young Children Using Themes, by Marjorie Kostelnik, ed. 1991. Glenview, IL: Good Year Books. 537p. $29.95 per copy.

This large, practical resource guide was written by teachers for teachers to respond to the following questions: What is theme teaching? What kinds of themes are most appropriate for preschoolers? How can theme teaching be used with kindergarten and first-grade students? Is there more than one way to carry out a theme? How long should each theme last? Twenty-four original thematic units are described, with over 1,400 child-centered learning activities.

The approach advocates for holistic, integrated, developmentally appropriate educational activities. *Teaching Young Children Using Themes* will provide both teachers new to the idea of theme teaching and those interested in using the Project Approach (see also chapter 9) with a valuable resource.

The Wonder Years: Kentucky's Primary School. Program Description I. 1991. ED 341 464. To order, contact the Kentucky State Department of Education, 1725 Capitol Plaza Tower, Frankfort, KY 40601.

Education reform in Kentucky included a radical restructuring from traditional education to the new primary school concepts. The guide outlines critical attributes of the program: developmentally appropriate practices, integrated curriculum, multi-age/multi-ability classrooms, continuous progress, authentic assessment, qualitative reporting methods, professional teamwork, and positive parent involvement. This document is an expanded position statement for a visionary approach to early childhood education.

Resource Books and Articles on Curriculum Development

Bredekamp, Sue, ed. 1987. *Developmentally Appropriate Practice in Early Childhood Programs Serving Young Children from Birth through Age 8.* Washington, DC: National Association for the Education of Young Children. ED 283 587.

Chard, Sylvia. 1992. *The Project Approach: A Practical Guide.* Edmonton, Alberta, Canada: University of Alberta. ED 340 518.

Cohen, Elizabeth. 1986. *Designing Groupwork: Strategies for the Heterogeneous Classroom.* New York: Teachers College Press.

Curtin, Helena, and Linda Martinez. 1989. *Integrating the Elementary School Curriculum into the Foreign Language Class: Hints for the FLES Teacher.* Los Angeles: University of California. ED 305 823.

Derman-Sparks, Louise, and The A.B.C. Task Force. 1989. *Anti-Bias Curriculum: Tools for Empowering Young Children.* Washington, DC: National Association for the Education of Young Children. ED 305 135.

DeVries, Rheta, and Lawrence Kohlberg. 1987. *Constructivist Early Education: Overview and Comparison with Other Programs.* Washington, DC: National Association for the Education of Young Children.

Fromberg, Doris. 1987. *The Full-Day Kindergarten.* New York: Teachers College Press.

Gareau, Marianne, and Colleen Kennedy. 1991. "Structure Time and Space To Promote

Pursuit of Learning in the Primary Grades." *Young Children* 46(4): 46–51. EJ 429 081.

Goffin, Stacie, and Delores Stegelin, eds. 1992. *Changing Kindergartens: Four Success Stories.* Washington, DC: National Association for the Education of Young Children.

Hirsch, Elizabeth, ed. 1986. *The Block Book.* Rev. ed. Washington, DC: National Association for the Education of Young Children.

Katz, Lilian. 1989. *Pedagogical Issues in Early Childhood Education.* Norwood, NJ: Ablex. ED 321 840.

Katz, Lilian, and Sylvia Chard. 1989. *Engaging Children's Minds: The Project Approach.* Norwood, NJ: Ablex.

Katz, Lilian, and Diane McClellan. 1991. 2d ed. *The Teacher's Role in the Social Development of Young Children.* Urbana, IL: ERIC Clearinghouse on Elementary and Early Childhood Education. ED 331 642.

Katz, Lilian, Demetra Evangelou, and Jeanette Hartman. 1990. *The Case for Mixed-Age Grouping in Early Education.* Washington, DC: National Association for the Education of Young Children. ED 326 302.

Klauke, A. 1988. "The Developmental Approach to Kindergarten: Profile of an Expert Teacher." *Oregon School Study Bulletin* 31(8). ED 294 679.

Kostelnik, Marjorie. 1992. "Myths Associated with Developmentally Appropriate Programs." *Young Children* 47(4): 17–23. EJ 447 666.

Lanser, Shirley, and Laura McDonnell. 1991. "Creating Quality Curriculum yet Not Buying out the Store." *Young Children* 47(1): 4–9. EJ 436 425.

Ministry of Education, Province of British Columbia. 1992. *Supporting Learning: Understanding and Assessing the Progress of Children in the Primary Program.* Victoria, British Columbia, Canada. ED 341 458.

Nachbar, Randa Roen. 1989. "A K/1 Class Can Work." *Young Children* 44(5): 67–71. EJ 394 073.

National Association of Elementary School Principals. 1989. *Early Childhood Education and the Elementary School Principal: Standards for Quality Programs for Young Children.* Alexandria, VA.

Peck, Johanne, Ginny McCaig, and Mary Ellen Sapp. 1988. *Kindergarten Policies: What's Best for Children?* Washington, DC: National Association for the Education of Young Children. ED 299 045.

Ramsey, Patricia. 1987. *Teaching and Learning in a Diverse World: Multi-Cultural Education for Young Children.* New York: Teachers College Press.

Rasala, Sue. 1989. "Assignment in Kindergarten: Introduce a New Curriculum." *Young Children* 44(5): 60–66. EJ 394 072.

Resnick, Lauren, and Leopold Klopfer. 1989. *Toward the Thinking Curriculum: Current Cognitive Research.* Alexandria, VA: Association for Supervision and Curriculum Development. ED 328 871.

Rogers, Cosby, and Janet Sawyers. 1988. *Play in the Lives of Children.* Washington, DC: National Association for the Education of Young Children.

Roopnarine, Jaipaul, and James Johnson. 1993. *Approaches to Early Childhood Education.* 2d ed. Columbus, OH: Merrill.

Seefeldt, Carol. 1987. *The Early Childhood Curriculum: A Review of Current Research.* New York: Teachers College Press.

Spodek, Bernard, ed. 1986. *Today's Kindergarten: Exploring the Knowledge Base, Expanding the Curriculum.* New York: Teachers College Press.

———. 1991. *Educationally Appropriate Kindergarten Practices.* Washington, DC: National Education Association. ED 338 436.

Spodek, Bernard, and Olivia Saracho. 1991. *Issues in Early Childhood Curriculum: Yearbook in Early Childhood Education,* vol. 2. New York: Teachers College Press.

Walker, Decker. 1990. *Fundamentals of Curriculum.* Orlando, FL: Harcourt Brace Jovanovich

Williams, Leslie, and Yvonne DeGaetano. 1985. *ALERTA: A Multicultural, Bilingual Approach to Teaching Young Children.* Reading, MA: Addison-Wesley.

Williams, Leslie, and Doris Fromberg, eds. 1992. *Encyclopedia of Early Childhood Education.* New York: Garland.

Zimiles, Herbert. 1991. "Diversity and Change in Young Children." In *Issues in Early Childhood Curriculum: Yearbook in Early Childhood Education,* ed. B. Spodek and O. Saracho, New York: Teachers College Press.

Literacy

Recent research suggests that children learn to read in ways similar to the way they learn to talk. This belief has led to an understanding that literacy is an emergent process, and that the whole-language approach to reading and writing provides a more meaningful learning experience for children than does one in which skills are decontextualized. To guide practice in early reading development, the position statement—*Literacy Development and Pre-First Grade: A Joint Statement of Concerns about Present Practices in Pre-First Grade Reading Instruction and Recommendations for Improvement*—was published in 1985. The following organizations support this position statement: the Association for Childhood Education International, the Association for Supervision and Curriculum Development, the International Reading Association, the National Association for the Education of Young Children, the National Association of Elementary School Principals, and the National Council of Teachers of English. Copies of the statement are available from the International Reading Association, 800 Balksdale Rd. P.O. Box 8139, Newark, DE 19714-8139.

The Answer Book: A Guide to Literacy in Reading, Language Arts, and Mathematics. 1988. Available from the State Department of Public Instruction, State Capitol Building, 600 Boulevard Avenue East, Bismarck, ND 58505.

Although it does not have all the answers, this book offers parents and teachers answers to the most commonly asked questions on teaching literacy and mathematics. It is useful for communicating with parents about curriculum as well as for guiding decisions on curriculum development.

Emerging Literacy: Young Children Learn To Read and Write, by Dorothy Strickland and Lesley Mandel Morrow. 1989. ED 305 602. Contact the National Council of Teachers of English, 111 Kenyan Road, Urbana, IL 61801. 161p. $14.95 per copy.

This well-respected text is filled with concrete ideas for encouraging literacy in young children. Examples of ways in which literacy knowledge changes from infancy through second grade is documented and described. Theory and practical suggestions are blended in this useful guide.

The Foundations of Literacy, by Don Holdaway. 1979. ED 263 540. New York: Ashton Scholastic. 232p. $9.95 per copy.

This was one of the first important books to explain why teachers should change from an isolated skills/textbook-driven method to a holistic, developmental approach to literacy. Beginning teachers, as well as those who have been frustrated by unsuccessful methods of teaching reading, will appreciate Holdaway's reasoned practical application of theory and practice into what has become known as the whole-language approach.

High/Scope K–3 Curriculum Series: Language & Literacy, by Jane M. Maehr. 1991. Available from High/Scope Press, 600 North River Street, Ypsilanti, MI 48198. 313-485-2000. $22.00 per copy.

The *Language and Literacy* volume of the High/Scope *Curriculum Series* begins with an extensive historical perspective on reading and a review of current trends in the field of literacy. The principles of planning activities around the key experiences (speaking, listening, writing, and reading), plan–do–review strategies, the importance of providing an appropriate learning environment, the active construction of learning, and assessment are detailed.

Appendices include resource lists of children's literature, selected computer software for language and literacy development, and writing/reading checklists and inventories. In addition to samples of children's emergent writing, and photographs of children engaged in reading and writing, passages from classic children's literature provide inspiration for the texts they accompany.

Joyful Learning: A Whole Language Kindergarten, by Bobbi Fisher. 1991. Portsmouth, NH: Heinemann. 222p.

Drawing on the rich experiences of her own kindergarten teaching, Bobbi Fisher relates how she implements a rich, experience-based, whole-language program throughout the kindergarten year. She offers insights on the theory of whole language as she has practiced it in her kindergarten classroom to implement shared reading, the reading and writing process, mathematics, dramatic play, assessment, and communication with parents.

The appendix includes reproducible forms for reading and writing activities and assessment, suggested supplies and materials for reading, writing, and dramatic play centers, and long lists of favorite children's literature and teacher resources.

Learning To Love Literature: Preschool through Grade 3, by Linda Lamme. ED 205 991. Urbana, IL: National Council of Teachers of English. 98p. $8.95 per copy.
The goal of this book is to assist primary teachers in developing a completely integrated curriculum with literature as its base. Several appealing children's books are recommended, and reproducible materials are offered. Topics include storytelling, reading aloud, and print and nonprint resources for a literature program.

Supporting Literacy: Developing Effective Learning Environments, by Catherine Loughlin and Mavis Martin. 1987. ED 284 176. New York: Teachers College Press.
Loughlin and Martin have written a guide to help teachers arrange classroom environments that encourage children's literacy development. Practical and specific suggestions and descriptions and examples on arranging an environment that supports literacy are detailed. Included are discussions of spatial organization, the functional use of print, the use of books, and strategies on analyzing and improving the learning environment.

The Whole Language Catalogue, by Kenneth Goodman, Lois Bird, and Yetta Goodman. 1990. Santa Rosa, CA: American School. 466p. $29.95 per copy.
Borrowing from the popular *Whole Earth Catalogue* concept, this rich resource is a compilation of more than 500 contributions from teachers, parents, administrators, and children about their whole-language ideas, values, and insights. There are seven sections: learning, literature, language, teaching, curriculum, community, and whole language. This comprehensive guide provides practical information on implementing whole-language strategies in the classroom.

The Whole Language Sourcebook: Grades K–2, and Whole Language Sourcebook: Moving On, Grades 3–4, by Jane Baskwell and Paulette Whitman. 1986–88. Available from Scholastic, P.O. Box 7502, Jefferson City, MO 65102. 800-325-6149. Each volume is 236p. $52.50 per copy per volume.

Two comprehensive support manuals provide a wealth of whole-language techniques, strategies, and organizational procedures, along with a history of successful classroom applications.

Literacy Resource Books and Articles

Cambourne, Brian. 1988. *The Whole Story: Natural Learning and the Acquisition of Literacy in the Classroom.* New York: Ashton Scholastic.

Goodman, Ken. 1986. *What's Whole in Whole Language?* Jefferson City, MO: Scholastic. ED 300 777.

Fields, Marjorie, and Dorris Lee. 1987. *Let's Begin Reading Right: A Developmental Approach to Beginning Literacy.* Columbus, OH: Merrill.

Hatch, Joan. 1992. "Improved Language Instruction in the Primary Grades: Strategies for Teacher-Controlled Change." *Young Children* 47(6): 54–59.

North Carolina State Department of Public Instruction. 1989. *Communication Skills, Grades 1 and 2 Assessment.* Raleigh, NC. ED 311 443.

Routman, Reggie. 1988. *Transitions: From Literature to Literacy.* Portsmouth, NH: Heinemann. ED 300 779.

Short, Kathy, and Carolyn Burke. 1991. *Creating Curriculum: A Primer To Be Read by Teachers in Preparation for Planning Curriculum.* Portsmouth, NH: Heinemann.

Teale, William H., and Elizabeth Sulzby, eds. 1986. *Emergent Literacy: Writing and Reading.* Norwood, NJ: Ablex. ED 280 004.

Throne, Jeanette. 1988. "Becoming a Kindergarten of Readers?" *Young Children,* 43(6): 10–16. EJ 376 680.

Trelease, Jim. 1989. *The New Read Aloud Handbook.* Newark, DE: International Reading Association. ED 316 858.

Mathematics

Curriculum and Evaluation Standards for School Mathematics. 1989. ED 304 336. Available from the National Council of Teachers of Mathematics, 1906 Association Drive, Reston, VA 22091.
The National Council of Teachers of Mathematics K–12 recommends thirteen curriculum

standards for teaching in grades K–4. The basic assumptions are that curriculum should be conceptually oriented, actively involve children in doing mathematics, emphasize the development of mathematical thinking and reasoning, emphasize the application of mathematics, include a broad range of content, and make ongoing use of calculators and computers.

The recommendations urge teachers to consider mathematics as a means to practice problem solving, communication, reasoning, connections, estimation, number sense and numeration, concepts of whole-number numeration, concepts of whole-number operations, whole-number computation, geometry and spatial sense, measurement, statistics and probability, fractions and decimals, and patterns and relationships.

The standards are consistent with current thinking within the early childhood profession on how young children learn and ways in which children should be taught. Reflecting a commitment to change from the traditional way of teaching mathematics to a more developmentally appropriate approach, the National Council of Teachers of Mathematics lists those practices that should receive increased and, conversely, decreased attention. Increased attention should be placed on number sense, meaning, estimation, word problems, study of patterns and relationships, manipulatives, cooperative work, and reading and writing about mathematics. Decreased attention should be given to symbolic learning, pencil-paper computation long division, rounding, clue words, rote memorization and practice, worksheets, one-word answers, and teaching by telling.

The standards were developed by committees of the Commission on Standards for School Mathematics as one way to improve the quality of school mathematics. Recommendations are also given for evaluating the quality of both the curriculum and student achievement.

Hands-On Math: Manipulative Math for Young Children, Ages 3–6, by Janet Stone. 1990. ED 309 962. Available through Scott, Foresman, 1900 East Lake Avenue, Glenview, IL 60025. 163p. $11.95 per copy.
This book provides 121 age-appropriate activities for helping young children understand and discover mathematics concepts through the use of inexpensive or free manipulative materials readily available around the home or classroom. Topics are sequenced, with recommendations to avoid more advanced activities for children younger than five or six. Included are shapes, sizes, one-to-one correspondence, counting with understanding, recognizing and ordering numerals, parts and wholes, joining and separating sets (addition and subtraction), and others. "Playsheets," referred to as improved worksheets, appear to be not that innovative.

High/Scope K–3 Curriculum Series: Mathematics, by Charles Hohmann. 1991. Available from High/Scope Press, 600 North River Street, Ypsilanti, MI 48198. 313-485-2000. 290p. $22.00 per copy.
Logical and mathematical learning and the development of children from five through nine years are the subjects of this volume. Based on the teachings of Jean Piaget and the idea that a child actively constructs knowledge, the concept of active learning through a broad range of experiences is detailed.

Recommended are a learning environment rich in appropriate active-learning materials, individual and small-group activities, the plan-do-review sequence of child choice of learning activities, and adult guidance and support. A section on current trends and research on learning mathematics provides teachers with a base for understanding the approach. Activities involving active learning and manipulatives are recommended around the key experiences: collecting, sorting, and ordering; one-to-one pairing; numerical operations; geometry and space; position and perspective; measurement; ordering, sequencing, and patterns; movement; time and speed; and language, symbols, and graphing.

The key experiences are also organized by grade level. The chapter on child assessment and program evaluation includes recommendations on assessing children's progress by combining a variety of observational checklists, anecdotal records, and work samples rather than relying on a single episode of standardized testing to measure learning.

An appendix includes an extensive list of selected computer software and activities for K–3 mathematics, including math workshop computer activities that address specific mathematics key experiences.

Mathematics for Every Young Child, by Karen Schultz, Ron Colarusso, and Virginia Strawderman. 1989. New York: Merrill/ Macmillan. 373p.

Written for teachers of children from three to eight years old, this thoughtful book supports the view that mathematical meanings are not passively obtained from the teacher but are constructed by the child. Teachers are encouraged to discover what mathematical understandings children have and to build upon them.

The first three chapters provide teachers with basic background by discussing the structures of learning, mathematics, and instructional planning. Mathematics content, arithmetic, geometry, and measurement are addressed in subsequent chapters. Included in each chapter are vocabulary for teachers and for children, content, a developmental learning perspective, and suggestions on planning for instruction. Problem solving, estimation, technology, reflective thinking, and children's construction of knowledge are emphasized throughout the book.

Mathematics Their Way: An Activity-Centered Mathematics Program for Early Childhood Education, by Mary Baratta-Lorton. 1976. Reading, MA: Addison-Wesley. 398p.

This book contains a sequential, hands-on, integrated approach to teaching mathematics from kindergarten through grade two. Teachers are advised on ways to make mathematics meaningful by creating an atmosphere of purposeful play and exploration of mathematical concepts through manipulatives. Suggestions are given for collections of concrete materials found around the home or school—such as buttons, macaroni, and modeling clay—and sources for purchasing materials such as Unifix cubes, geoboards, pattern blocks, and pegs. Topics include patterns, sorting and classifying, counting, comparing, graphing, numbers, place value, and free exploration. Recommendations on how to integrate mathematics experiences into other curriculum areas and encourage parents to extend mathematics learning in the home, plus lists of materials that correspond to the concepts, are also provided. The text is enhanced by many photographs and drawings of children participating in *Mathematics Their Way* activities. This program has generated a contagious enthusiasm among primary teachers,

which has increased the popularity of the approach. Families, communities, and entire schools have been caught up in such popular activities as the 100th Day, when children who have been counting days since the first day of school celebrate the milestone of the 100th day. Training workshops, courses, and a networking newsletter are available to teachers on the implementation of the *Mathematics Their Way* approach.

Mathematics Resource Books and Articles

Charlesworth, Rosalind, and Deanna Radeloff. 1990. *Experiences in Math for Young Children.* 2d ed. Albany, NY: Delmar.

Kamii, C. 1985. *Young Children Reinvent Arithmetic: Implications of Piaget's Theory.* New York: Teachers College Press. ED 262 980.

Lee, Carolyn. 1991. *Mathematics Education Programs that Work: A Collection of Proven Exemplary Educational Programs and Practices in the National Diffusion Network.* Washington, DC: Office of Educational Research and Improvement, United States Department of Education. ED 334 081.

National Council of Teachers of Mathematics. 1988. "Early Childhood Mathematics." Special issue. *Arithmetic Teacher* (February).

North Carolina State Department of Public Instruction. 1989. *Mathematics: Grades 1 and 2 Assessment.* Raleigh, NC. ED 312 127.

Social Studies

Charting a Course: Social Studies for the Twenty-First Century, by the National Commission on Social Studies in the Schools. 1989. ED 317 450. Available from the National Council for the Social Studies, 3501 Newark Street NW, Washington, DC 20016. 202-966-7840. 84p. $7.00 per copy.

The position of the National Commission on Social Studies for the twenty-first century is that "the coexistence of increasing diversity and cherished tradition require . . . courses to cultivate participatory citizenship and encourage the growth of independent, knowledgeable young adults who will conduct their lives in accord with democratic and ethical principles"

(p. 5). For grades K–3, recommendations include that the curriculum aim to avoid superficiality and be well defined and relevant to the needs and interests of young learners; maintain a balance of local, national, and global information and concepts; incorporate international and multicultural perspectives; and emphasize that each individual plays multiple and varied roles and that roles change as circumstances change. Concepts to be covered by the curriculum include relationships in family, neighborhood, and community; geography; heroes and heroines; and holidays—all integrated within reading, writing, and mathematics activities. This book is a helpful guide to conceptualizing goals for social studies education for grades K–12.

Early Childhood Social Studies, by Cynthia Sunal. 1990. Columbus, OH: Macmillan. 251p. $24.00 per copy.
By tracing a child's social learning from birth, this developmental approach searches for patterns in our social lives that can be explored in social studies in the primary grades. The author believes that children can learn the content of social studies while they develop processes through interaction with their physical and social environment.

Many practical suggestions are given on how to move away from textbooks and worksheets while inviting children to create their own curriculum through experiential learning. This book has several useful connections for teachers interested in using the Project Approach (see chapter 9).

Elementary School Social Studies: Research as a Guide to Practice (Bulletin No. 79), by Virginia Atwood, ed. 1986. Available from the National Council for the Social Studies, 3501 Newark Street NW, Washington, DC 20016. 202-966-7840. 176p. $14.95 per copy.
Beginning with the updated "Position Statement on Social Studies for Early Childhood and Elementary School Children," this document provides a sound rationale for planned and regular attention to social studies and makes readily accessible the most current and valid data on how and when children develop concepts, skills, and attitudes associated with social studies.

A Guide for Integrating Global Education across the Curriculum. 1989. ED 315 361. Available from Iowa Department of Education, Grimes State Office Building, Des Moines, IA 50319-0146. 40p.
Global education is a nationwide movement to recognize and teach about the realities of the global society. This document was developed to assist school districts in developing their own models of global education, thereby meeting Iowa's standard for teaching global education across the curriculum. Included in this guide are standards, definitions, a description of a thematic model, suggestions on infusing global perspectives into the curriculum, and an extensive list of resources including books, articles, and organizations to help in planning. This concise guide is useful for teachers looking to incorporate multicultural educational experiences into young children's education.

A Guide to Curriculum Planning in the Social Studies, by H. Michael Hartoonian. 1986. ED 268 038. Available from the Wisconsin Department of Public Instruction, 125 S. Webster Street, P.O. Box 7841, Madison, WI 53707-7841. 216p.
This guide is an excellent resource for integrating social studies into a curriculum suitable for children coming into the Information Age. The major themes recommended comprise cause and effect, celebration of pluralism, citizenship, community, culture, equal opportunity, freedom and justice, government and authority, human rights, independence and interdependence, peace, scarcity and choice, stewardship of natural and human resources, and survival issues and future alternatives. Suggested concepts/key ideas are outlined for each grade level:
kindergarten—self and family
first grade—family, school, and neighborhood
second grade—local communities
third grade—urban and rural communities around the world.
For each grade level, course descriptions, suggested objectives, and methods and activities are provided.

Social Studies Curriculum Planning Resources, by the National Council for the Social Studies. 1990. Available from Kendall/Hunt, 2450 Kerper Blvd., P.O. Box 539, Dubuque,

IA 52004-0539. 800-338-5578. $14.95 per copy.

This publication is designed to assist educators who are planning, evaluating, and revising a social studies program. Included are the NCSS position statements and guidelines that affect social studies curriculum, criteria for excellence in social studies, three model scope and sequence statements, guidelines for reviewing and evaluating a social studies curriculum, and a discussion of curriculum constants—the knowledge, skills, attitudes, and actions necessary for any social studies curriculum.

Social Studies for the Preschool–Primary Child, by Carol Seefeldt. 1993. 4th ed. New York: Merrill/Macmillan.

Carol Seefeldt has integrated the recommendations of the National Council for the Social Studies, the National Commission on Social Studies in the Schools, the National Association for the Education of Young Children, and the California State Department of Education into a timely guide for social studies curriculum planning. It is built around the knowledge, skills, and attitudes about the social studies which young children can learn. The text describes how children can acquire knowledge and key concepts in each of the social science disciplines: history, geography, economics, current topics (current events, conservation, and career education), and cross-cultural education. A section on teaching for concept formation introduces basic ideas about how children learn. Seefeldt describes the teacher's role in developing social skills and thinking skills, the end result being people thinking for themselves. She also addresses helping children develop attitudes and values that are also congruent with the democratic way of life.

Social Studies Resource Books and Articles

Billman, Jane. 1992. "The Native American Curriculum: Attempting Alternatives to Teepees and Headbands." *Young Children* 47(6): 22–25.

Carlsson-Paige, N., and D. Levin. N.d. *Helping Children Understand Peace, War, and the Nuclear Threat*. Washington DC: National Association for the Education of Young Children.

Fredericks, Anthony. 1991. *Social Studies through Children's Literature: An Integrated Approach*. Englewood, CO: Teacher Ideas Press.

Greenberg, Polly. 1992. "Teaching about Native Americans? Or Teaching about People, Including Native Americans?" *Young Children* 47(6): 27–30.

Harvey, Karen, Lisa Harjo, and Jane Jackson. 1990. *Teaching about Native Americans*. Bulletin no. 84. Washington, DC: National Council for the Social Studies. ED 325 413.

National Council for Geographic Education. 1987. *K–6 Geography: Themes, Key Ideas, and Learning Opportunities*. Geographic Education National Implementation Project. Macomb, IL: Western Illinois University. ED 288 807.

National Council for the Social Studies. 1992. "Curriculum Guidelines for Multicultural Education—A Position Statement." *Social Education* (September): 316–36.

Science

The National Science Teachers Association is launching a comprehensive change in strategy to help local school districts improve elementary science programs. *Standards Basic to Good Elementary School Science Teaching* are currently being developed.

An Early Start to Science, by Roy Richards, Margaret Collis, and Doug Kincaid. 1990. Hemel-Hempstead, UK: Macdonald Educational. Available from Teacher's Laboratory, Inc., P.O. Box 6480, Brattleboro, VT 05301-6480. 802-254-3457. 80p.

Although this colorful picture book is an activity book, it is unique. It contains an educationally appropriate, comprehensive collection of science experiences (observing, manipulating, comparing, organizing, questioning, testing, and looking for patterns), and recommends several ideas for themes and collections. This book can provide teachers with a broad array of ideas from which to begin to lead children toward an in-depth study of a topic (see chapter 9).

GrowLab: Activities for Growing Minds. 1990. Available from National Gardening Association, 180 Flynn Avenue, Burlington, VT 05401. 802-863-1308. 307p.

This K–8 curriculum guide was developed by the National Gardening Association for use with an indoor classroom garden. It is designed to stimulate an appreciation of the environment while involving children in hands-on, long-term projects. The experiences are built around four life-science concepts: the miracle of life from seed to plant, life cycles and plant reproduction, diversity of life, and interdependence in the global garden.

Activities are designed to reflect a variety of teaching styles, learning styles, and classroom conditions, with suggestions for both thematic units and long-term projects. Recommended grade ranges and integrated curriculum opportunities are also covered. Appendices include reproducibles in the whole-language tradition, such as graphing and keeping a journal; an annotated resource list of books for children and teachers; ordering information for seeds; and information on the network of GrowLab users and support partners.

High/Scope K–3 Curriculum Series: Science, by Frank Blackwell and Charles Hohmann. 1990. Available from High/Scope Press, 600 North River Street, Ypsilanti, MI 48198. 313-485-2000. 208p. $22.00 per copy.

This curriculum views science learning as an active process of doing and experiencing, based on the view that children construct knowledge during the process of active learning. The key experiences for science are observing; classifying and ordering; measuring, testing, and analyzing; observing, predicting, and controlling change; designing, building, fabricating, and modifying structures or materials; and reporting and interpreting data and results. The process of learning through the key experiences is centered on three broad themes: life and environment, structure and form, and energy and change.

The teacher uses both direct and indirect teaching strategies, allowing children to take responsibility for much of their learning through the plan–do–review process. Appendices include an extensive list of recommended materials for science and a checklist of progress through the key experiences. Each suggested learning activity includes a list of materials, the key experiences related to the activity, exten-

sions, additional possibilities, and related readings.

Hands-On Nature: Information and Activities for Exploring the Environment with Children, by Jenepher Linglebach. ED 278 558. For more information, contact the Vermont Institute of Natural Science, Woodstock, VT 05091.

The goal of this book is to promote successful teaching of environmental education through innovative integrated workshops for children. It is organized into four chapters: adaptations (insects, tooth types, frogs, thorns, and threats), habitats (field, forest floor, snow, streams), cycles (trees, winter weeds, bird songs), and designs of nature (snowflakes, camouflage, honeybees). Each chapter includes suggested activities such as field trips, visits by experts, puppet shows, stories to read aloud, and lists of children's books appropriate to each topic. A list of sources for materials, a glossary, and a bibliography are provided. *Hands-On Nature* offers a wide array of ideas from which to suggest long-term study of a topic.

Investigating Science with Young Children, by Rosemary Althouse. 1988. ED 302 399. Available from Teachers College Press, 1234 Amsterdam Avenue, New York, NY 10027. 200p. $17.95 per copy.

Althouse believes that process science is an open-ended approach, recognizing that the direction learning will take should be determined largely by the children. Part 1 gives concise background information on the importance of science, a summary of current understanding of how children learn, the possibilities that a topic offers for active learning, how to gain familiarity with suitable materials, and information about effective teaching methods. Part 2 presents eighty-five activities for topics such as water, pets, balance, foods, sand, motion, seeds, bubbles, and others. Lists of materials, procedures, and process skills are included for each activity. Many suggestions in this book, such as the study of boxes or setting objects in motion, may lend themselves to topics for long-term projects.

Science for Children: Resources for Teachers, by the National Science Resource Center. 1992. ED 303 320 (1988 ed.). Available from National Academy Press, 2101 Constitution Avenue NW, P.O. Box 285, Washington, DC 20055. 180p. $9.95 per copy. This comprehensive resource guide has been prepared as a joint effort of the National Academy of Sciences and the Smithsonian Institution.

There are sections for each of the content area categories of teaching science: life science, health and human biology, earth science, physical science, multidisciplinary, and applied science. The guide includes chapters on curriculum materials, supplementary resources (activity books, books on teaching science, and magazines for children and teachers), and sources of information and assistance (museums and science technology centers, professional associations, ideas for science projects, and lists of publishers and suppliers of science books and materials). For each annotated entry there is also ordering information, addresses and telephone numbers, recommended grade level, and price.

Life Lab Science Curriculum, Grades K–3. 1992. Available from Videodiscovery, Inc., 1700 Westlake Avenue N., Suite 600, Seattle, WA 98109-3021. $3,500.00 per copy.

Videodiscs and barcode scanners, hypercards and linkways! High technology in early childhood education! Although children and teachers can learn science using a garden as the framework at considerably less expense, the videodisc technology allows children to come as close to real experiences as possible through close-up video field trips that, for example, visit an open-air market; walk through a rain forest; observe timber being cut; watch an insect devour a leaf; or examine the workings of a commercial bakery, a recycling plant, and a tornado.

For each video field trip there are garden-related activities and experiences. Student lab books contain innovative worksheets with a whole-language flavor. Children are encouraged to write about or create with media their experiences and to do observational drawings of specific insects or animals as part of the learning process. Science concepts and process skills are developed as children study topics such as soil, water, seeds, plants, garden animals, climate and weather, life cycles, food

chains, and conservation. Year-long themes characterize each grade level: kindergarten, exploration; first grade, diversity and cycles; second grade, change; and third grade, structure and form. *The Life Lab Science Curriculum* is one of the programs recommended by the National Diffusion Network of the United States Department of Education.

The Young Child as Scientist, by Christine Chaille and Lory Britain. 1991. New York: HarperCollins. 166p.

The authors have combined research on cognitive and physical development with activities and techniques for developing science awareness. The text is designed to encourage meaningful intellectual exercises for young children. It includes hundreds of questions to stimulate thinking in the teacher before introducing an idea and for children while they are exploring.

Anecdotal examples of both appropriate and inappropriate experiences are provided. It is based on the constructivist perspective and treats the child as a theory builder. The process approach enables children to learn concepts and skills and to be challenged to think and process information in a useful manner. This book will be useful as a resource for the Project Approach (see chapter 9).

Science Resource Books and Articles

Gardner, Robert, and David Webster. 1987. *Science in Your Backyard.* New York: Simon & Schuster.

Holt, Bess-Gene. 1985. *Science with Young Children.* Washington, DC: National Association for the Education of Young Children.

Lind, Karen. 1990. *Exploring Science in Early Childhood: A Developmental Approach.* Albany, NY: Delmar.

Perdue, Peggy. 1989. *Small Wonders. Hands-on Science Activities for Young Children.* Glenview, IL: Good Year Books. ED 309 961.

———. 1991. *Schoolyard Science: Grades 2–4.* Glenview IL: Scott, Foresman. ED 324 221.

Rivkin, Mary, ed. 1992. "Science Is a Way of Life." *Young Children* 47(4): 4–8. EJ 447 664.

Rockwell, Robert, Elizabeth Sherwood, and Robert Williams. 1983. *Hug a Tree and Other Things To Do Outdoors with Young Children.* Mt. Rainier, MD: Gryphon.

———. 1992. *Everybody Has a Body: Science from Head to Toe.* Mt. Rainier, MD: Gryphon.

Siversten, Mary Lewis. 1990. *Science Education Programs that Work: A Collection of Proven Exemplary Educational Programs and Practices in the National Diffusion Network.* Washington, DC: Office of Educational Research and Improvement, U.S. Department of Education ED 327 376.

Smithsonian Family Learning Project. 1987. *Science Activity Book.* New York: GMG.

Sprung, Barbara, Merle Froschl, and Patricia Campbell. 1985. *What Will Happen If . . . Young Children and the Scientific Method.* U.S. Department of Education Women's Educational Equity Act Program. Mt. Rainier, MD: Gryphon. ED 275 513.

U.S. Department of Education. 1991. *Helping Your Child Learn Science.* Pueblo, CO: Consumer Information Center. ED 331 727.

Winnett, David, Robert Williams, Elizabeth Sherwood, and Robert Rockwell. In press. *Discovery Science: Explorations for the Early Years (Kindergarten).* San Francisco: Addison-Wesley.

The Arts

Children and the Arts: A Sourcebook of Arts Experiences for Pre-Kindergarten Early Intervention Programs. 1990. ED 330 454. Available from the Florida Department of Education, Educational Materials, Collins Building, Room B-1, Tallahassee, FL 32399-0400. 904-488-7101. 52p. $2.00 per copy.
Although this inexpensive "how-to" guide was written for prekindergarten children, it offers kindergarten and primary teachers with little or no experience in the arts an introduction to integrating the arts into the curriculum. Four areas are included: music, drama, dance/movement, and visual arts. Each art area provides age-appropriate activities, a dozen do's, lesson plans, recommended supplies, and a list of resources. A companion volume for school-age child care programs may provide teachers of older children with activities more appropriate for them. Information for teachers interested in workshops on implementation are available from the University of Central Florida College of Education.

Creative Drama in the Classroom: Grades 1–3, by June Cottrell. 1987. Lincolnwood, IL: National Textbook. 242p.
Teachers are taught to create a holistic, integrated, child-centered environment that includes drama. Topics covered include a rationale for studying theater arts, the creative drama process, strategies for leading, storytelling, terminology, creative movement, theater games involving nonverbal expression, pantomime, role playing, story dramatization, improvisation, and puppetry. Also covered are ways to integrate drama into the content areas using mathematics, science, literature, language arts, history, current events, and foreign language. A chapter on helping children become consumers of theater arts and the role and responsibilities of the child as a member of the audience is included, as well as insight on how to include children with special needs.

Creative Experiences: An Arts Curriculum for Young Children Including Those with Special Needs, by Belinda Broughton. 1986. ED 331 634. Available from Chapel Hill Training-Outreach Project, Lincoln Center, 800 Eastowne Drive, Suite 105, Chapel Hill, NC 27514. 253p. $25.00 per copy.
This curriculum guide provides 112 learning activities equally distributed across the areas of creative movement, drama, music, and the visual arts, and is correlated with the Learning Accomplishment Profile. It has been designed to be especially useful in mainstream classrooms, and includes suggestions for modifications in five areas of impairment: hearing, mental, physical, speech, and visual. Each activity is outlined by title, related skills, materials, procedure, suggested modifications, and variations for enrichment activities.

Current Issues in Art and Design Education: From Entertainment to Qualitative Experience, by Rob Barnes. 1989. *Journal of Art and Design Education* 8(3): 247-55.
Ways that quality art education can be fostered in primary schools are discussed in this article,

which specifies that curricula emphasizing disconnected activities and entertainment should be avoided. Several suggestions are made on how classroom teachers and art specialists can work together, such as by using shared teaching terminology.

Early Childhood ART: Activities, Resources, Techniques. 1991. Available from Binney and Smith, 1100 Church Lane, P.O. Box 431, Easton, PA 18045-0431. 215-253-6271. No charge.

This concise guide to visual art in early childhood addresses the need for developmentally appropriate art activities and provides ideas for integrating art throughout the curriculum. The topics encompass approaches to art, integrating art into the curriculum, involving parents as partners in art education, empowerment through art, using crayons, markers, paint, and fingerpaint, amazing art, and guidelines for selecting supplies.

Leading Young Children to Music, by B. Joan Haines and Linda Gerber. 1992. 4th ed. New York: Merrill/Macmillan.

Based on the belief that music is every child's birthright, this guide provides musical and music-related experiences for preschoolers through eight-year-olds. The materials can be used by music specialists and classroom teachers, and are adaptable to the abilities of the teacher and the children. Sections on children's development of music and background for teachers are followed by chapters on rhyme, singing, moving, playing instruments, and listening. New chapters include Music and Whole Language and Songs in Spanish. Several appendices provide additional background information on music notation, teaching strategies, the autoharp and the guitar, and sources and resources.

Music, A Way of Life for the Young Child, by Kathleen Bayless and Marjorie Ramsey. 1991. 4th ed. New York: Merrill/Macmillan.

This guide to music for children from infancy to kindergarten is based on the belief that music is a vital and necessary dimension in the lives of the very young. Musical concepts and activities are arranged by age level. Developmental levels, key ideas, songs, chants, rhythms, movement, activities, resources, and questions to consider are included for each age level. Suggestions are offered for establishing a music listening center for 4–6-year-olds. There are additional chapters on children with special needs, integrating music throughout the day, and music as a child's heritage. Included are appendices on musical terminology, resource materials, a practical approach to learning to play the autoharp, and fingering charts for guitar and soprano recorder. The book provides a rich resource of music content, but Bayless and Ramsey also stress the importance of encouraging children to have fun and be creative with music.

Learning from the Inside Out: The Expressive Arts, by Steve Hoffman, and Linda Lamme, eds. 1989. Urbana, IL: National Council of Teachers of English. 96p. $12.95 per copy.

This book highlights the powerful learning connections that can be made when cognitive and affective experiences blend with the expressive arts. Included are ways to involve children in story enactment, puppetry, dance, and other arts.

Arts Resource Books and Articles

Baker, David. 1990. "The Visual Arts in Early Childhood Education. *Design for Arts in Education* 91(6): 21–25. EJ 419 183.

Ballard, Dana. 1990. "Arts Every Day: The Public Elementary School Curriculum." *Design for Arts in Education* 91(6): 42–48. EJ 419 186.

Brown, Victoria. 1990. "Drama as an Integral Part of the Early Childhood Curriculum." *Design for Arts in Education* 91(6): 26–33. EJ 419 184.

Clemens, Sydney. 1991. "Art in the Classroom: Making Every Day Special." *Young Children* 46(2): 4–11. EJ 426 216.

Eisner, Elliot. 1991. "What Really Counts in Schools." *Educational Leadership* 48(5): 10–17. EJ 421 343.

Feierabend, John. 1990. "Music in Early Childhood." *Design for Arts in Education* 91(6): 15–20. EJ 419 182.

Szekely, G. 1990. "An Introduction to Art: Children's Books." *Childhood Education* 66(3): 132–38. EJ 410 743.

Stinson, Susan. 1990. "Dance Education in Early Childhood." *Design for Arts in Education* 91(6): 34–42. EJ 419 185.

Weikart, Phyllis. 1989. *Movement Plus Music: Activities for Children Ages 3 to 7.* 2d ed. Ypsilanti, MI: High/Scope Press.

Computer Software

High/Scope Buyer's Guide to Children's Software 1992, by William Buckleitner. Available from High/Scope Press, 600 N. River Street, Ypsilanti, MI 48198-2898. 313-485-2000. 268p. $19.95.

The annual survey of computer programs for children ages three to seven provides a review of more than five hundred software programs for use with preschool and primary children. In addition to a description, an explanation is given about why a program is developmentally appropriate for young children. Included are software descriptions, ratings, award-winning programs, listings of software by content area and brand, a glossary, and a directory of software producers.

Computer Learning for Young Children (videotape). 1989. Available from High/Scope Press, 600 North River Street, Ypsilanti, MI 48198-2898. $35 rental, $65 purchase. Color, 13 min.

This step-by-step guide to introducing children to computers covers purchasing hardware, selecting appropriate software, and integrating computers into the learning environment and daily routine.

Computer-Related
Resource Books and Articles

Burns, M. Susan, Laura Goin, and Jan Donlon. 1990. "A Computer in My Room." *Young Children* 45(2): 62–69. EJ 402 925.

Clements, Douglas. 1987. "Computers and Young Children: A Review of Research." *Young Children* 43(1): 34–44. EJ 363 920.

————. 1991. "Current Technology and the Early Childhood Curriculum." In *Issues in Early Childhood Curriculum: Yearbook in Early Childhood Education,* ed. B. Spodek and O. Saracho, vol. 2. New York: Teachers College Press.

Haugland, S., and D. Shade. 1990. *Developmental Evaluations Software for Young Children.* Albany, NY: Delmar.

Hohmann, Charles. 1990. *Young Children and Computers.* Ypsilanti, MI: High/Scope Press.

Merrill, P., et al. 1986. *Computers in Education.* Englewood Cliffs, NJ: Prentice-Hall.

Pea, Roy, and Karen Sheingold. 1987. *Mirrors of Minds: Patterns of Experience in Educational Computing.* Norwood, NJ: Ablex. ED 292 622.

Pennsylvania Department of Education. 1984. *Computers and Young Children: A Position Paper and Resource Guide.* Harrisburg, PA.

Schlenker, Richard. 1990. *Integrating Data Base into the Elementary School Science Program.* Washington, DC: Department of Defense Dependents Schools. ED 324 219.

Professional Journals
for Teachers of Young Children

Most professional organizations publish a journal of articles on topics of interest to members. Subscription to a journal is often a benefit of membership, but journals are also usually available individually for a fee (prices in the following descriptions are for one-year subscriptions, unless noted otherwise). The following list of publications have principally a practical focus rather than a research or theoretical one.

Art to Zoo: News from the Smithsonian Institution. A quarterly journal, each issue provides background information, a lesson plan, classroom activities, and resources for further information on a science, art, or social studies topic. Contact the Office of Elementary and Secondary Education, the Smithsonian Institution, Washington, DC 20560. No charge.

Arithmetic Teacher. Nine issues a year, September through May. For teachers K–8 and teacher educators. National Council of Teachers of Mathematics, 1906 Association Drive, Reston, VA 22091-1593. 703-620-9840. $40 individual, $45 institution.

Childhood Education. Issues affecting young children in public school settings from infancy through middle childhood. Articles range from practical to conceptual. Association for Childhood Education International, 11141 Georgia Avenue, Suite 200, Wheaton, MD 20902. 800-423-3563. $45 individual, $23 retired, $78 institution, $26 student.

High/Scope Extensions. Six issues a year, each 8p. This newsletter of the High/Scope Curriculum covers a range of curriculum issues, including timely information on the latest in early childhood and computer learning activities and programs. $30.

Journal of Computing in Childhood Education. A quarterly journal of the Association for the Advancement of Computers in Education. This journal is a refereed, noncommercial resource for early childhood-education teachers, curriculum developers, and administrators. It is a primary information source and forum in which to discuss practical suggestions and theoretical issues involving computer research and applications in preschool and primary education. Available from JCCE, P.O. Box 2966, Charlottesville, VA 22902. $36 individual, $58 institution.

Language Arts. A journal of the National Council of Teachers of English, 111 Kenyan Drive, Urbana, IL 61801. 217-328-3870. $40 individual, $50 institution.

Music Educators Journal. A publication of the Music Educators National Conference, 1902 Association Drive, Reston, VA 22091. 703-860-4000. $45.

Science and Children. This journal serves elementary science teachers but includes features of interest to early childhood education. Available from the National Science Teachers Association, 1742 Connecticut Avenue. NW, Washington, DC 20009. 202-328-5800. $50.

Smithsonian Spectrum. This annual publication describes services of the Smithsonian Institution's individual museum education departments. While targeted primarily at Washington, DC–area teachers (preK–12), it is also useful to teachers visiting the area. Includes information on field trips and gives addresses and phone numbers of museum education departments. Contact the Smithsonian Institution, Washington, DC 20560. No charge.

Social Studies and the Young Learner. A quarterly publication devoted to social studies from kindergarten through grade 6, it

provides teaching techniques designed to stimulate reading, writing, and critical thinking in children. Contact the National Council for the Social Studies, 3501 Newark Street. NW, Washington, DC 20016. 202-966-7840. $50 individual, $60 institution.

Teaching PreK–8. Published by Early Years, Inc., 40 Richards Avenue, Norwalk, CT 06854. No price available.

The Reading Teacher. From the International Reading Association, 800 Barksdale Road, Newark, DE 19714-8139. 302-731-1600. $38 individual, $41 institution.

Young Children. The official journal of NAEYC is published six times a year to provide a forum for discussion of major issues and ideas, provoke thought, and promote professional growth in the field of early childhood education and care. Available from the National Association for the Education of Young Children, 1509 16th Street NW, Washington, DC 20036. 800-424-2460 or 202-232-8777. $25 individual.

Other Resources for Curriculum Guides

Corporations

Many corporations have educational resources; for example, telephone companies often lend communications kits, including telephones, and hospitals provide field trips and print materials for teachers on topics related to health and careers in the medical field. Manufacturers often offer resources related to the product they produce, such as textiles, food products, or other consumer goods.

Museums, State Parks, and Zoos

These entities frequently have education departments with resource materials available, including study guides, newsletters for teachers, videotapes, computer software, and real objects to lend.

National Diffusion Network

This service offered by a branch of the U.S. Department of Education, makes exemplary educational programs available to schools, colleges, and other institutions. It does this by providing funds to exemplary programs called Dissemination Process Projects to make schools aware of their programs and to provide training, materials, and follow-up assistance to schools who implement them. Information can be obtained from the U.S. Department of Education, Recognition Division, 555 New Jersey Avenue NW, Washington, DC 20208-5645. 202-219-2134.

Public Libraries

Information on virtually any topic can be gleaned from public libraries; additional resources are available from libraries with interlibrary loan arrangements.

State Bureaus

Your state's and others' departments of energy and natural resources, conservation, historic preservation, transportation, health, education, and so forth can prove to be good sources of resource materials.

Smithsonian Institution— Resource Guide for Teachers

The biannual catalog from the Office of Elementary and Secondary Education lists the educational materials and resources (such as publications and audiovisual materials, preK–12) available from the Smithsonian's sixteen museums, the National Zoo, the Kennedy Center, the National Gallery of Art, and Reading Is Fundamental. For more information contact the Office of Elementary and Secondary Education, Arts & Industries Building—Room 1163, Washington, DC 20560. 202-357-3049. No charge.

PROJECTS IN THE EARLY CHILDHOOD CURRICULUM

Eileen Tracy Borgia
Doctoral Student in Early Childhood Education
University of Illinois at Urbana–Champaign, Urbana, Illinois

THE importance of using an integrated curriculum in early childhood education has received increased recognition in recent years, and the integrated curriculum has been recommended throughout this handbook. Features of such a curriculum include: open-ended, interactive, meaningful learning experiences that are drawn from, and built upon, the child's experience; activities in which the subject matter is interrelated rather than presented in discrete units of learning; activities that are educationally, developmentally, and culturally appropriate; and activities in which the processes of learning are valued as much as the acquisition of content or skills.

Most early childhood educators believe that young children learn by interacting with materials and people in an environment that supports their diverse developmental and intellectual abilities. There is also convincing evidence that children learn considerably by interacting with their peers as they develop skills of helping, negotiation, and cooperation. While there are many ways to integrate learning, the project approach offers some unique opportunities.

The Project Approach

Katz and Chard (1989) assert that children learn best when the content offered is meaningful for them, is authentic, is presented through firsthand experiences—in an informal environment of real materials and events—and is challenging enough that their minds are truly engaged. They suggest that one way to ensure that children have meaningful, interactive, and informal learning experiences is to encourage the long-term, in-depth study of a topic.

In the Project Approach children and teachers work together. They continuously plan and evaluate their work. Children are encouraged to make some of the major decisions about what is to be done, and they learn while investigating a topic of interest to them. The knowledge and skills expected of the children by the school district or state department of education are incorporated into the children's activities.

Some Examples

In *Explorers' Classrooms* (1992), Elizabeth Shores describes a variety of marvelous projects that have been completed recently by kindergarten and primary children in several elementary schools in five Southern states. For example, after reading *The Legend of Bluebonnet,* by Tomie DePaola, in which a child sacrifices a beloved doll to the Great Spirits in a prayer for rain, two children work together to create their own doll. This inspires other children to make a wizard doll based on the book, *How Much Is a Million?* In another classroom, a project on apples includes studying the gradual decay of an apple—measuring, weighing, and observing changes each day, making patterns of apples of different colors and sizes, and writing stories about apples.

Shores also reports on second graders in an Austin, Texas, school who created a xeriscape, a garden requiring very little water. They explored the life sciences (finding appropriate seeds, plants, and insects); moved gravel and timber; built a fence and a compost pile; and, in presenting their project, they practiced writing, public speaking, music, art, and photography. In addition, they learned about wind, weather, construction, the environment, planning, and cooperative work.

In another example, Shores tells of Travis and Nick, two students in Kelly Marcum's multi-age class who wrote *Our Boat,* their own book based both on their experiences and on their reading of a story called *My Boat.* Shores writes:

> Marcum's classroom schedule allowed Travis and Nick the time to work together and independently, researching marine life for their book, writing the story, illustrating it page by page, and finally "publishing" the book by making covers and binding the book. They worked on *Our Boat* for at least a week, perhaps first discovering *My Boat* when their teacher read it to the class, then working together and independently to draft and publish their own version. (57)

Projects and Play: Similar but Different

Educational experiences in early childhood include opportunities for children to play, because it is through the natural medium of play that children make sense of their world, increase competence, express feelings, commu-nicate, and grow and develop. Dramatic play, blocks, sand and water, art and music materials, climbing and wheel toys, and manipulatives support children's informal learning in ways that are meaningful and important.

Although there are similarities, project work is different than play. Katz and Chard (1989) believe that project work is more purposeful. Children's activity is more focused, and long periods of time are spent investigating the topic. The ways in which they inquire into the topic are meaningful and pleasurable. Children's participation is usually voluntary, providing opportunities for children to make choices and decisions. Projects frequently involve the materials of play—sand, clay, paint, wood, dramatic play props, small toys, blocks, books, and writing materials.

Benefits of the Project Approach

With the Project Approach, the teacher spends much of his/her time guiding and facilitating learning, and although children receive direct instruction as needed, it is less prominent than in traditional classrooms. Projects often last for a long time—more than a few days or weeks—depending on the age of the children and the amount of interest that is sustained. The idea for a project emerges from the dynamic interplay between the interests of the children and those of the teacher. Since they also provide continuous challenges for teachers, projects have potential for making a teacher's work interesting and professionally satisfying.

Webster (1990) points out that the use of project work is not new in early childhood education. Open Education, the Piagetian curriculum, Dewey's thematic activities, and the Bank Street model all include project work. The British Infant Schools used the approach as a central focus of curriculum during the Plowden years (late 60s to early 70s; see Plowden 1967). In American schools, however, projects have often been limited to an auxiliary activity that children can work on "after their work is completed," or as an extra-credit activity. Nevertheless, projects are beginning to emerge in early childhood classrooms as a major focus of the curriculum rather than as an addition.

When children are engaged in a project, they are challenged to use all of their senses and as many skills as possible in the process of learning. They might draw, write a report or a letter, interview an "expert," create a structure, write and perform a play, develop charts, graphs, or diagrams, speak to a group, or create an interesting display to share what they have learned with classmates and parents.

There are opportunities for children of varying abilities and age levels to have successful learning experiences through projects. Examples of children's work can be collected for assessment purposes, enabling teachers to accumulate samples and have a firsthand look at what a child is capable of doing. Using project work as a way of learning has been recommended by Howard Gardner (1992). He proposes that humans do not have one overall intelligence but are capable of at least seven different and independent forms of intellectual accomplishment: linguistic, logical-mathematical, spatial, musical, bodily-kinesthetic, interpersonal, and intrapersonal. He believes that one of the most effective ways for children to develop their various intelligences, work with peers, and present information in forms other than writing is by using the Project Approach.

Projects at Reggio Emilia

Recently, early childhood educators from throughout the world have traveled to Reggio Emilia, Italy, to see for themselves how in-depth projects have become a way of life for the children, their teachers, and the community in the preprimary schools administered by the municipality of Reggio Emilia.

Topics of interest to a few children, or to the entire school, are studied in depth and over long periods of time. Some projects are inspired by an interest of the children, and some of them evolve as a result of the teachers' persistent and insightful observation of the children and their educational needs.

Among the projects undertaken there recently are the study of the stone lions in the piazza; investigations of shadow, light, and shade; the planets; the life-forms that live in a field of wildflowers; and rain. A project involving the design of birdhouses extended into the full-blown construction of an "amusement park for birds" in the play yard of one of the schools.

Reflecting on her two early visits to Reggio Emilia, Lilian Katz (1990) wrote:

> I cannot recall having seen anywhere before, preschool children's work of such high quality as in Reggio Emilia. The dimensions of quality include the depth and thoroughness with which children explore a topic, and especially the attention to detail and the care with which their feelings, reactions, ideas, thoughts, observations, and findings are expressed and communicated; the variety of materials and media used for this is stunning. Teachers take an active role in encouraging and helping children explore the possibilities of a wide variety of materials and media. But most important, teachers do not underestimate children's capacities for sustained effort in achieving understanding of what they are exploring; nor do they underestimate children's abilities to capture and depict these understandings through a variety of art forms. (11)

Teachers and parents who are comfortable with the traditional, standard curriculum, whole-class, desks-in-rows, systematic instruction using textbooks, and similar one-dimensional materials models of classroom environment, may find it difficult to trust that learning through the Project Approach can be effective or feasible.

Stages of Project Work

Describing the stages of a project can highlight the learning potential inherent in the Project Approach. In Phase I, children and teachers discuss the topic. Using their own knowledge and experiences, they talk about, paint, draw, write, dramatize, and role play what they know about the topic. A *topic web* is developed to map the concepts the children already know about the subject. This forms a baseline of knowledge about a topic. (See Figure 1 for examples of topic webs.)

Firsthand experiences and the use of resource materials are important components of project work. The experiences should provide

FIGURE 1.   TOPIC WEBS

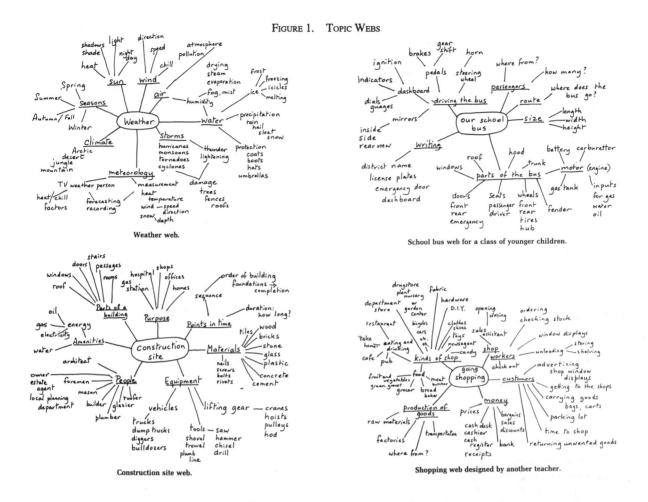

Weather web.

School bus web for a class of younger children.

Construction site web.

Shopping web designed by another teacher.

Source: Lilian G. Katz and Sylvia C. Chard, *Engaging Children's Minds:*
The Project Approach (Norwood, NJ: Ablex, 1989). Reproduced with permission.

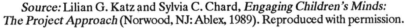

the children with new knowledge, rather than merely repeat things the children already know.

In Phase 2, fieldwork, children are involved in planning as well as in doing the project. Fieldwork includes many discussions and negotiations among the children, including development of questions based on what children are interested in knowing about the topic. Arrangements are made for children to interact with real objects and processes related to their topic of interest. Usually this is done by inviting an expert to meet with the children or by planning a field trip.

Experts—people with knowledge, skills, and experience related to the topic—are invited to come in to the school, or children visit them. They share their expertise with the students. A field trip might also be arranged. Children take field notes, make observational drawings, and photograph or videotape the people, events, objects, or processes they visit. When they

return to the classroom, they use the representational materials to continue the learning process long after a trip has taken place.

While they work on the project, children practice the skills that they are learning from more traditional areas of instruction, such as conversing, negotiating, interviewing, reading, writing, using mathematics, and doing library research. It is the additional experiences included in project work that make it unique. Children might engage in dramatic play; build a structure of wood, clay, or discarded materials; draw and paint what they have seen or learned; write a story; keep a journal; compose poetry or music; write letters; or develop a game, graph, chart or diagram. The products are displayed throughout the room and enhance the learning environment throughout the duration of the project.

In Phase 3, the work that has been accomplished is reviewed and evaluated, and representative samples of the work are selected. Children and teachers collaborate as samples of children's drawings, three-dimensional structures, music, plays, graphs, and other materials are arranged in an attractive display. Parents and children from other classes are invited to view the displayed work and listen while the children present reports about what they have learned during the project. (Katz and Chard 1989; Chard 1992b)

In the following vignette, Sylvia Chard (1992b) describes a class of kindergarten and first-grade children as they work on a project on the topic of rain. Note the traditional learning activities one would expect to find in any classroom of five- and six-year-olds, plus some that do not usually occur.

A Project on Rain
The children are working in groups and on their own, in different parts of the classroom and in the yard just outside. In the corner of the room is a dramatic play area which has been set up as a shop. There is a big notice the children have made which says, "The Rain Shop". Two children are arranging raincoats, hats, boots, and umbrellas on hangers and shelves. Another child is discussing prices with a "cashier" at the little checkout counter.

It has rained earlier in the day. By the window in the room, one child is writing a poem about the rain. She has first made a list of rain words, "falling, drops, pattering, windows, grey, puddles..." Three children are painting pictures of rainy scenes. Two children are drawing chalk lines around puddles in the yard and measuring the distance across the puddles in various directions. The puddles are drying up and at half hour intervals, these children draw new chalk lines recording the evaporation rate of the water during the morning. They also draw the puddles' decreasing circumferences on paper so that they will be able to tell the other children of their work at the class meeting at the end of the morning.

The teacher is working with six children at a table in the middle of the classroom. There are jars, bowls, elastic bands, pitchers of water, and several different kinds of material and fabric on the table. The children are experimenting to see which materials let the water through faster and which materials seem to be the most water proof. The teacher is encouraging close observation of the effect of the water on the fabrics. One of the children is writing down words used to describe what is happening. Another child has predicted that the water would be best kept out by very thick fabric. Testing that hypothesis leads to further study of absorbency. Someone investigates in a larger bowl how the more absorbent fabrics behave when squeezed and immersed in the water. The children are fascinated by the way the water is soaked up by a thick wooly mitten.

Several books on rain, water, and the weather have been borrowed from the library. A group of children sitting in the book area are reading to one another from the books and discussing what they are reading about. On a table nearby, there is an umbrella. Four children are drawing the umbrella with pencils and felt tip pens.

At the end of the morning, before the children leave the room for lunch they review the work they have been doing. One child tells of the book he was reading, another talks about events in "the rain shop". One of the group involved in the science activities with the teacher tells of their findings. The children measuring the shrinking puddles in the yard talk about their drawings. Later in the day there will be time for further review and for the story the teacher has planned to read about a family that gets caught in a rain storm while having a picnic by a lake. (3) (Reprinted with permission).

Criteria for Selecting Topics

Project work involves intensive investigation of a topic during which children gain knowledge while they practice skills. It is essential that the information the children accumulate be worthwhile and meaningful. Katz (1990b) suggests that the following criteria be considered when selecting a topic:

1. The subject matter is real, is related to the children's own everyday, first-hand experience, and will be useful to the children in later life experiences. It should be familiar enough that children can show initiative in exploring it and teachers can identify experts, plan field trips, and find resources for activities.

2. It is more suitable for learning *in* school than *out of school.*
3. It allows for integration of a range of subjects or disciplines, i.e., science, social studies, mathematics, music, art, reading, etc.
4. Real objects rather than abstract concepts are studied.
5. There is sufficient potential for exploration and investigation over a period of at least a week, ideally longer.
6. Opportunities are provided for problem solving, decision making, collaboration, cooperation, writing, drawing, using the computer, painting, making models, construction, and dramatic play.
7. Parents can contribute in some way.

Resources for Projects

There are distinctions between units or themes and projects. Projects are seldom repeated from year to year in exactly the same fashion, and they are rarely conceived exclusively by the teacher. It is less likely, therefore, that a specific resource book or unit will provide the information suited to a particular project. The best resources will be accumulated after the topic has been proposed and explored through Phase 1 (Chard 1992a).

Among the best resources for young children are the world around them, the school library, the public library, and experts—people who have information on a topic by virtue of their intense interest in it as a hobby or a livelihood. Encyclopedias and online data bases can be useful sources of information, and a well informed librarian will be most valuable in helping locate resources suited to the chosen topic. Many titles listed in chapter 8 of this handbook will also be useful. The following are additional resources for doing project work.

Project Work: A Short List of Annotated Resources

Abell, J., and J. Newman. 1988. *Learning Outdoors: Leader Guide, Grade 3, 4-H*

Discovery. Pullman, WA: Washington State University, Cooperative Extension Service. 47p. ED 315 290.
Although written as a leader's guide for 4-H groups, this book contains information and resources for conducting in-depth projects on the conservation of natural resources such as air, marine life, energy, forestry, range, soil, water, and wildlife. It includes suggestions for hiking, outdoor safety, keeping a field notebook, and outdoor manners.

Allison, Linda. 1989. *The Sierra Club Summer Book.* San Francisco: Sierra Club Books/ Little, Brown. Available from Sierra Club, 730 Polk Street, San Francisco, CA 94109.
This idea book suggests projects children might explore during the free time of summer vacation. Topics included are gardening, birds, insects, sleeping out, crafts, conservation, and trips. Many activities are clever and easy to do, such as making homemade "shades," sun dials, and stone sculptures, but there are also many ideas that can be the stimulus for the investigation of a topic as a long-term project.

Art to Zoo: News from the Smithsonian Institution. Washington, DC: Office of Elementary and Secondary Education. Smithsonian Institution, Washington, DC 20560.
Schools can be placed on the mailing list free of charge for this quarterly periodical, which provides teachers with current background information on topics such as rain forests, sculptures, animals, water, and the like. Each issue focuses on a science, art, or social studies topic selected for that issue, and provides background information, resources, photographs, and interesting activities.

Carter, Constance. May 1990. *Environmental Science Projects. LC Science Tracer Bullet.* Washington, DC: Library of Congress, Science and Technology Division. ED 324 209.
This literature guide compiled by the Library of Congress, primarily for junior and senior high school students and teachers, assists in planning, preparing, and executing science fair projects in the environmental sciences. Lists of books and resources are provided under the following headings: classroom experiments and activities, handbooks, manuals, bibliographies,

book/film reviews, journals, and selected materials. Although the material may be more suited to older children, it is included here since it might lead teachers to other more appropriate resources.

Chard, Sylvia. 1992. *The Project Approach: A Practical Guide for Teachers.* Edmonton: The University of Alberta. Available from Department of Elementary Education, B-117 Education North, University of Alberta, Edmonton, Alberta, Canada T6G 2G5. 70p. $9.00 per copy.
Sylvia Chard offers practical applications to the original book that she and Lilian Katz (1989) co-authored. Based on her actual work in classrooms, Chard uses a chart and list format to aid teachers in implementing the *Project Approach*. Among the issues addressed are distinctions between systematic instruction and project work; the classroom as a community of learners; distinctions between a project, a unit, and a theme; the process of making a topic web (with examples); a table to show the interaction of the phases, key events and children's work; and criteria for evaluating project work at each stage.
    Chard provides teachers with a useful reference guide, building on the theory and principles of teaching described so well in *Engaging Children's Minds: The Project Approach.* The book is geared more toward the implementation of projects for older children but will serve as a valuable resource to all teachers who are ready to try it.

Discovery. 1989. Washington, DC: The Education Resource Center. Available from the Office of Education P-700, National Air and Space Museum, Smithsonian Institution, Washington, DC 20560. 202-786-2109. 85p. ED 310 946.
This is one of several resource guides published by NASA. It presents project information for grades K–3 on the following topics related to flight: historical perspectives of flight; discovery vocabulary; previsit activities in preparation for a tour of the National Air and Space Museum; 48 classroom activities, including making models, time lines, puppets, dioramas, and other projects related to flight.

Also included is a list of Teacher Resource Centers established to provide educators with NASA-related materials, including publications, filmstrips, software, audiocassettes, videotapes, 35mm slides, and other reference materials.

Earthquakes: A Teacher's Package for Kindergarten–Grade 6. 1988. Available from the National Science Teachers Association, 1742 Connecticut Avenue, NW, Washington, DC 20009. 321p. $15.00 per copy. ED 304 306.
This series of hands-on experiences suggests materials readily available in classrooms and considers both scientific and folkloric explanations for earthquakes. It includes defining, recognizing, measuring, legends, theories, and earthquake safety and survival. Although this topic may be more suited to third grade and older children, the study of earthquakes might provide an interesting topic for a project.

The Earthworks Group. 1990. *Fifty Simple Things Kids Can Do to Save the Earth.* Kansas City, MO: Andrews and McMeel Publishers, A Universal Press Syndicate Company. 156p. $6.95 per copy.
This upbeat resource is written for children to encourage their involvement in making the earth a better place. A brief introduction sets the stage by describing the problems: acid rain, air pollution, water pollution, the greenhouse effect, the ozone hole, garbage, and disappearing animals. In general, kids can save the earth by guarding our natural resources, protecting animals, keeping the earth green, using energy wisely, and communicating the problems and solutions. Each of these could form the basis for a most interesting project.

Global Issues Education Set. 1990. Washington: Global Tomorrow Coalition.
Of special interest to primary teachers, it contains activities and lesson plans to inform students at the primary and secondary levels (grades 3–12) about such global issues as biological diversity, tropical forests, sustainable development, ocean and coastal resources, and the biosphere.

Katz, Lilian, and Sylvia Chard. 1989. *Engaging Children's Minds: The Project Approach.* Norwood, NJ: Ablex.

A book that is inspiring change in early childhood curriculum, it has led the way in helping teachers implement the Project Approach. The first chapter introduces the idea and aims of projects and reasons why they should be included in the curriculum. Chapter 2, Research and Principles of Practice, provides a theoretical foundation. It includes discussion of Katz's four categories of learning goals (knowledge, skills, dispositions and feelings) the role of informality, and the importance of interaction in learning. Project Work in Action describes several projects: the weather, a construction site, the school bus. The remaining chapters provide practical suggestions for conducting projects in classrooms, from getting started, doing a concept web, and presenting the results in culminating activities. Appendices include examples of topic webs for projects and a description of a delightful project based on simply taking a walk around the school. *Engaging Children's Minds* is a landmark work, a valuable resource for teachers who want to venture forth with the Project Approach.

Shores, Elizabeth. 1992. *Explorers' Classrooms: Good Practice for Kindergarten and the Primary Grades.* Available from the Southern Association on Children Under Six, P.O. Box 5403, Little Rock, AR 72215-5403. 95p. $10.00 per copy.

See chapter 8 for a review of this book as an example of a curriculum guide for preK-3. The book comes to life with anecdotes recorded during on-site visits, action photographs, and examples of actual projects undertaken by the children and teachers in elementary school classrooms in five Southern states. *Explorer's Classrooms* utilizes newspapers extensively, and ideas for visitors, trips, and projects themselves are often sparked by articles children discover while reading their daily newspaper. A study of foods, a project on the Arkansas State Fair, projects based on children's literature, and one called "Second Grade Life" are a few of those described in this timely and innovative resource.

Project Work: Additional Publications

Bergstrom, Joan, and Craig Bergstrom. 1992. *All the Best Contests for Kids.* Berkeley, CA: Ten Speed Press.

Chard, Sylvia. 1992a. "How Do I Integrate the Curriculum Using the Project Approach?" In *Project Construct: Understanding the Possibilities*, ed. D. Murphy and S. Goffin. Jefferson City, MO: Missouri Department of Elementary and Secondary Education.

————. 1992b. "Display in the Classroom." Unpublished manuscript.

Gardner, Howard. 1992. "Putting Research to Work: Multiple Intelligences." *Instructor* (July/August): 48-49.

Heacock, Grace. 1990. "The We-Search Process: Using the Whole Language Model of Writing To Learn Social Studies Content and Civic Competence." *Social Studies and the Young Learner* 2(3): 9-11.

Katz, Lilian. 1990a. "Impressions of Reggio Emilia Preschools." *Young Children* 45(6): 11-14.

————. 1990b. "Criteria for Selecting Project Topics." Unpublished manuscript.

Kayes, B., and J. Smentowski. 1987. "Student Pond Investigators." *Science Teacher* 54: 35-37.

Klein, Amelia. 1991. "All about Ants: Discovery Learning in the Primary Grades." *Young Children* 46(5): 23-27.

Laycock, G. 1990. "The Children's Crusade." *Wildlife Conservation* 93: 42-49.

National Science Resources Center. 1988. *Science for Children: Resources for Teachers.* Washington, DC: National Academy Press.

New, Rebecca. 1990. "Excellent Early Education: A City in Italy Has It." *Young Children* 45(6): 4-10.

————. 1991. "Projects and Provocations: Preschool Curriculum Ideas from Reggio Emilia." *Montessori Life* (Winter): 26-28.

Plowden, Bridget. 1967. *Children and Their Primary Schools: A Report of the Central Advisory Council for Education.* Vol. 1. London: Her Majesty's Stationery Office.

Schneider, M. 1984. "Setting Up An Outdoor Lab." *Science and Children* 21: 17-20.

Webster, Tupper. 1990. "Projects as Curriculum: Under What Conditions?" *Childhood Education* 67(1): 2-3.

White, Noel, Tina Blythe and Howard Gardner. 1992. *If Minds Matter: A Foreword to the Future.* Vol. 2. Palatine, IL: Skylight.

Whitlow, Fay, and Daniel Sidelnick. Spring 1991. "Integrating Geography Skills and Local History: A Third Grade Case Study." *Social Studies Journal* 20: 33–36.

RECOMMENDED TRADE BOOKS

Haldane Central School, Cold Spring, New York

T RADE books play an important role in the early childhood classroom. Trade books may be defined as noncommercialized children's literature. Contrary to the instructional textbooks, basal readers, and workbooks that are more commonly found in schoolrooms, good children's literature offers engaging stories, naturally rich vocabulary, and beautiful illustrations. The majority of trade books used with young children are picture books in which the brief text plays a secondary role to the illustrations. However, children's literature also includes biographies, informational books, poetry, fairy and folk tales, fables, myths and legends, and all other forms of fiction. Some educators and many parents may question the value of using trade books at this level when most children are nonreaders. However, no child is too young to benefit from quality literature. Even the youngest preschooler enjoys thumbing through the pages of a picture book or listening as the teacher reads a captivating story.

It is not unusual for early childhood educators to make the mistake of limiting the availability of books to the "library corner" of the classroom. They may also designate only a certain part of the day as "storytime." Although library corners and storytime have a place in the early childhood classroom, it is important to realize that books should be an integral part of each area of the room and each lesson of the day.

For example, the block area is the perfect place to display books like Byron Barton's *Building a House*, *Airport*, and *Trucks*. Students will sometimes refer to the pictures for construction designs. Books will often spark ideas and lead to lively discussions among children as they plan and build together. The housekeeping center should have a supply of children's cookbooks. It is also a good location for infants' board books and other non-narrative books that can be "read" to dolls by students role playing parents. The drama and/or puppet center should provide easy access to traditional stories such as *Goldilocks and the Three Bears*, *Little Red Riding Hood*, and *Mary Had a Little Lamb*, which lend themselves to simple retellings and reenactments.

Most books for this age group are fiction. However, in recent years there has been an increase in appropriate nonfiction for young children. Gail Gibbons is one author who specializes in nonfiction for youngsters. Her books, such as *The Milk Makers* and *The Seasons of Arnold's Apple Tree*, are full of factual information. When using nonfiction books with young children, the teacher must use her judgment as to whether the class is mature enough to attend to a reading of the text as printed, or whether it would be more appropriate for her to just show the illustrations and paraphrase the information. Unless otherwise noted, the nonfiction books listed in this chapter all have illustrations or photographs that make them appropriate for use with students in preschool through third grade.

When selecting trade books for use with early childhood students, it is important to ask the following questions:
1. Is the text developmentally appropriate in length and content for the target audience?
2. Are the illustrations or photographs appealing?
3. Is there a good match between the text and the illustrations?
4. If the book is to be read by the children, is the print clear and well spaced? Does it play a secondary role to the illustrations?

The predominant practice among early childhood educators is to integrate their curriculum through the study of a particular theme. This chapter will introduce a number of themes that are commonly encountered in preschool and primary-grade classrooms. The bibliography for each theme has been carefully compiled based on the above criteria. Each listing, unless otherwise noted, is appropriate for use with children in preschool, kindergarten, and first, second, and third grades. The books may be read aloud by the teacher or independently by the students, depending on the reading development of the targeted audience. It is incumbent upon the classroom teacher to preview any book she plans to use with her class and to judge its suitability, based on the ability and age of her students, as well as her teaching objectives.

In addition to the lists of thematically grouped trade books for children, this chapter will offer a bibliography of resources for early childhood educators. These books offer additional trade book titles and explore the uses of literature with young children.

Theme: The Alphabet

Alphabet books are one of the staples of any early childhood classroom library. Preschoolers begin to identify some letters, usually starting with those found in their names. The most suitable books for this age group are those that have one large letter per page paired with an easily identifiable picture. *Alphabet*, by Fiona Pragoff, and *Anno's Alphabet: An Adventure in Imagination*, by Mitsumasa Anno, are two such examples.

Kindergarten and first grade students need added practice in both letter recognition and identification. Children at this stage of development are also beginning to associate phonemes with letters. Therefore, books that show both the capital and lowercase forms of the letter, and that match these to an illustration with a descriptive word, are appropriate for this age group. Two books that fit these criteria are C. B. Falls's *ABC Book* and Lois Ehlert's *Eating the Alphabet: Fruits and Vegetables from A to Z*.

Second- and third-grade students have usually mastered letter recognition and identification skills. However, they will need reinforcement of phonemic concepts as a foundation for their newly developing spelling skills. Children in these grades enjoy reading alphabet books that present intricately detailed illustrations within which are hidden a number of objects and/or actions that begin with a particular letter sound. It becomes the reader's task to identify the words that are associated with the letter. Older primary students also enjoy a text that employs alliteration as a means of representing a letter. Books such as *Animalia*, by Graeme Base, and *On Market Street*, by Arnold Lobel, will entertain second- and third-graders for sustained periods of time. Creative teachers will use alphabet books as a jumping off point for lessons involving creative writing. Students in grades K–3 enjoy collaborating on creations such as "Our Winter Alphabet" or writing their own books that are modeled on the format of a favorite alphabet book, such as *Alphabatics*, by Suse MacDonald, or *All Butterflies*, by Marcia Brown.

ABC Book, by C. B. Falls (New York: Doubleday, 1923).
This classic book is a must for every early childhood class. Full-page woodcuts with contrasting colors illustrate each single-line page of text, which follows the "A is for antelope" pattern.

Alfred's Alphabet Walk, by Victoria Chess (New York: Greenwillow, 1979).
While taking a walk, Alfred learns all the letters of the alphabet from the sights that he sees. The brief text on each page uses alliteration and bold type to emphasize the letter being learned. Full-color, large illustra-

tions appear on each page, with text printed at bottom.

All Aboard ABC, by Doug Magee and Robert Newman (New York: Dutton, 1990).
This railroad alphabet book employs full-color photographs to introduce young readers to the world of trains. Each page contains both a capital and lowercase letter and a key word highlighted in red and used within a contextual sentence.

All Butterflies: An ABC Cut, by Marcia Brown (New York: Scribner's, 1974).
The beautifully colored, full-page woodcut illustrations are the focus of this book. Each two-page picture is accompanied by a clever two-word text that follows alphabetical order, from "**A**ll **B**utterflies" through "**Y**our **Z**oo."

Alphabatics, by Suse MacDonald (New York: Trumpet, 1986).
Through a series of boldly colored, clever illustrations, each letter of the alphabet is gradually transformed into an animal or object whose name begins with that letter. Most appropriate for students in grades 1–3, who will enjoy creating their own transformations.

Alphabet, by Fiona Pragoff (New York: Doubleday, 1985).
Big, bold, and brightly colored photographs of simple objects and actions illustrate the one-word text on each page. The glossy, spiral-bound, cardboard pages and simple format of this book make it ideal for use with preschoolers.

Animal Alphabet, by Bert Kitchen (New York: Dutton, 1984).
The reader is invited to guess the identity of twenty-six unusual animals representing the letters of the alphabet. The book has an oversized format and features warmly colored, richly detailed illustrations.

Animalia, by Graeme Base (New York: Abrams, 1986).
Each double-page spread of this oversized book holds an extremely detailed, full-color, collage-style painting depicting dozens of animals, objects, and actions that begin with the same letter. An alliterative sentence emphasizing the targeted letter is decoratively embedded within each illustration. This book is best suited for students in grades 1–3. Its intricate format lends itself to use with no more than three students at a time.

Animals A to Z, by David McPhail (New York: Scholastic, 1989).
This book uses a simple format of one capital letter per page, accompanied by a full-color, detailed, watercolor-and-ink illustration. Each picture contains a number of items that begin with that letter. Similar to *Animalia*, but less visually cluttered, the book is well suited for grades K–3.

Anno's Alphabet: An Adventure in Imagination, by Mitsumasa Anno (New York: Crowell, 1975).
Each letter of the alphabet, illustrated as if it had been carved from wood, is accompanied by a full-page color picture of an object whose name begins with that letter. The black pen-and-ink borders surrounding each page may go unnoticed by very young children, but older readers will find line drawings of related objects hidden within them.

Ben's ABC Day, by Terry Berger (New York: Lothrop, Lee & Shepard, 1982).
A small boy is shown performing activities beginning with each of the letters of the alphabet. Full-page color photos with one-word text below make this book ideal for grades preK–1.

Chicka Chicka Boom Boom, by Bill Martin, Jr., and John Archambault, ill. by Lois Ehlert (New York: Scholastic, 1989).
Rhythmic, rhyming text relates the mischief that the personified alphabet letters get into when they try to climb a coconut tree. Double-paged, boldly colored illustrations. A favorite of all ages.

Eating the Alphabet: Fruits and Vegetables from A to Z, by Lois Ehlert (New York: Harcourt Brace Jovanovich, 1989).
An alphabetical tour of the world of fruits and vegetables, from apricot to zucchini. The boldly

colored, eye-catching illustrations are accompanied by one-word labels printed in both capital and lowercase letters. A great nonfiction book for all ages.

Gretchen's abc, by Gretchen Dow Simpson (New York: Harper Collins, 1991).
Elegant full-color paintings illustrate each lowercase letter of the alphabet. Grades K-3.

The Ocean Alphabet Book, by Jerry Pallotta, ill. by Frank Mazzola, Jr. (Watertown, MA: Charlesbridge, 1986).
Each page features a capital and lowercase letter and an illustration of a sea-dwelling creature whose name begins with that letter. A paragraph of text describes each creature. The author has written a series of content-related alphabet books that follow the same format. They include: *The Icky Bug Alphabet Book, The Flower Alphabet Book, The Furry Animal Alphabet Book*, and *The Yucky Reptile Book*.

On Market Street, by Arnold Lobel, ill. by Anita Lobel (New York: Greenwillow, 1983).
A child buys presents from A to Z in shops along Market Street. Whimsically detailed pen-and-ink with watercolor illustrations inspired by seventeenth-century French trade engravings.

26 Letters and 99 Cents, by Tana Hoban (New York: Scholastic, 1987).
A two-in-one alphabet and number book. Full-color photos of capital and lowercase vinyl letters paired with a toy whose name begins with that letter. When flipped over and turned upside down, the book depicts vinyl numbers paired with coins that equal that amount of cents.

The Z Was Zapped, by Chris Van Allsburg (Boston: Houghton Mifflin, 1987).
This unique alphabet book uses a simple predictive text and photo-quality black, white, and gray illustrations to depict how each letter of the alphabet suffered a mishap. For example, A was in an avalanche, B was badly bitten, C was cut to ribbons, etc.

Theme: Numbers and Counting

Among the first kinds of books that young children enjoy reading are simple number books that let them practice their counting skills. Toddlers delight in pointing to the illustrations as they demonstrate their ability to count by rote from one to ten. Such finger-pointing helps to develop one-to-one correspondence, which is a very basic math concept. Older preschoolers and kindergarten students begin to associate a numeral with a number. Higher counting and more advanced numeral recognition skills are developed in first and second grade. Some counting books, such as *The Doorbell Rang*, by Pat Hutchins, and *How Much Is a Million?*, by David M. Schwartz, help primary students to develop more abstract math concepts and operations.

Adding: A Poem, by Christina Rossetta, ill. by Jan Balet (New York: Holt, Rinehart & Winston, 1964).
Simple verses that add twin numbers, e.g.—"1 and 1 are 2: That's for me and you"—are illustrated in colorful watercolor-and-ink pictures. This book is most suitable for grades 1-3.

Anno's Counting Book, by Mitsumasa Anno (New York: Crowell, 1975).
Beautiful watercolor illustrations introduce counting and numbers from 1 to 12 by showing mathematical relationships in nature. Margins on each double-page spread show a corresponding numeral paired with an appropriate amount of counting cubes.

Beginning To Learn about Numbers, by Richard L. Allington, ill. by Tom Garcia (Milwaukee: Raintree, 1979).
The numerals 1 to 10 are introduced through a counting game, with the correct number being determined by clues in the large, full-color illustrations. This selection is best for grades K-3.

Can You Imagine . . . ?, by Beau Gardner (New York: Dodd, Mean, 1987).
Brightly colored, full-page graphics match a whimsical rhyming text that asks the reader if

he can imagine "1 whale wearing a veil," "2 ducks driving trucks," etc. Older children will enjoy writing their own variations on the text.

Count, by Denise Fleming (New York: Henry Holt, 1992).
The antics of lively and colorful animals present the numbers 1 to 10, 20, 30, 40, and 50. Oversized and bright, these illustrations are great for whole-class sharing.

The Doorbell Rang, by Pat Hutchins (New York: Scholastic, 1986).
An increasing number of children want to share a dozen home-baked cookies. A fun story for younger children and a wonderful way for older primary grade students to learn simple division concepts.

How Many Snails?, by Paul Giganti, Jr., ill. by Donald Crews (New York: Greenwillow, 1988).
A young child takes walks to different places and wonders about the number and variety of things seen along the way. Large color illustrations and a questioning text make this book suitable for interactive reading with a whole-class group.

How Much Is a Million?, by David M. Schwartz, ill. by Steven Kellogg (New York: Lothrop, Lee & Shepard, 1985).
Text and pictures help children to try to conceptualize amounts of a million, a billion, and a trillion. The book is suitable for mature kindergartners and first- through third-graders.

Mouse Count, by Ellen Stoll Walsh (New York: Harcourt Brace Jovanovich, 1991).
As ten mice outsmart a hungry snake, the reader learns how to count from one to ten, and back to one again. Colorful collage illustrations are combined with an easy-to-read text.

Number Play, by John Burningham (New York: Viking, 1983).
The six non-narrative books in this series introduce basic math concepts to young children. The author uses colorful pen-and-ink and watercolor illustrations accompanied only by an occasional numeral, number word, or operational sign. Each of these board books is cleverly designed to fold out in two ways. They are appropriate for children in preK to first grade. *Pigs Plus* teaches simple addition, as a pig sets off for a rider in an old car and gains passengers along the way. *Read One* introduces number words matched to illustrations of some lively bears. *Five Down* teaches the reader to identify numerals by pairing them with the same number of objects. *Count Up* introduces the concept of number sets, as each successive illustration depicts a group that increases by one. *Just Cats* teaches students to classify groups of animals.

1, 2, 3, by Tana Hoban (New York: Greenwillow, 1985).
Two shoes, five fingers, ten toes—these are some of the familiar things presented to be counted in full-color photographs accompanied by a numeral, a number word, and a corresponding number of dots. This 6″ x 6″ board book is perfect for preK children.

One White Sail: A Caribbean Counting Book, by S. T. Garne, ill. by Lisa Etre (New York: Simon & Schuster, 1992).
Rhyming text counts the picturesque sights found on an island beach. Absolutely luminous watercolor illustrations.

The Right Number of Elephants, by Jeff Shepard, ill. by Felicia Bond (New York: HarperCollins, 1990).
A counting story in which a little girl relies on the help of some elephant friends. Readers learn to count backward from 10 to 1 as they enjoy the full-page, full-color illustrations.

Theme: Colors

One of the first lessons that young children learn is to identify colors. Since coloring and painting are important childhood activities, a knowledge of colors and their properties is fundamental to any early childhood program. The basic color words are usually among the first sight vocabulary that early readers develop.

Books such as Tana Hoban's *Of Colors and Things* help preschool children learn to name and discriminate colors. Kindergarten and first grade children enjoy learning how to mix their own colors from the primary colors red, blue, and yellow. *Do You Know Colors?*, by Miller and Howard, and *Mouse Paint*, by Ellen Stoll Walsh, are two appropriate books for introducing primary and secondary colors. The natural fascination that second- and third-grade students have for rainbows can lead to interesting lessons involving prisms and the bending of light into colors. *Light Experiments*, by Harry Sootin, is filled with easy-to-do classroom experiments that demonstrate the various principles of light and color. All children enjoy creating artwork and experimenting with the blending properties of colors by using various media, such as tempera, watercolors, chalk, markers, colored pencils, fingerpaints, and crayons.

Brown Bear, Brown Bear, What Do You See?, by Bill Martin, Jr., ill. by Eric Carle (New York: Holt, Rinehart & Winston, 1983).
In this simple, predictable text, children see a variety of animals, each one a different color. Youngsters love to "read" this book independently. Older primary students enjoy writing their own extensions of the text.

A Color of His Own, by Leo Lionni (New York: Pantheon, 1975).
A little chameleon is distressed because he does not have his own color like other animals. The story is illustrated with brilliant watercolor and collage illustrations.

Colors, by Richard L. Allington, ill. by Noel Spangler (Milwaukee: Raintree, 1979).
Simple text and tempera illustrations introduce twelve basic colors and explain how these colors can be combined to produce other colors. This is a good selection for grades K–3.

Color Zoo, by Lois Ehlert (New York: Trumpet, 1989).
The author/illustrator uses her trademark bold colors and cutout, overlapping shapes to create full-page animal faces. The animals and shapes are identified with a single word of text on each page. A second book, *Color Farm* (1990), follows the same format. PreK to first grade.

Do You Know Colors?, by J. P. Miller and Katherine Howard (New York: Random House, 1978).
Simple text and bright illustrations reveal how some colors are made from blending others. Depicts objects in each color with labels and can double as a picture dictionary for older students.

The Great Blueness and Other Predicaments, by Arnold Lobel (New York: Harper & Row, 1968).
This tale of a wizard who brought color to the world includes detailed pencil, ink, and watercolor wash illustrations. It is best for second- and third-graders because of the length of the story.

Hailstones and Halibut Bones: Adventures in Color, by Mary O'Neill, ill. by Leonard Weisgard (New York: Doubleday, 1961).
Twelve poems about various colors and what they suggest to the poet. This classic book should be part of every teacher's library. The poems offer an effective way to develop a child's imagination. Older students may enjoy writing their own color poems.

Light Experiments, by Harry Sootin, ill. by Frank Aloise (New York: Norton, 1963).
Easy-to-follow directions for a variety of experiments that may be done in school or at home with common materials. Simple line drawings help illustrate how to do the experiments. The book is suitable for use by students in grades 2 and 3 with adult supervision or by teachers of younger children for demonstration purposes.

Little Blue and Little Yellow, by Leo Lionni (New York: Obolensky, 1959).
This classic book teaches the basic color facts in a simple story of two friendly blobs of paint, one yellow and one blue, who hug each other and become green.

Mouse Paint, by Ellen Stoll Walsh (New York: Harcourt Brace Jovanovich, 1989).
Three white mice discover jars of red, blue, and yellow paints. Their discovery leads them to explore the world of color. A simple text is

matched with brilliantly colored cut-paper collage illustrations.

Of Colors and Things, by Tana Hoban (New York: Greenwillow, 1989).
Brightly colored objects are photographed and grouped together on pages that promote color identification. This non-narrative book is ideal for preschool and kindergarten children.

Rainbows and Frogs: A Story about Colors, by Joy Kim, ill. by Paul Harvey (Mahwah, NJ: Troll, 1981).
This book introduces the colors red, yellow, green, orange, and blue, and discusses how they make people feel. Illustrations are simple black line drawings with brilliant tempera color accents.

Rainbow Rhymes, by Virginia Parsons (New York: Golden, 1974).
Colorful, oversized illustrations accompany nursery rhymes for each color of the rainbow.

Red Bear, by Bodel Rikys (New York: Dial, 1992).
The individual color words form the only text in this preschool book that pairs the words with simply drawn pictures of a bear going about its daily activities.

Red, Blue, Yellow Shoe, by Tana Hoban (New York: Greenwillow, 1985).
Vibrantly colored photographs of common objects, with the name of each color printed in that color below each picture. This 6″ x 6″ board book is perfect for preschoolers but also well suited for students in grades K–1 who are learning to read the color words.

Red Day, Green Day, by Edith Kunhardt, ill. by Marylin Hafner (New York: Greenwillow, 1992).
Andrew and his kindergarten class learn about colors in a unique way. Children who hear this story will want to imitate the class in the book and make their own color collection.

Who Said Red?, by Mary Serfozo, ill. by Keiko Narahashi (New York: Scholastic, 1988).

Simple rhythmic text and warmly colored watercolor wash illustrations explore the basic colors discovered by a boy and his sister.

Theme: Shapes

The ability to discriminate and identify geometric shapes, like most other early childhood skills, develops over time with age and experience. Having a wide variety of trade books about shapes available can help to reinforce early recognition skills and lead to the development of an understanding of more advanced geometric concepts. Tana Hoban's non-narrative book *Circles, Triangles, and Squares* introduces preschoolers to the three most easily identified shapes. Rectangles, ovals, and diamonds present more of a challenge and are commonly introduced to children in kindergarten and first grade. At this age, the majority of students have also developed their fine motor skills sufficiently to be able to reproduce most of the six basic shapes. *Shapes*, by Richard L. Allington, and *Finding Out about Shapes*, by Mae Freeman, are good books for exploring these early-level skills. Since most first- through third-grade math programs include a study of basic geometric concepts such as fractions, perimeter, and area, in addition to shape identification, it is helpful to have a number of trade books on hand that explore these concepts. Three titles that suit this purpose are *Circles*, by Mindel and Harry Sitomer, *Exploring Triangles*, by Jo Phillips, and *Shapes*, by Jeanne Bendick.

Beginning To Learn about Shapes, by Richard L. Allington, ill. by Lois Ehlert (Milwaukee: Raintree, 1979).
This book introduces twenty geometric figures with activities that foster an understanding of shape and size relationships. It includes bold color illustrations.

Circles, by Mindel and Harry Sitomer, ill. by George Giusti (New York: Crowell, 1971).
This book explores the mathematical principles involved in circles. Simple color illustrations supplement a text that is most appropriate for advanced second- and third-graders or for teachers to use as a resource for related math issues.

Circles, Triangles, and Squares, by Tana Hoban (New York: Collier Macmillan, 1974).
Full-page black-and-white photographs of people and objects depict the three elementary shapes. This is an excellent book for promoting shape recognition in an interactive way.

Color Zoo, by Lois Ehlert (New York: Trumpet, 1989).
A variety of cutout shapes are ingeniously overlapped to create boldly colored animal faces. Each shape is labeled with a single word of text. A second book, *Color Farm* (1990), follows the same format. Both books are suitable for preK to first-grade students.

Exploring Triangles: Paper-Folding Geometry, by Jo Phillips, ill. by Jim Rolling (New York: Crowell, 1975).
This book explores the mathematical principles of triangles. The paper-folding activities may be too difficult for some students, but they provide an interesting way for teachers to demonstrate concepts. This is a good selection for grades 2–3.

Finding Out about Shapes, by Mae Freeman, ill. by Bill Morrison (New York: McGraw-Hill, 1969).
Simple, enjoyable text introduces lines and shapes in a captivating manner. Two-color illustrations are large and well matched to the text. This is an ideal choice for grades K–2.

If You Look around You, by Fulvio Testa (New York: Dial, 1983).
Geometric shapes are depicted in scenes of children indoors and outside. Full-page, brightly colored illustrations are matched with one line of text on the facing pages.

A Kiss Is Round, by Blossom Budney, ill. by Vladimer Bobri (New York: Lothrop, Lee & Shepard, 1954).
Rhyming text and colorful tempera-and-ink illustrations describe things that are round. Although simple enough for preschoolers, older students will also enjoy this book and will be inspired to create their own shape poems after reading it.

Look Around: A Book about Shapes, by Leonard Everett Fisher (New York: Viking, 1987).
Boldly colored, full-page illustrations present basic shapes in familiar scenes for the reader to identify. Simple, large-type text gives a brief description of each shape and asks interactive questions.

The Secret Birthday Message, by Eric Carle (New York: Crowell, 1972).
Tim finds a secret message under his pillow, which leads him along a path filled with a variety of shapes on his way to a discovery. Text includes rebus clues in the form of black silhouetted shapes. Illustrations make use of bright colors and cutout overlays of a variety of shapes.

The Sesame Street Book of Shapes, by Children's Television Workshop (New York: New American Library, 1971).
A combination of colored photographs and graphics are used to identify circles, rectangles, squares, and triangles. Several pages compare solid and plane geometric shapes. The small format of this 6″ x 4″ book lends itself to use by individuals or a small group.

Shapes, by Jeanne Bendick (New York: Franklin Watts, 1968).
This book introduces various kinds of shapes, both plane and solid, and tells about measurement, three-dimensional figures, and symmetry. It is most appropriately used as a teacher resource or for individual reading by more advanced second- and third-grade students.

Shapes and Things, by Tana Hoban (New York: Macmillan, 1970).
In this non-narrative book, unusual white-on-black silhouette photographs of everyday objects offer an innovative introduction to the beauty of pure shape.

Shapes, Sides, Curves, and Corners, by Illa Podendorf, ill. by Frank Rakoncay (Chicago: Children's Press, 1970).
Using simple color illustrations, this book teaches children to see basic shapes in the everyday things around them. The text asks many interactive questions about the things depicted in the illustrations.

Theme: Seasons

An understanding of seasons and the passing of time is a very difficult concept for young children. It is an extremely abstract idea that is beyond the comprehension of most preschoolers, who are at a very concrete stage of development. However, preK teachers can help build understanding by noting the daily weather and its effect on how children dress. *Clementine's Winter Wardrobe*, by Kate Spohn, and *The Jacket I Wear in the Snow*, by Shirley Neitzel, are well suited for this purpose. Kindergarten and first-grade students, who begin to develop a basic understanding of the calendar, are soon able to name the seasons and months of the year. They learn to associate certain kinds of weather, dress, activities, and environmental changes with specific seasons. Anne Rockwell's *First Comes Spring* and Lionni and Solomon's *Mouse Days* are two books that promote such learning at this age level. Primary-grade students are interested in the ways that the changing seasons affect the growth of plants and the habits of animals. Second- and third-grade children enjoy reading thermometers, keeping daily records of seasonal changes, and doing weather experiments.

A large variety of the trade books available on this theme, both fiction and nonfiction, deal with a specific season, such as *What Happens in the Spring*, by Kathleen Costello Beer, *Animals in Summer*, by Jane R. McCauley, *Winter's Coming*, by Eve Bunting, and *The Big Snow*, by Berta and Elmer Hader. The following bibliography includes only titles that deal with all four seasons.

Around the Seasons: Poems, by Eleanor Farjeon, ill. by Jane Paton (New York: H. Z. Walck, 1969).
Twenty poems with color illustrations describe the activities and pleasures that are a part of each season.

A Book of Seasons, by Alice Provenson (New York: Random House, 1976).
This easy-to-read description of the continuously changing seasons features brilliant watercolor-and-ink illustrations, with only one or two lines of well-matched text on each page.

Caps, Hats, Sock, and Mittens, by Louise Borden, ill. by Lillian Hoban (New York: Scholastic, 1989).
Proceeding season by season, the author describes the characteristic sights and activities for each time of year. Hoban's recognizable illustrations of children enjoying each season are done in colored pencil and watercolors.

First Comes Spring, by Anne Rockwell (New York: Crowell, 1985).
Bear Child notices that the clothes he wears, the things everyone does at work and play, and other parts of his world all change with the seasons. Brightly colored illustrations are a good match for the simple text, which offers some interactive questions relating to the pictures.

Four Stories for Four Seasons, by Tomie DePaola (New York: Prentice-Hall, 1977).
Four friends—a cat, a dog, a pig, and a frog—share the delights of each season. Features DePaola's distinctive illustrations.

From Spring to Spring, by Lois Duncan (n.p.: Westminster, 1982).
Arranged chronologically by seasons, this rich collection of poetry and photographs captures the joy of each time of year.

Mouse Days, by Leo Lionni and Hannah Solomon (New York: Pantheon, 1981).
A group of mice experiences the weather and activities characteristic of each month of the year. Illustrations are in soft colored-chalk and pencil.

My Favorite Time of Year, by Susan Pearson, ill. by John Wallner (New York: Harper & Row, 1988).
A family enjoys the weather and activities of every season. The watercolor brush illustrations are very expressive and cheerful. Text may be too long for some preschoolers, but the story can be easily paraphrased to match the pictures.

Ox-Cart Man, by Donald Hall, ill. by Barbara Cooney (New York: Viking, 1979).
This picture book describes day-to-day life for a nineteenth-century New England family throughout the changing seasons of the year.

The Seasons of Arnold's Apple Tree, by Gail
     Gibbons (New York: Harcourt Brace
     Jovanovich, 1984).
As the seasons pass, Arnold enjoys his special
place, the apple tree, in different ways. Detailed
full-color illustrations are matched with a text
that weaves factual information into the story.

This Year's Garden, by Cynthia Rylant, ill. by
     Mary Szilagyi (New York: Macmillan,
     1987).
Rylant's story follows the seasons of the year
as reflected in the growth, life, and death of the
garden of a rural family.

Weather Forecasting, by Gail Gibbons (New
     York: Four Winds, 1987).
Season by season, this book describes forecast-
ers at work in a weather station as they use
sophisticated equipment to track and gauge
weather changes. It will appeal to students in
grades 1–3.

What Comes in Spring, by Barbara Savadge
     Horton, ill. by Ed Young (New York: Knopf,
     1992).
A mother explains to her daughter how the
child grew inside her as the seasons changed,
bringing great happiness to her parents then and
now. Soft pastel illustrations capture the warm
relationship between the characters. This book
is suitable for grades K–3.

When Summer Ends, by Marisabina Russo, ill.
     by Susi Gregg Fowler (New York:
     Greenwillow, 1989).
A young child is sorry to see summer end until
she remembers all the good things that the
other seasons bring.

Yonder, by Tony Johnston, ill. by Lloyd Bloom
     (New York: Dial, 1988).
As the plum tree changes in the passing
seasons, so do the lives of a three-generation
farm family. Full-color tempera illustrations
capture the country feeling of this story.

Theme: Holidays

Holidays are exciting and special times for
young children. There is a wide variety of

opinions and administrative policies regarding
the teaching and celebration of holidays in
school. Most educators agree, however, that
students should develop an awareness of special
days and a tolerant respect for the various
traditions related to their observance.

   Occasionally, a favorite children's author
will publish a series of holiday books related to
a specific character. Here are a few examples:
   Norman Bridwell (Scholastic): *Clifford's
Halloween, Clifford's Christmas,* and *Clifford
We Love You* (Valentine's Day)
   Marc Brown (Little, Brown): *Arthur's Hal-
loween, Arthur's Thanksgiving, Arthur's Christ-
mas, Arthur's Valentine,* and *Arthur's April
Fool*
   Wende and Harry Devlin (Macmillan): *Cranberry Halloween, Cranberry Thanksgiving,
Cranberry Christmas,* and *Cranberry Valentine*
   Janice and Mariana (Lothrop, Lee &
Shepard): *Little Bear's Thanksgiving, Little
Bear's Christmas,* and *Little Bear Marches in
the St. Patrick's Day Parade*
   For virtually every holiday, there are
nonfiction books available that explain the
day's origin, its religious or historical significance, and the customs associated with its
observance. Unfortunately, with rare exceptions
such as Jean Marzollo's *In 1492* and Gail
Gibbons's *Thanksgiving Day,* most of these
books are not suitable for sharing aloud with
young children. However, early childhood
teachers should be encouraged to check their
library's holiday section (Dewey Decimal Number 394.2) for books that have background
information that may be helpful when preparing
lessons related to the holidays.

   The bibliography that follows was compiled
in order to present a sampling of children's
literature related to specific holidays, not to
provide sources of factual information about
them. The holidays were selected because of
their special interest to children and because
their observances fall within the school calendar year.

Halloween

The Biggest Pumpkin Ever, by Steven Kroll, ill.
     by Jeni Bassett (New York: Scholastic,
     1984).
Unbeknown to each other, two mice love and
care for the same pumpkin until it grows to

record size. The delightful story is enhanced by cheery watercolor illustrations.

Happy Halloween! Things To Make and Do, by Robyn Supraner, ill. by Renzo Barto (Mahwah, NJ: Troll, 1981).
This book has instructions for making Halloween decorations, games, disguises, and treats. Full-color illustrations and sequenced rebus pictures supplement the directions. Appropriate for independent readers in second and third grade, the book will also prove useful to teachers as a resource for Halloween projects and activities.

In a Dark, Dark Wood: An Old Tale with a New Twist, by David A. Carter (New York: Simon & Schuster, 1991).
The repetitive text of this traditional tale is illustrated line by line with oversized, full-color paintings. The last page reveals a huge pop-up ghost that leaps toward the reader.

It's Halloween, by Jack Prelutsky, ill. by Marylin Hafner (New York: Scholastic, 1977).
This collection of kooky and spooky Halloween poems is cleverly illustrated in autumn colors.

Pumpkin, Pumpkin, by Jeanne Titherington (New York: Scholastic, 1986).
Full-page, softly drawn colored-pencil illustrations accompany a brief text that describes the growth of a pumpkin, from seed to jack-o'lantern, as it is cared for by a young boy.

Scary, Scary Halloween, by Eve Bunting, ill. by Jan Brett (New York: Scholastic, 1986).
A rhyming text—printed in white against the darkly colored double-page illustrations—relates a delightfully mysterious Halloween story involving some costumed children and a family of frightened cats.

Spooky and the Ghost Cat, by Natalie Savage Carlson, ill. by Andrew Glass (New York: Lothrop, Lee & Shepard, 1985).
On Halloween night, Spooky, a black cat, rescues a ghost cat from a witch to whom he once belonged. The book includes richly textured, colorful pastel illustrations.

The Widow's Broom, by Chris Van Allsburg (Boston: Houghton Mifflin, 1992).
A widow discovers the magical powers of a witch's discarded broom. Van Allsburg's distinctively lifelike sepia-colored pencil illustrations add a mysteriously haunting feeling to the ironic text.

Thanksgiving

Arthur's Thanksgiving, by Marc Brown (Boston: Little, Brown, 1983).
Arthur finds his role as director of the Thanksgiving play a difficult one, especially since no one will agree to play the turkey. The lively, full-color illustrations are done in watercolor, pen and ink, and colored pencil. The book is best suited for grades 1 to 3 due to length of text.

Don't Eat Too Much Turkey!, by Miriam Cohen, ill. by Lillian Hoban (New York: Dell, 1987).
The first-grade students in Jim's class are preparing for Thanksgiving by drawing pictures, writing a play, and making a turkey costume together. Brightly colored illustrations enliven this story for grades K–2.

Over the River and through the Woods. by John Steven Gurney (New York: Scholastic, 1992).
The first verse of the traditional holiday song illustrated line by line with full-page, full-color paintings. Includes music and lyrics.

Thanksgiving at the Tappletons', by Eileen Spinelli, ill. by Maryann Cocca-Leffler (Reading, MA: Addison-Wesley, 1982).
Though calamity stalks every step of the preparations, the Tappleton family learns that there is more to Thanksgiving than turkey and trimmings. This is a delightful holiday treat for students in grades K–3.

Thanksgiving Day, by Gail Gibbons (New York: Holiday House, 1983).
The nonfiction text presents information about the first Thanksgiving and the way the holiday is celebrated today. The book contains full-page illustrations in bright autumn colors.

The Thanksgiving Story, by Alice Dagliesh, ill. by Helen Sewell (New York: Scribner's, 1954).
This classic book relates the story of one Pilgrim family, the hardships on the *Mayflower,* the struggle to survive the first winter, and the joy of the harvest. The sparse yet distinctive illustrations are reminiscent of early American artwork. The book is suitable for grades 1–3.

Christmas

Although Christmas is a religious day, it has developed as a secular holiday for many people. The entries listed here do not deal with the religious observance of the holiday.

Clifford's Christmas, by Norman Bridwell (New York: Scholastic, 1984).
Clifford the Big Red Dog and his owner, Emily Elizabeth, prepare for Christmas and help Santa out of a precarious situation. This children's classic contains color illustrations.

The Family Christmas Tree Book, by Tomie DePaola (New York: Holiday, 1980).
A family discusses the origin of the Christmas tree as they cut down and decorate their own. The text presents factual information in a colorfully illustrated format that makes use of speech balloons. The book is suitable for grades K–3.

I'm Santa Claus and I'm Famous, by Marjorie Weinman Sharmat, ill. by Marylin Hafner (New York: Trumpet, 1990).
Santa visits a school on Career Day and relates the story of his life and how he got his job. Full-color, cartoonlike illustrations utilize speech balloons in a comic book-style format. Since this book is not designed to be read aloud, it is best suited for independent readers in grades 1–3.

I Spy Christmas: A Book of Picture Riddles, by Jean Marzollo, photos by Walter Wick (New York: Scholastic, 1992).
Oversized full-color photographs of holiday collages invite the reader to find hidden objects described by the rhyming text.

Las Navidades: Popular Christmas Songs from Latin America, by Lulu Delacre (New York: Scholastic, 1990).
The music and lyrics (in English and Spanish) of twelve Latin American songs, one for each day from Christmas Eve to Epiphany. Accompanying the lyrics are bright watercolor and pencil illustrations with captions that serve as informative text on various holiday customs.

Merry Christmas, Strega Nona, by Tomie de Paola (New York: Scholastic, 1992).
As he tells this amusing story about "Grandma Witch" and her bumbling assistant Big Anthony, the author-illustrator weaves in many Italian traditions related to the celebration of Christmas. Grades K–3.

My First Kwanzaa Book, by Deborah M. Newton Chocolate, ill. by Cal Massey (New York: Scholastic, 1992).
This colorful book introduces the holiday in which African-Americans celebrate their cultural heritage during the time between Christmas and New Year's Day. Includes a simple text and large illustrations suitable for reading to very young children, as well as an informative glossary and afterword.

The Night after Christmas, by James Stevenson (New York: Greenwillow, 1981).
Tossed in garbage cans after they are replaced by new toys at Christmas, a teddy bear and a doll are befriended by a stray dog. The artist's characteristic watercolor-and-ink illustrations are eye-catching.

Pancho's Piñata, by Stefan Czernecki and Timothy Rhodes (New York: Hyperion Books for Children, 1992).
Brightly colored, full-page illustrations accompany the text of this legend that explains the origin of the piñata tradition and relates the story of a young Mexican boy who learns the true meaning of Christmas.

The Polar Express, by Chris Van Allsburg (Boston: Houghton Mifflin, 1985).
This Caldecott Medal book relates the story of a boy who takes a magical train ride to the North Pole on Christmas Eve to receive a special gift from Santa. Each warmly colored pastel drawing is an artistic masterpiece.

Tree of Cranes, by Allen Say (New York: Scholastic, 1992).
A young Japanese boy learns something about an American Christmas tradition from his mother who was born in California. Exquisite full-page, full-color watercolor and ink illustrations. Grades K–3.

The Twelve Days of Christmas, ill. by Claire Counihan (New York: Scholastic, 1989).
A traditional Christmas carol forms the text of this uniquely illustrated book. Facing each page of print is a photograph of a cake or confection that was baked and decorated by the artist to specifically illustrate one of the verses of the song. Included are a recipe for gingerbread cookies, the story of gingerbread, and the music and lyrics for "The Twelve Days of Christmas."

Chanukah

As with the Christmas bibliography above, the focus of the following books is on family celebration rather than on the religious significance of the holiday. Three of the seven trade books listed below are traditional Yiddish folktales that have been retold and illustrated specifically for children.

The Chanukah Guest, by Eric A. Kimmel, ill. by Giora Carmi (New York: Scholastic, 1988).
A funny tale about a nearsighted old woman who mistakes a bear for the rabbi she was expecting as her guest on the first night of the holiday.

Grandma's Latkes, by Malka Drucker, ill. by Eve Chwast (New York: Harcourt Brace Jovanovich, 1992).
A young girl learns the history and meaning of Hanukkah from her grandmother as they cook potato pancakes for the holiday. Grades K–3.

Hanukah!, by Roni Schotter, ill. by Marylin Hafter (Boston: Little, Brown, 1990).
This humorous story describes one family's evening of celebration. Beautifully colored illustrations capture the charm and appeal of the simple text.

Hanukah Money, by Sholem Aleichem, ill. by Uri Shulevitz (New York: Trumpet, 1978).

A classic tale about a poor European family's holiday celebration. Charmingly detailed pen-and-ink drawings rendered in earthy tones complement the lengthy text. The book includes a glossary of Yiddish terms. This is a good selection for grades 1–3.

Hershel and the Hanukkah Goblins, by Eric Kimmel, ill. by Trina Schart Hyman (New York: Scholastic, 1990).
This Caldecott Honor Book relates the story of how a poor but clever man saves an entire village by outwitting some wicked goblins who had forbidden the people to observe the holiday. Double-spread illustrations beautifully complement this story for grades K–3.

It's Chanukah!, by Ellie Gellman, ill. by Katherine Janus Kahn (Rockville, MD: Kar-Ben Copies, 1985).
This brightly colored board book reinforces color recognition, shape identification, and counting skills as the minimal text describes what Gila and her friends do to celebrate the holiday. The book is ideal for preK to first grade students.

Latkes and Applesauce: A Hanukkah Story, by Fran Manushkin, ill. by Robin Spowart (New York: Scholastic, 1990).
A family's traditional Hanukkah celebration is threatened by a sudden blizzard that covers all the apples and potatoes needed for their meal. Softly luminous full-color pastel illustrations accompany this text which is most suitable for children in grades 1-3.

My First Hanukkah Book, by Aileen Fisher, ill. by Priscilla Kiedrowski (Chicago: Children's Press, 1985).
This popular poet has written a cheerful collection of verses that relate to the fun aspects of the holiday and its historical origin. A full-page color illustration accompanies each poem.

Rainbow Candles: A Chanukah Counting Book, by Myra Shostak, ill. by Katherine Janus Kahn (Rockville, MD: Kar-Ben Copies, 1986).
A simple rhyming text and boldly colored illustrations count the nine candles in the menorah and describe some fun holiday activi-

ties. This 6″ x 6″ board book is perfect for
preK to first grade students.

Martin Luther King Day

Happy Birthday, Martin Luther King, by Jean
Marzollo, ill. by J. Brian Pinkney (New
York: Scholastic, 1993).
Colorful, full-sized scratchboard illustrations
accompany this simple story about the life and
work of Martin Luther King, Jr.

Martin Luther King Day, by Linda Lowery, ill.
by Hetty Mitchell (New York: Scholastic,
1989).
Primarily black-and-white pencil illustrations
highlight the text of this young reader's book
which describes the origin of the national
holiday as well as the life of Dr. King. Grades 2-3.

*Martin Luther King, Jr.: A Biography for
Young Children*, by Carol Hilgartner Schlank
and Barbara Metzger (New York: Rochester
Association for the Education of Young
Children, 1989).
Large, clearly drawn sepia-colored pencil
sketches illustrate the simple text of this brief
biography of Martin Luther King, Jr.

A Picture Book of Martin Luther King, Jr., by
David A. Adler, ill. by Robert Casilla (New
York: Scholastic, 1991).
Warm watercolor illustrations highlight this
children's biography of the great civil rights
leader. Grades K-3.

Valentine's Day

Four Valentines in a Rainstorm, by Felicia
Bond (New York: Harper & Row, 1990).
On the day it rains hearts, a little girl decides to
collect them and make valentine cards for four
of her friends. Colored pencil and black pen
illustrations accompany the brief text. The
small format is best suited for individual or
small group reading.

It's Valentine's Day, by Jack Prelutsky, ill. by
Yossi Abolafia (New York: Scholastic,
1983).

A collection of funny poems that present a
lighthearted look at the holiday and its customs
for students in grades K-3.

Little Mouse's Valentine, by Dave Ross (New
York: Morrow, 1986).
This colorfully illustrated book follows the
adventure of Little Mouse as he goes to buy a
valentine. One line of text per page and well-
matched, humorously expressive illustrations
make this an easy-to-read book.

One Zillion Valentines, by Frank Modell (New
York: Mulberry Books, 1981).
Two friends decide to make valentine cards for
everyone in their neighborhood. Watercolor and
blackline sketches colorfully complement the
brief text.

Things To Make and Do for Valentine's Day,
by Tomie DePaola (New York: Scholastic,
1967).
Projects, crafts, jokes, and games for the
holiday are colorfully illustrated. Step-by-step
directions are supplemented with rebus pictures
to make this book suitable for independent
readers in grades 1 to 3.

The Valentine Bears, by Eve Bunting, ill. by
Jan Brett (New York: Houghton Mifflin,
1983).
Despite the fact that they're usually hibernating
in February, Mrs. Bear plans a special Valentine's Day surprise for Mr. Bear. Softly
detailed, pencil drawings are highlighted with
yellow and red paint.

St. Patrick's Day

Clever Tom and the Leprechaun, by Linda
Shute (New York: Scholastic, 1988).
This traditional tale is about a poor Irishman
who captures a leprechaun and tries to trick
him into revealing the location of his pot of
gold. This book for grades K-3 includes
source notes on the origin of the tale.

The Hungry Leprechaun, by Mary Calhoun, ill.
by Roger Duvoisin (New York: William
Morrow, 1962).
During a famine in Ireland, a poor young man
catches Tippery, an equally poor leprechaun,
and convinces him to change a pot of dandelion

soup into a pot of gold. Tippery's magic fails, but the result is an unexpected blessing for all of Ireland. Two-color illustrations enhance the book for grades K–3.

Little Bear Marches in the St. Patrick's Day Parade, by Janice, ill. by Mariana (New York: Lothrop, Lee & Shepard, 1967).
Gray and green watercolor-wash illustrations accompany this story of Little Bear's parade adventure.

St. Patrick's Day in the Morning, by Eve Bunting, ill. by Jan Brett (New York: Clarion, 1990).
A wee Irish lad tries to prove that he is not too young to march in the St. Patrick's Day parade. The book includes intricately detailed, black pen-and-ink illustrations with green and yellow highlights.

Earth Day

Brother Eagle, Sister Sky, words by Chief Seattle, ill. by Susan Jeffers (New York: Dial, 1991).
A Suquamish Indian chief describes his people's respect and love for the earth and their concern about its destruction. The book includes double-spread, full-color artwork that is intricately detailed in fine-line pen. The text may be too sophisticated for some children, but even the youngest will enjoy the pictures.

50 Simple Things Kids Can Do To Save the Earth, by the Earth Works Group, ill. by Michele Montez (New York: Scholastic, 1990).
A handbook of ideas and activities that can help save energy, prevent pollution, and clean up the environment. Small line drawings illustrate the text. Teachers may want to share one or two ideas with their class each day during a unit related to Earth Day or the environment.

Heron Street, by Ann Turner, ill. by Lisa Desimini (New York: Scholastic, 1991).
This environmental story of a marsh's transformation from a wildlife habitat to a populated neighborhood is illustrated with large, richly colored paintings. Children will enjoy imitating the sounds represented in the story.

How Green Are You?, by David Bellamy, ill. by Penny Dann (New York: Clarkson N. Potter, 1991).
Written for children in grades 3 and up, this colorfully illustrated resource book is filled with projects that can save energy, protect wildlife, and fight pollution. It includes an index and listings of environmental organizations.

It Zwibble and the Greatest Cleanup Ever!, by Lisa V. Ross, ill. by Tom Ross (New York: Scholastic, 1991).
The fanciful characters in this story pitch in to rid their favorite swimming hole of garbage.

Just a Dream, by Chris Van Allsburg (Boston: Houghton Mifflin, 1990).
A boy begins to understand the importance of taking care of the earth after he has a dream about a future filled with pollution. The book is illustrated with classic Van Allsburg pastel pictures in full color.

A Tale of Antarctica, by Ulco Glimmerveen (New York: Scholastic, 1989).
A poignant story of a penguin family whose existence is threatened by the arrival of humans. Watercolor paintings complement this story.

Classic Children's Books

A classic story is one that has withstood the test of time by appealing to the hearts and imaginations of generations of children. For the purposes of this chapter, a classic book shall be defined as an author's original story, not a retelling of a traditional tale, that was first published prior to 1970 but continues to be available in print today. When choosing classic stories for children, the early childhood educator should keep in mind the age, attention span, language ability, and reading level of students.

Most of the authors represented in the following bibliography have written other wonderful books for children. Early childhood teachers may want to use this list as a starting point for developing their classroom libraries.

The bibliography that follows consists primarily of classic picture books that appeal to children in grades K–3. **Note:** Entries marked with an asterisk (*) are particularly appropriate for preschoolers because of the shorter length of their texts and their eye-catching illustrations; those titles marked with two asterisks (**) are chapter books that may be read independently by some third graders but that would be most appropriately read aloud by teachers, one or two chapters at a time, to younger primary students.

* *Alexander and the Wind-up Mouse*, by Leo Lionni (New York: Pantheon, 1969).

** *All-of-a-Kind Family*, ill. by Helen John (New York: Dell, 1951).

Babar the King, by Jean de Brunhoff (New York: Random House, 1935).

** *A Bear Called Paddington*, by Michael Bond, ill. by Peggy Fortnum (New York: Dell, 1958).

Bedtime for Frances, by Russell Hoban, ill. by Garth Williams (New York: Harper & Row, 1960).

The Big Snow, by Berta and Elmer Hader (New York: Collier, 1948).

The Biggest Bear, by Lynd Ward (Boston: Houghton Mifflin, 1953).

* *A Boy, A Dog, and A Frog*, by Mercer Mayer (New York: Dial, 1967).

* *Caps for Sale*, by Esphyr Slobodkina (New York: Scholastic, 1968).

** *Charlie and the Chocolate Factory*, by Roald Dahl, ill. by Joseph Schindelman (New York: Knopf, 1964).

** *Charlotte's Web*, by E. B. White, ill. by Garth Williams (New York: Harper & Row, 1952).

* *Clifford, the Big Red Dog*, by Norman Bridwell (New York: Scholastic, 1963).

Crow Boy, by Taro Yashima (New York: Viking/Penguin, 1955).

* *Curious George*, by H. A. Rey (New York: Scholastic, 1941).

** *Doctor Dolittle Tales,* by Hugh Lofting (New York: Lippincott, 1922).

** *Drummer Hoff*, by Barbara Emberly, ill. by Ed Emberly (New York: Prentice-Hall, 1967).

** *The Enormous Egg*, by Oliver Butterworth, ill. by Louis Darling (Boston: Little, Brown, 1956).

* *Goodnight, Moon*, by Margaret Wise Brown, ill. by Clement Hurd (New York: Harper & Row, 1947).

* *Harold and the Purple Crayon*, by Crockett Johnson (New York: Harper & Row, 1955).

Harry the Dirty Dog, by Gene Zion (New York: Harper & Row, 1956).

Horton Hatches the Egg, by Dr. Seuss (New York: Random House, 1940).

** *Just So Stories*, by Rudyard Kipling, ill. by J. M. Gleeson (New York: Doubleday, 1912).

Little Bear, by Else Holmelund Minarik (New York: Harper & Row, 1957).

* *The Little Engine that Could*, by Watty Piper (New York: Platt & Munk, 1930).

** *Little House on the Prairie*, by Laura Ingalls Wilder, ill. by Garth Williams (New York: Harper & Row, 1953).

The Little Island, by Golden MacDonald, ill. by Leonard Weisgard (New York: Doubleday, 1946).

Little Toot, by Hardie Gramatky (New York: Putnam, 1939).

Madeline, by Ludwig Bemelmans (New York: Viking, 1939).

Make Way for Ducklings, by Robert McCloskey (New York: Penguin, 1941).

Mike Mulligan and His Steam Shovel, by Virginea Lee Burton (New York: Scholastic, 1967).

* *Millions of Cats*, by Wand Ga'g (New York: Scholastic, 1928).

* *Mr. Rabbit and the Lovely Present*, by Charlotte Zolotow, ill. by Maurice Sendak (New York: Harper & Row, 1962).

* *Rosie's Walk*, by Pat Hutchins (New York: Macmillan, 1968).

* *The Snowy Day*, by Ezra Jack Keats (New York: Viking/Penguin, 1962).

The Story about Ping, by Marjorie Flack and Kurt Wiese (New York: Penguin, 1977).

The Story of Ferdinand, by Munro Leaf, ill. by Robert Lawson (New York: Penguin, 1988).

Strawberry Girl, by Lois Lenski (New York: Dell, 1945).

Sylvester and the Magic Pebble, by William Steig (New York: Simon & Schuster, 1969).

The Tale of Peter Rabbit, by Beatrix Potter (New York: Scholastic, 1989).

* *Where the Wild Things Are*, by Maurice Sendak (New York: Harper & Row, 1963).

* *Will I Have a Friend?*, by Miriam Cohen, ill. by Lillian Hoban (New York: Macmillan, 1967).

** *Winnie-the-Pooh*, by A. A. Milne, ill. by Ernest H. Shepard (New York: Dutton, 1954).

Teacher Resources

This section provides early childhood educators with a list of easily accessible professional books, journals, and magazines related to children's literature and literacy development. Each of the books listed includes its own annotated bibliographies. Many of them contain information on reading development and/or practical suggestions for using trade books in the classroom. This section concludes with a list of children's book clubs, which provide teachers, parents, and students the opportunity to purchase quality children's literature at affordable prices.

Teacher Resources: Books

Adventuring with Books: A Booklist for PreK–Grade 6, ed. by Diane L. Monson (Urbana, IL: National Council of Teachers of English, 1985).
As the title implies, this valuable reference book is an annotated bibliography of children's literature. There are well over one hundred lists, which are divided into the following topics: books for young children, traditional literature, modern fantasy, historical fiction, contemporary realistic fiction, poetry, language, social studies, biography, sciences, fine arts, crafts and hobbies, sports and games, and holidays. There is also a section on professional books. Each annotated listing includes an age recommendation. The text concludes with a directory of publishers, an author index, and a title index.

Babies Need Books, by Dorothy Butler (New York: Atheneum, 1985).
The six chapters of this text for parents and teachers cover the stages of reading development and the importance of literature for children from birth through age five. Each chapter contains an annotated bibliography of age-appropriate titles.

Books You Can Count On: Linking Mathematics and Literature, by Rachel Griffiths and

Margaret Clyne (Portsmouth, NH: Heinemann, 1988).

This very practical resource for teachers offers activities, ideas, and suggestions based on specific titles that relate well to the math concepts taught in primary classrooms. Ten chapters include an overview of mathematical topics, developing mathematical thinking, activities based on individual books, activities based on rhymes and poems, themes, counting books, classroom organization ideas, and assessment. Annotated booklists include the reading level of each book.

Children's Literature in the Reading Program, ed. by Bernice E. Cullinan (Newark, DE: International Reading Association, 1987).

Although this text covers children's literature at all grade levels, the first five chapters are specifically related to young children. Topics include inviting readers to literature, poetry, developing readers, and how to use literature with children. Each chapter concludes with a list of references and a bibliography of children's books. The book offers indexes of children's authors and children's books.

Children's Literature: Resource for the Classroom, ed. by Masha Kabakow Rudman (Boston: Christopher-Gordon, 1989).

The eleven chapters of this teacher reference book are divided into three parts: Context and Background for Using Children's Literature in the Classroom, Perspectives on Evaluation and Selection in Children's Literature, and Literature in and beyond the Classroom. Each chapter contains a list of references, and many offer bibliographies of children's books. Some of the bibliographies cover the following topics: multicultural literature, bibliotherapy, wordless books, and contemporary realistic fiction. There are also chapters devoted to literature-related videos and family–school partnerships.

Emerging Literacy: Young Children Learn To Read and Write, ed. by Dorothy S. Strickland and Lesley Mandel Morrow (Newark, DE: International Reading Association, 1989).

The twelve chapters of this book are written by a variety of experts in the field of literacy for young children. The content ranges from oral language and literacy development to family reading and from assessment to classroom designs. Each chapter includes a bibliography of professional resources. Specific titles for students are mentioned within the text and are often accompanied by teaching suggestions and activities.

Eyeopeners! How To Choose and Use Children's Books about Real People, Places, and Things, by Beverly Kobrin, with photographs by Richard Steinheimer and Shirley Burman (New York: Penguin, 1988).

This comprehensive guide to nonfiction books for children is readable, easy to use, and filled with practical tips and suggestions for using the more than five hundred titles included in its annotated bibliographies. Book lists are organized into dozens of subject areas ranging from ABC books and adoption to words and zoos. A Quick-Link Index provides the reader with theme-related, cross-referenced lists of titles. There is also an index of authors, illustrators, and book titles.

Focus Units in Literature: A Handbook for Elementary School Teachers, by Joy F. Moss (Urbana, IL: National Council of Teachers of English, 1984).

As the title implies, this text presents annotated bibliographies and suggested literature-based activities for a number of themes in grades 1–6. Focus units appropriate to grades 1–3 include toy animals, pig tales, the night, folktales, friendship, heroes and heroines, and giants and dragons. There is an appendix of professional references.

For Love of Reading: A Parent's Guide to Encouraging Young Readers from Infancy through Age 5, by Masha Kabakow Rudman, Anna Markus Pearce, and the editors of Consumer Reports Books (Mt. Vernon, NY: Consumers Union, 1988).

This valuable resource book for parents and teachers features an annotated bibliography of more than one thousand classic, award-winning, and contemporary books for children. Nine chapters offer information on reading development, age-appropriate literature, and books related to specific topics including death, divorce, and sibling relationships. Five appendices include a Selected List of Children's Book Awards, Organizations Providing Parents with Useful Information, Children's Book Clubs, List of Books by Age, and List of Wordless Books.

Invitation To Read: More Children's Literature in the Reading Program, ed. by Bernice E. Cullinan (Newark, DE: International Reading Association, 1992).

Written as a sequel to the author's first book, *Children's Literature in the Reading Program*, this text's fourteen chapters are divided into three sections: Genre Studies, Thematic Units, and Putting It All Together. Each chapter contains a list of references and a bibliography of children's books. The text concludes with indexes of children's authors and children's books.

Literacy Learning in the Early Years through Children's Eyes, by Linda Gibson (New York: Teachers College Press, 1989).

This text provides early childhood educators with an understanding of the process of learning to read and write. It combines the author's own theoretical perspective with anecdotal observations of teachers and children ages birth through eight years old. The book does not contain bibliographies, but it is a good reference book for those seeking a better understanding of reading development.

More than the ABCs: The Early Stages of Reading and Writing, by Judith A. Schickendanz (Washington, DC: National Association for the Education of Young Children, 1986).

This excellent resource book for parents and teachers provides a comprehensive description of reading and writing development in children from birth through age six years. It offer bibliographies of appropriate books for each stage.

Read On: A Conference Approach to Reading, by David Hornsby and Deborah Sukarna, with Jo-Ann Parry (Portsmouth, NH: Heinemann, 1986).

This text is a practical guide to implementing a literature-based program in the classroom. Fourteen chapters offer ideas of organization and planning, activities, ways of responding to reading, skills and strategies, reading aloud to children, record keeping, and evaluation. The appendix includes reproducible pages and a bibliography of teacher resources.

Story S-t-r-e-t-c-h-e-r-s: Activities To Expand Children's Favorite Books, by Shirley C. Raines and Robert J. Canaday (Mt. Rainier, MD: Gryphon, 1989).

This book is full of teaching ideas for literature-based early childhood activities. It will lend support to educators who are striving to create an atmosphere where young children can develop a love for books, poems, and songs. Each of the eighteen chapters is organized around a theme or unit commonly taught in preschool, kindergarten, or the primary grades. These include families, friendships, plants, grandparents, seasons, teddy bears, and transportation. Five titles are presented for each theme. For each title, the authors offer story stretchers for classroom centers such as art, block building, science and nature, workbench, music, housekeeping, and dress-up. This book was such a popular teacher resource that the authors have produced two sequels to it: *More Story S-t-r-e-t-c-h-e-r-s* (1991) and *Story S-t-r-e-t-c-h-e-r-s for the Primary Grades* (1992).

Transitions: From Literature to Literacy, by Regie Routman (Portsmouth, NH: Heinemann, 1988).

This resource text offers support, explanations, and ideas for teachers who are moving away from basal reading texts toward a whole-language, literature-based approach to reading. Approximately one-third of the book is devoted to resources for teachers, printed on blue pages. This section includes lists of professional books, journal articles, newsletters, literature extension activity resources, and an extensive list of recommended literature that is classified by grade, literary style, and degree of reading difficulty. Appendices offer sample lesson plans, program proposals, weekly schedules, vocabulary lists, parent communication suggestions, and much more.

Young Children and Picture Books, by Mary Renck Jalongo (Washington, DC: National Association for the Education of Young Children, 1988).

This is an exceptionally practical book that will help parents and educators learn how to use the best picture books with their children. Each of the six chapters concludes with a list of references and a bibliography of children's books. Four appendices present lists of outstanding picture book authors and illustrators, picture book classics, picture books that celebrate cultural diversity, and picture books on videocassette.

Teacher Resources: Journals and Magazines

Book Links is a bimonthly magazine connecting books, libraries, and classrooms. It is published by Booklist Publications, an imprint of the American Library Association, 50 East Huron Street, Chicago, IL 60611. This publication consists of annotated bibliographies related to various topics, themes, and current events. It also includes studies of authors and illustrators.

The Horn Book magazine is published six times a year by The Horn Book Incorporated, 14 Beacon Street, Boston, MA 02108. The magazine includes articles, annotated bibliographies, and indexes related to books for children and young adults.

Instructor magazine is published nine times annually by Scholastic Inc., 2931 East McCarty Street, P.O. Box 3710, Jefferson City, MO 65102-3710. This colorful publication provides a variety of ideas, suggestions, hands-on activities, and informational articles. A regular feature, "Literature Connection," offers three featured articles on "Learning with Literature," "Poetry Pages," and "Meet the Author." These articles frequently offer annotated bibliographies and literature-based activities.

Language Arts is published eight times a year, September through April, by the National Council of Teachers of English, 1111 Kenyon Road, Urbana, IL 61801. It contains original contributions on all facets of language arts learning and teaching, primarily concerning children in grades preK–6. Approximately one-half of each issue relates to a specific theme, such as "Writing in the Schools" (April 1992). The other half of the issue consists of articles related to regularly featured departments such as "Teacher's Notebook," "Research Directions," "Bookalogues," "Profile," and "Reviews and Reflections." References are noted for each article. The "Bookalogues" feature consists of annotated bibliographies related to a specific topic or theme.

The New Advocate is a journal for people involved with young people and literature. It is published in December, March, June, and September by Christopher-Gordon Publishers, Inc., 480 Washington St., Norwood, MA 02062. Regularly occurring features include "The Creative Process," "Concepts and Themes," "Practical Reflections," "Book Reviews Sampler," and "Reference Sampler." The first three features in each issue address different subject areas and themes. The "Book Review Sampler" offers an annotated bibliography of recently published children's books. The "Reference Sampler" keeps educators abreast of the latest research related to children's literature.

The Reading Teacher is the journal of the International Reading Association, 800 Barksdale Road, P.O. Box 8139, Newark, DE 19714-8139. It is published in nine issues per year. Half of the publication is devoted to regular departments, including "Children's Books," "Research," "Practice," "Reading to Learn," "Professional Resources," "Assessment," and "In the Classroom." The other half consists of articles related to literature and literacy.

Young Children is the journal of the National Association for the Education of Young Children, 1834 Connecticut Avenue NW, Washington, DC 20009-5786. It is published six times a year. Articles are aimed at keeping early childhood educators abreast of the latest developments in the field. The journal takes a scholarly approach to research, theory, and classroom practice. Three regularly featured departments related to literature are "New Books," "Book Review," and "Children's Books and Records."

Teacher Resources: Book Clubs

Carnival Book Club
P.O. Box 6035
Columbia, MO 65205

Children's Book-of-the-Month Club
P.O. Box 8813
Camp Hill, PA 17012

Parents Magazine Read-Aloud Book Club
685 Third Avenue
New York, NY 10017

Scholastic Book Clubs
P.O. Box 7502
Jefferson City, MO 65102

Troll Book Clubs
320 Route 17
Mahwah, NJ 07430

Trumpet Book Clubs
Dell Publishing Company
1 Dag Hammarskjold Plaza
New York, NY 10017

CURRICULUM MATERIAL PRODUCERS

THIS chapter provides information on publishers and producers of early childhood education materials, books, supplementary materials, software, and other items. For some of the larger publishers, we have provided a listing of early childhood series and book titles. For other companies, we provide a description of products. Much of the information in this chapter is based on the publishers' catalogues; for more details, you should contact the publishers and producers directly. The addresses and phone numbers given are for the offices that will supply catalogues and other promotion material; note that these phone numbers are not for the editorial offices.

ABC School Supply, Inc.
3312 North Berkeley Lake Road
P.O. Box 100019
Duluth, GA 30136-9419
800-669-4ABC

Infants, preschool. Learning materials, games, manipulatives, puzzles, music and instruments, blocks, movement education, resource books, big books, cassette read-alongs, videocassettes, whole language kits (readiness, perception), math kits (sorting, counting, classification), science activity kits

Academic Therapy Publications
20 Commercial Boulevard
Novato, CA 94949-6191
800-422-7249

Grades preK–12. Tests, supplementary curriculum materials, parent/teacher resources, remediation programs

Addison-Wesley Publishing Company
Jacob Way
Reading, MA 01867
800-447-2226

Happily Ever After (series)
PreK–grade 1. Complete literature-based early reading program. Big books classics package, teacher's guide, supplementary materials including English and Spanish audiocassette

Now Presenting: Classic Tales for Readers Theatre (series)
Elementary grades. Teacher's resource book, poster set

Superkids (series)
Grades K–1. Multi-level reading program. Student reader, teacher's resource kit, supplementary materials including audiocassettes

Teaching Language, Literature, and Culture (series)

Grades K–2. Multicultural early childhood program. Books, program binder, audiocassettes, posters

Grades K–3. Texts for natural science, mathematics, music, arts, cooking, social studies

Titles for parents: *Heart to Heart: Family Reading for Home and School, Right at Home: Family Experiences for Building Literacy, Growing Up With Language: How Children Learn to Talk*, and more. Titles for teachers: *Ten Best Ideas for Reading Teachers, Learning from Children: New Beginnings for Teaching Numerical Thinking, Pathways: Guidance Activities for Young Children, Infant and Toddler Programs: A Guide to Very Early Childhood Education* and more.

Agency for Instructional Technology (AIT)
Box A
Bloomington, IN 47402-0120
800-457-4509

Grades K–12. Videocassette series, interactive videodisc/instructional software (Apple/Macintosh), teacher's guides. For communication skills, literature, library skills

AGS (American Guidance Services)
Publishers' Building
Circle Pines, MN 55014-1796
800-328-2560

High Hat Early Reading Program
Preschool-Grade 1. Guides, workbook, software, High Hat puppet and cane

Listening to the World
Grades K–2. Manual, audiocassettes, sound book, song cards, game boards, plastic markers, rhythm instruments

The Adventures of Little Tune
Grades preschool to 2. Guides, big books, small books, audiocassettes

AGS® Language Decks (sequencing cards, cause and effect cards, association cards for preschool–adult); picture collections, articulation decks, games, language arts resources

KeyMath Teach and Practice (TAP)
Grades K–8. Lesson cards, blackline masters, teacher's guide

KeyMath Early Steps
Grades K–1. Teacher's guides, concepts and skills inventory, blackline masters

KeyMath Activity Pacs: Versatile manipulatives to enrich your math program
Grades K–6.

I Am Amazing: Promoting health, safety, and self-esteem
Grades preschool–K.

Fit For Me: Activities for Building Motor Skills in Young Children
Ages 3–6. Teacher's guide, activity cards, audiocassette

In health and science for preschoolers–2, *BodySkills: A Motor Development Curriculum for Children, Body Right* (A sexual abuse prevention program that instills confidence), *Drug Free* (series to prevent drug abuse and help students resist drugs)

In personal development, ages 0–7, *Small Wonder* (daily activities for babies and toddlers), *DUSO: Developing Understanding of Self and Others, Taking Part: Introducing Social Skills to Children,*

Grades K–12. Diagnostic tests, supplementary programs including software for language, speech and auditory development, reading

AIMS Education Foundation
P.O. Box 8120
Fresno, CA 93747-8120
209-255-4094

Grades K–9. Activity and investigation books on botany, the environment, seasons, energy sources, weather, basic physical science, magnetism, electricity

Albert Whitman & Company

6340 Oakton Street
Morton Grove, IL 60053-2723
800-255-7675

Preschool-grade 8. Supplemental reading to reading preparation and learning to read. Fiction, riddles, biographies, concept books (on abuse, AIDS, intergenerational, death, illnesses, families), holiday books, multicultural books

American Academy of Pediatrics

141 Northwest Point Boulevard
P.O. Box 927
Elk Grove Village, IL 60009-0927
800-433-9016

Emergency Medical Services for Children: The Role of the Primary Care Provider, Guidelines for Health Supervision, Health in Day Care and other theses on general child care.

American Association of School Administrators

1801 North Moore Street
Arlington, VA 22209-9988
703-875-0730

Guidelines for the teaching of reading and writing

American Chemical Society

1155 16th Street, NW
Room 810
Washington, DC 20036
202-872-6165

Grades K-6. Monthly publication, *WonderScience Magazine,* with physical science activities for elementary school science

American Coal Foundation

1130 Seventeenth Street, NW
Washington, DC 20036

Grades K-12. Curriculum materials relating to coal, electricity, land reclamation

American Education Publishing

3790 East Fifth Avenue
Columbus, OH 43219
800-542-7833

Distributes materials from Creative Education, The Child's World, Listening Library, and Milliken. Books, cassettes, posters

American Language Academy

Suite 550
1401 Rockville Pike, MD 20852
800-346-3469

Skills levels: beginning through advanced, ESL and EFL students. Software for Apple/IBM, teacher's handbooks, interactive sound/graphic programs. For grammar, reading, vocabulary

American Nuclear Society

555 North Kensington Avenue
La Grange Park, IL 60525
312-352-6611

Grades K-12. Curriculum guides and information booklets on nuclear energy, nuclear waste, energy alternatives; also audiovisual lending library

American School Publishers

SRA School Group
P.O. Box 5380
Chicago, IL 60680-5380
800-843-8855

Grades 1-12. Supplementary programs in whole language, reading, content area reading, test preparation, composition, grammar, writing (see also under SRA School group)

American Teaching Aids

4424 West 78th Street
Bloomington, MN 55435
800-526-9907

Grades preK–6. Resource books, badges, borders, calendars/accessories, charts, *Drill-It* workbooks, game pieces, incentive charts, interactive posters, stickers, teacher resources

Barnell-Loft

SRA School Group
P.O. Box 5380
Chicago, IL 60680-5380
800-843-8855

Grades preK–8. Supplementary programs for comprehension, phonics, specific skills, multiple skills, reading, spelling (see also under SRA School Group)

Barron's Educational Series, Inc.

P.O. Box 8040, 250 Wireless Boulevard
Hauppauge, NY 11788
800-645-3476

Children's books for all ages. Study guides for English/language arts and literature

Beacon Films
(Altschul Group Corporation)

930 Pitner Avenue
Evanston, IL 60202
800-323-5448

Videocassettes and films for language arts/ English, including *The Kids of DeGrassi Street Series, The Ray Bradbury Series, Storybook International Series, The Beacon Short Story Collection, Shakespeare from Page to Stage*

Beckley-Cardy

5 West First Street
Duluth, MN 55802
800-446-1477

Early childhood. Math manipulatives, math and language drills, *Family Day Care Activities from A to Z*, puzzles

BGR Publishing

4520 North 12th Street
Phoenix, AZ 85014
800-892-BOOK

Grades preK–6. Books and materials with emphasis on whole language and multiculturalism

Bo Peep Productions

P.O. Box 982
Eureka, MT 59917
800-532-0420

Action videos for toddlers and preschoolers. *Doing Things: Eating, Washing, In Motion, Bugs Don't Bug Us!, Good Morning, Good Night: A Day on the Farm, Moving Machines*

Book-Lab

P.O. Box 7316
500 74th Street
North Bergen, NJ 07047
800-654-4081

Instructional materials for language-delayed learners. Readers, spelling workbooks, and teacher's guides

Boyds Mills Press

910 Church Street
Honesdale, PA 18431
717-253-1164

Ages 2–5. Colorful illustrated classics and new titles

Branden

17 Station Street, Box 843
Brookline Village, MA 02147
617-734-2045

Classics, fiction, general nonfiction, computer software, women's studies, and biographies

Carolina Biological Supply

2700 York Road
Burlington, NC 27215
800-334-5551

Grades K-12. Equipment, apparatus, models, chemistry kits, rock and mineral collections and teaching aids for science classes

Carson-Dellosa

P.O. 35665
Greensboro, NC 27425
800-321-0943

Grades K-5. *Hands on Science, The Big Book of Scissor Skills, Everything for Language Arts,* game books for teaching whole language and stickers for all occasions

Celsa Learning Systems

120 Habersham Street
Savannah, GA 31401
912-232-6444

Preschool. Blocks with the alphabet and pictures on them

Chariot Software Group

3659 India Street, Suite 100C
San Diego, CA 92103
800-800-4540

Grades K-12. Macintosh educational software for English/language arts, including English grammar computer, grammar tutorials, linkword, pronunciation tutors, reading maze, *Sounds of English, Spell It Plus*

Charlesbridge Publishing

85 Main Street
Watertown, MA 02172
800-225-3214
617-926-0329

Thematic Big Book Sets
PreK-2. Theme selection of big books, small books and teaching notes.

Early Bird
PreK-K. Whole language approach includes teacher resource binder, big books, small books. Available in Spanish

Networks
Grades K-3. Whole language instruction for integrated learning.

Sunrise Phonics
Grades K-2.

Young Discovery Library (series)
Grades 3-6. Pocket-sized encyclopedias

Grades K-8. *Alphabet Books* (series), *Insights: Comprehension* (series) a reading-comprehension program, *Insights: Reading as Thinking* (series), *Sparks for Learning*, a special needs resource book, *Strategies for Language Expansion* (series)

CHEF (Comprehensive Health Education Foundation)

22323 Pacific Highway South
Seattle, WA 98198
800-323-2433

Grades K-2. *Primarily Health*™ units covered in basic health

Clarion Books

215 Park Avenue South
New York, NY 10003
800-225-3362

Preschool-grade 3. Illustrated fiction and nonfiction.

Communication Skill Builders

3830 East Bellevue
P.O. Box 42050
Tucson, AZ 85733
800-866-4446

Grades K-12. Culturally and linguistically diverse materials for speech and language therapy. Curriculum guides, teacher's manuals, assessment forms, activity books and kits, audio- and videocassettes, computer software

Community Playthings

Box 901
Rifton, NY 12471-0901
800-777-4244

Preschool. Product line includes toys for gross motor skills, active play, dramatic and social play

Compu-Teach™

78 Olive Street
New Haven, CT 06511
800-448-3224

Grades preK-6. Software for IBM/Macintosh/ Apple. In reading, story composition, writing

CONDUIT

The University of Iowa
Oakdale Campus
Iowa City, IA 52242
800-365-9774

Writer's Helper
Software for Windows™/Macintosh/Apple/ IBM-DOS. Prewriting and revising software includes teacher's manual, student edition, instructional videocassette

SEEN: Tutorials for Critical Reading Software for Apple/IBM. Includes teacher's manual

Constructive Playthings

1227 East 119th Street
Granview, MO 64030
800-448-4115

Preschool. Culturally diverse materials for antibias curriculums

Continental Press

520 East Bainbridge Street
Elizabethtown, PA 17022
800-233-0759

Grades K-12. Activity units, manipulative sets, skills series, literature-based reading, software, teacher's resource books, phonics programs, Spanish resources

Creative Education, Inc.

P.O. Box 227
Mankato, MN 56002-0227
507-388-6273

Investigating Science Series
Grades K-8. Blackline reproducible science books

Grades K-12. Illustrated children's literature

Creative Publications

5040 West 11th Street
Oak Lawn, IL 60453
800-624-0822

Grades preK-6. Teacher's resource books. Series titles include: *Themeworks, Language Through Literature, Early Childhood Language, Language Arts and Problem-Solving, Storytelling and Writing*

Creative Teaching Press

P.O. Box 6017
Cypress, CA 0630-0017
800-444-4CTP

Grades K-8. Resource guides, activity books, overhead transparencies, big book kits, shape book kits, *Learning about the United States* (series)

Critical Thinking Press & Software

Midwest Publications
P.O. Box 448
Pacific Grove, CA 93950
800-458-4849

Grades K-12. Remedial, average, gifted, at risk. Activity books, resource books, software, tests

Culver Company

Danvers House
130 Centre Street
Danvers, MA 01923
800-428-5837

Grades K–12. Activity booklets, films, video-cassettes concerning energy and natural resources

Curriculum Associates, Inc.

5 Esquire Road
North Billerica, MA 01862-2589
800-225-0248

Grades 2–adult ed. Handbooks, workbooks, teacher's guides, software in spelling, writing, language development, reading (available in Spanish)

Cusenaire Company of America

P.O. Box 5026
White Plains, NY 10602-5026
800-237-3142

Grades K–9. Measurement materials, teacher's resource materials, math, literature, environmental science, physical science, microscopes and magnifiers, life science, earth science, science equipment and supplies

D. C. Heath and Company

School Division
125 Spring Street
Lexington, MA 02173
800-235-3565
Literature

Explore-a-Story (series)
Grades K–5. Storybooks, software, activity books

Heath Reading (series)
Grades K–8. Textbooks, teacher's edition packages, teacher's resource materials, supplementary materials including audiocassettes, videocassettes, literature collections, software, Spanish resources

Dale Seymour Publications

P.O. Box 10888
Palo Alto, CA 94303-0879
800-USA-1100

Grades K–8. Teacher's source books, big books, story books and novels, activity books, self-study guides, reading kits, word games, software, microscopes, posters, science kits, teacher's resources

Dandy Lion Publications

3563 Sueldo
San Luis Obispo, CA 93401
800-776-8032

Literature, reading, poetry, and language workbooks, guides, and activity books

Davidson & Associates, Inc.

P.O. Box 2961
Torrance, CA 90509
800-545-7677

PreK–adult. Software for Apple/Macintosh/IBM/Tandy/Commodore, interactive (audio) programs, teacher materials. In grammar, spelling, journalism, reading

Davis-Grabowski, Inc.— Buki Toys (U.S.A.)Ltd.

P.O. Box 381994
Miami, FL 33138
305-751-3667

Infant–preschool. Educational games, imaginative and active play

Delmar Publishers, Inc.

2 Computer Drive West
P.O. Box 15015
Albany, NY 12212-5015
800-347-7707

Early childhood. *Growing Up with Literature, Early Childhood Experiences in Language Arts: Emerging Literacy, Introduction to Early Childhood Education* and other titles aimed toward caring for and teaching early childhood

Didax, Inc.

One Centennial Drive
Peabody, MA 01960
800-458-0024

Preschool, elementary, special needs. Speech
and language educational activities, reading
readiness materials, clearview materials, literature topical sets/whole language, ladybird
books, games, science kits, resource books,
activity books

Discount School Supply

P.O. Box 670
Capitola, CA 95010-0670
800-627-2829

Preschool–grade 3. Educational toys

Diskovery Educational Systems

1860 Old Okeechobee Road, Suite 105
West Palm Beach, FL 33409
800-331-5489

Grades preK–12. Software for Apple/IBM/
Macintosh/CD-ROM

DLM

P.O. Box 4000
One DLM Park
Allen, TX 75002
800-527-4747

Grades K–12. Alternative instructional materials for early childhood, reading, writing,
grammar, spelling, language development,
speech, remedial/basic skills

Econo-Clad Books

P.O. Box 1777
Topeka, KS 66601
800-255-3502

Grades preK–12. Literature-based and whole
language teaching materials. Literature collections, teacher's guides, teacher's resource packages, videocassettes

ECS Learning Systems, Inc.

P.O. Box 791437
San Antonio, TX 78279-1437
800-68-TEACH

Grades preK–12. Whole language learning
materials, language arts/English supplementary
materials, writing programs, reading resources,
novels units, teacher's resources, software

EDC Publishing

Div. of Educational Development
Corporation
P.O. Box 470663
Tulsa, OK 74147

Ages infants–14. Songbooks, first skills, first
languages, picture classics

EDL

P.O. Box 210726
Columbia, SC 29221
800-227-1606

Reading levels 1–13 (remedial). Vocabulary,
reading comprehension, fluency, and writing
programs. Student books, teacher's guides and
supplementary materials including audio- and
videocassettes, and software

Edmark

P.O. Box 3218
Redmond, WA 98073-3218
800-426-0856

Ages 3-9. Software for early childhood

Education Development Center, Inc.

55 Chapel Street
Newton, MA 02160
800-225-4276

Grades K-6. *Insights,* an inquiry-based,
hands-on science curriculum: includes units on
the environment, living things, the senses,
habitats, sound, skeletons, the human body

Educational Activities, Inc.

P.O. Box 392
Freeport, NY 11520
800-645-3739

Grades K–adult. Software for Apple/Macintosh/MS-DOS, voice-interactive programs, support materials. In English, basics, vocabulary, spelling, writing, simulation programs

Educational Development Specialists

5505 East Carson Street, Suite 250
Lakewood, CA 90713-3093
213-420-6814

Think Earth
Grades K–3. Environmental education program. Instructional units, teacher's guides, posters, reproducible masters, videocassette

Educational Insights

19560 S. Rancho Way
Dominguez Hills, CA 90220
800-933-3277

Preschool–grade 2. Phonics, signs, games, following directions, art, reading, mathematics and science touchable teaching aids

Edumate, Educational Materials

2231 Morena Boulevard
San Diego, CA 92110
619-275-7117

Ages 1–8. Ethnic learn to dress dolls, blocks, sound recognition tubes, masks, audiocassettes. Games in English and Spanish

Encyclopedia Britannica

310 South Michigan Avenue
Chicago, IL 60606
800-554-9862

The New 1993 Compton's Encyclopedia
Primary-junior high school grades. Encyclopedia available on computer

Compton's Precyclopedia
Preschool–grade 3. 16-volume encyclopedia, activities book, poster, worksheets

Polka-Dot Puppy Books (series)
Preschool–grade 2. Beginning reading concepts

Let's Take a Walk Books (series)
Grades K–2. Beginning reading concepts

Talk-Along Books (series)
Grades K–2. Beginning reading concepts

Magic Castle Readers (series)
Preschool–grade 2. Reading/language development in science, math, social science, creative arts and health safety. Available in Spanish

Sound Box Books (series)
Preschool–grade 2. Set of 26

I Love To Read Collection (series)
Grades K–4. Set of 24

Class Tales (series)
Grades K–2. Set of 30

Grades K–4. Series of stories, fantasies, fairy tales, mysteries, poems, magic monsters, safety, health, science, math, history, sports

Environmental Education for Preschoolers

c/o Center for Environmental Programs
Bowling Green State University
Bowling Green, OH 43403
419-372-7278

Fostering a Sense of Wonder During the Early Childhood Years
Early childhood. Guide and bibliography toward fostering environmental awareness

Facts On File, Inc.

460 Park Avenue South
New York, NY 10016-7382
800-322-8755

Reference materials in language arts and literature, including bibliographies and dictionaries

Fearon/Janus/Quercus
500 Harbor Boulevard
Belmont, CA 94002
800-877-4283

Special education/remedial programs. Language arts/reading softcover texts, curriculum guides, study guides, novels, audiocassettes, workbooks, magazines

1st Book Productions
P.O. Box 870128
New Orleans, LA 70128
504-242-2260

Ages 6 months to 1 year. Personalized beginning book for learning alphabet and numbers

Focus Media, Inc.
839 Stewart Avenue
P.O. Box 865
Garden City, NY 11530
800-645-8989

Grades preK-12. Software for Apple/MS-DOS/Macintosh/Commodore, support materials. In reading, writing, vocabulary, spelling

Frank Schaffer Publications, Inc.
23740 Hawthorne Boulevard
P.O. Box 2853, Dept. 444
Torrance, CA 90509-2853
800-421-5565

Early childhood. Floor puzzles and giant floor puzzles, games, seals and badges

Franklin Learning Resources
122 Burrs Road
Mt. Holly, NJ 08060
800-525-9673

Hand-held electronic learning products. Spelling, dictionary companion, language master, wordmaster, and encyclopedia series.

Gamco Industries, Inc.
P.O. Box 1862N1
Big Spring, TX 79721-1911
800-351-1404

Grades K-12. Software for Apple/MS-DOS/Macintosh, support materials. In phonics, spelling, vocabulary, reading comprehension, writing, grammar

Goldencraft
5440 North Cumberland Avenue
Chicago, IL 60656-1494
800-621-1115

Preschool-grade 3. Early childhood, easy reading

GoodYearBooks
1900 East Lake Avenue
Glenview, IL 60025
800-628-4480

Preschool-grade 6. Early childhood adventures, references including *Roget's Children's Thesaurus*, whole language, reading, building self-esteem, critical thinking, learning through art, multicultural, social studies, motivating math, and titles for teachers on classroom management

Graphic Learning
61 Mattatuck Heights Road
Waterbury, CT 06705
800-874-0029

Grades K-12. Integrated language arts/social studies programs. Student desk maps, activity pages, teacher's guides, workbooks, supplementary materials. Integrates geography, history, economics, politics, sociocultural concepts, map and globe skills, language/study skills, thinking skills

Gryphon House

P.O. Box 275
Mt. Rainier, MD 20712
800-638-0928

Ages 3–8. Early childhood book collection in multicultural, imagination, rhymes, feelings, self-esteem, Spanish, special days, science

H.P. Kopplemann, Inc.

Paperback Book Service
P.O. Box 145
Hartford, CT 06141-0145
800-243-7724

Grades K–12. Multicultural, literature based and whole language materials, software, video-cassettes, reading collections, teacher's guides, filmstrips, literature tests

Hammond Education Catalog

515 Valley Street
Maplewood, New Jersey 07040
800-526-4935

Grades K–12. Reading skills series. Classroom packs, softcover texts, teacher's answer key

Hand in Hand

Route 26
RR 1, Box 1425
Oxford, ME 04270
800-872-9745

Preschool. Toys for early lessons—play along, music, adjusting to siblings, early participation, curiosity

Harcourt Brace Jovanovich, Inc.

School Department
6277 Sea Harbor Drive
Orlando, FL 32821-9989
800-CALL-HBJ

Early Childhood

Bill Martin Big Books
Early childhood. Big books, audiocassettes, teacher's guides

Bright Start™
PreK. Themepacks include lap book and class library books, read-at-home books (available in Spanish), supplementary materials; teacher packs; teacher's resource video; parent partners program

The HBJ Kindergarten Literature Collection (series)
Grade K. Lap book, class library books, audiocassette

Handwriting

HBJ Handwriting (series)
Student editions, teacher's editions, teacher's resource materials, supplementary materials

Reading/Language

Basic Drills in English Skills I–IV
Grades 3-6. Workbooks, answer keys

Focus on Writing (series)
Grades 3-8. Workbooks

HBJ Language (series)
Grades K-8. Textbooks, teacher's editions, teacher's resource banks, supplementary materials include home activities (Spanish), audiocassettes, software

Imagination (series)
Grades K-6. Textbooks, teacher's editions, teacher's resource banks, supplementary materials including audiocassettes, software, video workshop

Impressions (series)
K-6. Readers, student anthologies, teacher resource books, supplementary materials including audiocassettes

Reading/Literature

HBJ Lectura (series)
Grades K-5. Spanish reading program. Textbooks, teacher's editions, supplementary materials

HBJ Reading Program (series)
Grades K-8. Textbooks, teacher's editions, teacher's resource banks, supplementary materials including audio- and videocassettes, software

HRW Reading: Reading Today and Tomorrow (series)
Grades K–8. Textbooks, teacher's editions, teacher's resource materials, supplementary materials including audiocassettes, software

Spelling

HBJ Spelling (series)
Levels 1–8. Student editions (consumable), teacher's editions, teacher's resource books, supplementary materials include audiocassettes, software

Harlan Davidson, Inc.
3110 North Arlington Heights Road
Arlington Heights, IL 60004-1592
312-253-9720

The Crofts Classics series contains classic works in English, American, and world literature; Goldentree bibliographies in language and literature

Hartley Courseware
133 Bridge Street
Dimondale, MI 48821
800-247-1380

Early learning. Educational software for reading and language, mathematics, science, social studies, problem solving

Heinemann Boynton/Cook
361 Hanover Street
Portsmouth, NH 03801-3959
800-541-2086

Teacher's resource books for reading, writing, literature, whole language, poetry, drama

Hoffman Educational Systems
1863 Business Center Drive
Duarte, CA 91010
800-472-2625

Laser Learning™ Barcode Application

Videodiscs, user's guides, laserdisc player, barcode reader. Videodisc reading program, process writing program

Holbrook-Patterson, Inc.
633 Race, P.O. Box 447
Coldwater, MI 49036
800-822-8121

Early childhood storage and play equipment including centers for small motor, large motor, science, art, role play, language

Houghton Mifflin
Department J
One Beacon Street
Boston, MA 02108-9971
800-323-5663

English

Houghton Mifflin English Levels K–8 (series)
Grades K–8. Textbooks, teacher's editions, teacher's resources, student workbooks, supplementary materials including audiocassettes, limited English proficiency activity masters

Grades K–8. Computer software including *FirstWriter, The Grolier Writer, Language Activities Courseware: Grammar and Study Skills, Microcourse Language Arts*

Reading/Literature

Houghton Mifflin Reading (series)
Grades K–8. Student readers, teacher's guides, teacher's resource file, supplementary materials

Houghton Mifflin Reading/Language Arts Program (series)
Grades K–8. Literary readers, teacher's guides, supplementary materials

Houghton Mifflin Reading: The Literature Experience (series)
Grades K–8. Student anthologies, theme books, read along books, teacher's editions, teacher's resource materials, supplementary materials including audiocassettes

Houghton Mifflin Transition
Grades K–8. Limited English-proficient student program. Student readers, workbooks, teacher's guides

Programa de lectura en español de Houghton Mifflin
Grades K–6. Literature-based reading program in Spanish. Spanish trade books, teacher's guides, student workbooks, supplementary materials

Grades K–8. Reading Resources literature collections, book and audiocassette programs, children's books and story plans, trade-author videocassettes, reading software

Vocabulary

Houghton Mifflin Spelling and Vocabulary (series)
Grades 1–8. Student books, teacher's editions, teacher's resource books, supplementary materials

Social Studies (General)

Houghton Mifflin Social Studies (series)
Grades 1–8. Textbooks, teacher's editions, Spanish editions, student text, supplementary materials including trade book sets

The National Proficiency Survey™ Series
Test booklets, answer sheets, technical manual, administrator's summary

Grades K–3. Illustrated multicultural, intergenerational fiction and nonfiction

Humanities Software, Inc.

408 Columbia Street, Suite 222
P.O. Box 950
Hood River, OR 97031
800-245-6737

Grades K–12. Software for IBM/Tandy/Apple/Macintosh, support materials. In writing, reading, whole language

I AM SPECIAL

200 Noll Plaza
Huntington, IN 46750
800-348-2440

Preschool to grade 3. Religious education materials, *A Teacher's Handbook for Children with Disabilities*

I/CT—Instructional/ Communications Technology, Inc.

10 Stepar Place
Huntington Station, NY 11746
516-549-3000

Grades K–adult. Software for Apple/MS-DOS and support materials, filmstrips, books, activity books, audiocassettes. For oral language development, visual efficiency, perceptual accuracy and efficiency, word recognition, decoding and spelling, vocabulary development, reading, comprehension skills, expressive skills, computer awareness

IBM Direct

PC Software Department 829
One Culver Road
Dayton, NJ 08810
800-222-7257

PreK–adult. Software for IBM, support materials, multimedia materials including CD-ROM, videodiscs, videocassettes. In reading comprehension, writing, spelling, grammar, vocabulary. Spanish program

Ideals Publishing Corporation

P.O. Box 140300
Nashville, TN 37214-0300
914-332-8500

Ages 3 to adult. Audiocassette collections of Christmas music, Appalachian folk songs, press-out Christmas decorations, animal Q-&-A series, activity books (models, games, puzzles, recipes), fiction and nonfiction

Insect Lore Products

P.O. Box 1535
Shafter, CA 93263
800-LIVE-BUG

Preschool–adult. Butterflies, ants, spiders and habitats. Videocassettes on insects, animals, environment. Illustrated fiction and nonfiction

Intellimation

Library for the Macintosh
Department 2SCK
P.O. Box 219
Santa Barbara, CA 93116-9954
800-346-8355

Grades K–12. Software for Macintosh, multi-media programs. In writing, grammar, spelling, literature

Interact

Box 997-H92
Lakeside, CA 92040
800-359-0961

Grades K–12. Simulation programs. Student guides, teacher's guides, supplementary materials including software. Topics include American literature, world literature, humanities, reading and editing skills, genealogy, poetry, media studies/mythology, public speaking, writing, geography, U.S. history, world history, government, economics, psychology, ecology

International Society for Technology in Education

1787 Agate Street
Eugene, OR 97403-1923
503-346-4414

Journals, books, courseware, teacher's guides to meet the needs of educators integrating computer technology in the classroom

IRI/Skylight Publishing, Inc.

200 East Wood Street, Suite 274
Palatine, IL 60067
800-348-4474

Grades K–12. Teacher's resource books, handbooks, videocassettes

J. Weston Walch, Publisher

321 Valley Street
P.O. Box 658
Portland, ME 04104-0658
800-341-6094

Materials for meeting literacy needs, whole language approaches, skills programs in reading and writing, story collections. Photocopy masters, activity cards, audiocassettes, student books, teacher's guides

J. L. Hammett Co.

P.O. Box 9057
Braintree, MA 02184
800-955-2200

Toys for infant and toddler play, manipulatives, language arts, science

Jamestown Publishers

P.O. Box 9168
Providence, RI 02940
800-USA-READ

Grades K–12. Anthologies, big books (English and Spanish), readers, skills series, literature programs, comprehension programs, classic author kits, reading the content fields kits

Jostens Learning Corporation

7878 North 16th Street
Suite 100
Phoenix, AZ 85020-4402
800-422-4339

PreK–grade 12. Software for Apple/IBM/Tandy. In language development (available in Spanish), reading, writing

Judy/Instructo

4424 West 78th Street
Bloomington, MN 55435
800-832-5228

Preschool–grade 2. Educational materials for English/language arts, including desk tapes, sorting boxes, picture cards, puzzles, alphabet wall charts

K-12 MicroMedia Publishing
6 Arrow Road
Ramsey, NJ 07446
201-825-8888

Grades 2–12. Software for Apple/Macintosh/
IBM/Tandy. For writing, literature

Kane/Miller Book Publishers
P.O. Box 8515
LaJolla, CA 92038-8515
718-624-5120

Ages 2–8. Illustrated fiction from around the
world. Available in Spanish

Kaplan
P.O. Box 609
Lewisville, NC 27023-0609
800-334-2014

Preschool–grade 3 and up. Toys for science,
art, social growth, language, music, gross motor
skills, manipulatives. Resources for curriculum
and parenting

Kelly Bear Books
Route 3, Box 99
Lafayette, AL 36862
205-864-8991

Kelly Bear Books (series)
Ages 3–9. Learn to share feelings, improve
behavior, be healthy

Knowledge Unlimited, Inc.
Box 52
Madison, WI 53701-0052
800-356-2303

Teacher's guides, filmstrips, audiocassettes for
poetry, journalism, composition; posters; videocassettes of literature classics

Krell Software
Flowerfield Building #7
Saint James, NY 11780-1502

Software for standardized-test preparation

Lakeshore Learning Materials
2695 East Dominquez Street
P.O. Box 6261
Carson, CA 90749
800-421-5354

Infants, preschool, elementary, special education. Arts and crafts, manipulatives, dramatic
play, active play, blocks, music, language skills,
mathematics readiness, science and nature

Laureate Learning Systems, Inc.
110 East Spring Street
Winooski, VT 05404-1837
800-562-6801

Talking software for special needs, compatible
with Apple/IBM/Tandy. For language development, concept development and processing,
reading and advanced cognitive skills

Lauri, Inc
P.O. Box F, Dept NL
Phillips-Avon, ME 04966

Ages 3–9. Manipulatives for all kinds of
occasions

Learning Links, Inc.
2300 Marcus Avenue
New Hyde Park, NY 11042
516-437-9071

Grades K–12. Literature-based study guides,
individual books, whole language sets, reading
books for social studies and science, thematic
units, read alouds, Spanish language books for
young readers

Learning Products Inc.

700 Fee Fee Road
Maryland Heights, MO 63043
314-997-6400

Preschool–grade 3. Games for teaching shapes, colors, forms, stacking, gross motor skills

LEGO Dacta

555 Taylor Road
Enfield, CT 06082
P.O. Box 1600
800-527-8339

Grades preK–2. Manipulatives, curriculum support materials. Scope and sequence includes cognitive development; transportation; animals and the environment; homes, family, and neighborhoods; problem solving and whole language; themes and project work

Live Oak Media

P.O. Box AL
Pine Plains, NY 12567
518-398-1010

Grades K–6. Media adaptations of outstanding children's books. Readalongs, recorded books, videos, sound filmstrips. Available in Spanish

Live Wire Video Publishers

3315 Sacramento Street
San Francisco, CA 94118
800-359-KIDS

Elementary school. Guidance videos enhancing life skills curriculums

Loyola University Press

3441 North Ashland Avenue
Chicago, IL 60657
800-621-1008

Voyages in English (series)
Grades 1–8. Text-workbooks, teacher's guides, test booklets

Macmillan/McGraw-Hill

School Division
220 East Danieldale Road
De Soto, Texas 75115-9990
800-442-9685

Reading

Connections (series)
Grades K–8. Thematic-literature units, teacher's editions, student workbooks, supplementary materials including in-service videotapes, software

McGraw-Hill Reading (series)
Grades K–8. Textbooks, teacher's editions, teacher's resource centers, student workbooks, supplementary materials

Reading Express (series)
Grades K–8. Textbooks, teacher's editions, teacher's resource centers, supplementary materials including software

Spanish Reading

Campanitas de Oro (series)
Grades K–6. Complete Spanish basal reading program. Textbooks, teacher's editions, teacher's resource packages, supplementary materials

Por el Mundo del Cuentro y la Aventura (series)
Grades K–6. Spanish basal-reading series. Textbooks, teacher's guides, workbooks

Early Childhood Programs: complete reading and language programs with supplementary materials. Includes *Big Books, Once upon a Time, Beginning To Read, Write and Listen, Superstart*

Language Arts

Language Arts Today (series)
Grades K–8. Integrated language arts program. Textbooks, teacher's editions, teacher's resource packages, supplementary materials including software

McGraw-Hill English (series)
Grades K–8. Textbooks, teacher's editions, teacher's resource packages, supplementary materials including software

McGraw-Hill Spelling (series)
Grades 1-8. Softcover texts, teacher's editions, teacher's resource packages, supplementary materials including software

Merrill Spelling
Grades K-8. Textbooks, teacher's editions, teacher's resource package, supplementary materials including software

Palmer Method Handwriting (series)
Grades K-8. Softcover texts, teacher's editions, teacher's resource package

Science

Science in Your World (series)
Grades K-6. Spanish/English bilingual edition available. Textbooks, teacher's editions, teacher's resource center, supplementary materials including audiocassettes and videocassettes, software, activity materials kits

Helping Your Child at Home . . . with Science (series)
Grades K-6. Available in Spanish. Activity books, teacher's guides

Social Studies

The World around Us Activity Program (series)
Grades K-2. Big books, project books, social studies anthology, teacher's editions, supplementary materials including audiocassettes

El Mundo que nos rodea programa de actividades (series)
Grades K-2. Spanish program. Big books, project books, social studies anthology, teacher's editions, supplementary materials including audiocassettes

The World around Us (series)
Grades K-7. Textbooks, teacher's editions, supplementary materials including software

World Atlas for Primary Students
Grades K-2. Text

Integrating Catholic Heritage (series)
Grades K-7. Supplementary texts

The MASTER Teacher
Leadership Lane
P.O. Box 1207
Manhattan, KS 66502
800-669-9633

PreK-grade 5. Videocassette series, software

MECC
6160 Summit Drive North
Minneapolis, MN 55430-4003
800-685-MECC

PreK-adult. Software for Macintosh/Apple/MS-DOS, multimedia materials. In reading, spelling, grammar, composition

Media Materials
P.O. Box 9971
Baltimore, MD 21224-0971
800-638-6470

Preschool, early childhood, elementary, special education. Whole language, early math, early learning, social studies cards, manipulatives, beads, puzzles, games

Merrill/Macmillan
SRA School Group
866 Third Avenue
New York, NY 10022
800-621-0476

Preschool-12. Supplementary programs in reading, phonics, grammar, composition, vocabulary. *The Very Young: Guiding Children from Infancy Through the Early Years, Developmentally appropriate Programs in Early Childhood Education, Early Childhood Curriculum, Social Studies for the Preschool/Primary Child, Approaches to Early Childhood Education*

Micrograms Publishing

1404 North Main Street
Rockford, IL 61103
800-338-4726

Grades K-6. Software for Apple. In reading, punctuation, capitalization, grammar, spelling

The Millbrook Press, Inc.

2 Old New Milford Road—Box 335
Brookfield, CT 06804
800-462-4703

Grades K-2, 4, and 8. Reading materials, including biographies and autobiographies

Milliken Publishing Company

1100 Research Boulevard
P.O. Box 21579
St. Louis, MO 63132-0579
800-643-0008

PreK-grade 8. Books, posters, teacher's resource guides, duplicating masters, blackline reproducibles, workbooks, filmstrips, videocassettes, whole language resource guides

Modern Curriculum Press

13900 Prospect Road
Cleveland, OH 44136
800-321-3106

Whole Language

Concept Science (series)
Grades K-3. Student books, big books, teacher's guides. Special teacher's guides for ESL/LEP students. Set themes include *Matter, Energy, The Universe, Animals, Plants, Our Earth.* Available in Spanish.

The Content Connection
Grades K-6. Read-a-loud books, student editions, audiocassettes. Grouped by theme

Folklore: On Stage
Grades 1-8. Dramatic adaptations of folk tales. Student scripts, director's handbook

Language Works: Developing Language
PreK-grade 1. Integrated program. Student books, teacher's reference book. Available in Spanish

Language Works: Exploring Our World
Grades K-4. Integration of science and social studies. Student books, teacher's reference book

Language Works: Folktales
Grades K-3. Integrated program. Student books, teacher's book

Language Works: Stories and Rhymes
Grades K-4. Integrated program. Student books, teacher's reference book

Poetry Works
PreK-grade 3. Posters, teacher's idea book, audiocassette

Swinging Out Language Development Program
Grade preK-1. Big books, books, mini-books, teacher's sourcebooks, supplementary materials

Reading Friends (series)
Grades K-3. Language acquisition. Story packs, organizer binders, puppet friends

What Do You Think? (series)
Grades K-2. Skills integration. Big books, student books, teacher's idea books, supplementary materials

The Writing Program (series)
Grades 1-9. Softcover texts, teacher's guides, writing folders

Yes, I Can! (series)
PreK-grade 1. Available in Spanish. Language acquisition. Big books, student books, teacher's guides

Young Explorers (series)
Grades K-4. Student books, big books, teaching companions, supplementary materials. Series themes include social studies, mathematics, science

Phonics

Discovery Phonics: An Integrated Approach to Decoding Strategies (series)
Grades K-2. Big books, small books, audiocassettes, teacher's resources

Literature First: Phonics with a Purpose (series)
Grades K-3. Softcover texts, teacher's guides, posters

Mortimer Moose Turns the Alphabet Loose (series)
PreK-grade 6. Student books, teacher's handbook, supplementary materials including audiocassettes, puppets

Grades K–4. Phonics Workbook Series including *Phonics First, Phonics Is Fun, Phonics Plus, Phonics Works, Schoolhouse Phonics, Starting off with Phonics*

Reading/Thinking Skills

Grades 1–3. Classroom Reading books, teacher's guides. Series includes *Beginning-to-Read Library, Just Beginning-To-Read Collection, Sharing and Caring Collection The Fantasy Collection, The Science and Technology Collection, The Social Awareness Collection, The Dragons and Dinosaurs Collection, Star Series Readers, The High Action Treasure Chest, The Books of Myths, MCP Endangered Species Readers*

Grades 1–8. Workbooks student workbooks, teacher's guides. Series includes *Keystones for Reading, Vocabulary Works, Reading in the Content Areas, Stepping into Reading: A Guide to Critical Thinking, Thinking about Reading, High Action Reading, Comprehension Plus, My Kindergraph, Skill-By-Skill Workbooks, Skill Stations*

Science

Concept Ecology (series)
Grades 1–6. Student books, teacher's guides. Series includes habitats, endangered animals, environmental challenges

Concept Science (series)
Grades K–3. Student books, big books, teacher's guides. Special teacher's guides for esl/lep students. Set themes include matter, energy, the universe, animals, plants, our earth

The MCP Science Series
Grades 1–6. Softcover texts, teacher's editions. Topics include life, health, earth, matter and energy, the universe. Available in Spanish

Science Workshop (series)
Grades 1–6. Activity books, teacher's editions

See How It Grows/See How It's Made
Grades K–1. Student books

Young Explorers in Science (series)
Grades K–4. Story books, big books, teaching companions

Social Studies

Maps, Charts, and Graphs (series)
Grades 1–8. Softcover texts, teacher's guide, transparencies

Young Explorers in Social Studies
Grades K–4. Story books, big books, teaching companions

Modern Educational Resource Guide
5000 Park Street North
St. Petersburg, FL 33709
800-243-6877

K–12. Free loan programs, free teaching materials, media for the classroom, videos for inservice training, computer and network-based programs, interactive learning systems, and filmstrips

Morrison School Supplies, Inc.
304 Industrial Way
San Carlos, CA 94070
800-950-4567

Early childhood. Touchables, wall enhancers, rhythm instruments, blocks, dinosaurs, games

My Friends
5844 Creek Valley Road
Edina, MN 55439-1212
612-941-1654

Early childhood. Dolls that indicate different emotions

National Association for the Education of Young Children
(NAEYC)
1834 Connecticut Avenue, NW
Washington, DC 20009-5786
800-424-2460

Early childhood. Resources in accreditation, curriculum for preschool, kindergarten, and primary, developmentally appropriate practice in preschool and primary, discipline, early childhood profession, for parents, infants and toddlers, multicultural education, physical environment, play, programs and schools, quality, compensation, affordability, teachers and caregivers

National Council of Teachers of English

1111 Kenyon Road
Urbana, IL 61801
217-328-3870

Grades K-college. Booklists, guidebooks, teacher's resource books, staff development materials, audiocassettes, videocassettes

National Resource Center for Middle Grades Education

University of South Florida
College of Education-EDU-118
Tampa, Florida 33620-5650
813-974-2530

Curriculum guides, resource books, reproducible interdisciplinary units, activity books for reading, writing, thinking skills, self-concept, study skills

National Science Teachers Association

Publication Sales
1742 Connecticut Avenue, NW
Washington, DC 20009
202-328-5800

Grades K-12. Curriculum guides and other publications for science teaching

New Dimensions in Education

61 Mattatuck Heights Road
Waterbury, CT 06705
800-227-9120

PreK-grade 3. Language immersion and reading readiness programs. Student readers, teacher's editions, supplementary materials including audio- and videocassettes

Newbridge Educational Programs

P.O. Box 965
Hicksville, NY 11802-0965
800-347-7829

Macmillan Early Skills Manipulatives
Preschool-grade 2. Skill-building activities in 12 units, 12-drawer box organizer and teaching guide

Macmillan Early Science Activities
Preschool-grade 2. Hands-on activities in 16 units, cards, teaching aids and storage box

Macmillan Early Skills Program
Preschool-grade 2. More than 2,500 ideas and activities in 24 units with index

Macmillan Seasonal Activity Packs
Preschool-grade 2. 32 units, over 3,200 ideas and activities, index and storage boxes

Novel Units

P.O. Box 1461, Dept. C
Palatine, IL 60078
708-253-8200

Grades K-12. Support materials for the study of literature. Also integrated whole language approach, including literature units, vocabulary, and writing materials

Open Court Publishing Company

315 Fifth Street
Peru, IL 61354
800-435-6850

The Headway Program (series)
Grades K-6. Readers, teacher's editions, workbooks, supplementary materials

Open Court Reading and Writing (series)
Grades K-6. Student workbooks, teacher's guides, teacher's resource books, supplementary materials

Grades K–6. Special Purpose Programs and Materials includes *Gifted and Talented Language Arts: The RISE Program, Reading Comprehension: Catching On, Remedial Reading: Breaking the Code, Skills Recovery Program: The Reading Connection.* Supplemental Reading Kits books grouped by grade and interest level. Magazines include *Ladybug Classroom Library, Cricket Classroom Library*

Orange Cherry/ Talking Schoolhouse Software

P.O. Box 390, Dept. S
Pound Ridge, NY 10576-0390
800-672-6002

PreK–grade 8. Software for Apple/Macintosh/ IBM/Tandy, support materials, multimedia programs. For phonics, reading, vocabulary, grammar, spelling

Parenting & Teaching Publications

16686 Meadowbrook Lane
Wayzata, MN 55391
612-473-1793

Self-Esteem for Tots to Teens
Parenting skills

Parenting Press, Inc.

P.O. Box 75267
Seattle, WA 98125
800-992-6657

Without Spanking or Spoiling
Ages 1–10. Guide to child raising

Ages 1–12. Resources on discipline, self-esteem, temperament, feelings, anger, siblings, sleep, stress, personal safety, difficult topics (e.g., death)

PCA Industries, Inc.

5642 Natural Bridge
St. Louis, MO 63120
800-727-8180

Preschool–lower elementary. Kitchen play, hand and eye development, gross motor skills

Peal Software, Inc.

P.O. Box 8188
Calabasas, CA 91372
800-541-1318

Grade preK. Software for early acquisition of language

Pegasus Learning Company

16 North Chestnut Street
Colorado Springs, CO 80905
719-634-4969

Grades K–8. *Frontiers of Science: Our Environment,* videodisc and resource manual with 60 activities on the environment, technology, energy, patterns, plants and animals; also *Insects: A Closer Look,* videodisc for grades 4–7

Peguis Publishers

520 Hargrave Street
Winnipeg, Manitoba
Canada R3A OX8
800-667-9673

Grades K–7. McCracken, whole language, and native literature programs; teacher's resource books, readers, classroom literature

Pelican Publishing Company

P.O. Box 189
Gretna, LA 70054
800-843-1724

Early childhood. Illustrated children's books

The Peoples Publishing Group, Inc.

P.O. Box 70
365 W. Passaic Street
Rochelle Park, NJ 07662
800-822-1080

Students-at-risk. Series in practical writing, survival reading, contemporary fiction

Perfection Learning™ Corporation

1000 North Second Avenue
Logan, IA 51546-1099
800-831-4190

Preschool–grade 12. Curriculum activities, manipulatives, videos, software and books for reading, writing, social studies and multiculturalism

Perry Publications, Inc.

P.O. Box 204
Whitewater, WI 53190
800-527-2966

Holding on to Childhood
Early childhood. Guide to the use of rhymes for very young children

Phoenix Learning Resources

468 Park Avenue South
New York, NY 10016
800-221-1274

Early childhood. Touchables, manipulatives, songs, games, books for stimulating learning in reading, language arts, mathematics, keyboarding, and social studies and low-cost videocassettes.

Players Press, Inc.

P.O. Box 1132
Studio City, CA 91614
818-784-8918

Play anthologies, activity books, teacher's guides. For drama, clowning and mime, costume reference, make-up, technical theatre, writing

Positive Images Children's Books

593A Macon Street
Brooklyn, NY 11233
800-662-READ

1–12. The best books and videocassettes in multicultural literature

The Putnam & Grosset Group

One Grosset Drive
Kirkwood, NY 13795
800-847-5515

Ages 1 and up. Illustrated children's literature from G.P. Putnam's Sons, Philomel Books, Sandcastle Books, Grosset & Dunlap, Platt & Munk, and Tuffy Books

Queue, Inc.

338 Commerce Drive
Fairfield, CT 06430
800-232-2224

Grades K–12. Software for Apple/IBM/Macintosh, support materials, multimedia materials. In creative writing, reading comprehension, writing skills, life skills, grammar, vocabulary, spelling

Rainbow Educational Video

170 Keyland Court
Bohemia, NY 11716
800-331-4047

Grades K–8. Videos on botany, geology, machines, natural science, animals, astronomy, electricity, weather, energy

Redco Science

11 Robinson Lane
Oxford, CT 06483
203-881-2016

Grades 10–12. Supplies for physics experiments: scales, bench meters, measurement equipment, timers, magnets

Redleaf Press

450 North Syndicate Suite 5
St. Paul, MN 55104-4125
800-423-8309

Family Day Caring
Early childhood. A magazine dealing with important issues for parenting

Time with Toddlers
Early childhood. Videocassette introduces typical toddler behaviors and helpful adult responses

Practical Solutions to Practically Every Problem: The Early Childhood Teacher's Manual

Preschool–early childhood. Curriculum resources using themes, building self-esteem, language, music, dramatic play, movement, games, science, art. Available in Spanish

Refhouse Publications
4356 College View Way
Carmichael, CA 95608-1614

Kinder Capers
Kindergarten. Curriculum, songbook, audiocassette

The Right Combination
Cornerstone Division
6025 Sandy Springs Circle
Atlanta, GA 30328
800-458-3219

Workbooks, blackline masters, teacher's guides for standardized test preparation

Rolf Learning Systems
15201 Roosevelt Boulevard, Suite 106
Clearwater, FL 34620
800-553-7653

Early childhood. Colorful manipulatives

Rutgers University Press
109 Church Street
New Brunswick, NJ 08901
908-932-7764

Learning about Family Life
Grades K–3. Text introducing family life, sexuality, relationships, self-respect, and acceptance. Big book, teacher's manual, and student journals

S & S
P.O. Box 513
Colchester, CT 06415-0513
800-243-9232

Early childhood. Flannelboards, manipulatives, rhythm instruments, puzzles, games

Scholastic, Inc.
2931 East McCarty Street
P.O. Box 7502
Jefferson City, MO 65102-9968
800-325-6149

Preschool

PreK Today Tips
Preschool. Safety, health, classroom management and curriculum

Parent Communication Tips
Preschool. Designed to strengthen home/preschool bond

Teacher Tips
Preschool. Room arrangement, classroom management, choosing books and videos, safety, curriculum

Director Tips
Preschool–early childhood. Big and little books with early childhood themes: accepting differences, conflict resolution, making friends, helping others, cooperation and caring for the environment, families and friends, self-esteem, children's literature, people and places, science through literature, and videocassettes

Elementary Language Arts/Reading

Basal Breaks: Applying Reading Strategies (series)
Grades 1–6. Grade units including paperback titles, teacher's guides

Bookshelf (series)
Grades K–2. Whole language libraries, teacher's resource books, audio packages

Innovations: Experiencing Literature in the Classroom
Grades K–9. Teaching guides for paperback literature

Scholastic Banners: Teaching with Themes (series)
Grades K-2. Big books, little books, read-a-loud books, audiocassettes, song charts, teaching theme folders

Scholastic Bookline (series)
Grades K-6. Science and social studies libraries with supplementary materials

Scholastic SuperPrint (series)
Grades K-12. Classroom publishing software, graphics activity packs, teacher's editions

Science

Science Explorers™
Grades 1-6. Software program includes teaching guide, activity sheets, glossaries
Science Magazine includes *SuperScience*, *ScienceWorld*, and *BIG Science*

School-Age Notes

P.O. Box 40205
Nashville, TN 37204
615-242-8464

Early childhood. *Caring Spaces, Learning Places: Children's Environments That Work, Early Childhood Programs and the Public Schools, Creative Play for the Developing Child* and publications on school-age care

The Science Lab, Inc.

75 Todd Pond Road
Lincoln, MA 01773
617-259-8929

Grades K-6. Science activity and project books, videos, and magic kits. Sea Life software, Dinosaur Zoo software, gem collections, sand collections

Shadow Play Records & Video

Educational Graphics Press, Inc.
P.O. Box 180476
Austin, TX 78718
800-274-8804

Early childhood. Audiocassettes teaching car safety, feelings, sensitivity

Silver Burdett and Ginn

4350 Equity Drive
P.O. Box 2649
Columbus, OH 43216
800-848-9500

Reading

World of Reading (series)
Grades K-8. Textbooks, teacher's editions, teacher's resource kits, early literacy program, supplementary materials including trade book collections, assessment materials, software, reader's journals and workbooks, and interactive teaching kits of audio- and videocassettes, posters, activity guides, theme cards

World of Language (series)
Grades K-8. Textbooks, teacher's editions, teacher's resource file, software, primary literature program, writing and spelling activity books, classroom libraries, assessment materials, multimedia resources including audio- and videocassettes

Social Studies

People in Time and Place (series)
Grades 1-junior high school. Textbooks, teacher's editions, teacher support systems, supplementary materials

People in Time and Place Activity Program
Grades K-2. Primary activity kits, poster book package

Silver Burdett & Ginn Estudios Sociales (series)
Grades 1-5. Textbooks, bilingual teacher's editions, teacher's resource files, supplementary materials including sound filmstrips

Soft-Kat

20630 Nordhoff Street
Chatsworth, CA 91311
800-641-1057

Grades K-12. Software for language arts—reading, spelling, writing, grammar, and vocabulary

Sound It Out Books
914 Laurie Drive
Madison, WI 53711
608-273-0037

Preschool. A natural start to reading with phonetic progression, diverse characters, simple structure, colorful pages

SRA School Group
American School Publishers
Barnell Loft-Merrill-SRA
P.O. Box 5380
Chicago, IL 60680-5380
800-843-8855

Grades K-12. Supplementary programs in reading, literature, life skills, comprehension, handwriting, composition-grammar, process writing, spelling, vocabulary

Steck-Vaughn Company
P.O. Box 26015
Austin, TX 78755
800-531-5015

Hooray, I'm Me!
Kindergarten. Social studies. Big books, little books, teacher's guide, audiocasettes with read-along and listening activities

Culture We Share
Kindergarten. Multicultural. Big books, little books, teachers's guide, audiocassettes with read-along and listening activities

Think, Do and Discover
Kindergarten. Science and technology. Big books, little books, teachers's guide, audiocassettes with read-along and listening activities

3 Cheers for Earth
Kindergarten. Earth. Big books, little books, teachers's guide, audiocassettes with read-along and listening activities

English
First-Time Phonics
Reading levels K-1. Student workbooks, picture cards, classroom library, teacher's editions

Phonics Readers (series)
Reading levels K-2. Readers, teacher's guides

Grades K-6. *Phonics and Sight Word Programs* includes *Building Sight Vocabulary, Power-Word Programs, Sounds, Words, and Meanings*

Whole Language
New Way: Learning with Literature (series)
PreK-3, reading levels 0-3. Big books, student books, teacher's guides, audiocassettes

Steck-Vaughn Writing Dictionary
Grades 1-2. Softcover workbook-dictionary

Steppingstone Stories (series)
Grades K-2. Student books, big books, teacher's guide

Social Studies
Portrait of America (series)
Grades K-12, reading level 4. Resource books on the 50 states and territories

Steck-Vaughn Social Studies (series)
Grades 1-6, reading levels 1-4. Softcover texts, teacher's editions

The Storyboard
P.O. Box 2650
Chino, CA 91708

Preschool-grade 2. Flannelboard stories, Mother Goose, songs, holidays, Aesop's fables

Sundance
P.O. Box 1326
Newton Road
Littleton, MA 01460
800-343-8204

PreK-grade 6. Early childhood materials, literature programs, developmental writing guides, thematic learning units, cross-curriculum units, classroom libraries, audio- and videocassettes

SVE—Society for Visual Education, Inc.

Department JT
1345 Diversey Parkway
Chicago, IL 60614-1299
800-829-1900

PreK-grade 9. Audio- and videocassettes, filmstrips, software, videodiscs. For children's literature, reading, writing, whole language skills

SWOOPE Program

Los Alamos National Laboratory
MS D447
Los Alamos, NM 87545
505-667-8950

Grades K-12. Students Watching Over Our Planet Earth, a hands-on environmental science program

T. S. Denison and Company, Inc.

9601 Newton Avenue South
Minneapolis, MN 55431
800-328-3831

Grades K-6. Kindergarten resource book for science; environmental resource book for grades 2-6; beginning science activity book

T. L. Clark Educational Products Group™

Unit of The Sierra Corporation™
P.O. Box 806
Fort Smith, Arkansas 72902
800-643-9768

Early Learning Concepts™ product line includes educational toys for gross motor skills, and manipulatives

Teacher Support Software

1035 Northwest 57th Street
Gainesville, Florida 32605-4486
800-228-2871

PreK-adult. Software for Apple/MS-DOS, support materials. For whole language, reading, writing, vocabulary

Teacher Ideas Press

Libraries Unlimited, Inc.
P.O. Box 3988
Englewood, CO 80155-3988
800-237-6124

Teacher's resource books, activity books for literature, reading, storytelling, research skills, writing, gifted and talented students

The Teachers' Laboratory

P.O. Box 6480
Brattleboro, VT 05302-6480
802-254-3457

Grades K-12. Distributes books, equipment, and teaching units for study of the environment, measurement, magnets, electricity, design, and technology

Texas Instruments

P.O. Box 10508 M/S 5724
Lubbock, TX 79408
800-TI-CARES

Preschool. Interactive, multisensory, bilingual electronic games

Tom Snyder Productions

90 Sherman Street
Cambridge, MA 02140
800-342-0236

Grades K-12. Software for Apple/Macintosh/IBM/Tandy/MS-DOS, support materials, multimedia materials. For grammar, writing

Unicorn Engineering, Inc

5221 Central Avenue, Suite 205
Richmond, CA 94804
800-899-6687

Intellikeys
Early childhood and elementary. Overlay for
keyboard to help children focus on using
software not searching for keys

United Learning, Inc.

6633 W. Howard Street
Niles, IL 60648-3305
800-424-0362

Grades K–12. Videocassettes, videostrips,
filmstrips, slides. In reading, literature, presentation skills, physical science, chemistry, earth
science, biology, and other subjects

Videodiscovery, Inc.

1700 Westlake Avenue North, Suite 600
Seattle, WA 98109-3012
800-548-3472

Grades K–12. Videodiscs, software for Macin-
tosh/Apple/MS-DOS. For reading, writing,
mythology, film, life science, earth science,
physical science, integrated science

Warren Publishing House, Inc.

P.O. Box 2250
Everett, WA 98203
800-344-4769

Preschool, kindergarten. Teaching themes,
music, language, *Totline*, a bi-monthly newsletter of ideas, *Super Snack News*, reproducible
information on nutritious snacks

Watten/Poe
Teaching Resource Center

P.O. Box 1509
14023 Catalina Street
San Leandro, CA 94577
800-833-3389

Integrated curriculum materials, teacher's
resource books, nursery rhyme strips, easels,
pocket charts and stands, theme kits, big books,
book/audiocassette packages, chalkboards,
markboards

Weaver Instructional Systems

6161 28th Street, Southeast
Grand Rapids, MI 49506
616-942-2891

Reading Efficiency System
Software for Apple/Franklin/Radio Shack/
Acorn/IBM/Atari/Commodore

English Grammar Instructional System
Grades 6 and above. Software for Apple/
Franklin/Radio Shack/Acorn/IBM/Atari/
Commodore

Weekly Reader Corporation

3000 Cindel Drive
P.O. Box 8037
Delran, NJ 08075

Weekly Reader Skills Books (series)
PreK–grade 9. Reading, writing, speech,
vocabulary, and library skills workbooks, science books, science readiness books, U.S.
history, geography, the 1992 elections, Christopher Columbus, supplementary materials

WICAT

The Learning Improvement Company
1875 South State Street
Orem, UT 84058
800-759-4228

Grades K–12. Software programs for capitalization, punctuation, grammar, usage and parts
of speech, writing, whole language writing
activity

William K. Bradford
Publishing Company

310 School Street
Acton, MA 01720
800-421-2009

Grades K–12. Software programs for reading,
language arts and science programs including
physical science simulation software; biology,

chemistry, and astronomy software, life and earth science simulation software; weather forecasting software

WINGS for Learning/Sunburst

1600 Green Hills Road
P.O. Box 660002
Scotts Valley, CA 95067-0002
800-321-7511

Grades K–college. Software for Apple/Macintosh/IBM/Tandy, multimedia materials. For reading, sequencing/categorization, handwriting, spelling, literature, writing

World Book Educational Products

101 Northwest Point Boulevard
Elk Grove Village, IL 60007
800-848-8170

The Early World of Learning
A readiness program using books, hands-on materials to help prepare for kindergarten

Write Source

Educational Publishing House
Box J
Burlington, WI 53105

Language arts handbooks, teacher's guides, activity books, workbooks, posters, literature collections

Zaner-Bloser

2200 West Fifth Avenue
P.O. Box 16764
Columbus, OH 43216-6764
800-421-3018

Day-by-Day Kindergarten Program
Cross-curriculum resource program. Teacher's resource book, student activity book, teacher's guide, supplementary materials

Developing Reading Power
Grades 1–8. Comprehension skills assessment program

Let's Read and Think (series)
Grades 1–3. Student text-workbooks, teacher's editions

Literacy Plus (series)
Grades K–8. Integrated language arts program. Teacher's guides, teacher's reference book, student reference book, student word books, trade book collections, supplementary materials including in-service videocassettes

Spelling Connections (series)
Grades 1–8. Textbooks, teacher's editions, teacher's resource binder, supplementary materials including in-service videocassettes, software

Zaner-Bloser Handwriting: A Way to Self-Expression
Grades K–8. Student workbooks, teacher's editions, teacher's resource binders, supplementary materials including in-service videocassettes

Zaner-Bloser Vocabulary Building (series)
Grades 1–9. Softcover texts, teacher's editions

Grades K–2. Kits, games, story books, and activity packets on environmental studies, conservation, waste management, electricity, energy, wildlife

Zephyr Press

3316 North Chapel Avenue
P.O. Box 13448-E
Tucson, AZ 85732-3448
800-350-0851

Grades K–12. Whole language source books, activity books

STATEWIDE TEXTBOOK ADOPTION

THERE are twenty-two states that have statewide adoption of textbooks and other instructional materials: Alabama, Arizona, Arkansas, California, Florida, Georgia, Idaho, Indiana, Kentucky, Louisiana, Mississippi, Nevada, New Mexico, North Carolina, Oklahoma, Oregon, South Carolina, Tennessee, Texas, Utah, Virginia, and West Virginia.

The policies and procedures for textbook adoption are similar in all twenty-two states, with some minor variations.

Textbook Advisory Committee

In general, the state board of education is responsible for developing guidelines and criteria for the review and selection of textbooks and for appointing members to a textbook advisory committee. However, in a few states, the appointment of committee members is the responsibility of the governor or of the Commissioner of Education.

The textbook advisory committee is usually composed of educators, lay citizens, and parents, and can have from nine to twenty-seven appointees, depending upon the state. Membership is weighted, however, toward individuals who are educators: elementary and secondary teachers in the subject areas in which textbooks are to be adopted, instructors of teacher education and curriculum from local universities and colleges, school administrators, and school board members. Lay citizens, in

order to sit on the committee, should be interested in and conversant with educational issues. An effort is made to select appointees who reflect the diversity of their state's population, and therefore decisions about appointments are often made with the purpose of having a wide representation of ethnic backgrounds and geographical residence within the state.

Adoption Process

The textbook and instructional materials adoption process takes approximately twelve months.

Once the textbook advisory committee is formed, the members conduct an organizational meeting to formulate policy on such issues as adoption subjects and categories; standards for textbook evaluation, allocation of time for publisher presentations, and location of regional sites for such; sampling directions for publishers; and publisher contact. The committee may appoint subcommittees, made up of curriculum and/or subject specialists, to assist them in developing criteria for evaluating instructional materials.

After these procedural matters are agreed upon, the committee issues an official textbook call or invitation to textbook publishers to submit their books. This document provides the publisher with adoption information and subject area criteria, which can be either the curriculum framework or essential skills list. Those publishers interested in having their materials considered for adoption submit their intention to bid, which shows the prices at which the publishers will agree to sell their material during the adoption period. Publishers usually bid current wholesale prices or lowest existing contract prices at which textbooks or other instructional materials are being sold elsewhere in the country.

If their bid has been accepted by the committee, the publishers submit sample copies of their textbooks for examination. The committee then hears presentations by the publishers. This meeting allows the publisher to present the texts submitted for adoption and to answer any questions the committee may have on the material. After publisher presentations, the textbooks are displayed in designated areas throughout the state for general public viewing. The committee then holds public hearings (usually two) which provide citizens with the opportunity to give an opinion on the textbooks offered for adoption. After much discussion and evaluation, the committee makes a recommendations for textbook adoption to the state board of education.

When the board of education approves the committee's recommendations, it negotiates the contract with the chosen publishers and disseminates the list of instructional materials to the school districts. The school districts will then make their textbook selections from this list. A few states also allow their school districts to use materials for the classroom that are not on the adoption list.

Textbook and Instructional Materials

There are two categories of instructional materials: basal and supplementary. Basal, or basic, materials address the goals, objectives, and content identified for a particular subject. Supplementary materials, used in conjunction with the basic text, enhance the teaching of the subject.

Instructional materials may include all or some of the following: hardcover books, softcover books, kits, workbooks, dictionaries, maps and atlases, electronic/computer programs, films, filmstrips, and other audiovisual materials.

The textbook adoption period generally runs from four to six years (California, the exception, has an eight-year contract period for K-8 only). The grade levels for adoption are usually K-12, with the following subject areas: English/language arts, social studies, foreign languages, English as a Second Language, science, mathematics, fine arts, applied arts, health education, physical education, vocational education, driver education, technology education, special education, home economics.

Textbooks and instructional materials are ultimately judged by how well they reflect the state curriculum framework and/or esential skills objectives. Materials are rated on the following criteria: organization, accuracy, and currency of subject content; correlation with grade-level requirements for the subject; adaptability for students with different abilities, backgrounds, and experiences; types of teacher aids provided; author's background and training; physical features; and cost.

In addition, some states have social content requirements that textbooks have to meet. For instance, textbooks should be objective in content and impartial in interpretation of the subject, and should not include offensive language or illustrations. American values (defined as democracy, the work ethic, and free enterprise), culture, traditions, and government should be presented in a positive manner. Respect for the individual's rights, and for the cultural and racial diversity of American society, can also be addressed in the text. Finally, some states declare that textbooks should not condone civil disorder, lawlessness, or deviance.

Kraus thanks the personnel we contacted at the state departments of education for their help in providing the states' textbook adoption lists.

List of Textbooks

Of the twenty-two states that have statewide adoption of instructional materials, New Mexico specifically adopts materials for early childhood and West Virginia adopts for combined subjects in kindergarten. Their materials are listed below; the title, grade level, publisher, and copyright date are provided. However, other states adopt textbooks and other instructional materials in specific subject areas

(English/language arts, social studies, science, etc.) that include prekindergarten through grade 3. Due to space considerations, we have not cited these listings here; please consult the curriculum resource handbooks in the specific subject areas for this information.

New Mexico

Logowriter, Site Licenses, Primary, IBM: Grades K-3
Logo Computer Systems, 1988
(Termination year: 1995)

Logowriter, Site Licenses, Primary, Apple: Grades K-3
Logo Computer Systems, 1988
(Termination year: 1995)

Early Childhood Activities: A Treasury of Ideas from Worldwide Sources: K-3
Humanics, 1982 (Termination year: 1995)

Reading Resource Book: Parents and Beginning Reading: Grades K-3
Humanics, 1986 (Termination year: 1995)

Humanics National Preschool Assessment Forms: Grade PreK
Humanics, 1982 (Termination year: 1995)

Teacher Aids (Grading Stamps, Pencil Border): Grades K-12
Center Enterprises, 1989
(Termination year: 1995)

Teacher Aids (Grading Stamps, Peace): Grades K-12
Center Enterprises, 1989
(Termination year: 1995)

Math/Time-Money & Fractions Rubber Stamps: Grade K
Center Enterprises, 1987
(Termination year: 1995)

$1, $5, $10 Rubber Stamp Kit: Grade K
Center Enterprises, 1988
(Termination year: 1995)

Banking Rubber Stamp Kit/Check Rubber Stamp: Grade K
Center Enterprises, 1987
(Termination year: 1995)

Mathematics Geoboards: Grade K
Center Enterprises, 1987
(Termination year: 1995)

Individual 10 Packs/Mammals: Grade K
Center Enterprises, 1988
(Termination year: 1995)

Teacher Aids-Primary Rainbow Stampers: Grades K-12
Center Enterprises, 1989
(Termination year: 1995)

All The Things You Don't Have To Write Again: Grades K-12
Center Enterprises, 1987
(Termination year: 1995)

This Is Homework, Rubber Stamp: Grades K-12
Center Enterprises, 1988
(Termination year: 1995)

General/Resource Material, Common Objects Rubber Stamps: Grade K
Center Enterprises, 1987
(Termination year: 1995)

Handwriting-Manuscript/Cursive Rubber Stamps: Grade K
Center Enterprises, 1987
(Termination year: 1995)

Language Development, Consonant Sounds Rubber Stamps: Grade K
Center Enterprises, 1988
(Termination year: 1995)

Imaginative Play Dinosaurs & Creative Color Rubber Stamps: Grade K
Center Enterprises, 1987
(Termination year: 1995)

Mathematics/Math Facts Rubber Stamps: Grade K
Center Enterprises, 1987
(Termination year: 1995)

Math/Numbers, Number Line & Shapes
Rubber Stamps: Grade K
Center Enterprises, 1987
(Termination year: 1995)

General-Resource Material, Fruits Rubber
Stamp: Grades K-12
Center Enterprises, 1987
(Termination year: 1995)

Teacher Aids-Grading Stamps, Love: Grades
K-12
Center Enterprises, 1989
(Termination year: 1995)

Teacher Aids-Grading Stamps, Super Home-
work Pencil: Grades K-12
Center Enterprises, 1989
(Termination year: 1995)

Teacher Aids-Grading Stamps, Afghan Hound:
Grades K -12
Center Enterprises, 1989
(Termination year: 1995)

Teacher Aids-Grading Stamps, Party Invita-
tion: Grades K-12
Center Enterprises, 1989
(Termination year: 1995)

Books Linking Math with Language: Grade K
Rigby Education, 1987 (Termination year: 1995)

More Books Linking Math with Language:
Grade 1
Rigby Education, 1987 (Termination year: 1995)

Traditional Tales, Rhymes, Stories:
Grades PreK-1
Rigby Education, 1987 (Termination year: 1995)

More Traditional Tales, Rhymes, Stories:
Grades K-3
Rigby Education, 1987 (Termination year: 1995)

Content Area Reading and Writing: Grades 1-3
Rigby Education, 1987 (Termination year: 1995)

Stories by Children: Grades 1-2
Rigby Education, 1987 (Termination year: 1995)

Traditional Tales, Rhymes, Stories:
Grades PreK-1
Rigby Education, 1988 (Termination year: 1995)

My Square Books, My Box of Rhymes, Set of 4
Books: Grades K-1
Ladybird Books, 1988 (Termination year: 1995)

My First Learning Book: Grades K-1
Ladybird Books, 1988 (Termination year: 1995)

My Baby Animals Box, Set of 4 Books: Grades
K-1
Ladybird Books, 1988 (Termination year: 1995)

Beginners Fairy Tales Box Set: Grades K-1
Ladybird Books, 1988 (Termination year: 1995)

Predictable Storybooks, Set 1: Grades Prek-1
DLM, 1985 (Termination year: 1995)

Bill Martin's Treasure Chest of Poetry:
Grades K-3
DLM, 1987 (Termination year: 1995)

Bridges to Understanding: Grades PreK-3
DLM, 1987 (Termination year: 1995)

Read Aloud Predictable Storybooks (also available in Spanish): Grades PreK-2
DLM, 1988 (Termination year: 1995)

Bobber Books-Small Books, Complete Sets
(also available in Spanish): Grades K-2
DLM, 1988 (Termination year: 1995)

Bobber Books-Big Books, Complete Sets (also
available in Spanish): Grades K-2
DLM, 1988 (Termination year: 1995)

Science Predictable Storybooks: Grades K-2
DLM, 1988 (Termination year: 1995)

Math Predictable Storybooks: Grades K-2
DLM, 1988 (Termination year: 1995)

Beginning Milestones: Grades PreK-K
DLM, 1987 (Termination year: 1995)

Springboards to Learning, Sunrise Edition (also
available in Spanish): Grade K
DLM, 1988 (Termination year: 1995)

Milestones, Material and Manipulatives (also available in Spanish): Grades PreK-K
DLM, 1988 (Termination year: 1995)

Crosscuts (also available in Spanish): Grades PreK-K
DLM, 1988 (Termination year: 1995)

Developmental Storybooks, Sets 1 & 2: Grades PreK-K
DLM, 1983 (Termination year: 1995)

Brigance Prescriptive Readiness: Grades K-1
Curriculum Associates, 1985
(Termination year: 1995)

Brigance Preschool Screen (includes screen, data forms and Spanish Direction Booklet):
Grade PreK
Curriculum Associates, 1985 (Termination year: 1995)

Brigance K & 1 Screen (includes screen, data forms and Spanish Direction Booklet):
Grades K-1
Curriculum Associates, 1987
(Termination year: 1995)

Story Pictures Plus, Assorted 3 Pack (Complete Set): Grades K-3
Curriculum Associates, 1988
(Termination year: 1995)

Story Pictures Plus, My Story Picture Book: Grades K-3
Curriculum Associates, 1988
(Termination year: 1995)

Muppet Learning Keys: Grades K-2
Sunburst Communications, 1986
(Termination year: 1995)

Goal: Beginners Social Studies: Grades PreK-2
Media Materials,1985 (Termination year: 1995)

Goal: Mathematical Concepts: Grades PreK-1
Media Materials, 1986 (Termination year: 1995)

Experience with Perception: Grades PreK-K
Media Materials, 1986 (Termination year: 1995)

Experience in Number Readiness:
Grades PreK-1
Media Materials, 1986 (Termination year: 1995)

Experience in Reading Readiness:
Grades PreK-K
Media Materials, 1986 (Termination year: 1995)

Goal Level 2: Language Development:
Grades 2-12
Media Materials, 1986 (Termination year: 1995)

Goal: Beginners Science: Grades PreK-3
Media Materials, 1985 (Termination year: 1995)

Goal: Beginners Health and Nutrition:
Grades PreK-2
Media Materials, 1985 (Termination year: 1995)

Goal: Level 1: Language Development:
Grades PreK-1
Media Materials, 1985 (Termination year: 1995)

Cubical Counting Blocks: Grades PreK-3
Media Materials, 1987 (Termination year: 1995)

Parquetry Design Blocks: Grades K-3
Media Materials, 1985 (Termination year: 1995)

Teddy Bear Manipulatives, Teddy Bear Search:
Grades PreK-1
Media Materials, 1989 (Termination year: 1995)

Development of Visual Motor Skills, Color Cubes & Pattern Cards: Grades PreK-3
Media Materials, 1989 (Termination year: 1995)

Teddy Bear Counters: Grades K-3
Media Materials, 1987 (Termination year: 1995)

Junior Unit Blocks (Manipulative Math Materials): Grades K-3
Cuisenaire, 1986 (Termination year: 1995)

100 Colored Blocks: Grades K-3
Cuisenaire, 1985 (Termination year: 1995)

Color Tiles Activities: Grades K-3
Cuisenaire, 1985 (Termination year: 1995)

Hundreds Boards: Grades K-3
Cuisenaire, 1985 (Termination year: 1995)

Cuisenaire Alphabet Book: Grades K-3
Cuisenaire, 1979 (Termination year: 1995)

Games & Activities, Books 1-2: Grades 1-4
Cuisenaire, 1987 (Termination year: 1995)

Homework: Grades K-2
Cuisenaire, 1987 (Termination year: 1995)

Blocks in a Box: Grades K-3
Cuisenaire, 1984 (Termination year: 1995)

Idea Book for Cuisenaire Rods: Grades K-2
Cuisenaire, 1977 (Termination year: 1995)

Cuisenaire Attribute Shapes: Grades K-3
Cuisenaire, 1984 (Termination year: 1995)

Pattern Animals: Grades 1-3
Cuisenaire, 1986 (Termination year: 1995)

Clock Dials: Grades K-3
Cuisenaire, 1986 (Termination year: 1995)

Swinging out Language Program: Grade K
Modern Curriculum, 1986
(Termination year: 1995)

The Word Book: Grades 1-3
Modern Curriculum, 1986
(Termination year: 1995)

The Schoolhouse Press Dictionary: Grades 1-3
Modern Curriculum, 1986
(Termination year: 1995)

Language Works, Language Works, Levels 1-3: Grades K-4
Modern Curriculum, 1988
(Termination year: 1995)

Stories To Share, Levels 1-3: Grades K-4
Modern Curriculum, 1988
(Termination year: 1995)

Language Works, How Many Shapes?:
Grades K-1
Modern Curriculum, 1989
(Termination year: 1995)

Language Works, The Hall of Mirrors:
Grades 1-2
Modern Curriculum, 1989
(Termination year: 1995)

Language Works, The Slippery, Slithery, Plump Pink Pig: Grades K-2
Modern Curriculum, 1989
(Termination year: 1995)

Language Works, The Giant and the Watchmaker's Wife: Grades 2-3
Modern Curriculum, 1989
(Termination year: 1995)

Language Works, Is There Room for Me? Big Book Pack: Grades 1-2
Modern Curriculum, 1989
(Termination year: 1995)

Red Jack Big Book Pack: Grades 2-3
Modern Curriculum, 1989
(Termination year: 1995)

Developing Language Set: Grades K-1
Modern Curriculum, 1989
(Termination year: 1995)

Folktales Set: Grades K-3
Modern Curriculum, 1989
(Termination year: 1995)

Stories and Rhymes, Levels A-B: Grades K-3
Modern Curriculum, 1989
(Termination year: 1995)

Exploring Our World, Levels A-B: Grades K-3
Modern Curriculum, 1989
(Termination year: 1995)

Poetry Posters: Grades K-3
Modern Curriculum, 1989
(Termination year: 1995)

Individual Story Packs, Level 2, *There's a Dragon in My Wagon:* Grades PreK-K
Modern Curriculum, 1989
(Termination year: 1995)

Reading Friends, (Levels 1-3) Complete
Collection: Grades PreK-2
Modern Curriculum, 1988
(Termination year: 1995)

Nuevo Amanecer Package: Grades K-3
National Textbook Company, 1985
(Termination year: 1995)

The Learning Center Idea Book: Grades K-3
National Textbook Company, 1985
(Termination year: 1995)

Circle Time Activity Book: Grades K-3
National Textbook Company, 1985
(Termination year: 1995)

People Who Keep You Safe: Grades K-2
National Textbook Company, 1987
(Termination year: 1995)

Safety at Home: Grades K-2
National Textbook Company, 1987
(Termination year: 1995)

Safety away from Home: Grades K-2
National Textbook Company, 1987
(Termination year: 1995)

Safety in Nature: Grades K-2
National Textbook Company, 1987
(Termination year: 1995)

Once upon a Time, Comprehensive Program:
Grade K
Macmillan/McGraw-Hill, 1988
(Termination year: 1995)

Little Books Library: Grade K
Macmillan/McGraw-Hill, 1988
(Termination year: 1995)

Big & Little Listening Library: Grade K
Macmillan/McGraw-Hill, 1988
(Termination year: 1995)

The Real Mother Goose: Grade K
Macmillan/McGraw-Hill, 1988
(Termination year: 1995)

Animal Kingdom: Primary Science, Class Set:
Grades 1-3
Trillium Press, 1988 (Termination year: 1995)

Social Concept and Affective Development
Cards: Grades K-3
Trillium Press, 1988 (Termination year: 1995)

Our Community: Primary Social Studies, Student Workbook: Grades 1-3
Trillium Press, 1986 (Termination year: 1995)

Drawing Discovery: Apple, Singled Packaged
Disk and Instruction: Grades K-3
Trillium Press, 1985 (Termination year: 1995)

Sunshine Days, Kindergarten Learning System
(also available in bilingual): Grade K
Scott, Foresman, 1988 (Termination year: 1995)

McGraw-Hill Superstart Teacher's Kit: Grades
K-3
McGraw-Hill, 1988 (Termination year: 1995)

McGraw-Hill Un Gran Comienzo, Teacher's
Kit: Grades K-3
McGraw-Hill, 1988 (Termination year: 1995)

Telling Time: Grades K-4
Gamco Industries, 1986 (Termination year: 1995)

Alphabet Express: Grades K-3
Gamco Industries, 1985 (Termination year: 1995)

Number Sea Hunt: Grades K-3
Gamco Industries, 1985 (Termination year: 1995)

Shape Starship: Grades K-3
Gamco Industries, 1985 (Termination year: 1995)

The Calendar: Grades 3-6
Gamco Industries, 1987 (Termination year: 1995)

Time Explorers: Grades K-4
Gamco Industries, 1986 (Termination year: 1995)

Clue in on Phonics: Grades K-3
Gamco Industries, 1988 (Termination year: 1995)

Singing Multiplication Tables 6-45 RPM:
Grades 1-6
Educational Activities, 1971
(Termination year: 1995)

Individualization in Movement and Music:
Grades K-3
Educational Activities, 1973
(Termination year: 1995)

Perceptual Motor Rhythm Games: Grades K-3
Educational Activities, 1973
(Termination year: 1995)

Learning Basic Skills Through Music, Volume
1 LP/Rec/GD: Grades K-3
Educational Activities, 1969
(Termination year: 1995)

Feelin' Free: Grades K-3
Educational Activities, 1972
(Termination year: 1995)

Simplified Folk Songs: Grades K-3
Educational Activities, 1969
(Termination year: 1995)

Patriotic and Morning Time Songs, LP/Rec/
GD: Grades K-3
Educational Activities, 1969
(Termination year: 1995)

Building Vocabulary, LP/Rec/GD: Grades K-3
Educational Activities, 1969
(Termination year: 1995)

Modern Tunes for Rhythms and Instruments:
Grades K-3
Educational Activities, 1970
(Termination year: 1995)

Folk Song Carnival, LP/Rec/GD: Grades K-3
Educational Activities, 1970
(Termination year: 1995)

Health and Safety, LP/Rec/GD: Grades K-3
Educational Activities, 1970
(Termination year: 1995)

Modern Marches, LP/Rec/GD: Grades K-3
Educational Activities, 1970
(Termination year: 1995)

Fingerplay Fun: Grades PreK-3
Educational Activities, 1979
(Termination year: 1995)

Creative Movement and Rhythmic Expression,
LP/Rec/GD: Grades K-3
Educational Activities, 1971
(Termination year: 1995)

Holiday Songs and Rhythms: Grades K-3
Educational Activities, 1973
(Termination year: 1995)

Math Readiness, Vocabulary and Concepts:
Grades 1-6
Educational Activities, 1972
(Termination year: 1995)

Math Readiness, Addition and Subtraction:
Grades 1-6
Educational Activities, 1972
(Termination year: 1995)

Getting To Know Myself: Grades K-3
Educational Activities, 1972
(Termination year: 1995)

Won't You Be My Friend?: Grades K-3
Educational Activities, 1972
(Termination year: 1995)

Homemade Band: Grades K-3
Educational Activities, 1973
(Termination year: 1995)

Movin': Grades K-3
Educational Activities, 1973
(Termination year: 1995)

I'm Not Small: Grades K-3
Educational Activities, 1974
(Termination year: 1995)

Ideas, Thoughts and Feelings: Grades K-3
Educational Activities, 1973
(Termination year: 1995)

Spin, Spider, Spin: Grades K-3
Educational Activities, 1973
(Termination year: 1995)

Walter the Waltzing Worm: Grades K-3
Educational Activities, 1982
(Termination year: 1995)

Everybody Cries Sometimes: Grades K-3
Educational Activities, 1975
(Termination year: 1995)

Pretend: Grades K-3
Educational Activities, 1975
(Termination year: 1995)

Rainy Day Dances, Rainy Day Songs:
Grades K-3
Educational Activities, 1975
(Termination year: 1995)

Witches' Brew: Grades K-4
Educational Activities, 1976
(Termination year: 1995)

I Can Do Anything: Grades K-3
Educational Activities, 1983
(Termination year: 1995)

Easy Does It: Grades K-4
Educational Activities, 1975
(Termination year: 1995)

Sea Gulls: Grades K-3
Educational Activities, 1978
(Termination year: 1995)

Learning with Circles and Sticks: Grades K-3
Educational Activities, 1979
(Termination year: 1995)

Tickly Toodle: Grades K-3
Educational Activities, 1981
(Termination year: 1995)

Animal Antics: Grades K-3
Educational Activities, 1987
(Termination year: 1995)

Sally the Swinging Snake: Grades K-3
Educational Activities, 1986
(Termination year: 1995)

Fingerplays and Footplays: Grades K-3
Educational Activities, 1987
(Termination year: 1995)

Backwards Land: Grades K-3
Educational Activities, 1987
(Termination year: 1995)

Do You Wanna Be Friends?: Grades K-3
Educational Activities, 1984
(Termination year: 1995)

Baby Song, LP Rec/GD: Grades PreK-2
Educational Activities, 1984
(Termination year: 1995)

Happy Hour: Grades K-3
Educational Activities, 1985
(Termination year: 1995)

Learning by Doing, Dancing and Discovering:
Grades PreK-3
Educational Activities, 1978
(Termination year: 1995)

It's Action Time, Let's Move: Grades PreK-3
Educational Activities, 1978
(Termination year: 1995)

Hand Jivin': Grades K-3
Educational Activities, 1980
(Termination year: 1995)

Motor Fitness Rhythm Games: Grades K-3
Educational Activities, 1981
(Termination year: 1995)

I'm a Very Special Person: Grades K-3
Educational Activities, 1982
(Termination year: 1995)

Safe Child, 1 cass/10 Wkbks/GD: Grades K-3
Educational Activities, 1987
(Termination year: 1995)

Hap Palmer's Favorites Songbook: Grades K-6
Educational Activities, 1981
(Termination year: 1995)

Hap Palmer's Movement Songbook: Grades K-6
Educational Activities, 1987
(Termination year: 1995)

Drugs and Poisons: Avoiding the Dangers
(Videocass, Act Master): Grades 1-4
Educational Activities, 1987
(Termination year: 1995)

Baby Songs, Videocassette #1: Grades PreK-K
Educational Activities, 1987
(Termination year: 1995)

Random House Phonics, Books 1-3: Grades 1-3
American School, 1988 (Termination year: 1995)

The Wolpert Program: Grades K-1
American School, 1988 (Termination year: 1995)

Number Fun, LP Rec: Grades PreK-3
Music Mart/Melody House, 1981 (Termination Date: 1995)

Mother Goose, LP Rec: Grades Prek-1
Music Mart/Melody House, 1979 (Termination Date: 1995)

Alphabet Soup, LP Rec: Grades PreK-1
Music Mart/Melody House, 1979 (Termination Date: 1995)

Channel Four, LP Rec: Grades PreK-1
Music Mart/Melody House, 1987 (Termination Date: 1995)

Channel Three, LP Rec: Grades PreK-K
Music Mart/Melody House, 1984 (Termination Date: 1995)

Kindergarten Carnival, LP Rec: Grade K
Music Mart/Melody House, 1987 (Termination Date: 1995)

Puppet Parade, LP Rec: Grades PreK-6
Music Mart/Melody House, 1986 (Termination Date: 1995)

Baby Can Too, LP Rec: Grades PreK-K
Music Mart/Melody House, 1982 (Termination Date: 1995)

Channel Two, LP Rec: Grades PreK-K
Music Mart/Melody House, 1983 (Termination Date: 1995)

Tempo For Tots, LP Rec: Grades PreK-K
Music Mart/Melody House, 1973 (Termination Date: 1995)

Follow the Clouds: Grades PreK-K
Music Mart/Melody House, 1982 (Termination Date: 1995)

Froggy Went a-Courtin', LP Rec: PreK-3
Music Mart/Melody House, 1986 (Termination Date: 1995)

Dynamic Dinosaurs, LP Rec & Book: Grades PreK-3
Music Mart/Melody House, 1985 (Termination Date: 1995)

Adventures in Sound, LP Rec: Grades PreK-3
Music Mart/Melody House, 1979 (Termination Date: 1995)

Boogie Woogie Bear, LP Rec: Grades PreK-3
Music Mart/Melody House, 1985 (Termination Date: 1995)

Creative Moods, LP Rec: Grades 1-6
Music Mart/Melody House, 1977 (Termination Date: 1995)

Color Me a Rainbow, LP Rec: Grades PreK-3
Music Mart/Melody House, 1973 (Termination Date: 1995)

For Everything a Season, LP Rec: Grades K-6
Music Mart/Melody House, 1979 (Termination Date: 1995)

Raindrops, LP Rec: Grades PreK-1
Music Mart/Melody House, 1975 (Termination Date: 1995)

Pretend To Be, LP Rec: Grades PreK-1
Music Mart/Melody House, 1977 (Termination Date: 1995)

My Playful Scarf, LP Rec: Grades K-3
Music Mart/Melody House, 1986 (Termination Date: 1995)

Rhythm and Rhyme, LP Rec: Grades PreK-3
Music Mart/Melody House, 1976 (Termination Date: 1995)

School Days, LP Rec: Grades PreK-3
Music Mart/Melody House, 1980 (Termination Date: 1995)

Safe Not Sorry, LP Rec: Grades PreK-3
Music Mart/Melody House, 1987 (Termination
Date: 1995)

My World Is Round, LP Rec: Grades PreK-K
Music Mart/Melody House, 1981 (Termination
Date: 1995)

Early Childhood Phonics, Set: 2 Cassettes/
Color Workbook: Grades PreK-1
Music Mart/Melody House, 1986 (Termination
Date: 1995)

Holiday Songs for All Occasions, LP Rec/
Words to Songs: Grades PreK-3
Music Mart/Kimbo, 1978
(Termination year: 1995)

It's Toddler Time, LP Rec/Guide: Grades PreK–K
Music Mart/Kimbo, 1978
(Termination year: 1995)

Fun Activities for Toddlers, LP Rec/Guide:
Grades PreK-K
Music Mart/Kimbo, 1982
(Termination year: 1995)

Shapes in Action, LP Rec/Guide: Grades PreK-2
Music Mart/Kimbo, 1980
(Termination year: 1995)

Walk Like the Animal, LP Rec/Guide:
Grades PreK-3
Music Mart/Kimbo, 1976
(Termination year: 1995)

Toes Up, Toes Down, LP Rec/Guide:
Grades PreK-2
Music Mart/Kimbo, 1976
(Termination year: 1995)

Heel, Toe, Away We Go, LP Rec/Guide:
Grades PreK-3
Music Mart/Kimbo, 1977
(Termination year: 1995)

Get a Good Start, LP Rec/Guide: Grades PreK-3
Music Mart/Kimbo, 1980
(Termination year: 1995)

Singable Nursery Rhymes, LP Rec/Guide:
Grades PreK-3
Music Mart/Kimbo, 1980
(Termination year: 1995)

Toddler on Parade, LP Rec/Guide: Grades
PreK-K
Music Mart/Kimbo, 1985
(Termination year: 1995)

Chidren's Games, LP Rec/Guide: Grades PreK-3
Music Mart/Kimbo, 1979
(Termination year: 1995)

Fun Activities for Perceptual Motor Skills, LP
Rec/Guide: Grades PreK-3
Music Mart/Kimbo, 1976
(Termination year: 1995)

Touch, Teach and Hug a Toddler, LP Rec/
Guide: Grades PreK-3
Music Mart/Kimbo, 1976
(Termination year: 1995)

Preschool Playtime Band, LP Rec/Guide:
Grades PreK-2
Music Mart/Kimbo, 1987
(Termination year: 1995)

Santa's Sack of Christmas Songs, LP Rec/
Guide: Grades K-6
Music Mart/Kimbo, 1987
(Termination year: 1995)

Homemade Games and Activities, LP Rec/
Guide: Grades PreK-3
Music Mart/Kimbo, 1987
(Termination year: 1995)

Animal Walks, LP Rec/Guide: Grades PreK-3
Music Mart/Kimbo, 1987
(Termination year: 1995)

Sweet Dreams, LP Rec/Guide: Grade PreK
Music Mart/Kimbo, 1988
(Termination year: 1995)

How Kids Deal with Love, Hate, Anger, Fear
(Videocassette): Grades 1-4
Music Mart/Kimbo, 1987
(Termination year: 1995)

Magical Tales from Other Lands (Videocassette): Grades PreK-3
Music Mart/Kimbo, 1987
(Termination year: 1995)

The New Kid on the Block: Grades 2-4
Music Mart/Listening Library, 1986
(Termination year: 1995)

Freckle Juice, Cass/Bk/Guide: Grades 2-3
Music Mart/Listening Library, 1982
(Termination year: 1995)

Amanda Pig & Her Big Brother Oliver, Cass/Bk/Guide: Grades 1-2
Music Mart/Listening Library, 1984
(Termination year: 1995)

Nate the Great, Cass/Bk/Guide: Grades 1-2
Music Mart/Listening Library, 1984
(Termination year: 1995)

The Gingerbread Boy, Cass/Bk/Guide: Grades PreK-2
Music Mart/Listening Library, 1984
(Termination year: 1995)

Little Red Riding Hood, Cass/Bk/Guide: Grades PreK-2
Music Mart/Listening Library, 1984
(Termination year: 1995)

Rapunzel, Cass/Bk/Guide: Grades PreK-2
Music Mart/Listening Library, 1984
(Termination year: 1995)

Teeny Tiny, Cass/Bk/Guide: Grades PreK-2
Music Mart/Listening Library, 1987
(Termination year: 1995)

There's a Nightmare in My Closet, Cass/Bk/Guide: Grades PreK-2
Music Mart/Listening Library, 1980
(Termination year: 1995)

The Little Engine that Could, Cass/Bk/Guide: Grades PreK-2
Music Mart/Listening Library, 1980
(Termination year: 1995)

Frog and Toad, 2 cassettes: Grades PreK-3
Music Mart/Listening Library, 1987
(Termination year: 1995)

Little Bear, 2 cassettes: Grades PreK-3
Music Mart/Listening Library, 1987
(Termination year: 1995)

Runaway Ralph, Cass/Bk/Guide: Grades 3-5
Music Mart/Listening Library, 1983
(Termination year: 1995)

How To Eat Fried Worms, Cass/Bk/Guide: Grades 2-3
Music Mart/Listening Library, 1981
(Termination year: 1995)

Ellen Tebbits, Cass/Bk/Guide: Grades 2-3
Music Mart/Listening Library, 1982
(Termination year: 1995)

Rookie Readers: Grades PreK-2
Childrens Press, 1988 (Termination year: 1995)

Just One More (12 titles): Grades PreK-2
Childrens Press, n.d. (Termination year: 1995)

Spanish Books (64 titles): Grades PreK-3
Childrens Press, n.d. (Termination year: 1995)

Share-A-Story TM Big Book Units: Grades PreK-2
Childrens Press, 1987 (Termination year: 1995)

Magic Castle Readers: Grades PreK-2
Childrens Press, 1989 (Termination year: 1995)

Green Tiger Storybooks: Grades PreK-4
Childrens Press, 1989 (Termination year: 1995)

Spanish Books: El libro de colores de azulin: Grades PreK-4
Childrens Press, 1986 (Termination year: 1995)

Beginning To Learn about Series: Grades 1-2
Raintree Pub/Steck-Vaughn, 1986
(Termination year: 1995)

Life Cycles Clippers: Grades 1-2
Raintree Pub/Steck-Vaughn, 1986
(Termination year: 1995)

Look at Science: Grade 2
Raintree Pub/Steck-Vaughn, 1988
(Termination year: 1995)

Raintree Rhymers, Books 1-4: Grade 1
Raintree Pub/Steck-Vaughn, 1988
(Termination year: 1995)

Teddies: Grade 1
Raintree Pub/Steck-Vaughn, 1988
(Termination year: 1995)

Spotlight: Grade 2
Raintree Pub/Steck-Vaughn, 1986
(Termination year: 1995)

*Introduction to Children's Literature: Nursery
Rhymes:* Grades K-3
Magnetic Way, 1988 (Termination year: 1995)

Introduction to Our World, Age of Dinosaurs:
Grades K-3
Magnetic Way, 1988 (Termination year: 1995)

West Virginia

Alpha Time Complete Program: Grade K
Arista, 1981 (Termination year: 1994)

Read to Me Library, Books A-Z: Grade K
Arista, 1978, 1985 (Termination year: 1994)

Springboards to Learning, Sunrise Edition:
Grade K
DLM, 1987 (Termination year: 1994)

Superstart (Big Books): Grade K
McGraw-Hill, 1988 (Termination year: 1994)

Sunshine Days-Learning System: Grade K
Scott, Foresman, 1988 (Termination year: 1994)

Beginning To Read, Write and Listen: Grade K
Scott, Foresman, 1978 (Termination year: 1994)

INDEX TO REVIEWS

THIS index cites reviews of recently published materials for use in early childhood classrooms, including curriculum guides, lesson plans, project books, software programs, videos, and filmstrips. The citations cover reviews from the past two years (up to August 1992), and they reflect a search of educational journals, magazines, and newsletters that would include reviews of early childhood materials. The journals chosen are those that are available in teacher college libraries, in other college and university collections, and in many public libraries. They also include the major publications sent to members of the appropriate educational organizations. The review for each item can be found under the following listings:

- the title of the item
- the author(s)
- the publisher or producer/distributor
- subject (a broad subject arrangement is used)
- special medium (for Software packages, Audiotape, Manipulatives, etc.)

ABC Bestiary
by Deborah Blackwell (New York: Farrar, Straus, and Giroux, 1989). Reviewed in: *Day Care and Early Education* 18, 1 (Fall 1990): 46

About Birds: A Guide for Children
by Catheryn Sill and illustrated by John Sill (Atlanta: Peachtree, 1991). Reviewed in: *School Library Journal* 38, no.2 (Feb. 1992): 84

Activities for Teaching K-6 Math/Science Concepts
by Walter A. Farmer and Margaret A. Farrell (Bowling Green, OH: School Science and Mathematics, 1989). Reviewed in: *Science and Children* 28, no.4 (Jan. 1991): 58

Adaptations
Software (Galesburg, MI: MCE, n.d.). Reviewed in: *Science and Children* 29, no.1 (Sept. 1991): 59

Advanced Ideas (publisher)
Stars and Planets, Software (Berkeley, CA: Advanced Ideas, n.d.). Reviewed in: *Science and Children* 28, no.7 (Apr. 1991): 53

Adventures in Clay Land: An Introduction to Clay
Film/Video (Fresno, CA: Margaret Hudson's Earth Arts Studio, n.d.). Reviewed in: *Arts and Activities* 110, no.4 (Dec. 1991): 14

Aesop
Animal Fables from Aesop (Boston: Godine, 1989). Reviewed in: *School Library Journal* 38, no.1 (Jan. 1992): 101

Aesop's Fables
Video (Los Angeles: Churchill Films, 1991). Reviewed in: *School Library Journal* 38, no.1 (Jan. 1992): 70

The Age of Dinosaurs
Film (Washington, DC: National Geographic Society, 1990). Reviewed in: *Media and Methods* 27, no.5 (May/June 1991): 43; *American Biology Teacher* 53, no.3 (Mar. 1991): 189

AIMS Media Film and Video
The Animal Life Series, Film/Video (Van Nuys, CA: AIMS Media Film and Video, 1991). Reviewed in: *Media and Methods* 28, no.1 (Sept./Oct. 1991): 46

The Airplane Book
by Cheryl Walsh Bellville (Minneapolis: Carolrhoda, 1991). Reviewed in: *School Library Journal* 38, no.2 (Feb. 1992): 80-81

Aladdin
Animals in Danger, by William McCay and illustrated by Wayne Ford (Riverside, NJ: Aladdin, 1990). Reviewed in: *Language Arts* 68, no.6 (Oct. 1991): 493; *Science and Children* 29, no.4 (Jan. 1992): 39

Aladdin Books
Magical Changes, by Graham Oakley (New York: Aladdin Books, 1987). Reviewed in: *Gifted Child Today* 15, no.2 (Mar.Apr. 1992): 59

Alcohol Abuse
Tell Someone, Video (n.p.: Landmark Films, 1987). Reviewed in: *School Library Journal* 37, no.1 (Jan. 1991): 53

Alexander, Heather
Look Inside Your Brain, by Heather Alexander and illustrated by Nicoletta Costa (New York: Grosset, 1991). Reviewed in: *School Library Journal* 38, no.1 (Jan. 1992): 101

Alfred Higgins Productions
My Brother Is Afraid of Just About Everything, Film/Video (North Hollywood, CA: Alfred Higgins Productions, 1990). Reviewed in: *Curriculum Review* 30, no.2 (Oct. 1990): 19

The Value of Being a Friend, Film (North Hollywood, CA: Alfred Higgins Productions, 1990). Reviewed in: *Curriculum Review* 30, no.1 (Sept. 1990): 24

The Value of Teamwork, Film/Video (North Hollywood, CA: Alfred Higgins Productions, 1990). Reviewed in: *School Library Journal* 37, no.1 (Jan. 1991): 54-55

The Value of Telling the Truth, Film (North Hollywood, CA: Alfred Higgins Productions, 1990). Reviewed in: *Curriculum Review* 30, no.1 (Sept. 1990): 24

All about Anger
Video (Pleasantville, NY: Sunburst Communications, 1990). Reviewed in: *Science Books and Films* 28, no.2 (Mar. 1992): 56

All about Birth and Growth
by Donna Bailey (Madison, NJ: Steck-Vaughn Library, 1991). Reviewed in: *Curriculum Review* 31, no.2 (Oct. 1991): 26-27

All about Trees
Video (Washington, DC: National Geographic Society, 1990). Reviewed in: *School Library Journal* 37, no.1 (Jan. 1991): 61

All about Where
by Tana Hoban (New York: William Morrow and Co., 1991). Reviewed in: *Arithmetic Teacher* 39, no.9 (May 1992): 5; *Young Children* 46, no.5 (July 1991): 66

All about Your Health and Blood
by Donna Bailey (Madison, NJ: Steck-Vaughn Library, 1991). Reviewed in: *Curriculum Review* 31, no.2 (Oct. 1991): 26-27

All about Your Senses
by Donna Bailey (Madison, NJ: Steck-Vaughn Library, 1991). Reviewed in: *Curriculum Review* 31, no.2 (Oct. 1991): 26-27

All about Your Skin, Hair, and Teeth
by Donna Bailey (Madison, NJ: Steck-Vaughn Library, 1991). Reviewed in: *Curriculum Review* 31, no.2 (Oct. 1991): 26-27

Alphabet books
Eight Hands Round: A Patchwork Alphabet, by Ann Whitford Paul and illustrated by Jeanette Winter (New York: HarperCollins, 1991). Reviewed in: *Childhood Education* 68, no.1 (Fall 1991): 46; *Language Arts* 69, no.3 (Mar. 1992): 217

Amazing Frogs and Toads
by Barry Clarke (New York: Random House, 1991). Reviewed in: *Curriculum Review* 31, no.1 (Sept. 1991): 30

Amazing Poisonous Animals
by Alexandra Parsons (New York: Knopf, 1990). Reviewed in: *Science Books and Films* 27, no.1 (Jan./Feb. 1991): 20

Amazing Science Experiments with Everyday Materials
by Richard Churchill and illustrated by Frances Zweifel (New York: Sterling, 1991). Reviewed in: *Science Books and Films* 27, no.4 (May 1991): 113

Amazing Things Animals Do: Books for World Explorers
by Susan McGrath (Washington, DC: National Geographic Society, 1989). Reviewed in: *American Biology Teacher* 53, no.5 (May 1991): 315

The American Flag
by Ann Armbruster (New York: Watts, 1991). Reviewed in: *School Library Journal* 38, no.1 (Jan. 1992): 117

American Gramaphone Records
Earth: Voices of a Planet, Audiotape/ Compact disc (Omaha, NE: American Gramaphone Records of Omaha, 1990). Reviewed in: *American Biology Teacher* 53, no.2 (Feb. 1991): 117

American School (publisher)
The Little Snowgirl, Video (Chicago: American School, n.d.). Reviewed in: *School Library Journal* 37, no.10 (Oct. 1991): 80

Following the Drinking Gourd, Video (Chicago: American School, n.d.). Reviewed in: *School Library Journal* 37, no.2 (Feb. 1991): 53-54

Andrews and McMeel
Fifty Simple Things Kids Can Do To Save the Earth, by the Earthworks Group (Kansas City, MO: Andrews and McMeel, 1990). Reviewed in: *Curriculum Review* 30, no.2 (Oct. 1990): 29

And the Green Grass Grew All Around
by Alvin Schwartz (New York: HarperCollins, 1992). Reviewed in: *School Library Journal* 38, no.6 (June 1992): 135

Animal Behavior: Babies and Their Parents
Video (Deerfield, IL: Coronet/MTI Film and Video, 1991). Reviewed in: *School Library Journal* 38, no.4 (Apr. 1992): 76

Animal Behavior: Partnerships
Video (Deerfield, IL: Coronet/MTI Film and Video, 1991). Reviewed in: *School Library Journal* 38, no.5 (May 1992): 75

Animal Fables from Aesop
(Boston: Godine, 1989). Reviewed in: *School Library Journal* 38, no.1 (Jan. 1992): 101

The Animal Life Series
Film/Video (Van Nuys, CA: AIMS Media Film and Video, 1991). Reviewed in: *Media and Methods* 28, no.1 (Sept./Oct. 1991): 46

Animals and Their World
by Judith E. Rinard, Gene S. Stuart, and Jennifer C. Urquhart (Washington, DC: National Geographic Society, 1990). Reviewed in: *Science and Children* 29, no.5 (Feb. 1992): 48

Animals, Animals: Fins, Feathers, Fur/ A Gaggle of Geese
Film/Video (Washington, DC: National Geographic Society, 1990). Reviewed in: *American Biology Teacher* 53, no.2 (Feb. 1991): 117

Animals in Danger
by William McCay and illustrated by Wayne Ford (Riverside, NJ: Aladdin, 1990). Reviewed in: *Language Arts* 68, no.6 (Oct. 1991): 493; *Science and Children* 29, no.4 (Jan. 1992): 39

Animals of the Night
by Mary Banks and illustrated by Ronald Himler (New York: Scribner's, 1990). Reviewed in: *Day Care and Early Education* 19, no.4 (Summer 1992): 43

Anno, Mitsumasa
Anno's Math Games III, by Mitsumasa Anno (New York: Philomel Books, 1991). Reviewed in: *Arithmetic Teacher* 39, no.3 (Nov. 1991): 58

Annunziata, Ed
Hop To It!, Software by Ed Annunziata and Stephen Birkelbach (Pleasantville, NY: Sunburst Communications, 1990). Reviewed in: *Arithmetic Teacher* 38, no.3 (Nov. 1990): 58; *Computing Teacher* 18, no.2 (Oct. 1990): 49; *Electronic Learning* 10, no.4 (Jan. 1991): 32; *School Library Journal* 37, no.1 (Jan. 1991): 47

Antarctica
by Helen Cowcher (New York: Farrar Straus and Giroux, 1990). Reviewed in: *Science and Children* 29, no.4 (Jan. 1992): 39

Arcade
Willy Can Count, by Anne Rockwell (New York: Arcade, 1989). Reviewed in: *Arithmetic Teacher* 38, no.2 (Oct. 1990): 53

Architecture
I Know That Building, by Jane D'Alelio (Washington, DC: Preservation Press, 1989). Reviewed in: *Gifted Child Today* 15, no.1 (Jan./Feb. 1992): 58

Spiderwebs to Skyscrapers: The Science of Structures, by David Darling (New York: Dillon, 1991). Reviewed in: *School Library Journal* 38, no.3 (Mar. 1992): 244

What It Feels Like To Be a Building, by Forrest Wilson (Washington, DC: Preservation Press, 1988). Reviewed in: *Gifted Child Today* 15, no.1 (Jan./Feb. 1992): 57-58

Ardley, Neil
The Science Book of Air, by Neil Ardley (San Diego: Gulliver Books, 1991). Reviewed in: *Language Arts* 68, no.6 (Oct. 1991): 494

The Science Book of Color, by Neil Ardley (San Diego: Gulliver Books, 1991). Reviewed in: *Language Arts* 68, no.6 (Oct. 1991): 494

The Science Book of Hot and Cold, by Neil Ardley (San Diego: Gulliver, 1992). Reviewed in: *Science Books and Films* 28, no.4 (May 1992): 110

The Science Book of Light, by Neil Ardley (San Diego: Gulliver Books, 1991). Reviewed in: *Language Arts* 68, no.6 (Oct. 1991): 494

The Science Book of the Senses, by Neil Ardley (San Diego: Gulliver, 1992). Reviewed in: *Science Books and Films* 28, no.4 (May 1992): 110

The Science Book of Water, by Neil Ardley (San Diego: Gulliver Books, 1991). Reviewed in: *Language Arts* 68, no.6 (Oct. 1991): 494

Armbruster, Ann
The American Flag, by Ann Armbruster (New York: Watts, 1991). Reviewed in: *School Library Journal* 38, no.1 (Jan. 1992): 117

Arnold, Tedd
My First Computer Book, Multimedia by David Schiller and David Rosenbloom, and illustrated by Tedd Arnold (New York: Workman, 1991). Reviewed in: *School Arts* 91, no.5 (Jan. 1992): 44

Arnosky, Jim
Otters under Water, by Jim Arnosky (New York: Putnam, 1992). Reviewed in: *School Library Journal* 38, no.8 (Aug. 1992): 150

Arragon: Winning Strategies for Math
Software by James Hsu and Linda C. Unger (Garden City, NY: Focus Media, 1989). Reviewed in: *Arithmetic Teacher* 38, no.1 (Sept. 1990): 42

Art activities

Art and Creative Development for Young Children, by R. Schirrmacher (New York: Delmar, 1988). Reviewed in: *Young Children* 46, no.2 (Jan. 1991): 83-85

Art Works, Multimedia (Orlando, FL: Harcourt Brace, n.d.). Reviewed in: *School Arts* 90, no.5 (Jan. 1991): 42-43

Draw! (Cincinnati, OH: Northlight Books, n.d.). Reviewed in: *School Arts* 91, no.6 (Feb. 1992): 44

Kid Pix, Software (San Rafael, CA: Broderbund Software, n.d.). Reviewed in: *Computing Teacher* 19, no.2 (Oct. 1991): 45-47; *Instructor* 101, no.5 (Jan. 1992): 73

Kid Pix Companion, Software (Navato, CA: Broderbund Software, n.d.). Reviewed in: *Computer Learning* 12, no.1 (Sept. 1992): 38

Make Gifts! (Cincinnati, OH: Northlight Books, n.d.). Reviewed in: *School Arts* 91, no.6 (Feb. 1992): 44

Make Prints! (Cincinnati, OH: Northlight Books, n.d.). Reviewed in: *School Arts* 91, no.6 (Feb. 1992): 44

Paint! (Cincinnati, OH: Northlight Books, n.d.). Reviewed in: *School Arts* 91, no.6 (Feb. 1992): 44

The Paper Zebra and Other Paper Possibilities, Video (Dallas, TX: Small Business Press, n.d.). Reviewed in: *Arts and Activities* 110, no.2 (Oct. 1991): 20

Running on Rainbows, Multimedia (Hainesport, NJ: Chroma Acrylics, n.d.). Reviewed in: *School Arts* 90, no.3 (Nov. 1990): 46

Art and Creative Development for Young Children

by R. Schirrmacher (New York: Delmar, 1988). Reviewed in: *Young Children* 46, no.2 (Jan. 1991): 83-85

Art appreciation

Colors, by Philip Yenawine (New York: Delacorte Press, n.d.). Reviewed in: *School Arts* 90, no.6 (Feb. 1991): 60-61

Come Look with Me: Enjoying Art with Children, by Gladys S. Blizzard (Charlottsville, VA: Thomasson Grant, 1990). Reviewed in: *School Arts* 91. no.7 (Mar. 1992): 50

Lines, by Philip Yenawine (New York: Delacorte Press, n.d.). Reviewed in: *School Arts* 90, no.6 (Feb. 1991): 60-61

Shapes, by Philip Yenawine (New York: Delacorte Press, n.d.). Reviewed in: *School Arts* 90, no.6 (Feb. 1991): 60-61

Stories, by Philip Yenawine (New York: Delacorte Press, n.d.). Reviewed in: *School Arts* 90, no.6 (Feb. 1991): 60-61

Talking with Artists, by Pat Cummings (New York: Bradbury, 1992). Reviewed in: *School Library Journal* 38, no.5 (May 1992): 120

Arts and crafts

Adventures in Clay Land: An Introduction to Clay, Film/Video (Fresno, CA: Margaret Hudson's Earth Arts Studio, n.d.). Reviewed in: *Arts and Activities* 110, no.4 (Dec. 1991): 14

Children's Book of Woodwork, by George Buchanan (North Pomfret, VT: Trafalgar Square/David and Charles, 1990). Reviewed in: *Arts and Activities* 108, no.5 (Jan. 1991): 55

A Fish That's a Box, by M. M. Esterman (Arlington, VA: Great Ocean Publishers, 1991). Reviewed in: *Arts and Activities* 110, no.1 (Sept. 1991): 51

Art Works

Multimedia (Orlando, FL: Harcourt Brace, n.d.). Reviewed in: *School Arts* 90, no.5 (Jan. 1991): 42-43

Asimov, Isaac

Why Does the Moon Change Shape? by Isaac Asimov (Milwaukee, WI: Gareth Stevens, 1991). Reviewed in: *School Library Journal* 38, no.3 (Mar. 1992): 226

Why Do Stars Twinkle? by Isaac Asimov (Milwaukee, WI: Gareth Stevens, 1991). Reviewed in: *School Library Journal* 38, no.3 (Mar. 1992): 226

Association for Supervision and Curriculum Development
  Renewing the Social Studies Curriculum, by Walter C. Parker (Alexandria, VA: Association for Supervision and Curriculum Development, 1991). Reviewed in: *Curriculum Review* 31, no.7 (Mar. 1992): 30

Astronomy
  Big Dipper and You, by E. C. Krupp (New York: Morrow, 1989). Reviewed in: *Science and Children* 28, no.2 (Oct. 1990): 56

  Galaxies, by Seymour Simon (New York: Morrow Junior Books, 1991). Reviewed in: *Reading Horizons* 32, no.1 (Oct. 1991): 79-80

  The Illustrated World of Space, by Iain Nicolson (New York: Simon and Schuster, 1991). Reviewed in: *Science Books and Films* 27, no.8 (Nov. 1991): 237

  Space: A Three-Dimensional Journey, by Brian Jones and illustrated by Richard Clifton-Dey (New York: Dial, 1991). Reviewed in: *Day Care and Early Education* 19, no.4 (Summer 1992): 43

  Stars and Planets, Software (Berkeley, CA: Advanced Ideas, n.d.). Reviewed in: *Science and Children* 28, no.7 (Apr. 1991): 53

  What Is a Shooting Star? by Isaac Asimov (Milwaukee, WI: Gareth Stevens, 1991). Reviewed in: *School Library Journal* 38, no.3 (Mar. 1992): 226

  Why Does the Moon Change Shape? by Isaac Asimov (Milwaukee, WI: Gareth Stevens, 1991). Reviewed in: *School Library Journal* 38, no.3 (Mar. 1992): 226

  Why Do Stars Twinkle? by Isaac Asimov (Milwaukee, WI: Gareth Stevens, 1991). Reviewed in: *School Library Journal* 38, no.3 (Mar. 1992): 226

AstroNUMBERS
  Software (Washington, DC: PC Gradeworks, 1990). Reviewed in: *Arithmetic Teacher* 39, no.1 (Sept. 1991): 46

Atheneum
  Samuel Todd's Book of Great Inventions, by E. L. Konigsburg (New York: Atheneum, 1991). Reviewed in: *Science and Children* 29, no.8 (May 1992): 36

The Atlantic Salmon
  by Bianca Lavies (New York: Dutton, 1992). Reviewed in: *School Library Journal* 38, no.4 (Apr. 1992): 139

Atlas Video
  Storyteller's Collection, Film/Video (n.p.: Atlas Video, 1991). Reviewed in: *Childhood Education* 69, no.1 (Fall 1992): 58

Atrium
  Fighting the Invisible Enemy: Understanding the Effects of Conditioning, by Terrence Webster-Doyle and illustrated by Rod Cameron (Ojai, CA: Atrium, 1990). Reviewed in: *Young Children* 46, no.4 (May 1990): 66

  Tug of War: Peace through Understanding Conflict, by Terrence Webster-Doyle and illustrated by Rod Cameron (Ojai, CA: Atrium, 1990). Reviewed in: *Young Children* 46, no.4 (May 1990): 66

At the Crack of the Bat: Baseball Poems
  by Lillian Morrison (New York: Hyperion, 1992). Reviewed in: *School Library Journal* 38, no.6 (June 1992): 134

Audiotape
  Call to the Wild, Audiotape (Masonville, CO: Wilderness Productions, 1989). Reviewed in: *American Biology Teacher* 53, no.2 (Feb. 1991): 117

  Earth: Voices of a Planet, Audiotape/Compact disc (Omaha, NE: American Gramaphone Records of Omaha, 1990). Reviewed in: *American Biology Teacher* 53, no.2 (Feb. 1991): 117

  First Concepts Read-along Book Bags, Audiotape (Mahwah, NJ: Troll Associates, 1992). Reviewed in: *School Library Journal* 38, no.6 (June 1992): 82

Audiotape *(cont'd)*

First Science Read-along Book Bags, Audiotape (Mahwah, NJ: Troll Associates, 1992). Reviewed in: *School Library Journal* 38, no.5 (May 1992): 80

Rap-Ability, Audiotapes by Mike and Suzanne Rossi (Lake Orion, MI: Aynn Visual, 1990). Reviewed in: *Arithmetic Teacher* 38, no.9 (May 1991): 49

Stories and Songs for Little Children, Audiotape by Pete Seeger (Fairview, NC: High Windy Audio, 1990). Reviewed in: *Young Children* 46, no.6 (Sept. 1991): 66

Axelroad, Alan

Songs of the Wild West, by Alan Axelroad (New York: Metropolitan Museum of Art, 1991). Reviewed in: *Childhood Education* 68, no.3 (Spring 1992): 178

Aynn Visual

Rap-Ability, Audiotapes by Mike and Suzanne Rossi (Lake Orion, MI: Aynn Visual, 1990). Reviewed in: *Arithmetic Teacher* 38, no.9 (May 1991): 49

Bailey, Brenda

KIDS: Keyboard Introductory Development Series, Software by Brenda Bailey (n.p.: Electronic Courseware Systems, 1989). Reviewed in: *American Music Teacher* 41, no.6 (June/July 1992): 10

Bailey, Donna

All about Birth and Growth, by Donna Bailey (Madison, NJ: Steck-Vaughn Library, 1991). Reviewed in: *Curriculum Review* 31, no.2 (Oct. 1991): 26-27

All about Your Health and Blood, by Donna Bailey (Madison, NJ: Steck-Vaughn Library, 1991). Reviewed in: *Curriculum Review* 31, no.2 (Oct. 1991): 26-27

All about Your Senses, by Donna Bailey (Madison, NJ: Steck-Vaughn Library, 1991). Reviewed in: *Curriculum Review* 31, no.2 (Oct. 1991): 26-27

All about Your Skin, Hair, and Teeth, by Donna Bailey (Madison, NJ: Steck-Vaughn Library, 1991). Reviewed in: *Curriculum Review* 31, no.2 (Oct. 1991): 26-27

Here We Live: Australia, by Donna Bailey (Austin, TX: Steck-Vaughn, 1990). Reviewed in: *Young Children* 46, no.1 (Nov. 1990): 66

Here We Live: Hong Kong, by Donna Bailey (Austin, TX: Steck-Vaughn, 1990). Reviewed in: *Young Children* 46, no.1 (Nov. 1990): 66

Here We Live: India, by Donna Bailey (Austin, TX: Steck-Vaughn, 1990). Reviewed in: *Young Children* 46, no.1 (Nov. 1990): 66

Here We Live: Trinidad, by Donna Bailey (Austin, TX: Steck-Vaughn, 1990). Reviewed in: *Young Children* 46, no.1 (Nov. 1990): 66

Nomads and Cities, by Donna Bailey (Austin, TX: Steck-Vaughn, 1990). Reviewed in: *Young Children* 46, no.1 (Nov. 1990): 66

Balka, Don

Exploring Fractions and Decimals with Manipulatives, Manipulatives by Don Balka (Peabody, MA: Didax, 1991). Reviewed in: *Arithmetic Teacher* 39, no.9 (May 1992): 53

Banks, Mary

Animals of the Night, by Mary Banks and illustrated by Ronald Himler (New York: Scribner's, 1990). Reviewed in: *Day Care and Early Education* 19, no.4 (Summer 1992): 43

Bare, Colleen Stanley

Never Kiss an Alligator, by Colleen Stanley Bare (New York: Dutton, 1989). Reviewed in: *Childhood Education* 66, no.5 (Annual 1990): 337

Barkan, Joanne

Creatures that Glow, by Joanne Barkan (New York: Doubleday, 1991). Reviewed in: *School Library Journal* 38, no.1 (Jan. 1992): 118-123

Barlin, A. L.
Hello Toes! Movement Games for Children, by A. L. Barlin and N. Kalev (Pennington, NJ: Princeton Book Company, 1989). Reviewed in: *Bulletin of the Council for Research in Music Education* 107 (Winter 1991): 75-76

Barney's Campfire Sing-Along
Video (n.p.: Lyons Group, 1990). Reviewed in: *School Library Journal* 37, no.1 (Jan. 1991): 53-54

Barnyard Babies
Video (n.p.: JVM Productions, 1990). Reviewed in: *School Library Journal* 37, no.3 (Mar. 1991): 151

Barrett, Norman
The Coral Reef, by Norman Barrett (New York: Watts, 1991). Reviewed in: *Science Books and Films* 27, no.4 (May 1991): 114

Picture Library Series, by Norman Barrett (New York: Franklin Watts, 1989). Reviewed in: *Science and Children* 28, no.1 (Sept. 1990): 79

Barrons
The Orchard, by Isidro Sanchez (New York: Barrons, 1991). Reviewed in: *Science Books and Films* 27, no.8 (Nov. 1991): 244

Barton, Harriett
Books and Libraries, by Jack Knowlton and illustrated by Harriett Barton (New York: HarperCollins, 1991). Reviewed in: *Childhood Education* 68, no.1 (Fall 1991): 45; *Language Arts* 69, no.2 (Feb. 1992): 139-140

Bash, Barbara
Urban Roosts: Where Birds Nest in the City, by Barbara Bash (San Francisco: Sierra Club, 1990). Reviewed in: *Language Arts* 68, no.6 (Oct. 1991): 494

Bash, Mary Ann S.
Think Aloud: Increasing Social and Cognitive Skills, by Bonnie Camp and Mary Ann S. Bash (Champaign, IL: Research Press, 1990). Reviewed in: *Science Books and Films* 27, no.2 (Mar. 1991): 45

Basic Reading Inventory
by Jerry L. Johns (Dubuque, IA: Kendall-Hunt, 1991). Reviewed in: *Reading Horizons* 32, no.2 (Dec. 1991): 158-159

Baskwill, Jane
Whole Language Source Book, by Jane Baskwill and Paulette Whitman (Ontario, Canada: Scholastic, 1986). Reviewed in: *Language Arts* 68, no.2 (Feb. 1991): 150

Battista, Michael
LOGO Geometry, Software by Michael Battista and Douglas H. Clements (Morristown, NJ: Simon and Schuster Education Group, 1991). Reviewed in: *Arithmetic Teacher* 40, no.1 (Sept. 1992): 56

Be a Better Writer
Software (Pleasantville, NY: Sunburst Communications, n.d.). Reviewed in: *Gifted Child Today* 15, no.3 (May/June 1992): 53

Bear in Mind: A Book of Bear Poems
by Bobbye S. Goldstein (New York: Puffin Books, 1991). Reviewed in: *Day Care and Early Education* 19, no.2 (Winter 1991): 36

Bell, Bob
Let's Pretend: Poems of Flight and Fancy, edited by Natalie S. Bober and illustrated by Bob Bell (New York: Viking Kestrel, 1986). Reviewed in: *Day Care and Early Education* 19, no.2 (Winter 1991): 35

Bellville, Cheryl Walsh
The Airplane Book, by Cheryl Walsh Bellville (Minneapolis: Carolrhoda, 1991). Reviewed in: *School Library Journal* 38, no.2 (Feb. 1992): 80-81

Bender, Lionel
Story of the Earth Series: Cave, by Lionel Bender (New York: Watts, 1989). Reviewed in: *Science and Children* 28, no.1 (Sept. 1990): 78

Berenbaum, May R.
Ninety-Nine Gnats, Nits, and Nibblers, by May R. Barenbaum (Champaign, IL: University of Illinois Press, 1989). Reviewed in: *American Biology Teacher* 53, no.5 (May 1991): 316

Berenstain Bears: Learn about Counting
Software (San Francisco: Britannica Software, 1990). Reviewed in: *School Library Journal* 37, no.1 (Jan. 1991): 47

Berger, Melvin
Discovering Science: As Old as the Hills, by Melvin Berger (Boston: Watts, 1989). Reviewed in: *Science and Children* 28, no.7 (Apr. 1991): 61

Bergman, Thomas
Finding a Common Language: Children Living with Deafness, by Thomas Bergman (Milwaukee, WI: Gareth Stevens, 1989). Reviewed in: *Teaching Exceptional Children* 24, no.3 (Spring 1992): 83-84

One Day at a Time: Children Living with Leukemia, by Thomas Bergman (Milwaukee, WI: Gareth Stevens, 1989). Reviewed in: *Teaching Exceptional Children* 24, no.3 (Spring 1992): 83-84

On Our Own Terms: Children Living with Physical Disabilities, by Thomas Bergman (Milwaukee, WI: Gareth Stevens, 1989). Reviewed in: *Teaching Exceptional Children* 24, no.3 (Spring 1992): 83-84

Seeing in Special Ways: Children Living with Blindness, by Thomas Bergman (Milwaukee, WI: Gareth Stevens, 1989). Reviewed in: *Teaching Exceptional Children* 24, no.3 (Spring 1992): 83-84

We Laugh, We Love, We Cry: Children Living with Mental Retardation, by Thomas Bergman (Milwaukee, WI: Gareth Stevens, 1989). Reviewed in: *Teaching Exceptional Children* 24, no.3 (Spring 1992): 83-84

Bet You Can! Science Possibilities To Fool You
by Vicki Cobb and Kathy Darling (New York, NY: Lothrop, Lee and Shepard, 1990). Reviewed in: *Science Books and Films* 27, no.1 (Jan./Feb. 1991): 15

Big and Little
Software (Pleasantville, NY: Sunburst Communications, n.d.). Reviewed in: *Computing Teacher* 19, no.1 (Aug./Sept. 1991): 44-46; *Instructor* 100, no.5 (Jan. 1991): 119

Big Book Maker: Favorite Fairy Tales and Nursery Rhymes
Software (Farmington, CT: Pelican Software, 1989). Reviewed in: *Instructor* 100, no.5 (Jan. 1991): 117

Big Dipper and You
by E. C. Krupp (New York: Morrow, 1989). Reviewed in: *Science and Children* 28, no.2 (Oct. 1990): 56

Big Time Bears
by Stephen Krensky (Boston: Little Brown, 1989). Reviewed in: *Arithmetic Teacher* 38, no.7 (Mar. 1991): 58-59; *Language Arts* 68, no.3 (Mar. 1991): 246

The Big Tree
by Bruce Hiscock (New York: Atheneum, 1991). Reviewed in: *Science Books and Films* 27, no.4 (May 1991): 115

Bird Watch
by Jane Yolen and illustrated by Ted Lewin (New York: Philomel, 1990). Reviewed in: *School Library Journal* 37, no.2 (Supplement to Feb. 1991): S-22

Birkelbach, Stephen
Hop To It!, Software by Ed Annunziata and Stephen Birkelbach (Pleasantville, NY: Sunburst Communications, 1990). Reviewed in: *Arithmetic Teacher* 38, no.3 (Nov. 1990): 58; *Computing Teacher* 18, no.2 (Oct. 1990): 49; *Electronic Learning* 10, no.4 (Jan. 1991): 32; *School Library Journal* 37, no.1 (Jan. 1991): 47

Birthday
Software (Pleasantville, NY: Sunburst Communications, 1991). Reviewed in: *Technology and Learning* 12, no.2 (Oct. 1991): 31

Bissinger, Kristen
Leap into Learning, by Kristen Bissinger and Nancy Renfro (Austin, TX: Nancy Renfro Studios, 1990). Reviewed in: *Curriculum Review* 31, no.7 (Mar. 1992): 25-26

Blackwell, Deborah
ABC Bestiary, by Deborah Blackwell (New York: Farrar, Straus, and Giroux, 1989). Reviewed in: *Day Care and Early Education* 18, 1 (Fall 1990): 46

Bruchac, Joseph
Keepers of the Animals: Native American Stories and Wildlife Activities for Children, by Michael J. Caduto and Joseph Bruchac (Golden, CO: Fulcrum, 1991). Reviewed in: *Curriculum Review* 31, no.8 (Apr. 1992): 28; *Young Children* 47, no.6 (Sept. 1992): 78

Keepers of the Earth, by Michael J. Caduto and Joseph Bruchac (Golden, CO: Fulcrum, 1991). Reviewed in: *Young Children* 47, Renfro, Nancyno.6 (Sept. 1992): 78

Brunn, Bertel
The Brain: What It Is, What It Does, by Ruth Dowling Brunn and Bertel Brunn, and illustrated by Bertel Brunn (New York: Greenwillow, 1989). Reviewed in: *Childhood Education* 66, no.5 (Annual 1990): 337

Brunn, Ruth Dowling
The Brain: What It Is, What It Does, by Ruth Dowling Brunn and Bertel Brunn, and illustrated by Bertel Brunn (New York: Greenwillow, 1989). Reviewed in: *Childhood Education* 66, no.5 (Annual 1990): 337

Buchanan, George
Children's Book of Woodwork, by George Buchanan (North Pomfret, VT: Trafalgar Square/David and Charles, 1990). Reviewed in: *Arts and Activities* 108, no.5 (Jan. 1991): 55

Building Elementary Reading Skills through Whole Language and Literature
by Donald C. Cushenbery (Springfield, IL: Charles C. Thomas, 1989). Reviewed in: *Curriculum Review* 30, no.3 (Nov. 1990): 27

Building Self-Esteem with Koala-Roo Can-Do
by Laura Fendel (Glenview, IL: Scott Foresman, 1989). Reviewed in: *Teaching Exceptional Children* 24, no.4 (Summer 1992): 83

Burgess, Anne
Ready, Set, Read: The Beginning Reader's Treasury, illustrated by Anne Burgess (New York: Doubleday, 1990). Reviewed in: *School Library Journal* 37, no.2 (Supplement Feb. 1991): S16

Burningham, John
Hey! Get Off Our Train, by John Burningham (New York: Crown, 1989). Reviewed in: *Arithmetic Teacher* 38, no.9 (May 1991): 45

Burns, Marilyn
The One-Dollar Word Riddle Book, by Marilyn Burns and illustrated by Martha Weston (New Rochelle, NY: Cuisenaire, 1990). Reviewed in: *Arithmetic Teacher* 39, no.2 (Oct. 1991): 51-52

The Button Box
by Margarette S. Reid (New York: Dutton Children's Books, 1990). Reviewed in: *Arithmetic Teacher* 38, no.9 (May 1991): 44

Butzow, Carol M.
Science through Children's Literature: An Integrated Approach, by Carol M. and John W. Butzow (Englewood, CO: Libraries Unlimited, n.d.). Reviewed in: *Curriculum Review* 30, no.1 (Sept. 1990): 30

Butzow, John W.
Science through Children's Literature: An Integrated Approach, by Carol M. and John W. Butzow (Englewood, CO: Libraries Unlimited, n.d.). Reviewed in: *Curriculum Review* 30, no.1 (Sept. 1990): 30

A Cache of Jewels
by Ruth Heller (New York: Putnam, 1989). Reviewed in: *Gifted Child Today* 15, no.1 (Jan./Feb. 1992): 58

Cactus Hotel
by Brenda Z. Guiberson and illustrated by Megan Lloyd (New York: Holt, 1991). Reviewed in: *Childhood Education* 68, no.1 (Fall 1991): 44; *Day Care and Early Education* 19, no.4 (Summer 1992): 43

Caduto, Michael J.
Keepers of the Animals: Native American Stories and Wildlife Activities for Children, by Michael J. Caduto and Joseph Bruchac (Golden, CO: Fulcrum, 1991). Reviewed in: *Curriculum Review* 31, no.8 (Apr. 1992): 28; *Young Children* 47, no.6 (Sept. 1992): 78

Caduto, Michael J. *(cont'd)*
Keepers of the Earth, by Michael J. Caduto and Joseph Bruchac (Golden, CO: Fulcrum, 1991). Reviewed in: *Young Children* 47, no.6 (Sept. 1992): 78; *Teaching Exceptional Children* 24, no.4 (Summer 1992): 83

California Neuropsychology Services
Talking Fingers, Software (San Rafael, CA: California Neuropsychology Services, n.d.). Reviewed in: *Technology and Learning* 13, no.1 (Sept. 1992): 16-17

Call to the Wild
Audiotape (Masonville, CO: Wilderness Productions, 1989). Reviewed in: *American Biology Teacher* 53, no.2 (Feb. 1991): 117

Cambridge University Press
Grammar Practice Activities: A Practical Guide for Teachers, by Penny Ur (Cambridge, UK: Cambridge University Press, 1986). Reviewed in: *TESL Canada Journal* 8, no.1 (Nov. 1990): 114-116

Cameron, Rod
Fighting the Invisible Enemy: Understanding the Effects of Conditioning, by Terrence Webster-Doyle and illustrated by Rod Cameron (Ojai, CA: Atrium, 1990). Reviewed in: *Young Children* 46, no.4 (May 1990): 66

Tug of War: Peace through Understanding Conflict, by Terrence Webster-Doyle and illustrated by Rod Cameron (Ojai, CA: Atrium, 1990). Reviewed in: *Young Children* 46, no.4 (May 1990): 66

Camp, Bonnie
Think Aloud: Increasing Social and Cognitive Skills, by Bonnie Camp and Mary Ann S. Bash (Champaign, IL: Research Press, 1990). Reviewed in: *Science Books and Films* 27, no.2 (Mar. 1991): 45

Candlewick
I Saw Esau: The School Child's Pocket Book, by Iona and Peter Opie and illustrated by Maurice Sendak (n.p.: Candlewick, 1992). Reviewed in: *School Library Journal* 38, no.6 (June 1992): 110

Capitals of the World (version 1.5)
Software by Keith Sutton (San Diego: K. Sutton, n.d.). Reviewed in: *Journal of Geography* 89, no.6 (Nov./Dec. 1990): 272

Caps, Hats, Socks, and Mittens
by Louise Borden and illustrated by Lillian Hoban (New York: Scholastic, 1989). Reviewed in: *Childhood Education* 66, no.5 (Annual 1990): 335

Caring for Our Water
by Carol Greene (Hillside, NJ: Enslow, 1991). Reviewed in: *Science and Children* 29, no.7 (Apr. 1992): 47

Carolrhoda
The Airplane Book, by Cheryl Walsh Bellville (Minneapolis: Carolrhoda, 1991). Reviewed in: *School Library Journal* 38, no.2 (Feb. 1992): 80-81

Cary, Helen H.
Raintree Science Adventures, by Helen H. Cary and Judith E. Greenberg (Milwaukee, WI: Raintree, 1990). Reviewed in: *Science and Children* 29, no.5 (Feb. 1992): 48

Categories
by C. F. Navarro (Alexandria, VA: Start Smart Books, 1990). Reviewed in: *Curriculum Review* 30, no.3 (Nov. 1990): 25-26

Cats, Big and Little
by Beatrice Fontanel (Ossining, NY: Young Discovery, 1991). Reviewed in: *Science Books and Films* 27, no.7 (Oct. 1991): 211

Cavanagh, Mary
Math in Brief, Manipulatives by Mary Cavanagh (Fort Collins, CO: Scott Resources, 1978). Reviewed in: *Arithmetic Teacher* 39, no.1 (Sept. 1991): 53

Chameleons: Dragons in the Trees
by James Martin (New York: Crown, 1991). Reviewed in: *Science and Children* 29, no.6 (Mar. 1992): 55

Charlesbridge
The Icky Bug Counting Book, by Jerry Pallotta and illustrated by Ralph Masiello (Watertown, MA: Charlesbridge, 1991). Reviewed in: *Science Books and Films* 28, no1 (Jan./Feb. 1992): 19

Charlesbridge *(cont'd)*
Will We Miss Them? Endangered Species, by Alexandra Wright and illustrated by Marshall Peck (Watertown, MA: Charlesbridge, 1992). Reviewed in: *Science Books and Films* 28, no.1 (Jan./Feb. 1992): 19

Charles C. Thomas
Building Elementary Reading Skills through Whole Language and Literature, by Donald C. Cushenbery (Springfield, IL: Charles C. Thomas, 1989). Reviewed in: *Curriculum Review* 30, no.3 (Nov. 1990): 27

Child abuse
It's OK To Tell, Film/Video (n.p.: Hi-Fidelity Films, 1990). Reviewed in: *School Library Journal* 37, no.1 (Jan. 1991): 51

Children's Activity Series
by Judith K. Scheer and Ana Matiella (Santa Cruz, CA: ETR Associates/Network Publications, 1990). Reviewed in: *Curriculum Review* 30, no.8 (Apr. 1991): 26-27

Children's Book of Woodwork
by George Buchanan (North Pomfret, VT: Trafalgar Square/David and Charles, 1990). Reviewed in: *Arts and Activities* 108, no.5 (Jan. 1991): 55

Chroma Acrylics
Running on Rainbows, Multimedia (Hainesport, NJ: Chroma Acrylics, n.d.). Reviewed in: *School Arts* 90, no.3 (Nov. 1990): 46

Chronicle Books
Ten Little Rabbits, by Virginia Grossman and illustrated by Sylvia Long (San Francisco: Chronicle Books, 1991). Reviewed in: *Arithmetic Teacher* 40, no.1 (Sept. 1992): 56-57

Churchill Films
Aesop's Fables, Video (Los Angeles: Churchill Films, 1991). Reviewed in: *School Library Journal* 38, no.1 (Jan. 1992): 70

Fall Brings Changes, Video (Los Angeles: Churchill Films, 1991). Reviewed in: *Science Books and Films* 28, no.4 (May 1992): 118

Growing, Growing, Film/Video (Los Angeles: Churchill Films, 1989). Reviewed in: *Childhood Education* 68, no.1 (Fall 1991): 54

I Once Had an Operation, Film (Los Angeles: Churchill Films, 1991). Reviewed in: *Media and Methods* 27, no.5 (May/June 1991): 42

Seeds and Seasons, Film/Video (Los Angeles: Churchill Films, 1987). Reviewed in: *Childhood Education* 68, no.1 (Fall 1991): 54

Spring Brings Changes, Video (Los Angeles: Churchill Films, 1991). Reviewed in: *Science Books and Films* 28, no.4 (May 1992): 119

Churchill, Richard
Amazing Science Experiments with Everyday Materials, by Richard Churchill and illustrated by Frances Zweifel (New York: Sterling, 1991). Reviewed in: *Science Books and Films* 27, no.4 (May 1991): 113

City Critters around the World
by Amy Goldman Koss (Los Angeles: Price, Stern, and Sloan, 1991). Reviewed in: *Young Children* 47, no.4 (May 1992): 85

Clarion Books
The Nonsense Poems of Edward Lear, by Edward Lear and illustrated by Leonard L. Brooke (New York: Clarion Books, 1991). Reviewed in: *Day Care and Early Education* 19, no.2 (Winter 1991): 36

Five Little Monkeys Jumping on the Bed, by Eileen Cristelow (New York: Clarion Books, 1989). Reviewed in: *Arithmetic Teacher* 38, no.7 (Mar. 1991): 59

Clark, Ann Nolan
In My Mother's House, by Ann Nolan Clark and illustrated by Velino Herrara (New York: Viking, 1991). Reviewed in: *Day Care and Early Education* 19, no.2 (Winter 1991): 36

Clarke, Barry
Amazing Frogs and Toads, by Barry Clarke (New York: Random House, 1991). Reviewed in: *Curriculum Review* 31, no.1 (Sept. 1991): 30

Clarkson Potter
Professor Curious and the Mystery of the Hiking Dinosaurs, by Yvonne Gil and illustrated by Bonnie Timmons (n.p.: Clarkson Potter, 1991). Reviewed in: *Language Arts* 68, no.6 (Oct. 1991): 492

Clearwater Detectives
Software (Minneapolis, MN: MECC, 1991). Reviewed in: *Science and Children* 29, no.5 (Feb. 1992): 36-39

Clement, Rod
Counting on Frank, by Rod Clement (Milwaukee, WI: Gareth Stevens, 1991). Reviewed in: *Science Books and Films* 28, no.2 (Mar. 1992): 50

Clements, Douglas H.
LOGO Geometry, Software by Michael Battista and Douglas H. Clements (Morristown, NJ: Simon and Schuster Education Group, 1991). Reviewed in: *Arithmetic Teacher* 40, no.1 (Sept. 1992): 56

Clifford's Big Book Publisher
Software (Jefferson City, MO: Scholastic, 1990). Reviewed in: *Instructor* 100, no.5 (Jan. 1991): 117-118; *Electronic Learning* 10, no.8 (May/June 1991): 40

Clifton-Day, Richard
Space: A Three-Dimensional Journey, by Brian Jones and illustrated by Richard Clifton-Dey (New York: Dial, 1991). Reviewed in: *Day Care and Early Education* 19, no.4 (Summer 1992): 43

Cobb, Vicki
Bet You Can! Science Possibilities To Fool You, by Vicki Cobb and Kathy Darling (New York: Lothrop, Lee and Shepard, 1990). Reviewed in: *Science Books and Films* 27, no.1 (Jan./Feb. 1991): 15

Feeding Yourself, Getting Dressed, Writing It Down, by Vicki Cobb (New York: Harper, 1989). Reviewed in: *Childhood Education* 66, no.5 (Annual 1990): 337-338

Cobblehill
Spring, by Ron Hirschi (New York: Cobblehill, 1990). Reviewed in: *Science Books and Films* 27, no.3 (Apr. 1991): 82

Winter, by Ron Hirschi (New York: Cobblehill, 1990). Reviewed in: *Science Books and Films* 27, no.3 (Apr. 1991): 82

Cobblehill/Dutton
In a Cabin in a Wood, by Darcie McNally and illustrated by Robin Michael Koontz (New York: Cobblehill/Dutton, 1991). Reviewed in: *Reading Horizons* 32, no.1 (Oct. 1991): 75-77

Cohen, Joy
GrowLab: Activities for Growing Minds, by Joy Cohen and Eve Pranis, and illustrated by Grant Urie (Burlington, VT: National Gardening Association, 1990). Reviewed in: *Science Books and Films* 27, no.2 (Mar. 1991): 49

Cole, Joanna
Magic School Bus on the Ocean Floor, by Joanna Cole and illustrated by Bruce Degen (New York: Scholastic, 1992). Reviewed in: *School Library Journal* 38, no.8 (Aug. 1992): 151

Colorcards
Manipulatives (Bicester, UK: Winslow Press, 1989). Reviewed in: *Child Language Teaching and Therapy* 7, no.3 (Oct. 1991): 361-362

Color Farm
by Lois Ehlert (New York: HarperCollins Children's Books, 1990). Reviewed in: *Arithmetic Teacher* 39, no.7 (Mar. 1992): 38

Colors
by Philip Yenawine (New York: Delacorte Press, n.d.). Reviewed in: *School Arts* 90, no.6 (Feb. 1991): 60-61

Come Look with Me: Enjoying Art with Children
by Gladys S. Blizzard (Charlottsville, VA: Thomasson Grant, 1990). Reviewed in: *School Arts* 91. no.7 (Mar. 1992): 50

Communication Skill Builders (publisher)
The FlipBook, by Brenda L. Hollingsworth and illustrated by Corey Zibleman (Tucson, AZ: Communication Skill Builders, 1989). Reviewed in: *Child Language Teaching and Therapy* 7, no.1 (Feb. 1991): 113

Communikeys
Software (Minneapolis, MN: MECC, 1989). Reviewed in: *Instructor* 101, no.7 (Mar. 1992): 66

Computation

AstroNUMBERS, Software (Washington, DC: PC Gradeworks, 1990). Reviewed in: *Arithmetic Teacher* 39, no.1 (Sept. 1991): 46

Counting on Frank, by Rod Clement (Milwaukee, WI: Gareth Stevens, 1991). Reviewed in: *Science Books and Films* 28, no.2 (Mar. 1992): 50

Exploring Measurement, Time, and Money: Levels One and Two, Software (Atlanta, GA: IBM Educational Systems, 1989). Reviewed in: *Arithmetic Teacher* 38, no.2 (Oct. 1990): 44; *Electronic Learning* 10, no.7 (Apr. 1991): 36

Funny Money, Game (Baltimore, MD: LML, 1986). Reviewed in: *Arithmetic Teacher* 38, no.1 (Sept. 1990): 52

Individualized Computer Motivated Math, Software by Max Maneral (n.p.: Max Maneral, 1988). Reviewed in: *Arithmetic Teacher* 38, no.4 (Dec. 1990): 59

Lollipop Dragon, Multimedia by Margo Turner (Chicago: SVE, 1989). Reviewed in: *Arithmetic Teacher* 38, no.3 (Nov. 1990): 47

Math Practice, Software (Cerritos, CA: Yhl Software, 1988). Reviewed in: *Arithmetic Teacher* 38, no.2 (Oct. 1990): 50

Maths at Play: Fun Ideas for 5-8 Year Olds, by Linn Maskell (Victoria, Australia: Dellasta, 1990). Reviewed in: *Arithmetic Teacher* 39, no.9 (May 1992): 51-52

Math Shop Junior, Software by Cary Hammer (New York: Scholastic, 1989). Reviewed in: *Arithmetic Teacher* 38, no.1 (Sept. 1990): 44

Math Smart, Game (Rochester, MN: GO Company of Rochester, 1987). Reviewed in: *Arithmetic Teacher* 38, no.1 (Sept. 1990): 52

Measuring: From Paces to Feet, Grades 3-4, by Rebecca B. Corwin and Susan Jo Russell (Palo Alto, CA: Dale Seymour, 1990). Reviewed in: *Arithmetic Teacher* 38, no.9 (May 1991): 48

Money and Time Workshop - Grades K-2, Software (Glenview, IL: Scott Foresman, 1991). Reviewed in: *Electronic Learning* 10, no.7 (Apr. 1991): 36; *Arithmetic Teacher* 39, no.1 (Sept. 1991): 48

Multiplication and Division Made Easy, by Catherine F. Debie (Artesia, CA: Scott Foresman, 1990). Reviewed in: *Arithmetic Teacher* 39, no.8 (Apr. 1992): 59

The Munchters Talk about Food, Manipulatives (Chicago: National Livestock and Meat Board, 1990). Reviewed in: *Journal of Nutritional Education* 23, no.4 (July/Aug. 1991): 198

New Math Blaster Plus, Software (Torrance, CA: Davidson and Associates, 1990). Reviewed in: *Instructor* 100, no.8 (April 1991): 74-75

Number Maze: Decimals and Fractions, Software (Scotts Valley, CA: Greatwave Software, n.d.). Reviewed in: *Electronic Learning* 10, no.5 (Feb. 1991): 36-37; *Media and Methods* 27, no.5 (May/June 1991): 60

Numbervision: Addition/Subtraction System, Software (Lexington, OH: Numbervision, 1990). Reviewed in: *Arithmetic Teacher* 39, no.2 (Oct. 1991): 50

The One-Dollar Word Riddle Book, by Marilyn Burns and illustrated by Martha Weston (New Rochelle, NY: Cuisenaire, 1990). Reviewed in: *Arithmetic Teacher* 39, no.2 (Oct. 1991): 51-52

Rap-Ability, Audiotapes by Mike and Suzanne Rossi (Lake Orion, MI: Aynn Visual, 1990). Reviewed in: *Arithmetic Teacher* 38, no.9 (May 1991): 49

Sidewalk Sneakers, Software (Pleasantville, NY: Sunburst Communications, 1991). Reviewed in: *School Library Journal* 38, no.7 (July 1992): 38

Talking Addition and Subtraction, Software (Pound Ridge, NY: Orange Cherry Software, 1989). Reviewed in: *Arithmetic Teacher* 38, no.7 (Mar. 1991): 56-57

Computation (*cont'd*)

Talking Money, Software (Pound Ridge, NY: Orange Cherry Software, 1989). Reviewed in: *Arithmetic Teacher* 38, no.1 (Sept. 1990): 44

Talking Multiplication and Division: Grades 3-6, Software (Pound Ridge, NY: Orange Cherry Software, 1990). Reviewed in: *Arithmetic Teacher* 39, no.3 (Nov. 1991): 57

Teaching Primary Math with Music, Multimedia by Esther Mardlesohn (Palo Alto, CA: Dale Seymour, 1990). Reviewed in: *Arithmetic Teacher* 39, no.1 (Sept. 1991): 53

Thinker Math: Developing Number Sense and Arithmetic Skills (Grades 3-4), by Carole Greenes, Linda Schulman, and Rika Spungin (Allen, TX: DLM, n.d.). Reviewed in: *Arithmetic Teacher* 38, no.2 (Oct. 1990): 54

We Love MATHS: Four Imaginative Themes for Early Primary Students, by Anne Marell and Susan Stajnko (Mount Waterly, Australia: Dellasta, 1990). Reviewed in: *Arithmetic Teacher* 39, no.1 (Sept. 1991): 53-54

Zero-in on Zero: Addition and Subtraction, Software (Allen, TX: DLM Software, 1990). Reviewed in: *Arithmetic Teacher* 38, no.7 (Mar. 1991): 57-58

Compu-Teach

Once upon a Time (Volume Three), Software (New Haven, CT: Compu-Teach, n.d.). Reviewed in: *Electronic Learning* 10, no.5 (Feb. 1991): 36-37

Computer activities

Birthday, Software (Pleasantville, NY: Sunburst Communications, 1991). Reviewed in: *Technology and Learning* 12, no.2 (Oct. 1991): 31

Kidware 2 - Learning Center, Software (n.p.: Mobius, 1991). Reviewed in: *Technology and Learning* 12, no.2 (Oct. 1991): 35

The Playroom, Software (San Rafael, CA: Broderbund Software, n.d.). Reviewed in: *Electronic Learning* 10, no.5 (Feb. 1991): 36-37; *Technology and Learning* 11, no.1 (Sept. 1990): 18

The Treehouse, Software (Novato, CA: Broderbund Software, n.d.). Reviewed in: *Technology and Learning* 12, no.5 (Feb. 1992): 10-12

Computer keyboard skills

Microtype: The Wonderful World of Paws, Software (Cincinnati, OH: South-Western Publications, 1992). Reviewed in: *Instructor* 101, no.7 (Mar. 1992): 66

Computer Painting

Easy Color Paint 1.1, Software (New Providence, NJ: Creative Software, n.d.). Reviewed in: *Computing Teacher* 18, no.7 (Apr. 1991): 45-47

Computer skills

Communikeys, Software (Minneapolis, MN: MECC, 1989). Reviewed in: *Instructor* 101, no.7 (Mar. 1992): 66

My First Computer Book, Multimedia by David Schiller and David Rosenbloom, and illustrated by Tedd Arnold (New York: Workman, 1991). Reviewed in: *School Arts* 91, no.5 (Jan. 1992): 44

New Print Shop, Software (San Rafael, CA: Broderbund Software, n.d.). Reviewed in: *Technology and Learning* 11, no.3 (Nov./ Dec. 1990): 34

Concept learning

All about Where, by Tana Hoban (New York: William Morrow and Co., 1991). Reviewed in: *Arithmetic Teacher* 39, no.9 (May 1992): 5; *Young Children* 46, no.5 (July 1991): 66

The Button Box, by Margarette S. Reid (New York: Dutton Children's Books, 1990). Reviewed in: *Arithmetic Teacher* 38, no.9 (May 1991): 44

Categories, by C. F. Navarro (Alexandria, VA: Start Smart Books, 1990). Reviewed in: *Curriculum Review* 30, no.3 (Nov. 1990): 25-26

Colorcards, Manipulatives (Bicester, UK: Winslow Press, 1989). Reviewed in: *Child Language Teaching and Therapy* 7, no.3 (Oct. 1991): 361-362

Concept learning *(cont'd)*
    Color Farm, by Lois Ehlert (New York: HarperCollins Children's Books, 1990). Reviewed in: *Arithmetic Teacher* 39, no.7 (Mar. 1992): 38

    Distinctions, by C. F. Navarro (Alexandria, VA: Start Smart Books, 1990). Reviewed in: *Curriculum Review* 30, no.3 (Nov. 1990): 25-26

    Exactly the Opposite, by Tana Hoban (New York: Greenwillow Books, 1990). Reviewed in: *Arithmetic Teacher* 39, no.1 (Sept. 1991): 51; *Young Children* 46, no.2 (Jan. 1991): 86

    In Common: Words and Things, Software (Pleasantville, NY: Sunburst Communications, 1991). Reviewed in: *Media and Methods* 27, no.5 (May/June 1991): 53

    Learning To Reason: Some, All, or None, Software (Kalamazoo, MI: MCE, 1988). Reviewed in: *Arithmetic Teacher* 39, no.1 (Sept. 1991): 47

    Mosaic Magic, Software (Encinitas, CA: Kinder Magic Software, 1990). Reviewed in: *Arithmetic Teacher* 39, no.1 (Sept. 1991): 48

    Of Colors and Things, by Tana Hoban (New York: Greenwillow Books, 1989). Reviewed in: *Arithmetic Teacher* 38, no.9 (May 1991): 44

    Patterns, Software (St. Paul, MN: MECC, 1988). Reviewed in: *Arithmetic Teacher* 38, no.2 (Oct. 1990): 50

    The Shapes Game, by Paul Rogers and illustrated by Sian Tucker (New York: Henry Holt, 1989). Reviewed in: *Arithmetic Teacher* 38, no.9 (May 1991): 45

    Time To. . ., (New York: Lothrop, Lee and Shepard, 1989). Reviewed in: *Arithmetic Teacher* 38, no.2 (Oct. 1990): 53

    Verbal Correspond, by C. F. Navarro (Alexandria, VA: Start Smart Books, 1990). Reviewed in: *Curriculum Review* 30, no.3 (Nov. 1990): 25-26

Conceptual Music Games
    Software by Thomas Gibson (n.p.: Temporal Acuity Products, Inc., 1991). Reviewed in: *American Music Teacher* 41, no.6 (June/July 1992): 10

Cooper, Gale
    Inside Animals, by Gale Cooper (San Diego: Mad Hatter Books, 1987). Reviewed in: *Gifted Child Today* 15, no.2 (Mar./Apr. 1992): 60

Cooperative Educational Service Agency
    Portage Classroom Curriculum, by J. Brinckerhoff (Portage, WI: Cooperative Educational Service Agency, 1987). Reviewed in: *Teaching Exceptional Children* 23, no.3 (Spring 1991): 72

The Coral Reef
    by Norman Barrett (New York: Watts, 1991). Reviewed in: *Science Books and Films* 27, no.4 (May 1991): 114

Coronet/MTI Film and Video
    Animal Behavior: Babies and Their Parents, Video (Deerfield, IL: Coronet/MTI Film and Video, 1991). Reviewed in: *School Library Journal* 38, no.4 (Apr. 1992): 76

    Animal Behavior: Partnerships, Video (Deerfield, IL: Coronet/MTI Film and Video, 1991). Reviewed in: *School Library Journal* 38, no.5 (May 1992): 75

    The Philharmonic Gets Dressed, Film/Video (Deerfield, IL: Coronet/MTI Film and Video, 1989). Reviewed in: *Media and Methods* 27, no.2 (Nov./Dec. 1990): 58

    Plants Are Different and Alike, Film/Video (Deerfield, IL: Coronet/MTI Film and Video, 1990). Reviewed in: *Childhood Education* 68, no.1 (Fall 1991): 54

    Sooper Puppy Drug Education Series: Flying High, Film/Video (Deerfield, IL: Coronet/MTI Film and Video, 1988). Reviewed in: *Childhood Education* 66, no.5 (Annual 1990): 349; *Media and Methods* 27, no.2 (Nov./Dec. 1990): 58-59

Coronet/MTI Film and Video *(cont'd)*
   What Is AIDS?, Film/Video (Purchase, NY:
   Coronet/MTI Film and Video, 1988).
   Reviewed in: *Day Care and Early Education*
   18, no.1 (Fall 1990): 42

Corwin, Rebecca B.
   *Measuring: From Paces to Feet, Grades 3-
   4,* by Rebecca B. Corwin and Susan Jo
   Russell (Palo Alto, CA: Dale Seymour,
   1990). Reviewed in: *Arithmetic Teacher* 38,
   no.9 (May 1991): 48

Costa, Nicoletta
   Look Inside Your Brain, by Heather Alexan-
   der and illustrated by Nicoletta Costa (New
   York: Grosset, 1991). Reviewed in: *School
   Library Journal* 38, no.1 (Jan. 1992): 101

*Counters: An Action Approach to Counting and
Arithmetic*
   Software (Scotts Valley, CA: Wings for
   Learning, 1990). Reviewed in: *Arithmetic
   Teacher* 39, no.3 (Nov. 1991): 56

Counting books
   Deep Down Underground, by Olivier Dunrea
   (Riverside, NJ: Macmillan, 1989). Reviewed
   in: *Arithmetic Teacher* 38, no.9 (May 1991): 45

   From One to One Hundred, by Teri Sloat
   (New York: Dutton, 1991). Reviewed in:
   Science Books and Films 27, no.9 (Dec.
   1991): 271-272

   Going Up!, by Peter Sis (New York:
   Greenwillow, 1989). Reviewed in: *Arithmetic
   Teacher* 38, no.2 (Oct. 1990): 52

   Hey! Get Off Our Train, by John
   Burningham (New York: Crown Publishers,
   1989). Reviewed in: *Arithmetic Teacher* 38,
   no.9 (May 1991): 45

   The Icky Bug Counting Book, by Jerry
   Pallotta and illustrated by Ralph Masiello
   (Watertown, MA: Charlesbridge, 1991). Re-
   viewed in: *Science Books and Films* 28, no.1
   (Jan./Feb. 1992): 19

   Just One More, by Michelle Koch (New
   York: Greenwillow Books, 1989). Reviewed
   in: *Arithmetic Teacher* 38, no.7 (Mar. 1991): 59

Nine Ducks Nine, by Sara Hayes (New York:
William Morrow, 1990). Reviewed in: *Arithmetic Teacher* 39, no.9 (May 1992): 51

Numbers at Play: A Counting Book, by
Charles Sullivan (New York: Rizzoli, 1992).
Reviewed in: *Childhood Education* 69, no.1
(Fall 1992): 49

*Numbers in Rhyme: Counting More and
More,* by Leland B. Jacobs (Allen, TX:
DLM, 1990). Reviewed in: *Arithmetic
Teacher* 38, no.2 (Oct. 1990): 57

Numbers in Rhyme: Counting One to Five,
by Leland B. Jacobs (Allen, TX: DLM,
1990). Reviewed in: *Arithmetic Teacher* 38,
no.2 (Oct. 1990): 57

Numbers in Rhyme: Counting Six to Ten, by
Leland B. Jacobs (Allen, TX: DLM, 1990).
Reviewed in: *Arithmetic Teacher* 38, no.2
(Oct. 1990): 57

*One Good Horse: A Cowpuncher's Counting
Book,* by Ann Herbert Scott (New York:
Greenwillow Books, 1990). Reviewed in:
Arithmetic Teacher 38, no.9 (May 1991): 45

One Special Star, by Anita McFadzean and
illustrated by Kate Jaspers (New York:
Simon and Schuster, 1991). Reviewed in:
Arithmetic Teacher 39, no.7 (Mar. 1992): 39

The Right Number of Elephants, by Jeff
Sheppard (New York: HarperCollins, 1990).
Reviewed in: *Arithmetic Teacher* 39, no.1
(Sept. 1991): 52

Sea Squares, by Joy N. Hulme and illustrated by Carol Schwartz (Waltham, MA:
Hyperion Books, 1991). Reviewed in: *Arithmetic Teacher* 40, no.1 (Sept. 1992): 56

Ten Little Rabbits, by Virginia Grossman
and illustrated by Sylvia Long (San Francisco: Chronicle Books, 1991). Reviewed in:
Arithmetic Teacher 40, no.1 (Sept. 1992):
56-57

*The Wildlife 1-2-3: A Nature Counting
Book,* by Jan Thornhill (New York: Simon
and Schuster Books for Young Readers,
1989). Reviewed in: *Arithmetic Teacher* 39,
no.7 (Mar. 1992): 39

Counting books *(cont'd)*
 Willy Can Count, by Anne Rockwell (New York: Arcade, 1989). Reviewed in: *Arithmetic Teacher* 38, no.2 (Oct. 1990): 53

Counting on Frank
 by Rod Clement (Milwaukee, WI: Gareth Stevens, 1991). Reviewed in: *Science Books and Films* 28, no.2 (Mar. 1992): 50

Counting on Math
 Manipulatives (Westminster, MD: Random House School Division, 1988). Reviewed in: *Arithmetic Teacher* 38, no.1 (Sept. 1990): 50

Counting skills
 Math, Money, and You: Count It Out, Film/Video (Washington, DC: National Geographic Society, 1989). Reviewed in: *Arithmetic Teacher* 38, no.4 (Dec. 1990): 61

 Talking Animals, Software (Pound Ridge, NY: Orange Cherry Software, 1989). Reviewed in: *Arithmetic Teacher* 38, no.4 (Dec. 1990): 60

 What Does It Cost?, Film (Washington, DC: National Geographic Society, 1989). Reviewed in: *Arithmetic Teacher* 38, no.4 (Dec. 1990): 61

Cowcher, Helen
 Antarctica, by Helen Cowcher (New York: Farrar Straus and Giroux, 1990). Reviewed in: *Science and Children* 29, no.4 (Jan. 1992): 39

Cranberries
 by William Jaspersohn (Boston: Houghton, Mifflin, 1991). Reviewed in: *Language Arts* 68, no.6 (Oct. 1991): 495

Crawford Productions
 Don't Touch That Gun (Part Two), Video (n.p.: Crawford Productions, 1990). Reviewed in: *School Library Journal* 37, no.1 (Jan. 1991): 59

Creative activities
 Fifty Creative Exercises- Book Two, by Baron Robert Nicolas (St. Paul, MN: Leonardo's Workshop, 1988). Reviewed in: *Gifted Child Today* 15, no.3 (May/June 1992): 50

The Look Again . . . and Again and Again and Again Book, by Beau Gardner (New York: Lothrop, Lee and Shepard, 1984). Reviewed in: *Gifted Child Today* 15, no.2 (Mar./Apr. 1992): 59

Magical Changes, by Graham Oakley (New York: Aladdin Books, 1987). Reviewed in: *Gifted Child Today* 15, no.2 (Mar./Apr. 1992): 59

T'NT - Talented and Thinking, by Fanny Forrest McAleer (Chatsworth, CA: Opportunities for Learning, 1987). Reviewed in: *Gifted Child Today* 15, no.5 (Sept./Oct. 1992): 41

What Is It? A Spin-About Book, by Beau Gardner (New York: G. P. Putnam's Sons, 1989). Reviewed in: *Gifted Child Today* 15, no.2 (Mar./Apr. 1992): 59

Creative Sciencing: Ideas and Activities for Teachers and Children
 by Alfred De Vito and Gerald H. Krockover (Glenview, IL: Scott Foresman, 1990). Reviewed in: *Science Books and Films* 27, no.1 (Jan./Feb. 1991): 15

Creative Software (publisher)
 Easy Color Paint 1.1, Software (New Providence, NJ: Creative Software, n.d.). Reviewed in: *Computing Teacher* 18, no.7 (Apr. 1991): 45-47

Creative writing
 Once upon a Time (Volume Three), Software (New Haven, CT: Compu-Teach, n.d.). Reviewed in: *Electronic Learning* 10, no.5 (Feb. 1991): 36-37

 Stories and More, Software (Boca Raton, FL: IBM, n.d.). Reviewed in: *Technology and Learning* 12, no.4 (Jan. 1992): 17-18

 Storybook Weaver, Software (St. Paul, MN: MECC, 1990). Reviewed in: *Instructor* 100, no.6 (Feb. 1991): 115

 Story Starters: Science, Software (Farmington, CT: Pelican Software, 1989). Reviewed in: *Science and Children* 29, no.2 (Oct. 1991): 47-48

Curriculum guides *(cont'd)*
Science through Children's Literature: An Integrated Approach, by Carol M. and John W. Butzow (Englewood, CO: Libraries Unlimited, n.d.). Reviewed in: *Curriculum Review* 30, no.1 (Sept. 1990): 30

Whole Language Source Book, by Jane Baskwill and Paulette Whitman (Ontario, Canada: Scholastic, 1986). Reviewed in: *Language Arts* 68, no.2 (Feb. 1991): 150

Cushenbery, Donald C.
Building Elementary Reading Skills through Whole Language and Literature, by Donald C. Cushenbery (Springfield, IL: Charles C. Thomas, 1989). Reviewed in: *Curriculum Review* 30, no.3 (Nov. 1990): 27

Cutchins, Judy
Slippery Babies: Young Frogs, Toads, and Salamanders, by Ginny Johnson and Judy Cutchins (New York: Morrow Junior Books, 1991). Reviewed in: *School Science and Mathematics* 92, no.3 (Mar. 1992): 165

D'Alelio, Jane
I Know That Building, by Jane D'Alelio (Washington, DC: Preservation Press, 1989). Reviewed in: *Gifted Child Today* 15, no.1 (Jan./Feb. 1992): 58

Dale Seymour (publisher)
Measuring: From Paces to Feet, Grades 3-4, by Rebecca B. Corwin and Susan Jo Russell (Palo Alto, CA: Dale Seymour, 1990). Reviewed in: *Arithmetic Teacher* 38, no.9 (May 1991): 48

Teaching Primary Math with Music, Multimedia by Esther Mardlesohn (Palo Alto, CA: Dale Seymour, 1990). Reviewed in: *Arithmetic Teacher* 39, no.1 (Sept. 1991): 53

Danny and the Dinosaur
Video (Weston, CT: Weston Woods, 1990). Reviewed in: *School Library Journal* 37, no.2 (Feb. 1991): 53

Darling, David
Spiderwebs to Skyscrapers: The Science of Structures, by David Darling (New York: Dillon, 1991). Reviewed in: *School Library Journal* 38, no.3 (Mar. 1992): 244

Darling, Kathy
Walrus on Location, by Kathy Darling (New York: Lothrop, Lee and Shepard, 1991). Reviewed in: *School Science and Mathematics* 92, no.5 (May/June 1992): 288

Davidson and Associates
New Math Blaster Plus, Software (Torrance, CA: Davidson and Associates, 1990). Reviewed in: *Instructor* 100, no.8 (April 1991): 74-75

Dawn to Dusk on the Galapagos
by Rita Golden Gelman (Boston: Little Brown, 1991). Reviewed in: *Science Books and Films* 27, no.5 (June/July 1991): 178

D. C. Heath
Explore-a-Story: Where Did My Toothbrush Go?, Software (Acton, MA: D. C. Heath, 1988). Reviewed in: *Instructor* 100, no.6 (Feb. 1991): 115-116

Debie, Catherine F.
Multiplication and Division Made Easy, by Catherine F. Debie (Artesia, CA: Scott Foresman, 1990). Reviewed in: *Arithmetic Teacher* 39, no.8 (Apr. 1992): 59

Deep Down Underground
by Olivier Dunrea (Riverside, NJ: Macmillan, 1989). Reviewed in: *Arithmetic Teacher* 38, no.9 (May 1991): 45

Degen, Bruce
Magic School Bus on the Ocean Floor, by Joanna Cole and illustrated by Bruce Degen (New York: Scholastic, 1992). Reviewed in: *School Library Journal* 38, no.8 (Aug. 1992): 151

Delacorte Press
Lines, by Philip Yenawine (New York: Delacorte Press, n.d.). Reviewed in: *School Arts* 90, no.6 (Feb. 1991): 60-61

Shapes, by Philip Yenawine (New York: Delacorte Press, n.d.). Reviewed in: *School Arts* 90, no.6 (Feb. 1991): 60-61

Stories, by Philip Yenawine (New York: Delacorte Press, n.d.). Reviewed in: *School Arts* 90, no.6 (Feb. 1991): 60-61

Distinctions
> by C. F. Navarro (Alexandria, VA: Start Smart Books, 1990). Reviewed in: *Curriculum Review* 30, no.3 (Nov. 1990): 25-26

Diving into Science: Hands-on Water-Related Experiments
> by Peggy K. Perdue (Glenview, IL: Scott Foresman, 1990). Reviewed in: *Science and Children* 28, no.7 (Apr. 1991): 60

DLM (publisher)
> *Numbers in Rhyme: Counting More and More,* by Leland B. Jacobs (Allen, TX: DLM, 1990). Reviewed in: *Arithmetic Teacher* 38, no.2 (Oct. 1990): 57

> *Numbers in Rhyme: Counting Six to Ten,* by Leland B. Jacobs (Allen, TX: DLM, 1990). Reviewed in: *Arithmetic Teacher* 38, no.2 (Oct. 1990): 57

> *Numbers in Rhyme: Counting One to Five,* by Leland B. Jacobs (Allen, TX: DLM, 1990). Reviewed in: *Arithmetic Teacher* 38, no.2 (Oct. 1990): 57

> *Thinker Math: Developing Number Sense and Arithmetic Skills (Grades 3-4),* by Carole Greenes, Linda Schulman, and Rika Spungin (Allen, TX: DLM, n.d.). Reviewed in: *Arithmetic Teacher* 38, no.2 (Oct. 1990): 54

DLM Software
> *Zero-in on Zero: Addition and Subtraction,* Software (Allen, TX: DLM Software, 1990). Reviewed in: *Arithmetic Teacher* 38, no.7 (Mar. 1991): 57-58

DLM Teaching Resources
> *On the Button in Math: Activities for Young Children,* by Carol A. Thornton and Judith K. Wells (Allen, TX: DLM Teaching Resources, 1990). Reviewed in: *Arithmetic Teacher* 38, no.9 (May 1991): 46

Doctor Zed's Science Surprises
> by Gordon Penrose (New York: Simon and Schuster, 1990). Reviewed in: *Science Books and Films* 27, no.1 (Jan./Feb. 1991): 15

Don't Touch That Gun (Part Two)
> Video (n.p.: Crawford Productions, 1990). Reviewed in: *School Library Journal* 37, no.1 (Jan. 1991): 59

Dorros, Arthur
> *Rain Forest Secrets,* by Arthur Dorros (New York: Scholastic, 1990). Reviewed in: *School Library Journal* 37, no.2 (Feb. 1991): 78

Do Touch: Instant, Easy, Hands-on Learning Experiences for Young Children
> by Labritta Gilbert (Mt. Rainier, MD: Gryphon House, 1989). Reviewed in: *Gifted Child Today* 15, no.5 (Sept./Oct. 1992): 40

Doubilet, Anne
> *Under the Sea from A to Z,* by Anne Doubilet (New York: Crown, 1991). Reviewed in: *Language Arts* 68, no.6 (Oct. 1991): 494

Doubleday
> *Creatures that Glow,* by Joanne Barkan (New York: Doubleday, 1991). Reviewed in: *School Library Journal* 38, no.1 (Jan. 1992): 118-123

> *Ready, Set, Read: The Beginning Reader's Treasury,* illustrated by Anne Burgess (New York: Doubleday, 1990). Reviewed in: *School Library Journal* 37, no.2 (Supplement Feb. 1991): S16

Down by the Bay
> by Raffi and illustrated by Nadine Westcott (New York: Crown, 1987). Reviewed in: *Reading Horizons* 32, no.1 (Oct. 1991): 75-77

Draw!
> (Cincinnati, OH: Northlight Books, n.d.). Reviewed in: *School Arts* 91, no.6 (Feb. 1992): 44

Drug education
> *Sooper Puppy Drug Education Series: Flying High,* Film/Video (Deerfield, IL: Coronet/MTI Film and Video, 1988). Reviewed in: *Childhood Education* 66, no.5 (Annual 1990): 349; *Media and Methods* 27, no.2 (Nov./Dec. 1990): 58-59

> *Spider-Man: What To Do about Drugs,* Video (n.p.: Learning Corporation of America, 1990). Reviewed in: *School Library Journal* 37, no.1 (Jan. 1991): 53

Dunrea, Olivier
Deep Down Underground, by Olivier Dunrea (Riverside, NJ: Macmillan, 1989). Reviewed in: *Arithmetic Teacher* 38, no.9 (May 1991): 45

Dutton
The Atlantic Salmon, by Bianca Lavies (New York: Dutton, 1992). Reviewed in: *School Library Journal* 38, no.4 (Apr. 1992): 139

El Enano Satarin, by Jacob Grimm and illustrated by Paul D. Zelinsky (New York: Dutton, 1992). Reviewed in: *Childhood Education* 69, no.1 (Fall 1992): 49

From One to One Hundred, by Teri Sloat (New York: Dutton, 1991). Reviewed in: *Science Books and Films* 27, no.9 (Dec. 1991): 271-272

Party Rhymes, by Marc Brown (New York: Dutton, 1989). Reviewed in: *Language Arts* 68, no.3 (Mar. 1991): 242

See How They Grow: Frog, by Kim Taylor (New York: Dutton, 1991). Reviewed in: *Childhood Education* 68, no.3 (Spring 1992): 178

Never Kiss an Alligator, by Colleen Stanley Bare (New York: Dutton, 1989). Reviewed in: *Childhood Education* 66, no.5 (Annual 1990): 337

Wild Animals of Africa ABC, by Hope Ryden (New York: Dutton, 1989). Reviewed in: *Day Care and Early Education* 18, no.1 (Fall 1990): 46

Dutton Children's Books
The Button Box, by Margarette S. Reid (New York: Dutton Children's Books, 1990). Reviewed in: *Arithmetic Teacher* 38, no.9 (May 1991): 44

Dyno-Quest
Software (Tucson, AZ: Mindplay/Methods and Solutions, 1984). Reviewed in: *Science and Children* 28, no.1 (Sept. 1990): 48

Early Geometry
by C. F. Navarro (Alexandria, VA: Start Smart Books, 1990). Reviewed in: *Curriculum Review* 30, no.3 (Nov. 1990): 25-26

Earth Alive
by Sandra Markle (New York: Lothrop, Lee and Shepard, 1991). Reviewed in: *Reading Horizons* 32, no.1 (Oct. 1991): 77-78

Earthquakes
by Seymour Simon (New York: Morrow Junior Books, 1991). Reviewed in: *Language Arts* 69, no.2 (Feb. 1992): 138-139; *Reading Horizons* 32, no.1 (Oct. 1991): 79-80

Earth Science for Every Kid: 101 Experiments That Really Work
by Janice Van Cleave (New York: John Wiley and Sons, 1991). Reviewed in: *Journal of Geography* 91, no.1 (Jan./Feb. 1992): 46

Earth sciences
Antarctica, by Helen Cowcher (New York: Farrar Straus and Giroux, 1990). Reviewed in: *Science and Children* 29, no.4 (Jan. 1992): 39

Discovering Science: As Old as the Hills, by Melvin Berger (Boston: Watts, 1989). Reviewed in: *Science and Children* 28, no.7 (Apr. 1991): 61

Earth Alive, by Sandra Markle (New York: Lothrop, Lee and Shepard, 1991). Reviewed in: *Reading Horizons* 32, no.1 (Oct. 1991): 77-78

Earthquakes, by Seymour Simon (New York: Morrow Junior Books, 1991). Reviewed in: *Language Arts* 69, no.2 (Feb. 1992): 138-139; *Reading Horizons* 32, no.1 (Oct. 1991): 79-80

Earthwatching III: An Environmental Reader with Teacher's Guide, by Tom Sinclair (Madison, WI: Institute for Environmental Studies, 1990). Reviewed in: *Journal of Environmental Education* 22, no.1 (Fall 1990): 44; *Science Teacher* 58, no.7 (Oct. 1991): 74

Eco-Saurus, Software (Torrance, CA: First Byte, 1991). Reviewed in: *Instructor* 101, no.8 (Apr. 1992): 108-110

Earth sciences *(cont'd)*

Fifty Simple Things Kids Can Do To Save the Earth, by the Earthworks Group (Kansas City, MO: Andrews and McMeel, 1990). Reviewed in: *Curriculum Review* 30, no.2 (Oct. 1990): 29

My First Green Book: A Life-Size Guide to Caring for Our Environment, by Angela Wilkes (New York: Random House, 1991). Reviewed in: *Curriculum Review* 32, no.1 (Sept. 1992): 28-29

Protecting Our Planet: Activities To Motivate Young Children to a Better Understanding of Our Environmental Problems, by Eva and Evelyn Deutsch (Carthage, IL: Good Apple, 1992). Reviewed in: *Curriculum Review* 32, no.1 (Sept. 1992): 27

The Restless Earth, by Francois Michel and Yves Lavor (New York: Viking, 1990). Reviewed in: *Language Arts* 68, no.6 (Oct. 1991): 494-495

The Science Book of Air, by Neil Ardley (San Diego: Gulliver Books, 1991). Reviewed in: *Language Arts* 68, no.6 (Oct. 1991): 494

The Science Book of Color, by Neil Ardley (San Diego: Gulliver Books, 1991). Reviewed in: *Language Arts* 68, no.6 (Oct. 1991): 494

The Science Book of Light, by Neil Ardley (San Diego: Gulliver Books, 1991). Reviewed in: *Language Arts* 68, no.6 (Oct. 1991): 494

The Science Book of Water, by Neil Ardley (San Diego: Gulliver Books, 1991). Reviewed in: *Language Arts* 68, no.6 (Oct. 1991): 494

Science Primer: Observing Air, Multimedia (Chicago: Society for Visual Education, 1989). Reviewed in: *Media and Methods* 27, no.3 (Jan./Feb. 1991): 52

Science Primer: Observing Earth, Multimedia (Chicago: Society for Visual Education, 1989). Reviewed in: *Media and Methods* 27, no.3 (Jan./Feb. 1991): 52

Science Primer: Observing Fire, Multimedia (Chicago: Society for Visual Education, 1989). Reviewed in: *Media and Methods* 27, no.3 (Jan./Feb. 1991): 52

Science Primer: Observing Water, Multimedia (Chicago: Society for Visual Education, 1989). Reviewed in: *Media and Methods* 27, no.3 (Jan./Feb. 1991): 52

Story of the Earth Series: Cave, by Lionel Bender (New York: Watts, 1989). Reviewed in: *Science and Children* 28, no.1 (Sept. 1990): 78

Water Cycle, Software (Galesburg, MI: MCE, n.d.). Reviewed in: *Science and Children* 29, no.4 (Jan. 1992): 35

Earth: Voices of a Planet
Audiotape/Compact disc (Omaha, NE: American Gramaphone Records of Omaha, 1990). Reviewed in: *American Biology Teacher* 53, no.2 (Feb. 1991): 117

Earthwatching III: An Environmental Reader with Teacher's Guide
by Tom Sinclair (Madison, WI: Institute for Environmental Studies, 1990). Reviewed in: *Journal of Environmental Education* 22, no.1 (Fall 1990): 44; *Science Teacher* 58, no.7 (Oct. 1991): 74

Easy Color Paint 1.1
Software (New Providence, NJ: Creative Software, n.d.). Reviewed in: *Computing Teacher* 18, no.7 (Apr. 1991): 45-47

EBEC (publisher)
The Guinea Pig, Video (n.p.: EBEC, 1990). Reviewed in: *School Library Journal* 37, no.2 (Feb. 1991): 56

Eco-Saurus
Software (Torrance, CA: First Byte, 1991). Reviewed in: *Instructor* 101, no.8 (Apr. 1992): 108-110

Educational Activities (publisher)
Talk to Me, Software (Freeport, NY: Educational Activities, 1990). Reviewed in: *Computing Teacher* 18, no.4 (Dec. 1990/Jan. 1991): 44-46

Educational Computing (publisher)
Grammar Monsters, Software (n.p.: Educational Computing, 1991). Reviewed in: *School Library Journal* 37, no.7 (July 1991): 33-34

Educational Insights
Geo-Safari, Software (Dominguez Hills, CA: Educational Insights, n.d.). Reviewed in: *Journal of Geography* 91, no.1 (Jan./Feb. 1992): 49

Eight Hands Round: A Patchwork Alphabet by Ann Whitford Paul and illustrated by Jeanette Winter (New York: HarperCollins, 1991). Reviewed in: *Childhood Education* 68, no.1 (Fall 1991): 46; *Language Arts* 69, no.3 (Mar. 1992): 217

Electronic Courseware Series
KIDS: Keyboard Introductory Development Series, Software by Brenda Bailey (n.p.: Electronic Courseware Systems, 1989). Reviewed in: *American Music Teacher* 41, no.6 (June/July 1992): 10

Musical Stairs - MIDI, Software by Steve Walker (n.p.: Electronic Courseware Systems, 1987). Reviewed in: *American Music Teacher* 40, no.3 (Dec. 1990/Jan. 1991): 10

El Enano Satarin
by Jacob Grimm and illustrated by Paul D. Zelinsky (New York: Dutton, 1992). Reviewed in: *Childhood Education* 69, no.1 (Fall 1992): 49

Enslow (publisher)
Caring for Our Water, by Carol Greene (Hillside, NJ: Enslow, 1991). Reviewed in: *Science and Children* 29, no.7 (Apr. 1992): 47

Esterman, M. M.
A Fish That's a Box, by M. M. Esterman (Arlington, VA: Great Ocean Publishers, 1991). Reviewed in: *Arts and Activities* 110, no.1 (Sept. 1991): 51

ETR Associates/Network Publications
Children's Activity Series, by Judith K. Scheer and Ana Matiella (Santa Cruz, CA: ETR Associates/Network Publications, 1990). Reviewed in: *Curriculum Review* 30, no.8 (Apr. 1991): 26-27

European Folk Tales
Video (Chatsworth, CA: Aims Media, 1990). Reviewed in: *School Library Journal* 37, no.10 (Oct. 1991): 73

Everything Grows
by Raffi (New York: Crown Publishers, 1989). Reviewed in: *Arithmetic Teacher* 39, no.1 (Sept. 1991): 51

Exactly the Opposite
by Tana Hoban (New York: Greenwillow Books, 1990). Reviewed in: *Arithmetic Teacher* 39, no.1 (Sept. 1991): 51; *Young Children* 46, no.2 (Jan. 1991): 86

Explore-a-Classic: "Stone Soup"
Software (Concord, MA: William Bradford, 1989). Reviewed in: *Instructor* 100, no.3 (Oct. 1990): 53

Explore-a-Classic: "The Princess and the Pea"
Software (Concord, MA: William Bradford, 1989). Reviewed in: *Instructor* 100, no.3 (Oct. 1990): 53

Explore-a-Classic: "The Three Little Pigs"
Software (Concord, MA: William Bradford, 1989). Reviewed in: *Instructor* 100, no.3 (Oct. 1990): 53

Explore-a-Story: Where Did My Toothbrush Go?
Software (Acton, MA: D. C. Heath, 1988). Reviewed in: *Instructor* 100, no.6 (Feb. 1991): 115-116

Exploring Fractions and Decimals with Manipulatives
Manipulatives by Don Balka (Peabody, MA: Didax, 1991). Reviewed in: *Arithmetic Teacher* 39, no.9 (May 1992): 53

Exploring Mathematics: Activities for Concept and Skill Development, K-3
by Jean M. Sham (Glenview, IL: Scott Foresman, 1990). Reviewed in: *Arithmetic Teacher* 38, no.1 (Sept. 1990): 46

Exploring Measurement, Time, and Money:
Levels One and Two
  Software (Atlanta, GA: IBM Educational
  Systems, 1989). Reviewed in: *Arithmetic*
  Teacher 38, no.2 (Oct. 1990): 44; *Electronic*
  Learning 10, no.7 (Apr. 1991): 36

Exploring Sound
  Video (San Diego: Media Guild, 1990).
  Reviewed in: *Science Books and Films* 27,
  no.5 (June/July 1991): 150

Exploring with Color Tiles: Grades K-3
  Manipulatives by Judi Magarian-Gold and
  Sandra Mogensen (New Rochelle, NY:
  Cuisenaire, 1990). Reviewed in: *Arithmetic*
  Teacher 38, no.8 (Apr. 1991): 56

Fairy Tale Rap: "Jack and the Beanstalk" and
Other Stories
  Multimedia adapted by Barbara Leeds
  (Miramonte, CA: Miramonte Press, 1990).
  Reviewed in: *International Journal of In-*
  structional Media 18, no.1 (n.d.): 96-97;
  Teaching Exceptional Children 24, no.4
  (Summer 1992): 83

Fall Brings Changes
  Video (Los Angeles: Churchill Films, 1991).
  Reviewed in: *Science Books and Films* 28,
  no.4 (May 1992): 118

Farm Animals
  Video (Geneva, IL: Stage Fright Productions,
  n.d.). Reviewed in: *Science Books and Films*
  27, no.7 (Oct. 1991): 217

Farmer, Walter A.
  Activities for Teaching K-6 Math/Science
  Concepts, by Walter A. Farmer and Margaret
  A. Farrell (Bowling Green, OH: School
  Science and Mathematics, 1989). Reviewed
  in: *Science and Children* 28, no.4 (Jan.
  1991): 58

Farrar, Straus, and Giroux
  ABC Bestiary, by Deborah Blackwell (New
  York: Farrar, Straus, and Giroux, 1989).
  Reviewed in: *Day Care and Early Education*
  18, 1 (Fall 1990): 46

  Antarctica, by Helen Cowcher (New York:
  Farrar Straus and Giroux, 1990). Reviewed
  in: *Science and Children* 29, no.4 (Jan.
  1992): 39

Farrell, Margaret A.
  Activities for Teaching K-6 Math/Science
  Concepts, by Walter A. Farmer and Margaret
  A. Farrell (Bowling Green, OH: School
  Science and Mathematics, 1989). Reviewed
  in: *Science and Children* 28, no.4 (Jan.
  1991): 58

Fearon Teacher Aids
  Gardening Fun, by Jean Stangl (Carthage,
  IL: Fearon Teacher Aids, 1992). Reviewed
  in: *Curriculum Review* 32, no.1 (Sept. 1992): 27

Feeding Yourself, Getting Dressed, Writing It
Down
  by Vicki Cobb (New York: Harper, 1989).
  Reviewed in: *Childhood Education* 66, no.5
  (Annual 1990): 337-338

Fendel, Laura
  Building Self-Esteem with Koala-Roo Can-
  Do, by Laura Fendel (Glenview, IL: Scott
  Foresman, 1989). Reviewed in: *Teaching*
  Exceptional Children 24, no.4 (Summer
  1992): 83

Fifty Creative Exercises—Book Two
  by Baron Robert Nicolas (St. Paul, MN:
  Leonardo's Workshop, 1988). Reviewed in:
  Gifted Child Today 15, no.3 (May/June
  1992): 50

Fifty Simple Things Kids Can Do To Save the
Earth
  by the Earthworks Group (Kansas City, MO:
  Andrews and McMeel, 1990). Reviewed in:
  Curriculum Review 30, no.2 (Oct. 1990): 29

Fighting the Invisible Enemy: Understanding
the Effects of Conditioning
  by Terrence Webster-Doyle and illustrated
  by Rod Cameron (Ojai, CA: Atrium, 1990).
  Reviewed in: *Young Children* 46, no.4 (May
  1990): 66

Film/Video
  Adventures in Clay Land: An Introduction to
  Clay, Film/Video (Fresno, CA: Margaret
  Hudson's Earth Arts Studio, n.d.). Reviewed
  in: *Arts and Activities* 110, no.4 (Dec. 1991): 14

  Aesop's Fables, Video (Los Angeles:
  Churchill Films, 1991). Reviewed in: *School*
  Library Journal 38, no.1 (Jan. 1992): 70

Film/Video *(cont'd)*

The Age of Dinosaurs, Film (Washington, DC: National Geographic Society, 1990). Reviewed in: *Media and Methods* 27, no.5 (May/June 1991): 43; *American Biology Teacher* 53, no.3 (Mar. 1991): 189

All about Anger, Video (Pleasantville, NY: Sunburst Communications, 1990). Reviewed in: *Science Books and Films* 28, no.2 (Mar. 1992): 56

All about Trees, Video (Washington, DC: National Geographic Society, 1990). Reviewed in: *School Library Journal* 37, no.1 (Jan. 1991): 61

Animal Behavior: Babies and Their Parents, Video (Deerfield, IL: Coronet/MTI Film and Video, 1991). Reviewed in: *School Library Journal* 38, no.4 (Apr. 1992): 76

Animal Behavior: Partnerships, Video (Deerfield, IL: Coronet/MTI Film and Video, 1991). Reviewed in: *School Library Journal* 38, no.5 (May 1992): 75

The Animal Life Series, Film/Video (Van Nuys, CA: AIMS Media Film and Video, 1991). Reviewed in: *Media and Methods* 28, no.1 (Sept./Oct. 1991): 46

Animals, Animals: Fins, Feathers, Fur/A Gaggle of Geese, Film/Video (Washington, DC: National Geographic Society, 1990). Reviewed in: *American Biology Teacher* 53, no.2 (Feb. 1991): 117

Barney's Campfire Sing-Along, Video (n.p.: Lyons Group, 1990). Reviewed in: *School Library Journal* 37, no.1 (Jan. 1991): 53-54

Barnyard Babies, Video (n.p.: JVM Productions, 1990). Reviewed in: *School Library Journal* 37, no.3 (Mar. 1991): 151

Danny and the Dinosaur, Video (Weston, CT: Weston Woods, 1990). Reviewed in: *School Library Journal* 37, no.2 (Feb. 1991): 53

Don't Touch That Gun (Part Two), Video (n.p.: Crawford Productions, 1990). Reviewed in: *School Library Journal* 37, no.1 (Jan. 1991): 59

European Folk Tales, Video (Chatsworth, CA: Aims Media, 1990). Reviewed in: *School Library Journal* 37, no.10

Explore-a-Classic: "The Princess and the Pea", Software (Concord, MA: William Bradford, 1989). Reviewed in: *Instructor* 100, no.3 (Oct. 1990): 53

Exploring Sound, Video (San Diego: Media Guild, 1990). Reviewed in: *Science Books and Films* 27, no.5 (June/July 1991): 150

Fall Brings Changes, Video (Los Angeles: Churchill Films, 1991). Reviewed in: *Science Books and Films* 28, no.4 (May 1992): 118

Farm Animals, Video (Geneva, IL: Stage Fright Productions, n.d.). Reviewed in: *Science Books and Films* 27, no.7 (Oct. 1991): 217

A First Look at Electricity and Magnetism, Film (Washington, DC: National Geographic Society, 1990). Reviewed in: *Media and Methods* 27, no.5 (May/June 1991): 42-43

Following the Drinking Gourd, Video (Chicago: American School, n.d.). Reviewed in: *School Library Journal* 37, no.2 (Feb. 1991): 53-54

The Fool and the Flying Ship, Video (Universal City, CA: UNI, 1991). Reviewed in: *School Library Journal* 37, no.12 (Dec. 1991): 63

Growing, Growing, Film/Video (Los Angeles: Churchill Films, 1989). Reviewed in: *Childhood Education* 68, no.1 (Fall 1991): 54

The Guinea Pig, Video (n.p.: EBEC, 1990). Reviewed in: *School Library Journal* 37, no.2 (Feb. 1991): 56

The Happy Lion, Video (Weston, CT: Weston Woods, 1991). Reviewed in: *School Library Journal* 37, no.1 (Jan. 1991): 56-57

Hexagons, Video (Evanston, IL: Journal Films, 1990). Reviewed in: *Science Books and Films* 27, no.4 (May 1991): 121

Infinity, Video (Evanston, IL: Journal Films, 1990). Reviewed in: *Science Books and Films* 27, no.4 (May 1991): 121

Film/Video *(cont'd)*

I Once Had an Operation, Film (Los Angeles: Churchill Films, 1991). Reviewed in: *Media and Methods* 27, no.5 (May/June 1991): 42

It's OK To Tell, Film/Video (n.p.: Hi-Fidelity Films, 1990). Reviewed in: *School Library Journal* 37, no.1 (Jan. 1991): 51

Josephine's Imagination, Video (n.p.: Fireworks Films, 1991). Reviewed in: *Childhood Education* 69, no.1 (Fall 1992): 58

A Kid's Guide to Getting Organized, Film (n.p.: Learning Tree, 1990). Reviewed in: *School Library Journal* 37, no.3 (Mar. 1991): 156

Let's Be Friends, Video (Seattle, WA: Tickle Tune Typhoon, 1989). Reviewed in: *Young Children* 46, no.6 (Sept. 1991): 66

Let's Get a Move On! Video (n.p.: Kidvidz, 1990). Reviewed in: *School Library Journal* 37, no.1 (Jan. 1991): 54

The Listener, Video (Boca Raton, FL: Social Issues Resources Series, 1987). Reviewed in: *Music Educator's Journal* 77, no.7 (Mar. 1991): 52

The Little Snowgirl, Video (Chicago: American School, n.d.). Reviewed in: *School Library Journal* 37, no.10 (Oct. 1991): 80

Madeline and the Bad Hat, Video (Weston, CT: Weston Woods, 1991). Reviewed in: *School Library Journal* 37, no.3 (Mar. 1991): 150

Math, Money, and You: Count It Out, Film/Video (Washington, DC: National Geographic Society, 1989). Reviewed in: *Arithmetic Teacher* 38, no.4 (Dec. 1990): 61

Max's Library: Beginning To Write, Video (Chicago: SVE, 1991). Reviewed in: *School Library Journal* 37, no.9 (Sept. 1991): 212-213

Miss Carolyn's Magical Music Shoppe: A Special Halloween, Video (Stillwater, OH: Giant Blueberry Music, 1988). Reviewed in: *Music Educator's Journal* 77, no.1 (Sept. 1990): 15

My Brother Is Afraid of Just About Everything, Film/Video (North Hollywood, CA: Alfred Higgins Productions, 1990). Reviewed in: *Curriculum Review* 30, no.2 (Oct. 1990): 19

Number Nine, Video (Evanston, IL: Journal Films, 1990). Reviewed in: *Science Books and Films* 27, no.4 (May 1991): 121

The Paper Zebra and Other Paper Possibilities, Video (Dallas, TX: Small Business Press, n.d.). Reviewed in: *Arts and Activities* 110, no.2 (Oct. 1991): 20

The Philharmonic Gets Dressed, Film/Video (Deerfield, IL: Coronet/MTI Film and Video, 1989). Reviewed in: *Media and Methods* 27, no.2 (Nov./Dec. 1990): 58

Plants Are Different and Alike, Film/Video (Deerfield, IL: Coronet/MTI Film and Video, 1990). Reviewed in: *Childhood Education* 68, no.1 (Fall 1991): 54

Problem Solving, Video (Atlanta, GA: Silver Burdett and Ginn, 1991). Reviewed in: *Arithmetic Teacher* 39, no.2 (Oct. 1991): 52-53

Ready, Set, Go: How Animals Move, Film (Washington, DC: National Geographic Society, 1989). Reviewed in: *American Biology Teacher* 52, no.8 (Nov./Dec. 1990): 514

Seeds and Seasons, Film/Video (Los Angeles: Churchill Films, 1987). Reviewed in: *Childhood Education* 68, no.1 (Fall 1991): 54

Smoke Detectives, Video (Chicago: Smoke Detectives, 1990). Reviewed in: *Curriculum Review* 30, no.5 (Jan. 1991): 26-27

Sooper Puppy Drug Education Series: Flying High, Film/Video (Deerfield, IL: Coronet/MTI Film and Video, 1988). Reviewed in: *Childhood Education* 66, no.5 (Annual 1990): 349; *Media and Methods* 27, no.2 (Nov./Dec. 1990): 58-59

Spider-Man: What To Do about Drugs, Video (n.p.: Learning Corporation of America, 1990). Reviewed in: *School Library Journal* 37, no.1 (Jan. 1991): 53

First Science Read-along Book Bags
Audiotape (Mahwah, NJ: Troll Associates, 1992). Reviewed in: *School Library Journal* 38, no.5 (May 1992): 80

A Fish That's a Box
by M. M. Esterman (Arlington, VA: Great Ocean Publishers, 1991). Reviewed in: *Arts and Activities* 110, no.1 (Sept. 1991): 51

Five Little Monkeys Jumping on the Bed
by Eileen Cristelow (New York: Clarion Books, 1989). Reviewed in: *Arithmetic Teacher* 38, no.7 (Mar. 1991): 59

Fleming, Denise
In the Tall, Tall Grass, by Denise Fleming (New York: Holt, 1991). Reviewed in: *Day Care and Early Education* 19, no.4 (Summer 1992): 43

The FlipBook
by Brenda L. Hollingsworth and illustrated by Corey Zibleman (Tucson, AZ: Communication Skill Builders, 1989). Reviewed in: *Child Language Teaching and Therapy* 7, no.1 (Feb. 1991): 113

Focus Media
Arragon: Winning Strategies for Math, Software by James Hsu and Linda C. Unger (Garden City, NY: Focus Media, 1989). Reviewed in: *Arithmetic Teacher* 38, no.1 (Sept. 1990): 42

Follow the Dream: The Story of Christopher Columbus
by Peter Sis (New York: Knopf, 1991). Reviewed in: *Childhood Education* 68, no.3 (Spring 1992): 178; *Language Arts* 69, no.3 (Mar. 1992): 216

Following the Drinking Gourd
Video (Chicago: American School, n.d.). Reviewed in: *School Library Journal* 37, no.2 (Feb. 1991): 53-54

Fontanel, Beatrice
Cats, Big and Little, by Beatrice Fontanel (Ossining, NY: Young Discovery, 1991). Reviewed in: *Science Books and Films* 27, no.7 (Oct. 1991): 211

Food Chains
Software (Galesburg, MI: MCE, n.d.). Reviewed in: *Science and Children* 29, no.2 (Oct. 1991): 46

The Fool and the Flying Ship
Video (Universal City, CA: UNI, 1991). Reviewed in: *School Library Journal* 37, no.12 (Dec. 1991): 63

Ford, Wayne
Animals in Danger, by William McCay and illustrated by Wayne Ford (Riverside, NJ: Aladdin, 1990). Reviewed in: *Language Arts* 68, no.6 (Oct. 1991): 493; *Science and Children* 29, no.4 (Jan. 1992): 39

Four Winds Press
If You Were a Writer, by Joan L. Nixon (New York: Four Winds Press, 1988). Reviewed in: *Gifted Child Today* 15, no.1 (Jan./Feb. 1992): 58

Frog Went A-Courting
by Wendy Watson (New York: Lothrop, Lee and Shepard, 1990). Reviewed in: *Language Arts* 68, no.3 (Mar. 1991): 243

From One to One Hundred
by Teri Sloat (New York: Dutton, 1991). Reviewed in: *Science Books and Films* 27, no.9 (Dec. 1991): 271-272

Fulcrum (publisher)
Keepers of the Earth, by Michael J. Caduto and Joseph Bruchac (Golden, CO: Fulcrum, 1991). Reviewed in: *Young Children* 47, no.6 (Sept. 1992): 78; *Teaching Exceptional Children* 24, no.4 (Summer 1992): 83

Keepers of the Animals: Native American Stories and Wildlife Activities for Children, by Michael J. Caduto and Joseph Bruchac (Golden, CO: Fulcrum, 1991). Reviewed in: *Curriculum Review* 31, no.8 (Apr. 1992): 28; *Young Children* 47, no.6 (Sept. 1992): 78

George, William T.
Box Turtle at Long Pond, by William T.
George and illustrated by Lindsay Barrett
George (New York: Greenwillow, 1989).
Reviewed in: *Childhood Education* 66, no.5
(Annual 1990): 338

Geo-Safari
Software (Dominguez Hills, CA: Educational
Insights, n.d.). Reviewed in: *Journal of
Geography* 91, no.1 (Jan./Feb. 1992): 49

Giant Blueberry Music
*Miss Carolyn's Magical Music Shoppe: A
Special Halloween,* Video (Stillwater, OH:
Giant Blueberry Music, 1988). Reviewed in:
Music Educator's Journal 77, no.1 (Sept.
1990): 15

Gibson, Thomas
Conceptual Music Games, Software by Tho-
mas Gibson (n.p.: Temporal Acuity Products,
Inc., 1991). Reviewed in: *American Music
Teacher* 41, no.6 (June/July 1992): 10

Gil, Yvonne
*Professor Curious and the Mystery of the
Hiking Dinosaurs,* by Yvonne Gil and
illustrated by Bonnie Timmons (n.p.:
Clarkson Potter, 1991). Reviewed in: *Lan-
guage Arts* 68, no.6 (Oct. 1991): 492

Gilbert, Labritta
*Do Touch: Instant, Easy, Hands-on Learn-
ing Experiences for Young Children,* by
Labritta Gilbert (Mt. Rainier, MD: Gryphon
House, 1989). Reviewed in: *Gifted Child
Today* 15, no.5 (Sept./Oct. 1992): 40

GO Company of Rochester
Math Smart, Game (Rochester, MN: GO
Company of Rochester, 1987). Reviewed in:
Arithmetic Teacher 38, no.1 (Sept. 1990): 52

Godine
Animal Fables from Aesop (Boston: Godine,
1989). Reviewed in: *School Library Journal*
38, no.1 (Jan. 1992): 101

Going Up!
by Peter Sis (New York: Greenwillow,
1989). Reviewed in: *Arithmetic Teacher* 38,
no.2 (Oct. 1990): 52

Goldstein, Bobbye S.
Bear in Mind: A Book of Bear Poems, by
Bobbye S. Goldstein (New York: Puffin
Books, 1991). Reviewed in: *Day Care and
Early Education* 19, no.2 (Winter 1991): 36

Good Apple
*Protecting Our Planet: Activities To Moti-
vate Young Children to a Better Understanding of Our Environmental Problems,* by Eva
and Evelyn Deutsch (Carthage, IL: Good
Apple, 1992). Reviewed in: *Curriculum
Review* 32, no.1 (Sept. 1992): 27

Gottlieb, Joan
The Human Body, by Joan Gottlieb (Austin
TX: Steck-Vaughn, 1990). Reviewed in:
Science Books and Films 27, no.1 (Jan./Feb.
1991): 18

G. P. Putnam's Sons
What Is It? A Spin-About Book, by Beau
Gardner (New York: G. P. Putnam's Sons,
1989). Reviewed in: *Gifted Child Today* 15,
no.2 (Mar./Apr. 1992): 59

Grammar
The FlipBook, by Brenda L. Hollingsworth
and illustrated by Corey Zibleman (Tucson,
AZ: Communication Skill Builders, 1989).
Reviewed in: *Child Language Teaching and
Therapy* 7, no.1 (Feb. 1991): 113

Grammar Monsters, Software (n.p.: Educational Computing, 1991). Reviewed in:
School Library Journal 37, no.7 (July 1991):
33-34

*Grammar Practice Activities: A Practical
Guide for Teachers,* by Penny Ur (Cambridge, UK: Cambridge University Press,
1986). Reviewed in: *TESL Canada Journal*
8, no.1 (Nov. 1990): 114-116

Many Luscious Lollipops, by Ruth Heller
(New York: Grosset and Dunlap, 1989).
Reviewed in: *Gifted Child Today* 15, no.1
(Jan./Feb. 1992): 59

Up, Up and Away: A Book about Adverbs,
by Ruth Heller (New York: Grosset, 1991).
Reviewed in: *School Library Journal* 38,
no.2 (Feb. 1992): 82

Grossman, Virginia
Ten Little Rabbits, by Virginia Grossman and illustrated by Sylvia Long (San Francisco: Chronicle Books, 1991). Reviewed in: *Arithmetic Teacher* 40, no.1 (Sept. 1992): 56-57

Growing, Growing
Film/Video (Los Angeles: Churchill Films, 1989). Reviewed in: *Childhood Education* 68, no.1 (Fall 1991): 54

GrowLab: Activities for Growing Minds
by Joy Cohen and Eve Pranis, and illustrated by Grant Urie (Burlington, VT: National Gardening Association, 1990). Reviewed in: *Science Books and Films* 27, no.2 (Mar. 1991): 49

Gryphon House
Do Touch: Instant, Easy, Hands-on Learning Experiences for Young Children, by Labritta Gilbert (Mt. Rainier, MD: Gryphon House, 1989). Reviewed in: *Gifted Child Today* 15, no.5 (Sept./Oct. 1992): 40

Guiberson, Brenda Z.
Cactus Hotel, by Brenda Z. Guiberson and illustrated by Megan Lloyd (New York: Holt, 1991). Reviewed in: *Childhood Education* 68, no.1 (Fall 1991): 44; *Day Care and Early Education* 19, no.4 (Summer 1992): 43

The Guinea Pig
Video (n.p.: EBEC, 1990). Reviewed in: *School Library Journal* 37, no.2 (Feb. 1991): 56

Gulliver Books
The Science Book of Air, by Neil Ardley (San Diego: Gulliver Books, 1991). Reviewed in: *Language Arts* 68, no.6 (Oct. 1991): 494

The Science Book of Color, by Neil Ardley (San Diego: Gulliver Books, 1991). Reviewed in: *Language Arts* 68, no.6 (Oct. 1991): 494

The Science Book of Hot and Cold, by Neil Ardley (San Diego: Gulliver, 1992). Reviewed in: *Science Books and Films* 28, no.4 (May 1992): 110

The Science Book of Light, by Neil Ardley (San Diego: Gulliver Books, 1991). Reviewed in: *Language Arts* 68, no.6 (Oct. 1991): 494

The Science Book of the Senses, by Neil Ardley (San Diego: Gulliver, 1992). Reviewed in: *Science Books and Films* 28, no.4 (May 1992): 110

The Science Book of Water, by Neil Ardley (San Diego: Gulliver Books, 1991). Reviewed in: *Language Arts* 68, no.6 (Oct. 1991): 494

Guthrie, Woody
Woody's Twenty Grow-Big Songs, by Woody Guthrie (New York: HarperCollins, 1992). Reviewed in: *School Library Journal* 38, no.7 (July 1992): 68

Hammer, Cary
Math Shop Junior, Software by Cary Hammer (New York: Scholastic, 1989). Reviewed in: *Arithmetic Teacher* 38, no.1 (Sept. 1990): 44

Hands-on Math: Volumes One and Two
Software (Newbury Park, CA: Ventura Educational Systems, 1988). Reviewed in: *Arithmetic Teacher* 38, no.2 (Oct. 1990): 46-48; *Instructor* 100, no.8 (Apr. 1991): 74

The Happy Lion
Video (Weston, CT: Weston Woods, 1991). Reviewed in: *School Library Journal* 37, no.1 (Jan. 1991): 56-57

Harcourt Brace Jovanovich
Art Works, Multimedia (Orlando, FL: Harcourt Brace, n.d.). Reviewed in: *School Arts* 90, no.5 (Jan. 1991): 42-43

One Hundred Words about My House, Multimedia (Orlando, FL: Harcourt Brace Jovanovich, 1990). Reviewed in: *School Library Journal* 37, no.1 (Jan. 1991): 62

One Hundred Words about Working, Multimedia (Orlando, FL: Harcourt Brace Jovanovich, 1990). Reviewed in: *School Library Journal* 37, no.1 (Jan. 1991): 62

Harper and Row/HarperCollins
And the Green Grass Grew All Around, by Alvin Schwartz (New York: HarperCollins, 1992). Reviewed in: *School Library Journal* 38, no.6 (June 1992): 135

Books and Libraries, by Jack Knowlton and illustrated by Harriett Barton (New York: HarperCollins, 1991). Reviewed in: *Childhood Education* 68, no.1 (Fall 1991): 45; *Language Arts* 69, no.2 (Feb. 1992): 139-140

Color Farm, by Lois Ehlert (New York: HarperCollins Children's Books, 1990). Reviewed in: *Arithmetic Teacher* 39, no.7 (Mar. 1992): 38

Eight Hands Round: A Patchwork Alphabet, by Ann Whitford Paul and illustrated by Jeanette Winter (New York: HarperCollins, 1991). Reviewed in: *Childhood Education* 68, no.1 (Fall 1991): 46; *Language Arts* 69, no.3 (Mar. 1992): 217

Feeding Yourself, Getting Dressed, Writing It Down, by Vicki Cobb (New York: Harper, 1989). Reviewed in: *Childhood Education* 66, no.5 (Annual 1990): 337-338

The Right Number of Elephants, by Jeff Sheppard (New York: HarperCollins, 1990). Reviewed in: *Arithmetic Teacher* 39, no.1 (Sept. 1991): 52

There's a Hole in the Bucket, by Nadine Bernard Westcott (New York: Harper and Row, 1990). Reviewed in: *Language Arts* 68, no.3 (Mar. 1991): 243

Whales, by Seymour Simon (New York: Harper, 1989). Reviewed in: *Chilhood Education* 66, no.5 (Annual 1990): 338-339

Woody's Twenty Grow-Big Songs, by Woody Guthrie (New York: HarperCollins, 1992). Reviewed in: *School Library Journal* 38, no.7 (July 1992): 68

Hayes, Sara
Nine Ducks Nine, by Sara Hayes (New York: William Morrow, 1990). Reviewed in: *Arithmetic Teacher* 39, no.9 (May 1992): 51

Health activities
Children's Activity Series, by Judith K. Scheer and Ana Matiella (Santa Cruz, CA: ETR Associates/Network Publications, 1990). Reviewed in: *Curriculum Review* 30, no.8 (Apr. 1991): 26-27

Health sciences
I Once Had an Operation, Film (Los Angeles: Churchill Films, 1991). Reviewed in: *Media and Methods* 27, no.5 (May/June 1991): 42

Thumbs Up for Kids: AIDS Education, Film/Video (Purchase, NY: Media Express, 1989). Reviewed in: *Day Care and Early Education* 18, no.1 (Fall 1990): 42

What Is AIDS?, Film/Video (Purchase, NY: Coronet/MTI Film and Video, 1988). Reviewed in: *Day Care and Early Education* 18, no.1 (Fall 1990): 42

Heinemann
Literacy through Literature, by Terry D. Johnson and Daphne R. Louis (Portsmouth, NH: Heinemann, 1987). Reviewed in: *TESOL Quarterly* 24, no.4 (Winter 1990): 730-731

Heller, Ruth
A Cache of Jewels, by Ruth Heller (New York: Putnam, 1989). Reviewed in: *Gifted Child Today* 15, no.1 (Jan./Feb. 1992): 58

Many Luscious Lollipops, by Ruth Heller (New York: Grosset and Dunlap, 1989). Reviewed in: *Gifted Child Today* 15, no.1 (Jan./Feb. 1992): 59

Hello Toes! Movement Games for Children by A. L. Barlin and N. Kalev (Pennington, NJ: Princeton Book Company, 1989). Reviewed in: *Bulletin of the Council for Research in Music Education* 107 (Winter 1991): 75-76

Here We Live: Australia by Donna Bailey (Austin, TX: Steck-Vaughn, 1990). Reviewed in: *Young Children* 46, no.1 (Nov. 1990): 66

Here We Live: Greece
by Jenny Vaughn (Madison, NJ: Steck-Vaughn, 1990). Reviewed in: *Young Children* 46, no.1 (Nov. 1990): 66

Here We Live: Hong Kong
by Donna Bailey (Austin, TX: Steck-Vaughn, 1990). Reviewed in: *Young Children* 46, no.1 (Nov. 1990): 66

Here We Live: India
by Donna Bailey (Austin, TX: Steck-Vaughn, 1990). Reviewed in: *Young Children* 46, no.1 (Nov. 1990): 66

Here We Live: Russia
by Jenny Vaughn (Madison, NJ: Steck-Vaughn, 1990). Reviewed in: *Young Children* 46, no.1 (Nov. 1990): 66

Here We Live: Trinidad
by Donna Bailey (Austin, TX: Steck-Vaughn, 1990). Reviewed in: *Young Children* 46, no.1 (Nov. 1990): 66

Herman, M. L.
Teaching Kids To Love the Earth, by M. L. Herman (n.p.: Pfeifer-Hamilton, 1991). Reviewed in: *Science and Children* 29, no.7 (Apr. 1992): 46

Herrara, Velino
In My Mother's House, by Ann Nolan Clark and illustrated by Velino Herrara (New York: Viking, 1991). Reviewed in: *Day Care and Early Education* 19, no.2 (Winter 1991): 36

Hexagons
Video (Evanston, IL: Journal Films, 1990). Reviewed in: *Science Books and Films* 27, no.4 (May 1991): 121

Hey! Get Off Our Train
by John Burningham (New York: Crown Publishers, 1989). Reviewed in: *Arithmetic Teacher* 38, no.9 (May 1991): 45

Hi-Fidelity Films
It's OK To Tell, Film/Video (n.p.: Hi-Fidelity Films, 1990). Reviewed in: *School Library Journal* 37, no.1 (Jan. 1991): 51

High Windy Audio
Stories and Songs for Little Children, Audiotape by Pete Seeger (Fairview, NC: High Windy Audio, 1990). Reviewed in: *Young Children* 46, no.6 (Sept. 1991): 66

Himler, Ronald
Animals of the Night, by Mary Banks and illustrated by Ronald Himler (New York: Scribner's, 1990). Reviewed in: *Day Care and Early Education* 19, no.4 (Summer 1992): 43

Hirschi, Ron
Spring, by Ron Hirschi (New York: Cobblehill, 1990). Reviewed in: *Science Books and Films* 27, no.3 (Apr. 1991): 82

Winter, by Ron Hirschi (New York: Cobblehill, 1990). Reviewed in: *Science Books and Films* 27, no.3 (Apr. 1991): 82

Hiscock, Bruce
The Big Tree, by Bruce Hiscock (New York: Atheneum, 1991). Reviewed in: *Science Books and Films* 27, no.4 (May 1991): 115

History
The Airplane Book, by Cheryl Walsh Bellville (Minneapolis: Carolrhoda, 1991). Reviewed in: *School Library Journal* 38, no.2 (Feb. 1992): 80-81

The American Flag, by Ann Armbruster (New York: Watts, 1991). Reviewed in: *School Library Journal* 38, no.1 (Jan. 1992): 117

Discovery of the Americas, by Betsy Maestro and Giulio Maestro (New York: Lothrop, Lee and Shepard, 1991). Reviewed in: *Reading Horizons* 32, no.1 (Oct. 1991): 79-80

Following the Drinking Gourd, Video (Chicago: American School, n.d.). Reviewed in: *School Library Journal* 37, no.2 (Feb. 1991): 53-54

Follow the Dream: The Story of Christopher Columbus, by Peter Sis (New York: Knopf, 1991). Reviewed in: *Childhood Education* 68, no.3 (Spring 1992): 178; *Language Arts* 69, no.3 (Mar. 1992): 216

Hulme, Joy N.
   Sea Squares, by Joy N. Hulme and illustrated by Carol Schwartz (Waltham, MA:
   Hyperion Books, 1991). Reviewed in: *Arithmetic Teacher* 40, no.1 (Sept. 1992): 56

The Human Body
   by Joan Gottlieb (Austin TX: Steck-Vaughn,
   1990). Reviewed in: *Science Books and
   Films* 27, no.1 (Jan./Feb. 1991): 18

The Human Body and How It Works
   by Angela Royston (New York: Warwick
   Press, 1991). Reviewed in: *Science Books
   and Films* 28, no.1 (Jan./Feb. 1992): 21

Humanities Software
   Reader's Quest, Software (Hood River, OR:
   Humanities Software, 1991). Reviewed in:
   Electronic Learning 10, no.8 (May/June
   1991): 40

   Story Tailor Library, Software (Hood River,
   OR: Humanities Software, n.d.). Reviewed
   in: *Technology and Learning* 11, no.5 (Feb.
   1991): 25-28

Hunt, Joyce
   A First Look at Ducks, Geese, and Swans,
   by Millicent E. Selsam and Joyce Hunt, and
   illustrated by Harriett Springer (New York:
   Walker, 1990). Reviewed in: *Language Arts*
   68, no.6 (Oct. 1991): 493-494

Hyperion
   At the Crack of the Bat: Baseball Poems, by
   Lillian Morrison (New York: Hyperion,
   1992). Reviewed in: *School Library Journal*
   38, no.6 (June 1992): 134

Hyperion Books
   Sea Squares, by Joy N. Hulme and illustrated by Carol Schwartz (Waltham, MA:
   Hyperion Books, 1991). Reviewed in: *Arithmetic Teacher* 40, no.1 (Sept. 1992): 56

I Bet You Didn't Know That
   by Carol Iverson (Minneapolis: Lerner,
   1990). Reviewed in: *Science and Children*
   29, no.6 (Mar. 1992): 55

IBM
   Stories and More, Software (Boca Raton,
   FL: IBM, n.d.). Reviewed in: *Technology
   and Learning* 12, no.4 (Jan. 1992): 17-18

IBM Educational Systems
   *Exploring Measurement, Time, and Money:
   Levels One and Two,* Software (Atlanta:
   IBM Educational Systems, 1989). Reviewed
   in: *Arithmetic Teacher* 38, no.2 (Oct. 1990):
   44; *Electronic Learning* 10, no.7 (Apr.
   1991): 36

I Can Write
   Software (Pleasantville, NY: Sunburst Com-
   munications, n.d.). Reviewed in: *Gifted Child
   Today* 15, no.3 (May/June 1992): 53

The Icky Bug Counting Book
   by Jerry Pallotta and illustrated by Ralph
   Masiello (Watertown, MA: Charlesbridge,
   1991). Reviewed in: *Science Books and
   Films* 28, no1 (Jan./Feb. 1992): 19

Ideals (publisher)
   Survival: Could You Be a Frog? by John
   Norris Wood (Nashville, TN: Ideals, 1990).
   Reviewed in: *Science Books and Films* 27,
   no.3 (Apr. 1991): 84

   Survival: Could You Be a Mouse? by John
   Norris Wood (Nashville, TN: Ideals, 1990).
   Reviewed in: *Science Books and Films* 27,
   no.3 (Apr. 1991): 84

If You Were a Writer
   by Joan L. Nixon (New York: Four Winds
   Press, 1988). Reviewed in: *Gifted Child
   Today* 15, no.1 (Jan./Feb. 1992): 58

I Know That Building
   by Jane D'Alelio (Washington, DC: Preservation Press, 1989). Reviewed in: *Gifted
   Child Today* 15, no.1 (Jan./Feb. 1992): 58

The Illustrated World of Space
   by Iain Nicolson (New York: Simon and
   Schuster, 1991). Reviewed in: *Science Books
   and Films* 27, no.8 (Nov. 1991): 237

In a Cabin in a Wood
   by Darcie McNally and illustrated by Robin
   Michael Koontz (New York: Cobblehill/
   Dutton, 1991). Reviewed in: *Reading Horizons* 32, no.1 (Oct. 1991): 75-77

In Common: Words and Things
   Software (Pleasantville, NY: Sunburst Com-
   munications, 1991). Reviewed in: *Media and
   Methods* 27, no.5 (May/June 1991): 53

Johnson, Ginny
Slippery Babies: Young Frogs, Toads, and Salamanders, by Ginny Johnson and Judy Cutchins (New York: Morrow Junior Books, 1991). Reviewed in: *School Science and Mathematics* 92, no.3 (Mar. 1992): 165

Johnson, Terry D.
Literacy through Literature, by Terry D. Johnson and Daphne R. Louis (Portsmouth, NH: Heinemann, 1987). Reviewed in: *TESOL Quarterly* 24, no.4 (Winter, 1990): 730-731

Jones, Brian
Space: A Three-Dimensional Journey, by Brian Jones and illustrated by Richard Clifton-Dey (New York: Dial, 1991). Reviewed in: *Day Care and Early Education* 19, no.4 (Summer 1992): 43

Josephine's Imagination
Video (n.p.: Fireworks Films, 1991). Reviewed in: *Childhood Education* 69, no.1 (Fall 1992): 58

Journal Films
Hexagons, Video (Evanston, IL: Journal Films, 1990). Reviewed in: *Science Books and Films* 27, no.4 (May 1991): 121

Infinity, Video (Evanston, IL: Journal Films, 1990). Reviewed in: *Science Books and Films* 27, no.4 (May 1991): 121

Number Nine, Video (Evanston, IL: Journal Films, 1990). Reviewed in: *Science Books and Films* 27, no.4 (May 1991): 121

Jungle Safari
Software (Pound Ridge, NY: Orange Cherry Software, 1990). Reviewed in: *Science and Children* 29, no.4 (Jan. 1992): 35-36

Just Grandma and Me
Software (Novato, CA: Broderbund Software, n.d.). Reviewed in: *Technology and Learning* 13, no.1 (Sept. 1992): 17-20

Just One More
by Michelle Koch (New York: Greenwillow Books, 1989). Reviewed in: *Arithmetic Teacher* 38, no.7 (Mar. 1991): 59

JVM Productions
Barnyard Babies, Video (n.p.: JVM Productions, 1990). Reviewed in: *School Library Journal* 37, no.3 (Mar. 1991): 151

Kalev, N.
Hello Toes! Movement Games for Children, by A. L. Barlin and N. Kalev (Pennington, NJ: Princeton Book Company, 1989). Reviewed in: *Bulletin of the Council for Research in Music Education* 107 (Winter 1991): 75-76

Kaminski, Robert
Multicultural Folktales: Stories To Tell Young Children, by Judy Sierra and Robert Kaminski (Phoenix, AZ: Oryx Press, 1991). Reviewed in: *Young Children* 47, no.2 (Jan. 1992): 71

Katie's Farm
Software (Galesburg, MI: Lawrence Productions, n.d.). Reviewed in: *Science and Children* 28, no.3 (Nov./Dec. 1990): 44

Keepers of the Animals: Native American Stories and Wildlife Activities for Children
by Michael J. Caduto and Joseph Bruchac (Golden, CO: Fulcrum, 1991). Reviewed in: *Curriculum Review* 31, no.8 (Apr. 1992): 28; *Young Children* 47, no.6 (Sept. 1992): 78

Keepers of the Earth
by Michael J. Caduto and Joseph Bruchac (Golden, CO: Fulcrum, 1991). Reviewed in: *Young Children* 47, no.6 (Sept. 1992): 78; *Teaching Exceptional Children* 24, no.4 (Summer 1992): 83

Kendall-Hunt
Basic Reading Inventory, by Jerry L. Johns (Dubuque, IA: Kendall-Hunt, 1991). Reviewed in: *Reading Horizons* 32, no.2 (Dec. 1991): 158-159

A Kettle of Hawks and Other Wildlife Groups
(New York: Lothrop, Lee and Shepard, 1990). Reviewed in: *Language Arts* 68, no.2 (Feb. 1991): 145-146

Kid Pix
Software (San Rafael, CA: Broderbund Software, n.d.). Reviewed in: *Computing Teacher* 19, no.2 (Oct. 1991): 45-47; *Instructor* 101, no.5 (Jan. 1992): 73

Kuhn, Dwight
More Than Just a Garden, by Dwight Kuhn (Englewood Cliffs, NJ: Silver Burdett, 1990). Reviewed in: *Science and Children* 29, no.2 (Oct. 1991): 53

Kunitz, Sharon Lohse
Maestroscope Theory Readiness B and C, Software by Sharon Lohse Kunitz (n.p.: Maestro Music, 1989). Reviewed in: *American Music Teacher* 41, no.6 (June/July 1992): 10

The Lady with the Alligator Purse by Nadine Westcott (Boston: Little Brown, 1989). Reviewed in: *Reading Horizons* 32, no.1 (Oct. 1991): 75-77

Landmark Films
Tell Someone, Video (n.p.: Landmark Films, 1987). Reviewed in: *School Library Journal* 37, no.1 (Jan. 1991): 53

Language acquisition
Windows on Science (Spanish Edition), Software (Warren, NJ: Optical Data, n.d.). Reviewed in: *Computing Teacher* 18, no.4 (Dec. 1990/Jan. 1991): 53

Language arts
Big and Little, Software (Pleasantville, NY: Sunburst Communications, n.d.). Reviewed in: *Computing Teacher* 19, no.1 (Aug./Sept. 1991): 44-46; *Instructor* 100, no.5 (Jan. 1991): 119

Language skills
One Hundred Words about My House, Multimedia (Orlando, FL: Harcourt Brace Jovanovich, 1990). Reviewed in: *School Library Journal* 37, no.1 (Jan. 1991): 62

One Hundred Words about Working, Multimedia (Orlando, FL: Harcourt Brace Jovanovich, 1990). Reviewed in: *School Library Journal* 37, no.1 (Jan. 1991): 62

Talk to Me, Software (Freeport, NY: Educational Activities, 1990). Reviewed in: *Computing Teacher* 18, no.4 (Dec. 1990/Jan. 1991): 44-46

Truck, by Donald Crews (New York: Greenwillow Books, 1980). Reviewed in: *Instructor* 100, no.4 (Nov./Dec. 1990): 66

Lauber, Patricia
How We Learned the Earth Is Round, by Patricia Lauber and illustrated by Megan Lloyd (n.p.: Thomas Y. Crowell, 1990). Reviewed in: *Language Arts* 68, no.2 (Feb. 1991): 146

Laughing Time: Collected Nonsense by William Smith and illustrated by Jay F. Krahn (New York: Sunburst, 1990). Reviewed in: *Day Care and Early Education* 19, no.2 (Winter 1991): 36

Laureate Learning Systems
The Sentence Master, Software (Winooski, VT: Laureate Learning Systems, n.d.). Reviewed in: *Computing Teacher* 18, no.4 (Dec. 1990/Jan. 1991): 50-51

Lavies, Bianca
The Atlantic Salmon, by Bianca Lavies (New York: Dutton, 1992). Reviewed in: *School Library Journal* 38, no.4 (Apr. 1992): 139

Lavor, Yves
The Restless Earth, by Francois Michel and Yves Lavor (New York: Viking, 1990). Reviewed in: *Language Arts* 68, no.6 (Oct. 1991): 494-495

Lawrence, R. D.
Wolves, by R. D. Lawrence (Boston: Little Brown, 1990). Reviewed in: *Language Arts* 69, no.4 (Apr. 1992): 301

Lawrence Productions
Katie's Farm, Software (Galesburg, MI: Lawrence Productions, n.d.). Reviewed in: *Science and Children* 28, no.3 (Nov./Dec. 1990): 44

Nigel's World, Software (Galesburg, MI: Lawrence Productions, n.d.). Reviewed in: *Computing Teacher* 20, no.1 (Aug./Sept. 1992): 44-47

Leap into Learning
by Kristen Bissinger and Nancy Renfro (Austin, TX: Nancy Renfro Studios, 1990). Reviewed in: *Curriculum Review* 31, no.7 (Mar. 1992): 25-26

Lear, Edward
The Nonsense Poems of Edward Lear, by Edward Lear and illustrated by Leonard L. Brooke (New York: Clarion Books, 1991). Reviewed in: *Day Care and Early Education* 19, no.2 (Winter 1991): 36

Learn about Insects
Software (Pleasantville, NY: Sunburst Communications, n.d.). Reviewed in: *Science and Children* 28, no.8 (May 1991): 31

Learn about Plants
Software (Scotts Valley, CA: WINGS for Learning, n.d.). Reviewed in: *Computing Teacher* 18, no.8 (May 1991): 41-45

Learning activities
Hello Toes! Movement Games for Children, by A. L. Barlin and N. Kalev (Pennington, NJ: Princeton Book Company, 1989). Reviewed in: *Bulletin of the Council for Research in Music Education* 107 (Winter 1991): 75-76

Leap into Learning, by Kristen Bissinger and Nancy Renfro (Austin, TX: Nancy Renfro Studios, 1990). Reviewed in: *Curriculum Review* 31, no.7 (Mar. 1992): 25-26

Learning Company
Reader Rabbit 2, Software (Fremont, CA: Learning Company, n.d.). Reviewed in: *Technology and Learning* 12, no.7 (Apr. 1992): 7-10

Super Solvers Spellbound, Software (Fremont, CA: Learning Company, 1991). Reviewed in: *Technology and Learning* 12, no.6 (Mar. 1992): 11-14

The Writing Center - School Edition, Software (Fremont, CA: Learning Company, n.d.). Reviewed in: *Technology and Learning* 12, no.3 (Nov./Dec. 1991): 9

Learning Corporation of America
Spider-Man: What To Do about Drugs, Video (n.p.: Learning Corporation of America, 1990). Reviewed in: *School Library Journal* 37, no.1 (Jan. 1991): 53

Learning skills
Feeding Yourself, Getting Dressed, Writing It Down, by Vicki Cobb (New York: Harper, 1989). Reviewed in: *Childhood Education* 66, no.5 (Annual 1990): 337-338

A Kid's Guide to Getting Organized, Film (n.p.: Learning Tree, 1990). Reviewed in: *School Library Journal* 37, no.3 (Mar. 1991): 156

Once inside the Library, by Barbara A. Huff and illustrated by Iris Van Rynback (Boston: Little Brown, 1990). Reviewed in: *Science Books and Films* 27, no.2 (Mar. 1991): 45

Project Zoo, Software (Washington, DC: National Geographic Society, 1987). Reviewed in: *School Science and Mathematics* 190, no.6 (Nov. 1990): 652

Talking Alpha Chimp, Software (Pound Ridge, NY: Orange Cherry Software, 1989). Reviewed in: *Arithmetic Teacher* 38, no.4 (Dec. 1990): 59; *Instructor* 100, no.3 (Oct. 1990): 53

Talking Classroom: Grades Pre-K to Four, Software (Pound Ridge, NY: Orange Cherry Software, 1990). Reviewed in: *Arithmetic Teacher* 39, no.3 (Nov. 1991): 57

Talking Clock, Software (Pound Ridge, NY: Orange Cherry Software, n.d.). Reviewed in: *Media and Methods* 27, no.1 (Sept./Oct. 1990): 71-77

Talking Dinosaurs, Software (Pound Ridge, NY: Orange Cherry Software, n.d.). Reviewed in: *Media and Methods* 27, no.1 (Sept./Oct. 1990): 71-77

Talking Reading Railroad, Software (Pound Ridge, NY: Orange Cherry Software, n.d.). Reviewed in: *Media and Methods* 27, no.1 (Sept./Oct. 1990): 71-77

Talking School Bus, Software (Pound Ridge, NY: Orange Cherry Software, 1989). Reviewed in: *Arithmetic Teacher* 38, no.1 (Sept. 1990): 44

Learning To Reason: Some, All, or None
Software (Kalamazoo, MI: MCE, 1988).
Reviewed in: *Arithmetic Teacher* 39, no.1
(Sept. 1991): 47

Learning Tree (publisher)
A Kid's Guide to Getting Organized, Film
(n.p.: Learning Tree, 1990). Reviewed in:
School Library Journal 37, no.3 (Mar.
1991): 156

Leder, Dora
I Was So Mad! by Norma Simon and
illustrated by Dora Leder (Morton Grove, IL:
Whitman, 1992). Reviewed in: *Science
Books and Films* 28, no.3 (Apr. 1992): 80

Leeds, Barbara
*Fairy Tale Rap: "Jack and the Beanstalk"
and Other Stories,* Multimedia adapted by
Barbara Leeds (Miramonte, CA: Miramonte
Press, 1990). Reviewed in: *International
Journal of Instructional Media* 18, no.1
(n.d.): 96-97; *Teaching Exceptional Child-
ren* 24, no.4 (Summer 1992): 83

Legacy Software
Mutanoid Math Challenge, Software
(Northridge, CA: Legacy Software, n.d.).
Reviewed in: *Technology and Learning* 12,
no.8 (May/June 1992): 11-12

Leonardo's Workshop (publisher)
Fifty Creative Exercises- Book Two, by
Baron Robert Nicolas (St. Paul, MN:
Leonardo's Workshop, 1988). Reviewed in:
Gifted Child Today 15, no.3 (May/June
1992): 50

Lerner (publisher)
I Bet You Didn't Know That, by Carol
Iverson (Minneapolis, MN: Lerner, 1990).
Reviewed in: *Science and Children* 29, no.6
(Mar. 1992): 55

Let's Be Friends
Video (Seattle, WA: Tickle Tune Typhoon,
1989). Reviewed in: *Young Children* 46,
no.6 (Sept. 1991): 66

Let's Get a Move On!
Video (n.p.: Kidvidz, 1990). Reviewed in:
School Library Journal 37, no.1 (Jan. 1991): 54

Let's Pretend: Poems of Flight and Fancy
edited by Natalie S. Bober and illustrated by
Bob Bell (New York: Viking Kestrel, 1986).
Reviewed in: *Day Care and Early Education*
19, no.2 (Winter 1991): 35

Lewin, Ted
Bird Watch, by Jane Yolen and illustrated by
Ted Lewin (New York: Philomel, 1990).
Reviewed in: *School Library Journal* 37,
no.2 (Supplement to Feb. 1991): S-22

Lewis, James
*Measure, Pour and Mix: Kitchen Science
Tricks,* by James Lewis (New York:
Meadowbrook Press, 1990). Reviewed in:
Science Books and Films 27, no.3 (Apr.
1991): 79

Libraries Unlimited
*Science through Children's Literature: An
Integrated Approach,* by Carol M. and John
W. Butzow (Englewood, CO: Libraries
Unlimited, n.d.). Reviewed in: *Curriculum
Review* 30, no.1 (Sept. 1990): 30

Life Cycles
Software (Galesburg, MI: MCE, n.d.). Re-
viewed in: *Science and Children* 29, no.1
(Sept. 1991): 58-59

Life science
About Birds: A Guide for Children, by
Catheryn Sill and illustrated by John Sill
(Atlanta: Peachtree, 1991). Reviewed in:
School Library Journal 38, no.2 (Feb. 1992): 84

Adaptations, Software (Galesburg, MI: MCE,
n.d.). Reviewed in: *Science and Children* 29,
no.1 (Sept. 1991): 59

The Age of Dinosaurs, Film (Washington,
DC: National Geographic Society, 1990).
Reviewed in: *Media and Methods* 27, no.5
(May/June 1991): 43; *American Biology
Teacher* 53, no.3 (Mar. 1991): 189

All about Birth and Growth, by Donna
Bailey (Madison, NJ: Steck-Vaughn Library,
1991). Reviewed in: *Curriculum Review* 31,
no.2 (Oct. 1991): 26-27

Life science *(cont'd)*

All about Trees, Video (Washington, DC: National Geographic Society, 1990). Reviewed in: *School Library Journal* 37, no.1 (Jan. 1991): 61

All about Your Health and Blood, by Donna Bailey (Madison, NJ: Steck-Vaughn Library, 1991). Reviewed in: *Curriculum Review* 31, no.2 (Oct. 1991): 26-27

All about Your Senses, by Donna Bailey (Madison, NJ: Steck-Vaughn Library, 1991). Reviewed in: *Curriculum Review* 31, no.2 (Oct. 1991): 26-27

All about Your Skin, Hair, and Teeth, by Donna Bailey (Madison, NJ: Steck-Vaughn Library, 1991). Reviewed in: *Curriculum Review* 31, no.2 (Oct. 1991): 26-27

Amazing Frogs and Toads, by Barry Clarke (New York: Random House, 1991). Reviewed in: *Curriculum Review* 31, no.1 (Sept. 1991): 30

Amazing Poisonous Animals, by Alexandra Parsons (New York: Knopf, 1990). Reviewed in: *Science Books and Films* 27, no.1 (Jan./ Feb. 1991): 20

Amazing Things Animals Do: Books for World Explorers, by Susan McGrath (Washington, DC: National Geographic Society, 1989). Reviewed in: *American Biology Teacher* 53, no.5 (May 1991): 315

Animal Behavior: Babies and Their Parents, Video (Deerfield, IL: Coronet/MTI Film and Video, 1991). Reviewed in: *School Library Journal* 38, no.4 (Apr. 1992): 76

Animal Behavior: Partnerships, Video (Deerfield, IL: Coronet/MTI Film and Video, 1991). Reviewed in: *School Library Journal* 38, no.5 (May 1992): 75

The Animal Life Series, Film/Video (Van Nuys, CA: AIMS Media Film and Video, 1991). Reviewed in: *Media and Methods* 28, no.1 (Sept./Oct. 1991): 46

Animals and Their World, by Judith E. Rinard, Gene S. Stuart, and Jennifer C. Urquhart (Washington, DC: National Geographic Society, 1990). Reviewed in: *Science and Children* 29, no.5 (Feb. 1992): 48

Animals, Animals: Fins, Feathers, Fur/ A Gaggle of Geese, Film/Video (Washington, DC: National Geographic Society, 1990). Reviewed in: *American Biology Teacher* 53, no.2 (Feb. 1991): 117

Animals in Danger, by William McCay and illustrated by Wayne Ford (Riverside, NJ: Aladdin, 1990). Reviewed in: *Language Arts* 68, no.6 (Oct. 1991): 493; *Science and Children* 29, no.4 (Jan. 1992): 39

Animals of the Night, by Mary Banks and illustrated by Ronald Himler (New York: Scribner's, 1990). Reviewed in: *Day Care and Early Education* 19, no.4 (Summer 1992): 43

The Atlantic Salmon, by Bianca Lavies (New York: Dutton, 1992). Reviewed in: *School Library Journal* 38, no.4 (Apr. 1992): 139

Barnyard Babies, Video (n.p.: JVM Productions, 1990). Reviewed in: *School Library Journal* 37, no.3 (Mar. 1991): 151

The Big Tree, by Bruce Hiscock (New York: Atheneum, 1991). Reviewed in: *Science Books and Films* 27, no.4 (May 1991): 115

Bird Watch, by Jane Yolen and illustrated by Ted Lewin (New York: Philomel, 1990). Reviewed in: *School Library Journal* 37, no.2 (Supplement to Feb. 1991): S-22

Books for Young Explorers: Set XVI (Washington, DC: National Geographic Society, 1989). Reviewed in: *American Biology Teacher* 53, no.5 (May 1991): 314

Box Turtle at Long Pond, by William T. George and illustrated by Lindsay Barrett George (New York: Greenwillow, 1989). Reviewed in: *Childhood Education* 66, no.5 (Annual 1990): 338

Life science *(cont'd)*

The Brain: What It Is, What It Does, by Ruth Dowling Brunn and Bertel Brunn, and illustrated by Bertel Brunn (New York: Greenwillow, 1989). Reviewed in: *Childhood Education* 66, no.5

Cactus Hotel, by Brenda Z. Guiberson and illustrated by Megan Lloyd (New York: Holt, 1991). Reviewed in: *Childhood Education* 68, no.1 (Fall 1991): 44; *Day Care and Early Education* 19, no.4 (Summer 1992): 43

Cats, Big and Little, by Beatrice Fontanel (Ossining, NY: Young Discovery, 1991). Reviewed in: *Science Books and Films* 27, no.7 (Oct. 1991): 211

Chameleons: Dragons in the Trees, by James Martin (New York: Crown, 1991). Reviewed in: *Science and Children* 29, no.6 (Mar. 1992): 55

City Critters around the World, by Amy Goldman Koss (Los Angeles: Price, Stern, and Sloan, 1991). Reviewed in: *Young Children* 47, no.4 (May 1992): 85

The Coral Reef, by Norman Barrett (New York: Watts, 1991). Reviewed in: *Science Books and Films* 27, no.4 (May 1991): 114

Cranberries, by William Jaspersohn (Boston: Houghton, Mifflin, 1991). Reviewed in: *Language Arts* 68, no.6 (Oct. 1991): 495

Creatures that Glow, by Joanne Barkan (New York: Doubleday, 1991). Reviewed in: *School Library Journal* 38, no.1 (Jan. 1992): 118-123

Creepy Crawlies: Ladybugs, Lobsters, and Other Amazing Arthropods, (New York: Sterling Publishing Co., 1991). Reviewed in: *Curriculum Review* 31, no.2 (Oct. 1991): 30

Dawn to Dusk on the Galapagos, by Rita Golden Gelman (Boston: Little Brown, 1991). Reviewed in: *Science Books and Films* 27, no.5 (June/July 1991): 178

Dyno-Quest, Software (Tucson, AZ: Mindplay/Methods and Solutions, 1984). Reviewed in: *Science and Children* 28, no.1 (Sept. 1990): 48

Fall Brings Changes, Video (Los Angeles: Churchill Films, 1991). Reviewed in: *Science Books and Films* 28, no.4 (May 1992): 118

Farm Animals, Video (Geneva, IL: Stage Fright Productions, n.d.). Reviewed in: *Science Books and Films* 27, no.7 (Oct. 1991): 217

A First Look at Ducks, Geese, and Swans, by Millicent E. Selsam and Joyce Hunt, and illustrated by Harriett Springer (New York: Walker, 1990). Reviewed in: *Language Arts* 68, no.6 (Oct. 1991): 493-494

Food Chains, Software (Galesburg, MI: MCE, n.d.). Reviewed in: *Science and Children* 29, no.2 (Oct. 1991): 46

Gardening Fun, by Jean Stangl (Carthage, IL: Fearon Teacher Aids, 1992). Reviewed in: *Curriculum Review* 32, no.1 (Sept. 1992): 27

Geo-Safari, Software (Dominguez Hills, CA: Educational Insights, n.d.). Reviewed in: *Journal of Geography* 91, no.1 (Jan./Feb. 1992): 49

Growing, Growing, Film/Video (Los Angeles: Churchill Films, 1989). Reviewed in: *Childhood Education* 68, no.1 (Fall 1991): 54

The Guinea Pig, Video (n.p.: EBEC, 1990). Reviewed in: *School Library Journal* 37, no.2 (Feb. 1991): 56

The Human Body, by Joan Gottlieb (Austin, TX: Steck-Vaughn, 1990). Reviewed in: *Science Books and Films* 27, no.1 (Jan./Feb. 1991): 18

The Human Body and How It Works, by Angela Royston (New York: Warwick Press, 1991). Reviewed in: *Science Books and Films* 28, no.1 (Jan./Feb. 1992): 21

Inside Animals, by Gale Cooper (San Diego: Mad Hatter Books, 1987). Reviewed in: *Gifted Child Today* 15, no.2 (Mar./Apr. 1992): 60

In the Tall, Tall Grass, by Denise Fleming (New York: Holt, 1991). Reviewed in: *Day Care and Early Education* 19, no.4 (Summer 1992): 43

Life science *(cont'd)*

Jungle Safari, Software (Pound Ridge, NY: Orange Cherry Software, 1990). Reviewed in: *Science and Children* 29, no.4 (Jan. 1992): 35-36

Katie's Farm, Software (Galesburg, MI: Lawrence Productions, n.d.). Reviewed in: *Science and Children* 28, no.3 (Nov./Dec. 1990): 44

A Kettle of Hawks and Other Wildlife Groups (New York: Lothrop, Lee and Shepard, 1990). Reviewed in: *Language Arts* 68, no.2 (Feb. 1991): 145-146

Learn about Insects, Software (Pleasantville, NY: Sunburst Communications, n.d.). Reviewed in: *Science and Children* 28, no.8 (May 1991): 31

Learn about Plants, Software (Scotts Valley, CA: WINGS for Learning, n.d.). Reviewed in: *Computing Teacher* 18, no.8 (May 1991): 41-45

Life Cycles, Software (Galesburg, MI: MCE, n.d.). Reviewed in: *Science and Children* 29, no.1 (Sept. 1991): 58-59

Look Inside Your Brain, by Heather Alexander and illustrated by Nicoletta Costa (New York: Grosset, 1991). Reviewed in: *School Library Journal* 38, no.1 (Jan. 1992): 101

Look! The Ultimate Spot the Difference Book, illustrated by April Wilson (New York: Dial Books for Young Readers, 1990). Reviewed in: *Language Arts* 68, no.6 (Oct. 1991): 493; *Young Children* 47, no.3 (Feb. 1992): 75

Magic School Bus on the Ocean Floor, by Joanna Cole and illustrated by Bruce Degen (New York: Scholastic, 1992). Reviewed in: *School Library Journal* 38, no.8 (Aug. 1992): 151

Mammals: A Multimedia Encyclopedia, Multimedia (Washington, DC: National Geographic Society, n.d.). Reviewed in: *Science and Children* 30, no.1 (Sept. 1992): 55-56

Manatee on Location (New York: William Morrow, 1991). Reviewed in: *Language Arts* 69, no.4 (Apr. 1992): 301

More Than Just a Garden, by Dwight Kuhn (Englewood Cliffs, NJ: Silver Burdett, 1990). Reviewed in: *Science and Children* 29, no.2 (Oct. 1991): 53

My First Look at Nature (New York: Random House, 1991). Reviewed in: *Science Books and Films* 27, no.8 (Nov. 1991): 236

Never Kiss an Alligator, by Colleen Stanley Bare (New York: Dutton, 1989). Reviewed in: *Childhood Education* 66, no.5 (Annual 1990): 337

New Questions and Answers about Dinosaurs, by Seymour Simon and illustrated by Jennifor Dewey (New York: Morrow Junior Books, 1990). Reviewed in: *Language Arts* 68, no.6 (Oct. 1991): 492

A Night and a Day in the Desert, by Jennifer Dewey (Boston: Little Brown, 1991). Reviewed in: *Language Arts* 69, no.2 (Feb. 1992): 138

Ninety-Nine Gnats, Nits, and Nibblers, by May R. Barenbaum (Champaign, IL: University of Illinois Press, 1989). Reviewed in: *American Biology Teacher* 53, no.5 (May 1991): 316

The Orchard, by Isidro Sanchez (New York: Barrons, 1991). Reviewed in: *Science Books and Films* 27, no.8 (Nov. 1991): 244

Otters under Water, by Jim Arnosky (New York: Putnam, 1992). Reviewed in: *School Library Journal* 38, no.8 (Aug. 1992): 150

Our Vanishing Farm Animals: Saving America's Rare Breeds, by Catherine Paladino (Boston: Little Brown, 1991). Reviewed in: *Language Arts* 68, no.6 (Oct. 1991): 495

Pet Gerbils, by Jerome Wexler (Morton Grove, IL: Albert Whitman, 1990). Reviewed in: *Science and Children* 29, no.6 (Mar. 1992): 55

Plants Are Different and Alike, Film/Video (Deerfield, IL: Coronet/MTI Film and Video, 1990). Reviewed in: *Childhood Education* 68, no.1 (Fall 1991): 54

Life science *(cont'd)*

Professor Curious and the Mystery of the Hiking Dinosaurs, by Yvonne Gil and illustrated by Bonnie Timmons (n.p.: Clarkson Potter, 1991). Reviewed in: *Language Arts* 68, no.6 (Oct. 1991): 492

Project Classify: Dinosaurs, Software (Washington, DC: National Geographic Society, 1990). Reviewed in: *Instructor* 101, no.4 (Nov./Dec. 1991): 83; *Media and Methods* 27, no.3 (Jan./Feb. 1991): 62-63

Rain Forest Secrets, by Arthur Dorros (New York: Scholastic, 1990). Reviewed in: *School Library Journal* 37, no.2 (Feb. 1991): 78

Ready, Set, Go: How Animals Move, Film (Washington, DC: National Geographic Society, 1989). Reviewed in: *American Biology Teacher* 52, no.8 (Nov./Dec. 1990): 514

A Sea Full of Sharks, by Betty Maestro and illustrated by Guilio Maestro (New York: Scholastic, 1990). Reviewed in: *Language Arts* 69, no.4 (Apr. 1992): 299-300

Seeds and Seasons, Film/Video (Los Angeles: Churchill Films, 1987). Reviewed in: *Childhood Education* 68, no.1 (Fall 1991): 54

See How They Grow: Frog, by Kim Taylor (New York: Dutton, 1991). Reviewed in: *Childhood Education* 68, no.3 (Spring 1992): 178

Slippery Babies: Young Frogs, Toads, and Salamanders, by Ginny Johnson and Judy Cutchins (New York: Morrow Junior Books, 1991). Reviewed in: *School Science and Mathematics* 92, no.3 (Mar. 1992): 165

Spring, by Ron Hirschi (New York: Cobblehill, 1990). Reviewed in: *Science Books and Films* 27, no.3 (Apr. 1991): 82

Spring Brings Changes, Video (Los Angeles: Churchill Films, 1991). Reviewed in: *Science Books and Films* 28, no.4 (May 1992): 119

Survival: Could You Be a Frog? by John Norris Wood (Nashville, TN: Ideals, 1990). Reviewed in: *Science Books and Films* 27, no.3 (Apr. 1991): 84

Survival: Could You Be a Mouse? by John Norris Wood (Nashville, TN: Ideals, 1990). Reviewed in: *Science Books and Films* 27, no.3 (Apr. 1991): 84

Under the Sea from A to Z, by Anne Doubilet (New York: Crown, 1991). Reviewed in: *Language Arts* 68, no.6 (Oct. 1991): 494

Urban Roosts: Where Birds Nest in the City, by Barbara Bash (San Francisco: Sierra Club, 1990). Reviewed in: *Language Arts* 68, no.6 (Oct. 1991): 494

Walrus on Location, by Kathy Darling (New York: Lothrop, Lee and Shepard, 1991). Reviewed in: *School Science and Mathematics* 92, no.5 (May/June 1992): 288

Wetlands, Software (Warren, NJ: Optical Data, n.d.). Reviewed in: *Science and Children* 29, no.7 (Apr. 1992): 40-41

Whales, by Seymour Simon (New York: Harper, 1989). Reviewed in: *Chilhood Education* 66, no.5 (Annual 1990): 338-339

What Neat Feet, by Hana Machotka (New York: Morrow Junior Books, 1991). Reviewed in: *Reading Horizons* 32, no.1 (Oct. 1991): 79-80; *School Science and Mathematics* 92, no.4 (Apr. 1992): 228; *Language Arts* 69, no.4 (Apr. 1992): 302

When the Woods Hum, by Joanne Ryder and illustrated by Catherine Stock (New York: Morrow Junior Books, 1990). Reviewed in: *Reading Horizons* 32, no.1 (Oct. 1991): 77-78; *School Science and Mathematics* 92, no.3 (Mar. 1992): 165

Who Lives Here? Animals in and around Ponds, Film (Washington, DC: National Geographic Society, 1990). Reviewed in: *American Biology Teacher* 52, no.7 (Oct. 1990): 443

Who Lives Here? Animals in the Backyard, Film (Washington, DC: National Geographic Society, 1990). Reviewed in: *American Biology Teacher* 52, no.7 (Oct. 1990): 443

Life science *(cont'd)*

Who Lives Here? Animals in the Desert, Film (Washington, DC: National Geographic Society, 1990). Reviewed in: *American Biology Teacher* 52, no.7 (Oct. 1990): 443

Who Lives Here? Animals of the Sea, Film (Washington, DC: National Geographic Society, 1990). Reviewed in: *American Biology Teacher* 52, no.7 (Oct. 1990): 443

Wildlife at Risk: Bears, by Malcom Penny (n.p.: Bookright, 1990). Reviewed in: *Science and Children* 29, no.4 (Jan. 1992): 39

Wild Places: Rocky Mountain Meadow, Film/Video (Deerfield, IL: Coronet/MTI Film and Video, 1990). Reviewed in: *School Library Journal* 37, no.1 (Jan. 1991): 59

Will We Miss Them? Endangered Species, by Alexandra Wright and illustrated by Marshall Peck (Watertown, MA: Charlesbridge, 1992). Reviewed in: *Science Books and Films* 28, no.1 (Jan./Feb. 1992): 19

Winter, by Ron Hirschi (New York: Cobblehill, 1990). Reviewed in: *Science Books and Films* 27, no.3 (Apr. 1991): 82

Wolves, by R. D. Lawrence (Boston: Little Brown, 1990). Reviewed in: *Language Arts* 69, no.4 (Apr. 1992): 301

Life science activities

Nature All Year Long, by Clare Walker Leslie (New York: Greenwillow Books, 1991). Reviewed in: *Young Children* 47, no.4 (May 1992): 85

Life science (sounds)

Call to the Wild, Audiotape (Masonville, CO: Wilderness Productions, 1989). Reviewed in: *American Biology Teacher* 53, no.2 (Feb. 1991): 117

Earth: Voices of a Planet, Audiotape/Compact disc (Omaha, NE: American Gramaphone Records of Omaha, 1990). Reviewed in: *American Biology Teacher* 53, no.2 (Feb. 1991): 117

Lines

by Philip Yenawine (New York: Delacorte Press, n.d.). Reviewed in: *School Arts* 90, no.6 (Feb. 1991): 60-61

Liquid and Buoyancy

by Barbara Taylor (New York: Watts, 1990). Reviewed in: *Science Books and Films* 27, no.1 (Jan./Feb. 1991): 17

The Listener

Video (Boca Raton, FL: Social Issues Resources Series, 1987). Reviewed in: *Music Educator's Journal* 77, no.7 (Mar. 1991): 52

Literacy through Literature

by Terry D. Johnson and Daphne R. Louis (Portsmouth, NH: Heinemann, 1987). Reviewed in: *TESOL Quarterly* 24, no.4 (Winter, 1990): 730-731

Little Brown

Big Time Bears, by Stephen Krensky (Boston: Little Brown, 1989). Reviewed in: *Arithmetic Teacher* 38, no.7 (Mar. 1991): 58-59; *Language Arts* 68, no.3 (Mar. 1991): 246

Dawn to Dusk on the Galapagos, by Rita Golden Gelman (Boston: Little Brown, 1991). Reviewed in: *Science Books and Films* 27, no.5 (June/July 1991): 178

The Lady with the Alligator Purse, by Nadine Westcott (Boston: Little Brown, 1989). Reviewed in: *Reading Horizons* 32, no.1 (Oct. 1991): 75-77

A Night and a Day in the Desert, by Jennifer Dewey (Boston: Little Brown, 1991). Reviewed in: *Language Arts* 69, no.2 (Feb. 1992): 138

Once inside the Library, by Barbara A. Huff and illustrated by Iris Van Rynback (Boston: Little Brown, 1990). Reviewed in: *Science Books and Films* 27, no.2 (Mar. 1991): 45

Our Vanishing Farm Animals: Saving America's Rare Breeds, by Catherine Paladino (Boston: Little Brown, 1991). Reviewed in: *Language Arts* 68, no.6 (Oct. 1991): 495

Puss in Boots, by Charles Perrault and illustrated by Alain Vaes (Boston: Little Brown, 1992). Reviewed in: *School Library Journal* 38, no.4 (Apr. 1992): 108-109

Skip to My Lou, by Nadine Westcott (Boston: Little Brown, 1987). Reviewed in: *Reading Horizons* 32, no.1 (Oct. 1991): 75-77

Little Brown *(cont'd)*
The Wheels on the Bus, by Maryann Kovalski (Boston: Little Brown, 1987). Reviewed in: *Reading Horizons* 32, no.1 (Oct. 1991): 75-77

Wolves, by R. D. Lawrence (Boston: Little Brown, 1990). Reviewed in: *Language Arts* 69, no.4 (Apr. 1992): 301

The Little Snowgirl
Video (Chicago: American School, n.d.). Reviewed in: *School Library Journal* 37, no.10 (Oct. 1991): 80

Live Oak Media
Picture Book of Abraham Lincoln, Multimedia (Ancramdale, NY: Live Oak Media, 1990). Reviewed in: *School Library Journal* 37, no.1 (Jan. 1991): 63

Picture Book of George Washington, Multimedia (Ancramdale, NY: Live Oak Media, 1990). Reviewed in: *School Library Journal* 37, no.1 (Jan. 1991): 63

Lloyd, Megan
Cactus Hotel, by Brenda Z. Guiberson and illustrated by Megan Lloyd (New York: Holt, 1991). Reviewed in: *Childhood Education* 68, no.1 (Fall 1991): 44; *Day Care and Early Education* 19, no.4 (Summer 1992): 43

How We Learned the Earth Is Round, by Patricia Lauber and illustrated by Megan Lloyd (n.p.: Thomas Y. Crowell, 1990). Reviewed in: *Language Arts* 68, no.2 (Feb. 1991): 146

LML (publisher)
Funny Money, Game (Baltimore, MD: LML, 1986). Reviewed in: *Arithmetic Teacher* 38, no.1 (Sept. 1990): 52

Lodestar (publisher)
Temperature and You, by Betsy Maestro and illustrated by Guilio Maestro (New York: Lodestar, 1990). Reviewed in: *School Library Journal* 37, no.2 (Feb. 1991): 84

LOGO Geometry
Software by Michael Battista and Douglas H. Clements (Morristown, NJ: Simon and Schuster Education Group, 1991). Reviewed in: *Arithmetic Teacher* 40, no.1 (Sept. 1992): 56

Lollipop Dragon
Multimedia by Margo Turner (Chicago: SVE, 1989). Reviewed in: *Arithmetic Teacher* 38, no.3 (Nov. 1990): 47

Long, Sylvia
Ten Little Rabbits, by Virginia Grossman and illustrated by Sylvia Long (San Francisco: Chronicle Books, 1991). Reviewed in: *Arithmetic Teacher* 40, no.1 (Sept. 1992): 56-57

The Look Again . . . and Again and Again and Again Book
by Beau Gardner (New York: Lothrop, Lee and Shepard, 1984). Reviewed in: *Gifted Child Today* 15, no.2 (Mar./Apr. 1992): 59

Look Inside Your Brain
by Heather Alexander and illustrated by Nicoletta Costa (New York: Grosset, 1991). Reviewed in: *School Library Journal* 38, no.1 (Jan. 1992): 101

Look! The Ultimate Spot the Difference Book
illustrated by April Wilson (New York: Dial Books for Young Readers, 1990). Reviewed in: *Language Arts* 68, no.6 (Oct. 1991): 493; *Young Children* 47, no.3 (Feb. 1992): 75

Lothrop, Lee and Shepard
Bet You Can! Science Possibilities To Fool You, by Vicki Cobb and Kathy Darling (New York: Lothrop, Lee and Shepard, 1990). Reviewed in: *Science Books and Films* 27, no.1 (Jan./Feb. 1991): 15

Discovery of the Americas, by Betsy Maestro and Giulio Maestro (New York: Lothrop, Lee and Shepard, 1991). Reviewed in: *Reading Horizons* 32, no.1 (Oct. 1991): 79-80

Earth Alive, by Sandra Markle (New York: Lothrop, Lee and Shepard, 1991). Reviewed in: *Reading Horizons* 32, no.1 (Oct. 1991): 77-78

A Kettle of Hawks and Other Wildlife Groups (New York: Lothrop, Lee and Shepard, 1990). Reviewed in: *Language Arts* 68, no.2 (Feb. 1991): 145-146

Madeline and the Bad Hat
Video (Weston, CT: Weston Woods, 1991).
Reviewed in: *School Library Journal* 37,
no.3 (Mar. 1991): 150

Mad Hatter Books
Inside Animals, by Gale Cooper (San Diego:
Mad Hatter Books, 1987). Reviewed in:
Gifted Child Today 15, no.2 (Mar./Apr.
1992): 60

Maestro, Betsy
Discovery of the Americas, by Betsy Maestro
and Giulio Maestro (New York: Lothrop,
Lee and Shepard, 1991). Reviewed in:
Reading Horizons 32, no.1 (Oct. 1991): 79-80

A Sea Full of Sharks, by Betsy Maestro and
illustrated by Giulio Maestro (New York:
Scholastic, 1990). Reviewed in: *Language
Arts* 69, no.4 (Apr. 1992): 299-300

Temperature and You, by Betsy Maestro and
illustrated by Giulio Maestro (New York:
Lodestar, 1990). Reviewed in: *School Library Journal* 37, no.2 (Feb. 1991): 84

Maestro, Giulio
Discovery of the Americas, by Betsy Maestro
and Giulio Maestro (New York: Lothrop,
Lee and Shepard, 1991). Reviewed in:
Reading Horizons 32, no.1 (Oct. 1991): 79-80

A Sea Full of Sharks, by Betsy Maestro and
illustrated by Giulio Maestro (New York:
Scholastic, 1990). Reviewed in: *Language
Arts* 69, no.4 (Apr. 1992): 299-300

Temperature and You, by Betsy Maestro and
illustrated by Giulio Maestro (New York:
Lodestar, 1990). Reviewed in: *School Library Journal* 37, no.2 (Feb. 1991): 84

Maestro Music
Maestroscope Theory Readiness B and C,
Software by Sharon Lohse Kunitz (n.p.:
Maestro Music, 1989). Reviewed in: *Ameri-
can Music Teacher* 41, no.6 (June/July
1992): 10

Maestroscope Theory Readiness B and C
Software by Sharon Lohse Kunitz (n.p.:
Maestro Music, 1989). Reviewed in: *American Music Teacher* 41, no.6 (June/July
1992): 10

Magarian-Gold, Judi
Exploring with Color Tiles: Grades K-3,
Manipulatives by Judi Magarian-Gold and
Sandra Mogensen (New Rochelle, NY:
Cuisenaire, 1990). Reviewed in: *Arithmetic
Teacher* 38, no.8 (Apr. 1991): 56

Magic School Bus on the Ocean Floor
by Joanna Cole and illustrated by Bruce
Degen (New York: Scholastic, 1992). Reviewed in: *School Library Journal* 38, no.8
(Aug. 1992): 151

*Magic Slate: The Word Processor That Grows
with You*
Software (Pleasantville, NY: Sunburst Communications, n.d.). Reviewed in: *Gifted Child
Today* 15, no.3 (May/June 1992): 53

Magic Slate II (20 Column)
Software (Pleasantville, NY: Sunburst Com-
munications, n.d.). Reviewed in: *Childhood
Education* 68, no.1 (Fall 1991): 56

Magical Changes
by Graham Oakley (New York: Aladdin
Books, 1987). Reviewed in: *Gifted Child
Today* 15, no.2 (Mar.Apr. 1992): 59

Make Gifts!
(Cincinnati, OH: Northlight Books, n.d.).
Reviewed in: *School Arts* 91, no.6 (Feb.
1992): 44

Make Prints!
(Cincinnati, OH: Northlight Books, n.d.).
Reviewed in: *School Arts* 91, no.6 (Feb.
1992): 44

Mammals: A Multimedia Encyclopedia
Multimedia (Washington, DC: National Geographic Society, n.d.). Reviewed in: *Science
and Children* 30, no.1 (Sept. 1992): 55-56

Manatee on Location
(New York: William Morrow, 1991). Reviewed in: *Language Arts* 69, no.4 (Apr.
1992): 301

Maneral, Max
Individualized Computer Motivated Math,
Software by Max Maneral (n.p.: Max
Maneral, 1988). Reviewed in: *Arithmetic
Teacher* 38, no.4 (Dec. 1990): 59

Manipulatives

Colorcards, Manipulatives (Bicester, UK: Winslow Press, 1989). Reviewed in: *Child Language Teaching and Therapy* 7, no.3 (Oct. 1991): 361-362

Exploring Fractions and Decimals with Manipulatives, Manipulatives by Don Balka (Peabody, MA: Didax, 1991). Reviewed in: *Arithmetic Teacher* 39, no.9 (May 1992): 53

Exploring with Color Tiles: Grades K-3, Manipulatives by Judi Magarian-Gold and Sandra Mogensen (New Rochelle, NY: Cuisenaire, 1990). Reviewed in: *Arithmetic Teacher* 38, no.8 (Apr. 1991): 56

Math in Brief, Manipulatives by Mary Cavanagh (Fort Collins, CO: Scott Resources, 1978). Reviewed in: *Arithmetic Teacher* 39, no.1 (Sept. 1991): 53

MathMats: Hands-on Activities for Young Children - Set Two, Manipulatives by Carol A. Thornton and Judith K. Wells (Allen, TX: Teaching Resources, 1990). Reviewed in: *Arithmetic Teacher* 39, no.7 (Mar. 1992): 44

Stick and Score: The Good Food Game, Manipulatives (St. Paul, MN: Stick and Score, 1990). Reviewed in: *Journal of Nutritional Education* 23, no.3 (May/June 1991): 142-143

Many Luscious Lollipops
by Ruth Heller (New York: Grosset and Dunlap, 1989). Reviewed in: *Gifted Child Today* 15, no.1 (Jan./Feb.): 59

Mardlesohn, Esther
Teaching Primary Math with Music, Multimedia by Esther Mardlesohn (Palo Alto, CA: Dale Seymour, 1990). Reviewed in: *Arithmetic Teacher* 39, no.1 (Sept. 1991): 53

Marell, Anne
We Love MATHS: Four Imaginative Themes for Early Primary Students, by Anne Marell and Susan Stajnko (Mount Waterly, Australia: Dellasta, 1990). Reviewed in: *Arithmetic Teacher* 39, no.1 (Sept. 1991): 53-54

Margaret Hudson's Earth Arts Studio
Adventures in Clay Land: An Introduction to Clay, Film/Video (Fresno, CA: Margaret Hudson's Earth Arts Studio, n.d.). Reviewed in: *Arts and Activities* 110, no.4 (Dec. 1991): 14

Markle, Sandra
Earth Alive, by Sandra Markle (New York: Lothrop, Lee and Shepard, 1991). Reviewed in: *Reading Horizons* 32, no.1 (Oct. 1991): 77-78

Martin, James
Chameleons: Dragons in the Trees, by James Martin (New York: Crown, 1991). Reviewed in: *Science and Children* 29, no.6 (Mar. 1992): 55

Marzollo, Jean
In 1492, by Jean Marzollo (New York: Scholastic, 1991). Reviewed in: *Childhood Education* 68, no.3 (Spring 1992): 178

Masiello, Ralph
The Icky Bug Counting Book, by Jerry Pallotta and illustrated by Ralph Masiello (Watertown, MA: Charlesbridge, 1991). Reviewed in: *Science Books and Films* 28, no1 (Jan./Feb. 1992): 19

Maskell, Linn
Maths at Play: Fun Ideas for 5-8 Year Olds, by Linn Maskell (Victoria, Australia: Dellasta, 1990). Reviewed in: *Arithmetic Teacher* 39, no.9 (May 1992): 51-52

Mathematical activities
Counting on Math, Manipulatives (Westminster, MD: Random House School Division, 1988). Reviewed in: *Arithmetic Teacher* 38, no.1 (Sept. 1990): 50

Developing Graph Comprehension: Elementary and Middle School Activities, by Frances R. Curcio (Reston, VA: National Council of Teachers of Mathematics, 1989). Reviewed in: *Mathematics Teacher* 83, no.6 (Sept. 1990): 480

Exploring Fractions and Decimals with Manipulatives, Manipulatives by Don Balka (Peabody, MA: Didax, 1991). Reviewed in: *Arithmetic Teacher* 39, no.9 (May 1992): 53

Mathematical activities *(cont'd)*
    Exploring Mathematics: Activities for Concept and Skill Development, K-3, by Jean M. Sham (Glenville, IL: Scott Foresman, 1990). Reviewed in: *Arithmetic Teacher* 38, no.1 (Sept. 1990): 46

    Mutanoid Math Challenge, Software (Northridge, CA: Legacy Software, n.d.). Reviewed in: *Technology and Learning* 12, no.8 (May/June 1992): 11-12

    On the Button in Math: Activities for Young Children, by Carol A. Thornton and Judith K. Wells (Allen, TX: DLM Teaching Resources, 1990). Reviewed in: *Arithmetic Teacher* 38, no.9 (May 1991): 46

Mathematical concepts
    Hexagons, Video (Evanston, IL: Journal Films, 1990). Reviewed in: *Science Books and Films* 27, no.4 (May 1991): 121

    Infinity, Video (Evanston, IL: Journal Films, 1990). Reviewed in: *Science Books and Films* 27, no.4 (May 1991): 121

    Number Nine, Video (Evanston, IL: Journal Films, 1990). Reviewed in: *Science Books and Films* 27, no.4 (May 1991): 121

Mathematical skills
    Anno's Math Games III, by Mitsumasa Anno (New York: Philomel Books, 1991). Reviewed in: *Arithmetic Teacher* 39, no.3 (Nov. 1991): 58

    Arragon: Winning Strategies for Math, Software by James Hsu and Linda C. Unger (Garden City, NY: Focus Media, 1989). Reviewed in: *Arithmetic Teacher* 38, no.1 (Sept. 1990): 42

    Big Time Bears, by Stephen Krensky (Boston: Little Brown, 1989). Reviewed in: *Arithmetic Teacher* 38, no.7 (Mar. 1991): 58-59; *Language Arts* 68, no.3 (Mar. 1991): 246

    Counters: An Action Approach to Counting and Arithmetic, Software (Scotts Valley, CA: Wings for Learning, 1990). Reviewed in: *Arithmetic Teacher* 39, no.3 (Nov. 1991): 56

Early Geometry, by C. F. Navarro (Alexandria, VA: Start Smart Books, 1990). Reviewed in: *Curriculum Review* 30, no.3 (Nov. 1990): 25-26

Exploring with Color Tiles: Grades K-3, Manipulatives by Judi Magarian-Gold and Sandra Mogensen (New Rochelle, NY: Cuisenaire, 1990). Reviewed in: *Arithmetic Teacher* 38, no.8 (Apr. 1991): 56

Geometry Workshop, Grades 3-8, Software (Glenview, IL: Scott Foresman, 1991). Reviewed in: *Arithmetic Teacher* 39, no.8 (Apr. 1992): 58

Graphing and Probability Workshop, Grades 3-8, Software (Glenview, IL: Scott Foresman, 1991). Reviewed in: *Arithmetic Teacher* 39, no.3 (Nov. 1991): 56

Hands-on Math: Volumes One and Two, Software (Newbury Park, CA: Ventura Educational Systems, 1988). Reviewed in: *Arithmetic Teacher* 38, no.2 (Oct. 1990): 46-48; *Instructor* 100, no.8 (Apr. 1991): 74

Hop to It!, Software by Ed Annunziata and Stephen Birkelbach (Pleasantville, NY: Sunburst Communications, 1990). Reviewed in: *Arithmetic Teacher* 38, no.3 (Nov. 1990): 58; *Computing Teacher* 18, no.2 (Oct. 1990): 49; *Electronic Learning* 10, no.4 (Jan. 1991): 32; *School Library Journal* 37, no.1 (Jan. 1991): 47

LOGO Geometry, Software by Michael Battista and Douglas H. Clements (Morristown, NJ: Simon and Schuster Education Group, 1991). Reviewed in: *Arithmetic Teacher* 40, no.1 (Sept. 1992): 56

Math in Brief, Manipulatives by Mary Cavanagh (Fort Collins, CO: Scott Resources, 1978). Reviewed in: *Arithmetic Teacher* 39, no.1 (Sept. 1991): 53

MathMats: Hands-on Activities for Young Children - Set Two, Manipulatives by Carol A. Thornton and Judith K. Wells (Allen, TX: Teaching Resources, 1990). Reviewed in: *Arithmetic Teacher* 39, no.7 (Mar. 1992): 44

Mathematical skills *(cont'd)*

Muppet Labs, Software (Pleasantville, NY: Sunburst Communications, 1992). Reviewed in: *School Library Journal* 38, no.5 (May 1992): 61

Muppet Math, Software (Pleasantville, NY: Sunburst Communications, 1991). Reviewed in: *School Library Journal* 38, no.2 (Feb. 1992): 49-50

Mystery Castle: Strategies for Problem Solving (Level One), Software (Acton, MA: William K. Bradford, 1990). Reviewed in: *Arithmetic Teacher* 39, no.3 (Nov. 1991): 57

Primary Geometry Workshop (Grades K-2), Software (Glenview, IL: Scott Foresman, 1991). Reviewed in: *Arithmetic Teacher* 39, no.8 (Apr. 1992): 58

Problem Solving, Video (Atlanta, GA: Silver Burdett and Ginn, 1991). Reviewed in: *Arithmetic Teacher* 39, no.2 (Oct. 1991): 52-53

Puzzlers, by Suse MacDonald (New York: Dial, 1989). Reviewed in: *Childhood Education* 66, no.5 (Annual 1990): 335

Reading Higher: A Problem-solving Approach to Elementary School Mathematics, Multimedia (Reston, VA: NCTE, 1990). Reviewed in: *Curriculum Review* 31, no.7 (Mar. 1992): 26-27

Super, Super Superwords, by Bruce McMillan (New York: Lothrop, Lee and Shepard, 1989). Reviewed in: *Arithmetic Teacher* 38, no.2 (Oct. 1990): 52

Mathematical skills (basic)

Berenstain Bears: Learn about Counting, Software (San Francisco: Britannica Software, 1990). Reviewed in: *School Library Journal* 37, no.1 (Jan. 1991): 47

Five Little Monkeys Jumping on the Bed, by Eileen Cristelow (New York: Clarion Books, 1989). Reviewed in: *Arithmetic Teacher* 38, no.7 (Mar. 1991): 59

What Comes in Two's, Three's, and Fours, (New York: Simon and Schuster, 1990). Reviewed in: *Instructor* 102, no.2 (Sept. 1992): 80

Math in Brief

Manipulatives by Mary Cavanagh (Fort Collins, CO: Scott Resources, 1978). Reviewed in: *Arithmetic Teacher* 39, no.1 (Sept. 1991): 53

MathMats: Hands-on Activities for Young Children - Set Two

Manipulatives by Carol A. Thornton and Judith K. Wells (Allen, TX: Teaching Resources, 1990). Reviewed in: *Arithmetic Teacher* 39, no.7 (Mar. 1992): 44

Math, Money, and You: Count It Out

Film/Video (Washington, DC: National Geographic Society, 1989). Reviewed in: *Arithmetic Teacher* 38, no.4 (Dec. 1990): 61

Math Practice

Software (Cerritos, CA: Yhl Software, 1988). Reviewed in: *Arithmetic Teacher* 38, no.2 (Oct. 1990): 50

Maths at Play: Fun Ideas for 5-8 Year Olds

by Linn Maskell (Victoria, Australia: Dellasta, 1990). Reviewed in: *Arithmetic Teacher* 39, no.9 (May 1992): 51-52

Math Shop Junior

Software by Cary Hammer (New York: Scholastic, 1989). Reviewed in: *Arithmetic Teacher* 38, no.1 (Sept. 1990): 44

Math Smart

Game (Rochester, MN: GO Company of Rochester, 1987). Reviewed in: *Arithmetic Teacher* 38, no.1 (Sept. 1990): 52

Matiella, Ana

Children's Activity Series, by Judith K. Scheer and Ana Matiella (Santa Cruz, CA: ETR Associates/Network Publications, 1990). Reviewed in: *Curriculum Review* 30, no.8 (Apr. 1991): 26-27

Max Maneral (publisher)

Individualized Computer Motivated Math, Software by Max Maneral (n.p.: Max Maneral, 1988). Reviewed in: *Arithmetic Teacher* 38, no.4 (Dec. 1990): 59

Max's Library: Beginning To Write

Video (Chicago: SVE, 1991). Reviewed in: *School Library Journal* 37, no.9 (Sept. 1991): 212-213

MCE (publisher)
Adaptations, Software (Galesburg, MI: MCE, n.d.). Reviewed in: *Science and Children* 29, no.1 (Sept. 1991): 59

Food Chains, Software (Galesburg, MI: MCE, n.d.). Reviewed in: *Science and Children* 29, no.2 (Oct. 1991): 46

Learning To Reason: Some, All, or None, Software (Kalamazoo, MI: MCE, 1988). Reviewed in: *Arithmetic Teacher* 39, no.1 (Sept. 1991): 47

Life Cycles, Software (Galesburg, MI: MCE, n.d.). Reviewed in: *Science and Children* 29, no.1 (Sept. 1991): 58-59

An Ocean of Air, Software (Galesburg, MI: MCE, n.d.). Reviewed in: *Science and Children* 29, no.2 (Oct. 1991): 47

Water Cycle, Software (Galesburg, MI: MCE, n.d.). Reviewed in: *Science and Children* 29, no.4 (Jan. 1992): 35

Meadowbrook Press
Measure, Pour and Mix: Kitchen Science Tricks, by James Lewis (New York: Meadowbrook Press, 1990). Reviewed in: *Science Books and Films* 27, no.3 (Apr. 1991): 79

Measure, Pour and Mix: Kitchen Science Tricks by James Lewis (New York: Meadowbrook Press, 1990). Reviewed in: *Science Books and Films* 27, no.3 (Apr. 1991): 79

Measuring: From Paces to Feet, Grades 3-4 by Rebecca B. Corwin and Susan Jo Russell (Palo Alto, CA: Dale Seymour, 1990). Reviewed in: *Arithmetic Teacher* 38, no.9 (May 1991): 48

MECC (publisher)
Clearwater Detectives, Software (Minneapolis, MN: MECC, 1991). Reviewed in: *Science and Children* 29, no.5 (Feb. 1992): 36-39

Communikeys, Software (Minneapolis, MN: MECC, 1989). Reviewed in: *Instructor* 101, no.7 (Mar. 1992): 66

Paper Plane Pilot, Software (Minneapolis, MN: MECC, 1991). Reviewed in: *Science and Children* 29, no.2 (Oct. 1991): 46

Patterns, Software (St. Paul, MN: MECC, 1988). Reviewed in: *Arithmetic Teacher* 38, no.2 (Oct. 1990): 50

Spelling Puzzles and Tests, Software (St. Paul, MN: MECC, 1990). Reviewed in: *School Library Journal* 37, no.3 (Mar. 1991): 142-144

Storybook Weaver, Software (St. Paul, MN: MECC, 1990). Reviewed in: *Instructor* 100, no.6 (Feb. 1991): 115

Sun and Seasons, Software (St. Paul, MN: MECC, 1990). Reviewed in: *Science and Children* 28, no.7 (Apr. 1991): 52-53

Woolly Bounce, Software (Minneapolis, MN: MECC, 1991). Reviewed in: *Science and Children* 29, no.4 (Jan. 1992): 34

Media Express
Thumbs Up for Kids: AIDS Education, Film/Video (Purchase, NY: Media Express, 1989). Reviewed in: *Day Care and Early Education* 18, no.1 (Fall 1990): 42

Media Guild
Exploring Sound, Video (San Diego: Media Guild, 1990). Reviewed in: *Science Books and Films* 27, no.5 (June/July 1991): 150

Meteorology
An Ocean of Air, Software (Galesburg, MI: MCE, n.d.). Reviewed in: *Science and Children* 29, no.2 (Oct. 1991): 47

Sun and Seasons, Software (St. Paul, MN: MECC, 1990). Reviewed in: *Science and Children* 28, no.7 (Apr. 1991): 52-53

Weatherwatch, by Valerie Wyatt (Reading, MA: Wesley, 1990). Reviewed in: *Curriculum Review* 30, no.5 (Jan. 1991): 30

Methods and Solutions (publisher)
Safety First! Software (Stoneham, MA: Methods and Solutions, 1985). Reviewed in: *Gifted Child Today* 15, no.3 (May/June 1992): 54

Morrow *(cont'd)*

Manatee on Location (New York: William Morrow, 1991). Reviewed in: *Language Arts* 69, no.4 (Apr. 1992): 301

New Questions and Answers about Dinosaurs, by Seymour Simon and illustrated by Jennifer Dewey (New York: Morrow Junior Books, 1990). Reviewed in: *Language Arts* 68, no.6 (Oct. 1991): 492

Nine Ducks Nine, by Sara Hayes (New York: William Morrow, 1990). Reviewed in: *Arithmetic Teacher* 39, no.9 (May 1992): 51

Slippery Babies: Young Frogs, Toads, and Salamanders, by Ginny Johnson and Judy Cutchins (New York: Morrow Junior Books, 1991). Reviewed in: *School Science and Mathematics* 92, no.3 (Mar. 1992): 165

What Neat Feet, by Hana Machotka (New York: Morrow Junior Books, 1991). Reviewed in: *Reading Horizons* 32, no.1 (Oct. 1991): 79-80; *School Science and Mathematics* 92, no.4 (Apr. 1992): 228; *Language Arts* 69, no.4 (Apr. 1992): 302

When the Woods Hum, by Joanne Ryder and illustrated by Catherine Stock (New York: Morrow Junior Books, 1990). Reviewed in: *Reading Horizons* 32, no.1 (Oct. 1991): 77-78; *School Science and Mathematics* 92, no.3 (Mar. 1992): 165

Mosaic Magic

Software (Encinitas, CA: Kinder Magic Software, 1990). Reviewed in: *Arithmetic Teacher* 39, no.1 (Sept. 1991): 48

Multicultural Folktales: Stories To Tell Young Children

by Judy Sierra and Robert Kaminski (Phoenix, AZ: Oryx Press, 1991). Reviewed in: *Young Children* 47, no.2 (Jan. 1992): 71

Multimedia

Art Works, Multimedia (Orlando, FL: Harcourt Brace, n.d.). Reviewed in: *School Arts* 90, no.5 (Jan. 1991): 42-43

Fairy Tale Rap: "Jack and the Beanstalk" and Other Stories, Multimedia adapted by Barbara Leeds (Miramonte, CA: Miramonte Press, 1990). Reviewed in: *International Journal of Instructional Media* 18, no.1 (n.d.): 96-97; *Teaching Exceptional Children* 24, no.4 (Summer 1992): 83

Lollipop Dragon, Multimedia by Margo Turner (Chicago: SVE, 1989). Reviewed in: *Arithmetic Teacher* 38, no.3 (Nov. 1990): 47

Mammals: A Multimedia Encyclopedia, Multimedia (Washington, DC: National Geographic Society, n.d.). Reviewed in: *Science and Children* 30, no.1 (Sept. 1992): 55-56

Music! Words! Opera! (Level One), Multimedia by Sandra Purrington and Carroll Rinehart (St. Louis, MO: MMB Music, 1990). Reviewed in: *Music Educator's Journal* 78, no.4 (Dec. 1991): 16-18

One Hundred Words about My House, Multimedia (Orlando, FL: Harcourt Brace Jovanovich, 1990). Reviewed in: *School Library Journal* 37, no.1 (Jan. 1991): 62

One Hundred Words about Working, Multimedia (Orlando, FL: Harcourt Brace Jovanovich, 1990). Reviewed in: *School Library Journal* 37, no.1 (Jan. 1991): 62

Picture Book of Abraham Lincoln, Multimedia (Ancramdale, NY: Live Oak Media, 1990). Reviewed in: *School Library Journal* 37, no.1 (Jan. 1991): 63

Picture Book of George Washington, Multimedia (Ancramdale, NY: Live Oak Media, 1990). Reviewed in: *School Library Journal* 37, no.1 (Jan. 1991): 63

Reading Higher: A Problem-solving Approach to Elementary School Mathematics, Multimedia (Reston, VA: NCTE, 1990). Reviewed in: *Curriculum Review* 31, no.7 (Mar. 1992): 26-27

Running on Rainbows, Multimedia (Hainesport, NJ: Chroma Acrylics, n.d.). Reviewed in: *School Arts* 90, no.3 (Nov. 1990): 46

Multimedia *(cont'd)*
Science Primer: Observing Air, Multimedia (Chicago: Society for Visual Education, 1989). Reviewed in: *Media and Methods* 27, no.3 (Jan./Feb. 1991): 52

Science Primer: Observing Earth, Multimedia (Chicago: Society for Visual Education, 1989). Reviewed in: *Media and Methods* 27, no.3 (Jan./Feb. 1991): 52

Science Primer: Observing Fire, Multimedia (Chicago: Society for Visual Education, 1989). Reviewed in: *Media and Methods* 27, no.3 (Jan./Feb. 1991): 52

Science Primer: Observing Water, Multimedia (Chicago: Society for Visual Education, 1989). Reviewed in: *Media and Methods* 27, no.3 (Jan./Feb. 1991): 52

Teaching Primary Math with Music, Multimedia by Esther Mardlesohn (Palo Alto, CA: Dale Seymour, 1990). Reviewed in: *Arithmetic Teacher* 39, no.1 (Sept. 1991): 53

Multiplication and Division Made Easy
by Catherine F. Debie (Artesia, CA: Scott Foresman, 1990). Reviewed in: *Arithmetic Teacher* 39, no.8 (Apr. 1992): 59

The Munchters Talk about Food
Manipulatives (Chicago: National Livestock and Meat Board, 1990). Reviewed in: *Journal of Nutritional Education* 23, no.4 (July/Aug. 1991): 198

Muppet Labs
Software (Pleasantville, NY: Sunburst Communications, 1992). Reviewed in: *School Library Journal* 38, no.5 (May 1992): 61

Muppet Math
Software (Pleasantville, NY: Sunburst Communications, 1991). Reviewed in: *School Library Journal* 38, no.2 (Feb. 1992): 49-50

Muppet Slate
Software (Pleasantville, NY: Sunburst Communications, 1990). Reviewed in: *Gifted Child Today* 15, no.3 (May/June 1992): 53; *Instructor* 100, no.5 (Jan. 1991): 119

Musical skills
Pick the Pitch, Software by Brian R. Moore (n.p.: Temporal Acuity Products, 1988). Reviewed in: *American Music Teacher* 40, no.4 (Feb./Mar. 1991): 10

Musical skills (basic)
Conceptual Music Games, Software by Thomas Gibson (n.p.: Temporal Acuity Products, Inc., 1991). Reviewed in: *American Music Teacher* 41, no.6 (June/July 1992): 10

Music appreciation
The Listener, Video (Boca Raton, FL: Social Issues Resources Series, 1987). Reviewed in: *Music Educator's Journal* 77, no.7 (Mar. 1991): 52

Music! Words! Opera! (Level One), Multimedia by Sandra Purrington and Carroll Rinehart (St. Louis, MO: MMB Music, 1990). Reviewed in: *Music Educator's Journal* 78, no.4 (Dec. 1991): 16-18

The Philharmonic Gets Dressed, Film/Video (Deerfield, IL: Coronet/MTI Film and Video, 1989). Reviewed in: *Media and Methods* 27, no.2 (Nov./Dec. 1990): 58

Musical Stairs - MIDI
Software by Steve Walker (n.p.: Electronic Courseware Systems, 1987). Reviewed in: *American Music Teacher* 40, no.3 (Dec. 1990/Jan. 1991): 10

Music! Words! Opera! (Level One)
Multimedia by Sandra Purrington and Carroll Rinehart (St. Louis, MO: MMB Music, 1990). Reviewed in: *Music Educator's Journal* 78, no.4 (Dec. 1991): 16-18

Mutanoid Math Challenge
Software (Northridge, CA: Legacy Software, n.d.). Reviewed in: *Technology and Learning* 12, no.8 (May/June 1992): 11-12

M. V. Egan (publisher)
Spelling Strategies You Can Teach, by Mary Tarasoff (Victoria, Canada: M. V. Egan, 1990). Reviewed in: *Curriculum Review* 30, no.3 (Nov. 1990): 27

My Brother Is Afraid of Just About Everything
Film/Video (North Hollywood, CA: Alfred Higgins Productions, 1990). Reviewed in: *Curriculum Review* 30, no.2 (Oct. 1990): 19

My First Computer Book
Multimedia by David Schiller and David Rosenbloom, and illustrated by Tedd Arnold (New York: Workman, 1991). Reviewed in: *School Arts* 91, no.5 (Jan. 1992): 44

My First Green Book: A Life-Size Guide to Caring for Our Environment
by Angela Wilkes (New York: Random House, 1991). Reviewed in: *Curriculum Review* 32, no.1 (Sept. 1992): 28-29

My First Look at Nature
(New York: Random House, 1991). Reviewed in: *Science Books and Films* 27, no.8 (Nov. 1991): 236

My First Science Book
by Angela Wilkes (New York: Knopf, 1990). Reviewed in: *Science Books and Films* 27, no. 2 (Mar. 1991): 47

Mystery Castle: Strategies for Problem Solving (Level One)
Software (Acton, MA: William K. Bradford, 1990). Reviewed in: *Arithmetic Teacher* 39, no.3 (Nov. 1991): 57

Nancy Renfro Studios
Leap into Learning, by Kristen Bissinger and Nancy Renfro (Austin, TX: Nancy Renfro Studios, 1990). Reviewed in: *Curriculum Review* 31, no.7 (Mar. 1992): 25-26

National Council of Teachers of English (publisher)
Reading Higher: A Problem-solving Approach to Elementary School Mathematics, Multimedia (Reston, VA: NCTE, 1990). Reviewed in: *Curriculum Review* 31, no.7 (Mar. 1992): 26-27

National Council of Teachers of Mathematics (publisher)
Developing Graph Comprehension: Elementary and Middle School Activities, by Frances R. Curcio (Reston, VA: National Council of Teachers of Mathematics, 1989). Reviewed in: *Mathematics Teacher* 83, no.6 (Sept. 1990): 480

National Gardening Association (publisher)
GrowLab: Activities for Growing Minds, by Joy Cohen and Eve Pranis, and illustrated by Grant Urie (Burlington, VT: National Gardening Association, 1990). Reviewed in: *Science Books and Films* 27, no.2 (Mar. 1991): 49

National Geographic Society
The Age of Dinosaurs, Film (Washington, DC: National Geographic Society, 1990). Reviewed in: *Media and Methods* 27, no.5 (May/June 1991): 43; *American Biology Teacher* 53, no.3 (Mar. 1991): 189

All about Trees, Video (Washington, DC: National Geographic Society, 1990). Reviewed in: *School Library Journal* 37, no.1 (Jan. 1991): 61

Amazing Things Animals Do: Books for World Explorers, by Susan McGrath (Washington, DC: National Geographic Society, 1989). Reviewed in: *American Biology Teacher* 53, no.5 (May 1991): 315

Animals and Their World, by Judith E. Rinard, Gene S. Stuart, and Jennifer C. Urquhart (Washington, DC: National Geographic Society, 1990). Reviewed in: *Science and Children* 29, no.5 (Feb. 1992): 48

Animals, Animals: Fins, Feathers, Fur/ A Gaggle of Geese, Film/Video (Washington, DC: National Geographic Society, 1990). Reviewed in: *American Biology Teacher* 53, no.2 (Feb. 1991): 117

Books for Young Explorers: Set XVI, (Washington, DC: National Geographic Society, 1989). Reviewed in: *American Biology Teacher* 53, no.5 (May 1991): 314

A First Look at Electricity and Magnetism, Film (Washington, DC: National Geographic Society, 1990). Reviewed in: *Media and Methods* 27, no.5 (May/June 1991): 42-43

Mammals: A Multimedia Encyclopedia, Multimedia (Washington, DC: National Geographic Society, n.d.). Reviewed in: *Science and Children* 30, no.1 (Sept. 1992): 55-56

National Geographic Society *(cont'd)*
Math, Money, and You: Count It Out, Film/
Video (Washington, DC: National Geographic Society, 1989). Reviewed in: *Arithmetic Teacher* 38, no.4 (Dec. 1990): 61

Project Classify: Dinosaurs, Software
(Washington, DC: National Geographic Society, 1990). Reviewed in: *Instructor* 101, no.4
(Nov./Dec. 1991): 83; *Media and Methods*
27, no.3 (Jan./Feb. 1991): 62-63

Project Zoo, Software (Washington, DC:
National Geographic Society, 1987). Reviewed in: *School Science and Mathematics*
190, no.6 (Nov. 1990): 652

Ready, Set, Go: How Animals Move, Film
(Washington, DC: National Geographic Soci-
ety, 1989). Reviewed in: *American Biology
Teacher* 52, no.8 (Nov./Dec. 1990): 514

*Who Lives Here? Animals in and around
Ponds,* Film (Washington, DC: National
Geographic Society, 1990). Reviewed in:
American Biology Teacher 52, no.7 (Oct.
1990): 443

Who Lives Here? Animals in the Backyard,
Film (Washington, DC: National Geographic
Society, 1990). Reviewed in: *American
Biology Teacher* 52, no.7 (Oct. 1990): 443

Who Lives Here? Animals in the Desert,
Film (Washington, DC: National Geographic
Society, 1990). Reviewed in: *American
Biology Teacher* 52, no.7 (Oct. 1990): 443

Who Lives Here? Animals of the Sea, Film
(Washington, DC: National Geographic Soci-
ety, 1990). Reviewed in: *American Biology
Teacher* 52, no.7 (Oct. 1990): 443

National Livestock and Meat Board (publisher)
The Munchters Talk about Food,
Manipulatives (Chicago: National Livestock
and Meat Board, 1990). Reviewed in:
Journal of Nutritional Education 23, no.4
(July/Aug. 1991): 198

Nature All Year Long
by Clare Walker Leslie (New York:
Greenwillow Books, 1991). Reviewed in:
Young Children 47, no.4 (May 1992): 85

Navarro, C. F.
Categories, by C. F. Navarro (Alexandria,
VA: Start Smart Books, 1990). Reviewed in:
Curriculum Review 30, no.3 (Nov. 1990):
25-26

Distinctions, by C. F. Navarro (Alexandria,
VA: Start Smart Books, 1990). Reviewed in:
Curriculum Review 30, no.3 (Nov. 1990):
25-26

Early Geometry, by C. F. Navarro (Alexandria, VA: Start Smart Books, 1990). Reviewed in: *Curriculum Review* 30, no.3
(Nov. 1990): 25-26

Verbal Correspond, by C. F. Navarro
(Alexandria, VA: Start Smart Books, 1990).
Reviewed in: *Curriculum Review* 30, no.3
(Nov. 1990): 25-26

Never Kiss an Alligator
by Colleen Stanley Bare (New York: Dutton,
1989). Reviewed in: *Childhood Education*
66, no.5 (Annual 1990): 337

New Math Blaster Plus
Software (Torrance, CA: Davidson and
Associates, 1990). Reviewed in: *Instructor*
100, no.8 (April 1991): 74-75

New Print Shop
Software (San Rafael, CA: Broderbund
Software, n.d.). Reviewed in: *Technology
and Learning* 11, no.3 (Nov./Dec. 1990): 34

New Questions and Answers about Dinosaurs
by Seymour Simon and illustrated by Jennifer Dewey (New York: Morrow Junior
Books, 1990). Reviewed in: *Language Arts*
68, no.6 (Oct. 1991): 492

Nicolas, Baron Robert
Fifty Creative Exercises- Book Two, by
Baron Robert Nicolas (St. Paul, MN:
Leonardo's Workshop, 1988). Reviewed in:
Gifted Child Today 15, no.3 (May/June
1992): 50

Nicolson, Iain
The Illustrated World of Space, by Iain
Nicolson (New York: Simon and Schuster,
1991). Reviewed in: *Science Books and
Films* 27, no.8 (Nov. 1991): 237

Nigel's World
Software (Galesburg, MI: Lawrence Productions, n.d.). Reviewed in: *Computing Teacher* 20, no.1 (Aug./Sept. 1992): 44-47

A Night and a Day in the Desert
by Jennifer Dewey (Boston: Little Brown, 1991). Reviewed in: *Language Arts* 69, no.2 (Feb. 1992): 138

Nine Ducks Nine
by Sara Hayes (New York: William Morrow, 1990). Reviewed in: *Arithmetic Teacher* 39, no.9 (May 1992): 51

Ninety-Nine Gnats, Nits, and Nibblers
by May R. Barenbaum (Champaign, IL: University of Illinois Press, 1989). Reviewed in: *American Biology Teacher* 53, no.5 (May 1991): 316

Nixon, Joan L.
If You Were a Writer, by Joan L. Nixon (New York: Four Winds Press, 1988). Reviewed in: *Gifted Child Today* 15, no.1 (Jan./Feb. 1992): 58

Nomads and Cities
by Donna Bailey (Austin, TX: Steck-Vaughn, 1990). Reviewed in: *Young Children* 46, no.1 (Nov. 1990): 66

The Nonsense Poems of Edward Lear
by Edward Lear and illustrated by Leonard L. Brooke (New York: Clarion Books, 1991). Reviewed in: *Day Care and Early Education* 19, no.2 (Winter 1991): 36

Northlight Books
Draw! (Cincinnati, OH: Northlight Books, n.d.). Reviewed in: *School Arts* 91, no.6 (Feb. 1992): 44

Make Gifts! (Cincinnati, OH: Northlight Books, n.d.). Reviewed in: *School Arts* 91, no.6 (Feb. 1992): 44

Make Prints! (Cincinnati, OH: Northlight Books, n.d.). Reviewed in: *School Arts* 91, no.6 (Feb. 1992): 44

Paint! (Cincinnati, OH: Northlight Books, n.d.). Reviewed in: *School Arts* 91, no.6 (Feb. 1992): 44

Number Maze: Decimals and Fractions
Software (Scotts Valley, CA: Greatwave Software, n.d.). Reviewed in: *Electronic Learning* 10, no.5 (Feb. 1991): 36-37; *Media and Methods* 27, no.5 (May/June 1991): 60

Number Nine
Video (Evanston, IL: Journal Films, 1990). Reviewed in: *Science Books and Films* 27, no.4 (May 1991): 121

Numbers at Play: A Counting Book
by Charles Sullivan (New York: Rizzoli, 1992). Reviewed in: *Childhood Education* 69, no.1 (Fall 1992): 49

Numbers in Rhyme: Counting More and More
by Leland B. Jacobs (Allen, TX: DLM, 1990). Reviewed in: *Arithmetic Teacher* 38, no.2 (Oct. 1990): 57

Numbers in Rhyme: Counting One to Five
by Leland B. Jacobs (Allen, TX: DLM, 1990). Reviewed in: *Arithmetic Teacher* 38, no.2 (Oct. 1990): 57

Numbers in Rhyme: Counting Six to Ten
by Leland B. Jacobs (Allen, TX: DLM, 1990). Reviewed in: *Arithmetic Teacher* 38, no.2 (Oct. 1990): 57

Numbervision: Addition/Subtraction System
Software (Lexington, OH: Numbervision, 1990). Reviewed in: *Arithmetic Teacher* 39, no.2 (Oct. 1991): 50

Nutrition
Stick and Score: The Good Food Game, Manipulatives (St. Paul, MN: Stick and Score, 1990). Reviewed in: *Journal of Nutritional Education* 23, no.3 (May/June 1991): 142-143

Oakley, Graham
Magical Changes, by Graham Oakley (New York: Aladdin Books, 1987). Reviewed in: *Gifted Child Today* 15, no.2 (Mar./Apr. 1992): 59

An Ocean of Air
Software (Galesburg, MI: MCE, n.d.). Reviewed in: *Science and Children* 29, no.2 (Oct. 1991): 47

Oehlkers, William J.
  Tales for Thinking, by William J. Oehlkers and Ezra Stieglitz (North Billerica, MA: Curriculum Associates, 1991). Reviewed in: *Curriculum Review* 31, no.1 (Sept. 1991): 28

Of Colors and Things
  by Tana Hoban (New York: Greenwillow Books, 1989). Reviewed in: *Arithmetic Teacher* 38, no.9 (May 1991): 44

Once inside the Library
  by Barbara A. Huff and illustrated by Iris Van Rynback (Boston: Little Brown, 1990). Reviewed in: *Science Books and Films* 27, no.2 (Mar. 1991): 45

Once upon a Time (Volume Three)
  Software (New Haven, CT: Compu-Teach, n.d.). Reviewed in: *Electronic Learning* 10, no.5 (Feb. 1991): 36-37

One Day at a Time: Children Living with Leukemia
  by Thomas Bergman (Milwaukee, WI: Gareth Stevens, 1989). Reviewed in: *Teaching Exceptional Children* 24, no.3 (Spring 1992): 83-84

The One-Dollar Word Riddle Book
  by Marilyn Burns and illustrated by Martha Weston (New Rochelle, NY: Cuisenaire, 1990). Reviewed in: *Arithmetic Teacher* 39, no.2 (Oct. 1991): 51-52

One Good Horse: A Cowpuncher's Counting Book
  by Ann Herbert Scott (New York: Greenwillow Books, 1990). Reviewed in: *Arithmetic Teacher* 38, no.9 (May 1991): 45

One Hundred Words about My House
  Multimedia (Orlando, FL: Harcourt Brace Jovanovich, 1990). Reviewed in: *School Library Journal* 37, no.1 (Jan. 1991): 62

One Hundred Words about Working
  Multimedia (Orlando, FL: Harcourt Brace Jovanovich, 1990). Reviewed in: *School Library Journal* 37, no.1 (Jan. 1991): 62

One Special Star
  by Anita McFadzean and illustrated by Kate Jaspers (New York: Simon and Schuster, 1991). Reviewed in: *Arithmetic Teacher* 39, no.7 (Mar. 1992): 39

On Our Own Terms: Children Living with Physical Disabilities
  by Thomas Bergman (Milwaukee, WI: Gareth Stevens, 1989). Reviewed in: *Teaching Exceptional Children* 24, no.3 (Spring 1992): 83-84

On the Button in Math: Activities for Young Children
  by Carol A. Thornton and Judith K. Wells (Allen, TX: DLM Teaching Resources, 1990). Reviewed in: *Arithmetic Teacher* 38, no.9 (May 1991): 46

Opie, Iona and Peter
  I Saw Esau: The School Child's Pocket Book, by Iona and Peter Opie and illustrated by Maurice Sendak (n.p.: Candlewick, 1992). Reviewed in: *School Library Journal* 38, no.6 (June 1992): 110

Opportunities for Learning (publisher)
  T'NT - Talented and Thinking, by Fanny Forrest McAleer (Chatsworth, CA: Opportunities for Learning, 1987). Reviewed in: *Gifted Child Today* 15, no.5 (Sept./Oct. 1992): 41

Optical Data (publisher)
  Wetlands, Software (Warren, NJ: Optical Data, n.d.). Reviewed in: *Science and Children* 29, no.7 (Apr. 1992): 40-41

  Windows on Science (Spanish Edition), Software (Warren, NJ: Optical Data, n.d.). Reviewed in: *Computing Teacher* 18, no.4 (Dec. 1990/Jan. 1991): 53

Orange Cherry Software
  Jungle Safari, Software (Pound Ridge, NY: Orange Cherry Software, 1990). Reviewed in: *Science and Children* 29, no.4 (Jan. 1992): 35-36

  Talking Alpha Chimp, Software (Pound Ridge, NY: Orange Cherry Software, 1989). Reviewed in: *Arithmetic Teacher* 38, no.4 (Dec. 1990): 59; *Instructor* 100, no.3 (Oct. 1990): 53

Orange Cherry Software *(cont'd)*
   Talking Animals, Software (Pound Ridge, NY: Orange Cherry Software, 1989). Reviewed in: *Arithmetic Teacher* 38, no.4 (Dec. 1990): 60

   Talking Classroom: Grades Pre-K to Four, Software (Pound Ridge, NY: Orange Cherry Software, 1990). Reviewed in: *Arithmetic Teacher* 39, no.3 (Nov. 1991): 57

   Talking Clock, Software (Pound Ridge, NY: Orange Cherry Software, n.d.). Reviewed in: *Media and Methods* 27, no.1 (Sept./Oct. 1990): 71-77

   Talking Dinosaurs, Software (Pound Ridge, NY: Orange Cherry Software, n.d.). Reviewed in: *Media and Methods* 27, no.1 (Sept./Oct. 1990): 71-77

   Talking Money, Software (Pound Ridge, NY: Orange Cherry Software, 1989). Reviewed in: *Arithmetic Teacher* 38, no.1 (Sept. 1990): 44

   Talking Multiplication and Division: Grades 3-6, Software (Pound Ridge, NY: Orange Cherry Software, 1990). Reviewed in: *Arithmetic Teacher* 39, no.3 (Nov. 1991): 57

   Talking Reading Railroad, Software (Pound Ridge, NY: Orange Cherry Software, n.d.). Reviewed in: *Media and Methods* 27, no.1 (Sept./Oct. 1990): 71-77

   Talking School Bus, Software (Pound Ridge, NY: Orange Cherry Software, 1989). Reviewed in: *Arithmetic Teacher* 38, no.1 (Sept. 1990): 44

The Orchard
   by Isidro Sanchez (New York: Barrons, 1991). Reviewed in: *Science Books and Films* 27, no.8 (Nov. 1991): 244

Oryx Press
   Multicultural Folktales: Stories To Tell Young Children, by Judy Sierra and Robert Kaminski (Phoenix, AZ: Oryx Press, 1991). Reviewed in: *Young Children* 47, no.2 (Jan. 1992): 71

Otters under Water
   by Jim Arnosky (New York: Putnam, 1992). Reviewed in: *School Library Journal* 38, no.8 (Aug. 1992): 150

Our Vanishing Farm Animals: Saving America's Rare Breeds
   by Catherine Paladino (Boston: Little Brown, 1991). Reviewed in: *Language Arts* 68, no.6 (Oct. 1991): 495

Paint!
   (Cincinnati, OH: Northlight Books, n.d.). Reviewed in: *School Arts* 91, no.6 (Feb. 1992): 44

Paladino, Catherine
   Our Vanishing Farm Animals: Saving America's Rare Breeds, by Catherine Paladino (Boston: Little Brown, 1991). Reviewed in: *Language Arts* 68, no.6 (Oct. 1991): 495

Pallotta, Jerry
   The Icky Bug Counting Book, by Jerry Pallotta and illustrated by Ralph Masiello (Watertown, MA: Charlesbridge, 1991). Reviewed in: *Science Books and Films* 28, no1 (Jan./Feb. 1992): 19

Paper Plane Pilot
   Software (Minneapolis, MN: MECC, 1991). Reviewed in: *Science and Children* 29, no.2 (Oct. 1991): 46

The Paper Zebra and Other Paper Possibilities
   Video (Dallas, TX: Small Business Press, n.d.). Reviewed in: *Arts and Activities* 110, no.2 (Oct. 1991): 20

Parker, Walter C.
   Renewing the Social Studies Curriculum, by Walter C. Parker (Alexandria, VA: Association for Supervision and Curriculum Development, 1991). Reviewed in: *Curriculum Review* 31, no.7 (Mar. 1992): 30

Parsons, Alexandra
   Amazing Poisonous Animals, by Alexandra Parsons (New York: Knopf, 1990). Reviewed in: *Science Books and Films* 27, no.1 (Jan./Feb. 1991): 20

Party Rhymes
   by Marc Brown (New York: Dutton, 1989). Reviewed in: *Language Arts* 68, no.3 (Mar. 1991): 242

Philomel Books *(cont'd)*
Bird Watch, by Jane Yolen and illustrated by Ted Lewin (New York: Philomel, 1990). Reviewed in: *School Library Journal* 37, no.2 (Supplement to Feb. 1991): S-22

Physical sciences
Exploring Sound, Video (San Diego: Media Guild, 1990). Reviewed in: *Science Books and Films* 27, no.5 (June/July 1991): 150

Liquid and Buoyancy, by Barbara Taylor (New York: Watts, 1990). Reviewed in: *Science Books and Films* 27, no.1 (Jan./Feb. 1991): 17

Machines and Movement, by Barbara Taylor (New York: Watts, 1990). Reviewed in: *Science Books and Films* 27, no.1 (Jan./Feb. 1991): 17

Shadows and Reflections, by Barbara Taylor (New York: Watts, 1990). Reviewed in: *Science Books and Films* 27, no.1 (Jan./Feb. 1991): 17

Sound and Music, by Barbara Taylor (New York: Watts, 1990). Reviewed in: *Science Books and Films* 27, no.1 (Jan./Feb. 1991): 17

Temperature and You, by Betsy Maestro and illustrated by Guilio Maestro (New York: Lodestar, 1990). Reviewed in: *School Library Journal* 37, no.2 (Feb. 1991): 84

Physics (basic)
A First Look at Electricity and Magnetism, Film (Washington, DC: National Geographic Society, 1990). Reviewed in: *Media and Methods* 27, no.5 (May/June 1991): 42-43

Physics for Kids: 49 Easy Experiments with Acoustics
by Robert W. Wood (Blue Ridge Summit, PA: TAB, 1990). Reviewed in: *Science Books and Films* 27, no.3 (Apr. 1991): 80

Physics for Kids: 49 Easy Experiments with Electricity and Magnetism
by Robert W. Wood (Blue Ridge Summit, PA: TAB, 1990). Reviewed in: *Science Books and Films* 27, no.3 (Apr. 1991): 80

Physics for Kids: 49 Easy Experiments with Optics
by Robert W. Wood (Blue Ridge Summit, PA: TAB, 1990). Reviewed in: *Science Books and Films* 27, no.3 (Apr. 1991): 80

Pick the Pitch
Software by Brian R. Moore (n.p.: Temporal Acuity Products, 1988). Reviewed in: *American Music Teacher* 40, no.4 (Feb./Mar. 1991): 10

Picture Atlas of the World
(Chicago: Rand McNally, 1991). Reviewed in: *Science Books and Films* 27, no.7 (Oct. 1991): 213

Picture Book of Abraham Lincoln
Multimedia (Ancramdale, NY: Live Oak Media, 1990). Reviewed in: *School Library Journal* 37, no.1 (Jan. 1991): 63

Picture Book of George Washington
Multimedia (Ancramdale, NY: Live Oak Media, 1990). Reviewed in: *School Library Journal* 37, no.1 (Jan. 1991): 63

Picture Library Series
by Norman Barrett (New York: Franklin Watts, 1989). Reviewed in: *Science and Children* 28, no.1 (Sept. 1990):79

Plants Are Different and Alike
Film/Video (Deerfield, IL: Coronet/MTI Film and Video, 1990). Reviewed in: *Childhood Education* 68, no.1 (Fall 1991): 54

The Playroom
Software (San Rafael, CA: Broderbund Software, n.d.). Reviewed in: *Electronic Learning* 10, no.5 (Feb. 1991): 36-37; *Technology and Learning* 11, no.1 (Sept. 1990): 18

PlayWrite
Software (Pleasantville, NY: Sunburst Communications, 1991). Reviewed in: *Electronic Learning* 10, no.8 (May/June 1991): 40; *Technology and Learning* 11, no.8 (May/June 1991): 6

PODD
Software (Pleasantville, NY: Sunburst Communications, n.d.). Reviewed in: *Computing Teacher* 18, no.3 (Nov. 1990): 46-47

Poetry

And the Green Grass Grew All Around, by Alvin Schwartz (New York: HarperCollins, 1992). Reviewed in: *School Library Journal* 38, no.6 (June 1992): 135

At the Crack of the Bat: Baseball Poems, by Lillian Morrison (New York: Hyperion, 1992). Reviewed in: *School Library Journal* 38, no.6 (June 1992): 134

Bear in Mind: A Book of Bear Poems, by Bobbye S. Goldstein (New York: Puffin Books, 1991). Reviewed in: *Day Care and Early Education* 19, no.2 (Winter 1991): 36

In My Mother's House, by Ann Nolan Clark and illustrated by Velino Herrara (New York: Viking, 1991). Reviewed in: *Day Care and Early Education* 19, no.2 (Winter 1991): 36

I Saw Esau: The School Child's Pocket Book, by Iona and Peter Opie and illustrated by Maurice Sendak (n.p.: Candlewick, 1992). Reviewed in: *School Library Journal* 38, no.6 (June 1992): 110

Laughing Time: Collected Nonsense, by William Smith and illustrated by Jay F. Krahn (New York: Sunburst, 1990). Reviewed in: *Day Care and Early Education* 19, no.2 (Winter 1991): 36

Let's Pretend: Poems of Flight and Fancy, edited by Natalie S. Bober and illustrated by Bob Bell (New York: Viking Kestrel, 1986). Reviewed in: *Day Care and Early Education* 19, no.2 (Winter 1991): 35

The Nonsense Poems of Edward Lear, by Edward Lear and illustrated by Leonard L. Brooke (New York: Clarion Books, 1991). Reviewed in: *Day Care and Early Education* 19, no.2 (Winter 1991): 36

Portage Classroom Curriculum
by J. Brinckerhoff (Portage, WI: Cooperative Educational Service Agency, 1987). Reviewed in: *Teaching Exceptional Children* 23, no.3 (Spring 1991): 72

Pranis, Eve

GrowLab: Activities for Growing Minds, by Joy Cohen and Eve Pranis, and illustrated by Grant Urie (Burlington, VT: National Gardening Association, 1990). Reviewed in: *Science Books and Films* 27, no.2 (Mar. 1991): 49

Preservation Press

What It Feels Like To Be a Building, by Forrest Wilson (Washington, DC: Preservation Press, 1988). Reviewed in: *Gifted Child Today* 15, no.1 (Jan./Feb. 1992): 57-58

Price, Stern, and Sloan

City Critters around the World, by Amy Goldman Koss (Los Angeles: Price, Stern, and Sloan, 1991). Reviewed in: *Young Children* 47, no.4 (May 1992): 85

Primary Geometry Workshop (Grades K-2)
Software (Glenview, IL: Scott Foresman, 1991). Reviewed in: *Arithmetic Teacher* 39, no.8 (Apr. 1992): 58

Princeton Book Company

Hello Toes! Movement Games for Children, by A. L. Barlin and N. Kalev (Pennington, NJ: Princeton Book Company, 1989). Reviewed in: *Bulletin of the Council for Research in Music Education* 107 (Winter 1991): 75-76

Problem Solving
Video (Atlanta, GA: Silver Burdett and Ginn, 1991). Reviewed in: *Arithmetic Teacher* 39, no.2 (Oct. 1991): 52-53

Professor Curious and the Mystery of the Hiking Dinosaurs
by Yvonne Gil and illustrated by Bonnie Timmons (n.p.: Clarkson Potter, 1991). Reviewed in: *Language Arts* 68, no.6 (Oct. 1991): 492

Project Classify: Dinosaurs
Software (Washington, DC: National Geographic Society, 1990). Reviewed in: *Instructor* 101, no.4 (Nov./Dec. 1991): 83; *Media and Methods* 27, no.3 (Jan./Feb. 1991): 62-63

Project Zoo
   Software (Washington, DC: National Geographic Society, 1987). Reviewed in: *School Science and Mathematics* 190, no.6 (Nov. 1990): 652

Protecting Our Planet: Activities To Motivate Young Children to a Better Understanding of Our Environmental Problems
   by Eva and Evelyn Deutsch (Carthage, IL: Good Apple, 1992). Reviewed in: *Curriculum Review* 32, no.1 (Sept. 1992): 27

Puffin Books
   Bear in Mind: A Book of Bear Poems, by Bobbye S. Goldstein (New York: Puffin Books, 1991). Reviewed in: *Day Care and Early Education* 19, no.2 (Winter 1991): 36

Purrington, Sandra
   Music! Words! Opera! (Level One), Multimedia by Sandra Purrington and Carroll Rinehart (St. Louis, MO: MMB Music, 1990). Reviewed in: *Music Educator's Journal* 78, no.4 (Dec. 1991): 16-18

Putnam (publisher)
   A Cache of Jewels, by Ruth Heller (New York: Putnam, 1989). Reviewed in: *Gifted Child Today* 15, no.1 (Jan./Feb. 1992): 58

   Otters under Water, by Jim Arnosky (New York: Putnam, 1992). Reviewed in: *School Library Journal* 38, no.8 (Aug. 1992): 150

Queue (publisher)
   The World of Reading, Software (n.p.: Queue, 1989). Reviewed in: *Curriculum Review* 30, no.4 (Dec. 1990): 28

Rain Forest Secrets
   by Arthur Dorros (New York: Scholastic, 1990). Reviewed in: *School Library Journal* 37, no.2 (Feb. 1991): 78

Raintree (publisher)
   Raintree Science Adventures, by Helen H. Cary and Judith E. Greenberg (Milwaukee, WI: Raintree, 1990). Reviewed in: *Science and Children* 29, no.5 (Feb. 1992): 48

Raintree Science Adventures
   by Helen H. Cary and Judith E. Greenberg (Milwaukee, WI: Raintree, 1990). Reviewed in: *Science and Children* 29, no.5 (Feb. 1992): 48

Rand McNally
   Picture Atlas of the World (Chicago: Rand McNally, 1991). Reviewed in: *Science Books and Films* 27, no.7 (Oct. 1991): 213

Random House
   Amazing Frogs and Toads, by Barry Clarke (New York: Random House, 1991). Reviewed in: *Curriculum Review* 31, no.1 (Sept. 1991): 30

   Counting on Math, Manipulatives (Westminster, MD: Random House School Division, 1988). Reviewed in: *Arithmetic Teacher* 38, no.1 (Sept. 1990): 50

   My First Green Book: A Life-Size Guide to Caring for Our Environment, by Angela Wilkes (New York: Random House, 1991). Reviewed in: *Curriculum Review* 32, no.1 (Sept. 1992): 28-29

   My First Look at Nature (New York: Random House, 1991). Reviewed in: *Science Books and Films* 27, no.8 (Nov. 1991): 236

Random House Encyclopedia
   Software (Pittsford, NY: Microlytics, 1990). Reviewed in: *Science and Children* 29, no.6 (Mar. 1992): 49-50

Rap-Ability
   Audiotapes by Mike and Suzanne Rossi (Lake Orion, MI: Aynn Visual, 1990). Reviewed in: *Arithmetic Teacher* 38, no.9 (May 1991): 49

Reader Rabbit 2
   Software (Fremont, CA: Learning Company, n.d.). Reviewed in: *Technology and Learning* 12, no.7 (Apr. 1992): 7-10

Reader's Digest Children's World Atlas
   (New York: Reader's Digest, 1991). Reviewed in: *Science Books and Films* 27, no.8 (Nov. 1991): 244

Reading skills (music)
KIDS: Keyboard Introductory Development Series, Software by Brenda Bailey (n.p.: Electronic Courseware Systems, 1989). Reviewed in: *American Music Teacher* 41, no.6 (June/July 1992): 10

Maestroscope Theory Readiness B and C, Software by Sharon Lohse Kunitz (n.p.: Maestro Music, 1989). Reviewed in: *American Music Teacher* 41, no.6 (June/July 1992): 10

Musical Stairs - MIDI, Software by Steve Walker (n.p.: Electronic Courseware Systems, 1987). Reviewed in: *American Music Teacher* 40, no.3 (Dec. 1990/Jan. 1991): 10

Ready, Set, Go: How Animals Move
Film (Washington, DC: National Geographic Society, 1989). Reviewed in: *American Biology Teacher* 52, no.8 (Nov./Dec. 1990): 514

Ready, Set, Read: The Beginning Reader's Treasury
illustrated by Anne Burgess (New York: Doubleday, 1990). Reviewed in: *School Library Journal* 37, no.2 (Supplement Feb. 1991): S16

Reference books
Picture Atlas of the World (Chicago: Rand McNally, 1991). Reviewed in: *Science Books and Films* 27, no.7 (Oct. 1991): 213

Picture Library Series, by Norman Barrett (New York: Franklin Watts, 1989). Reviewed in: *Science and Children* 28, no.1 (Sept. 1990): 79

Random House Encyclopedia, Software (Pittsford, NY: Microlytics, 1990). Reviewed in: *Science and Children* 29, no.6 (Mar. 1992): 49-50

Reader's Digest Children's World Atlas (New York: Reader's Digest, 1991). Reviewed in: *Science Books and Films* 27, no.8 (Nov. 1991): 244

Reid, Margarette S.
The Button Box, by Margarette S. Reid (New York: Dutton Children's Books, 1990). Reviewed in: *Arithmetic Teacher* 38, no.9 (May 1991): 44

Renewing the Social Studies Curriculum
by Walter C. Parker (Alexandria, VA: Association for Supervision and Curriculum Development, 1991). Reviewed in: *Curriculum Review* 31, no.7 (Mar. 1992): 30

Research Press
Think Aloud: Increasing Social and Cognitive Skills, by Bonnie Camp and Mary Ann S. Bash (Champaign, IL: Research Press, 1990). Reviewed in: *Science Books and Films* 27, no.2 (Mar. 1991): 45

The Restless Earth
by Francois Michel and Yves Lavor (New York: Viking, 1990). Reviewed in: *Language Arts* 68, no.6 (Oct. 1991): 494-495

The Right Number of Elephants
by Jeff Sheppard (New York: HarperCollins, 1990). Reviewed in: *Arithmetic Teacher* 39, no.1 (Sept. 1991): 52

Rinard, Judith E.
Animals and Their World, by Judith E. Rinard, Gene S. Stuart, and Jennifer C. Urquhart (Washington, DC: National Geographic Society, 1990). Reviewed in: *Science and Children* 29, no.5 (Feb. 1992): 48

Rinehart, Carroll
Music! Words! Opera! (Level One), Multimedia by Sandra Purrington and Carroll Rinehart (St. Louis, MO: MMB Music, 1990). Reviewed in: *Music Educator's Journal* 78, no.4 (Dec. 1991): 16-18

Rizzoli (publisher)
Numbers at Play: A Counting Book, by Charles Sullivan (New York: Rizzoli, 1992). Reviewed in: *Childhood Education* 69, no.1 (Fall 1992): 49

Rockwell, Anne
Willy Can Count, by Anne Rockwell (New York: Arcade, 1989). Reviewed in: *Arithmetic Teacher* 38, no.2 (Oct. 1990): 53

Rogers, Paul
The Shapes Game, by Paul Rogers and illustrated by Sian Tucker (New York: Henry Holt, 1989). Reviewed in: *Arithmetic Teacher* 38, no.9 (May 1991): 45

Scholastic (publisher) *(cont'd)*
Clifford's Big Book Publisher, Software (Jefferson City, MO: Scholastic, 1990). Reviewed in: *Instructor* 100, no.5 (Jan. 1991): 117-118; *Electronic Learning* 10, no.8 (May/June 1991): 40

In 1492, by Jean Marzollo (New York: Scholastic, 1991). Reviewed in: *Childhood Education* 68, no.3 (Spring 1992): 178

Magic School Bus on the Ocean Floor, by Joanna Cole and illustrated by Bruce Degen (New York: Scholastic, 1992). Reviewed in: *School Library Journal* 38, no.8 (Aug. 1992): 151

Math Shop Junior, Software by Cary Hammer (New York: Scholastic, 1989). Reviewed in: *Arithmetic Teacher* 38, no.1 (Sept. 1990): 44

Rain Forest Secrets, by Arthur Dorros (New York: Scholastic, 1990). Reviewed in: *School Library Journal* 37, no.2 (Feb. 1991): 78

Science Explorers (Volumes One and Two), Software (Jefferson City, MO: Scholastic, 1990). Reviewed in: *Science Books and Films* 27, no.6 (Aug./Sept. 1991): 187

A Sea Full of Sharks, by Betty Maestro and illustrated by Guilio Maestro (New York: Scholastic, 1990). Reviewed in: *Language Arts* 69, no.4 (Apr. 1992): 299-300

Whole Language Source Book, by Jane Baskwill and Paulette Whitman (Ontario, Canada: Scholastic, 1986). Reviewed in: *Language Arts* 68, no.2 (Feb. 1991): 150

School Science and Mathematics (publisher)
Activities for Teaching K-6 Math/Science Concepts, by Walter A. Farmer and Margaret A. Farrell (Bowling Green, OH: School Science and Mathematics, 1989). Reviewed in: *Science and Children* 28, no.4 (Jan. 1991): 58

Schoolyard Science
by Peggy Perdue (Glenview, IL: Scott Foresman, 1991). Reviewed in: *Curriculum Review* 30, no.3 (Nov. 1990): 30

Schulman, Linda
Thinker Math: Developing Number Sense and Arithmetic Skills (Grades 3-4), by Carole Greenes, Linda Schulman, and Rika Spungin (Allen, TX: DLM, n.d.). Reviewed in: *Arithmetic Teacher* 38, no.2 (Oct. 1990): 54

Schwartz, Alvin
And the Green Grass Grew All Around, by Alvin Schwartz (New York: HarperCollins, 1992). Reviewed in: *School Library Journal* 38, no.6 (June 1992): 135

Schwartz, Carol
Sea Squares, by Joy N. Hulme and illustrated by Carol Schwartz (Waltham, MA: Hyperion Books, 1991). Reviewed in: *Arithmetic Teacher* 40, no.1 (Sept. 1992): 56

Science activities
Activities for Teaching K-6 Math/Science Concepts, by Walter A. Farmer and Margaret A. Farrell (Bowling Green, OH: School Science and Mathematics, 1989). Reviewed in: *Science and Children* 28, no.4 (Jan. 1991): 58

Amazing Science Experiments with Everyday Materials, by Richard Churchill and illustrated by Frances Zweifel (New York: Sterling, 1991). Reviewed in: *Science Books and Films* 27, no.4 (May 1991): 113

Bet You Can! Science Possibilities To Fool You, by Vicki Cobb and Kathy Darling (New York: Lothrop, Lee and Shepard, 1990). Reviewed in: *Science Books and Films* 27, no.1 (Jan./Feb. 1991): 15

Caring for Our Water, by Carol Greene (Hillside, NJ: Enslow, 1991). Reviewed in: *Science and Children* 29, no.7 (Apr. 1992): 47

Clearwater Detectives, Software (Minneapolis, MN: MECC, 1991). Reviewed in: *Science and Children* 29, no.5 (Feb. 1992): 36-39

Creative Sciencing: Ideas and Activities for Teachers and Children, by Alfred De Vito and Gerald H. Krockover (Glenview, IL: Scott Foresman, 1990). Reviewed in: *Science Books and Films* 27, no.1 (Jan./Feb. 1991): 15

Science activities *(cont'd)*

Science for Kids: 39 Easy Chemistry Experiments, by Robert W. Wood (Blue Ridge Summit, PA: TAB, 1991). Reviewed in: *Science and Children* 29, no.8 (May 1992): 36

Science for Kids: 39 Easy Meteorology Experiments, by Robert W. Wood (Blue Ridge Summit, PA: TAB, 1991). Reviewed in: *Science and Children* 29, no.8 (May 1992): 36

Science Is an Action Word! by Peggy K. Perdue and illustrated by Karen Disorbo (Glenview, IL: Scott Foresman, 1991). Reviewed in: *Science Books and Films* 27, no.2 (Mar. 1991): 46

Science Magic For Kids: 68 Simple and Safe Experiments, by William R. Wellnitz (n.p.: 1990). Reviewed in: *Science and Children* 29, no.6 (Mar. 1992): 55

Teaching Kids To Love the Earth, by M. L. Herman (n.p.: Pfeifer-Hamilton, 1991). Reviewed in: *Science and Children* 29, no.7 (Apr. 1992): 46

Woolly Bounce, Software (Minneapolis, MN: MECC, 1991). Reviewed in: *Science and Children* 29, no.4 (Jan. 1992): 34

The Science Book of Air
by Neil Ardley (San Diego: Gulliver Books, 1991). Reviewed in: *Language Arts* 68, no.6 (Oct. 1991): 494

The Science Book of Color
by Neil Ardley (San Diego: Gulliver Books, 1991). Reviewed in: *Language Arts* 68, no.6 (Oct. 1991): 494

The Science Book of Hot and Cold
by Neil Ardley (San Diego: Gulliver, 1992). Reviewed in: *Science Books and Films* 28, no.4 (May 1992): 110

The Science Book of Light
by Neil Ardley (San Diego: Gulliver Books, 1991). Reviewed in: *Language Arts* 68, no.6 (Oct. 1991): 494

The Science Book of the Senses
by Neil Ardley (San Diego: Gulliver, 1992). Reviewed in: *Science Books and Films* 28, no.4 (May 1992): 110

The Science Book of Water
by Neil Ardley (San Diego: Gulliver Books, 1991). Reviewed in: *Language Arts* 68, no.6 (Oct. 1991): 494

Science Explorers (Volumes One and Two)
Software (Jefferson City, MO: Scholastic, 1990). Reviewed in: *Science Books and Films* 27, no.6 (Aug./Sept. 1991): 187

Science for Kids: 39 Easy Animal Biology Experiments
by Robert W. Wood (Blue Ridge Summit, PA: TAB, 1991). Reviewed in: *Science and Children* 29, no.8 (May 1992): 36

Science for Kids: 39 Easy Chemistry Experiments
by Robert W. Wood (Blue Ridge Summit, PA: TAB, 1991). Reviewed in: *Science and Children* 29, no.8 (May 1992): 36

Science for Kids: 39 Easy Meteorology Experiments
by Robert W. Wood (Blue Ridge Summit, PA: TAB, 1991). Reviewed in: *Science and Children* 29, no.8 (May 1992): 36

Science (general)
First Science Read-along Book Bags, Audiotape (Mahwah, NJ: Troll Associates, 1992). Reviewed in: *School Library Journal* 38, no.5 (May 1992): 80

I Bet You Didn't Know That, by Carol Iverson (Minneapolis, MN: Lerner, 1990). Reviewed in: *Science and Children* 29, no.6 (Mar. 1992): 55

Samuel Todd's Book of Great Inventions, by E. L. Konigsburg (New York: Atheneum, 1991). Reviewed in: *Science and Children* 29, no.8 (May 1992): 36

Science Is an Action Word!
by Peggy K. Perdue and illustrated by Karen Disorbo (Glenview, IL: Scott Foresman, 1991). Reviewed in: *Science Books and Films* 27, no.2 (Mar. 1991): 46

Science Magic For Kids: 68 Simple and Safe Experiments
by William R. Wellnitz (n.p.: 1990). Reviewed in: *Science and Children* 29, no.6 (Mar. 1992): 55

Science Primer: Observing Air
Multimedia (Chicago: Society for Visual Education, 1989). Reviewed in: *Media and Methods* 27, no.3 (Jan./Feb. 1991): 52

Science Primer: Observing Earth
Multimedia (Chicago: Society for Visual Education, 1989). Reviewed in: *Media and Methods* 27, no.3 (Jan./Feb. 1991): 52

Science Primer: Observing Fire
Multimedia (Chicago: Society for Visual Education, 1989). Reviewed in: *Media and Methods* 27, no.3 (Jan./Feb. 1991): 52

Science Primer: Observing Water
Multimedia (Chicago: Society for Visual Education, 1989). Reviewed in: *Media and Methods* 27, no.3 (Jan./Feb. 1991): 52

Science through Children's Literature: An Integrated Approach
by Carol M. and John W. Butzow (Englewood, CO: Libraries Unlimited, n.d.). Reviewed in: *Curriculum Review* 30, no.1 (Sept. 1990): 30

Scott, Ann Herbert
One Good Horse: A Cowpuncher's Counting Book, by Ann Herbert Scott (New York: Greenwillow Books, 1990). Reviewed in: *Arithmetic Teacher* 38, no.9 (May 1991): 45

Scott Foresman
Building Self-Esteem with Koala-Roo Can-Do, by Laura Fendel (Glenview, IL: Scott Foresman, 1989). Reviewed in: *Teaching Exceptional Children* 24, no.4 (Summer 1992): 83

Creative Sciencing: Ideas and Activities for Teachers and Children, by Alfred De Vito and Gerald H. Krockover (Glenview, IL: Scott Foresman, 1990). Reviewed in: *Science Books and Films* 27, no.1 (Jan./Feb. 1991): 15

Diving into Science: Hands-on Water-Related Experiments, by Peggy K. Perdue (Glenview, IL: Scott Foresman, 1990). Reviewed in: *Science and Children* 28, no.7 (Apr. 1991): 60

Exploring Mathematics: Activities for Concept and Skill Development, K-3, by Jean M. Sham (Glenview, IL: Scott Foresman, 1990). Reviewed in: *Arithmetic Teacher* 38, no.1 (Sept. 1990): 46

Geometry Workshop, Grades 3-8, Software (Glenview, IL: Scott Foresman, 1991). Reviewed in: *Arithmetic Teacher* 39, no.8 (Apr. 1992): 58

Graphing and Probability Workshop, Grades 3-8, Software (Glenview, IL: Scott Foresman, 1991). Reviewed in: *Arithmetic Teacher* 39, no.3 (Nov. 1991): 56

Money and Time Workshop - Grades K-2, Software (Glenview, IL: Scott Foresman, 1991). Reviewed in: *Electronic Learning* 10, no.7 (Apr. 1991): 36; *Arithmetic Teacher* 39, no.1 (Sept. 1991): 48

Multiplication and Division Made Easy, by Catherine F. Debie (Artesia, CA: Scott Foresman, 1990). Reviewed in: *Arithmetic Teacher* 39, no.8 (Apr. 1992): 59

Primary Geometry Workshop (Grades K-2), Software (Glenview, IL: Scott Foresman, 1991). Reviewed in: *Arithmetic Teacher* 39, no.8 (Apr. 1992): 58

Schoolyard Science, by Peggy Perdue (Glenview, IL: Scott Foresman, 1991). Reviewed in: *Curriculum Review* 30, no.3 (Nov. 1990): 30

Scott Resources
Math in Brief, Manipulatives by Mary Cavanagh (Fort Collins, CO: Scott Resources, 1978). Reviewed in: *Arithmetic Teacher* 39, no.1 (Sept. 1991): 53

Scribner's
Animals of the Night, by Mary Banks and illustrated by Ronald Himler (New York: Scribner's, 1990). Reviewed in: *Day Care and Early Education* 19, no.4 (Summer 1992): 43

A Sea Full of Sharks
by Betty Maestro and illustrated by Guilio Maestro (New York: Scholastic, 1990). Reviewed in: *Language Arts* 69, no.4 (Apr. 1992): 299-300

Sea Squares
by Joy N. Hulme and illustrated by Carol Schwartz (Waltham, MA: Hyperion Books, 1991). Reviewed in: *Arithmetic Teacher* 40, no.1 (Sept. 1992): 56

Seeds and Seasons
Film/Video (Los Angeles: Churchill Films, 1987). Reviewed in: *Childhood Education* 68, no.1 (Fall 1991): 54

See How They Grow: Frog
by Kim Taylor (New York: Dutton, 1991). Reviewed in: *Childhood Education* 68, no.3 (Spring 1992): 178

Seeing in Special Ways: Children Living with Blindness
by Thomas Bergman (Milwaukee, WI: Gareth Stevens, 1989). Reviewed in: *Teaching Exceptional Children* 24, no.3 (Spring 1992): 83-84

Selsam, Millicent E.
A First Look at Ducks, Geese, and Swans, by Millicent E. Selsam and Joyce Hunt, and illustrated by Harriett Springer (New York: Walker, 1990). Reviewed in: *Language Arts* 68, no.6 (Oct. 1991): 493-494

Sendak, Maurice
I Saw Esau: The School Child's Pocket Book, by Iona and Peter Opie and illustrated by Maurice Sendak (n.p.: Candlewick, 1992). Reviewed in: *School Library Journal* 38, no.6 (June 1992): 110

The Sentence Master
Software (Winooski, VT: Laureate Learning Systems, n.d.). Reviewed in: *Computing Teacher* 18, no.4 (Dec. 1990/Jan. 1991): 50-51

Shadows and Reflections
by Barbara Taylor (New York: Watts, 1990). Reviewed in: *Science Books and Films* 27, no.1 (Jan./Feb. 1991): 17

Sham, Jean M.
Exploring Mathematics: Activities for Concept and Skill Development, K-3, by Jean M. Sham (Glenview, IL: Scott Foresman, 1990). Reviewed in: *Arithmetic Teacher* 38, no.1 (Sept. 1990): 46

Shapes
by Philip Yenawine (New York: Delacorte Press, n.d.). Reviewed in: *School Arts* 90, no.6 (Feb. 1991): 60-61

The Shapes Game
by Paul Rogers and illustrated by Sian Tucker (New York: Henry Holt, 1989). Reviewed in: *Arithmetic Teacher* 38, no.9 (May 1991): 45

Sheppard, Jeff
The Right Number of Elephants, by Jeff Sheppard (New York: HarperCollins, 1990). Reviewed in: *Arithmetic Teacher* 39, no.1 (Sept. 1991): 52

Sidewalk Sneakers
Software (Pleasantville, NY: Sunburst Communications, 1991). Reviewed in: *School Library Journal* 38, no.7 (July 1992): 38

Sierra, Judy
Multicultural Folktales: Stories To Tell Young Children, by Judy Sierra and Robert Kaminski (Phoenix, AZ: Oryx Press, 1991). Reviewed in: *Young Children* 47, no.2 (Jan. 1992): 71

Sierra Club (publisher)
Urban Roosts: Where Birds Nest in the City, by Barbara Bash (San Francisco: Sierra Club, 1990). Reviewed in: *Language Arts* 68, no.6 (Oct. 1991): 494

Sill, Catheryn
About Birds: A Guide for Children, by Catheryn Sill and illustrated by John Sill (Atlanta: Peachtree, 1991). Reviewed in: *School Library Journal* 38, no.2 (Feb. 1992): 84

Sill, John
About Birds: A Guide for Children, by Catheryn Sill and illustrated by John Sill (Atlanta: Peachtree, 1991). Reviewed in: *School Library Journal* 38, no.2 (Feb. 1992): 84

Silver Burdett
More Than Just a Garden, by Dwight Kuhn (Englewood Cliffs, NJ: Silver Burdett, 1990). Reviewed in: *Science and Children* 29, no.2 (Oct. 1991): 53

Silver Burdett (cont'd)
Problem Solving, Video (Atlanta, GA: Silver Burdett and Ginn, 1991). Reviewed in: *Arithmetic Teacher* 39, no.2 (Oct. 1991): 52-53

Simon, Norma
I Was So Mad! by Norma Simon and illustrated by Dora Leder (Morton Grove, IL: Whitman, 1992). Reviewed in: *Science Books and Films* 28, no.3 (Apr. 1992): 80

Simon, Seymour
Earthquakes, by Seymour Simon (New York: Morrow Junior Books, 1991). Reviewed in: *Language Arts* 69, no.2 (Feb. 1992): 138-139; *Reading Horizons* 32, no.1 (Oct. 1991): 79-80

Galaxies, by Seymour Simon (New York: Morrow Junior Books, 1991). Reviewed in: *Reading Horizons* 32, no.1 (Oct. 1991): 79-80

New Questions and Answers about Dinosaurs, by Seymour Simon and illustrated by Jennifer Dewey (New York: Morrow Junior Books, 1990). Reviewed in: *Language Arts* 68, no.6 (Oct. 1991): 492

Whales, by Seymour Simon (New York: Harper, 1989). Reviewed in: *Chilhood Education* 66, no.5 (Annual 1990): 338-339

Simon and Schuster
Doctor Zed's Science Surprises, by Gordon Penrose (New York: Simon and Schuster, 1990). Reviewed in: *Science Books and Films* 27, no.1 (Jan./Feb. 1991): 15

The Illustrated World of Space, by Iain Nicolson (New York: Simon and Schuster, 1991). Reviewed in: *Science Books and Films* 27, no.8 (Nov. 1991): 237

One Special Star, by Anita McFadzean and illustrated by Kate Jaspers (New York: Simon and Schuster, 1991). Reviewed in: *Arithmetic Teacher* 39, no.7 (Mar. 1992): 39

What Comes in Two's, Three's, and Fours, (New York: Simon and Schuster, 1990). Reviewed in: *Instructor* 102, no.2 (Sept. 1992): 80

The Wildlife 1-2-3: A Nature Counting Book, by Jan Thornhill (New York: Simon and Schuster Books for Young Readers, 1989). Reviewed in: *Arithmetic Teacher* 39, no.7 (Mar. 1992): 39

Simon and Schuster Education Group
LOGO Geometry, Software by Michael Battista and Douglas H. Clements (Morristown, NJ: Simon and Schuster Education Group, 1991). Reviewed in: *Arithmetic Teacher* 40, no.1 (Sept. 1992): 56

Sinclair, Tom
Earthwatching III: An Environmental Reader with Teacher's Guide, by Tom Sinclair (Madison, WI: Institute for Environmental Studies, 1990). Reviewed in: *Journal of Environmental Education* 22, no.1 (Fall 1990): 44; *Science Teacher* 58, no.7 (Oct. 1991): 74

Sis, Peter
Follow the Dream: The Story of Christopher Columbus, by Peter Sis (New York: Knopf, 1991). Reviewed in: *Childhood Education* 68, no.3 (Spring 1992): 178; *Language Arts* 69, no.3 (Mar. 1992): 216

Going Up!, by Peter Sis (New York: Greenwillow, 1989). Reviewed in: *Arithmetic Teacher* 38, no.2 (Oct. 1990): 52

Skip to My Lou
by Nadine Westcott (Boston: Little Brown, 1987). Reviewed in: *Reading Horizons* 32, no.1 (Oct. 1991): 75-77

Slippery Babies: Young Frogs, Toads, and Salamanders
by Ginny Johnson and Judy Cutchins (New York: Morrow Junior Books, 1991). Reviewed in: *School Science and Mathematics* 92, no.3 (Mar. 1992): 165

Sloat, Teri
From One to One Hundred, by Teri Sloat (New York: Dutton, 1991). Reviewed in: *Science Books and Films* 27, no.9 (Dec. 1991): 271-272

Small Business Press
The Paper Zebra and Other Paper Possibilities, Video (Dallas, TX: Small Business Press, n.d.). Reviewed in: *Arts and Activities* 110, no.2 (Oct. 1991): 20

Smith, William
Laughing Time: Collected Nonsense, by William Smith and illustrated by Jay F. Krahn (New York: Sunburst, 1990). Reviewed in: *Day Care and Early Education* 19, no.2 (Winter 1991): 36

Smoke Detectives
Video (Chicago: Smoke Detectives, 1990). Reviewed in: *Curriculum Review* 30, no.5 (Jan. 1991): 26-27

Social Issues Resources Series
The Listener, Video (Boca Raton, FL: Social Issues Resources Series, 1987). Reviewed in: *Music Educator's Journal* 77, no.7 (Mar. 1991): 52

Social skills
All about Anger, Video (Pleasantville, NY: Sunburst Communications, 1990). Reviewed in: *Science Books and Films* 28, no.2 (Mar. 1992): 56

Building Self-Esteem with Koala-Roo Can-Do, by Laura Fendel (Glenview, IL: Scott Foresman, 1989). Reviewed in: *Teaching Exceptional Children* 24, no.4 (Summer 1992): 83

Fighting the Invisible Enemy: Understanding the Effects of Conditioning, by Terrence Webster-Doyle and illustrated by Rod Cameron (Ojai, CA: Atrium, 1990). Reviewed in: *Young Children* 46, no.4 (May 1990): 66

Finding a Common Language: Children Living with Deafness, by Thomas Bergman (Milwaukee, WI: Gareth Stevens, 1989). Reviewed in: *Teaching Exceptional Children* 24, no.3 (Spring 1992): 83-84

I Was So Mad! by Norma Simon and illustrated by Dora Leder (Morton Grove, IL: Whitman, 1992). Reviewed in: *Science Books and Films* 28, no.3 (Apr. 1992): 80

Let's Be Friends, Video (Seattle, WA: Tickle Tune Typhoon, 1989). Reviewed in: *Young Children* 46, no.6 (Sept. 1991): 66

Let's Get a Move On! Video (n.p.: Kidvidz, 1990). Reviewed in: *School Library Journal* 37, no.1 (Jan. 1991): 54

My Brother Is Afraid of Just About Everything, Film/Video (North Hollywood, CA: Alfred Higgins Productions, 1990). Reviewed in: *Curriculum Review* 30, no.2 (Oct. 1990): 19

One Day at a Time: Children Living with Leukemia, by Thomas Bergman (Milwaukee, WI: Gareth Stevens, 1989). Reviewed in: *Teaching Exceptional Children* 24, no.3 (Spring 1992): 83-84

On Our Own Terms: Children Living with Physical Disabilities, by Thomas Bergman (Milwaukee, WI: Gareth Stevens, 1989). Reviewed in: *Teaching Exceptional Children* 24, no.3 (Spring 1992): 83-84

Seeing in Special Ways: Children Living with Blindness, by Thomas Bergman (Milwaukee, WI: Gareth Stevens, 1989). Reviewed in: *Teaching Exceptional Children* 24, no.3 (Spring 1992): 83-84

Think Aloud: Increasing Social and Cognitive Skills, by Bonnie Camp and Mary Ann S. Bash (Champaign, IL: Research Press, 1990). Reviewed in: *Science Books and Films* 27, no.2 (Mar. 1991): 45

Tug of War: Peace through Understanding Conflict, by Terrence Webster-Doyle and illustrated by Rod Cameron (Ojai, CA: Atrium, 1990). Reviewed in: *Young Children* 46, no.4 (May 1990): 66

The Value of Being a Friend, Film (North Hollywood, CA: Alfred Higgins Productions, 1990). Reviewed in: *Curriculum Review* 30, no.1 (Sept. 1990): 24

The Value of Teamwork, Film/Video (North Hollywood, CA: Alfred Higgins Productions, 1990). Reviewed in: *School Library Journal* 37, no.1 (Jan. 1991): 54-55

Software packages *(cont'd)*

Berenstain Bears: Learn about Counting, Software (San Francisco: Britannica Software, 1990). Reviewed in: *School Library Journal* 37, no.1 (Jan. 1991): 47

Big and Little, Software (Pleasantville, NY: Sunburst Communications, n.d.). Reviewed in: *Computing Teacher* 19, no.1 (Aug./Sept. 1991): 44-46; *Instructor* 100, no.5 (Jan. 1991): 119

Big Book Maker: Favorite Fairy Tales and Nursery Rhymes, Software (Farmington, CT: Pelican Software, 1989.) Reviewed in: *Instructor* 100, no.5 (Jan. 1991): 117

Birthday, Software (Pleasantville, NY: Sunburst Communications, 1991). Reviewed in: *Technology and Learning* 12, no.2 (Oct. 1991): 31

Capitals of the World (Version 1.5), Software by Keith Sutton (San Diego: K. Sutton, n.d.). Reviewed in: *Journal of Geography* 89, no.6 (Nov./Dec. 1990): 272

Clearwater Detectives, Software (Minneapolis, MN: MECC, 1991). Reviewed in: *Science and Children* 29, no.5 (Feb. 1992): 36-39

Clifford's Big Book Publisher, Software (Jefferson City, MO: Scholastic, 1990). Reviewed in: *Instructor* 100, no.5 (Jan. 1991): 117-118; *Electronic Learning* 10, no.8 (May/June 1991): 40

Communikeys, Software (Minneapolis, MN: MECC, 1989). Reviewed in: *Instructor* 101, no.7 (Mar. 1992): 66

Conceptual Music Games, Software by Thomas Gibson (n.p.: Temporal Acuity Products, Inc., 1991). Reviewed in: *American Music Teacher* 41, no.6 (June/July 1992): 10

Counters: An Action Approach to Counting and Arithmetic, Software (Scotts Valley, CA: Wings for Learning, 1990.) Reviewed in: *Arithmetic Teacher* 39, no.3 (nov. 1991): 56

Counting on Math, Manipulatives (Westminster, MD: Random House School Division, 1988). Reviewed in: *Arithmetic Teacher* 38, no.1 (Sept. 1990): 50

Designasaurus II, Software (San Francisco: Britannica Software, 1990). Reviewed in: *Science and Children* 29, no.1 (Sept. 1991): 59

Dyno-Quest, Software (Tucson, AZ: Mindplay/Methods and Solutions, 1984). Reviewed in: *Science and Children* 28, no.1 (Sept. 1990): 48

Easy Color Paint 1.1, Software (New Providence, NJ: Creative Software, n.d.). Reviewed in: *Computing Teacher* 18, no.7 (Apr. 1991): 45-47

Eco-Saurus, Software (Torrance, CA: First Byte, 1991). Reviewed in: *Instructor* 101, no.8 (Apr. 1992): 108-110

Explore-a-Classic: "Stone Soup", Software (Concord, MA: William Bradford, 1989). Reviewed in: *Instructor* 100, no.3 (Oct. 1990): 53

Explore-a-Classic: "The Three Little Pigs", Software (Concord, MA: William Bradford, 1989). Reviewed in: *Instructor* 100, no.3 (Oct. 1990): 53

Explore-a-Story: Where Did My Toothbrush Go?, Software (Acton, MA: D. C. Heath, 1988). Reviewed in: *Instructor* 100, no.6 (Feb. 1991): 115-116

Exploring Measurement, Time, and Money: Levels One and Two, Software (Atlanta, GA: IBM Educational Systems, 1989). Reviewed in: *Arithmetic Teacher* 38, no.2 (Oct. 1990): 44; *Electronic Learning* 10, no.7 (Apr. 1991): 36

Food Chains, Software (Galesburg, MI: MCE, n.d.). Reviewed in: *Science and Children* 29, no.2 (Oct. 1991): 46

Geo-Safari, Software (Dominguez Hills, CA: Educational Insights, n.d.). Reviewed in: *Journal of Geography* 91, no.1 (Jan./Feb. 1992): 49

Geometry Workshop, Grades 3-8, Software (Glenview, IL: Scott Foresman, 1991). Reviewed in: *Arithmetic Teacher* 39, no.8 (Apr. 1992): 58

Software packages *(cont'd)*

Magic Slate II (20 Column), Software (Pleasantville, NY: Sunburst Communications, n.d.). Reviewed in: *Childhood Education* 68, no.1 (Fall 1991): 56

Magic Slate: The Word Processor That Grows with You, Software (Pleasantville, NY: Sunburst Communications, n.d.). Reviewed in: *Gifted Child Today* 15, no.3 (May/June 1992): 53

Math Practice, Software (Cerritos, CA: Yhl Software, 1988). Reviewed in: *Arithmetic Teacher* 38, no.2 (Oct. 1990): 50

Math Shop Junior, Software by Cary Hammer (New York: Scholastic, 1989). Reviewed in: *Arithmetic Teacher* 38, no.1 (Sept. 1990): 44

Mickey's Crossword Puzzle Maker, Software (Burbank, CA: Walt Disney Computer Software, n.d.). Reviewed in: *Technology and Learning* 11, no.6 (Mar. 1991): 9

Microtype: The Wonderful World of Paws, Software (Cincinnati, OH: South-Western Publications, 1992). Reviewed in: *Instructor* 101, no.7 (Mar. 1992): 66

Money and Time Workshop - Grades K-2, Software (Glenview, IL: Scott Foresman, 1991). Reviewed in: *Electronic Learning* 10, no.7 (Apr. 1991): 36; *Arithmetic Teacher* 39, no.1 (Sept. 1991): 48

Mosaic Magic, Software (Encinitas, CA: Kinder Magic Software, 1990). Reviewed in: *Arithmetic Teacher* 39, no.1 (Sept. 1991): 48

The Munchters Talk about Food, Manipulatives (Chicago: National Livestock and Meat Board, 1990). Reviewed in: *Journal of Nutritional Education* 23, no.4 (July/Aug. 1991): 198

Muppet Labs, Software (Pleasantville, NY: Sunburst Communications, 1992). Reviewed in: *School Library Journal* 38, no.5 (May 1992): 61

Muppet Math, Software (Pleasantville, NY: Sunburst Communications, 1991). Reviewed in: *School Library Journal* 38, no.2 (Feb. 1992): 49-50

Muppet Slate, Software (Pleasantville, NY: Sunburst Communications, 1990). Reviewed in: *Gifted Child Today* 15, no.3 (May/June 1992): 53; *Instructor* 100, no.5 (Jan. 1991): 119

Musical Stairs - MIDI, Software by Steve Walker (n.p.: Electronic Courseware Systems, 1987). Reviewed in: *American Music Teacher* 40, no.3 (Dec. 1990/Jan. 1991): 10

Mutanoid Math Challenge, Software (Northridge, CA: Legacy Software, n.d.). Reviewed in: *Technology and Learning* 12, no.8 (May/June 1992): 11-12

Mystery Castle: Strategies for Problem Solving (Level One), Software (Acton, MA: William K. Bradford, 1990). Reviewed in: *Arithmetic Teacher* 39, no.3 (Nov. 1991): 57

New Math Blaster Plus, Software (Torrance, CA: Davidson and Associates, 1990). Reviewed in: *Instructor* 100, no.8 (April 1991): 74-75

New Print Shop, Software (San Rafael, CA: Broderbund Software, n.d.). Reviewed in: *Technology and Learning* 11, no.3 (Nov./Dec. 1990): 34

Nigel's World, Software (Galesburg, MI: Lawrence Productions, n.d.). Reviewed in: *Computing Teacher* 20, no.1 (Aug./Sept. 1992): 44-47

Number Maze: Decimals and Fractions, Software (Scotts Valley, CA: Greatwave Software, n.d.). Reviewed in: *Electronic Learning* 10, no.5 (Feb. 1991): 36-37; *Media and Methods* 27, no.5 (May/June 1991): 60

Numbervision: Addition/Subtraction System, Software (Lexington, OH: Numbervision, 1990). Reviewed in: *Arithmetic Teacher* 39, no.2 (Oct. 1991): 50

An Ocean of Air, Software (Galesburg, MI: MCE, n.d.). Reviewed in: *Science and Children* 29, no.2 (Oct. 1991): 47

Once upon a Time (Volume Three), Software (New Haven, CT: Compu-Teach, n.d.). Reviewed in: *Electronic Learning* 10, no.5 (Feb. 1991): 36-37

South-Western Publications
Microtype: The Wonderful World of Paws,
Software (Cincinnati, OH: South-Western
Publications, 1992). Reviewed in: *Instructor*
101, no.7 (Mar. 1992): 66

Space: A Three-Dimensional Journey
by Brian Jones and illustrated by Richard
Clifton-Dey (New York: Dial, 1991).
Reviewed in: *Day Care and Early Education*
19, no.4 (Summer 1992): 43

Special Writer Coach
Software (Cambridge, MA: Tom Snyder
Productions, n.d.). Reviewed in: *Computing
Teacher* 19, no.2 (Oct. 1991): 49-52

Spelling
Mickey's Crossword Puzzle Maker, Software
(Burbank, CA: Walt Disney Computer Soft-
ware, n.d.). Reviewed in: *Technology and
Learning* 11, no.6 (Mar. 1991): 9

Spelling Puzzles and Tests, Software (St.
Paul, MN: MECC, 1990). Reviewed in:
School Library Journal 37, no.3 (Mar.
1991): 142-144

Spelling Strategies You Can Teach, by Mary
Tarasoff (Victoria, Canada: M. V. Egan,
1990). Reviewed in: *Curriculum Review* 30,
no.3 (Nov. 1990): 27

Super Solvers Spellbound, Software
(Fremont, CA: Learning Company, 1991).
Reviewed in: *Technology and Learning* 12,
no.6 (Mar. 1992): 11-14

Spelling Puzzles and Tests
Software (St. Paul, MN: MECC, 1990).
Reviewed in: *School Library Journal* 37,
no.3 (Mar. 1991): 142-144

Spelling Strategies You Can Teach
by Mary Tarasoff (Victoria, Canada: M. V.
Egan, 1990). Reviewed in: *Curriculum Review* 30, no.3 (Nov. 1990): 27

Spider-Man: What To Do about Drugs
Video (n.p.: Learning Corporation of Amer-
ica, 1990). Reviewed in: *School Library
Journal* 37, no.1 (Jan. 1991): 53

*Spiderwebs to Skyscrapers: The Science of
Structures*
by David Darling (New York: Dillon, 1991).
Reviewed in: *School Library Journal* 38,
no.3 (Mar. 1992): 244

Spring
by Ron Hirschi (New York: Cobblehill,
1990). Reviewed in: *Science Books and
Films* 27, no.3 (Apr. 1991): 82

Spring Brings Changes
Video (Los Angeles: Churchill Films, 1991).
Reviewed in: *Science Books and Films* 28,
no.4 (May 1992): 119

Springer, Harriett
A First Look at Ducks, Geese, and Swans,
by Millicent E. Selsam and Joyce Hunt, and
illustrated by Harriett Springer (New York:
Walker, 1990). Reviewed in: *Language Arts*
68, no.6 (Oct. 1991): 493-494

Stage Fright Productions
Farm Animals, Video (Geneva, IL: Stage
Fright Productions, n.d.). Reviewed in: *Sci-
ence Books and Films* 27, no.7 (Oct. 1991): 217

Stajnko, Susan
*We Love MATHS: Four Imaginative Themes
for Early Primary Students,* by Anne Marell
and Susan Stajnko (Mount Waterly, Australia: Dellasta, 1990). Reviewed in: *Arithmetic Teacher* 39, no.1 (Sept. 1991): 53-54

Stangl, Jean
Gardening Fun, by Jean Stangl (Carthage,
IL: Fearon Teacher Aids, 1992). Reviewed
in: *Curriculum Review* 32, no.1 (Sept. 1992): 27

Stars and Planets
Software (Berkeley, CA: Advanced Ideas,
n.d.). Reviewed in: *Science and Children* 28,
no.7 (Apr. 1991): 53

Start Smart Books
Categories, by C. F. Navarro (Alexandria,
VA: Start Smart Books, 1990). Reviewed in:
Curriculum Review 30, no.3 (Nov. 1990):
25-26

Distinctions, by C. F. Navarro (Alexandria,
VA: Start Smart Books, 1990). Reviewed in:
Curriculum Review 30, no.3 (Nov. 1990):
25-26

Start Smart Books *(cont'd)*
  Early Geometry, by C. F. Navarro (Alexandria, VA: Start Smart Books, 1990). Reviewed in: *Curriculum Review* 30, no.3 (Nov. 1990): 25-26

  Verbal Correspond, by C. F. Navarro (Alexandria, VA: Start Smart Books, 1990). Reviewed in: *Curriculum Review* 30, no.3 (Nov. 1990): 25-26

Steck-Vaughn
  All about Birth and Growth, by Donna Bailey (Madison, NJ: Steck-Vaughn Library, 1991). Reviewed in: *Curriculum Review* 31, no.2 (Oct. 1991): 26-27

  All about Your Health and Blood, by Donna Bailey (Madison, NJ: Steck-Vaughn Library, 1991). Reviewed in: *Curriculum Review* 31, no.2 (Oct. 1991): 26-27

  All about Your Senses, by Donna Bailey (Madison, NJ: Steck-Vaughn Library, 1991). Reviewed in: *Curriculum Review* 31, no.2 (Oct. 1991): 26-27

  All about Your Skin, Hair, and Teeth, by Donna Bailey (Madison, NJ: Steck-Vaughn Library, 1991). Reviewed in: *Curriculum Review* 31, no.2 (Oct. 1991): 26-27

  Here We Live: Australia, by Donna Bailey (Austin, TX: Steck-Vaughn, 1990). Reviewed in: *Young Children* 46, no.1 (Nov. 1990): 66

  Here We Live: Greece, by Jenny Vaughn (Madison, NJ: Steck-Vaughn, 1990). Reviewed in: *Young Children* 46, no.1 (Nov. 1990): 66

  Here We Live: Hong Kong, by Donna Bailey (Austin, TX: Steck-Vaughn, 1990). Reviewed in: *Young Children* 46, no.1 (Nov. 1990): 66

  Here We Live: India, by Donna Bailey (Austin, TX: Steck-Vaughn, 1990). Reviewed in: *Young Children* 46, no.1 (Nov. 1990): 66

  Here We Live: Russia, by Jenny Vaughn (Madison, NJ: Steck-Vaughn, 1990). Reviewed in: *Young Children* 46, no.1 (Nov. 1990): 66

  Here We Live: Trinidad, by Donna Bailey (Austin, TX: Steck-Vaughn, 1990). Reviewed in: *Young Children* 46, no.1 (Nov. 1990): 66

  The Human Body, by Joan Gottlieb (Austin TX: Steck-Vaughn, 1990). Reviewed in: *Science Books and Films* 27, no.1 (Jan./Feb. 1991): 18

  Nomads and Cities, by Donna Bailey (Austin, TX: Steck-Vaughn, 1990). Reviewed in: *Young Children* 46, no.1 (Nov. 1990): 66

Sterling (publisher)
  Amazing Science Experiments with Everyday Materials, by Richard Churchill and illustrated by Frances Zweifel (New York: Sterling, 1991). Reviewed in: *Science Books and Films* 27, no.4 (May 1991): 113

  Creepy Crawlies: Ladybugs, Lobsters, and Other Amazing Arthropods, (New York: Sterling Publishing Co., 1991). Reviewed in: *Curriculum Review* 31, no.2 (Oct. 1991): 30

Stick and Score: The Good Food Game Manipulatives (St. Paul, MN: Stick and Score, 1990). Reviewed in: *Journal of Nutritional Education* 23, no.3 (May/June 1991): 142-143

Stieglitz, Ezra
  Tales for Thinking, by William J. Oehlkers and Ezra Stieglitz (North Billerica, MA: Curriculum Associates, 1991). Reviewed in: *Curriculum Review* 31, no.1 (Sept. 1991): 28

Stock, Catherine
  When the Woods Hum, by Joanne Ryder and illustrated by Catherine Stock (New York: Morrow Junior Books, 1990). Reviewed in: *Reading Horizons* 32, no.1 (Oct. 1991): 77-78; *School Science and Mathematics* 92, no.3 (Mar. 1992): 165

Stories
  Aesop's Fables, Video (Los Angeles: Churchill Films, 1991). Reviewed in: *School Library Journal* 38, no.1 (Jan. 1992): 70

  Animal Fables from Aesop (Boston: Godine, 1989). Reviewed in: *School Library Journal* 38, no.1 (Jan. 1992): 101

Sunburst Communications *(cont'd)*
 PlayWrite, Software (Pleasantville, NY: Sunburst Communications, 1991). Reviewed in: *Electronic Learning* 10, no.8 (May/June 1991): 40

 PODD, Software (Pleasantville, NY: Sunburst Communications, n.d.). Reviewed in: *Computing Teacher* 18, no.3 (Nov. 1990): 46-47; *Technology and Learning* 11, no.8 (May/June 1991): 6

 Sidewalk Sneakers, Software (Pleasantville, NY: Sunburst Communications, 1991). Reviewed in: *School Library Journal* 38, no.7 (July 1992): 38

 You Can Say No and Mean It, Video (Pleasantville, NY: Sunburst Communications, 1990). Reviewed in: *Science Books and Films* 28, no.2 (Mar. 1992): 56

Super Solvers Spellbound
 Software (Fremont, CA: Learning Company, 1991). Reviewed in: *Technology and Learning* 12, no.6 (Mar. 1992): 11-14

Super, Super Superwords
 by Bruce McMillan (New York: Lothrop, Lee and Shepard, 1989). Reviewed in: *Arithmetic Teacher* 38, no.2 (Oct. 1990): 52

Supplementary materials
 Funny Money, Game (Baltimore, MD: LML, 1986). Reviewed in: *Arithmetic Teacher* 38, no.1 (Sept. 1990): 52

 Math Smart, Game (Rochester, MN: GO Company of Rochester, 1987). Reviewed in: *Arithmetic Teacher* 38, no.1 (Sept. 1990): 52

Survival: Could You Be a Frog?
 by John Norris Wood (Nashville, TN: Ideals, 1990). Reviewed in: *Science Books and Films* 27, no.3 (Apr. 1991): 84

Survival: Could You Be a Mouse?
 by John Norris Wood (Nashville, TN: Ideals, 1990). Reviewed in: *Science Books and Films* 27, no.3 (Apr. 1991): 84

Sutton, Keith
 Capitals of the World (Version 1.5), Software by Keith Sutton (San Diego: K. Sutton, n.d.). Reviewed in: *Journal of Geography* 89, no.6 (Nov./Dec. 1990): 272

SVE (publisher)
 Lollipop Dragon, Multimedia by Margo Turner (Chicago: SVE, 1989). Reviewed in: *Arithmetic Teacher* 38, no.3 (Nov. 1990): 47

 Max's Library: Beginning To Write, Video (Chicago: SVE, 1991). Reviewed in: *School Library Journal* 37, no.9 (Sept. 1991): 212-213

TAB (publisher)
 Physics for Kids: 49 Easy Experiments with Acoustics, by Robert W. Wood (Blue Ridge Summit, PA: TAB, 1990). Reviewed in: *Science Books and Films* 27, no.3 (Apr. 1991): 80

 Physics for Kids: 49 Easy Experiments with Electricity and Magnetism, by Robert W. Wood (Blue Ridge Summit, PA: TAB, 1990). Reviewed in: *Science Books and Films* 27, no.3 (Apr. 1991): 80

 Physics for Kids: 49 Easy Experiments with Optics, by Robert W. Wood (Blue Ridge Summit, PA: TAB, 1990). Reviewed in: *Science Books and Films* 27, no.3 (Apr. 1991): 80

 Science for Kids: 39 Easy Animal Biology Experiments, by Robert W. Wood (Blue Ridge Summit, PA: TAB, 1991). Reviewed in: *Science and Children* 29, no.8 (May 1992): 36

 Science for Kids: 39 Easy Chemistry Experiments, by Robert W. Wood (Blue Ridge Summit, PA: TAB, 1991). Reviewed in: *Science and Children* 29, no.8 (May 1992): 36

 Science for Kids: 39 Easy Meteorology Experiments, by Robert W. Wood (Blue Ridge Summit, PA: TAB, 1991). Reviewed in: *Science and Children* 29, no.8 (May 1992): 36

Tales for Thinking
 by William J. Oehlkers and Ezra Stieglitz (North Billerica, MA: Curriculum Associates, 1991). Reviewed in: *Curriculum Review* 31, no.1 (Sept. 1991): 28

Talking Addition and Subtraction
 Software (Pound Ridge, NY: Orange Cherry Software, 1989). Reviewed in: *Arithmetic Teacher* 38, no.7 (Mar. 1991): 56-57

Teaching Resources (publisher)
MathMats: Hands-on Activities for Young Children - Set Two, Manipulatives by Carol A. Thornton and Judith K. Wells (Allen, TX: Teaching Resources, 1990). Reviewed in: *Arithmetic Teacher* 39, no.7 (Mar. 1992): 44

Tell Someone
Video (n.p.: Landmark Films, 1987). Reviewed in: *School Library Journal* 37, no.1 (Jan. 1991): 53

Temperature and You
by Betsy Maestro and illustrated by Guilio Maestro (New York: Lodestar, 1990). Reviewed in: *School Library Journal* 37, no.2 (Feb. 1991): 84

Temporal Acuity Products
Conceptual Music Games, Software by Thomas Gibson (n.p.: Temporal Acuity Products, Inc., 1991). Reviewed in: *American Music Teacher* 41, no.6 (June/July 1992): 10

Pick the Pitch, Software by Brian R. Moore (n.p.: Temporal Acuity Products, 1988). Reviewed in: *American Music Teacher* 40, no.4 (Feb./Mar. 1991): 10

Ten Little Rabbits
by Virginia Grossman and illustrated by Sylvia Long (San Francisco: Chronicle Books, 1991). Reviewed in: *Arithmetic Teacher* 40, no.1 (Sept. 1992): 56-57

There's a Hole in the Bucket
by Nadine Bernard Westcott (New York: Harper and Row, 1990). Reviewed in: *Language Arts* 68, no.3 (Mar. 1991): 243

Think Aloud: Increasing Social and Cognitive Skills
by Bonnie Camp and Mary Ann S. Bash (Champaign, IL: Research Press, 1990). Reviewed in: *Science Books and Films* 27, no.2 (Mar. 1991): 45

Thinker Math: Developing Number Sense and Arithmetic Skills (Grades 3-4)
by Carole Greenes, Linda Schulman, and Rika Spungin (Allen, TX: DLM, n.d.). Reviewed in: *Arithmetic Teacher* 38, no.2 (Oct. 1990): 54

Thomas Y. Crowell (publisher)
How We Learned the Earth Is Round, by Patricia Lauber and illustrated by Megan Lloyd (n.p.: Thomas Y. Crowell, 1990). Reviewed in: *Language Arts* 68, no.2 (Feb. 1991): 146

Thomasson Grant (publisher)
Come Look with Me: Enjoying Art with Children, by Gladys S. Blizzard (Charlottsville, VA: Thomasson Grant, 1990). Reviewed in: *School Arts* 91. no.7 (Mar. 1992): 50

Thomson, Ruth
Indians of the Plains, by Ruth Thomson (New York: Watts, 1991). Reviewed in: *School Library Journal* 38, no.2 (Feb. 1992): 105-106

Thornhill, Jan
The Wildlife 1-2-3: A Nature Counting Book, by Jan Thornhill (New York: Simon and Schuster Books for Young Readers, 1989). Reviewed in: *Arithmetic Teacher* 39, no.7 (Mar. 1992): 39

Thornton, Carol A.
MathMats: Hands-on Activities for Young Children - Set Two, Manipulatives by Carol A. Thornton and Judith K. Wells (Allen, TX: Teaching Resources, 1990). Reviewed in: *Arithmetic Teacher* 39, no.7 (Mar. 1992): 44

On the Button in Math: Activities for Young Children, by Carol A. Thornton and Judith K. Wells (Allen, TX: DLM Teaching Resources, 1990). Reviewed in: *Arithmetic Teacher* 38, no.9 (May 1991): 46

Thumbs up for Kids: AIDS Education
Film/Video (Purchase, NY: Media Express, 1989). Reviewed in: *Day Care and Early Education* 18, no.1 (Fall 1990): 42

Tickle Tune Typhoon (publisher)
Let's Be Friends, Video (Seattle, WA: Tickle Tune Typhoon, 1989). Reviewed in: *Young Children* 46, no.6 (Sept. 1991): 66

Timeliner
Software (Cambridge, MA: Tom Snyder Productions, 1986). Reviewed in: *Instructor* 100, no.4 (Nov./Dec. 1990): 82

Ur, Penny
Grammar Practice Activities: A Practical Guide for Teachers, by Penny Ur (Cambridge, UK: Cambridge University Press, 1986). Reviewed in: *TESL Canada Journal* 8, no.1 (Nov. 1990): 114-116

Urban Roosts: Where Birds Nest in the City by Barbara Bash (San Francisco: Sierra Club, 1990). Reviewed in: *Language Arts* 68, no.6 (Oct. 1991): 494

Urie, Grant
GrowLab: Activities for Growing Minds, by Joy Cohen and Eve Pranis, and illustrated by Grant Urie (Burlington, VT: National Gardening Association, 1990). Reviewed in: *Science Books and Films* 27, no.2 (Mar. 1991): 49

Vaes, Alain
Puss in Boots, by Charles Perrault and illustrated by Alain Vaes (Boston: Little Brown, 1992). Reviewed in: *School Library Journal* 38, no.4 (Apr. 1992): 108-109

The Value of Being a Friend
Film (North Hollywood, CA: Alfred Higgins Productions, 1990). Reviewed in: *Curriculum Review* 30, no.1 (Sept. 1990): 24

The Value of Teamwork
Film/Video (North Hollywood, CA: Alfred Higgins Productions, 1990). Reviewed in: *School Library Journal* 37, no.1 (Jan. 1991): 54-55

The Value of Telling the Truth
Film (North Hollywood, CA: Alfred Higgins Productions, 1990). Reviewed in: *Curriculum Review* 30, no.1 (Sept. 1990): 24

Van Allsburg, Chris
The Z Was Zapped, by Chris Van Allsburg (Boston: Houghton Mifflin, 1987). Reviewed in: *Gifted Child Today* 15, no.1 (Jan./Feb. 1992): 59

Van Cleave, Janice
Earth Science for Every Kid: 101 Experiments That Really Work, by Janice Van Cleave (New York: John Wiley and Sons, 1991). Reviewed in: *Journal of Geography* 91, no.1 (Jan./Feb. 1992): 46

Van Rynback, Iris
Once inside the Library, by Barbara A. Huff and illustrated by Iris Van Rynback (Boston: Little Brown, 1990). Reviewed in: *Science Books and Films* 27, no.2 (Mar. 1991): 45

Vaughn, Jenny
Here We Live: Russia, by Jenny Vaughn (Madison, NJ: Steck-Vaughn, 1990). Reviewed in: *Young Children* 46, no.1 (Nov. 1990): 66

Ventura Educational Systems
Hands-on Math: Volumes One and Two, Software (Newbury Park, CA: Ventura Educational Systems, 1988). Reviewed in: *Arithmetic Teacher* 38, no.2 (Oct. 1990): 46-48; *Instructor* 100, no.8 (Apr. 1991): 74

Verbal Correspond
by C. F. Navarro (Alexandria, VA: Start Smart Books, 1990). Reviewed in: *Curriculum Review* 30, no.3 (Nov. 1990):

Viking (publisher)
In My Mother's House, by Ann Nolan Clark and illustrated by Velino Herrara (New York: Viking, 1991). Reviewed in: *Day Care and Early Education* 19, no.2 (Winter 1991): 36

The Restless Earth, by Francois Michel and Yves Lavor (New York: Viking, 1990). Reviewed in: *Language Arts* 68, no.6 (Oct. 1991): 494-495

Viking Kestrel (publisher)
Let's Pretend: Poems of Flight and Fancy, edited by Natalie S. Bober and illustrated by Bob Bell (New York: Viking Kestrel, 1986). Reviewed in: *Day Care and Early Education* 19, no.2 (Winter 1991): 35

Vocabulary
A Cache of Jewels, by Ruth Heller (New York: Putnam, 1989). Reviewed in: *Gifted Child Today* 15, no.1 (Jan./Feb. 1992): 58

Walker, Steve
Musical Stairs - MIDI, Software by Steve Walker (n.p.: Electronic Courseware Systems, 1987). Reviewed in: *American Music Teacher* 40, no.3 (Dec. 1990/Jan. 1991): 10

Webster-Doyle, Terrence *(cont'd)*
Tug of War: Peace through Understanding Conflict, by Terrence Webster-Doyle and illustrated by Rod Cameron (Ojai, CA: Atrium, 1990). Reviewed in: *Young Children* 46, no.4 (May 1990): 66

We Laugh, We Love, We Cry: Children Living with Mental Retardation
by Thomas Bergman (Milwaukee, WI: Gareth Stevens, 1989). Reviewed in: *Teaching Exceptional Children* 24, no.3 (Spring 1992): 83-84

Wellnitz, William R.
Science Magic For Kids: 68 Simple and Safe Experiments, by William R. Wellnitz (n.p.: 1990). Reviewed in: *Science and Children* 29, no.6 (Mar. 1992): 55

Wells, Judith K.
MathMats: Hands-on Activities for Young Children - Set Two, Manipulatives by Carol A. Thornton and Judith K. Wells (Allen, TX: Teaching Resources, 1990). Reviewed in: *Arithmetic Teacher* 39, no.7 (Mar. 1992): 44

On the Button in Math: Activities for Young Children, by Carol A. Thornton and Judith K. Wells (Allen, TX: DLM Teaching Resources, 1990). Reviewed in: *Arithmetic Teacher* 38, no.9 (May 1991): 46

We Love MATHS: Four Imaginative Themes for Early Primary Students
by Anne Marell and Susan Stajnko (Mount Waterly, Australia: Dellasta, 1990). Reviewed in: *Arithmetic Teacher* 39, no.1 (Sept. 1991): 53-54

Wesley (publisher)
Weatherwatch, by Valerie Wyatt (Reading, MA: Wesley, 1990). Reviewed in: *Curriculum Review* 30, no.5 (Jan. 1991): 30

Westcott, Nadine
Down by the Bay, by Raffi and illustrated by Nadine Westcott (New York: Crown, 1987). Reviewed in: *Reading Horizons* 32, no.1 (Oct. 1991): 75-77

The Lady with the Alligator Purse, by Nadine Westcott (Boston: Little Brown, 1989). Reviewed in: *Reading Horizons* 32, no.1 (Oct. 1991): 75-77

Skip to My Lou, by Nadine Westcott (Boston: Little Brown, 1987). Reviewed in: *Reading Horizons* 32, no.1 (Oct. 1991): 75-77

There's a Hole in the Bucket, by Nadine Bernard Westcott (New York: Harper and Row, 1990). Reviewed in: *Language Arts* 68, no.3 (Mar. 1991): 243

Weston, Martha
The One-Dollar Word Riddle Book, by Marilyn Burns and illustrated by Martha Weston (New Rochelle, NY: Cuisenaire, 1990). Reviewed in: *Arithmetic Teacher* 39, no.2 (Oct. 1991): 51-52

Weston Woods (publisher)
Danny and the Dinosaur, Video (Weston, CT: Weston Woods, 1990). Reviewed in: *School Library Journal* 37, no.2 (Feb. 1991): 53

The Happy Lion, Video (Weston, CT: Weston Woods, 1991). Reviewed in: *School Library Journal* 37, no.1 (Jan. 1991): 56-57

Madeline and the Bad Hat, Video (Weston, CT: Weston Woods, 1991). Reviewed in: *School Library Journal* 37, no.3 (Mar. 1991): 150

Wetlands
Software (Warren, NJ: Optical Data, n.d.). Reviewed in: *Science and Children* 29, no.7 (Apr. 1992): 40-41

Wexler, Jerome
Pet Gerbils, by Jerome Wexler (Morton Grove, IL: Albert Whitman, 1990). Reviewed in: *Science and Children* 29, no.6 (Mar. 1992): 55

Whales
by Seymour Simon (New York: Harper, 1989). Reviewed in: *Chilhood Education* 66, no.5 (Annual 1990): 338-339

What Comes in Twos, Threes, and Fours
(New York: Simon and Schuster, 1990). Reviewed in: *Instructor* 102, no.2 (Sept. 1992): 80

What Does It Cost?
Film (Washington, DC: National Geographic Society, 1989). Reviewed in: *Arithmetic Teacher* 38, no.4 (Dec. 1990): 61

The Wildlife 1-2-3: A Nature Counting Book
by Jan Thornhill (New York: Simon and
Schuster Books for Young Readers, 1989).
Reviewed in: *Arithmetic Teacher* 39, no.7
(Mar. 1992): 39

Wild Places: Rocky Mountain Meadow
Film/Video (Deerfield, IL: Coronet/MTI
Film and Video, 1990). Reviewed in: *School
Library Journal* 37, no.1 (Jan. 1991): 59

Wiley and Sons
Earth Science for Every Kid: 101 Experi-
ments That Really Work, by Janice Van
Cleave (New York: Wiley and Sons, 1991).
Reviewed in: *Journal of Geography* 91, no.1
(Jan./Feb. 1992): 46

Wilkes, Angela
My First Green Book: A Life-Size Guide to
Caring for Our Environment, by Angela
Wilkes (New York: Random House, 1991).
Reviewed in: *Curriculum Review* 32, no.1
(Sept. 1992): 28-29

My First Science Book, by Angela Wilkes
(New York: Knopf, 1990). Reviewed in:
Science Books and Films 27, no. 2 (Mar.
1991): 47

William Bradford (publisher)
Explore-a-Classic: "Stone Soup", Software
(Concord, MA: William Bradford, 1989).
Reviewed in: *Instructor* 100, no.3 (Oct.
1990): 53

Explore-a-Classic: "The Three Little Pigs",
Software (Concord, MA: William Bradford,
1989). Reviewed in: *Instructor* 100, no.3
(Oct. 1990): 53

Explore-a-Classic: "The Princess and the
Pea", Software (Concord, MA: William
Bradford, 1989). Reviewed in: *Instructor*
100, no.3 (Oct. 1990): 53

Mystery Castle: Strategies for Problem
Solving (Level One), Software (Acton, MA:
William K. Bradford, 1990). Reviewed in:
Arithmetic Teacher 39, no.3 (Nov. 1991): 57

Will We Miss Them? Endangered Species
by Alexandra Wright and illustrated by
Marshall Peck (Watertown, MA:
Charlesbridge, 1992). Reviewed in: *Science
Books and Films* 28, no.1 (Jan./Feb. 1992): 19

Willy Can Count
by Anne Rockwell (New York: Arcade,
1989). Reviewed in: *Arithmetic Teacher* 38,
no.2 (Oct. 1990): 53

Wilson, April
Look! The Ultimate Spot the Difference
Book, illustrated by April Wilson (New
York: Dial Books for Young Readers, 1990).
Reviewed in: *Language Arts* 68, no.6 (Oct.
1991): 493; *Young Children* 47, no.3 (Feb.
1992): 75

Wilson, Forrest
What It Feels Like To Be a Building, by
Forrest Wilson (Washington, DC: Preserva-
tion Press, 1988). Reviewed in: *Gifted Child
Today* 15, no.1 (Jan./Feb. 1992): 57-58

Windows on Science (Spanish Edition)
Software (Warren, NJ: Optical Data, n.d.).
Reviewed in: *Computing Teacher* 18, no.4
(Dec. 1990/Jan. 1991): 53

Wings for Learning
Counters: An Action Approach to Counting
and Arithmetic, Software (Scotts Valley, CA:
Wings for Learning, 1990). Reviewed in:
Arithmetic Teacher 39, no.3 (Nov. 1991): 56

Learn about Plants, Software (Scotts Valley,
CA: Wings for Learning, n.d.). Reviewed in:
Computing Teacher 18, no.8 (May 1991):
41-45

Winslow Press
Colorcards, Manipulatives (Bicester, UK:
Winslow Press, 1989). Reviewed in: *Child
Language Teaching and Therapy* 7, no.3
(Oct. 1991): 361-362

Winter
by Ron Hirschi (New York: Cobblehill,
1990). Reviewed in: *Science Books and
Films* 27, no.3 (Apr. 1991): 82

Winter, Jeanette
Eight Hands Round: A Patchwork Alphabet, by Ann Whitford Paul and illustrated by Jeanette Winter (New York: HarperCollins, 1991). Reviewed in: *Childhood Education* 68, no.1 (Fall 1991): 46; *Language Arts* 69, no.3 (Mar. 1992): 217

Wolves
by R. D. Lawrence (Boston: Little Brown, 1990). Reviewed in: *Language Arts* 69, no.4 (Apr. 1992): 301

Wood, Audrey
Into the Napping House, by Audrey Wood and illustrated by Don Wood (San Diego: Harcourt Brace Jovanovich, 1990). Reviewed in: *Music Educator's Journal* 77, no.3 (Nov. 1990): 19

Wood, Don
Into the Napping House, by Audrey Wood and illustrated by Don Wood (San Diego: Harcourt Brace Jovanovich, 1990). Reviewed in: *Music Educator's Journal* 77, no.3 (Nov. 1990): 19

Wood, John Norris
Survival: Could You Be a Mouse? by John Norris Wood (Nashville, TN: Ideals, 1990). Reviewed in: *Science Books and Films* 27, no.3 (Apr. 1991): 84

Survival: Could You Be a Frog? by John Norris Wood (Nashville, TN: Ideals, 1990). Reviewed in: *Science Books and Films* 27, no.3 (Apr. 1991): 84

Wood, Robert W.
Science for Kids: 39 Easy Meteorology Experiments, by Robert W. Wood (Blue Ridge Summit, PA: TAB, 1991). Reviewed in: *Science and Children* 29, no.8 (May 1992): 36

Physics for Kids: 49 Easy Experiments with Electricity and Magnetism, by Robert W. Wood (Blue Ridge Summit, PA: TAB, 1990). Reviewed in: *Science Books and Films* 27, no.3 (Apr. 1991): 80

Physics for Kids: 49 Easy Experiments with Optics, by Robert W. Wood (Blue Ridge Summit, PA: TAB, 1990). Reviewed in: *Science Books and Films* 27, no.3 (Apr. 1991): 80

Science for Kids: 39 Easy Animal Biology Experiments, by Robert W. Wood (Blue Ridge Summit, PA: TAB, 1991). Reviewed in: *Science and Children* 29, no.8 (May 1992): 36

Physics for Kids: 49 Easy Experiments with Acoustics, by Robert W. Wood (Blue Ridge Summit, PA: TAB, 1990). Reviewed in: *Science Books and Films* 27, no.3 (Apr. 1991): 80

Science for Kids: 39 Easy Chemistry Experiments, by Robert W. Wood (Blue Ridge Summit, PA: TAB, 1991). Reviewed in: *Science and Children* 29, no.8 (May 1992): 36

Woody's Twenty Grow-Big Songs
by Woody Guthrie (New York: HarperCollins, 1992). Reviewed in: *School Library Journal* 38, no.7 (July 1992): 68

Woolly Bounce
Software (Minneapolis, MN: MECC, 1991). Reviewed in: *Science and Children* 29, no.4 (Jan. 1992): 34

Workman (publisher)
My First Computer Book, Multimedia by David Schiller and David Rosenbloom, and illustrated by Tedd Arnold (New York: Workman, 1991). Reviewed in: *School Arts* 91, no.5 (Jan. 1992): 44

The World of Reading
Software (n.p.: Queue, 1989). Reviewed in: *Curriculum Review* 30, no.4 (Dec. 1990): 28

Wright, Alexandra
Will We Miss Them? Endangered Species, by Alexandra Wright and illustrated by Marshall Peck (Watertown, MA: Charlesbridge, 1992). Reviewed in: *Science Books and Films* 28, no.1 (Jan./Feb. 1992): 19

Writing activities

Big Book Maker: Favorite Fairy Tales and Nursery Rhymes, Software (Farmington, CT: Pelican Software, 1989). Reviewed in: *Instructor* 100, no.5 (Jan. 1991): 117

Clifford's Big Book Publisher, Software (Jefferson City, MO: Scholastic, 1990). Reviewed in: *Instructor* 100, no.5 (Jan. 1991): 117-118; *Electronic Learning* 10, no.8 (May/June 1991): 40

Explore-a-Story: Where Did My Toothbrush Go?, Software (Acton, MA: D. C. Heath, 1988). Reviewed in: *Instructor* 100, no.6 (Feb. 1991): 115-116

The Writing Center - School Edition Software (Fremont, CA: Learning Company, n.d.). Reviewed in: *Technology and Learning* 12, no.3 (Nov./Dec. 1991): 9

Writing skills

Be a Better Writer, Software (Pleasantville, NY: Sunburst Communications, n.d.). Reviewed in: *Gifted Child Today* 15, no.3 (May/June 1992): 53

I Can Write, Software (Pleasantville, NY: Sunburst Communications, n.d.). Reviewed in: *Gifted Child Today* 15, no.3 (May/June 1992): 53

Magic Slate: The Word Processor That Grows with You, Software (Pleasantville, NY: Sunburst Communications, n.d.). Reviewed in: *Gifted Child Today* 15, no.3 (May/June 1992): 53

Magic Slate II (20 Column), Software (Pleasantville, NY: Sunburst Communications, n.d.). Reviewed in: *Childhood Education* 68, no.1 (Fall 1991): 56

Max's Library: Beginning To Write, Video (Chicago: SVE, 1991). Reviewed in: *School Library Journal* 37, no.9 (Sept. 1991): 212-213

Muppet Slate, Software (Pleasantville, NY: Sunburst Communications, 1990). Reviewed in: *Gifted Child Today* 15, no.3 (May/June 1992): 53; *Instructor* 100, no.5 (Jan. 1991): 119

PlayWrite, Software (Pleasantville, NY: Sunburst Communications, 1991). Reviewed in: *Electronic Learning* 10, no.8 (May/June 1991): 40; *Technology and Learning* 11, no.8 (May/June 1991): 6

PODD, Software (Pleasantville, NY: Sunburst Communications, n.d.). Reviewed in: *Computing Teacher* 18, no.3 (Nov. 1990): 46-47

Reader Rabbit 2, Software (Fremont, CA: Learning Company, n.d.). Reviewed in: *Technology and Learning* 12, no.7 (Apr. 1992): 7-10

Reader's Quest, Software (Hood River, OR: Humanities Software, 1991). Reviewed in: *Electronic Learning* 10, no.8 (May/June 1991): 40

Special Writer Coach, Software (Cambridge, MA: Tom Snyder Productions, n.d.). Reviewed in: *Computing Teacher* 19, no.2 (Oct. 1991): 49-52

The Writing Center - School Edition, Software (Fremont, CA: Learning Company, n.d.). Reviewed in: *Technology and Learning* Social Skills 12, no.3 (Nov./Dec. 1991): 9

You Can Say No and Mean It, Video (Pleasantville, NY: Sunburst Communications, 1990). Reviewed in: *Science Books and Films* 28, no.2 (Mar. 1992): 56

Wyatt, Valerie
Weatherwatch, by Valerie Wyatt (Reading, MA: Wesley, 1990). Reviewed in: *Curriculum Review* 30, no.5 (Jan. 1991): 30

Yenawine, Philip
Colors, by Philip Yenawine (New York: Delacorte Press, n.d.). Reviewed in: *School Arts* 90, no.6 (Feb. 1991): 60-61

Lines, by Philip Yenawine (New York: Delacorte Press, n.d.). Reviewed in: *School Arts* 90, no.6 (Feb. 1991): 60-61

Shapes, by Philip Yenawine (New York: Delacorte Press, n.d.). Reviewed in: *School Arts* 90, no.6 (Feb. 1991): 60-61

KRAUS CURRICULUM
DEVELOPMENT LIBRARY CUSTOMERS

T HE following list shows the current subscribers to the Kraus Curriculum Development Library (KCDL), Kraus's annual program of curriculum guides on microfiche. Customers marked with an asterisk (*) do not currently have standing orders to KCDL, but do have recent editions of the program. This information is provided for readers who want to use KCDL for models of curriculum in particular subject areas or grade levels.

Alabama

Auburn University
Ralph Brown Draughton Library/Serials
Mell Street
Auburn University, AL 36849

Jacksonville State University
Houston Cole Library/Serials
Jacksonville, AL 36265

University of Alabama at Birmingham
Mervyn H. Sterne Library
University Station
Birmingham, AL 35294

*University of Alabama at Tuscaloosa
University Libraries
204 Capstone Drive
Tuscaloosa, AL 35487-0266

Alaska

*University of Alaska—Anchorage
Library
3211 Providence Drive
Anchorage, AK 99508

Arizona

Arizona State University, Phoenix
Fletcher Library/Journals
West Campus
4701 West Thunderbird Road
Phoenix, AZ 85069-7100

Arizona State University, Tempe
Library/Serials
Tempe, AZ 85287-0106

Northern Arizona University
University Library
Flagstaff, AZ 86011

University of Arizona
Library/Serials
Tuson, AZ 85721

Arkansas

Arkansas State University
Dean B. Ellis Library
State University, AR 72467

Southern Arkansas University
The Curriculum Center
SAU Box 1389
Magnolia, AR 71753

*University of Arkansas at Monticello
Library
Highway 425 South
Monticello, AR 71656

University of Central Arkansas
The Center for Teaching & Human
Development
Box H, Room 104
Conway, AR 72032

California

California Polytechnic State University
Library/Serials
San Luis Obispo, CA 93407

California State Polytechnic University
Library/Serials
3801 West Temple Avenue
Pomona, CA 91768

California State University at Chico
Meriam Library
Chico, CA 95929-0295

*California State University, Dominguez Hills
Library
800 East Victoria Street
Carson, CA 90747

California State University at Fresno
Henry Madden Library/Curriculum Department
Fresno, CA 93740

California State University at Fresno
College of the Sequoia Center
5241 North Maple, Mail Stop 106
Fresno, CA 93740

California State University at Fullerton
Library Serials BIC
Fullerton, CA 92634

California State University at Long Beach
Library/Serials Department
1250 Bellflower Boulevard
Long Beach, CA 90840

*California State University at Sacramento
Library
2000 Jed Smith Drive
Sacramento, CA 95819

California State University, Stanislaus
Library
801 West Monte Vista Avenue
Turlock, CA 95380

*La Sierra University
Library
Riverside, CA 92515

Los Angeles County Education Center
Professional Reference Center
9300 East Imperial Highway
Downey, CA 90242

National University
Library
4007 Camino del Rio South
San Diego, CA 92108

San Diego County Office of Education
Research and Reference Center
6401 Linda Vista Road
San Diego, CA 92111-7399

San Diego State University
Library/Serials
San Diego, CA 92182-0511

*San Francisco State University
J. Paul Leonard Library
1630 Holloway Avenue
San Francisco, CA 94132

San Jose State University
Clark Library, Media Department
San Jose, CA 95192-0028

*Stanford University
Cubberly Library
School of Education
Stanford, CA 94305

*University of California at Santa Cruz
Library
Santa Cruz, CA 95064

Colorado

Adams State College
Library
Alamosa, CO 81102

University of Northern Colorado
Michener Library
Greeley, CO 80639

Connecticut

*Central Connecticut State University
Burritt Library
1615 Stanley Street
New Britain, CT 06050

District of Columbia

The American University
Library
Washington, DC 20016-8046

*United States Department of Education/OERI
Room 101
555 New Jersey Avenue, N.W., C.P.
Washington, DC 20202-5731

*University of the District of Columbia
Learning Resource Center
11100 Harvard Street, N.W.
Washington, DC 20009

Florida

*Florida Atlantic University
Library/Serials
Boca Raton, FL 33431-0992

Florida International University
Library/Serials
Bay Vista Campus
North Miami, FL 33181

Florida International University
Library/Serials
University Park
Miami, FL 33199

Marion County School Board
Professional Library
406 S.E. Alvarez Avenue
Ocala, FL 32671-2285

*University of Central Florida
Library
Orlando, FL 32816-0666

University of Florida
Smathers Library/Serials
Gainesville, FL 32611-2047

*University of North Florida
Library
4567 St. Johns Bluff Road South
Jacksonville, FL 32216

*University of South Florida
Library/University Media Center
4202 Fowler Avenue
Tampa, FL 33620

University of West Florida
John C. Pace Library/Serials
11000 University Parkway
Pensacola, FL 32514

Georgia

*Albany State College
Margaret Rood Hazard Library
Albany, GA 31705

Atlanta University Center in Georgia
Robert W. Woodruff Library
111 James P. Brawley Drive
Atlanta, GA 30314

*Columbus College
Library
Algonquin Drive
Columbus, GA 31993

Kennesaw College
TRAC
3455 Frey Drive
Kennesaw, GA 30144

University of Georgia
Main Library
Athens, GA 30602

Guam

*University of Guam
Curriculum Resources Center
College of Education
UOG Station
Mangilao, GU 96923

Idaho

*Boise State University
Curriculum Resource Center
1910 University Drive
Boise, ID 83725

Illinois

Community Consolidated School District 15
Educational Service Center
505 South Quentin Road
Palatine, IL 60067

Illinois State University
Milner Library/Periodicals
Normal, IL 61761

Loyola University
Instructional Materials Library
Lewis Towers Library
820 North Michigan Avenue
Chicago, Illinois 60611

National—Louis University
Library/Technical Services
2840 North Sheridan Road
Evanston, IL 60201

Northeastern Illinois University
Library/Serials
5500 North St. Louis Avenue
Chicago, IL 60625

*Northern Illinois University
Founders Memorial Library
DeKalb, IL 60115

Southern Illinois University
Lovejoy Library/Periodicals
Edwardsville, IL 62026

*University of Illinois at Chicago
Library/Serials
Box 8198
Chicago, IL 60680

University of Illinois at Urbana—Champaign
246 Library
1408 West Gregory Drive
Urbana, IL 61801

Indiana

Indiana State University
Cunningham Memorial Library
Terre Haute, IN 47809

Indiana University
Library/Serials
Bloomington, IN 47405-1801

Kentucky

Cumberland College
Instructional Media Library
Williamsburg, KY 40769

*Jefferson County Public Schools
The Greens Professional Development
Academy
4425 Preston Highway
Louisville, KY 40213

Maine

University of Maine
Raymond H. Fogler Library/Serials
Orono, ME 04469

Maryland

*Bowie State University
Library
Jericho Park Road
Bowie, MD 20715

*University of Maryland
Curriculum Laboratory
Building 143, Room 0307
College Park, MD 20742

Western Maryland College
Hoover Library
2 College Hill
Westminster, MD 21157

Massachusetts

*Barnstable Public Schools
230 South Street
Hyannis, MA 02601

Boston College
Educational Resource Center
Campion Hall G13
Chestnut Hill, MA 02167

Bridgewater State College
Library
3 Shaw Road
Bridgewater, MA 02325

Framingham State College
Curriculum Library
Henry Whittemore Library
Box 2000
Framingham, MA 01701

Harvard University
School of Education
Monroe C. Gutman Library
6 Appian Way
Cambridge, MA 02138

*Lesley College
Library
30 Mellen Street
Cambridge, MA 02138

*Salem State College
Professional Studies Resource Center
Library
Lafayette Street
Salem, MA 01970

Tufts University
Wessell Library
Medford, MA 02155-5816

*University of Lowell
OLeary Library
Wilder Street
Lowell, MA 01854

*Worcester State College
Learning Resource Center
486 Chandler Street
Worcester, MA 01602

Michigan

*Grand Valley State University
Library
Allendale, MI 49401

*Wayne County Regional Educational Services
Agency
Technical Services
5454 Venoy
Wayne, MI 48184

Wayne State University
Purdy Library
Detroit, MI 48202

*Western Michigan University
Dwight B. Waldo Library
Kalamazoo, MI 49008

Minnesota

Mankato State University
Memorial Library
Educational Resource Center
Mankato, MN 56002-8400

Moorhead State University
Library
Moorhead, MN 56563

University of Minnesota
170 Wilson Library/Serials
309 19th Avenue South
Minneapolis, MN 55455

Winona State University
Maxwell Library/Curriculum Laboratory
Sanborn and Johnson Streets
Winona, MN 55987

Mississippi

Mississippi State University
Mitchell Memorial Library
Mississippi State, MS 39762

University of Southern Mississippi
Cook Memorial Library/Serials
Box 5053
Hattiesburg, MS 39406-5053

Missouri

Central Missouri State University
Ward Edwards Library
Warrensburg, MO 64093-5020

Missouri Southern State College
George A. Spiva Library
3950 Newman Road
Joplin, MO 64801-1595

Northeast Missouri State University
Pickler Library/Serials
Kirksville, MO 63501

Southwest Baptist University
ESTEP Library
Bolivar, MO 65613-2496

Southwest Missouri State University
#175 Library
Springfield, MO 65804-0095

*University of Missouri at Kansas City
Instructional Materials Center
School of Education
5100 Rockhill Road
Kansas City, MO 64110-2499

University of Missouri at St. Louis
Library
St. Louis, MO 63121

Webster University
Library
470 East Lockwood Avenue
St. Louis, MO 63119-3194

Nebraska

Chadron State College
Library
10th and Main Streets
Chadron, NE 69337

University of Nebraska
University Libraries
Lincoln, NE 68588

University of Nebraska at Kearney
Calvin T. Ryan Library/Serials
Kearney, NE 68849-0700

*University of Nebraska at Omaha
Education Technology Center/Instructional
Material
Kayser Hall, Room 522
Omaha, NE 68182-0169

Nevada

*University of Nevada, Las Vegas
Materials Center—101 Education
Las Vegas, NV 89154

*University of Nevada, Reno
Library (322)
Reno, NV 89557-0044

New Hampshire

Plymouth State College
Herbert H. Lamson Library
Plymouth, NH 03264

New Jersey

Caldwell College
Library
9 Ryerson Avenue
Caldwell, NJ 07006

Georgian Court College
Farley Memorial Library
Lakewood, NJ 08701

Jersey City State College
Forrest A. Irwin Library
2039 Kennedy Boulevard
Jersey City, NJ 07305

*Kean College of New Jersey
Library
Union, NJ 07083

Paterson Board of Education
Media Center
823 East 28th Street
Paterson, NJ 07513

*Rutgers University
Alexander Library/Serials
New Brunswick, NJ 08903

St. Peters College
George F. Johnson Library
Kennedy Boulevard
Jersey City, NJ 07306

Trenton State College
West Library
Pennington Road CN4700
Trenton, NJ 08650-4700

William Paterson College
Library
300 Pompton Road
Wayne, NJ 07470

New Mexico

University of New Mexico
General Library/Serials
Albuquerque, NM 87131

New York

*BOCES—REPIC
Carle Place Center Concourse
234 Glen Cove Road
Carle Place, NY 11514

*Canisius College
Curriculum Materials Center
Library
2001 Main Street
Buffalo, NY 14208

Fordham University
Duane Library
Bronx, NY 10458

Hofstra University
Library
1000 Hempstead Turnpike
Hempstead, NY 11550

*Hunter College
Library
695 Park Avenue
New York, NY 10021

*Lehman College
Library/Serials
Bedford Park Boulevard West
Bronx, NY 10468

*New York University
Bobst Library
70 Washington Square South
New York, NY 10012

*Niagara University
Library/Serials
Niagara, NY 14109

Queens College
Benjamin Rosenthal Library
Flushing, NY 11367

St. Johns University
Library
Grand Central and Utopia Parkways
Jamaica, NY 11439

State University of New York at Albany
University Library/Serials
1400 Washington Avenue
Alany, NY 12222

State University of New York, College at
Buffalo
E. H. Butler Library
1300 Elmwood Avenue
Buffalo, NY 14222

State University of New York, College at
Cortland
Teaching Materials Center
Cortland, NY 13045

State University of New York, College at
Oneonta
James M. Milne Library
Oneonta, NY 13820

Teachers College of Columbia University
Millbank Memorial Library/Serials
525 West 120th Street
New York, NY 10027

North Carolina

*Appalachian State University
Instructional Materials Center
Belk Library
Boone, NC 28608

Charlotte–Mecklenburg Schools
Curriculum Resource Center
Staff Development Center
428 West Boulevard
Charlotte, NC 28203

*East Carolina University
Joyner Library
Greenville, NC 27858-4353

North Carolina A&T State University
F. D. Bluford Library
Greeensboro, NC 27411

North Carolina State University
D. H. Hill Library
Box 7111
Raleigh, NC 27695-7111

University of North Carolina at Chapel Hill
Davis Library/Serials
Campus Box 3938
Chapel Hill, NC 27599-3938

University of North Carolina at Charlotte
Atkins Library
UNCC Station
Charlotte, NC 28223

University of North Carolina at Wilmington
William M. Randall Library
601 South College Road
Wilmington, NC 28403-3297

*Western Carolina University
Hunter Library/Acquisitions
Cullowhee, NC 28723

Ohio

Bowling Green State University
Curriculum Center
Jerome Library
Bowling Green, OH 43403-0177

Miami University
Library
Oxford, OH 45056

*Ohio State University
2009 Millikin Road
Columbus, OH 43210

University of Akron
Bierce Library/Serials
Akron, OH 44325

*University of Rio Grande
Davis Library
Rio Grande, OH 45674

*Wright State University
Educational Resource Center
Dayton, OH 45435

Oklahoma

Southwestern Oklahoma State University
Al Harris Library
809 North Custer Street
Weatherford, OK 73096

*University of Tulsa
McFarlin Library
600 South College
Tulsa, OK 74104

Oregon

Oregon State University
Kerr Library/Serials
Corvallis, OR 97331-4503

Portland State University
Library/Serials
Portland, OR 97207

University of Oregon
Knight Library/Serials
Eugene, OR 97403

Pennsylvania

*Bucks County Intermediate Unit #22
705 Shady Retreat Road
Doylestown, PA 18901

*Cheyney University
Library
Cheyney, PA 19319

East Stroudsburg University of Pennsylvania
Library
East Stroudsburg, PA 18301

Holy Family College
Grant and Frankford Avenues
Philadelphia, PA 19114

*Indiana University of Pennsylvania
Media Resource Department
Stapleton Library
Indiana, PA 15705

Kutztown University
Curriculum Materials Center
Rohrbach Library
Kutztown, PA 19530

La Salle College
Instructional Materials Center
The Connelly Library
Olney Avenue at 20th Street
Philadelphia, PA 19141

Lock Haven University of Pennsylvania
Library
Lock Haven, PA 17745

*Millersville University
Ganser Library
Millersville, PA 17551-0302

*Pennsylvania State University
Pattee Library/Serials
University Park, PA 16802

*Shippensburg University of Pennsylvania
Ezra Lehman Library
Shippensburg, PA 17257-2299

*Slippery Rock University
Bailey Library
Instructional Materials Center
Slippery Rock, PA 16057

University of Pittsburgh
Hillman Library/Serials
Pittsburgh, PA 15260

West Chester University
Francis H. Green Library
West Chester, PA 19383

Rhode Island

Rhode Island College
Curriculum Resources Center
600 Mt. Pleasant Avenue
Providence, RI 02908

South Dakota

Northern State University
Williams Library
Aberdeen, SD 57401

University of South Dakota
I. D. Weeks Library
414 East Clark
Vermillion, SD 57069

Tennessee

Tennessee Technological University
Library
Cookeville, TN 38505

Trevecca Nazarene College
Curriculum Library
Mackey Library
33 Murfreesboro Road
Nashville, TN 37210-2877

*University of Tennessee at Chattanooga
Library/Serials
Chattanooga, TN 37403

*University of Tennessee at Martin
Instructional Improvement
Gooch HallRoom 217
Martin, TN 38238

*Vanderbilt University
Curriculum Laboratory
Peabody Library
Peabody Campus, Magnolia Circle
Nashville, TN 37203-5601

Texas

Baylor University
School of Education
Waco, TX 76798-7314

East Texas State University
Curriculum Library
Commerce, TX 75429

*East Texas State University
Library
Texarkana, TX 75501

*Houston Baptist University
Moody Library
7502 Fondren Road
Houston, TX 77074

*Incarnate Word College
Library
4301 Broadway
San Antonio, TX 78209

*Sam Houston State University
Library
Huntsville, TX 77341

*Southern Methodist University
Fondren Library
Dallas, TX 75275-0135

Stephen F. Austin State University
Library/Serials
Box 13055 SFA Station
Nacogdoches, TX 75962

Texas A&M University
Library/Serials
College Station, TX 77843-5000

*Texas Tech University
Library
Lubbock, TX 79409

Texas Womans University
Library
Box 23715 TWU Station
Denton, TX 76204

University of Houston—University Park
University of Houston Library
Central Serial
4800 Calhoun
Houston, TX 77004

University of North Texas
Library
Denton, TX 76203

*University of Texas at Arlington
Library
702 College Street
Arlington, TX 76019-0497

University of Texas at Austin
General Libraries/Serials
Austin, TX 78713-7330

University of Texas at El Paso
Library
El Paso, TX 79968-0582

*University of Texas—Pan American
School of Education
1201 West University Drive
Edinburg, TX 78539

Utah

Utah State University
Educational Resources Center
College of Education
Logan, UT 84322-2845

Vermont

University of Vermont
Guy W. Bailey Library/Serials
Burlington, VT 05405

Virginia

Longwood College
Dabney Lancaster Library
Farmville, VA 23909-1897

*Regent University
Library
Virginia Beach, VA 23464-9877

University of Virginia
Alderman Library
Serials/Periodicals
Charlottesville, VA 22901

*Virginia Beach Public Schools
Instruction and Curriculum
School Administration Building
2512 George Mason Drive
Virginia Beach, VA 23456

Washington

Central Washington University
Library/Serials
Ellensburg, WA 98926

University of Puget Sound
Collins Library
Tacoma, WA 98416

University of Washington
Library/Serials
Seattle, WA 98195

Washington State University
Library
Pullman, WA 99164-5610

Western Washington University
Wilson Library
Bellingham, WA 98225

Wisconsin

University of Wisconsin—Eau Claire
Instructional Media Center
Eau Claire, WI 54702-4004

University of Wisconsin—Madison
Instructional Materials Center
225 North Mills
Madison, Wisconsin 53706

University of Wisconsin—Oshkosh
F. R. Polk Library
Oshkosh, WI 54901

University of Wisconsin—Platteville
Library
One University Plaza
Platteville, WI 53818-3099

University of Wisconsin—Whitewater
Learning Resources
Whitewater, WI 53190

Wyoming

*University of Wyoming
Coe Library
15th and Lewis
Laramie, WY 82071

AUSTRALIA

Griffith University
Library
Mount Gravatt Campus
Nathan, Queensland 4111

CANADA

The Ontario Institute for Studies in Education
Library
252 Bloor Street West
Toronto, Ontario M5S 1V6

Queens University
Education Library
McArthur Hall
Kingston, Ontario K7L 3H6

*University of New Brunswick
Harriet Irving Library/Serials
Fredericton, New Brunswick E3B 5H5

University of Regina
Library/Serials
Regina, Saskatchewan S4S 0A2

University of Saskatchewan
Library
Saskatoon, Saskatchewan S7N 0W0

University of Windsor
Leddy Library/Serials
Windsor, Ontario N9B 3P4

*Vancouver School Board
Teachers Professional Library
123 East 6th Avenue
Vancouver, British Columbia V5T 1J6

HONG KONG

*The Chinese University of Hong Kong
University Library
Shatin, N.T.

KOREA

*Kyungpook National University
Department of Education
Taegu 702-701, Korea

THE NETHERLANDS

National Institute for Curriculum Development
(Stichting voor de Leerplanontwikkeling)
7500 CA Enschede

APPENDIX:
CURRICULUM GUIDE REPRINT

CURRICULUM developers can often find ideas and models by studying curriculum guides. Chapter 8, "Annotated List of Curriculum Guides" is a reference chapter to lead you to many of the guides available for early childhood. In this chapter, we have reprinted segments of the following exemplary curriculum guide as a model:

Explorations with Young Children: A Curriculum Guide from The Bank Street College of Education. 1992. Mt. Ranier, MD: Gryphon House.

Unable to reprint the guide in its entirety, we have selected, in addition to the front matter (reprinted chapters are indicated with a check mark in the Table of Contents), chapters 1, 7, 8, 10, and 17.

Chapter 1, "Principles of the Bank Street Approach," begins with Bank Street's theoretical roots and proceeds through its principles and goals to a description of educational concepts. Chapter 7, "Valuing Diversity," discusses the concept of diversity in its many forms, going into how and why to incorporate it into early childhood. Chapter 8, "Creating Curriculum in Early Childhood," delves into their definition of curriculum, and how to develop it. Chapter 10, "Integrated Curriculum for Four- through Eight-Year-Olds," discusses the what, why, and how of integrated curriculum. Finally, Chapter 17, "A Study of Bread and Bakeries: An Example of Integrated Curriculum," follows on Chapter 10's heels with a concrete example of that discussion.

Each chapter concludes with exercises and a list of resources. We include this reprint to provide an example of a superior curriculum guide, to aid you in developing your own curriculum or guide. To obtain a complete copy of this guide (total 309pp), contact Gryphon House, Inc., 3706 Otis Street, Mt. Ranier, MD, 20712; 800-638-0928; list price $19.95.

Explorations

with

Young Children

A Curriculum Guide from
The Bank Street College of Education

Edited by Anne Mitchell and Judy David

Sara, Age 5

gryphon house
Mt. Rainier, Maryland

Published by Gryphon House, Inc., 3706 Otis Street, Mt. Rainier, MD 20712
ISBN: 0-87659-160-8

Library of Congress Catalog Number: 92-74062

Illustrations: Debby Dixler, Nina Woldin, Catherine Minor, Joan Auclair
Cover Design: Beverly Hightshoe

Publisher's Cataloging in Publication
(Prepared by Quality Books Inc.)

Explorations with young children : a curriculum guide from Bank Street
    College of Education / editors-in-chief, Judy David, Anne Mitchell.
      p.cm.
      Includes bibiographical references and index.
      ISBN 0-87659-160-8

    1. Education, Preschool—United States—Curricula.   2. Education, Pri-
mary—United States—Curricula.   I. David, Judith A., 1945- II. Mitchell,
Anne W., 1950-   III. Bank Street College of Education

Contents

Foreword

From its founding in 1916 as the Bureau of Educational Experiments to this last decade of the twentieth century, Bank Street College has held a distinctive position in the field of education, influencing educational practices in the city, across the nation, and around the world. Founded by Lucy Sprague Mitchell and Harriet Johnson, the Bureau was initially characterized by a diversity of interests that grew out of the context of early progressivism—educational testing, rural schools, vocational education, day nurseries, public school nutrition. By 1919, the Bureau staff had established a focus for its work that continues to this day: to understand through study, experimentation, and research the complex development of children, and to create environments that support and promote their development.

Combining research, practice, publishing, and outreach, Bank Street is now composed of a Graduate School of Education, a model School for Children and Family Center, a Division of Continuing Education, a Publications Group, and a Research Division. Through the efforts of all these divisions, Bank Street works to improve the education of young children by preparing teachers and educational leaders; demonstrating our approach in programs for children at Bank Street and in many other educational settings; conducting research; and creating materials in various media for teachers, children, and parents.

Explorationns with Young Children: A Curriculum Guide from Bank Street College of Education is a logical extension of these efforts—our way of reaching out to all those who work with young children and their families. The plan for putting together this Guide and making the companion videotape, *Social Studies: A Way to Integrate Curriculum for Four- and Five-Year-Olds*, originally emerged from a College-wide strategic planning process begun in 1988 with support from the W. Alton Jones Foundation. We asked ourselves: What would really help people who are trying to create quality programs for young children? Making the Bank Street approach to early childhood education accessible to many more people than we can reach directly through our programs in New York City seemed to be the answer.

Thus, we decided that our priority would be the production of a set of materials (written and audiovisual) that could be disseminated widely. The Ford Foundation supported this phase of our work. Planning involved many of our current and former colleagues at

5

Bank Street—the Bank Street Advisory Group—as well as colleagues from the larger early childhood community—the National Advisory Panel. They reviewed the early drafts of materials and commented on them. Their contributions were invaluable, and we thank them again.

National Advisory Panel

Don Bolce
National Head Start Association

Sue Bredekamp
National Association for the Education of Young Children

Peggy Crichton
American Association of Community College Early Childhood Educators

Harriet Egertson
National Association of Early Childhood Specialists in State Departments of Education

Kay Hollestelle
The Children's Foundation;
National Association for Family Day Care

Deborah Jordan
Council for Early Childhood Professional Recognition

Pauline Koch
National Association of Regulatory Administration

Peggy Pizzo
National Center for Clinical Infant Programs

Tutti Sherlock
National Association of Child Care Resource and Referral Agencies

Margaret Spencer
Division of Educational Studies, Emory University

Bank Street College Advisory Panel

Nancy Balaban	Bill Hooks
Harriet Cuffaro	Maritza Macdonald
Dick Feldman	Ann-Marie Mott
Sam Gibbon	Edna Shapiro
Susan Ginsberg	Sal Vascellaro
Judith Gold	Eileen Wasow
Laura Guarino	

Writing the Guide and making the companion videotape were collaborative processes that brought together the skills and talents of colleagues from every part of the College. The writers, reviewers, editors, illustrators, photographers, typists, and administrators among us all contributed their best to bring these materials into being. As the materials were nearing completion, they were also being field tested in a variety of early childhood settings and reviewed by staff developers, trainers, and other teachers of adults. Our work during this period was generously supported by the NYNEX Foundation and the East Coast Migrant Head Start Project.

We hope these materials will enrich the important and valuable work you do every day with young children and their families. The process of creating them has been a deeply rewarding learning experience for us at Bank Street. We hope that using them will be the same kind of experience for you.

Anne Mitchell, Editor-in-Chief
  and Project Director
  (July 1989-July 1991)

Joan Cenedella, Vice President
  for Academic Affairs
  Bank Street College

7

Introduction

*E*xplorations with Young Children: A Curriculum Guide from Bank Street College of Education is written for early childhood professionals who are serving infants, toddlers, preschoolers, and young school-age children (6 to 8 years old) in a variety of educational settings—family day care homes, center-based care, Head Start, and public schools. By early childhood professionals, we mean teachers, caregivers, staff developers, teacher trainers. (We use the words "teacher" and "caregiver" interchangeably throughout the Guide, eschewing the common distinction that one teaches and the other cares for. We believe that *all* early childhood professionals both care for children and educate them.) Teachers and caregivers will find the Guide and its companion videotape, *Social Studies: A Way to Integrate Curriculum for Four- and Five-Year-Olds*, helpful in planning and putting into practice every aspect of their program; staff developers and education directors will find the materials useful supplements to their inservice work with staff; and college instructors and Child Development Associate (CDA) trainers will be able to incorporate chapters from the Guide into their courses (see Appendix A). Finally, for those readers, whether educators or not, who have an interest in the theoretical roots of the Bank Street approach (also referred to as the developmental-interaction approach), the Guide presents an overview and examples of how theory is translated into practice.

Whatever your setting, as an early childhood professional you are a vital part of your children's early, critical years of learning and growth. Our goal in writing this curriculum guide is to offer a framework for planning and carrying out work with young children. At Bank Street, we believe that a sound framework based on an understanding of how children grow and learn—rather than a series of lesson plans and specific curricula—is the best guide for those working with children. The curricula, the lessons, the pacing—these will grow out of the particulars of the school or setting, the needs and interests of the children, and the professional's own strengths and interests.

This Guide offers a way of thinking about, or helping others to think about, program issues and make decisions on what to teach and how to teach it. It is meant to encourage early childhood professionals to develop their own curricula based on a few important principle, which, together, we think of as a framework for educators, no matter who they are or in what setting they work with

Who is this Guide for?

9

children. These principles, extensively developed in the Guide, include the following:

- Your work with children is based on knowledge of child development, and especially of the interdependence of social, emotional, physical, and intellectual growth.

- You learn about your particular children through observation and recording, through children's works or products, through children's families, and through others who have worked with them.

- You create a physical environment for children that encourages their active participation in their own learning.

- You create a social/emotional environment that encourages a sense of community and of the value of each individual in the community.

These principles are discussed in the first seven chapters of the Guide; the remaining chapters give examples of how these principles can be applied in your program and in specific areas of curriculum. The examples throughout the book come from many different schools and settings. Some, but by no means all, come from Bank Street's Family Center and School for Children; some come from schools and child care settings that Bank Street works with; others come from settings where Bank Street places graduate students for field placements; still others come from settings our faculty have worked in. The settings are private, public, suburban, urban, and rural. We have deliberately included a wide diversity of settings to make the point that the framework can work in many different situations. (The principles of the Bank Street approach are applicable to children with special needs. However, the Guide does not address issues specific to their disabilities.)

How can the Guide be used?

We urge you to make this Guide yours, to use it in the way that best suits your needs and interests. For many readers, this will mean reading the Guide from beginning to end, chapter by chapter. This strategy would immerse you initially in the theoretical bases and general framework of the Bank Street approach, as described in the chapters "Principles of the Bank Street Approach," "Child Development," and "Observing and Recording Children's Behavior." With a grounding in the underlying theory and ideas of the Guide, you would then see how they can be put into action as you read about planning the learning environment, valuing diversity, developing curriculum, working with families, fulfilling your role as teacher, and conducting assessment.

For some readers, it may make sense to review the Table of Contents and then begin by reading the chapter that addresses a particular concern or interest. For staff whose priority is to involve families in the program, the chapter on "Working with Families" would be relevant. If you are thinking about general curriculum issues—for example, what developmentally appropriate practice means for your setting—then a good starting point would be one of these curriculum chapters: "Creating Curriculum," "Planning for Infants, Toddlers, and Threes," or "Integrated Curriculum for Four-through Eight-Year-Olds." Ideas about how to enrich a curriculum area, such as math or music, and how to integrate it with other curriculum areas are presented in the respective chapters. Although you can begin by reading any one chapter in the Guide, we do recommend that, at some time, you look at the initial chapters, which provide the framework for the Bank Street approach.

In general, the chapters in the Guide have a similar format. The topic or subject is first defined; for example, what is child development, discipline and management, or science in early childhood? Then a rationale is presented—why incorporate movement into the curriculum or why value diversity? The third section is "how to"; for example, how to observe and record, support emerging literacy, develop an integrated curriculum, or assess through the curriculum. This section provides guidelines and recommendations, not fail-safe recipes. (At the heart of the Bank Street approach is the recognition that the specifics of any early childhood program will reflect unique characteristics of the children, families, and staff.) The next section provides vivid examples of what caregivers and teachers do to implement a curriculum area (e.g., art or movement) with different age groups—infants and toddlers, preschoolers, young school-age children—and with families. Each chapter concludes with a series of exercises for you to try and a list of resources for further reading. Throughout the Guide, Bank Street's respect for diversity is reflected in references to males and females from many ethnic and cultural backgrounds.

One of the reasons we at Bank Street wanted to create the Guide was to support current national efforts to improve the quality of programs for young children and to reform schools. The ideas in the Guide support these efforts in numerous ways.

Our materials are consistent with the efforts of the National Association for the Education of Young Children (NAEYC) to define "developmentally appropriate practice" and with NAEYC's standards for accrediting programs (1987). The Bank Street approach is characterized by its emphasis on age-appropriateness and individual appropriateness in early childhood programs. *The Guidelines for Appropriate Curriculum Content and Assessment in Programs Serving Children Ages 3 through 8*, published by NAEYC in 1991, focuses on

How does the Guide support current efforts to improve programs?

11

the "what" and "when" issues of teaching and learning, and on assessment. Here are two important examples of how the Guide is consistent with NAEYC's guidelines:

The first curriculum guideline is:

> The curriculum has an articulated description of its theoretical base that is consistent with prevailing professional opinion and research on how children learn (p. 29).

The first chapter in the Guide, "Principles of the Bank Street Approach," describes our theoretical base and its relevance to research on children's growth and learning.

The sixth guideline is:

> Curriculum content reflects and is generated by the needs and interests of individual children within the group. Curriculum incorporates a wide variety of learning experiences, materials and equipment, and instructional strategies to accommodate a broad range of children's individual differences in prior experience, maturation rates, styles of learning, needs, and interests (p. 30).

The Bank Street approach is an integrated curriculum rooted in social studies. As you will see in the chapters, "Creating Curriculum" and "An Integrated Curriculum for Four- through Eight-Year-Olds," these studies are designed to arise from children's interests and are developed to meet individual children's needs. Other chapters, including "Observing and Recording Children's Behavior" and "Valuing Diversity," also reflect this guideline. Throughout the Guide and highlighted in the chapter "Assessment through the Curriculum," the curriculum approach we present is consistent with this important guideline.

In 1988, the National Association of State Boards of Education (NASBE) convened a Task Force on Early Childhood Education, Their report, *Right from the Start*, called on schools to recognize the early childhood years (ages 4-8) as a distinct period, and to restructure teaching in those years on the basis of child development and the child in context of family and community (1988). The themes of child development, diversity, and families which run through every chapter in the Guide will make it a useful tool for schools working to implement the recommendations of the report.

The Guide is also consistent with the standards put forth by the National Association of Elementary School Principals (NAESP) for programs serving 3- through 8-year-olds (1990). The chapters focusing on curriculum, assessment, and working with families are particularly relevant.

In an effort to improve programs for very young children and their families, the National Center for Clinical Infant Programs has identified core concepts for professional practice (1990). The core concepts of developmental processes and the interrelationship and transaction between the infant and the environment are addressed in the chapters "Child Development," "The Learning Environment," and "Planning for Infants, Toddlers, and Threes." Nearly every chapter of the Guide includes sections on infants and toddlers and on families.

Thus, the approach to early childhood education articulated in the Guide supports all the current major national efforts to improve the education of young children. This is true, despite the fact that the essential principles of the Bank Street approach were developed in the late teens and early twenties of this century. Indeed, much of what is perceived today as "new" in early childhood education was part of Bank Street's theory and practice some seventy years ago. We are delighted to have so many influential allies in our ongoing efforts to provide the best possible education for young children in all the settings in which they grow and learn. And we hope this Guide will add valuable momentum to the movement toward child-centered, developmentally appropriate programs for our nation's children.

Anne Mitchell, Editor-in-Chief
and Project Director
(July 1989-July 1991)

Judy David, Editor-in-Chief
and Project Director
(August 1991-June 1992)

Joan Cenedella, Vice President
for Academic Affairs, Bank Street College

Resources

Bredekamp, S. (Ed.). (1987). *Developmentally appropriate practice in early childhood programs serving children from birth through age 8.* Washington, DC: National Association for the Education of Young Children.

National Association for the Education of Young Children and the National Association of Early Childhood Specialists in State Departments of Education. (1991). Position Statement: Guidelines for appropriate curriculum content and assessment in programs serving children ages 3 through 8. *Young Children*, 46(3), 21-38.

National Association of Elementary School Principals. (1990). *Early childhood programs and the elementary school principal: Standards for quality programs for young children.* Alexandria, VA: Author.

National Association of State Boards of Education Task Force on Early Childhood Education. (1988). *Right from the start.* Alexandria, VA: Author.

National Center for Clinical Infant Programs. (1990). *Preparing practitioners to work with infants, toddlers and their families.* Washington, DC: Author.

1 | Principles of the Bank Street Approach

The way we teach reflects the way we think people learn. Over the years, many philosophers, psychologists, and educators have devised ideal educational systems that follow from their images of what human beings are like and theories about how we become the people we are. Theories about development are not a luxury or an add-on to practice; theory governs action, even when we are not fully aware of why we do what we do. The principles of Bank Street's approach to education are based on a coherent set of values and goals for optimum development and anchored in knowledge of processes of growth.

Bank Street was founded in 1916 and was originally called the Bureau of Educational Experiments, a name that reflected the idea that educational practice should be based on studying children to better understand their development. Lucy Sprague Mitchell, the founder of Bank Street, like others of her time, believed strongly in the power of education to affect and improve society. Education takes place in a social context and has profound consequences for the larger society.

Bank Street's approach to education is not limited to any one educational institution. But while the general outlines and theoretical bases are shared by a number of other educators and psychologists, Bank Street has a uniquely long-term experience in putting the theory into practice.

Theoretical roots

The approach flows from three main sources: (1) the dynamic psychology of Freud and his followers, especially those who were concerned with development in a social context, for example, Anna Freud and Erik Erikson; (2) developmental psychologists like Jean Piaget and Heinz Werner, whose theories focused primarily on cognitive development but who were not especially concerned with education; and (3) educational theorists and practitioners like John Dewey, Harriet Johnson (the founding director of Bank Street's early education program), Susan Isaacs, and Lucy Sprague Mitchell. These have been the main theoretical sources. However, there are many other psychologists and educators whose ideas are compatible with Bank Street's approach to education, and who have influenced its continuing development and refinement, for example, Kurt Lewin, Lois Murphy, Lev Vygotsky. Barbara Biber, a psychologist who had a long and distinguished career at Bank Street in research and

15

teaching, helped to define the connections between psychology and educational philosophy and practice.

As we already have said, Bank Street's approach is not unique to Bank Street, and therefore we wanted to give it a name that indicated its generality, and also its distinctiveness from other educational models. We have called it the developmental-interaction approach. Developmental refers to the patterns of growth and ways of understanding and responding that characterize children and adults as they mature. Interaction points, first, to an emphasis on interaction with the environment, an environment of children, adults, and the material world. And, second, it points to the interaction of cognitive and affective development; that is, thinking and emotion are not seen as separate but as interconnected spheres of development.

These concepts apply to the education of children and adults of all ages. However, a basic principle is that one has to understand the stage of development of those one is teaching. Therefore, concepts need to be adapted or translated for children and adults of different ages, capabilities, and cultures. Perhaps most important, children are different from adults. They are not just a smaller version, or even a smaller, less-knowing version; their ways of taking in and relating to the world, their ways of thinking and expressing themselves are different from those of adults. In these chapters, we are focusing on the way the developmental-interaction approach relates to the education of young children, from birth through the primary years, through age eight.

Governing principles

Six general principles of development are basic to understanding the Bank Street approach.

1. Development is not a simple path from less to more; and it is not an unfolding, like the unfolding of a flower. Development involves changes or shifts in the way a person organizes experience and copes with the world, generally moving from simpler to more complex, from single to multiple and integrated ways of responding. The concept of stages of development is crucial, and is also a convenient way of talking and thinking about developmental change and growth. Stages are approximate and are only loosely related to age.

   This leads to a second principle:

2. Individuals are never at a fixed point on a straight line of development, but operate within a range of possibilities. Earlier ways of organizing experience are not erased, but become integrated into more advanced systems. While people will want to function at the highest possible level, they are also able to use less mature ways appropriately. (Even after a child knows how to hop and jump, there are times when it is a good idea to crawl; even adults find

moments when it is appropriate to be silly.)

One of the biggest puzzles of development is how one moves from one stage to the next. No one really understands the process, but one aspect is clear:

3. Developmental progress involves a mix of stability and instability. A central task for the educator is to find a balance between helping a child consolidate new understandings and offering challenges that will promote growth.

The fundamental concept that development involves the interaction of the individual with the environment leads to our fourth principle:

4. The motivation to engage actively with the environment—to make contact, to have an impact, and to make sense of experience—is built into human beings. The growing child gradually adds more ways of actively engaging with the world as she develops. Generally, the progression is from more physical, body-centered ways of responding to perceptual and then more conceptual, symbolic ways.

Probably one of the most agreed-upon principles of development is the importance of developing a sense of self as a unique and independent individual:

5. The child's sense of self is built up from his experiences with other people and with objects; knowledge of the self is based on repeated awareness and testing of one's self in interaction.

Finally, an equally important principle:

6. Growth and maturing involve conflict—conflict within the self, and conflict with others. Conflict is necessary for development. The way conflicts are resolved depends on the nature of the interaction with significant figures in the child's life and the demands of the culture.

Educational goals

The educational system is seen as responsible for fostering the child's development in a broad sense; the aim is not simply to promote specific learnings but to provide many opportunities for physical, social, and emotional as well as cognitive development. A fundamental principle of the developmental-interaction approach is that cognitive growth cannot be separated from the growth of personal and social processes. Further, the school should be an active community, connected to the social world of which it is a part, rather than an isolated place for "learning lessons." This means that the school shares responsibility with children's families and with other neighborhood institutions.

Educational goals are conceived in terms of developmental processes, not as specific achievements. The school is responsible for fostering the individual's ability to deal effectively with her environment. The development of competence is central. Competence means being as able as possible in all areas of development, and being motivated to use one's abilities. A second goal is the development of a sense of autonomy and individuality. This involves a strong sense of identity, the ability to act on your own, to make choices, take risks, and be able to accept help.

Coupled with this is the development of social relatedness and connectedness. This means caring about others, learning to feel part of larger social groups, being able to form friendships, cherishing diversity, developing awareness of human interconnectedness, and seeing human beings in an ecological context.

The encouragement of creativity is a fourth goal. Creativity does not focus only on the product but honors the processes of making. It involves having a range of means for expressing feelings and ideas-logical, intuitive, subjective. Children's (and adults') creative work can take many forms—physical movement; drawing, painting, sculpting; spoken and written words; melody or rhythm; dramatic enactment; mathematical and scientific ideas. Finally, the school promotes integration rather than compartmentalization. Integration means pulling together different ways of experiencing the world—joining thinking and feeling, making connections between how one feels and how others might feel, communicating in both original and conventional ways, connecting the self to the world.

It is critical to understand that these broadly stated goals need to be thought of and made concrete in terms that are appropriate to the child's developmental stage, and also to the cultural context.

Educational concepts

How does this translate into educational practice? How do we put the theory into action?

The Teacher's Role

The teacher creates the climate of the young child's learning environment. Within the constraints of what is possible, she structures the physical and psychological atmosphere. Teachers vary in personal style, temperament, cultural background, and the kinds of experience they bring to teaching. In enacting the developmental-interaction approach, the teacher's personal qualities do matter; in this way of teaching, the teacher does not leave her personal self at the classroom door. This framework is compatible with a wide range of personal and teaching styles. The essential and overriding principle, however, is that the teacher should respond and relate to each child with respect. The task is to enable the child to have trust in himself, and in the adult caregiver and teacher. This means that the teacher herself must be trustworthy.

It is the teacher's responsibility to know the children in her charge as individuals. Knowing means understanding patterns of child development, and knowing each child—her talents and weaknesses, her tolerance for frustration, her pace of learning, her sources of pride and concerns about inadequacy, and her family. A good deal of this knowledge is based on close, careful, and frequent observation of the children in a range of different situations, an essential part of the educator's task.

Work and Play

Adults make a major distinction between work and play; young children learn these concepts from us. There are activities children like and those they don't like, or "hate," but the difference has nothing to do with what we consider work or play. Learning and play can and should be joyful and fun, a source of pleasure. Play offers ways of trying out new ideas, new combinations, of expressing emotions, of taking different roles, and of repeating known ways of enjoyment.

Learning, especially in the early years, is active, physical exploration—touching, tasting, hearing, seeing, moving. An infant drops something to see what happens. The sequence of learning moves from open exploration to more structured engagement with materials and ideas. Children learn through active doing, through experimenting with materials, with language; they learn from each other and from adults. Even very young children are capable of sustained concentration when their interest is captured. Unless they are taught otherwise, they enjoy learning, discovering, and mastering.

The Educational Environment as a Community

Every child, every person, is part of a number of communities—family (or families), neighborhood(s), cultural and ethnic group(s). Programs for children are another kind of community that children become part of. They learn how to relate to others in the group, they learn the "rules of the game" of the center, the preschool, the elementary school; they learn from and teach each other. Positive experiences of belonging, of cooperating with others, of being a group member, of dealing with differences of opinion and styles of interaction are necessary for functioning well in a democratic society.

Connections with the Larger World

A good part of children's learning takes place at home, and in the neighborhood—that is, outside of the "formal" educational environment. Sometimes there is continuity between home and school in the kinds of learning that are valued, the expectations of appropriate behavior, and the customs. More often, in this country of diverse national and ethnic groups, there are sharp breaks between the cultures of school and home. Educators must connect with the child's world, both in the sense of knowing the child's experience and also as interpreters of educational programs and goals. Educators should

19

be a resource to parents and others who also are responsible for the child's welfare and development.

There is no simple recipe for fostering children's development. If you believe that all you have to do is "lay out the facts" and the child will learn, then you can say, "too bad," and blame the child or the family when she doesn't. But if you believe that the educator needs to meet the children where they are, then you have to find out where they are. If you want genuine and mutual trust and respect, you have to give as well as receive. You have to be willing to join with the children in an exploration of possibilities, to accept that what worked yesterday may not work tomorrow. Like the children, you have to learn from experience. But first, you have to give such learning a chance. The chapters that follow give practical information about how to put the Bank Street approach to work in your program. It is not always easy, but when it works, you will find much pleasure and satisfaction in enhancing the development of the children you care for.

Resources

Antler, J. (1987). *Lucy Sprague Mitchell: The making of a modern woman.* New Haven, CT: Yale University Press.

Biber, B. (1977). A developmental-interaction approach: Bank Street College of Education. In M. C. Day & R. K. Parker (Eds.), *Preschool in action: Exploring early childhood programs* (2nd ed.). Boston: Allyn & Bacon.

Biber, B. (1984). *Early education and psychological development.* New Haven, CT: Yale University Press.

Biber, B., Shapiro, E., & Wickens, D. (1977). *Promoting cognitive growth: A developmental-interaction point of view* (2nd ed.). Washington, DC: National Association for the Education of Young Children.

Cuffaro, H. K. (1977). *The developmental-interaction approach.* In B. D. Boeghehold, H. K. Cuffaro, W. H. Hooks, & G. J. Klopf (Eds.), *Education before five.* New York: Bank Street College.

Gilkeson, E., & Bowman, G. W. (1976). *The focus is on children: The Bank Street approach to early childhood education as enacted in Follow Through.* New York: Bank Street College.

Shapiro, E., & Biber, B. (1972). The education of young children: A developmental-interaction point of view. *Teachers College Record, 74,* 55-79.

Zimiles, H. (1987). The Bank Street approach. In J. L. Roopnarine & J. E. Johnson (Eds.), *Approaches to early childhood education.* Columbus, OH: Charles E. Merrill.

About the Authors:

Edna Shapiro, Ph.D., a senior researcher in the Research Division at Bank Street College, is a developmental psychologist interested in the application of psychological principles to educational thoery and practice. Dr. Shapiro is the author of a number of articles in psychological and educational journals, and is co-author of The Psychological Impact of School Experience, *with Patricia Minuchin, Barbara Biber, and Herbert Zimiles (Basic Books, 1969), and co-editor with Evelyn Weber of* Cognitive and Affective Growth: Developmental Interaction *(Erlbaum, 1981).*

Anne Mitchell, M.S., is an early childhood policy researcher at Bank Street College where she did a national study of public schools as providers of programs for children under six and then developed the Early Childhood Curriculum Project. She has taught Education Policy and is the founder of Bank Street's master's program in Early Childhood Leadership. She has been a trainer and consultant with early childhood teachers and family day care providers, and was the director of two child care centers where she worked with toddlers, preschoolers, and children with special needs.

7 | Valuing Diversity

Diversity means the range of differences among people that we need to take into account if we are to work effectively with children, families, and communities. The concept of diversity includes the perspectives of multiculturalism and nonsexist and antibias education. Diversity encompasses children's individual interests and capabilities, racial and cultural differences, age and gender differences, and language differences. It also includes the social realities that affect children and communities, including availability of economic resources, access to technology, health and safety concerns, demographic make-up, and locale.

What is diversity?

Think about the concept of "family," which is a universal human experience, and consider the diverse meanings it may have for children:

- For one child, "family" may mean a mom and a dad and siblings; for another, "family" may mean the grandmother and aunt who raised her; for a third, the two dads who adopted him.

- "Family" may be a mom or a dad, or two households where a child divides his week—mom's house some days, and dad and his new wife's house other days.

- In some situations, "family" may include a person who is hired to care for a child when parents travel or work away from home; in others, "family" may describe three generations who live in the same building and speak a language other than English.

Knowing and recognizing the diversity of family experiences affects the way in which caregivers and teachers make decisions in planning appropriate programs. Some decisions may affect how you think and relate to the children and families in the program; others may affect the content of the curriculum choices. To value these diverse family experiences, you need to think about:

- when and how to speak to children about families;

- which households should receive school notices;

- how, when, and with whom to plan family conferences;

- in what language to communicate with the children's families;

- how families prefer to describe themselves to their children and others;

- how to interpret children's play, especially around family themes

- how to select materials that reflect different kinds of families.

Diversity represents the richness and uniqueness of human life. It is something we want to value and share with the children we work with.

Why include diversity in early childhood?

There are many reasons to include consideration of diversity as a central theme in early childhood programs. When you value diversity, you maximize the positive impact of your program for all your children by:

- building children's positive self-esteem (*when you do this you give them the confidence to reach out to new learning experiences*);

- affirming children's identities with regard to race, ethnicity, gender, religion, handicapping conditions, class (*when you do this you pave the way for children—who are ever fascinated with how they are alike and different from one another—to appreciate human differences as a natural part of life*);

- strengthening ties with families (*when you do this you promote families' involvement with their children's early childhood programs*).

Further, when you include diversity in your work with children, you are preparing them for citizenship in a society where people speak different languages, practice different customs, and embrace different values. By starting in early childhood, you will be helping individuals learn to work together, communicate across their differences, and value just and fair treatment for all. You will also be preparing children to fight bias and discrimination directed toward themselves or other members of society. Preparing children for active participation in a democracy is one of the educational goals proposed by Dewey and early Bank Street leaders (as discussed in the chapter "Principles of the Bank Street Approach").

Making consideration of diversity a major part of your program is particularly important in early childhood because it is during this period, and especially between the ages of 2 and 5, that children become aware of gender, race, ethnicity, disabilities, and other differences among people. Because young children are aware of diversity, you need to be prepared to address it in your work with them. You need to treat their questions and comments seriously and respectfully, just as you would if they were expressing curiosity about nature or other phenomena. Young children also acquire attitudes and values from their families and society about which differences are positive and which are not. How you respond to the ideas they express will influence the feelings and judgments they will form.

When you value diversity, you too become a learner. You learn about the children you work with and the communities they live in. You may also learn about the educational theories, practices, and policies that will strengthen your program's response to diversity. For example, you might choose to learn about second language acquisition or legislation pertaining to low-income or handicapped children. As a teacher or caregiver, you need to be aware of the laws that challenge unequal practices and policies and promote equal educational opportunity.

If you work with children and families from diverse cultural and linguistic backgrounds, the opportunities for valuing diversity in the curriculum may be quite apparent. But if you are working with children from similar backgrounds, you also need to address diversity in the curriculum. You may need to counter stereotypes or misconceptions they have. All children need to be exposed to new experiences and broaden their understanding of how people live.

There are many ways for caregivers and teachers to help children learn about human differences. Margarita, a teacher of 4- and 5-year-olds, encounters chronic illness for the first time in her class. Two children have diabetes and three others have severe allergies. At first, she worries about how to remember who can eat or drink what kinds of things. She thinks of her curriculum and how she can incorporate these aspects of diversity into the children's learning experiences. She begins with a class discussion of favorite foods; she writes down children's responses on a chart "Our favorite foods." Then she leads the children into further discussion about their eating habits, and from these emerge other charts: "Snacks some of us should not have" and "Snacks we can all have." The charts are put up in the room for all to see and are a reminder of the similarities and differences in this group of children. With these charts as a beginning, Margarita develops a curriculum study around health and nutrition, helping the children learn to take good care of themselves and each other.

Underlying a commitment to diversity is a set of beliefs and values. Caregivers and teachers like Margarita share these:

- a sense of trust in others;
- a sense of justice;
- a belief in cooperation and shared learning;
- a belief that all children can be competent;
- a belief that all children can be proud of their culture and heritage;
- a belief that all children can be curious about and learn to accept human similarities and differences;
- a sense of the individuality of each child;

105

- a sense that a group of children is a small society where there is fairness, opportunity, caring, and satisfaction for all its members.

When you value diversity, you are addressing the needs of the "whole child" and promoting both affective and cognitive development. You are recognizing that children live in diverse social and physical environments. You are imparting a sense of shared humanity.

How can you incorporate diversity into early childhood?

First, you need to spend time thinking about your own beliefs, behaviors, and knowledge about diversity. Next, think about the lives and experiences of your children and their families and communities. Then you will be ready to plan curricula that expand your own vision, capitalize on children's experiences, and provide new learning experiences. Finally, you need to consider your role as a policy maker and how the policies in your program respond to issues of diversity.

You as Caregiver or Teacher

There are many ways to begin thinking about how to incorporate diversity into your early childhood setting:

- For some caregivers and teachers, gender difference is a comfortable starting point. They think seriously about how boys and girls are influenced by teaching decisions, by the arrangement of the environment, and by new experiences that encourage initiative and competence in both sexes.

- For others, the starting point may be their understanding of racial and economic differences. They might choose experiences that help balance and strengthen educational opportunities for children of different racial, cultural, and economic backgrounds.

- Others count on their knowledge of different languages to help all children learn other languages and about other cultures.

- Many teachers wish to understand more about diversity because they feel a strong desire to foster fairness, interdependence, and peace among individuals. They wish to have those values influence their work with children.

- For yet others, the starting point is the challenge of understanding and nurturing different learning styles. As a result, they might find it more comfortable to begin by learning how to observe, document, and assess learning from this perspective.

No matter where you begin, you will have to think about the beliefs and attitudes about human beings that you want to promote in your program. Related to this, is the necessity of assessing your own behavior and looking at what you say and do to communicate to children that you value diversity. Children look to you as a model of how they should act toward others. Here are some guidelines:

- Monitor the language you use to describe situations so that your words carry a message of inclusion, knowledge, and acceptance of others. You might say, "speakers of another language" rather than "non-English speakers," or "we teach children who come from many places" rather than "we teach immigrants."

- Explicitly counter prejudice and bias. Young children do notice differences. When a 4-year-old says his Chinese friend talks "funny," explain, "Mark is learning English. He also speaks Chinese because his family does. That's why he sounds different. Maybe he can teach us some Chinese words." Think about how to intervene when you hear a remark like, "I don't want to sit next to you because your face is black." Make it clear that prejudiced remarks or discriminatory behavior hurt other people's feelings and are not allowed in your group.

- Study anti-bias curricula which can expand your understanding of stereotypes and racial, gender, and cultural differences and similarities. They can provide you with ways to develop anti-bias materials and change discriminatory behavior (Derman-Sparks, 1989; Williams et al., 1985).

The way you are treated as a member of a racial or ethnic group, as a man or woman, is likely to affect how you treat others. It is important, then, to become aware of ways in which your own individuality and diverse experiences are valued. Ask yourself:

- What kinds of practices and policies at work or elsewhere are supportive of me? What other opportunities would I like?

- Where do I myself encounter discrimination or bias? What can I do to change it?

The Children

Ask yourself if children find their images, interests, or experiences reflected in your program and its environment.

- Do boys and girls feel free to play and work in all the areas of the room? If you have children of diverse economic backgrounds, is their range of experience represented in the curriculum? In a study of families, for example, you can ask children, "What is your favorite part of where you live?" which emphasizes the child's use of space, rather than, "How many rooms are there?"

- Examine your selection of books, pictures, tapes, and stories. Do they represent diverse cultures, races, ages, and the interests of the children in your group. Do they avoid stereotypes?

- Does your study of the community include services and institutions used by people of different socioeconomic levels, such as free medical clinics and used clothing stores, and those used by people of different cultural backgrounds, such as bodegas and synagogues?

Think about what you know about your children's styles of learning and expressing what they know. Providing opportunities for learning, and for demonstrating what is learned, in diverse ways is the essence of educating children, as individuals and as members of a group.

Do you know which children engage with learning by approaching materials first, which children engage first with other children and usually undertake tasks with a friend, which children need to spend a little time with you or with another adult before joining in? It is important to observe and document a child's strengths and interests and build on them as you lead him to new learnings. When you recognize that one child learns best through music and movement, that another child newly arrived in the United States is fascinated with the airplanes that transported him, and that a child in a wheelchair is a leader in the class, you can build individually appropriate curriculum. (You can read more about observational techniques in the chapter "Observing and Recording Children's Behavior.")

Consider the individual circumstances of the children's lives as you plan ways in which your program can nurture them. You may confront such issues as overindulgence, complicated divorce arrangements, lack of adult supervision, and over-scheduling. Your sensitivity to the different circumstances and needs of the children in your program can be reflected in numerous ways:

- In some cases, nurturing comes from a daily bag of fruit and cheese you may have in the class; in other cases, it is the extra rest time for the child who does not get enough sleep at home.

- For another child, the nurturing may come in reassuring him which day of the week it is, and to which household he goes on that day.

- Perhaps you will lend one child a book from the class library to keep him company at bedtime, or send a note home to say that the child lost a tooth today and it is in an envelope in the backpack.

Apply your knowledge of child development to help children learn about and appreciate diversity.

- **Preschoolers** are interested in their own emotional lives and have the capacity to empathize, although from an egocentric perspective. They comfort a friend who is crying or offer a stuffed animal to a sick parent. Preschoolers cannot understand the socioeconomic and political causes of homelessness, but they can understand how people might feel when they do not have a place to live or put their belongings.

- **Young school-age children** are better able than preschoolers to understand people who differ from them. They may be interested in the scientific explanation of different skin colors and fascinated with different ways of speaking and writing. Issues of fairness and justice in the classroom, on the playground, and at home engage the young school-age child's capacity to think in logical and nonegocentric ways. This ability can serve as a basis for exposing 5- through 8-year-olds to social conditions that give rise to discrimination, inequity, and injustice. In discussions, you follow their lead, using their questions or events in the classroom as a springboard for further exploration. For example, when a 7-year-old observes that it is not fair that some people do not have enough to eat, you use this as an opportunity to explore and extend children's thinking about social issues. Keep in mind that young school-age children are still limited in their ability to understand complex cause-and-effect relationships and abstract notions.

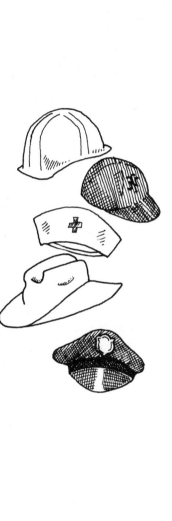

The Family and the Community

Think about what you know about the social influences in your children's lives. What is their community like, and how can you incorporate it into your curriculum?

- **Work.** It is important to find out about the work your families do, since it shapes their experiences and their lives. Children need to learn that all kinds of workers—lawyers, seamstresses, computer programmers, migrant workers, secretaries, doctors, clergymen, pilots, bus drivers, construction workers, sanitation workers, nurses, teachers, butchers—make a community that serves everyone.

- **Demographics.** In the last ten years, there have been demographic changes that have made many communities more diverse. Knowing about population changes in your students' communities helps you think about different languages, different traditions, different family structures, different experiences with schooling, and different expectations about the relationships between families and teachers. In some cultural groups, for example, school and home relationships are more formal than those common in America, and there is no expectation that home and school should create partnerships in making school decisions. If you are unaware of these cultural

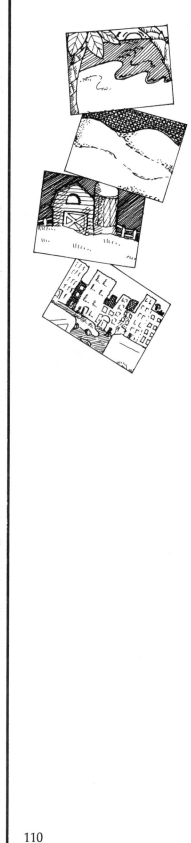

differences, you may misunderstand parents' seeming lack of involvement in their children's lives in school.

- **Urban, suburban, and rural locales.** Every location has its advantages and disadvantages. The urban teacher longs for children to be able see chickens being born and crops picked each season. The teacher of migrant children wishes for trips to museums, airports, and high bridges. The suburban teacher struggles with finding activities that are less homogeneous and predictable in order to immerse her children in a very different experience. All these teachers who are eager to offer something different are on the right track. Begin by understanding what you do have, and capitalize on the learning value inherent in your own community, and then continue your search for the live chicks, the museums, and the unpredictable subway ride as means for expanding everyone's world.

- **Economic conditions.** Issues of poverty, neglect, abuse, and poor health are of major import in many programs that serve young children. These concerns, largely economic in origin, are also part of sensitivity to diversity: all children, at whatever economic level, require careful educational decisions and a curriculum that enables them to feel confident and competent. They need access to toys, books, and age-appropriate materials that will stimulate them and help them learn; for some children, such access may come only in their early childhood education setting. Broken toys, torn books, and pencils that do not write convey the message "you are not valued." As a caregiver or teacher, you need to be aware of socioeconomic conditions as you work with parents or other family members who care for the children, and as you think of the services which may be available to them within or outside of the school.

- **Holidays and celebrations.** The ideas in this Guide discourage the use of holidays as the main source for curriculum decisions, and encourage you instead to select content that includes looking at diversity within the context of a study. For example, if the children are making books about themselves as part of a study, you might suggest that they give the books to their families on a special day of their choice. One child might give the book as a Christmas present; another may choose a birthday; a third may select Father's Day; and yet another may select Chanukah. You can also discuss holidays with children to explore their understanding of why they do not have school or why a particular day is important to some people. These discussions can be part of "social studies" or "study of people," and can help balance the misinformation, commercialization, and media hype that surround most holidays. They also deal with the "here and now" concerns of the young child: "Why is there school tomorrow?"

Another strategy for dealing with holidays and celebrations is to focus on seasonal changes as a way of including and responding to diverse traditions. In the fall, a Harvest Fair can include different traditions centered around this time: baking, canning, sharing meals, dancing, reading scary stories, singing harvest songs, raking leaves, making prints, moving to another migrant community, and making warmer clothes. A winter celebration may include a cluster of traditions that focus on the changes brought in by the cold, the shortest day of the year, winter sports, and family celebrations of many sorts. In spring, the sense of renewal and rebirth can be a catalyst for other celebrations and give rise to studies related to natural sciences, such as the hatching of chicks and the preservation of resources and the environment. These ideas can serve as the basis for including holidays and celebrations in your curriculum; however, it is important that you adapt them to serve the individual needs, values, and traditions of your program and your community.

You as Policy Maker

Think about what you know about cultures, languages, races, geographic influences, history, literature, and art that are different from your own experiences.

- Be aware of what you know and what you do not know. This is the first step in finding out what kind of help and resources you may need in order to serve diverse populations of children. This important step will highlight your own strengths, and it will help you decide when to turn to your community, your families, the library, a film, or a resource book to provide new knowledge you may need to expand the children's possibilities—and your own. Gathering resource materials will also allow you to build a reference library to help you make decisions about many issues related to diversity.

- Invite others to come to your program to share their knowledge and experiences. This, too, is a good starting point because it teaches the children that all people have something to offer, and it provides *you* with an easy way to learn.

- Share ideas with other caregivers and teachers who work with children from similar linguistic and cultural backgrounds. In this way, you will be expanding the resources available to you and creating a community of learners. After a series of staff meetings to discuss curriculum ideas for migrant school children in their classes, one of the teachers said, "I just realized that

111

we have no local people to pick the crops, so we'd better be less prejudiced about the migrant laborers. I now appreciate how important they are to all of our lives." As you deal with issues of diversity, you may also find that you are struggling with issues of economic, social, and educational equity, as these teachers did.

Think about policies in your program and think about how they serve your families needs. The following examples will help you think of and examine other policies in your own programs.

家庭

My Family MI FAMILIA

הַמִשְׁפָּחָה שֶׁלִי

MIO 3.A.MIGLIA

- **Family conferences.** Most teachers and programs plan conferences with parents. Yet, in many cases, other adults, such as grandparents or aunts, may be involved in raising the child. It is more inclusive and respectful of diversity to plan "family" rather than "parent" conferences. Think about how you set up family conferences. Are they scheduled at convenient times? Will families need to make special work or child care arrangements to meet with you? Can you offer a choice of schedules?

- **Home language.** Parents may need—or want—to speak to their children in the language and manner native to their culture. If your program uses a language of instruction different from the children's native language, it is important to encourage families to be natural and authentic with their children and to communicate in ways they find comfortable. Reassure them that knowing two languages is not only possible but desirable, and will come in time.

- **New families.** Each program has its own system for entering newcomers. When you have new families, do not assume that their previous experience was in a program similar to yours. Encourage visits before enrolling, collect pictures of your program in action, prepare tours or information sessions about your program. When you work with families who are new to your community, prepare information packets and encourage their participation in field trips, which will help them learn about places to take their children in the future. In some cases, families new to the country may need guidance in relation to community resources, such as doctors, jobs, community services, language courses, recreational facilities, and transportation.

- **Children with disabilities.** Legislation—and good educational practice—requires that children with disabilities be placed in the "least restrictive environment" that can still provide them with appropriate education. How you think about children with special needs is important in your acquiring the knowledge and seeking the resources to help them gain the compe-

112

tence, pride, interest in learning, and respect that are the right of all the children in the program. Understanding a specific disability, and knowing the educational practices that are most helpful in addressing it, might affect the way you arrange your program materials or classroom, the conversations you will have with other children when their curiosity gives rise to questions or comments, and how you go about obtaining the parental input that is required for making individualized educational plans for special needs children.

Valuing diversity is a challenge. It requires attention to who you are as a caregiver or teacher, who your children, families, and communities are, and what your program is like. It offers opportunities to learn about yourself and to help children value themselves and others.

Infants and Toddlers

Anna Walters and Susan Fein work in an infant-toddler center located in a suburban hospital. They care for children of hospital staff, many of whom come from other countries with diverse child-rearing practices and languages. Anna and Susan plan ways of learning about these differences, about how children and families communicate, and about how to make this knowledge explicit and public so that the families can learn about each other.

They first ask the families to write down the words their children use when they need something. They want to ensure that they can understand the children and respond to their needs. Anna and Susan post a chart in the room with this information on it:

> **Our children's favorite words when they need something:**
>
> Lucy: "No tete"   means "no bottle"
> Paco: "Oto"   means "otro" or "another one"
> Katie: "Uppy"   means "pick me up"
> Lin: "Sto"   means "stop" and "no more"
> Scott: "Baba juice"   means "bottle of juice"
> Andy: "No pamper"   means "I am going to the potty by myself"

Later on in the year, they continue this practice by collecting information on the children's favorite music, stories, and toys. All this is written down on charts for the caregivers and families to see. By the end of the year, they have learned a great deal. Lucy started using the cup when she came to the center. Paco's mother is a pediatric nurse who works with Spanish-speaking families; she uses Spanish when talking to Paco to foster his bilingual development.

Putting what you know about diversity into action

113

Katie has several older siblings who love carrying her around. Lin is from Taiwan and her father will work at the hospital for two years before returning to Taiwan. Scott loves taking his juice from a bottle and other liquids from a cup. Andy stopped using diapers last summer, before coming to the program.

They have also learned that some of the families take long airplane trips to return home for important holidays. So the center has toy airplanes and pictures of families going on trips. Anna and Susan help prepare the children for these trips by talking about them. They take photos of all the children, the room, and themselves and put them in a small album for the departing child to take on the trip. They have learned that some of the families address them (the caregivers) by their first names, Anna and Susan, while others, coming from more formal traditions, call them Miss Walters and Mrs. Fein. They have also learned to work with families to make labels for the classroom materials and to write notices in several languages.

In this infant/toddler program, valuing diversity means building close ties with families. It all started with the teachers' invitation to the families to "Tell us what it means when we don't understand your child." To the families new to the community and the program, this said, "Welcome, we think that your language, ideas, and lifestyles are important to share with us and with others."

Preschoolers

In her classroom of 3- and 4-year-olds, Akiko has children from several cultural backgrounds, some born in the United States, some from other countries. They have been studying their families, and talking about whom they live with, what they like to do at home, and the kinds of foods their families eat. Discussions about younger siblings and visits by babies to the program have provoked a lot of interest. Akiko has decided to collect a variety of clothes (including kimonos and dashikis), dolls, and baby clothes for the dramatic play area. She has also put up magazine photos of families from many parts of the world.

Zack and Cindy are involved in their favorite activity, playing "Mommy and Daddy." Zack places two dolls in a backpack and puts it on. Cindy wraps a scarf around her head and another around her hips. She looks at a photo on the wall, as if to make sure she has got the placing of the scarves right. Then she unties the scarf on her hips, places a doll inside, and ties it up again. She and Zack put a few more dolls in the baby carriage and push it toward Akiko, who comments, "Isn't it great how parents carry babies in so many different ways!" Zack smiles and says, "I really like the backpack. My daddy has one for my little sister." Cindy adds, "I like scarves for *everything*. I'm going to get one to put around my neck!"

Akiko smiles, seeing that the children's play reflects their understanding of diversity. She feels she has worked hard to include materials and to arrange the room in ways that encourage many kinds of play. She also knows that with children of this age, the best place to begin is with their interest in families and their own experiences.

Young School-Age Children

A first grade teacher, Jean-Marie, thinks about the characteristics of her group and her community as she plans the direction and content of the curriculum study of libraries and bookstores. The program is located in a suburban community which has several bookstores, a town library, and a community college with a library and a store that sells secondhand books. She plans activities that will differentiate between the concepts of making books, borrowing books, and buying new and used books.

Jean-Marie plans to help the children read, express their ideas through illustration and writing, classify different types of books, and learn about bookmaking, printing, and illustrating. But she also decides to include the diverse language experiences of her students and to build on their individual strengths in drawing, writing, and bookmaking. As she develops the curriculum, she comes up with the following activities:

- having a meeting with the children to ask them what they know about libraries and bookstores, and what new things they may want to know *(this helps the teacher learn what previous experiences with books the children have had and to determine what they understand about libraries and bookstores)*;

- organizing the classroom library to include books written in the native languages of some of the children, and books in English that depict children of diverse cultural or racial backgrounds *(this helps reinforce a sense of belonging for all class members)*;

- asking parents to take dictation of stories in their native languages when children are writing *(this recognizes that all children can express their thinking best in the language they are most familiar with)*;

- asking family members to share a story they heard or read when they were children *(this includes oral as well as written traditions, and expands everyone's understanding of stories)*;

- taking field trips to libraries, bookstores, secondhand bookstores, and developing trip-boards to record these experiences *(this offers common experiences for the whole group and fosters group life)*;

115

- having children work in teams of writers, illustrators, and bookmakers in order to have children share each other's different strengths *(this allows each child to contribute his or her skill and experience)*;

- inviting book sellers, writers, and librarians to come and talk about their different jobs *(this provides opportunities to talk about different careers and the skills and training needed for each job)*;

- building play libraries and bookstores in the block area to understand the concepts of borrowing and selling, and the use of money and library cards *(this integrates several curriculum areas)*;

- collecting fairy tales from different cultural traditions and finding their similarities and differences *(this emphasizes the common humanity portrayed in folk literature)*;

- making charts to illustrate where books were printed or the languages in which they are written *(this fosters understanding that books are made in many parts of the world)*. The chart might look like this:

Name of Book	Author's Last Name	Language Written	Place Printed
Joseph had a Little Overcoat	Taback	English	Colombia
Toad is the Uncle of Heaven	Lee	English	Japan
The Giving Tree	Silverstein	English	UnitedStates
El Cuento de Ferdinando	Leaf	Spanish	United States
El Gusto	Rius and Puig	Spanish	Spain
Le Prince et la Souris Blanche	Coulibaly	French	Cote d'Ivoire

Jean-Marie also considers what kind of culminating activity would be appropriate. She thinks that sharing the classroom library with other first graders would give her children a sense of accomplishment and expose the others to cultural and linguistic diversity in literature.

Families

Mr. and Mrs. Clark have just had a conference at their children's school, where the reading/writing process and invented spelling are part of the curriculum. They are very concerned, because this curriculum approach is new to them and so different from the way they were taught in school. They wonder whether their children are learning what they need to know to succeed in school and later in life. The Clarks know that their children, Nicky, 5 years, and Jason, 7 years, are interested in reading. They see them reading cereal boxes, sports books, cassette labels, and birthday cards at home. They want to understand better what the teachers are telling them about the curriculum. The school has suggested that all parents talk to their children about what they read or write in school. The teachers have also suggested that parents call or send a note if they have further concerns.

During the next few weeks, the Clarks ask Nicky and Jason to tell them about what they are writing in school. Nicky explains that he sometimes just writes down his ideas the way they sound. At other times, he dictates to a teacher or into a tape recorder, which later he transcribes into in his writing book. Jason, who is in second grade, describes how his class dictated a letter to the lady at the museum who had shown them the fossils. He says,

> The teacher wrote down what we said on the chart. When she was finished, she told us that the names of people and places begin with capital letters and that thank-you letters are important to send to people who helped us. She also asked us to pick two words from the thank-you letter and put them in our writing book to remember them later. I picked the words "fossil" and "subway" because they both have "s" sounds, like the one in the middle of my name, Jason.

Mr. and Mrs. Clark intend to continue to ask the school about their sons' work, but they are beginning to understand what the teachers mean about children finding ideas that are interesting to them and expressing them in letters, stories, and tapes. They are impressed with Jason's knowledge about thank-you letters, capitals, and "s" sounds.

The teachers are trying to communicate with all parents about the different ways they teach literacy. The school recognizes how important it is to keep the dialogue open between parents and teachers if they are to succeed at educating children.

Exercises

Here are some exercises for you to do by yourself or with colleagues to help you apply what you have learned about diversity and young children.

1. Ask yourself which is your preferred mode for learning. Do you have to be actively involved and then read about it, or do you gather a lot of reading material first and then apply it? Do you like trying new things by yourself, or with a peer, or with a group of people? Think about your favorite part of your own teaching day. Is it when you read stories to children, or do you prefer the walks

117

to the local park when the children ask questions about nature, or do you thrive on the type of logic they use to settle an argument? Do you look forward to the quiet time when they write, or the outdoor time when they hang from their feet on the jungle-gym? Now summarize what you know about your own preferred way of learning and teaching.

2. Now ask yourself similar questions about the children with whom you work. Which parts of the day and what kinds of activities do individual children prefer? Do you tend to notice the children who are more like you or different from you? Use this information to think about your group and about your curriculum. Is it flexible and varied enough to offer opportunities to foster initiative and competence?

3. Next, shift your focus to your school, program, and community. Is there any aspect of diversity that makes your program different from most others? Consider family types, cultures, economic issues, languages, health concerns, and access to technology. How do the mission and the policies of your program respond to different aspects of diversity?

4. Think about experiences outside of school that will foster a respect for diversity. Plan field trips that will help you create common experiences. Trips to museums or radio stations and access to magazines, like *National Geographic*, or newspapers in different languages can validate experiences for some and expand horizons for others.

5. Review the reasons why valuing diversity is important. Make up your own list of why you want to incorporate diversity in your early childhood setting. Brainstorm with a colleague.

6. Keep informed on advances in technology that provide you with access to information, or resources that will enrich your knowledge about other fields and their impact on education.

7. Think about your own experiences and the times when you could express your individuality. Then, recall the times when you felt that you were not respected or that you were being stereotyped. Were you able to alter the discriminatory behavior? Reflecting on our own experiences helps us empathize with children and respect their individuality.

8. Be vigilant about the ways in which you model behavior or affect others. How do your behaviors, attitudes, curriculum choices, and use of resources demonstrate respect for children, as individuals and as members of groups? Share your insights with a colleague, and together think of ways to broaden your own understanding and appreciation of diversity.

Banks, J., & Banks, C. M. (Eds.). (1989). *Multicultural education: Issues and perspectives.* Boston: Allyn & Bacon.

Comer, J. (1989). Racism and the education of young children. In F. Rust & L. Williams (Eds.), *The care and education of young children: Expanding contexts, sharpening focus.* New York: Teachers College Press.

Cuffaro, H. (1975). Reevaluating basic premises: Curricula free of sexism. *Young Children, 30,* 469-478.

Derman-Sparks, L., & A.B.C. Task Force Staff. (1989). *The anti-bias curriculum: Tools for empowering young children.* Washington, DC: National Association for the Education of Young Children.

Dewey, J. (1956). *The child and the curriculum and the school and society.* Chicago: The University of Chicago Press.

Gardner, H. (1983). *Frames of mind: The theory of multiple intelligences.* New York: Basic Books.

Grant, C. (1989). Equity, equality, and classroom life. In W. G. Secada (Ed.), *Equity in education.* London: Falmer Press.

Moll, L. (1990). Creating zones of possibilities: Combining social contexts for instruction. In L. Moll (Ed.), *Vygotsky and education: Instructional implications and applications of sociohistorical psychology.* Cambridge: Cambridge University Press.

Ramsey, P. G. (1987). *Teaching and learning in a diverse world: Multicultural education for young children.* New York: Teachers College Press.

Williams, L. R., & De Gaetano, Y. (1985). *Alerta: A multicultural, bilingual approach to teaching young children.* Menlo Park, CA: Addison-Wesley.

Resources

About the Author:

Maritza B. Macdonald , M.S., is a faculty member in the Graduate School at Bank Street College. She directs the Preservice Program and teaches curriculum courses for teachers and administrators. Mrs. Macdonald is a doctoral candidate at Teachers College, Columbia University. Her professional interests include issues of diversity, accountability, and bilingualism.

8 | Creating Curriculum in Early Childhood

What is curriculum?

At Bank Street, we think of curriculum not as a series of recipes for activities, but rather as the opportunities for experience you offer children that help them deepen their understanding of the world. The curriculum is the sum of those opportunities and it is created through a dynamic process of planning and decision making.

When you plan curriculum, every decision you make affects what children learn and how they feel about themselves as learners. Every day, you make important decisions about how children use the physical environment, materials, and time, and about how they work with each other. In doing that, you are developing your curriculum. These decisions are based on your understanding of how children grow and learn, and on your special knowledge of the individual children in your class or program. Let us look at some examples of the kinds of decisions you make:

- The physical space of your program is the laboratory for children's learning; it is where you help them ask and answer their questions and work out their thinking. Decisions you make about room arrangement can support children's learning. For instance, Luis, a kindergarten teacher, has learned from experience that putting the art supplies across the room from the sink makes it difficult for children to assume responsibility for a project from beginning to end. Inevitably, spills and messes occur during clean-up. By placing the art table next to the sink, with painting supplies on clearly labeled shelves close by, Luis teaches children to be in charge of their work, which includes clean-up.

- The materials you decide to make available are tools of the curriculum. Materials children can touch and move like blocks, playdough, paint, collage, clay, sand, and water provide children with opportunities to re-create and symbolize their observations of the world. Such materials can be used by children of varying ages, although they will be used differently. Thus, blocks can be used by 16-month-old Martha to load and empty a "fill and dump can," by 4-year-old Jenny to construct tall buildings, and by 6-year-old Marcus to recreate the airport visited earlier in the week.

- Decisions you make about the daily schedule also shape curriculum. For example, in her family day care home, Sandra

121

alternates active and quiet times during the day; after the playground time, she reads stories to the children and plays soft music. Mrs. James, teacher of a multi-age group of 5- and 6-year-olds, knows that children this age benefit from a long, uninterrupted work period to explore materials. Therefore, she plans an extended work period from 9:15 to 10:45 a.m. each day, during which children may choose several activities. (You can read more about physical environment, materials, and schedule in the chapter "The Learning Environment.")

- Helping children develop social relationships is also part of curriculum planning. Rose, a preschool teacher, knows that working in small groups enables 4-year-olds to handle both taking turns and their emerging friendships. For this reason, she invites a parent volunteer to help out with small-group cooking activities on Thursday mornings. (You can read more about social relationships in the chapter "The Group Process.")

All of these decisions are curriculum decisions. In this chapter, we discuss why a dynamic approach to curriculum planning is important and how you do it, and then give you some examples of curriculum experiences for different age groups. There are exercises for you to do with your colleagues to help you understand better how to develop curriculum.

Why is it important for you to be a curriculum planner?

You and the children both benefit from a dynamic approach to curriculum development. By dynamic, we mean an approach that allows you to change and modify your plans easily in response to things that happen in the course of the day—an unexpected question that can lead to an interesting discussion, an opportunity to have a parent share a special skill with the children. This approach allows you to look carefully at children and create a flexible program that meets their needs.

Like many caregivers or teachers, you may have to work within curriculum structures based on federal, state, or local mandates. The framework we provide will help you tailor prescribed curriculum to the needs of your program and individual children. As curriculum creator rather than consumer of pre-packaged curriculum materials, you can feel good about curriculum decisions you make because they will be based on your knowledge of the children in your program and will thus be appropriate for them.

Because you observe the children, you are able to make subtle changes in your program to meet individual or group needs. Consider these examples:

- A caregiver of toddlers, wanting children to feel competent and knowing that they often get impatient waiting for a turn to pour juice, provides several small pitchers at snack time.

- Noticing that the children have lost interest in dramatic play, a preschool teacher introduces new props, thus extending their ideas for play.
- A teacher of young school-age children plans a second trip to the bus station because the children are trying to accurately construct, in the classroom, a bus station made of crates and cardboard.

These are all curriculum decisions, facilitated by the flexible framework of a dynamic approach.

A dynamic approach to curriculum development forces you to think about what you do and why you do it, rather than simply following a prescribed series of activities. You make your curriculum decisions on the basis of what you believe is important about children at this stage of development, the individual children in your program, learning, and the function of education in society. You alter or modify your plans on the basis of what actually happens in the classroom. Assuming the role of decision maker enhances the sense of purpose you feel about your work.

Bank Street has always viewed the caregiver or teacher as a curriculum developer. When you assume a leadership role in developing curriculum for your program, everyone benefits—teaching is more exciting for you, and children's learning is deeper and more exciting for them. Carefully planning your work with children makes you a better teacher.

How do you develop curriculum?

Curriculum development is guided by what you know about how children grow and learn. This includes knowing how children develop, knowing that social influences affect them, that children learn by active exploration, that certain content is particularly engaging for children of a given age, and that emotional development plays a central part in children's growth and learning. It also includes listening carefully to the children themselves. Children's questions are what enliven and give direction to your curriculum. Many of these questions may be thought of as leading to investigations in the social studies curriculum. Later on, we describe how social studies can be used to integrate other learning experiences. Let us look at how your knowledge of children's growth and learning shapes curriculum decisions.

Curriculum planning must be based on your knowledge of child development.

Laura, a family day care provider, knows each child in her group is behaving appropriately for his or her age in the sandbox when she observes Jason, age 2, filling and dumping sand in a pail, while 3-year-old Tory imitates two 4-year-olds busily making "blueberry pies," and Josh, also 3 years old but not yet aware of the consequences

123

of his actions, happens to push his truck right through the middle of everyone's play. Laura also knows that children develop at different rates. Although both Tory and Josh are 3 years old, Tory is beginning to engage in cooperative play, while Josh continues to play alongside others, but is not yet capable of sustained interaction.

Caregivers and teachers provide opportunities for learning, knowing that children's ability to make sense of the world is different at each stage of development. For example, 5-month-old Pete experiences the world through his senses and bodily movements as he grasps, sucks, and pats the soft blocks his caregiver has placed on his blanket in front of him. Ricky, 4 years old, clarifies and refines his ideas about the world in his play. After a visit to the pet store, he builds a store out of blocks and pretends to be the "man who sells fish and puppies." Eight-year-old Becky, guided by her teacher, first molds plasticene in a pan and then pours water in, observing how islands exist beneath the water. At her stage of development, Becky can begin to think in logical ways; she decides to "test out" how a volcano can form an island.

Knowing that social influences affect children in your program helps you plan curriculum that is sensitive to their personal experiences and interests.

Social influences affecting children include family life, cultural background, and community issues and concerns. For example, Margaret, a first grade teacher, knows that 6-year-old Celia, recently arrived from the Philippines, is homesick for family and friends. A conversation with Celia's mother about holidays in the Philippines helps Margaret make a plan to welcome Celia's family into the classroom. Celia's mother will come to school on the Patron Saint's Day in the family's hometown to make Suman (a rice treat) with the class. Think about the children in your program. What are their cultural backgrounds, languages, and family structures?

By observing, listening, and questioning, you can learn about children, their lives, and their families, and use that knowledge to make curriculum decisions that engage children's interests. For example, Ms. Burton spoke with Ramon's father yesterday about Ramon's work in the classroom and learned that next week, Ramon will visit his grandfather in Puerto Rico for the first time. Because of this, at story time she reads a book about a boy taking a plane trip.

Children's daily lives are an important factor in curriculum decisions. The locale of your program affects your planning. When they wake up in the morning, do children in your program hear sirens, traffic, or birds chirping? Children's interests and concerns come from what they see and hear each day.

As you make curriculum decisions, think about children's everyday experiences as these teachers did: Wanting to show children how print is used in the environment, Janice takes her class of urban first graders to observe and photograph traffic signs on the busy street outside their school, while Margie, teaching in a suburb, takes children from her second grade class to a nearby railroad station where they study train schedules and billboards. (To learn more about the social influences that affect children, you can read the chapter "Valuing Diversity.")

Knowing that children learn through firsthand observation, play, and direct experience influences decisions you make about curriculum.

Children need to take hold of an idea and make it their own. For example, Brenda is a teacher in an interage class of 5- through 7-year-olds in a nongraded elementary school. She knows that children learn best when they first observe, and then, through dramatic play, painting, construction, and discussion, re-create and reveal what they know and what they are confused about, thereby suggesting next steps for curriculum planning. For a study of the marketplace, Brenda plans a trip to the apple orchard nearby. On the trip, children talk with workers, pick apples, and bring several baskets full of apples back to school. Afterwards, they choose their own ways of recreating the experience. When they do this, children engage in active thinking about what they have seen. Some children reconstruct the orchard trip with blocks, using different colors of plasticene for apples and cardboard for trees; others paint a colorful mural. Small groups of children take turns making applesauce. Brenda plans some additional cooking experiences so that they can think more about how cooking affects apples.

As children learn about their world through concrete experiences, they discover how things and ideas relate to each other.

This happens best when you plan experiences that build on each other. While on a neighborhood walk, Mr. Rosco and his preschoolers see a letter carrier transferring letters from a mailbox to her truck. The children ask many questions such as "Where are you taking the letters?" "Are there any magazines there?" and "Is there a letter for me?" Back in the classroom, Mr. Rosco and the children discuss what they saw. He records all the children's questions about the letter carrier and the mail on a chart. Then he plans a visit to the post office so children can gather firsthand information to answer their questions. Following the trip, the children use hollow blocks to recreate the post office, with Mr. Rosco providing props (a plastic mail carrier's hat, a mailbox, and some mailbags) to stimulate their play. He has placed many kinds of paper, envelopes, stamps, and ink pads on the writing table so that the children can "write" letters with scribbles and invented spelling to mail in their post office. Taking the spontaneous experience of seeing the letter carrier, Mr. Rosco ex-

125

tends it so children can ask new questions, make discoveries, and construct meaning out of the connections and relationships they see. Thus, out of the children's questions and interests, their teacher has developed a social studies unit.

Addressing children's emotions is also part of curriculum development.

Young children have very strong feelings. By observing children and listening to them as they talk with you and their peers, you can begin to understand how they feel inside and identify their questions and confusions. You can use this information to figure out how to be sensitive to children's emotional lives in your curriculum.

Young children do have fears. No matter how much you wish you could shelter them, children encounter frightening scenes as they watch TV and walk down a city street. Their fears may center around experiences they have had or someone they know has had. Some fears may be imagined, although nightmares and monsters seem very real to young children, who cannot always distinguish fantasy from reality. They may be frightened of bad weather, racial unrest, or death.

Curriculum includes discussions about why the class guinea pig has died, what a hurricane is, or why people go to war. Preschoolers and young school-age children may want to talk about what makes friends angry at each other and ways they can deal with their feelings. They need opportunities to express their concerns through dramatic play, story writing, art, and other areas of the curriculum. When one of their classmates is hospitalized, a group of 4-year-olds begin asking questions about hospitals and why people get sick. This is the time for their teacher to think about taking a field trip to a hospital, inviting parents who work in the health field to talk with the class about their jobs, and adding a doctor's kit and related props to the dramatic play area.

Children's emotional lives also include moments of joy, excitement, and exuberance. It is important to build these into your curriculum, for example, by celebrating a new baby in a child's family, talking about an impending trip, or creating a dance to show how a puppy walks. When first graders cannot stop talking about the warm spring weather and the "greening" of the drab winter landscape, you may decide to plant seeds indoors or outdoors and study seasonal changes.

Throughout early childhood, children are learning about themselves and their social world.

The following overview of children's interest and abilities at different ages will help you develop curriculum that engages them in learning. (This information will be familiar to you if you have read the chapter "Child Development.") These general descriptions of infants through 8-year-olds can serve as a guide to planning curriculum, supplemented by knowledge of your individual children and their relevant experiences.

- **Infants** are learning through their senses—seeing, hearing, tasting, smelling—and through their physical activity. Their initial activities, such as sucking on their fingers and kicking their feet, are focused on themselves. In a few months, more of their activity is directed toward the external world as they reach for things and smile at familiar people. As they become independently mobile—crawling and eventually walking—they explore the world even more. They are learning all the time, as they go through the daily routines of sleeping, eating, and diapering, and as they establish trusting relationships with adults.

- **Toddlers** demonstrate increased autonomy and mobility, as well as beginning language and abstract thought. They explore their immediate environment in active, physical ways. They use their large muscles to climb and run or explore materials by splashing water, pounding playdough, or drawing big circles. As toddlers get older, the world of self expands to include other things and people—the neighbor's dog, the shop where snack is purchased, a favorite cousin. Familiar activities may be expressed in pretend play. Daily routines and primary relationships continue to be at the core of their learning and constitute the essence of their curriculum.

- **Three- and four-year-olds** focus many of their interests on the world they know best—their family relationships. They take on family roles in their play, pretending to be a parent at home or at work, a baby, or a grandparent. They are interested in learning about what families do, how they shop, cook, get around, and have fun. They are interested in the work of adults, such as the fireman, hairdresser, librarian, or bus driver. They work hard to make sense of the world, based on what they already know. A 4-year-old tells her teacher that on the way to school she saw a nurse. When her teacher asks how she knew the person was a nurse, she replies, "She was wearing white shoes." This explanation makes sense to the child, who had recently visited a hospital where she saw many nurses wearing white shoes. Preschoolers' questions concern everyday life. They use their senses to examine and investigate, as they observe the environment piece by piece. Through their play, they try out roles, express their concerns, and clarify their ideas. It is helpful to think of the child's expanding world in terms of concentric circles; as the circle gets wider to include more people and more relationships, earlier interests still remain important.

- **Five-year-olds**, pleased with their competence, are curious about work—how people and things work. They are eager to explore the working world of their neighborhood in systematic, planful ways. Studies of stores, farms, transportation, post offices, and police stations are some ways 5-year-olds begin to understand how people do their work. The blurring of reality and fantasy, characteristic of 3- and 4- year-olds' role play, gives way to more realistic and accurate depictions. Their block buildings are visual reconstructions of what they see, feel, and think about. Block building is early geography. Think about how you might incorporate the 5-year-old's interest in jobs and workers in the community into your curriculum plans.

- **Six-year-olds** think about how things fit together, the interrelationships of workers and jobs, machines and workers, and services and people. For example, a class of suburban first graders are studying their neighborhood. First, they look at all the services people need to live in the town. They find out who does these jobs by taking trips and interviewing workers. Later, when they build a model of their city, they decide to include the street lights using batteries and bulbs. This leads to a study of the electric company. Some of their questions are: why the streets need lights, how you decide where to place street lights, how the lights work, and how electricity gets from the electric company to the street light in the neighborhood. They make maps of the neighborhood, the city or town where they live.

- **Seven-year-olds**, more flexible in their thinking, look at what is familiar and gradually think about the past. Concrete experiences help them answer their questions. For instance, a group of 7- and 8-year-olds make personal timelines of their lives, recording one important event to mark each year. Their questions about the past include: "Were there cars when our grandparents were little?" "When were computers invented?" "What were schools like in the past?" They interview parents, grandparents, and other older relatives or neighbors and create timelines of *their* lives. Comparing the lengths of the timelines helps them visualize "long ago." The children write stories of the childhood memories they learned about in the interviews and, in this way, gain knowledge and answers to their questions about life in the past, as well as insights into the historian's methods.

- **Eight-year-olds** learn about "distant and long ago" still linked to "here and now." Gradually moving from concrete to more abstract thinking, 8-year-olds might begin a study of environ-

ments by thinking about environments they have visited and creating dioramas of these places. Next, they might create homes for snails or other small creatures they could keep in their classroom. As they move on to a study of the people in a particular area long ago, they are already deeply engaged in thinking about environments. They can gather information from museums, myths and stories, diaries, timetables, maps, and pictures. Through crafts, construction, and plays, they can make generalizations and abstractions about new ideas.

All these factors—child development, social influences, active learning, engaging children's interests, listening to children—are elements in curriculum planning. By using a dynamic approach to curriculum development, you can take each of the factors into account and create a program that builds on what children know, what their interests are, and what you know is important for them to learn. In this way, you engage them as active and eager learners.

Infants and Toddlers

Joan, a family day care provider for infants and toddlers, knows her children learn from events that occur during the daily routine. She takes advantage of a learning opportunity on the day the paper towels run out. Two-year-old Sandra comes running over to Joan, saying, "No towels!" Joan kneels down to Sandra's level and responds, "The towels are all gone. We will have to get some more from the pantry. Shall we go?" Hand in hand, they go off down the hall to get more towels.

Once in the pantry, Sandra points to the box of paper towels and Joan reads the label to her. They return to the kitchen and Joan pulls over a chair for Sandra to climb on; together they replace the towels in the paper towel holder. By involving Sandra in solving a problem, Joan has helped her gain a sense of order about how things work. She is also supporting early literacy, helping Sandra make a connection between print and what it stands for.

Preschoolers

Preschoolers, curious about their immediate world, use materials in the room to recreate their experiences. A group of 4-year-olds uses cardboard boxes, chairs, and some blocks to re-create and dramatize their recent visit to a car repair shop. Carla, their teacher, supports their play by providing some props: coveralls and some child-sized tools. Some children create a sign, using scribbles and invented spelling, to label their shop.

Carla observes Daryl and Tanya as they change a tire on a make-believe car made of several chairs pushed together. Wanting to extend their play, she suggests they jack it up with some tools and

Putting curriculum development into action

reminds them of the jacks they saw on their trip. The children go off to find something that will work to jack up their car. They return with some long blocks which they push under one chair leg. Their play continues. Meanwhile, two other 4-year-olds have put on dresses and are having a party right beside the car repair shop. Carla comes over to them and asks, "Did your car break down on the way to the party? Do you need a ride home?" In this way, she supports their ideas while engaging them in the work of the other children.

Young School-Age Children

Don, a teacher of 6-year-olds, knows his children are interested in reading and creating stories, but have different levels of skills. He has helped children feel comfortable with their abilities by providing many different reading and writing choices.

During reading/writing workshop, the following activities take place in the room, indicating that all children are participating at their own levels: Don listens to Rico read his story written in invented spelling. Two small groups of children sit nearby at tables using markers and pencils; they are drawing and writing in writing folders, helping one another with invented spelling and listening to each other's work. In another part of the room, a group of children uses props to act out a story they have written collaboratively and will perform later for the class. Curled up on pillows, four children read picture books and several others read chapter books. (For more information on how to help children work in small groups, see the chapter "Discipline and Management"; the chapter "Literacy in Early Childhood" describes ways to promote children's interest in reading and writing.)

Families

Sarah works in a day care center where many children are transported on the bus provided by the program. As a way of helping parents understand her curriculum and feel a part of what is happening in the classroom, she takes pictures of the children at play and includes these with the newsletter she sends home every month.

Sarah makes frequent home visits to the families. Her conversations with parents during visits are similar to the informal chats she might have with them if they were able to bring and pick up their children each day. Once a month, the staff at Sarah's center hosts a parent breakfast from 7:15 to 8:15 a.m. Sometimes the breakfasts are purely social; at other times, there is a brief meeting or workshop planned.

Sometimes, Sarah also arranges to ride the bus back and forth. This gives her a chance to observe the children in a context outside the classroom and stimulates her to think about how to incorporate the bus ride into her curriculum planning.

Our goal in this chapter has been to offer you a framework for thinking about curriculum. We encourage you to look carefully at your children and plan your program accordingly. Collaboration with colleagues is both helpful and supportive as you create curriculum. It provides opportunities for shared perspectives, other opinions, and new ideas.

Here are some exercises that you can try with colleagues to help you think about a dynamic approach to curriculum planning:

Exercises

1. Observe a child for at least five minutes and record your observations. Look over your observations and think about what the child was doing. What experiences could you provide for that child to extend his or her learning?

2. Imagine that a child in your program has told you that her older sister is having a baby. You can tell from her comments that she is very interested in and curious about the upcoming event. What are some ways you might help her (and her friends, with whom she has also discussed this event) answer her questions. Depending on the age of the child, would a story be best, props for dramatic play, a visit from the sister, or perhaps a class discussion in which children could share common experiences?

3. Have a conversation with a parent in your program. Ask questions about the family's culture and how it is a part of their family life. Think of some ways you can incorporate what you learn into the program. Share the conversation with a colleague and see if you can come up with more ideas.

4. Observe three different children doing a similar activity during a work/play time. From the way each of them does the activity, what can you tell about their interests, their abilities? Are there ways you can build on each child's experience with the activity?

5. Think about an upcoming event or holiday that is recognized or celebrated in different ways by families in your program. Find pictures, objects, stories, and books to have in your classroom that represent the differences (and highlight similarities). Plan ways you can share these materials with children.

Resources

Bredekamp, S. (Ed.). (1991). *Developmentally appropriate practice in early childhood programs serving children from birth through age 8* (rev. ed.). Washington, DC: National Association for the Education of Young Children.

Christensen, D., Feeney, S., & Moravcik, E. (1987). *Who am I in the lives of children?* Columbus, OH: Charles E. Merrill.

Derman-Sparks, L., & A.B.C. Task Force Staff. (1989). *The anti-bias curriculum: Tools for empowering young children.* Washington, DC: National Association for the Education of Young Children.

Dewey, J. (1956). *The child and the curriculum and the school and society.* Chicago: University of Chicago Press.

Duckworth, E. (1987). *"The having of wonderful ideas" and other essays on teaching and learning.* New York: Teachers College Press.

Goodlad, J. I., & Anderson, R. H. (1987). *The non-graded elementary school* (2nd rev. ed.). New York: Teachers College Press.

Katz, L. G., & Chard, S. C. (1989). *Engaging children's minds: The project approach.* Norwood, NJ: Ablex.

Pratt, C. (1984). *I learn from children.* New York: Simon & Schuster.

Ramsey, P. G. (1987). *Teaching and learning in a diverse world: Multicultural education for young children.* New York: Teachers College Press.

Scales, B., Almy, M., Nicolopoulou, A., & Ervin-Tripp, S. (Eds.) (1991). *Play and the social context of development in early care and education.* New York: Teachers College Press.

Seefeldt, C. (1989). *Social studies for the preschool-primary child* (3rd ed.). Columbus, OH: Charles E. Merrill.

Williams, L. R., & De Gaetano, Y. (1985). *Alerta: A multicultural, bilingual approach to teaching young children.* Menlo Park, CA: Addison-Wesley.

About the Author:

Judy R. Jablon, M.S., is a curriculum consultant who works with teachers in Head Start and public school programs. She has been a primary grade teacher in public and private schools, including Bank Street School for Children. She has taught courses in curriculum development at Bank Street College.

10 | Integrated Curriculum for Four- through Eight-Year-Olds

At Bank Street, we call the work children do to understand their world "social studies." Social studies means seeing connections between self, family, and community. Using social studies topics as a framework, teachers provide opportunities for experiences that help children learn concepts about the social world and master important skills. It is through the social studies that you build an integrated curriculum, one that helps children use the skills they are learning throughout your program in a meaningful context.

Most often, skills are taught in isolation. Using an integrated approach to curriculum helps children see the direct application of these skills in their learning. For example, as the 7-year-old writes down how many and what kinds of workers she observes at the produce market, she employs writing and math skills in a useful context.

Social studies topics range from a study of families to the study of a river, depending on the age and interests of children, where they live, and the skills and concepts you want them to master. The constant element within any study is that children have experiences in art, movement, building, cooking, science, reading, writing, math, dramatics, and music. Experiences planned in an integrated way help children make sense of their world.

With infants, toddlers, and 3-year-olds, the question of teaching "subjects" does not come up in the way that it does in later childhood. As children mature, however, they are increasingly ready and need to learn skills and disciplines that traditionally have been compartmentalized into discrete areas or subjects, such as the three "Rs." Yet children 4 through 8 years of age need to continue to learn from organizing experiences in their own, more holistic ways.

Experiences are meaningful for children when they build on each other and lead to new experiences and further learning. We have found that the most effective way for children to understand how and why the human and physical world works is to allow them to act upon this information in their own way. Children need to experience things first. Then they gather meaning from what they have experienced by re-creating it. This re-creation includes discussion, dramatization, and construction. As a caregiver or teacher, you need to provide a wide variety of opportunities for children to re-create and

What is an integrated curriculum?

Why use an integrated approach to curriculum?

process what they encounter in the world around them.

An integrated curriculum supports children's learning because it provides ample time for experimentation, speculation, and discussion in order for children to become deeply engaged in content. This way, over time, they see subtle relationships and make connections. In-depth thinking does not happen when children gather disconnected bits of knowledge or learn in compartmentalized packages.

Children are motivated to learn when content is interesting to them. Cohen (1972) says that children "mix science, math, poetry, body movement, and feelings with total ease in the examination of problems that concern them." When the content of a study is rich, it will engage your interest as well as theirs. You can have satisfaction seeing children master meaningful content from a study you created.

In an integrated curriculum, you integrate:

- a variety of curriculum experiences, including music, reading, writing, math, dramatics, and art around a core study of a social studies topic;

- all aspects of children's development—physical, social, emotional, cognitive;

- firsthand experience with opportunities to re-create them;

- children's experiences at home and in the world with their work in the early childhood setting.

How can you integrate curriculum?

In this section we offer a framework to use as you develop an integrated curriculum. Do not think of this as a rigid system, but rather as an outline to help you with your planning. As you read this section and consider the examples, keep in mind that there are many ways to approach every study; each teacher is different and every environment and group of children suggest rich and creative possibilities. At the end of this section, we suggest techniques some teachers use to integrate curriculum. The following is a guideline for planning; each step will be described in detail:

- Think of a study in relation to the children in your program.

- Consider concepts.

- Learn about the subject.

- Gather resources.

- Plan opportunities for experiences.

- Involve families.

- Plan a culminating activity.

- Evaluate the study.

Think of a topic for study.

You select a topic for an integrated study based on what you know about the children in your program—their age, their interests, where they live, and what they see each day. A good topic provides opportunities for the children in your program to make sense of their immediate world, their families, and their communities. Choose a study that offers variety—you want it to appeal to the different interests and talents of children in your program. At the beginning of the study, children's questions may appear superficial, but as they gather information and spend time with projects, their questions become deeper and more subtle.

- Be sure the topic challenges children's thinking but does not ask too much of them. When we ask 4-, 5-, even 6-year-olds to study a place different from where they live—a group of children in a large city studying farm animals, for example—the study has less meaning for them. It would be more meaningful for urban children to study transportation, or apartment buildings, or stores in their neighborhood because of what they see and use each day.

- Emphasize tangible experiences connected to the children's lives. Four-year-olds are deeply interested in their own families, the foods they eat at home, and the ways their families celebrate holidays. This could be the basis of a rich study around Thanksgiving. A focus on the historical facts is inappropriate for this age group. On the other hand, 7- and 8-year-olds can study the historical story of "the Pilgrims and the Indians" and use it as an opportunity to evaluate stereotypical portrayals of these groups. You can also broaden their knowledge of other celebrations related to harvest and fall activities. (You can read more about holiday celebrations in the chapter "Valuing Diversity.")

- Select a topic that offers children many possibilities for investigation. For instance, a study of their city by a first grade class might include visits to a bus station, police station, firehouse, hospital, harbor, and sanitation department. Follow-up activities include block building, dramatic play, sketching and painting scenes from their trips, and reading and writing stories.

  The study of the city also demonstrates how a study helps children organize their learning. First, children have chances to observe—to collect information by seeing, handling, smelling and tasting, and listening. After they observe, they re-create these observations. Children use art and drama to symbolize and represent their firsthand experiences. They act on what they have learned. They use movement, art, math, and writing to make connections.

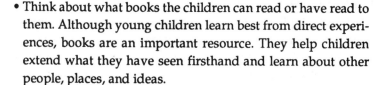

- Think about what books the children can read or have read to them. Although young children learn best from direct experiences, books are an important resource. They help children extend what they have seen firsthand and learn about other people, places, and ideas.

- Choose a topic that offers opportunities for children to talk and think about differences. Through a study of families, for example, 4-year-olds can begin to think about diversity of language, celebrations, foods, family size and structure, and music.

- Be sure the topic appeals to your own interests. You have to be challenged by the subject in order to help the children explore it. For a study to be meaningful to children, you have to put together a great deal of knowledge first, and that takes time and energy.

Consider concepts.

Think about concepts you want children to learn and the big ideas you want them to think about. Concepts are the important questions children will think about—the relationships they can discover. When children put two facts together to make a new fact, they are thinking. They are seeing connections and making generalizations. These generalizations lead children toward further knowledge and promote the ability to think, reason, and solve problems.

Think about what you want children to know *during* the study as well as at the end of the study. Taba (1971) tells us that concepts are the teacher's starting point of a study and the children's ending point—after they have done a variety of activities, had many experiences, posed and answered many questions.

Consider this example: Bart, a teacher of 8-year-olds studying Native Americans of the Eastern Woodlands, brings dried corn and a mortar and pestle to the classroom. He wants the children to think about what kinds of tools the Native Americans used and how they did their work. The children begin to grind the corn. They work each day and by the end of the week, one child observes, "All we have is a tiny bit of cornmeal and it isn't even powder like the cornmeal we bought at the store." Another child adds, "We do not make things from scratch. The Native Americans did. We go to the store and buy flour, butter, and eggs and think that this is baking from scratch. Well, it isn't." These children are learning about many relationships. They discover the relationship between corn, cornmeal, the mortar and pestle, and hard work. Bart understands that by letting the children re-create the Native American experience of grinding corn, the children will draw comparisons between long ago and the present, and they have. Could these children learn and fully appreciate these concepts from reading a textbook?

Learn about the subject.

Lucy Sprague Mitchell (1934) says that, as a curriculum developer, you yourself must explore the environment. Take a walk to capture the child's-eye view; look for ways for children to begin to see relationships between people and the environment. Mrs. Alvarez teaches second graders in a fishing town beside a river; her class will study how the river is used by the community. First, she herself takes several walks along the river. She visits the harbor to talk with the fishermen and climb on their boats; she reads the history of the river and learns some of the science and geography about how rivers are formed.

To learn more about the subject, go to your local library for books about your study. Books with vivid pictures are especially helpful. Look for folktales and poems that relate to the topic and are appropriate for your age group. Museums and bookstores can also be a good place to find materials. As you look in card catalogs, computer files, and bibliographies, you may get additional ideas. Or you may discover that you have to rethink your idea because there is not enough appropriate material available.

When, at last, you feel like an expert on the subject, your hardest job is to keep what you know to yourself, allowing the children to make their own discoveries. It is through these discoveries that children learn.

Collect resources.

For the children, the study is an investigation. You provide them with resources and opportunities for experiences that stimulate questions, speculations, and hypotheses, but the discoveries they make and the knowledge they acquire are their own. Having yourself been an investigator, you have greater sensitivity to their questions and to problems they may want to solve.

Think of resources that will deepen, expand, and extend children's knowledge of a topic, and always keep in mind the age of the children in your program. You will want to:

- identify appropriate trips;
- collect props for dramatic play;
- gather block accessories;
- choose books to have in the library;
- find recipes;
- locate pictures, posters, films, and maps;
- gather artifacts;
- find poems;
- invite people who can talk with your class about the topic.

149

Studies for older children that focus on the past depend more on books and museums as sources of information. Children can use atlases, old diaries, myths, and legends to help them gather information about people. These materials give children raw facts and let them draw some of their own conclusions, whereas encyclopedias and textbooks present conclusions already drawn. Listening to a Native American myth about creation gave 8-year-olds studying "environments" clues about famines, celebrations, and religious beliefs. Pictures from magazines like *National Geographic* provide children with visual details of a culture they cannot observe firsthand.

As you plan the resources of the study, include books and pictures that help children observe differences in ethnicity, color, lifestyles, and gender roles.

Plan opportunities for experiences.
Plan opportunities for experiences that help the study come alive; trips are especially valuable when children can have firsthand experiences relevant to the study. Keep in mind that children's understanding of a topic deepens when they can see it from a variety of perspectives.

Begin a study by asking children what they know about a subject and what they want to find out. This helps you assess your group as well as engage their curiosity.

Trips, in small groups or with the whole group, provide children with firsthand opportunities to observe and question. Experiences children have following a trip help them to relive and process it. Construction with blocks, clay, or other open-ended materials allows the initiative for play and the reconstruction of their experience to come from children. The relationship thinking that children act out in their play can be extended through discussions and stories.

Simple trips, like taking a few preschoolers to the local grocery store to purchase snacks, stimulate discussion and dramatic play. Each environment suggests its own trips. A class of 6-year-olds in a suburban school visits the railroad station where their parents take the train each day to go to work. They bring back train schedules from the trip. They make block buildings and cardboard constructions of trains. They draw clocks.

Trip sheets for 5- through 8-year-olds encourage children to record what they see, as well as directing their attention to a particular part of the trip. Mr. Bickel makes a trip sheet for the 5-year-olds he takes on a neighborhood walk; he has drawn and labeled columns so they can record how many cars, buses, and trucks they see (see Figure 1). They will use this information to make graphs back in the classroom. Ms. Roth helps her third graders, who are visiting the museum, by including some detailed questions about blacksmith tools and a place to sketch what they see.

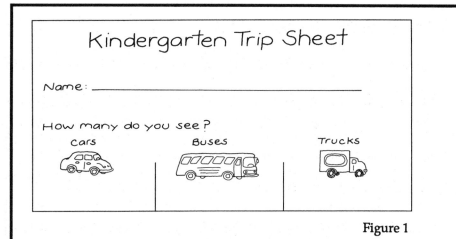

Figure 1

As you plan opportunities for experiences, think carefully about sequence. The experiences of your curriculum are building blocks of children's learning. Always ask yourself: "Why do I want the children to do this? What learning will take place? What experiences can it lead to? What questions might children ask?" Attention to sequence helps children organize their thinking and fosters in-depth thinking. As the following example illustrates, each experience connects logically to the one that came before and prepares children for the next one.

A group of 4- and 5-year-old children visit a shoe store in the neighborhood. When they return, they talk about what they see. The teacher makes sure that the children take the lead; she listens to what is interesting to them, rather than directs them. Through discussion, she sees what they know and what confusions they have. Several children remark that some stores sell only children's shoes; Tanya adds that she buys her shoes at the same place she buys clothes. Shiwon asks, "Why does the man measure your foot?" Allison thinks he is weighing her foot.

Some children draw pictures and dictate stories about the trip. Their drawings are visual representations of what caught their interest. As they write and converse with each other, they experiment with new vocabulary and concepts. The teacher makes a list of words about the shoe store for the children to refer to. Through constant discussion and play with new language, the children learn words like cashier and merchandise.

Spontaneous play emerges in the block area, where some 5-year-olds build a shoe store and use the block people to act out the roles of salesperson, customer, and cashier. The children make signs for the shoe store. To encourage others to join in, the teacher adds shoe boxes, shoes, and a stool to the dramatic play area.

It is important to use open-ended questions when children have new experiences. An open-ended question has many answers and no

151

I love this farm.
I am glad I went
And these are
pumpkins.

Eli   Figure 2

We Went
on A hAy
ride. It Was
fun. I heard
birds CrY.

Yuta   Figure 3

single right answer. It allows children to do their own thinking. Before the trip to the shoe store, the teacher asks, "What do you think you will see?" This question helps the children anticipate and lets the teacher know what previous experiences her children have.

You constantly make decisions about when to extend children's thinking. For example, later in the shoe store study, the teacher introduces a foot measurer to the children's shoe store and a series of measurement experiences begin. Think of some other activities you could offer to children to extend the experience of visiting the shoe store.

As you develop curriculum, plan opportunities for the whole group, for small groups, and for individuals. Children learn differently in each of these circumstances. And consider the complete spectrum of learning—have you included activities in your study that let children think mathematically and scientifically? Are there musical and artistic possibilities? Have they cooked? Have they read lots of stories? Have they written or dictated their own stories? (For examples of stories written and illustrated by 6- and 7-year-olds after a class trip to a pumpkin farm, see Figures 2 and 3).

Involve families.
As you plan, think about how you will involve families in the study. At what point should you invite parents to visit? Parents and other relatives can be a wonderful resource for children's learning.

Jenny is 5. Her father works on a boat in the harbor. Jenny's teacher invites him to come and visit the children to talk about his work. The children ask him many questions. After the visit, some of the children make boats to use in the water table.

Nick's grandmother is coming in to make guacamole with his class. Nick is very excited. Nick's teacher has called ahead for the recipe, which she has written on a big chart in the classroom (see Figure 4). Some of the children help shop for the ingredients at a local bodega (Hispanic grocery store).

Sending home weekly or monthly newsletters describing your study lets parents know what is happening in their child's program. In the newsletters, suggest ways for parents to be involved and welcome other ideas. Having an updated bulletin board near the door to your classroom or center is another way to keep families informed.

Plan a culminating activity.
It is difficult to say how long a study should go on. Sometimes a study takes one month and sometimes it takes three. The length of time depends on the age and interest of the children. Children's enthusiasm or boredom can be effective measures of how long the study should continue. It is better to end it sooner than planned than to

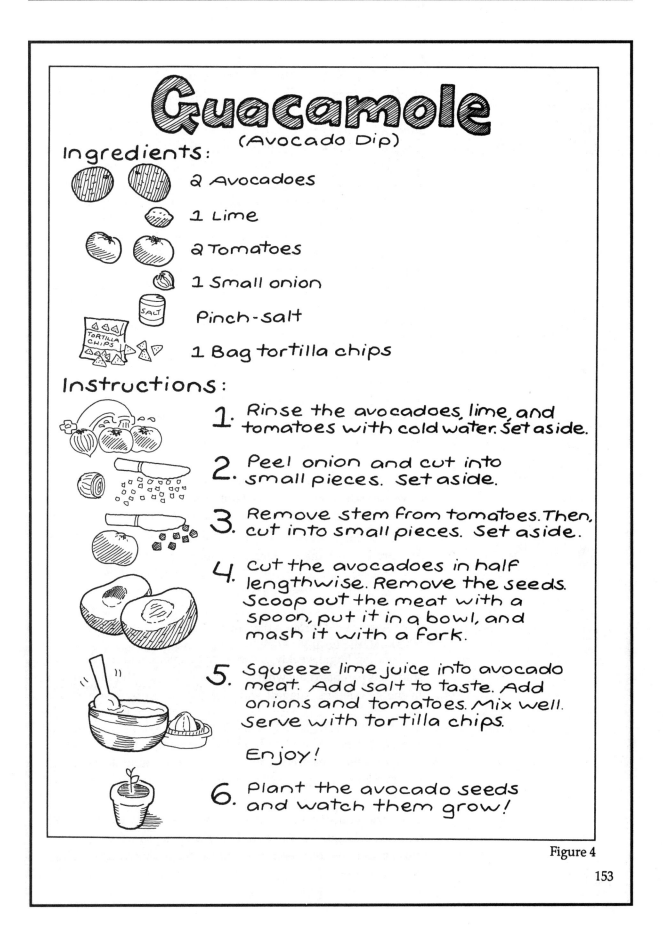

Guacamole
(Avocado Dip)

Ingredients:

2 Avocadoes

1 Lime

2 Tomatoes

1 Small onion

Pinch-salt

1 Bag tortilla chips

Instructions:

1. Rinse the avocadoes, lime, and tomatoes with cold water. Set aside.

2. Peel onion and cut into small pieces. Set aside.

3. Remove stem from tomatoes. Then, cut into small pieces. Set aside.

4. Cut the avocadoes in half lengthwise. Remove the seeds. Scoop out the meat with a spoon, put it in a bowl, and mash it with a fork.

5. Squeeze lime juice into avocado meat. Add salt to taste. Add onions and tomatoes. Mix well. Serve with tortilla chips.

   Enjoy!

6. Plant the avocado seeds and watch them grow!

Figure 4

153

continue when interest has faded.

However long they last, all studies must have closure. Part of planning is deciding on an ending, a culminating experience for a study. The ending is the organizing experience—the thing that brings all the learning together. Think of the ending as a way for the group to celebrate their collaborative efforts and their cumulative learning. For you as the teacher, the culminating experience is a way of evaluating your work and the work of children. The kind of culminating experience you choose depends on the age of your children and the nature of your study.

Your ending may be a class book, a mural, a play, or the re-creation of a store in the classroom. Preschoolers studying families make a class book with pictures and stories about their families. They have a potluck supper with family members to share their book. Eight-year-olds studying the history of the river in their town make a permanent model, using clay, wood, soil, sticks, and other found materials, to depict life along the river one hundred years ago. The model is the synthesis of the children's learning. They donate the model to the local public library for the community to enjoy. Think about ways you can bring a study to closure. Remember, each of these examples is only one of many possible ways.

Observe and evaluate.

How you observe and evaluate children during a study is another part of the planning process. A content approach to curriculum such as we have described does not lend itself readily to tests or other standard measures of evaluation. These guidelines may be useful:

- Constant observing and recording are essential. As children prepare for the culminating experience, it is important to observe and record what they have learned and also to keep track of misunderstandings that still exist. (You can review the chapters "Observing and Recording Children's Behavior" and "Assessment through the Curriculum" for methods.)

- Listening to the children as they build in blocks, construct a model, or talk to a friend lets you know what they have synthesized and what confusions they still have. Follow up on their confusions with group discussion, individual experiences, or a one-to-one conversation.

- Saving examples of children's work is important. Creating a portfolio for each child allows you to assess growth over time, and is especially helpful in talking with parents during conferences.

Teachers find it helpful, whenever possible, to work with at least one other colleague to plan a study. By working as a team, you can think about ideas collaboratively, ask each other questions, try ideas out, share successes, and ponder failures together. Some questions for you to think about are:

- What are the interests and abilities of the children in the program?

- What resources does our community offer?

- How might we involve parents?

- What special strengths do each of us, as teachers, bring to this study? Sharing materials and resources, as well as dividing research tasks, reduces the amount of work teachers have when they plan studies for the first time.

As you become more experienced with developing studies, you may use different techniques or develop your own to help you conceptualize a study. In the early stages of planning, some teachers find "webbing" an effective strategy for exploring the range of possibilities a study can offer. Even if you do the study independently, do the brainstorming with other people; it will help you extend your thinking. Webbing helps you identify all of a study's possibilities. These are the steps:

1. Write down as many words related to your topic as you can think of on small pieces of paper. Be as inventive as you can. For a study of breads, you might write words such as flour, work, good smells, pizza.

2. Group the words to make categories of similar words and label the categories. Categories might be workers, ingredients, utensils.

3. Transfer your categories to a large piece of paper for a permanent record. For a study of breads, your record may look something like Figure 5.

Large monthly planning calendars can be used to help you plot curriculum plans. Using the steps described earlier in the chapter, think about how and when to begin the study and record it on the calendar. Put in specific dates (or the week) you plan to take trips. Consider the logical sequence of trips as well as when appointments are available. Record experiences and activities you plan as follow-up to the trips. Jot down notes for open-ended discussion questions you will use in group meetings before and after trips and projects. If you have found stories that fit with specific parts of the study, add them to the calendar.

Curriculum wheels help you see that your curriculum is complete. They are divided into subject areas; teachers list possibilities for experiences and activities according to subjects (see Figure 6). Often activities overlap subjects; for example, a graphing experience about favorite types of donuts might be a math activity as well as a writing experience as children record data during a survey and print labels on the actual graph. Although some teachers find using

155

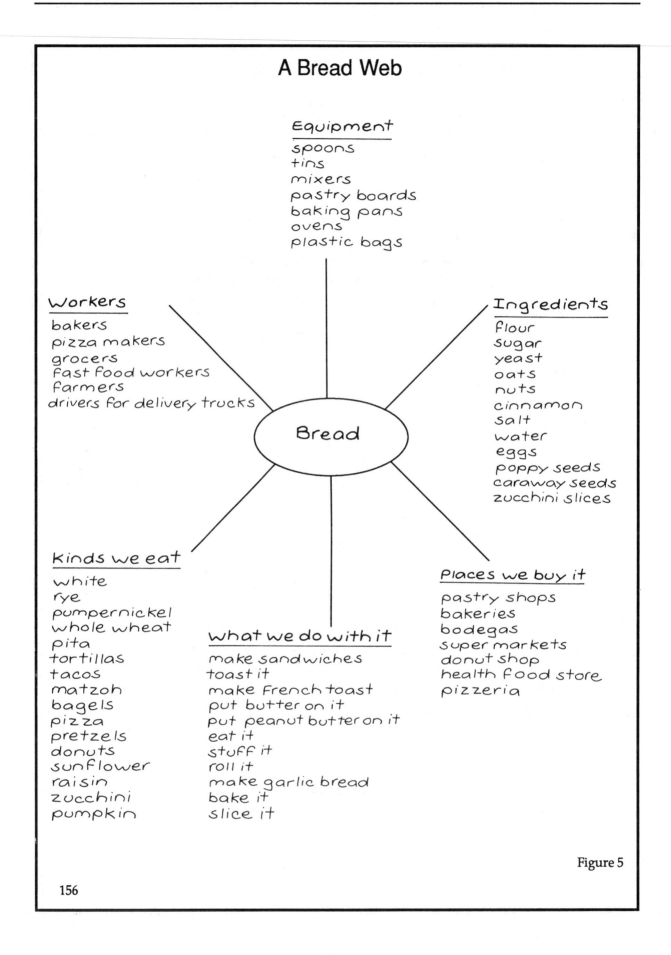

A Bread Web

Equipment
spoons
tins
mixers
pastry boards
baking pans
ovens
plastic bags

Workers
bakers
pizza makers
grocers
fast food workers
farmers
drivers for delivery trucks

Ingredients
flour
sugar
yeast
oats
nuts
cinnamon
salt
water
eggs
poppy seeds
caraway seeds
zucchini slices

Bread

Kinds we eat
white
rye
pumpernickel
whole wheat
pita
tortillas
tacos
matzoh
bagels
pizza
pretzels
donuts
sunflower
raisin
zucchini
pumpkin

What we do with it
make sandwiches
toast it
make French toast
put butter on it
put peanut butter on it
eat it
stuff it
roll it
make garlic bread
bake it
slice it

Places we buy it
pastry shops
bakeries
bodegas
super markets
donut shop
health food store
pizzeria

Figure 5

156

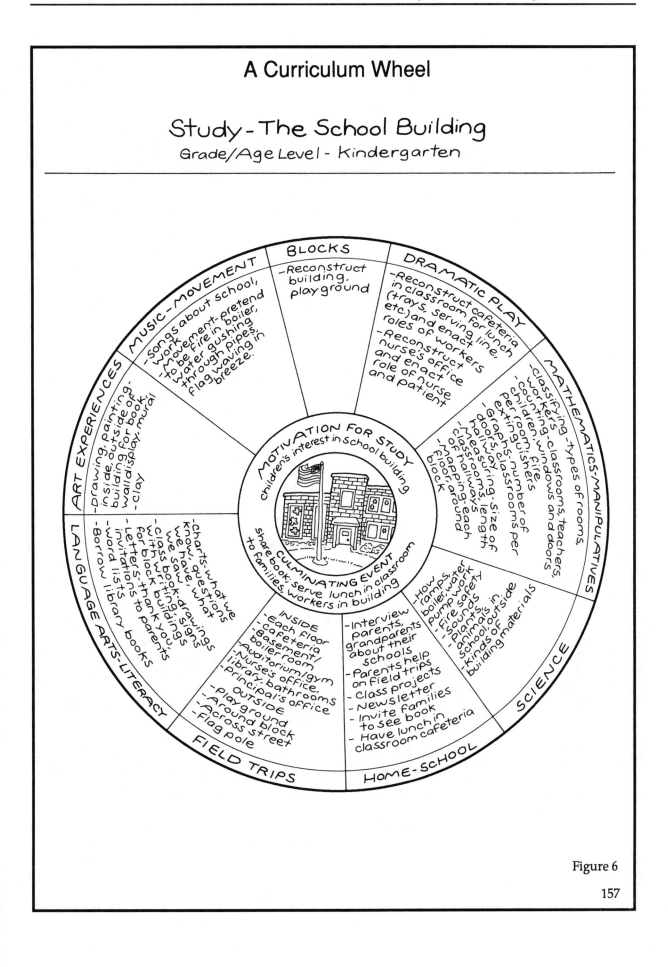

A Curriculum Wheel

Study - The School Building
Grade/Age Level - Kindergarten

BLOCKS
- Reconstruct building, playground

MUSIC-MOVEMENT
- Songs about school, work
- Movement-pretend to be fire in boiler, water gushing through pipes, flag waving in breeze.

DRAMATIC PLAY
- Reconstruct cafeteria in classroom for lunch (trays, serving line, etc.) and enact roles of workers
- Reconstruct nurse's office and enact role of nurse and patient

ART EXPERIENCES
- Drawing, painting inside, outside of building for book
- Wall display, mural
- clay

MATHEMATICS-MANIPULATIVES
- classifying - types of rooms, workers
- counting - classrooms, teachers, children, windows and doors
- extinguishers, fire per room
- graphs - number of doors, classrooms per hallways
- measuring - length, size of classrooms, each block
- Mapping - around off - floor

MOTIVATION FOR STUDY
Children's interest in school building

CULMINATING EVENT
share book, serve lunch in classroom to families, workers in building

SCIENCE
- How ramps, boiler, water pump work
- Fire safety
- Sounds
- Plants, animals in school, outside
- Kinds of building materials

LANGUAGE ARTS-LITERACY
- charts - what we know, questions we have, what we saw
- class book - drawings with writing, signs for block buildings
- Letters - thank you's, invitations to parents
- word lists
- Borrow library books

FIELD TRIPS
INSIDE
- Each floor
- Cafeteria
- Basement/ boiler room
- Auditorium/gym
- Nurse's office, library, bathrooms
- Principal's office
OUTSIDE
- Play ground
- Around block
- Across street
- Flag pole

HOME-SCHOOL
- Interview parents, grandparents about their schools
- Parents help on field trips
- Class projects
- Newsletter
- Invite families to see book
- Have lunch in classroom cafeteria

Figure 6

157

curriculum wheels helpful, be careful not to make up gimmicky ideas simply to fill the wheel; be sure the activities you plan really enhance children's learning.

All teachers have different styles, and you will find the technique that works best for you. A good study must be well planned but should also remain flexible to include the spontaneous ideas that come from children, other colleagues, parents, a visitor, or you. In the chapter "A Study of Bread and Bakeries: An Example of Integrated Curriculum," you can read about how a teacher of 5- and 6-year-olds developed a study. As you read it, keep in mind that this is one teacher and one study. There are many ways to develop a study and many topics that are appropriate for each age group.

Exercises

Here are some exercises for you to try alone or with colleagues to help you understand how to integrate curriculum.

1. Think of an idea for a study you might do with children in your program. Is it appropriate for their age, their environment? What are some trips you could take with children to help them gather information about the topic? Think about ways to follow up on children's experiences on the trip. What are some open-ended discussion questions you could use to help children think about the study? Discuss your ideas with a colleague.

2. Imagine you are doing a study of a topic with a multi-aged group of 4-, 5-, and 6-year-olds. With a few other colleagues, create a web about a topic that fits your neighborhood. Think about how the same study can be adapted to meet the interests of each of these age groups in a multi-aged setting.

3. Create a web or wheel for a study of the same topic for three different age groups; each age group will work in its own classroom. How will the study differ for each age group? Does this exercise influence your thinking about Exercise 2? Discuss your findings with colleagues.

4. Make a curriculum wheel for the study you began planning in Exercise 1.

5. Draft a letter to parents about this study, inviting them to share their ideas and participate in some way.

Resources

Cohen, D. H. (1972). *The learning child*. New York: Schocken Books.

Gamberg, R., Kwak, W., Hutchings, M., & Altheim, J. (1988). *Learning and loving it: Theme studies in the classroom*. Portsmouth, NH: Heinemann.

Katz, L. G., & Chard, S. C. (1989). *Engaging children's minds: The project approach*. Norwood, NJ: Ablex.

Mitchell, L. S. (1991). *Young geographers* (4th ed.). New York: Bank Street College of Education. (Originally published in 1934 by The John Day Company.)

Taba, H., Durken, M., Fraenkel, J., & McNaughton, A. (1971). *A teacher's handbook to elementary social studies: An inductive approach* (2nd ed.). Reading, MA: Addison-Wesley.

About the Author:

Judy R. Jablon, M.S., is a curriculum consultant who works with teachers in Head Start and public school programs. She has been a primary grade teacher in public and private schools, including Bank Street School for Children. She has taught courses in curriculum development at Bank Street College.

17 | A Study of Bread and Bakeries: An Example of Integrated Curriculum

The task of developing curriculum is a challenging one and can seem overwhelming at first. However, it helps to think of yourself as a learner embarking on a learning experience with your children. In this section, you will look at an example of a study to see how one teacher uses a social studies topic to integrate curriculum. As you read, think about other age groups, other environments, and other studies. This example is not a recipe; all effective studies reflect the individual thinking of the teachers who design them.

Mrs. Lyons, a teacher of a mixed-age group of 23 kindergarten and first grade children in an urban public school, chooses a study of breads and bakeries as a vehicle for helping her children think about how people do their jobs. She wants her children to understand that people have specific jobs and that it takes many different workers to produce our food. From a scientific perspective, she wants the children to think about physical change, and bread provides interesting content for experiments, observations, and discussions. The school's neighborhood has many ethnic bakeries and supermarkets, and bakeries are filled with interesting machines and devices that appeal to children. Mrs. Lyons likes this study topic because bread is common to virtually all cultures. At the same time, it comes in many different forms. The varieties of bread available in the neighborhood will lead naturally to discussions of different families and cultures. The children will have ample opportunities to appreciate diversity while recognizing commonalities.

Before we go on, think of your setting and age group. What are the interests of the children? What resources does the community provide? Keep your answers in mind as you read through the example.

Prior to the study, Mrs. Lyons talks with another teacher about her plans. She finds this helps her generate ideas and clarify her thinking. They discuss how the children will see wheat and grind it (activities that help children understand where bread comes from), and how they will see and taste different kinds of breads, such as donuts, pretzels, tortillas, and pita. This discussion helps her consider the range of possibilities for the study. What other ideas can you think of for a study of bread for 5- and 6-year-olds?

She begins organizing trips to stores, interviews with workers, discussions with family members about recipes—all experiences children need to gather information. She anticipates ways they can

241

recreate their learning: block buildings of bakeries and pizza stores, songs about bakers and bread, dramatic play about bakeries, murals, cookbooks, science experiments, measurement activities during cooking, story books, wheat grinding, baking and eating.

Before beginning the study with children, Mrs. Lyons visits a pastry shop, a bagel store, a pizza shop, a Latino bakery, and a natural foods store. She explains to local merchants that her class will study breads and bakeries and asks if they can visit. The shopkeepers are receptive to her requests.

Now it is time to begin. One afternoon, she opens up discussion by asking the class, "What did you have for lunch today?" The children talk about what they have eaten and Mrs. Lyons records answers on a chart. Many of the children say they ate sandwiches for lunch. She asks them to describe the kinds of bread used in their sandwiches: white, whole wheat, pita, raisin bread. The chart remains on the wall throughout the study.

The next day she has a grain grinder and wheat berries on the table for the children to look at as they come into the room. Some children ask, "Where do wheat berries come from?" Mrs. Lyons is prepared for this question and has a book from the library with text and pictures of wheat and wheat fields. She asks the children to think about their question and lets them know they will discuss it later on. At the morning meeting, Mrs. Lyons says, "Today we will talk about flour. What is flour?" Many of the children are not sure. One child's question reveals some confusion about "flowers" and "flour." Children share stories about baking with parents and grandparents.

During the morning work period, some children use the grinder and taste the flour. They draw pictures and write (or dictate) about the grain grinder and the flour they have made. By week's end, everyone has had a chance to grind flour and to draw and write about the experience. Mrs. Lyons mounts the children's stories and drawings on pieces of construction paper. Using metal binder rings, she compiles these into a class book. The following week, Mrs. Lyons reads the book to the class during story time and then the book is added to the class library.

Knowing that the experience of making bread will stimulate the children's thinking and questions, Mrs. Lyons prepares a recipe for whole wheat bread. A parent brings in her favorite recipe for challah, a kind of egg bread, and helps the children make it. After a visit to the pizza shop, the baker gives the children the recipe for pizza dough.

Mrs. Lyons has asked a parent to bring in a small oven that the class can use during the study. She also brings her toaster oven from home. As children begin baking, they ask why bread rises. They want to know how dough changes from something sticky to something firm that can be sliced. Experiments using yeast and baking soda help them find answers to their questions.

The class takes a trip each week to different bakeries or bread shops in the neighborhood. Mrs. Lyons sometimes takes children on trips in half-groups, enlisting the support of parent volunteers.

First, they go to a bagel store. During the trip, Mrs. Lyons listens to children's questions and conversations; she records anecdotes in her notebook. Danielle asks, "Is a donut a bagel?" Mrs. Lyons acknowledges her inquiry by saying the question is interesting and Danielle should think more about it.

The next day, Mrs. Lyons presents the question to the class. She uses an open-ended statement to begin the discussion: "Yesterday, Danielle observed similarities between bagels and donuts. Let's talk about donuts and bagels." The children begin sharing stories about both foods. One child says that a bagel is bread and a donut is cake. Another child observes that both are round with holes. Mrs. Lyons's role in this discussion is facilitator; she does not give answers. Rather, she uses opportunities like these to help children learn ways to solve problems. They learn how to test their hypotheses. She wants to help Danielle think through her question. Mrs. Lyons tells the class they will bake both donuts and bagels and compare the recipe charts for similarities and differences.

The first trip to the bagel store is the basis for many experiences and many discussions. The children bring back bagels to taste and make a graph of their favorite kinds. Some children make paintings of machines and workers they saw in the bagel store.

After their paintings are completed, Mrs. Lyons talks with children about their work and listens carefully to their discussions. Through her informal conversations with children, she evaluates their learning and assesses their need for additional experiences.

The class makes a book about their trip. Each child contributes a drawing and a piece of writing. Again, some dictate stories and others write by themselves, using invented spelling. One child depicts his experience at the "bread shop" like this:

Several children build a bakery in the block corner while others construct a model of a bread factory, using boxes and milk cartons of different sizes. They use masking tape to hold them together and to tape them to a large piece of flat cardboard. Important learning is taking place here as the children discover the relationships between workers, machines, and the environment.

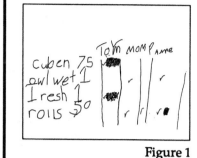

Figure 1

As the class bakes different kinds of bread, charts are hung around the room with the names of breads and recipes. Children discover their families have different names for the same bread. Around the classroom, books are displayed containing stories and poetry about breads, pies, bakers, and other related subjects, representing many cultures and customs. Some children have surveyed other classes to learn about the favorite kinds of breads of other children. Their graph, with its invented spellings, is also on display. One child prepares a shopping list. She asks her father (Tom) and her mother what kind of bread each of them would like and records their choices along with the prices (see Figure 1).

Although the study of bakeries and breads is the focal point of the classroom for several weeks, other work in the room—reading, writing process, art, music, math activities—continue as usual. The bakery study provides a rich context in which children can use their skills and knowledge from these other areas, and adds to their growing skills and knowledge in all areas.

The study that began in October will end in late November. Mrs. Lyons plans a bakery in the classroom for the culminating experience. Parents and other adults in school will be invited. She notifies parents of her plans in the monthly newsletter. Can you think of other appropriate culminating experiences?

Organizing the bakery is a big job for both Mrs. Lyons and the children. There is much planning and discussion and lots of excitement. Some items will be baked at school in small ovens in the classroom; others are baked in the large oven in the school's kitchen. Several parents take items prepared at school and bake them at home.

The bakery project sparks many new math experiences: the children keep track of ingredients used, items baked, and how many times each child has a turn as baker. They keep records of who serves, bakes, and is cashier. Real money is collected and counted. The children are ready for this because play money was used extensively in the make-believe bakery they built with blocks. Mrs. Lyons extended children's learning by designing additional math activities using play money. Now the children apply the math skills they have learned throughout the study in their real bakery.

The children are very proud of what they have learned and eager to share it with their parents. They set up a display inside the classroom including their trip books, stories, graphs and other art work for parents to see when they come to the bakery. The bakery is planned for the week before Thanksgiving. The children will sell their baked goods early in the morning when their parents bring them to school. Many parents buy breads and cakes to serve during the holiday. The bakery is a wonderful success.

Throughout the study, Mrs. Lyons reflects on how and what her

244

children are learning. In addition to her extensive anecdotal records, she has drawings and writing from the children. She takes pictures of block buildings and constructions to help her with parent conferences and report writing.

As you read about Mrs. Lyons's study, you probably had many ideas of your own. There is no one way to create a social studies curriculum. Every group of children, every teacher, changes the quality of a study. Imagine that Mrs. Lyons teaches in a rural environment where there are no local bakeries or food shops. How might she give children firsthand experiences with other workers and their jobs?

Looking at integrated curriculum for other age groups

We looked at a study for 5- and 6-year-olds. Let us consider the ways this study might change if the group of children were somewhat younger or older.

Four year-olds might well be interested in the jobs they observe people doing and will recreate trips through extensive dramatic play. While a 5- or 6-year-old makes her own baker's hat if she needs one for her play, a younger child grabs the baker's hat you place in the dramatic play area to begin her play as baker. As much as 4-year-olds enjoy mixing and kneading real bread, they are equally enthusiastic about making playdough cupcakes and pies and pizza, having serious and involved discussions as they work. An appropriate culminating experience for 4-year-olds might be a breakfast for parents and children with muffins prepared the day before. A long-range project like the one Mrs. Lyons planned would frustrate younger children because they find it hard to wait and plan far in advance.

Now that you have read about how to put a study into action, think about other topics for 4-year-olds in your community.

For older children, the study includes more writing, reading, and recording, but it continues to be rich in building, making, and dramatizing experiences. Seven- and eight-year-olds might study baking techniques used now and long ago and think about the history of baking ovens, from the fires of American Indians to the brick ovens of the early settlers, to the solar-powered ovens of today. They could build an oven using a light bulb, or make a solar-powered oven to experiment with heat and temperature. They might prepare a recipe book of breads.

A historical study of machinery and equipment used for wheat production and bread making could be a way to investigate how technology has changed through history. Older children love inventions. Through questions, speculations, and rich experiences, they begin to develop an appreciation of how people's lives have changed as a result of changes in technology.

The history of bread or baking equipment is one way to approach

245

a study of long ago that begins with something from the here and now. Can you think of other topics that might be relevant to your children and your environment? A study for 7- and 8-year-olds will include visits to historical places and museums. Are there places in your community that have collections of historical material? Older children like to reenact the roles of people long ago in skits and plays. They can design costumes and write scripts for plays. These experiences provide meaningful opportunities for research and writing. Stories that they read or hear help them to imagine the lifestyles of people long ago. Films and video help to bring history to life as well.

About the Author:

Judy R. Jablon, M.S., is a curriculum consultant who works with teachers in Head Start and public school programs. She has been a primary grade teacher in public and private schools, including Bank Street School for Children. She has taught courses in curriculum development at Bank Street College.

INDEX

CURRICULUM RESOURCE HANDBOOK SURVEY

As Kraus International Publications develops its new book series, CURRICULUM RESOURCE HAND-BOOKS, your evaluation of this handbook will prove invaluable. Please take time after having reviewed or used the *Handbook* to answer the following questions, then fold, seal, and mail the postage-paid form.

1a. Which sections of the handbook are most useful? Please circle the appropriate response for EACH section.

1b. Should the amount of material in each section be changed? Please check ( ) the appropriate response for EACH section.

SECTION	MOST USEFUL			LEAST USEFUL		NO OPINION	INCREASE	DECREASE	NO CHANGE
Introduction	1	2	3	4	5	6	____	____	____
Overview of Trends	1	2	3	4	5	6	____	____	____
Curriculum Design	1	2	3	4	5	6	____	____	____
Topical Outline	1	2	3	4	5	6	____	____	____
State Guidelines	1	2	3	4	5	6	____	____	____
List of Publishers	1	2	3	4	5	6	____	____	____
List of Curriculum Guides	1	2	3	4	5	6	____	____	____
Guide Reprints	1	2	3	4	5	6	____	____	____
Special Project Ideas	1	2	3	4	5	6	____	____	____
Discussion of Trade Books	1	2	3	4	5	6	____	____	____
State Text Adoption	1	2	3	4	5	6	____	____	____
Index to Reviews	1	2	3	4	5	6	____	____	____
KCDL Customer List	1	2	3	4	5	6	____	____	____

2. For the sections that you indicated in Question 1b should be changed, please describe any specific way the material could be improved.

_____

_____

_____

_____

3. How is this handbook to be used? Indicate your PRIMARY use with a "1" and check ( ) all others that apply:
_____ For developing curriculum
_____ For general reference
_____ For text adoption information
_____ For publisher information
_____ For guidelines and requirements
_____ Other (please cite)

_____

4. Including yourself, who will use this Handbook in your school or district?
_____ Curriculum Specialist
_____ Department Chair
_____ Classroom Teacher
_____ Media Specialist
_____ Librarian
_____ Other (please specify)

_____

5. The update frequency for the EARLY CHILDHOOD CURRICULUM RESOURCE HANDBOOK is now scheduled for a new edition every two years. Is this sufficient?
_____ Yes
_____ No, update every year
_____ No, update every three years
_____ Just update the timely chapters, and offer in looseleaf format

6. Please indicate those subject areas in which you think handbooks are needed. Please indicate the MOST IMPORTANT with a "1" and check ( ) all others that apply. Feel free to add subject areas.
_____ Adult Basic Education   _____ AIDS/Family Life
_____ Consumer Education   _____ Environmental Studies
_____ Foreign Languages   _____ Gifted/Talented Education
_____ Home Economics   _____ Industrial Arts
_____ Mathematics   _____ Physical Education
_____ Special Education   _____ Technology in Education
_____ Visual/Performing Arts   _____ Vocational Education
_____ Other (please specify)

_____

7. Please indicate the content arrangement you would prefer for future handbooks:
_____ Current handbook arrangement (one subject covering grades K–12)
_____ One subject with one book covering K–6 and one book covering 7–12
_____ Combining related subjects with one book for K–6 and another for 7–12 (e.g., humanities; science/technology/society; etc.)

8. Please indicate which of the following might be of interest to you:
_____ Textbook review service (periodic publication with original, critical reviews of newly published textbooks in all subject areas, K-12)
_____ Topic/Resource service (monthly newsletter devoted to a current topic of interest, with background and resources for teaching)
_____ Curriculum materials ordering service (centralized source for ordering instructional materials cited in CURRICULUM RESOURCE HANDBOOKS.)
_____ Complete lesson plan packets (subject:_____)
_____ Other (please specify:_____)

9. Any specific comments concerning the contents of the EARLY CHILDHOOD CURRICULUM RESOURCE HANDBOOK are welcome here.

_____

_____

_____

_____

_____

 SPECIAL DISCOUNT OFFER

Your comments are very valuable. When we receive your completed questionnaire, we will send you a 10% DISCOUNT COUPON toward your next purchase of a CURRICULUM RESOURCE HANDBOOK or another select Kraus International Publications title. Please provide address information below.

Respondent's Name _____

Title _____

School _____

Address _____

City, State, Zip _____

Telephone/FAX _____

THANK YOU!